Successful Writing at Work

Oregon State University

Custom Edition

Philip Kolin

CENGAGE
Learning·

Australia • Brazil • Japan • Korea • Mexico • Singapore • Spain • United Kingdom • United States

CENGAGE
Learning

Successful Writing at Work: Oregon State University, Custom Edition

Successful Writing at Work, Concise Fourth Edition
Philip C. Kolin
© 2015, 2012, 2009 Cengage Learning. All rights reserved.

Successful Writing at Work, Tenth Edition
Philip C. Kolin
© 2013, 2010, 2007 Cengage Learning. All rights reserved.

Senior Manager, Student Engagement:
Linda deStefano

Manager, Student Engagement:
Julie Dierig

Marketing Manager:
Rachael Kloos

Manager, Premedia:
Kim Fry

Manager, Intellectual Property Project Manager:
Brian Methe

Senior Manager, Production:
Donna M. Brown

Manager, Production:
Terri Daley

For product information and technology assistance, contact us at
Cengage Learning Customer & Sales Support, 1-800-354-9706
For permission to use material from this text or product,
submit all requests online at **cengage.com/permissions**
Further permissions questions can be emailed to
permissionrequest@cengage.com

This book contains select works from existing Cengage Learning resources and was produced by Cengage Learning Custom Solutions for collegiate use. As such, those adopting and/or contributing to this work are responsible for editorial content accuracy, continuity and completeness.

Compilation © 2014 Cengage Learning

ISBN: 9781305295667

WCN: 01-100-101

Cengage Learning

20 Channel Center Street
Boston, MA 02210
USA

Cengage Learning is a leading provider of customized learning solutions with office locations around the globe, including Singapore, the United Kingdom, Australia, Mexico, Brazil, and Japan. Locate your local office at:
www.international.cengage.com/region.
Cengage Learning products are represented in Canada by Nelson Education, Ltd.

For your lifelong learning solutions, visit **www.cengage.com /custom.**

Visit our corporate website at **www.cengage.com.**

Brief Contents

Welcome to Business Writing at Oregon State University.

We are delighted that you have joined this class. As college students, you are preparing for a job market driven by new technologies, a changed economy, and the need to communicate effectively with different audiences from all over the globe. This textbook has been customized for your success in this class.

The ability to write clearly and effectively for a wide range of purposes and audiences will be a vital skill in your future, regardless of your field of work. This course will develop your understanding of the rhetorical situation, your audience and purpose, and the professional conventions needed to advance your communication skills.

Through a range of practical assignments, you will produce typical workplace documents that will prepare you for future careers. You will focus on the clear and effective writing skills that you need to be successful in a variety of workplaces.

WR 214 meets OSU's Baccalaureate Core Writing II requirement. In this course you will fulfill those WR II outcomes to:

- Apply multiple theories, concepts, and techniques for creating and evaluating written communication.
- Write effectively for diverse audiences within a specific area or discipline using appropriate standards and conventions.
- Apply critical thinking to writing and writing process, including revision.

When you finish this course, you will have a professional resume and job application letter you can use right away as well as important job hunting skills and sophisticated workplace knowledge. What a great reason to take this course!

GO BEAVS!
Sara Jameson
Assistant Director of Writing

Preface

Overview

Successful Writing at Work, Concise Fourth Edition, is a practical introductory text for students in business, professional, and occupational writing courses. As readers of the full-length edition of this text have found, *Successful Writing at Work* clearly helps students develop and master key communication skills vital for success in the global workplace. The *Concise Fourth Edition* serves the same purpose, but it is designed for those readers who prefer a more compact text, one that covers nearly as many business writing topics but is more streamlined and focuses on the most essential skills and strategies for writing successfully on the job. Whereas the full-length edition includes 16 chapters, the *Concise Fourth Edition* contains 10 chapters, yet these fully cover a range of workplace communications technologies and a variety of e-communications from essential considerations such as audience analysis and ethics, to writing increasingly more complex business documents (letters, instructions, procedures, proposals, short and long reports), to making presentations, to preparing a résumé and interviewing for a job.

Versatility of New *Concise Fourth Edition*

As with the earlier concise editions, this *Concise Fourth Edition* is designed for a variety of educational settings where business writing is taught and practiced. It is versatile enough for a full semester or trimester course, or it can be used successfully in a shorter course, such as on a quarter system. It can also meet the diverse goals of varied educational settings, including online, webinars, distance education, continuing education, and week-long intensive courses, as well as in-house training programs, workshops, and conferences.

Successful Writing at Work, Concise Fourth Edition, provides students with easy-to-understand guidelines for writing and designing clear, well-organized, and readable documents. Along with user-friendly guidelines, this edition provides students with realistic models of the precise kinds of documents and e-communications they will be asked to write on the job. In addition, this text can serve as a ready reference that readers can easily carry with them to the workplace. Students will quickly find that this book includes many practical applications, which are useful to those who have little or no job experience as well as those with years of experience in the world of work.

Distinctive Features of *Successful Writing at Work, Concise Fourth Edition*

The distinctive features that have made *Successful Writing at Work, Concise Edition*, a user-friendly text in the contemporary workplace continue to be emphasized and expanded in this new, fourth edition. These features, emphasizing up-to-date approaches to teaching business writing, can be found throughout this edition:

1. **Approaching writing as a problem-solving activity.** The *Concise Fourth Edition* continues to approach writing not merely as a set of rules and formats but as a problem-solving activity in which employees meet the needs of their employers, co-workers, customers, clients, community groups, and vendors worldwide by getting to the bottom line. This approach to writing, introduced in Chapter 1 and carried throughout the text, helps students to think through the writing process by asking the key questions of *who* (who is the audience?), *why* (why do they need this document?), *what* (what is the message?), and *how* (how can the writer present the most appropriate style, tone, and format?). As in earlier editions, this new edition teaches students how to develop the critical skills necessary for planning, drafting, revising, editing, and formatting a variety of documents—from emails, instant messages (IMs), tweets, texts, blogs, letters, instructions, and proposals, to short and long reports. In addition, numerous case studies and figures demonstrate how writers answer these key questions to solve problems in the business world.

2. **Writing for the global marketplace.** In today's international workplace, effective employees must be consistently aware of how to write for a variety of readers, both in the United States and across the globe. Consequently, this new *Concise Fourth Edition* throughout emphasizes writing for international readers and non-native speakers of English. The needs and expectations of these international audiences receives special attention starting with Chapter 1 in the section "Writing for the Global Marketplace" and continues with coverage of writing letters for international speakers of English in Chapter 4, designing appropriate visuals and documents for this audience in Chapter 6, preparing clear instructions in Chapter 7, and making presentations for global audiences in Chapter 10. Especially important is the long report in Chapter 9 on the role international workers play in a corporation that must meet their needs and those of a global marketplace.

3. **Viewing student readers as business professionals.** To encourage students in their job-related writing, this new *Concise Fourth Edition* treats them as professionals seeking success at different phases of their business. Students are asked to place themselves in the workplace setting (or, in the case of Chapter 5, in the role of job seekers) as they approach each topic, to understand the differences between workplace and academic writing better. In Chapter 1, they are given the kinds of orientation to company culture and protocols that they might find in the early days of their employment. Students are then asked to see themselves

as members of a collaborative team drafting and developing an important workplace document (Chapter 2); workers writing routine e-communications and documents (Chapters 3 and 4); employees designing and writing more complex documents, such as instructions, proposals, and reports (Chapters 7, 8, and 9); co-workers designing documents, visuals, and websites (Chapter 6); and company representatives making presentations before co-workers and potential clients worldwide (Chapter 10).

4. **Using the latest workplace technologies.** This new edition offers the most current coverage of communication technologies for writing successfully in the rapidly changing world of work, including social media such as Facebook and Twitter, LinkedIn, email, instant messaging, texts, wikis, document tracking systems, and Google Docs (used to collaboratively draft, revise, and edit reports), business blogs, videoconferencing tools, and presentation software such as PowerPoint and Prezi. Coverage of these technologies is integrated into each chapter. Easy-to-understand explanations and annotated models throughout this edition assist students to discover the *hows* as well as the *whys* of writing and using visuals for the digital world of work.

5. **Being an ethical employee.** Companies and agencies expect their employees to behave and write ethically. As in earlier editions, the *Concise Fourth Edition* reinforces the importance of ethical workplace writing. Beginning with enhanced coverage of ethical writing and solving ethical dilemmas at work, Chapter 1 further stresses ethics in the workplace with a section titled "Ethical Writing in the Workplace." Special attention to ethics continues in sections of Chapter 2 on avoiding sexism and biased language in the workplace; Chapter 3 draws students' attention to the ethical choices they have to make when writing e-communications, including email, IMs, tweets, texts, and blogs. Ethics coverage continues with drafting diplomatic letters in Chapter 4, preparing honest and realistic résumés and web folios in Chapter 5, constructing unbiased and unaltered visuals and websites in Chapter 6, preparing safe and effective instructions in Chapter 7, writing honest and accurate proposals and reports in Chapters 8 and 9, and making clear and accurate presentations in Chapter 10.

New and Updated Material in *Successful Writing at Work: Concise Fourth Edition*

To help students in today's growing and changing global workplace, this new concise version is one of the most extensively revised editions of *Successful Writing at Work*. It has been carefully streamlined and updated to help students excel in the workplace. Throughout this new *Concise Fourth Edition*, there is expanded coverage of key topics, such as social and professional networking, new communication technologies, greening the workplace, guidelines for effective writing, and a wealth of new annotated examples of workplace documents, plus many new case studies.

With its new, full-color palette, the *Concise Fourth Edition* also exemplifies a wide range of professional design and layout choices that writers make in the world of work, thus giving students models to help them prepare their own documents. Not only has the layout of the text been redesigned, but many of the examples and figures have also benefited from the full-color adaptation and have been revised to show the variety of layouts, logos, and visual designs found in workplace documents.

Chapter-by-Chapter Updates

Here, then, chapter-by-chapter, are the new additions/features for the *Concise Fourth Edition*.

Chapter 1 Getting Started: Writing and Your Career

- *New* section on how writing relates to other skills in the world of work
- Revised case study on adapting technical information to meet the needs of diverse audiences within a corporate setting
- Expanded discussion, "Ethical Requirements on the Job"
- Further attention to solving ethical dilemmas in the workplace
- Additional exercises on diversity in the workplace and on audience analysis

Chapter 2 The Writing Process and Collaboration at Work

- Enhanced coverage of drafting, revising, and editing on the job
- Expanded case study, "A 'Before' and 'After' Revision of a Short Report"
- Additional advice on avoiding stereotypical language, including eliminating sexism
- Increased emphasis on being a team player in the world of work
- Greater attention to collaborative communication technologies
- Revised sections and figures illustrating the use of Track Changes in Microsoft Word and Google Docs for collaborative writing
- Updated discussion of conferencing tools
- *New* section on preparing for and conducting a meeting at work—setting an agenda, taking notes, summarizing ethically, and writing the minutes
- *New* section on videoconferencing with Skype

(New) Chapter 3 E-Communications at Work

- *Brand new* chapter brings together the major types of workplace e-communications and addresses crucial questions about the differences among them
- Discusses the importance of and differences among emails, IMs, tweets, texts, and blogs
- Substantially revised sections on emails and instant messaging in the workplace
- Expanded discussion of business blogs and job-related texting
- *New* section on the use of Twitter in the workplace

Chapter 4 Preparing Correspondence: Some Basics for Writing to Audiences Worldwide

- Further emphasis on the importance of letters and memos in the Internet Age
- Strengthened discussions of the business contexts for correspondence
- *New* section on cover letters
- Numerous redesigned business letters and memos
- Revised sections on writing different types of correspondence
- Greater attention to needs of international readers with an enhanced case study on adapting letters to international readers

Chapter 5 How to Get a Job: Searches, Networking, Dossiers, Portfolios/Webfolios, Résumés, Transitioning to a Civilian Job, Letters, and Interviews

- Expanded section on identifying and emphasizing marketable job skills
- Updated coverage on where to look for a job, with further examples of and advice on using job-posting sites
- *New* section "Using Online Social and Professional Networking Sites in Your Job Search"
- *New* section on LinkedIn with a new annotated figure of a LinkedIn profile with detailed commentary
- *New* section, "Transitioning to the Civilian Workforce," aimed at helping veterans prepare successful job application materials; includes new annotated skills résumé
- Updated and redesigned letters and résumés throughout the chapter
- Eight different résumés for print and digital formats presented as models for students
- Greater attention to online résumés, with two new model résumés
- *New* case study, "Creating an Online Resume for a Job Search"
- Expanded coverage of interview Do's and Don'ts
- Updated, practical advice on finding salary ranges and inquiring about salary
- Additional exercises on preparing online résumés and application letters
- Revised section on questions to expect at a job interview

Chapter 6 Designing Successful Documents, Visuals, and Websites

- Expanded section "Using Appropriate Visuals for International Audiences"
- Greater attention to documenting and citing visuals in written work
- *New* section on using infographs
- Several new figures of maps, pie charts, and edited photographs
- Enhanced discussion of using visuals for international readers
- Greater attention to creating ethical visuals
- *New* section on creating and incorporating reader-friendly headings and sub-headings in a document
- Further attention to understanding differences between writing for a print document and writing for the Web

Chapter 7 Writing Instructions and Procedures

- Increased coverage of preparing legally and ethically proper instructions and procedures
- Greater attention to writing, formatting, and illustrating online instructions
- Several *new*, annotated examples of online and print instructions
- *New*, fully annotated model of a set of lengthy instructions on assembling and using an all-in-one printer, illustrating the use of both print and online formats
- Enhanced discussion of how to write concise, clear, and effective workplace procedures
- Additional updated exercises

Chapter 8 Writing Effective Short Reports and Proposals

- Expanded discussion of how and why different audiences read a report
- Additional coverage of designing reader-friendly reports
- *New* case study on preparing a periodic report
- *New* section on "Employee Activity/Performance Reports" with a *new* carefully annotated model report
- Updated examples of sales and internal proposals
- *New* section on legal and ethical issues to consider when writing a proposal
- *New* sample internal proposal on purchasing inventory tracking software with helpful annotations
- Additional coverage of doing research an collaborating in writing short reports and proposals
- *New* exercises

Chapter 9 Documenting and Writing Careful Long Reports

- Revised discussion of transmittal letters
- *New* section on paginating a long report
- Additional coverage on developing and documenting conclusions and recommendations
- Coverage of latest MLA and APA documentation styles, with additional guidelines and updated examples
- Completely revised and updated model long report on meeting the needs of multinational workers

Chapter 10 Making Successful Presentations at Work

- Enhanced section on informal briefings with a new figure instructing bank employees how to detect and report counterfeit currency
- Revised advice and slides for a PowerPoint presentation
- *New* section on using Prezi software
- *New* section on specific audience needs for different types of presentations
- Revised discussion on evaluating a presentation

Additional Resources

Resources for Students   CENGAGE **brain**.com

On **CengageBrain.com** students will be able to save up to 60 percent on their course materials through our full spectrum of options. Students will have the option to rent their textbooks or purchase print textbooks, e-textbooks, or individual e-chapters and audio books, all for substantial savings over average retail prices. **CengageBrain.com** also includes access to Cengage Learning's broad range of homework and study tools and features a selection of free content.

English CourseMate. Cengage Learning's English CourseMate brings course concepts to life with interactive learning, study, and exam-preparation tools that support the printed textbook. CourseMate includes the following:

- The **MindTap Reader** is more than a digital version of a textbook. It is an interactive, learning resource that was built from the ground up to create a digital reading experience based on how students assimilate information in an online environment. **MindTap Reader** allows learners to make notes, highlight text, and even find definitions right from the page.
- Interactive teaching and learning tools, including
  - Interactive quizzes for each chapter in the text
  - Online exercises that help students enhance their understanding of chapter topics and improve their technology skills
  - Simulations that provide practice handling typical workplace situations
  - Documents for analysis
  - Web links that expand on topics in the text

Learn more at **www.cengage.com/coursemate**.

Resources for Instructors

Instructor's Edition (IE). Examination and desk copies of the Instructor's Edition of *Successful Writing at Work, Concise Fourth Edition*, are available upon request.

Online Instructor's Resource Manual. The Instructor's Manual contains resources designed to streamline and maximize the effectiveness of your course preparation. This helpful manual provides a sample course syllabus; suggestions for teaching job-related writing, with ideas for simulating real-world experience in the classroom; suggested approaches to exercises; and test items for each chapter.

Instructor's Website. This password-protected website includes chapter-level PowerPoint lecture slides, as well as the Online Instructor's Resource Manual, available for download.

English CourseMate. Cengage Learning's English CourseMate brings course concepts to life with interactive learning, study, and exam-preparation tools that support the printed textbook. CourseMate includes the following:

- The **MindTap Reader** is more than a digital version of a textbook. It is an interactive, learning resource that was built from the ground up to create a digital reading experience based on how students assimilate information in an online environment. **MindTap Reader** allows learners to make notes, highlight text, and even find definitions right from the page.

- Interactive teaching and learning tools, including
  - Interactive quizzes for each chapter in the text
  - Online exercises that help students enhance their understanding of chapter topics and improve their technology skills
  - Simulations that provide practice handling typical workplace situations
  - Documents for analysis
  - Web links that expand on topics in the text
- Engagement Tracker, a first-of-its-kind tool that monitors student engagement in the course

Learn more at **www.cengage.com/coursemate**.

Write Experience. Write Experience is a new technology product that allows you to assess written communication skills without adding to your workload. Write Experience utilizes artificial intelligence to not only score student writing instantly and accurately but also provide students with detailed revision goals and feedback on their writing to help them improve. Two key features of Write Experience, MYTutor and MYEditor, provide students with real-time, simultaneous feedback in their native language while they write! Learn more at **www.cengage .com/writeexperience**.

Please contact your local Cengage sales representative for more information, to evaluate examination copies of any of these instructor or student resources, or for product demonstrations. You may also contact the Cengage Learning Academic Resource Center at 800-423-0563, or visit us at **www.cengagebrain.com**.

Acknowledgments

In a very real sense, the *Successful Writing at Work, Concise Fourth Edition,* has profited from my collaboration with various reviewers. I am, therefore, honored to thank the following individuals who have helped me improve this edition significantly with their helpful comments: Jenny Billings Beaver, English Division Chair, *Rowan-Cabarrus Community College*; Ann E. Biswas, *University of Dayton*; William Carney, *Cameron University*; Darin Cozzens, *Surry Community College*; Terry Dale, *King Fahd University of Petroleum & Minerals*, Saudi Arabia; Carlos Evia, Director of Professional Writing at *Virginia Polytechnic Institute and State University*; Traci HalesVass, *San Juan College*; and Suba Subbarao, *Oakland Community College*.

I am also thankful for the reviewers of the last two editions of this book, whose comments also helped shape the revisions and new material added for this edition: Sonya Compton Borton, *University of Louisville*; Kristin Dietsche, *Northern Kentucky University*; Scott Downing, *DePaul University*; Eileen M. Finelli, *Northampton Community College*; Christy L. Kinnion, *Wake Technical Community*

College; Mary Mullaly, *Washtenaw Community College*; Ronald G. Mullins, *Bronx Community College*; Cynthia Murrell, *New Mexico State University*; Becky Newman, *Dixie Applied Technology College*; Linda Nicole Patino, *Surry Community College*; Andrea Penner, *San Juan College*; Catherine Ramsden, *DePaul University*; Lourdes Rassi, *Florida International University*; Leticia Slabaugh, *Arizona State University–Tempe*; David R. Swarts, *Clinton Community College*; and Carol Whittaker, *Pennsylvania State University*.

My thanks also go to the following individuals at the University of Southern Mississippi for their help—Linda Allen, Jeremy DeFatta, Sarah Taylor, Nikita Core, Danielle Sypher-Haley, Anna Beth Williams, chair Eric Tribunella (Department of English); David Tisdale (University Communications), Ann Branton (Cook Library), Mary Lux (Department of Medical Laboratory Science), Cliff Burgess (Department of Computer Science), Sandra Leal (Department of Biological Sciences), and Daniel Miles (Department of Biochemistry). I am especially grateful to Steven R. Moser, Dean of the College of Arts and Letters, for his continued appreciation of my work.

My gratitude also goes to Terri Smith Ruckel, Jianqing Zheng at Mississippi Valley State University, and Erin Smith at the University of Tennessee–Knoxville.

Several individuals from the business world also gave me wise counsel, for which I am deeply grateful—Sally Eddy at Georgia Pacific; Kirk Woodward at Visiting Nurses Services of New York; Jimmy Stockstill at Petro Automotive; Carrie Logan and Nancy Steen from Adelman & Steen, LLP; Teresa Rogers and Rachel Sullivan at Regents Bank, Inc.; Rick Leal; and Brig. General Steve Parham, U.S. Army.

I am also especially grateful to Father Michael Tracey for his counsel and contributions to Chapter 6 on document and website design.

My thanks go to the team at Cengage Learning for their assistance, encouragement, and friendship—Kate Derrick, Maggie Cross, Erin Bosco, Janine Tangney, Lydia LeStar, and Rebecca Donahue, and to content developer Ed Dodd for his always helpful assistance. I want to thank Ed Dionne at MPS Limited for his cooperation through the painstaking production cycle. I am also grateful to Jessica Elias at Cengage, and Sarah Andrews and Padma Priya at PreMedia Global, who handled the permissions for *Successful Writing at Work, Concise Fourth Edition*.

I thank my extended family—Margie and Al Parish, Sister Carmelita Stinn, SFCC, and Sister Annette Seymour, RSM, and Mary and Ralph Torrelli—for their prayers and love.

Finally, I am deeply grateful to my son, Eric, and my daughter-in-law, Theresa, for their enthusiastic and invaluable assistance as I prepared this edition; to my grandson, Evan Philip, and granddaughters, Megan Elise and Erica Marie, for their love and encouragement. My daughter, Kristin, also merits loving praise for her help throughout this new edition by doing various searches and revisions and by offering her knowledgeable, practical advice on successful writing at work.

P.C.K.
January 2014

CHAPTER 1

Getting Started

Writing and Your Career

Writing—An Essential Job Skill

Writing is a part of every job, from your initial letter of application conveying first impressions to memos, emails, blogs, letters, websites, proposals, instructions, and reports. Writing keeps businesses moving. It allows employees to communicate with one another, with management, and with the customers, clients, and agencies a company must serve to stay in business. A survey conducted by the McKinsey Global Insitute found that workers spend more than 2½ hours a day just reading and answering their emails.

How Writing Relates to Other Skills

Almost everything you do at work is related to your writing ability. Deborah Price, a human resource director with thirty years of experience, stresses that "without the ability to write clearly an employee cannot perform the other duties of the job, regardless of the company he or she works for." Here is a list of the common tasks you will be expected to perform in the workplace that will require clear and concise writing to get them done well.

- Assess a situation, a condition, a job site, etc.
- Research and record the results accurately.
- Summarize information concisely and identify main points quickly.
- Work as part of a team to collect, to share, and to evaluate information.
- Tackle and solve problems and explain how and why you did.
- Display cultural sensitivity in the workplace.
- Network with individuals in diverse fields outside your company and across the globe.
- Answer customer questions and meet their needs.
- Prepare and test instructions and procedures.
- Justify financial, personnel, or other actions and decisions.
- Make persuasive presentations to co-workers, employers, and clients.

To perform each of these essential workplace tasks, you have to be an effective writer—clear, concise, accurate, ethical, and persuasive.

The High Cost of Effective Writing

Clearly, then, writing is an essential skill for employees and employers alike. According to Don Bagin, a communications consultant, most people need an hour or more to write a typical business letter. If an employer is paying someone $30,000 a year, one letter costs $14 of that employee's time; for someone who earns $50,000 a year, the cost for the average letter jumps to $24. Mistakes in letters are costly for workers as well as for employers. As David Noble cautions in his book *Gallery of Best Cover Letters*, "The cost of a cover letter (in applying for a job, for instance) might be as much as a third of a million dollars—even more if you figure the amount of income and benefits you don't receive, say, in a 10-year period for a job you don't get because of an error that got you screened out."

Unfortunately, as the Associated Press (AP) reported in a recent survey, "Most American businesses say workers need to improve their writing . . . skills." Yet that same report cited a survey of more than 400 companies that identified writing as "the most valuable skill employees can have." In fact, the employers polled in that AP survey indicated that 80 percent of their workforce needed to improve their writing. Beyond a doubt, your success as an employee will depend on your success as a writer. The higher you advance in an organization, the more and better writing you will be expected to do. Promotions, and other types of job recognition, are often based on an employee's writing skills.

How This Book Will Help You

This book will show you, step by step, how to write clearly and efficiently the job-related communications you need for success in the world of work. Chapter 1 gives you some basic information about writing in the global marketplace and raises major questions you need to ask yourself to make the writing process easier and the results more effective. It also describes the basic functions of on-the-job writing and introduces you to one of the most important requirements in the business world—writing ethically.

Writing for the Global Marketplace

The Internet, teleconferencing, digital communications, and m-commerce have shrunk the world into a global village. Accordingly, it is no longer feasible to think of business in exclusively regional or even national terms. Many companies are multinational corporations with offices throughout the world. In fact, many U.S. businesses are branches of international firms. A large, multinational corporation may have its equipment designed in Japan; built in Bangladesh; and sold in Detroit, Atlanta, and Los Angeles. Its stockholders may be in Mexico City as well as Saudi Arabia—in fact, anywhere. In this global economy, every country is affected by every other one, and all of them are connected by the Internet.

Competing for International Business

Companies must compete for international sales to stay in business. Every business, whether large or small, has to appeal to diverse international markets to be competitive. Each year a larger share of the U.S. gross national product (GNP) depends on global markets. Some U.S. firms estimate that 50 to 60 percent of their business is conducted outside of the United States. Walmart, for example, has opened hundreds of stores in mainland China, and General Electric has plants in more than fifty countries. In fact, estimates suggest that 75 percent of the global Internet population lives outside the United States. If your company, however small, has a website, then it is an international business.

Communicating with Global Audiences

To be a successful employee in this highly competitive global market, you have to communicate clearly and diplomatically with a host of readers from different cultural backgrounds. Adopting a global perspective on business will help you communicate and build goodwill with the customers you write to, no matter where they live—across town, in another state, or on other continents, miles and time zones away. As a result, don't presume that you will be writing only to native speakers of American English. As a part of your job, you may communicate with readers in Singapore, Jamaica, and South Africa, for example, who speak varieties of English quite different from American English. You will also very likely be writing to readers for whom English is not their first (or native) language. Your international readers will have varying degrees of proficiency in English, from a fairly good command (as with many readers in India and the Philippines, where English is widely spoken), to little comprehension without the use of a foreign language dictionary and a grammar book. Non-native speakers, who may reside either in the United States or in a foreign country, will constitute a large and important audience for your work.

Seeing the World Through the Eyes of Another Culture

Writing to international readers with proper business etiquette means first learning about their cultural values and assumptions—what they value and also what they regard as communication taboos. They may not conduct business exactly the way it is done in the United States, and to think they should is wrong. Your international audience is likely to have different expectations of how they want a letter addressed or written to them, whether they allow you to use their first name, how they wish a business meeting to be conducted, or how they think questions should be asked and agreements reached. Their concepts of time, family, money, the world, the environment, managers, and communication itself may be nothing like those in the United States. Visuals, including icons, that are easily understood in the United States may be baffling elsewhere in the world. If you misunderstand your audience's culture and inadvertently write, create, or say something inappropriate, it can cost your company a contract and you your job.

Cultural Diversity at Home

Cultural diversity exists inside as well as outside the company you work for. Don't conclude that your boss or co-workers are all native speakers of English, either, or that they come from the same cultural background that you do. In the next decade, as much as 40 to 50 percent of the U.S. skilled workforce may be composed of recent immigrants who bring their own traditions and languages with them. These are highly educated, multicultural, and multinational individuals who have acquired English as a second or even a third language.

For the common good of your company, you need to be respectful of your international colleagues. In fact, multinational employees can be tremendously important for your company in making contacts in their native country and in helping your firm understand and appreciate ethical and cultural differences among customers. The model long report in Chapter 9 (pages 367–380) describes some ways in which a company can both acknowledge and respect the different cultural traditions of its international employees. Businesses want to emphasize their international commitments. A large corporation such as Citibank, for instance, is eager to promote its image of helping customers worldwide, as Figure 1.1 shows.

Using International English

Whether your international readers are customers or colleagues, you need to adapt your writing to respect their language needs and cultural protocols. To communicate with non-native speakers, use "international English," a way of writing that is easily understood, culturally appropriate, and diplomatic. International English is user friendly in terms of the words, sentences, formats, and visuals you choose.

To write international English means you re-examine your own writing. The words, idioms, phrases, and sentences you select instinctively for U.S. readers may not be appropriate for an audience for whom English is a second, or even a third, language. If you find the set of instructions accompanying your software package confusing, imagine how much more intimidating such a document would be for non-native speakers of English. You can eliminate such confusion by making your message clear, straightforward, and appropriately polite for readers who are not native speakers.

Here are some basic guidelines to help you write international English:

- Use clear, easy-to-understand sentences, not rambling, complex ones. That does not mean you write insultingly short and simple sentences but that you take into account that readers will find your message easier to translate if your sentences do not exceed fifteen to twenty words.
- Do not try to pack too much information into a single sentence; consider using two or more sentences instead (see pages 46–50).
- Avoid jargon, idioms (e.g., "to line one's pockets"), and abbreviations (e.g., "FEMA") that international readers may not know.
- Choose clear, commonly used words that unambiguously translate into the non-native speaker's language. Avoid flowery or pretentious language (e.g., "amend" for "change").

FIGURE 1.1 A Company's Dedication to Globalization

How Citigroup Meets Banking Needs Around the World

WITH A BANKING EMPIRE that spans more than 100 countries, Citigroup is experienced at meeting the diverse financial services needs of businesses, individuals, customers, and governments. The bank is headquartered in New York City but has offices in Africa, Asia, Central and South America, Europe, the Middle East, as well as throughout North America. Live or work in Japan? You can open a checking account at Citigroup's Citibank branch in downtown Tokyo. How about Mexico? Visit a Grupo Financiero Banamex-Accival branch, owned by Citigroup. Citigroup owns European American Bank and has even bought a stake in a Shanghai-based bank with an eye toward attracting more of China's $1 trillion in bank deposits. Between acquisitions and long-established branches, Citigroup covers the globe from the Atlantic to the Pacific and the Indian Oceans.

AP Photo/Greg Baker

Citigroup is active in communities around the world through . . . financial literacy seminars, volunteerism, and supplier diversity programs. This financial services giant strives for the best of both worlds, wielding its global presence and resources to meet banking needs locally, one customer at a time.

Source: From PRIDE, Business, 8E. © 2005 Cengage Learning

- Select visuals and icons that are free from cultural bias and that are not taboo in the non-native speaker's country. (For more on this, see pages 253–256.)
- When in doubt, consult someone from the native speaker's country—a co-worker or an instructor, for example.

Because it is so important, international English is discussed in greater detail on pages 141–146. Later chapters of this book will also give you additional practical guidelines on writing correspondence, instructions, proposals, reports, websites, PowerPoint presentations, and other work-related documents suitable for a global audience.

Four Keys to Effective Writing

Effective writing on the job is carefully planned, thoroughly researched, and clearly presented. Its purpose is always to accomplish a specific goal and to be as persuasive as possible. Whether you send a routine email to a co-worker in Cincinnati or Shanghai or a commissioned report to the president of the company, your writing will be more effective if you ask yourself these four questions:

1. Who will read what I write? (Identify your audience.)
2. Why should they read what I write? (Establish your purpose.)
3. What do I have to say to them? (Formulate your message.)
4. How can I best communicate? (Select an appropriate style and tone.)

The questions *who*, *why*, *what*, and *how* do not function independently; they are all related. You write (1) for a specific audience (2) with a clearly defined purpose in mind (3) about a topic your readers need to understand (4) in language appropriate for the occasion. Once you answer the first question, you are off to a good start toward answering the other three. Now let's examine each of the four questions in detail.

Identifying Your Audience

Knowing *who* makes up your audience is one of your most important responsibilities as a writer. Keep in mind that you are not writing for yourself but for a specific reader or group of readers. Expect to analyze your audience throughout the composing process.

Look at the advertisements in Figures 1.2, 1.3, and 1.4. The main purpose of all three documents is the same—to discourage people from smoking. The underlying message in each ad—smoking is dangerous to your health—is also the same. But note how the different details—words, photographs, situations—have been selected to appeal to three different audiences.

The advertisement in Figure 1.2 is aimed at fathers who smoke. As you can see, it shows an image of a father smoking next to his son, who is reaching for his pack of cigarettes. Note how the headline "Will your child follow in your footsteps?" plays on the fact that the father and son are both literally sitting on steps, but at the same time it implies that the son will imitate his father's behavior as a smoker. The statistic at the bottom of the advertisement reinforces both the headline and the image, hitting home the point that parental behavior strongly influences children's behavior. The child in the photograph already is following his father by showing a clear interest in smoking, picking up his father's pack of cigarettes.

The advertisement in Figure 1.3, however, is aimed at an audience of pregnant women and shows a member of this audience with a lit cigarette. The words on the advertisement appeal to a mother's sense of responsibility, encouraging pregnant women to stop smoking to avoid harm to their unborn children.

Figure 1.4 (page 8) is directed toward still another audience: young athletes. The word *smoke* in this advertisement is aimed directly at their game and their goal. The headline includes a pun. The writer aptly made the goal the same for the game as well as for the players' lives. Note, too, how this image with its four photos is suitable for an international audience.

FIGURE 1.2 No-Smoking Advertisement Aimed at Fathers Who Smoke

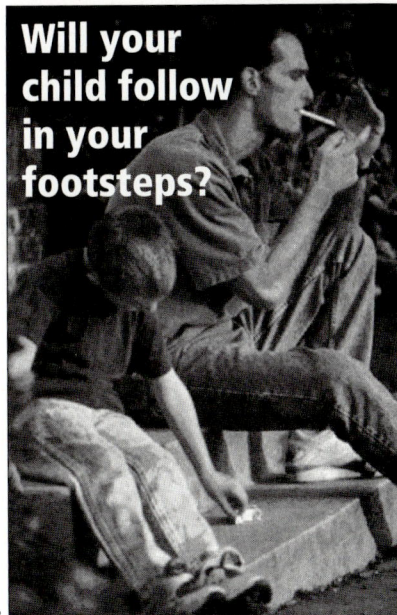

Will your child follow in your footsteps?

Children whose parents smoke are 50% more likely to start smoking than children whose parents don't smoke.

Peter Poulides/Getty Images

FIGURE 1.3 No-Smoking Advertisement Directed at Pregnant Women

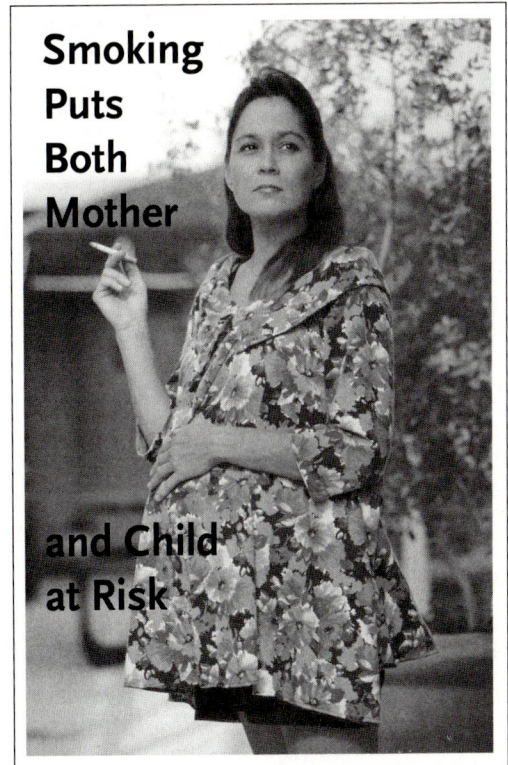

Smoking Puts Both Mother and Child at Risk

Photo by Bill Crump/Brand X Pictures/Fotosearch/Royalty-Free Image

FIGURE 1.4 No-Smoking Advertisement Appealing to Young Athletes

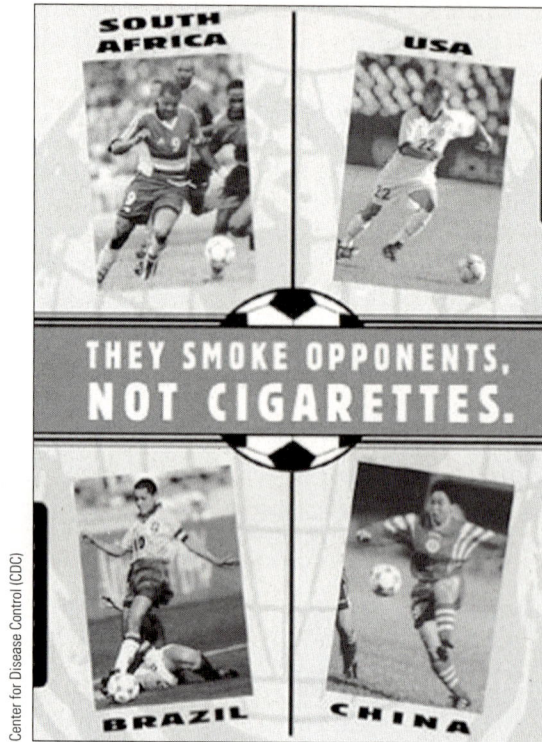

Center for Disease Control (CDC)

The copywriters who created these advertisements have chosen appropriate details—words, pictures, captions, and so on—to persuade each audience not to smoke. With their careful choices, they successfully answered the question "How can we best communicate with each audience?" Note that details relevant for one audience (athletes, for example) could not be used as effectively for another audience (such as fathers).

The three advertisements in Figures 1.2, 1.3, and 1.4 illustrate some fundamental points you need to keep in mind when identifying your audience:

- Members of each audience differ in their backgrounds, experiences, and needs.
- How you picture your audience will determine what you say to them.
- Viewing something from the audience's perspective will help you to select the most relevant details for that audience.

Some Questions to Ask About Your Audience

You can form a fairly accurate picture of your audience by asking yourself key questions before you write. For each audience you need to reach, consider the following questions:

1. **Who is my audience?** What individual(s) will most likely be reading my work?

   If you are writing for colleagues or managers at work:

   - What is my reader's job title? Is he or she a co-worker? Immediate supervisor? Vice president?
   - What kinds of job experience, education, and interests does my reader have?

   If you are writing for clients or consumers (a very large, often diverse audience):

   - How can I find out about their interest in my product or service?
   - How much will this audience know about my company? About me?

2. **How many people will make up my audience?**

   - Will just one individual read what I write (the nurse on the next shift, the production manager), or will many people read it (all the consumers of my company's product or service)?
   - Will my boss want to see my work (say, a letter to a consumer in response to a complaint) to approve it?
   - Will I be sending my message to a large group of people sharing a similar interest in my topic?

3. **How well does my audience understand English?**

   - Are all my readers native speakers of English?
   - Will I be communicating with people around the globe?
   - Will some of my readers speak English as a second or even a third language and thereby require extra sensitivity on my part to their needs?
   - Will some of my readers speak no English and instead use an English grammar book, a foreign language dictionary, or perhaps an online translator, such as Google Translate, for email or webpages where you just copy and paste the text into the translate window?

4. **How much does my audience already know about my topic?**

   - Will my readers know as much as I do about the particular problem or issue, or will they need to be briefed, be given background information, or be updated?
   - Are my readers familiar with, and do they expect me to use, technical terms and descriptions, or will I have to provide definitions and easy-to-understand, nontechnical wording and visuals?

5. **What is my audience's reason for reading my work?**

   - Is my communication part of their routine duties, or are they looking for information to solve a problem or make a decision?
   - Am I writing to describe benefits that another writer or company cannot offer?
   - Will my readers expect complete details, or will a short summary be enough?
   - Are they looking at my work to make an important decision affecting a co-worker, a client, a community, government agency, or the environment?
   - Are they reading something I write because they must (a legal notification or an incident report, for instance)?

Writing to Different Audiences in a Large Corporation

Jan Melius works in the Communication Department of GrandCo, a firm that manufactures large heavy-duty equipment. As a regular part of her job, Melius has to prepare documents for several different audiences, including the management and staff at GrandCo, current and potential customers, and the greater community of Fairfield where the company is located. Each group of her readers will have different requirements and expectations, and she has to understand those differences if she wants to meet their needs. Often the documents that she prepares are a result of her collaborations with individuals (accountants, engineers, safety and security) at GrandCo as well as at other companies (suppliers) and community leaders. She also has to decide on the right type of document (e.g., brochure, email, memo, report, blog) to send to her readers.

    Below is a list of the audiences that Melius writes for or to, along with the kinds of documents they need with examples of appropriate information found in these documents.

Audience	Types of Information/Documents to Supply
Customer	Ads, websites, proposals urging customers to buy a GrandCo model, stressing its state-of-the-art advantages over the competition's and the specific benefits GrandCo offers (cost, service, quality, efficiency)
Owner or Principal Executive	Short and long reports on sales, cash flow, productivity, market trends; research about potential competition
Production Engineer	Reports on design and manufacturing models, including spec sheets, diagrams, etc., on transmissions, strength of materials; status reports following Environmental Protection Agency (EPA) or Occupational Safety and Health Administration (OSHA) guidelines
Production Supervisor	Service reports about schedules, staffing needs, and employee activity reports; availability of parts from vendors
Operator	Instructions in manuals on operating equipment safely and responsibly; warnings about any type of precautions; information on necessary special training
Maintenance Worker	Reports and guidelines about maintenance procedures; schedules; checklists of items to be inspected; troubleshooting procedures
Community Residents	News releases about GrandCo's sponsoring events, offering tours or demonstrations; blogs on how GrandCo is greening the workplace; articles on GrandCo's dedication to community environment and safety; hiring notices

As these examples show, to succeed in the world of work, give each reader the details he or she needs to accomplish a given job.

6. **What are my audience's expectations about my written work?**

   - Do they want an email, or will they expect a formal letter?
   - Will they expect me to follow a company format and style?
   - Are they looking for a one-page memo or for a comprehensive report?
   - Should I use a formal tone or a more relaxed and conversational style?

7. **What is my audience's attitude toward me and my work?**

   - Will I be writing to a group of disgruntled and angry customers or vendors about a sensitive issue (a product recall, the discontinuation of a service, a refusal of credit, or a shipment delay)?
   - Will I have to be sympathetic while at the same time give firm, convincing reasons for my company's (or my) decision?
   - Will my readers be skeptical, indifferent, or accepting about what I write?
   - Will my readers feel guilty that they have not answered an earlier message of mine, not paid a bill now overdue, or not kept a commitment?

8. **What do I want my audience to do after reading my work?**

   - Do I want my readers to purchase something from me, approve my plan, or send me additional documentation?
   - Do I expect my readers to acknowledge my message, save it for future reference, or review and email it to another individual or office?
   - Do my readers have to take immediate action, or do they have several days or weeks to respond?
   - Do I simply want my readers to get my message and not respond at all?

As your answers to these questions will show, you may have to communicate with many different audiences on your job. Each group of readers will have different expectations and requirements; you need to understand those audience differences if you want to supply relevant information.

Establishing Your Purpose

By knowing *why* you are writing, you will communicate better and find the writing process itself to be easier. The reader's needs and your goal in communicating will help you to formulate your purpose. It will guide you in determining exactly what you can and must say.

Make sure you follow the most important rule in occupational writing: *Get to the point right away*. At the beginning of your message, state your goal clearly. Don't feel as if you have to entertain or impress your reader.

> I want new employees to know how to log on to the computer.

Think over what you have written. Rewrite your purpose statement until it states precisely why you are writing and what you want your readers to do or to know.

> I want to teach new employees the security code for logging on to the company computer.

Since your purpose controls the amount and order of information you include, state it clearly at the beginning of every email, memo, letter, and report.

> This email will acquaint new employees with the security measures they must take when logging on to the company computer.

In the opening purpose statement that follows, note how the author clearly informs the reader what the report will and will not cover.

> As you requested at last month's organizational meeting, I have conducted a survey of how well our websites advertise our products. This survey describes users' responses but does not prioritize them.

Formulating Your Message

Your message is the sum of the facts, responses, and recommendations you put into writing. A message includes the scope and details of your communication.

- *Scope* refers to how much information you give readers about key details.
- *Details* are the key points you think readers need to know.

Some messages will consist of one or two phrases or sentences: "Do not touch; wet paint." "Order #756 was sent this afternoon by express shipment. It should arrive at your office on March 22." At the other extreme, messages may extend over many pages. Messages may carry good news or bad news. They may deal with routine matters, or they may handle changes in policy, special situations, or problems.

Keep in mind that you will need to adapt your message to fit your audience. For some audiences, such as engineers or technicians, you may have to supply a complete report with every detail noted or contained in an appendix. For other readers—busy executives, for example—include only a summary of financial or managerial significance. (See page 369 for an example of an abstract.)

Selecting Your Style and Tone

Style

Style refers to *how* something is written rather than what is written. Style helps to determine how well you communicate with an audience and how well your readers understand and receive your message. It involves the choices you make about

- the construction of your paragraphs
- the length and patterns of your sentences
- your choice of words

You will have to adapt your style to take into account different messages, different purposes, and different audiences. Your words, for example, will certainly vary with your audience. If all your readers are specialists in your field, you may safely use the technical language and symbols of your profession. Nonspecialists, however, will be confused and annoyed if you write to them in the same way. The average consumer, for example, will not know what a potentiometer is; but if you write "volume control on a radio" instead, you will be using words that the general public can understand. And as we saw, when you write for an international audience you have to take into account their proficiency in English and choose your words and sentences with their needs in mind (see pages 3–6).

Tone

Tone in writing, like tone of voice, expresses your attitude toward a topic and toward your audience. Your tone can range from formal and impersonal (a scientific report) to informal and personal (an email to a friend or a how-to article for consumers). Your tone can be unprofessionally sarcastic or diplomatically agreeable.

Tone, like style, is indicated in part by the words you choose. For example, saying that someone is "interested in details" conveys a more positive tone than saying the person is a "nitpicker." The word *economical* is more positive than *stingy* or *cheap*.

Case Study

Adapting a Description of Heparin for Two Different Audiences

In the workplace you will often be faced with the problem of presenting the same information to two completely different audiences. To better understand the impact that style and tone can have when you have to solve this problem, read the following two descriptions of heparin, a drug used to prevent blood clots. In both descriptions, the message is basically the same. Yet because the audiences differ, so do the style and the tone.

The first description of heparin appears in a reference work for physicians and other health care providers and is written in a highly technical style with an impersonal tone appropriate for the contexts in which this medicine is discussed.

The writer has made the appropriate stylistic choices for the audience, the purpose, and the message. Health care providers understand and expect the jargon and the scientific explanations, which enable them to prescribe or administer heparin correctly. The writer's authoritative, impersonal tone is coldly clinical, which, of course, is also appropriate because the purpose is to convey the accurate, complete scientific facts about this drug, not the writer's or reader's personal opinions or beliefs. The writer sounds both knowledgeable and objective.

Technical Description

Heparin Sodium Injection, USP Sterile Solution

Description: Heparin Sodium Injection, USP is a sterile solution of heparin sodium derived from bovine lung tissue, standardized for anticoagulant activity.

Each ml of the 1,000 and 5,000 USP units per ml preparations contains heparin sodium 1,000 or 5,000 USP units; 9 mg sodium chloride; 9.45 mg benzyl alcohol added as preservative. Each ml of the 10,000 USP units per ml preparations contains heparin sodium 10,000 units; 9.45 mg benzyl alcohol added as a preservative.

When necessary, the pH of Heparin Sodium Injection, USP was adjusted with hydrochloric acid and/or sodium hydroxide. The pH range is 5.0–7.5.

(Continued)

Clinical pharmacology: Heparin inhibits reactions that lead to the clotting of blood and the formation of fibrin clots both *in vitro* and *in vivo*. Heparin acts at multiple sites in the normal coagulation system. Small amounts of heparin in combination with antithrombin III (heparin cofactor) can inhibit thrombosis by inactivating activated Factor X and inhibiting the conversion of prothrombin to thrombin.

Dosage and administration: Heparin sodium is not effective by oral administration and should be given by intermittent intravenous injection, intravenous infusion, or deep subcutaneous (intrafrat, i.e., above the iliac crest or abdominal fat layer) injection. **The intramuscular route of administration should be avoided because of the frequent occurrence of hematoma at the injection site.**[1]

The second description of heparin below, however, is written in a nontechnical style and with an informal, caring tone. This description is similar to those found on information sheets given to patients about the medications they are receiving in a hospital.

The writer of this patient-centered description has also made appropriate choices for nonspecialists, such as patients or their families, who do not need elaborate descriptions of the origin and composition of the drug. Using familiar words and adopting a personal, friendly tone help to win the patients' confidence and enable them to understand why and how they should take the drug.

Nontechnical Description

Patient Information Sheet

Your doctor has prescribed a drug called *heparin* for you. This drug will prevent any new blood clots from forming in your body. Since heparin cannot be absorbed from your stomach or intestines, you will not receive it in a capsule or tablet. Instead, it will be given into a vein or the fatty tissue of your abdomen. After several days, when the danger of clotting is past, your dosage of heparin will be gradually reduced. Then another medication you can take by mouth will be started.

The tone of your writing is especially important in occupational writing because it reflects the image you project to your readers and thus determines how they will respond to you, your work, and your company. Depending on your tone, you can appear sincere and intelligent or angry and uninformed. Of course, in all your written work, you need to sound professional and knowledgeable. The wrong tone

---

[1] *Source: Physicians' Desk Reference*® 45th edition, 1991, published by Medical Economics, Montvale, NJ 07645.

in a letter or a proposal might cost you a customer. Sarcastic or hostile language will alienate you from your readers, as the letters in Figures 4.5 and 4.10 demonstrate (see pages 109 and 120).

Characteristics of Job-Related Writing

Job-related writing characteristically serves six basic functions: (1) to provide practical information, (2) to give facts rather than impressions, (3) to supply visuals to clarify and condense information, (4) to give accurate measurements, (5) to state responsibilities precisely, and (6) to persuade and offer recommendations. These six functions tell you what kind of writing you will produce after you successfully answer the *who, why, what,* and *how.*

1. Providing Practical Information

On-the-job writing requires a practical "here's what you need to do or to know" approach. One such practical approach is *action oriented.* You instruct the reader to do something—assemble a ceiling fan, test for bacteria, perform an audit, or create a website. Another practical approach of job-related writing is *knowledge oriented.* You explain what you want the reader to understand—why a procedure was changed, what caused a problem or solved it, how much progress was made on a job site, or why a new piece of equipment should be purchased.

The following description of the Energy Efficiency Ratio combines both the action-oriented and knowledge-oriented approaches of practical writing.

> Whether you are buying window air-conditioning units or a central air-conditioning system, consider the performance factors and efficiency of the various units on the market. Before you buy, determine the Energy Efficiency Ratio (EER) of the units under consideration. The EER is found by dividing the BTUs (units of heat) that the unit removes from the area to be cooled by the watts (amount of electricity) the unit consumes. The result is usually a number between 5 and 12. The higher the number, the more efficiently the unit will use electricity.[2]

2. Giving Facts, Not Impressions

Occupational writing is concerned with what can be seen, heard, felt, tasted, or smelled. The writer uses *concrete language* and specific details. The emphasis is on facts rather than on the writer's feelings or guesses.

The discussion below, addressed to a group of scientists about the sources of oil spills and their impact on the environment, is an example of writing with objectivity. It describes events and causes without anger or tears. Imagine how much emotion would have been packed into a paragraph by the residents of the coastal states who watched massive spills come ashore recently.

> The most critical impact results from the escapement of oil into the ecosystem, both crude oil and refined fuel oils, the latter coming from sources such as marine traffic. Major oil spills occur as a result of accidents such as blowout, pipeline breakage, etc.

---

[2] *Source:* New Orleans Public Services, Inc.

Technological advances coupled with stringent regulations [can] reduce the chances of such major spills; however, there is [still] a chronic low-level discharge of oil associated with normal drilling and production operations. Waste oils discharged through the river systems and practices associated with tanker transports dump more significant quantities of oils into the ocean, compared to what is introduced by the offshore oil industry. All of this contributes to the chronic low-level discharge of oil into world oceans. The long-range cumulative effect of these discharges is possibly the most significant threat to the ecosystem.[3]

3. Supplying Visuals to Clarify and Condense Information

Visuals are indispensable partners of words in conveying information to your readers. On-the-job writing makes frequent use of visuals—such as tables, charts, photographs, flow charts, diagrams, and drawings—to clarify and condense information. Thanks to various software packages, you can easily create and insert visuals into your writing. The use of visuals is discussed in detail in Chapter 6, and PowerPoint and Prezi presentations are covered in Chapter 10.

Visuals play an important role in the workplace. Note how the photograph in Figure 1.5 can help computer users to better understand and follow the accompanying written ergonomics guidelines. A visual like this, reproduced in an employee handbook or displayed on a website, can significantly reduce physical stress and increase a worker's productivity.

The following graphic devices in your letters, reports, and websites can also make your writing easier to read and follow:

- headings, such as "Four Keys to Effective Writing" or "Characteristics of Job-Related Writing"
- subheadings to divide major sections into parts, such as "Providing Practical Information" or "Giving Facts, Not Impressions"
- numbers within a paragraph, or even a line, such as (1) this, (2) this, and (3) also this
- different types of s p a c i n g
- CAPITALIZATION (use sparingly only when necessary)
- *italics* (easily made by a word processing command or indicated in typed copy by underscoring)
- **boldface** (darker print for emphasis)
- symbols (visual markers such as →)
- hypertext (Internet links, often presented underscored, in boldface, or in a different color)
- asterisks (*) to separate items or to note key information
- lists with bullets (like those before each entry in this list)

Keep in mind that graphic devices should be used carefully and in moderation, not to decorate a letter or report. When used properly, they can help you to

- organize, arrange, and emphasize your ideas
- make your work easier to read and to recall

---

[3] *Source:* The Offshore Ecology Investigation.

FIGURE 1.5 Use of a Visual to Convey Information

Using Your Computer Safely

By following the bulleted guidelines below, and illustrated in the photo to the right, you can avoid workplace injuries when using your computer.

- **To reduce the possibility of eye damage**, maintain a distance of 18 to 24 inches between your eyes and the computer screen and always make sure to keep your work area well lit.

- **To minimize neck strain**, position your computer screen so that the top of the screen is at or just below your eye level.

- **To avoid back and shoulder strain**, sit up straight at a right angle in your chair with your shoulders relaxed and your lower back firmly supported (with a cushion, if necessary).

- **To lessen leg and back strain**, adjust your chair height so that your upper body and your legs form a 90-degree angle and that your feet are either flat on the floor or on a footrest.

18"–24"

90-degree angle

Footrest

Ergo Concepts, LLC

© Cengage Learning

- preview and summarize your ideas, for example, through boldface headings
- list related items to help readers distinguish, follow, compare, and recall them—as this bulleted list does

4. Giving Accurate Measurements

Much of your work will depend on measurements—acres, bytes, calories, kilometers, centimeters, degrees, dollars and cents, grams, percentages, pounds, square feet, and so on. Numbers are clear and convincing. However, you must be sensitive to which units of measurement you use when writing to international readers. Not every culture computes in dollars or records temperatures in degrees Fahrenheit.

The following discussion of mixing colored cement for a basement floor would be useless to readers if it did not supply accurate quantities:

Including permanent color in a basement floor is a good selling point. One way of doing this is by incorporating commercially pure mineral pigments in a topping mixture placed to a 1-inch depth over a normal base slab. The topping mix should range in volume between 1 part portland cement, 1¼ parts sand, and 1¼ parts gravel or crushed stone and 1 part portland cement, 2 parts sand, and 2 parts gravel or crushed stone. Maximum size gravel or crushed stone should be ⅜ inch.

Mix cement and pigment before aggregate and water are added and be very thorough to secure uniform dispersion and the full color value of the pigment. The proportion varies from 5 to 10 percent of pigment by weight of cement, depending on the shade desired. If carbon black is used as a pigment to obtain grays or black, a proportion of from ½ to 1 percent will be adequate. Manufacturers' instructions should be followed closely; care in cleanliness, placing, and finishing are also essential. Colored topping mixes are available from some suppliers of ready mixed concrete.[4]

5. Stating Responsibilities Precisely

Because it is directed to a specific audience, your job-related writing should make absolutely clear what it expects of, or can do for, that audience. Misunderstandings waste time, cost money, and can result in injuries. Directions on order forms, for example, should indicate how and where information is to be listed and how it is to be routed and acted on. The following directions show readers how to perform different tasks:

- Enter agency code numbers in the message box.
- Items 1 through 16 of this form should be completed by the injured employee or by someone acting on his or her behalf, whenever an injury is sustained on the job. The term *injury* includes occupational disease caused by the employment. The form should be given to the employee's official superior within 12–24 hours following the injury. The official superior is that individual having responsible supervision over the employee.

Other kinds of job-related writing deal with the writer's responsibilities rather than the reader's, for example, "Tomorrow I will meet with the district sales manager to discuss (1) July's sales, (2) the opportunities of expanding our market, and (3) next fall's production schedule. I will send a PDF of our discussion by August 3."

6. Persuading and Offering Recommendations

Persuasion is a crucial part of writing on the job. In fact, it is one of the most crucial skills you can learn in the business world. Persuasion means trying to convince your reader(s) to accept your ideas, approve your recommendations, or order your products. Convincing your reader to accept your interpretation or ideas is at the heart of the world of work, whether you are writing to someone outside or inside your company.

Writing Persuasively to Clients and Customers

Much of your writing in the business world will promote your company's image by persuading customers and clients (a) to buy a product or service, (b) to adopt a plan of action endorsed by your employer, or (c) to support a particular cause or campaign that affects a community. You will have to convince readers that you (and your company)—your products and services—can save them time and money, increase efficiency, reduce risks, or improve their image and that you can do this better than your competitors can.

---

[4] *Source: Concrete Construction Magazine*, World of Concrete Center, 426 S. Westgate, Addison, IL 60101.

Expect also to be called on to write convincingly about your company's image, as in the case of product recalls, customer complaints, or damage control after a corporate mistake affecting the environment. You may also have to convince customers around the globe that your company respects cultural diversity and upholds specific ethnic values.

A large part of being a persuasive writer is supporting your claims with evidence. You will have to conduct research; provide logical arguments; supply appropriate facts, examples, and statistics; and identify the most relevant information for your particular audience(s). Notice how the advertisement in Figure 1.6 offers a bulleted list of persuasive reasons—based on cost, time, efficiency, safety, and convenience—to convince correctional officials that they should use General Medical's services rather than those of a hospital or clinic.

Writing Persuasively to In-House Personnel

As much as 70 percent of your writing may be directed to individuals you work with and for. In fact, your very first job-related writing will likely be a persuasive letter of application to obtain a job interview with a potential employer.

On the job, you may have to persuade a manager to buy a new technology or lobby for a change in your office or department. To be successful, you will have to evaluate various products or options by studying, analyzing, and deciding on the

FIGURE 1.6 An Advertisement Employing Persuasive Arguments to Convince Potential Customers to Use a Service

Visual stresses the need for a more efficient way to transport prisoners for medical attention

GENERAL MEDICAL WILL STOP THE UNNECESSARY TRANSPORTING OF YOUR INMATES.

- We'll bring our X-ray services to your facility, 7 days a week, 24 hours a day.
- We can reduce your X-ray costs by a minimum of 28%. X-ray cost includes radiologist's interpretation and written report.
- Same-day service with immediate results telephoned to your facility.
- Save correctional officers' time, thereby saving your facility money.
- Avoid chance of prisoner's escape and possible danger to the public.
- Avoid long waits in overcrowded hospitals.
- Reduce your insurance liabilities.
- Other Services Available: Ultrasound, Two-Dimensional Echocardiogram, C.T. Scan, EKG, Blood Lab and Holter Monitor.

Bulleted list conveniently and persuasively uses factual data to convince

General Medical Services Corp.
A subsidiary of

Federal Medical Industries, Inc. O.T.C.
950 S.W. 12th Avenue, 2nd Floor Suite, Pompano, Florida 33069
(305) 942-1111   FL WATS: 1-800-654-8282

General Medical Is Your On-Site Medical Problem Solver

Encourages readers to use this service

© Cengage Learning 2013

most relevant one(s) for your boss. Your reader will expect you to offer clear-cut, logical, and convincing reasons for your choice, backed up with persuasive facts.

As part of your job, too, you will be asked to write convincing memos, emails, letters, blogs, and websites to boost employee morale, encourage them to be more productive, and compliment them on a job well done.

Figure 1.7 is a persuasive email from an employee to a manager reporting a payroll mistake and persuading the reader to correct it. The email contains many of the other characteristics of job-related writing we have discussed. Note how the

FIGURE 1.7   A Persuasive Email from an Employee to a Business Manager

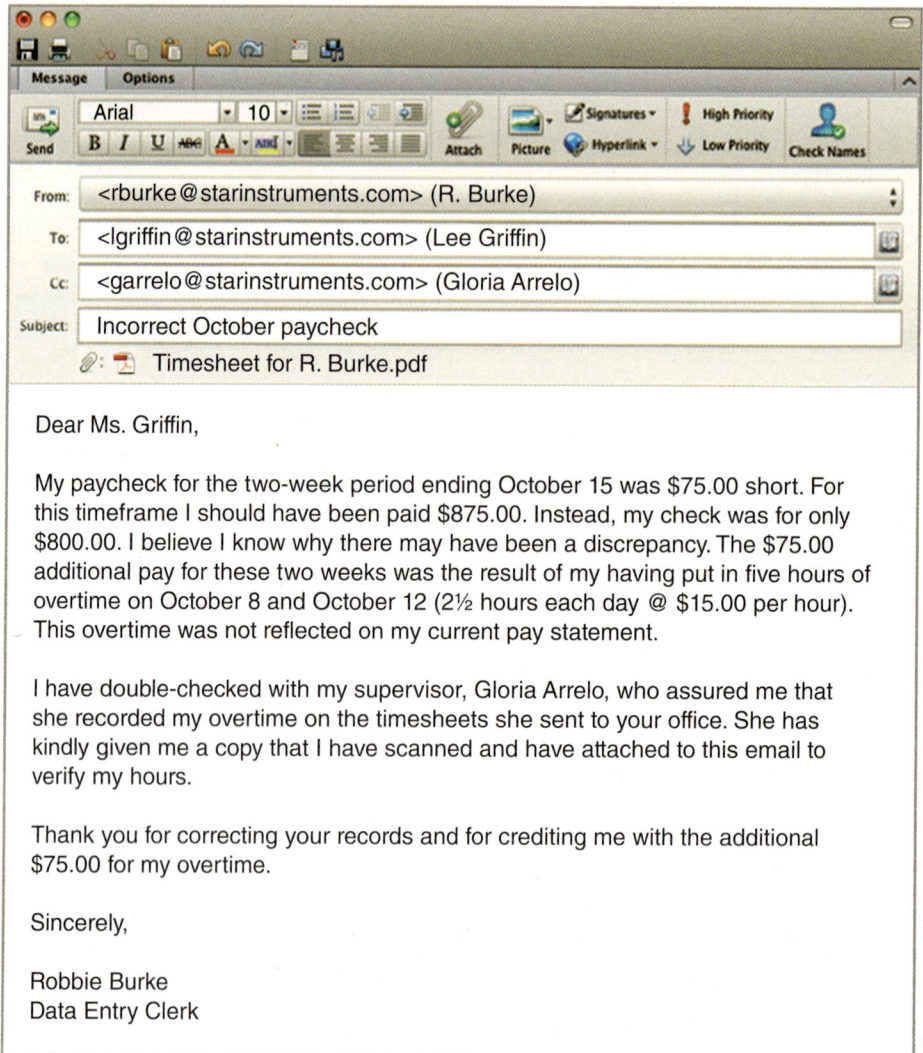

From:	<rburke@starinstruments.com> (R. Burke)
To:	<lgriffin@starinstruments.com> (Lee Griffin)
Cc:	<garrelo@starinstruments.com> (Gloria Arrelo)
Subject:	Incorrect October paycheck
	Timesheet for R. Burke.pdf

Dear Ms. Griffin,

Clearly explains and documents the problem

My paycheck for the two-week period ending October 15 was $75.00 short. For this timeframe I should have been paid $875.00. Instead, my check was for only $800.00. I believe I know why there may have been a discrepancy. The $75.00 additional pay for these two weeks was the result of my having put in five hours of overtime on October 8 and October 12 (2½ hours each day @ $15.00 per hour). This overtime was not reflected on my current pay statement.

Offers further evidence in attachment

I have double-checked with my supervisor, Gloria Arrelo, who assured me that she recorded my overtime on the timesheets she sent to your office. She has kindly given me a copy that I have scanned and have attached to this email to verify my hours.

Closes politely with specific request

Thank you for correcting your records and for crediting me with the additional $75.00 for my overtime.

Sincerely,

Robbie Burke
Data Entry Clerk

writer provides factual, not subjective, information; attaches a PDF of his timesheet (a type of visual); gives accurate details; and identifies her own and her immediate supervisor's responsibilities. The writer's tone is suitably polite yet direct.

Ethical Writing in the Workplace

One of your most important job responsibilities is to ensure that your writing and behavior are ethical. Writing ethically means choosing language that is right and fair, honest, and complete in all documents prepared for your employer, co-workers, and customers. Your reputation and character plus your employer's corporate image will depend on your following an ethical course of action.

Many of the most significant phrases in the world of business reflect an ethical commitment to honesty and fairness: *accountability*, *public trust*, *equal opportunity employer*, *core values*, *global citizenship*, *good-faith effort*, *truth in lending*, *fair play*, *honest advertising*, *full disclosure*, *high professional standards*, *fair trade*, *community involvement*, and *corporate responsibility*.

Unethical business dealings, conversely, are stigmatized in *cover-ups*, *dodges*, *stonewalling*, *shady deals*, *spin-doctoring*, *foul play*, *bid rigging*, *employee raiding*, *misrepresentations*, *kickbacks*, *hostile takeovers*, *planned obsolescence*, *price gouging*, and *unfair advantage*. Those are the activities that make customers angry and that local, state, and federal agencies may investigate.

Employers Insist on and Monitor Ethical Behavior

Ethical behavior is crucial to your success in the workplace. Your employer will insist that you are honest, follow professional standards, show integrity, and exhibit loyalty in your professional relationships with clients, co-workers, supervisors, and vendors. You will be expected to know and comply with your company policies and procedures, as outlined in the employee or agency handbook (see pages 295–297), and you will also have to follow the professional codes, regulations, and methods that affect your job.

On the job, employers can legally monitor their employees' work — electronically, through cameras, or by personal visits. Some of these visits are not announced (such as the "secret shoppers" who report on the customer service they receive). How many times have you made a call to an organization and heard, "This call may be monitored for quality assurance"? According to a survey conducted by the American Management Association, monitoring employees has risen 45 percent in the past few years and extends to their voicemail, email, IMs, and Internet use.

Employers monitor the behavior of their employees for several reasons:

- to determine if a worker is doing his or her job correctly
- to identify employee wrongdoing
- to improve service, production, communication, or transportation
- to ensure compliance with federal, state, and municipal codes
- to limit company liability
- to adhere to and even strengthen security measures

Monitoring gives management solid facts about employee training, performance reviews, and promotions. But working with integrity means doing the right thing—even when no one is watching.

Ethical Requirements on the Job

In the workplace, you will be expected to meet the highest ethical standards by fulfilling the following eleven requirements:

1. Supplying honest and up-to-date information about yourself in your résumé and job applications. The résumé and your portfolio/webfolio (see pages 173–197). are key places where you must make ethical decisions about your qualifications for a job.
2. Respecting co-workers, customers, and suppliers in conduct that avoids bullying, discrimination, or any other unfair or unprofessional behavior.
3. Refusing to use language that makes false claims or tries to deceive readers with ambiguous words, jargon, or misleading statistics and visuals (see pages 27–29 and 249–253).
4. Avoiding language that excludes others on the basis of gender, race, national origin, religion, age, physical ability, or sexual orientation (see pages 50–55).
5. Maintaining accurate and current records at work. Remember: "If it isn't written, it didn't happen."
6. Complying with all local, state, and federal regulations, especially those ensuring a safe, healthy work environment, products, and/or services, for example, following the Occupational Safety and Health Administration guidelines.
7. Adhering to your profession's code or standard of ethics, internal audits, licenses, and certificate requirements.
8. Following your company's policies and procedures.
9. Honoring guarantees and warranties and meeting customers' needs impartially.
10. Cooperating fairly and on a timely basis with your collaborative team.
11. Respecting all copyright obligations and privileges.

Following these guidelines is not only an ethical requirement; it could also be a legal one. For example, doing personal (or outside consulting) work on company time is unethical and illegal. It would also be neglectful and unethical to allow an unsafe product to stay on the market simply to spare your company the expense and embarrassment of a product recall.

Computer Ethics

Computer ethics are essential in the world of e-commerce. A good rule to follow is never to do anything online that you wouldn't do offline. For instance, never use a company computer for any activity not directly related to your job. Moreover, it would be grossly unethical to erase a computer program intentionally, violate a software licensing agreement, or misrepresent (by fabrication or exaggeration) the scope of a database. Also, posting anything that attacks a competitor, a colleague, your boss, or your company is considered unethical. Follow the Ten Commandments of Computer Ethics prepared by the Computer Ethics Institute listed in Figure 1.8.

You are also ethically bound to protect your computer at work from security risks and possible system malfunctions. Never be afraid to ask for advice from a co-worker or someone in your firm's IT department who knows what to do if there is a computer emergency.

Here are some other specific guidelines to follow when using your computer at work:

- Protect passwords that allow access to your company's documents as well as its proprietary databases, templates, and other customized applications. Do not share your password, and never use a password belonging to someone else.
- Always save sensitive emails, IMs, blogs, memos, letters, and so on, that you or your employer may need to document decisions.
- Protect your computer from viruses, spyware, and malware by making sure the most recent updates to your antivirus programs are installed on your computer.
- Be especially careful in opening attachments or anything you suspect may be infected, such as spam. Never forward a document you think may have a virus.
- Do not use your work email account for personal emails (see pages 81–83). Instead, use an alternate email address (for example, Yahoo!, Gmail). If you cannot access your email on the job because of a computer emergency, you can use an alternate email address until the problem is solved.

FIGURE 1.8 The Ten Commandments of Computer Ethics

1. Thou shalt not use a computer to harm other people.
2. Thou shalt not interfere with other people's computer work.
3. Thou shalt not snoop around in other people's computer files.
4. Thou shalt not use a computer to steal.
5. Thou shalt not use a computer to bear false witness.
6. Thou shalt not copy or use proprietary software for which you have not paid.
7. Thou shalt not use other people's computer resources without authorization or proper compensation.
8. Thou shalt not appropriate other people's intellectual output.
9. Thou shalt think about the social consequences of the program you are writing or the system you are designing.
10. Thou shalt always use a computer in ways that ensure consideration and respect for your fellow humans beings.

Source: Computer Ethics Institute, London.

"Thinking Green": Making Ethical Choices About the Environment

Be respectful of the environment—whether at the office, at a work site, in the community, or in the global marketplace. Many companies are proud of their ethical commitments to the environment. Starbucks, for example, tells customers that its "10 percent post-consumer recycled . . . paper cups helped conserve enough energy to supply your homes for a year and save approximately 110,000 trees."

Like Starbucks, companies around the globe have adopted a green philosophy, encouraging their employees to avoid polluting the environment, save energy, and protect endangered species.

You can "think green" in several ways. At your office, conserve energy by turning off all computers, copiers, and other machines when you leave work; replace incandescent lightbulbs with energy-efficient ones; recycle paper; copy and print your documents on both sides of paper; view documents on your computer screen instead of printing them; adjust thermostats when you are gone for the day or weekend, and car pool to and from work. You can also reduce toxic chemicals in the atmosphere by using soy-based ink, by inspecting vehicles regularly, and by maintaining them properly to reduce or eliminate pollution.

Some Guidelines to Help You Reach Ethical Decisions

The workplace presents conflicts over who is right and who is wrong, what is best for the company and what is not, and whether a service or product should be changed and why. You will be asked to make a decision and justify it. While this book cannot cover all kinds of ethical problems, here are a few guidelines to help you respond ethically on the job.

1. Follow your conscience and "to thine own self be true." You cannot authorize something that you believe is wrong, dangerous, unfair, contradictory, or incomplete. But don't be hasty. Leave plenty of room for diplomacy and for careful questioning and researching. Don't blow a small matter out of proportion.

2. Be suspicious of convenient (and false) appeals that go against your beliefs. Watch out for red flags that anyone places in the way of your conscience: "No one will ever know." "It's OK to cut corners every once in a while." "We got away with it last time." "Don't rock the boat." "No one's looking." "As long as the company makes money, who cares?" These rationalizations are traps you must avoid.

3. Meet your obligations to your employer, your co-workers, your customers, and the global community. Keeping information from a co-worker who needs it, omitting a fact, justifying unnecessary expenses, concealing something risky about a product or service from an international customer that you otherwise would disclose to a U.S. consumer—all of these are unethical acts.

4. Take responsibility for your actions. Saying "I do not know" when you do know can constitute a serious ethical violation. Keep your records up-to-date and accurate, sign and date your work, and never backdate a document to delete information or to fix an error that you made. Failing to test a set of instructions thoroughly, for example, might endanger readers around the globe.

5. **Honor confidentiality at work.** Never share sensitive/confidential information with individuals who are *not* entitled to see or hear it. You violate corporate trust by telling others about your company's marketing strategies, sales records, personnel decisions, or customer/client interactions. You also have to respect an individual's right to privacy laws. For example, according to the Health Insurance Portability and Accountability Act (HIPPA) guidelines, heath care professionals are not allowed to share a patient's records with unauthorized individuals. It is equally unethical to divulge personal information that a co-worker or supervisor has asked you to keep confidential.

6. **Document your work carefully and honestly.** Rely on hard evidence: company records, tests, testimony, valid precedents. Do your homework by studying codes, specifications, books and agency handbooks; confer with a customer or a co-worker when you are in doubt about an issue. Familiarize yourself with your company's protocols, methods, and materials. Make sure your documents are accurate and comply with appropriate city, state, federal, and international regulations.

7. **Keep others in the loop.** Confer regularly with your collaborative writing team (see Chapter 2, pages 56–57) and report to your boss as often as you are instructed to give progress reports and to alert him or her about problems. If you experience a problem at work, don't wait until it gets worse to tell your supervisor and/or co-workers. Prompt and honest notifications are essential to the safety, security, morale, progress, and success of a company. Also, never keep a co-worker, customer, or vendor waiting; call in advance if you are going to be delayed.

8. **Treat company property respectfully.** Use company supplies, networks/computers, equipment, technology, and vehicles responsibly and only for work-related business. Taking supplies home, charging non–work-related expenses (meals, clothes, travel) on a company credit card, surfing the Internet when you are at work—these are just a few instances of unethical behavior.

9. **Weigh all sides before you commit to a conclusion.** Research what you write and communicate orally. Do your homework by conferring with co-workers, checking the history of a transaction or other corporate decision, and familiarizing yourself with company policies. Don't rely on office gossip or create problems where there are none. Give people the benefit of the doubt until you have hard evidence (for example, dates, costs, names, frequency, etc.) to the contrary.

Ethical Dilemmas: Some Scenarios

Sometimes in the workplace you will face situations where there is no clear-cut right or wrong choice. Here are a few scenarios, similar to ones in which you may find yourself, that are gray areas, ethically speaking, along with some possible solutions.

- You work with an office bully who often intimidates co-workers, including you, by talking down to them, interrupting them, or insulting them for their suggestions. At times, this bully has even sent sarcastic emails and IMs. You are upset that this behavior has not been reported to management. But you are concerned that if the bully finds out that you have reported the situation the entire office may suffer. How should you handle the problem?

You cannot allow such rude, insulting behavior to go unreported. But first you need to provide documentation about where, when, and how often the bullying has occurred. You may want to speak directly to the bully, but if you feel uncomfortable doing this, go directly to your boss, report how the bully's actions have negatively affected the workplace, and ask for assistance. You may also get help from your company's employee assistance program or from someone in human resources. In accordance with state and federal laws, companies must provide a safe work environment, free from intimidation, harassment, or threats of dismissal for reporting bullying.

- You work very closely with an individual who takes frequent extended lunch breaks, often comes in late and leaves early, and even misses deadlines. Sometimes you cover for him when he is not at the office to answer questions. But your department is under minimal supervision from an off-site manager, so there is no boss looking over your colleague's shoulder. You like your co-worker and do not want him to be fired, but he is taking advantage of your friendship and unfairly expecting you to cover for him. What should you do?

The best route is to take your co-worker aside and speak with him before informing management. Let him know you value working with him, but firmly explain that you no longer will cover for him or take on his workload. If he does not agree with you, let him know that you will be forced to discuss the problem with your manager. If the problem persists, and you go to your boss, bring documentation—dates, duties not performed, and so on—with you.

- You see an opening for a job in your area, but the employer wants someone with a minimum of two years of field experience. You have just completed an internship and had one summer's experience, which together total almost seven months. Should you apply for the job, describing yourself as "experienced"?

Yes, but honestly state the type and the extent of your field experience and the conditions under which you obtained it.

- You work for a company that usually assigns commissions to the salesperson for whom the customer asks. One afternoon a customer asks for a salesperson who happens to have the day off. You assist the customer all afternoon and even arrange to have an item shipped overnight so that she can have it in the morning. When you ring up the sale, should you list your employee number for the commission or the off-duty employee's?

You probably should defer crediting the sale to either of you until you speak to the absent employee and suggest a compromise—splitting the commission, for instance.

- A piece of IT equipment, scheduled for delivery to your customer the next day, arrives with a damaged part. You decide to replace it at your store before the customer receives it. Should you inform the customer?

  Yes, but assure the customer that the equipment is still under the same warranty and that the replacement part is new and also under the same warranty. If the customer protests, agree to let him or her use the computer until a new unit arrives.

As these brief scenarios suggest, sometimes you have to make concessions and compromises to be ethical in the world of work.

Writing Ethically on the Job

Your writing as well as your behavior must be ethical. Words, like actions, have implications and consequences. If you slant your words to conceal the truth or to gain an unfair advantage, you are not being ethical. False reporting and advertising are unethical. Bias and omission of facts are wrong. Strive to be fair, reliable, and accurate in reporting products, services, events, environmental issues, statistics, and trends.

Unethical writers are usually guilty of one or more of the following faults, which can conveniently be listed as the three *M*'s: misquotation, misrepresentation, and manipulation. Here are nine examples:

1. Plagiarism is stealing someone else's words and claiming them as your own without documenting the source. Do not think that by changing a few words of someone else's writing here and there you are not plagiarizing. Give proper credit to your source, whether in print, in person (through an interview), or online. The penalties for plagiarism are severe—a reprimand or even the loss of your job. See pages 355–357 for further advice on how to avoid plagiarism.

2. Selective misquoting deliberately omits damaging or unflattering comments to paint a better (but untruthful) picture of you or your company. By picking and choosing only a few words from a quotation, you unethically misrepresent what the speaker or writer originally intended.

Selective Misquotation:	I've enjoyed . . . our firm's association with Technology, Inc. The quality of their service was . . . excellent.
Full Quotation:	I've enjoyed at times our firm's association with Technology, Inc., although I was troubled by the uneven quality of their service. At times, it was excellent while at others it was far less so.

The spaced dots, called *ellipses*, unethically suggest that only extraneous or unimportant details were omitted.

3. Skewing numbers unethically misrepresents, by increasing or decreasing percentages or other numbers, statistical or other information. It is unethical to stretch the differences between competing plans or proposals to gain an unfair advantage or to express accurate figures in an inaccurate way.

> **Embellishment:** An overwhelming majority of residents voted for the new plan.
>
> **Ethical:** The new plan was passed by a vote of 53 to 49.
>
> **Embellishment:** Our competitor's sales volume increased by only 10 percent in the preceding year, while ours doubled.
>
> **Ethical:** Our competitor controls 90 percent of the market, yet we increased our share of that market from 5 percent to 10 percent last year.

4. Omitting key information, service, or location intentionally deprives readers of the facts they need to reach a decision.

> **Omitting Information:** You will save thousands of dollars when buying the Model 2400T, the least expensive four-wheeler on the market.
>
> **Key Information Supplied:** Although the model 2400T is the least expensive four-wheeler you can purchase, it is the most expensive to operate and to repair, making it the most costly four-wheeler to choose.

5. Manipulating information or context, which is closely related to the embellishment of numbers, is the misrepresentation of events, usually to put a good face on a bad situation. The writer here unethically uses slanted language and intentionally misleading euphemisms to misinterpret events for readers.

> **Manipulation:** Looking ahead to 2016, the United Funds Group is exceptionally optimistic about its long-term prospects in an expanding global market. We are happy to report steady to moderate activity in an expanding sales environment last year. The United Funds Group seeks to build on sustaining investment opportunities beneficial to all subscribers.
>
> **Ethical:** Looking ahead to 2016, the United Funds Group is optimistic about its long-term prospects in an expanding global market. Though the market suffered from inflation this year, the United Funds Group hopes to recoup its losses in the year ahead.

The writer who manipulates information minimizes the negative effects of inflation by calling it "an expanding sales environment."

6. Using fictitious benefits to promote a product or service seemingly promises customers advantages but delivers none. Saying a product is environmentally safe when that claim is unproven is unethical, as is neglecting to point out that results may vary greatly when advertising a weight-loss program or home care product.

> **False Benefit:** Our bottled water is naturally hydrogenated from clear underground springs.
>
> **Truth:** All water is hydrogenated because it contains hydrogen.
>
> **False Benefit:** All our homes come with construction-grade fixtures.
>
> **Truth:** Construction-grade fixtures are the least expensive and least durable a builder can use.

7. **Exaggerating or minimizing** hiring or firing conditions is unethical.

Unethical:	One of the benefits of working for Spelco is the double pay you earn for overtime.
Truth:	Overtime is assigned on the basis of seniority.
Unethical:	Our corporate restructuring will create a more efficient and streamlined company, benefiting management and workers alike.
Truth:	Downsizing has led to 150 layoffs this quarter.

Companies faced with laying off employees want to protect their corporate image and maintain their stockholders' good faith, so they often put the best face on such an action.

8. **Misleading international readers** by adopting a condescending view of their culture and economy is unethical.

Unethical:	Since our product has appealed to U.S. customers for the last sixteen months, there's no doubt that it will be popular in your country as well.
Fair:	Please let us know if any changes in product design or construction may be necessary for customers in your country.

9. **Using a distorted or slanted visual** is one of the most common types of unethical writing. Making a visual appear bigger, smaller, or more or less favorable is all too easy with graphics software. Printing warning or caution statements the same size and type font as ingredients or directions or enlarging advertising hype ("Double Your Money Back") is also unethical if major points are then reduced to small print. (See pages 249–253 in Chapter 6 for guidelines on how to prepare ethical visuals.)

Ethical writing is clear, accurate, fair, and honest. These are among the most important goals of any workplace communication. Because ethics is such an important topic in writing for the business world, it will be emphasized throughout this book.

Successful Employees Are Successful Writers

As this chapter has stressed, being a successful employee means being a successful writer at work. The following ten guidelines, which summarize the key points of this chapter, will help you to be both:

1. Know your job—assignments, roles, responsibilities, goals, what you need to write, and what you *shouldn't*.
2. Analyze your audience's needs and what they will expect to find in your writing.
3. Be prepared to give and to receive feedback from co-workers, managers, vendors, and customers.
4. Work toward and meet all deadlines.
5. Be sensitive to the needs of a multicultural audience.
6. Make sure your written work is accurate, relevant, and practical, and include culturally appropriate visuals to help readers understand your message.
7. Document, document, document. Submit everything you write with clear-cut evidence based on factual details and persuasive, logical interpretations.

8. Use your computer only for company business. Never share your password, and protect your computer from viruses.
9. Follow your company's policy, and promote your company's image, culture, and traditions.
10. Be ethical in what you say, write, illustrate, and do.

✓ # Revision Checklist

At the end of each chapter you'll find a checklist to review before you submit the final copy of your work, either to your instructor or to your boss. The checklists specify the types of research, planning, drafting, editing, and revising you should do to ensure the success of your work. Regard each checklist as a summary of the main ideas in the chapter as well as a handy guide to quality control. You may find it helpful to check each box as you verify that you have performed the necessary revision and review. Effective writers are also careful editors.

☐ Showed respect for and appropriately shaped my message for a global audience.
☐ Identified my audience—background, knowledge of English, reason for reading my work, and likely response to my work and me.
☐ Tailored my message to my audience's needs and background, giving them neither too little nor too much information.
☐ Pushed to the main point right away; did not waste my readers' time.
☐ Selected the most appropriate language, technical level, tone, and level of formality.
☐ Did not waste my readers' time with unsupported generalizations or opinions; instead gave them accurate measurements, dates, and carefully researched material.
☐ Selected appropriate visuals to make my work easier for my audience to understand and follow.
☐ Used persuasive reasons and data to convince my readers to accept my plan or work.
☐ Ensured that my writing and visuals are ethical—accurate, fair, honest, a true reflection of the situation or condition I am explaining or describing, for U.S. as well as global audiences.
☐ Followed the Ten Commandments of Computer Ethics.
☐ Adhered to the ethical codes of my profession as well as the policies and regulations set down by my employer.
☐ Gave full and complete credit to any sources I used, including resource people.
☐ Avoided plagiarism and unfair or dishonest use of copyrighted materials, both written and visual, including all electronic media.

Exercises

1. Write a memo (see pages 133–141 for format) addressed to a prospective supervisor to introduce yourself. Your memo should have four headings: **Education**—including goals and accomplishments; **Job Information**—where you have worked and your responsibilities; **Community Service**—volunteer work, church work, youth groups; and **Writing Experience**—your strengths and weaknesses as a writer, the types of writing you have done, and the audiences for whom you have written.

2. Bring to class a set of printed instructions, a memo, a sales letter, a brochure, or the printout of a company's or organization's home page. Comment on how well the example answers the following questions:
   a. Who is the audience?
   b. Why was the material written?
   c. What is the message?
   d. Are the style and tone appropriate for the audience, the purpose, and the message? Explain.
   e. Discuss the use of any visuals and color in the document. For instance, how does color (or the lack of it) affect an audience's response to the message?

3. Find an advertisement in a print source or online that contains a drawing or photograph. Bring the ad to class along with a paragraph of your own (75–100 words) describing how the message of the ad is directed to a particular audience and commenting on how the drawing or photo is appropriate for that audience.

4. Select one of the following topics, and write two descriptions of it. In the first description, use technical details and vocabulary. In the second, use language and details suitable for the general public.

   a. iPad
   b. blood pressure cuff
   c. flash drive
   d. energy drinks
   e. Bluetooth headset
   f. legal contract
   g. electric sander
   h. firewalls
   i. muscle
   j. protein
   k. smartphone
   l. cloud computing
   m. bread
   n. money
   o. all-in-one printer
   p. soap
   q. blogging
   r. computer virus
   s. swine flu
   t. thermostat
   u. trees
   v. mobile app
   w. earthquake
   x. recycling

5. Select another topic from Exercise 4, and write two more descriptions as a collaborative writing project.

6. Select one article from a daily newspaper online and one article from a professional e- or print journal in your major field or from one of the following journals:

Advertising Age, American Journal of Nursing, Business Marketing, Businessweek, Computer, Computer Design, Construction Equipment, Criminal Justice Review, E-Commerce, Food Service Marketing, Journal of Forestry, Journal of Soil and Water Conservation, National Safety News, Nutrition Action, Office Machines, Park Maintenance, Scientific American. State how the two articles you selected differ in terms of audience, purpose, message, style, and tone.

7. Assume that you work for Appliance Rentals, Inc., a company that rents TVs, microwave ovens, refrigerators, and the like. Write a persuasive letter to the members of a campus organization or civic club urging them to rent an appropriate appliance or appliances. Include details in your letter that might have special relevance to members of this specific organization.

8. How do the visuals and the text of the Digital World Technologies advertisement on page 33 stress to current (and potential) employees, customers, and stockholders that the company is committed to diversity in the workplace? Also explain how the ad illustrates the functions of on-the-job writing as defined on pages 15–21.

9. Write a letter to a cell phone provider that has mistakenly billed you for a text-messaging plan that you never ordered or used.

10. The following statements contain embellishments, selected misquotations, false benefits, omitted key information, and other types of unethical tactics. Revise each statement to eliminate the unethical aspects. Make up details as needed.
    a. Storm damage done to water filtration plant #3 was minimal. While we had to shut down temporarily, service resumed to meet residents' needs.
    b. All customers qualify for the maximum discount available.
    c. "The service contract . . . on the whole . . . applied to upgrades."
    d. We followed the protocols precisely with test results yielding further opportunities for experimentation.
    e. All our costs were within fair-use guidelines.
    f. Customers' complaints have been held to a minimum.
    g. All the lots we are selling offer relatively easy access to the lake.
    h. Factory-trained technicians respond to all our calls.

11. You work for a large international company, and a co-worker tells you that he has no plans to return to his job after he takes his annual two-week vacation. You know that your department cannot meet its deadlines shorthanded and that your company will need at least two or three weeks to recruit and hire a qualified replacement. You also know that it is your company's policy not to give paid vacations to employees who do not agree to work for at least three months following their return. What should you do? What points would you make in a confidential email to your boss? What points would you raise to your co-worker?

12. Your company is regulated and inspected by the Environmental Protection Agency (EPA). In 90 days, the EPA will relax a regulation about dumping

WE ARE

Digital World

TECHNOLOGIES

Excellence

Accountability

Teamwork

Integrity

WE ARE committed to providing our clients worldwide with superior service. Our diverse, talented workforce shares our vision to offer you the latest and most effective solutions for all your digital security needs. We have helped thousands of companies like yours with our innovative technical assistance and our broad knowledge of what it takes to do business around the globe.

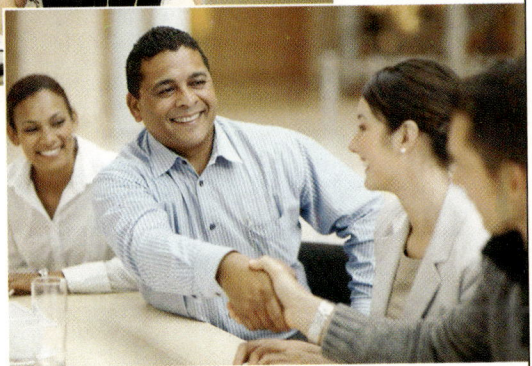

digitalworldtx.com
800-555-0120

occupational waste. Your company's management is considering cutting costs by relaxing the standard now, before the new, less demanding regulation is in place. You know that the EPA inspector probably will not return before the 90-day period elapses. What do you recommend to management?

13. You and your co-workers have been intimidated by an office bully, a twelve-year employee who has seniority. As a collaborative writing project (see pages 55–57), draft a letter to the head of your human resources department documenting instances of the bully's actions and asking for advice on how to proceed.

14. Write a 50- to 200-word email to your boss about one of the following unethical activities you have witnessed in your workplace. Your email must be carefully documented, fair, and persuasive—in short, ethical.

a. bullying
b. surfing pornography websites
c. using workplace technology for personal matters (shopping, dating, buying stocks)
d. falsifying compensatory or travel time
e. telling sexist, off-color jokes
f. concealing the use of company funds for personal gifts for fellow employees
g. misdating or backdating company records

h. sharing privileged information with individuals outside your department or company
i. fudging the number of hours worked
j. exaggerating a workplace-related injury
k. not reporting a second job to avoid scheduled weekend work
l. misrepresenting, by minimizing, a client's complaint

CHAPTER 2

The Writing Process and Collaboration at Work

In Chapter 1 you learned about the different functions of writing for the world of work and also explored some basic concepts all writers must master. To be a successful writer, you need to

- identify your audience's needs
- determine your purpose in writing to that audience
- make sure your message meets your audience's needs
- use the most appropriate style and tone for your message
- format your work so that it clearly reflects your message to your audience

Just as significant to your success is knowing how effective writers actually create their work for their audiences. This chapter gives you practical information about the strategies and techniques careful writers use when they work. These procedures are a vital part of what is known as the *writing process*. This process involves such matters as how writers gather information, how they transform their ideas into written form, and how they organize and revise what they have written to make it relevant for their audiences. This chapter will also show you how writers in the world of work collaborate on creating a document.

What Writing Is and Is Not

As you begin your study of writing for the world of work, it might be helpful to identify some notions about what writing is and what it is not.

What Writing Is

- **The writing process is dynamic; it is not static.** It enables you to discover and evaluate your thoughts as you draft and revise.
- **A piece of writing changes as your thoughts and information change and as your view of the material changes.**

- **Writing takes time.** Some people think that revising and polishing are too time consuming. But poor writing actually takes more time and costs more money in the end. It can lead to misunderstandings, lost sales, product recalls, and even damage to your reputation and that of your company.
- **Writing means making a number of judgment calls.**
- **Writing grows sometimes in bits and pieces and sometimes in great spurts.** It needs many revisions; an early draft is never a final copy.

What Writing Is Not

- **Writing is not a mysterious process, known only to a few.** Even if you have not done much writing before, you can learn to do it effectively.
- **Writing is not simply following a magical formula.** Successful writing requires hard work and thoughtful effort, not simply following a formula, as if you were painting by numbers. Writing does not proceed in some predictable way, in which introductions are always written first and conclusions last.
- **Writing is not completed in a first attempt.** Just because you put something down on paper or on a computer screen does not mean it is unchangeable. Writing means *rewriting*, *revising*, and *rethinking*. The better a piece of writing is, the more the writer has reworked it.

The Writing Process

The writing process we have just discussed is something fluid, not static. Think of it as a back and forth process rather than following a formula—do this, then do that. To move from a blank sheet of paper or computer screen to a successful piece of writing, you need to follow a process. The parts of that process include researching, planning, drafting, revising, and editing.

Researching

Before you start to compose any email, memo, letter, report, proposal, or website, you'll need to do research. Research is crucial because it enables you to obtain the right information for your audience. Information must be factually correct and relevant. The world of work is based on conveying information—the logical presentation and sensible interpretation of facts. Chapter 9 will introduce you to the variety of research strategies and tools you can expect to use in the world of work.

Don't ever think you are wasting time by doing some research before starting to write any document. Actually, you will waste time and risk doing a poor job if you do not find out as much as possible about your topic (and your audience's interest in it). Find out about your readers' needs and how to meet them.

Then you can determine the kind of research you must do to gather and interpret the information your audience needs. Depending on the length and scope of your written work and on your audience's needs, your research may include

- interviewing people inside and outside your company
- reviewing similar or related company documents
- consulting notes from conferences or meetings
- collaborating in person, by email, or by instant messaging (IM)
- doing Internet searches
- locating and evaluating websites
- reading current periodicals, trade journals, reports, and other documents
- evaluating reports, products, and services
- conferring with co-workers, customers, or vendors
- participating in a focus group
- surveying customers' views
- visiting a work site

Keep in mind that research is not confined to just the beginning of the writing process; it is an ongoing process.

Planning

At this stage in the writing process your goal is to get something—anything—down on paper or on your computer screen. For most writers, getting started is the hardest part of the job. But you will feel more comfortable and confident once you begin to see your ideas written down before your eyes. It is always easier to clarify and criticize something you can see.

Getting started is also easier if you have researched your topic, because you have something concrete to say and to build on. Each part of the process relates to and supports the next. Careful research prepares you to begin writing.

Still, getting started is not easy. Take advantage of a number of widely used strategies that can help you to develop, organize, and tailor the right information for your audience. Use any one of the following techniques, alone or in combination.

1. Clustering. In the middle of a sheet of paper, write the word or phrase that best describes your topic, and then start writing other words or phrases that come to mind. (It is also possible to do this on your computer screen using a "mind mapping" software program such as FreeMind, XMind, or iMindMap to create clusters.) As you write, circle each word or phrase and connect it to the word from which it sprang. Note the clustered grouping in Figure 2.1 (page 38) for a report encouraging a manager to switch to flextime—a system in which employees can work on a flexible time schedule within certain limits. The resulting diagram gives the writer a rough sense of some of the major divisions of the topic and where they may belong in the report.

2. Brainstorming. At the top of a sheet of paper or your computer screen, describe your topic in a word or phrase and then list any information you know or found out about that topic—in any order and as quickly as you can. Brainstorming is like thinking aloud except that you are recording your thoughts.

FIGURE 2.1 Clustering of Ideas to Prepare a Report on Flextime

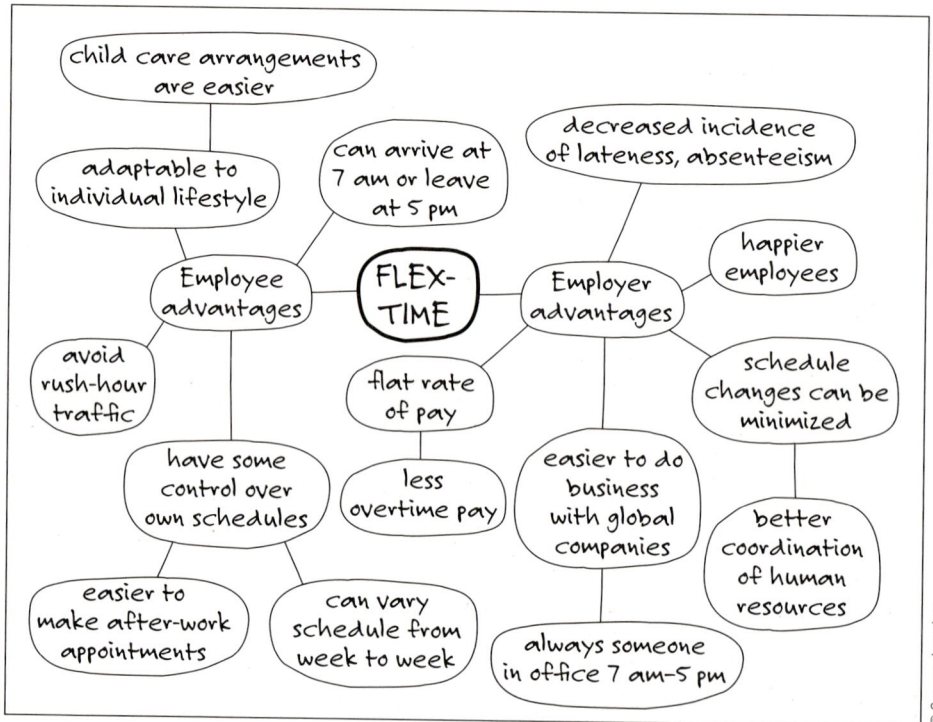

© Cengage Learning

- Don't stop to delete, rearrange, or rewrite anything, and don't dwell on any one item.
- Don't worry about spelling, punctuation, grammar, or whether you are using words and phrases instead of complete sentences.
- Keep the ideas flowing. The result may well be an odd assortment of details, comments, and opinions.
- After stepping away from the list for a few minutes (or hours) and returning with fresh eyes, expect to add and delete some ideas or combine or rearrange others as you start to develop your topic in more detail.

Figure 2.2 shows Marcus Weekley's initial brainstormed list for a report to his boss on purchasing a new color laser all-in-one printer. After he began to revise it, he realized that some items were not relevant for his audience (6, 8, and 13). He also recognized that some items were repetitious (1, 2, and 11). Further investigation revealed that his company could purchase a printer for far less than his initial high guess (17). As Weekley continued to work on his list and the overall topic became clearer to him, he added and deleted points.

3. Outlining. This process may be the easiest and most comfortable way to begin or to continue planning a report or letter. Outlines can go through stages,

FIGURE 2.2 Marcus Weekley's Initial, Unrevised Brainstormed List

1. combines four separate pieces of equip—printer, copier, fax, and scanner

2. more comprehensive than our current configuration of four pieces of equip

3. would coordinate with office furniture

4. energy efficiency increased due to fewer machines being used

5. more scalable fonts

6. one machine interfaces with all others in same-case housing

7. scanner makes photographic-quality pictures

8. print capabilities are a real contribution to technology

9. increased communication abilities through fax machine

10. new scanner picture quality better than current scanner

11. only have to buy one machine as opposed to four

12. speed of fax allows quick response time

13. stock is doing better on Wall Street compared to other equities

14. reducing our advertising costs through use of color printer

15. increased work area available

16. would help us do our work better

17. top-of-line models can be bought for $4,500

List is not organized but simply records writer's initial ideas about possible topics

1, 2, and 11 are repetitious

6, 8, and 13 are not relevant for audience or purpose

4, 9, 12, and 14 are of special interest to decision makers concerned about costs

Research will show cost estimate is too high

© Cengage Learning 2013

so don't worry if your first attempt is brief and messy. It does not have to be formal (with lots of Roman and Arabic numerals), complete, or pretty. It is intended for no one's eyes but yours. Use your preliminary outline as a quick way to sketch in some ideas, a convenient container into which you can put information. You might simply jot down a few major points and identify a few subpoints. Note how Weekley organized his revised brainstormed list into an outline seen below in Figure 2.3.

FIGURE 2.3 Marcus Weekley's Early Outline After Revising His Brainstormed List

I. Convenience/capabilities of all-in-one laser printer

    A. Would reduce number of machines having to be serviced

    B. Can be configured easily for our network system

    C. Easy to install and to operate

    D. 33.6 Kbps fax machine would increase our communication

    E. 2,400 × 1,200 dpi copier means better copy quality

    F. 4,800 × 4,800 dpi scanner means higher quality pictures than current scanner provides

II. Time/efficiency

    A. 40 ppm color printer is nearly twice as fast as current printer

    B. 33.6 Kbps fax allows quick response time

    C. Greater graphics capability—130 scalable fonts

    D. Scanner compatible with our current PhotoEdit imaging/graphics software

    E. 100,000-page monthly duty cycle means less maintenance

III. Money

    A. Costs less overall for multitasking printer than combined four machines

    B. Reduced monthly power bill by using one machine rather than four

    C. Wi-fi capability means no need to buy new software to network office computers

    D. Save on service costs

    E. Reduced advertising costs through printer's 50–400% enlargement/ reduction options, which allow for more in-house advertising

Outline form helps writer group ideas/ topics and go to next step in the process

Headings correspond to major sections of report

Outline reflects scope and details of writer's research

Last section of outline also functions as a conclusion

Drafting

If you have planned carefully, you will find it easier to start your first draft. When you draft, you convert the words and phrases from your outline, brainstormed list, or clustered grouping into paragraphs. During drafting, as elsewhere in the writing process, you will see some overlap as you look back over your list or outline to shape your text.

Don't expect to wind up with a polished, complete version of your letter or report after working on only one draft. In most cases, you will have to work through many drafts, but each draft should be less rough and more acceptable than the preceding one.

Key Questions to Ask as You Draft

As you work on your drafts, ask yourself the following questions about your content and organization:

- Am I giving my readers too much or too little information?
- Do I need to do more research—where and why?
- Should I confer further with my boss or co-workers?
- Does this point belong where I have it, or would it more logically follow or precede something else?
- Is this point necessary and relevant?
- Am I repeating or contradicting myself?
- Have I ended appropriately for my audience?

To answer the questions successfully, you may have to continue researching your topic and reexamining your audience's needs. But, in the process, new and even better ideas may come to you, and the ideas you originally thought were essential may in time appear to be unworkable and unnecessary.

Guidelines for Successful Drafting

Following are some suggestions to help your drafting go more smoothly and efficiently.

- In an early draft, write the easiest part first. Some writers feel more comfortable drafting the body (or middle) of their work first. See the differences between the short report in Figures 2.4 and 2.5 (pages 44–45).
- As you work on a later draft, write straight through. Do not worry about spelling, punctuation, or the way a word or sentence sounds. Save those concerns for later stages.
- Allow enough time between drafts so that you can evaluate your work with fresh eyes and a clear mind.
- Get frequent outside opinions. Show, email, or fax a draft to a co-worker or a supervisor for comment. A new pair of eyes will see things you missed. As we'll see, collaboration is essential in the workplace (see pages 55–56).
- Consider whether visuals would enhance the quality of your work and, if so, decide on what types and where best to insert them.

Revising

Revision is an essential stage in the writing process. It requires more than giving your work another quick glance. Do not be tempted to skip the revision stage just because you have written the required number of words or sections or because you think you have put in too much time already. Revision is done *after* you produce a draft that you think conveys the appropriate message for your audience. The quality of your memo, letter, or report depends on the revisions you make now.

Allow Enough Time to Revise

Like planning or drafting, revision is not done well in one big push. It evolves over a period of time. Make sure you budget enough time to do it carefully.

- Avoid drafting and revising in one sitting. If possible, wait at least a day before you start to revise. (In the busy work world, waiting a couple of hours may have to suffice.)
- Ask a co-worker or friend familiar with your topic to comment on your work.
- Plan to read your revised work more than once.

Revision Is Rethinking

When you revise, you *resee*, *rethink*, and *reconsider* your entire document. You ask questions about the major issues of content, organization, tone, and format (see pages 217–227). Revision involves going back and repeating earlier steps in the writing process.

Revision means asking again the questions you have already asked and answered during the planning and drafting stages. During the process, you will discover gaps to fill, points to change, and errors to correct in your draft. Revision gives you a second (or third or fourth) chance to get things right for your audience. Take advantage of the document tracking options (see pages 60–61) such as *Track Changes* and *Edit* that allow you to see your additions, cuts, and moves in a different color.

Key Questions to Ask as You Revise

By asking and successfully answering the following questions as you revise, you can discover gaps or omissions, points to change, and errors to correct in your draft.

Content

1. Is it accurate? Are my facts (figures, names, addresses, dates, costs, references, warranty terms, statistics) correct?

2. Is it relevant for my audience and purpose? Have I included information that is unnecessary, too technical, concrete or inappropriate?
3. Have I given enough concrete evidence to explain things adequately and to persuade my readers? (Too little information will make readers skeptical about what you are describing or proposing.) Have I left anything out?

Organization

1. Have I clearly identified my main points and shown readers why those points are important?
2. Is everything in the right, most effective order? Should anything be switched or moved closer to the beginning or the end of my document?
3. Am I spending too much (or too little) effort on one section? Do I repeat myself? What can be cut? Where and why?
4. Have I grouped related items in the same part of my report or letter, or have I scattered details that need to appear in one paragraph or section?

Tone

1. How do I sound to my readers—professional and sincere, or arrogant and unreliable? What attitude/tone do my words or expressions convey?
2. How will my readers, native speakers as well as an international audience, think I perceive them—honest and intelligent or unprofessional and uncooperative?

Case Study

A "Before" and "After" Revision of a Short Report

Mary Fonseca, a staff member at Seacoast Labs, was asked by her supervisor to prepare a short report for the general public on the Labs' most recent experiments. Conferring with her supervisor, Fonseca learned that the report was intended to attract favorable publicity for the Labs' commitment to conserving energy and lowering marine fuel costs.

When she began to revise her first draft (seen in Figure 2.4 on page 44), Fonseca realized that it lacked focus. It jumped back and forth between drag on ships and drag on airplanes. Because Seacoast Labs did not work on planes, she wisely decided to drop that idea. She also understood that the information on the effects of drag was so important it deserved a separate paragraph. In light of this key idea, she knew that her explanation of molecules, eddies, and drag needed to be made more reader-friendly, and so she added the analogy about spoons/ships and honey/drag. Researching further, she decided to add a new paragraph on the causes and effects of drag, which became paragraph 2 in her second draft (seen in Figure 2.5 on page 45).

Yet by pulling ideas about drag and its effects from the long first paragraph in Figure 2.4, Fonseca had to find an opening for this section of her report. Buried in her original opening paragraph was the idea that we cannot always see the forces of nature, but we can feel them.

*Information
hard to follow
and not
relevant for
audience*

*Does not
explain
process
very well*

*Important
point not
developed*

Drag is an important concept in the world of science and technology. It has many implications. Drag occurs when a ship moves through the water and eddies build up. Ships on the high seas have to fight the eddies, which results in drag. In the same way, an airplane has to fight the winds at various altitudes at which it flies; these winds are very forceful, moving at many knots per hour. All these forces of nature are around us. Sometimes we can feel them, too. We get tired walking against a strong wind. The eddies around a ship are the same thing. These eddies form various barriers around the ship's hull. They come from a combination of different molecules around the ship's hull and exert quite a force. Both types of molecules pull against the ship. This is where the eddies come in.

Scientists at Seacoast Labs are concerned about drag. Dr. Karen Runnels, who joined Seacoast about three years ago, is the chief investigator. She and her team of highly qualified experts have constructed some fascinating multilevel water tunnels. These tunnels should be useful to ship owners. Drag wastes a ship's fuel.

© Cengage Learning 2013

She thought this comparison of walking against the wind and fighting drag would work better for her audience than the original wooden remarks she had started with.

Although her organization and ideas were far better in her second draft than in her "before" draft in Figure 2.4, she concluded she had said very little about her employer, Seacoast Labs, and the corporate image it wanted to project through its experiments. Doing more research, she found additional information about Seacoast's experiments and why they were so important in conserving fuel and saving money. This information was far more significant and relevant than saying that Dr. Runnels had been at Seacoast for three years.

Through revision and further research, then, Mary Fonseca transformed two poorly organized and incomplete paragraphs into three separate yet logically connected ones that highlighted her employer's work. In her revision (Figure 2.5), she came up with three very helpful headings—"What Is Drag?," "How Drag Works," and "Reducing Drag"—for her non-specialist readers.

What Is Drag?

We cannot see or hear many of the forces around us, but we can certainly detect their presence. Walking or running into a strong wind, for example, requires a great deal of effort and often quickly leaves us feeling tired. When a ship sails through the water, it also experiences these opposing forces known as **drag**. Overcoming drag causes a ship to reduce its energy efficiency, which leads to higher fuel costs.

Effective use of headings and definition

How Drag Works

It is not easy for a ship to fight drag. As the ship moves through the water, it drags the water molecules around its hull at the same rate the ship is moving. Because of the cohesive force of those molecules, other water molecules immediately outside the ship's path get pulled into its way. All the molecules become tangled rather than simply sliding past each other. The result is an **eddy**, or small circling burst of water around the ship's hull, which intensifies the drag. Dr. Jorge Fröes, a highly respected structural engineer, explains the process using this analogy: "When you put a spoon in honey and pull it out, half the honey comes out with the spoon. That's what is happening to ships. The ship is moving and at the same time dragging the ocean with it."

Describes cause and effect of drag in concise, easy to understand terms

Reducing Drag

At Seacoast Labs, scientists are working to find ways to reduce drag on ships. Dr. Karen Runnels, the principal investigator, and a team of researchers have constructed water tunnels to simulate the movement of ships at sea. The drag a ship encounters is measured from the tiny air bubbles emitted in the water tunnel. Dr. Runnels's team has also developed the use of polymers, or long carbon chain molecules, to reduce drag. The polymers act like a slimy coating for the ship's hull to help it glide through the water more easily. When asbestos fibers were added to the polymer solutions, the investigators measured a 90 percent reduction in drag. The team has also experimented with an external pump attached to the hull of a ship, which pushes the water away from a ship's path, saving even more energy and time.

Supplies an easy-to-follow analogy for her audience

Clearly explains the Labs' research and its importance for readers concerned about the economy and environment

Editing

Editing is quality control for your reader. This last stage in the writing process might be compared to detailing an automobile—the preparation a dealer goes through to ready a new car for prospective buyers. Editing is done only after you are completely satisfied that you have made all of the big decisions about content, organization, and format—that you have said what you wanted to, where and how you intended, for your audience.

When you edit, you will check your work to make sure it is readable and correct. At this stage, pay close attention to

- sentences
- word choices
- punctuation

- spelling
- grammar and usage
- tone

As you edit, check to be sure your message is clear and concise so that readers will be able to understand it quickly and find it persuasive. The sentences you write and the words and tone you choose play a major role in how your message is received.

As with revising, don't skip or rush through the editing process, thinking that once your ideas are down, your work is done. If your work is hard to read or contains mistakes in spelling or punctuation, readers will think that your ideas and your research are also faulty.

The following sections will give you basic guidelines about what to look for when you edit your sentences and words. "A Writer's Brief Guide to Paragraphs, Sentences, and Words," found in the Appendix on pages A-1–A-19, also contains helpful suggestions on using correct spelling and punctuation.

Editing Guidelines for Writing Lean and Clear Sentences

Here are four of the most frequent complaints readers voice about poorly edited writing in the world of work:

- **The sentences are too long.** I could not follow the writer's ideas easily.
- **The sentences are too complex,** making it hard to understand what the writer meant the first time I read the work; I had to reread it several times.
- **The sentences are unclear.** Even after I reread them, I was not sure I understood the writer's message.
- **The sentences are too short and simplistic.** The writing felt "dumbed down."

Writing clear, readable sentences is not always easy. It takes effort, but the time you spend editing will pay off in rich dividends for you and your readers. The seven guidelines that follow should help with the editing phase of your work.

  1. Avoid needlessly complex or lengthy sentences. Do not pile words on top of words. Instead, edit one overly long sentence into two or even three more manageable ones.

> Too long: The planning committee decided that the awards banquet
>   should be held on March 15 at 6:30, since the other two
>   dates (March 7 and March 22) suggested by the hospitality

committee conflict with local sports events, even though one of those events could be changed to fit our needs.

Edited for easier reading: The planning committee has decided to hold the awards banquet on March 15 at 6:30. The other dates suggested by the hospitality committee—March 7 and March 22—conflict with two local sports events. Although the date of one of those sports events could be changed, the planning committee still believes that March 15 is our best choice.

2. Combine short, choppy sentences. Don't shorten long, complex sentences, only to turn them into choppy, simplistic ones. A memo, an email, or a letter written exclusively in short, staccato sentences sounds immature.

When you find yourself looking at a series of short, blunt sentences, as in the following example, combine them where possible and use connective words similar to those italicized in the edited version.

Choppy: Medical transcriptionists have many responsibilities. Their responsibilities are important. They must be familiar with medical terminology. They must listen to dictation. Sometimes physicians talk very fast. Then the transcriptionist must be quick to transcribe what is heard. Words could be missed. Transcriptionists must forward reports. These reports have to be approved. This will take a great deal of time and concentration. These final reports are copied and stored properly for reference.

Edited: Medical transcriptionists have many important responsibilities. *These* include transcribing physicians' orders using correct medical terminology. *When* physicians dictate rapidly, transcriptionists have to keyboard accurately *so* that no words are omitted. *Among their most demanding* duties are keyboarding and forwarding transcriptions *and then*, after approval, storing copies properly for future reference.

3. Edit sentences to tell who does what to whom or what. The clearest sentence pattern in English is the subject-verb-object (s-v-o) pattern.

s   v   o

Sue booted the computer.

               s   v   o

Our website contains a link to key training software programs.

Readers find this pattern easiest to understand because it provides direct and specific information about the action. Hard-to-read sentences obscure or scramble information about the subject, the verb, or the object. In the following unedited sentence, the subject is hidden in the middle rather than being placed in the most crucial subject position.

Who is responsible for taking action? What action must they take? For whom is such action taken?

Unclear: The control of the ceiling limits of glycidyl ethers on the part of the employers for the optimal safety of workers in the workplace is necessary.

Edited: Employers must control the ceiling limits of glycidyl ethers for workers' safety.

4. **Use strong, active verbs rather than verb phrases.** In trying to sound important, many bureaucratic writers avoid using simple, graphic verbs. Instead, these writers use a weak verb phrase (for example, *provide maintenance of* instead of *maintain, work in cooperation with* instead of *cooperate*). Such verb phrases imprison the active verb inside a noun format and slow readers down. Note how the edited version here rewrites the weak verb phrases.

> Weak: The city provided the employment of two work crews to assist the strengthening of the dam.
> Strong: The city employed two work crews to strengthen the dam.

5. **Avoid piling modifiers in front of nouns.** Putting too many modifiers (words used as adjectives) in the readers' path to the noun is confusing for readers, who will have trouble deciphering how one modifier relates to another modifier or to the noun.

> Crowded: The vibration noise control heat pump condenser quieter can make your customer happier.
> Readable: The quieter on the condenser for the heat pump will make your customer happier by controlling noise and vibrations.

Twenty-one words of the original sentence—everything after "areas for"—have been reduced to four words: "resident and commuter students."

6. **Replace wordy phrases or clauses with one- or two-word synonyms.**

> Wordy: The college has parking zones for different areas for people living on campus as well as for those who do not live on campus and who commute to school.
> Edited: The college has different parking zones for resident and commuter students.

This revision combines three sentences into one, condenses twenty-four words into fourteen, and joins three related thoughts.

7. **Combine sentences beginning with the same subject or ending with an object that becomes the subject of the next sentence.**

> Wordy: Homeowners want to buy low-maintenance bushes. These low-maintenance bushes include the ever-popular holly and boxwood varieties. These bushes are also inexpensive.
> Edited: Homeowners want to buy low-maintenance and inexpensive bushes such as holly and boxwood.

Editing Guidelines for Cutting Out Unnecessary Words

Too many people in business think the more words, the better. Nothing could be more self-defeating. Your readers are busy; unnecessary words slow them down. Make every word work. Cut out any words you can from your sentences. If the sentence still makes sense and reads correctly, you have eliminated wordiness.

1. **Replace wordy phrases with precise ones.** See how in Table 2.1 wordy phrases on the left are replaced with their much more concise equivalents on the right. Many of these wordy phrases have slowed business writing down for decades.

2. **Use concise, not redundant, phrases.** Another kind of wordiness comes from using redundant expressions—saying the same thing a second time, only in different words. "Fellow colleague," "component parts," "corrosive acid," and "free gift" are phrases that contain this kind of double speech; a fellow *is* a colleague, a component

TABLE 2.1   Wordy Phrases and Their Concise Equivalents

Wordy	Concise	Wordy	Concise
at a slow rate	slowly	in connection with	about
at an early date	soon	in the event that	if
at this point in time	now	in the month of May	in May
based on the fact	because	in the neighborhood of	approximately, about
be in agreement with	agree	it is often the case that	often
bring to a conclusion	conclude, end	look something like	resemble
come to terms with	agree, accept	of the opinion that	think
due to the fact that	because	on the grounds that	because
during the course of	during	until such time as	until
express an opinion that	affirm	with reference to	regarding, about
for the period of	for	with the result that	so

© Cengage Learning 2015

is a part, acid *is* corrosive, and a gift *is* free. In the following examples, the suggested changes on the right are preferable to the redundant phrases on the left.

Redundant	Concise
absolutely essential	essential
advance reservations	reservations
basic necessities	necessities, needs
close proximity	proximity, nearness
end result	result
final conclusions/final outcome	conclusions/outcome
first and foremost	first
full and complete	full, complete
personal opinion	opinion
tried-and-true	tried, proven

© Cengage Learning 2015

3. Watch for repetitive words, phrases, or clauses within a sentence. Sometimes one sentence or one part of a sentence needlessly duplicates another.

Redundant: To provide more room for employees' cars, the security department is studying ways to expand the employees' parking lot.

Edited: The security department is studying ways to expand the employees' parking lot.

Because the first phrase says nothing that the reader does not know from the independent clause, it can be cut.

4. Avoid unnecessary prepositional phrases. Adding a prepositional phrase can sometimes contribute to redundancy. The italicized words in the following list are unnecessary. Be on the lookout for these phrases and delete them.

audible *to the ear*　　light *in weight*　　short *in duration*
bitter *in taste*　　loud *in volume*　　soft *in texture*
fly *through the air*　　orange *in color*　　tall *in height*
hard *to the touch*　　rectangular *in shape*　　twenty *in number*
honest *in character*　　second *in sequence*　　visible *to the eye*

Figure 2.6 below shows an email that Trudy Wallace wants to send to her boss, Lee Chadwick, about issuing tablets to the sales force. Her unedited work is bloated with unnecessary words, expendable phrases, and repetitious ideas.

FIGURE 2.6 A Wordy, Unedited Email

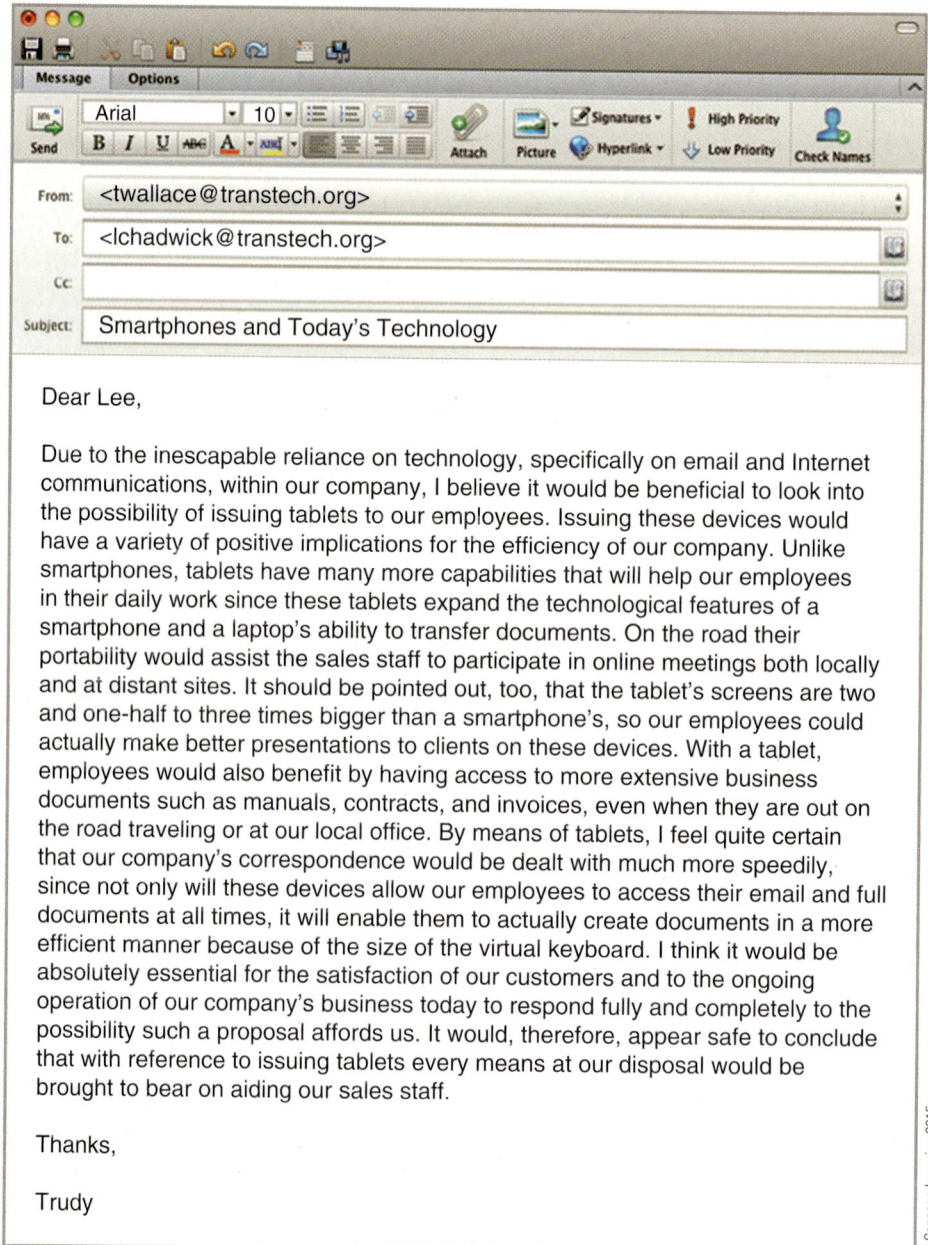

Wordy and unfocused subject

One long, unbroken paragraph is hard to follow

Repeats same idea in two or three sentences

Uses awkward and wordy sentences

Does not specify what writer will do about problem

From: <twallace@transtech.org>

To: <lchadwick@transtech.org>

Cc:

Subject: Smartphones and Today's Technology

Dear Lee,

Due to the inescapable reliance on technology, specifically on email and Internet communications, within our company, I believe it would be beneficial to look into the possibility of issuing tablets to our employees. Issuing these devices would have a variety of positive implications for the efficiency of our company. Unlike smartphones, tablets have many more capabilities that will help our employees in their daily work since these tablets expand the technological features of a smartphone and a laptop's ability to transfer documents. On the road their portability would assist the sales staff to participate in online meetings both locally and at distant sites. It should be pointed out, too, that the tablet's screens are two and one-half to three times bigger than a smartphone's, so our employees could actually make better presentations to clients on these devices. With a tablet, employees would also benefit by having access to more extensive business documents such as manuals, contracts, and invoices, even when they are out on the road traveling or at our local office. By means of tablets, I feel quite certain that our company's correspondence would be dealt with much more speedily, since not only will these devices allow our employees to access their email and full documents at all times, it will enable them to actually create documents in a more efficient manner because of the size of the virtual keyboard. I think it would be absolutely essential for the satisfaction of our customers and to the ongoing operation of our company's business today to respond fully and completely to the possibility such a proposal affords us. It would, therefore, appear safe to conclude that with reference to issuing tablets every means at our disposal would be brought to bear on aiding our sales staff.

Thanks,

Trudy

After careful editing, Trudy Wallace streamlined her email seen in Figure 2.7. She pruned wordy expressions and combined sentences to cut out duplication. The revised version is only 127 words, as opposed to the 299 words in the draft. Not only has Wallace shortened her message, but she has also made it easier to read.

Editing Guidelines to Eliminate Sexist Language

Editing involves far more than just making sure that your sentences are readable. It also reflects your professional style—how you see and characterize the world of

FIGURE 2.7 A Concise Version of the Wordy Email in Figure 2.6

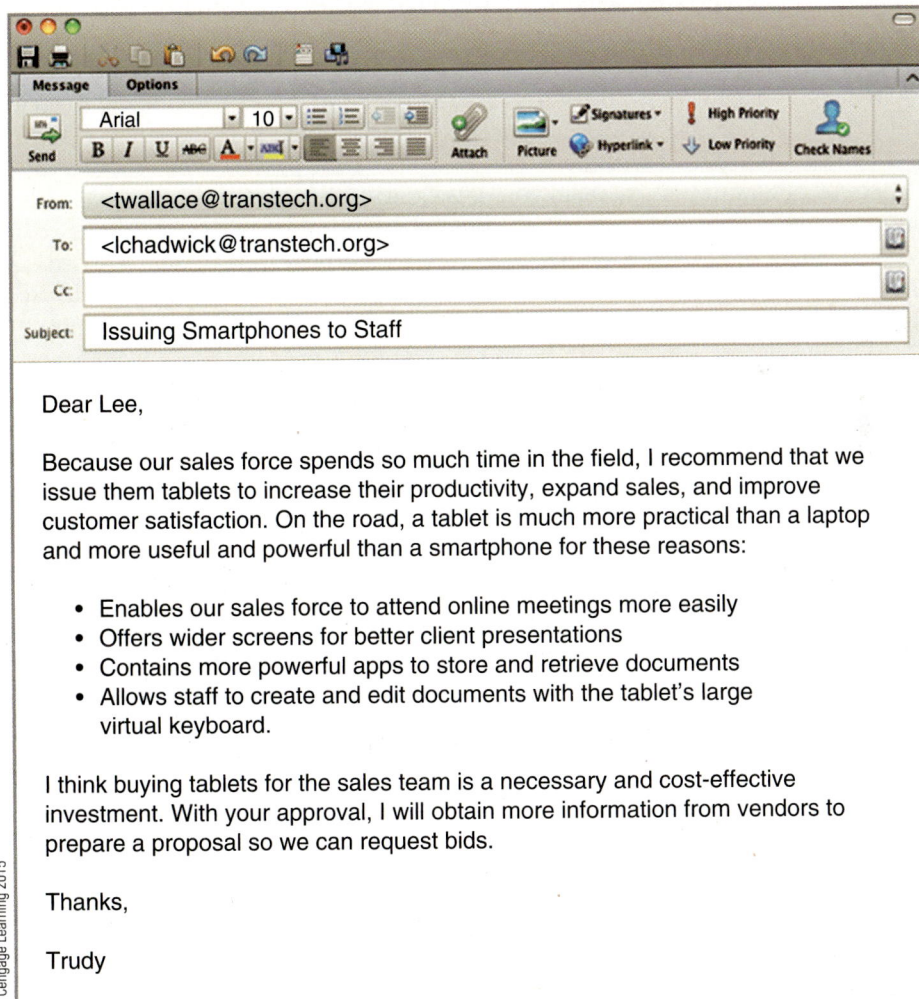

From: <twallace@transtech.org>
To: <lchadwick@transtech.org>
Cc:
Subject: Issuing Smartphones to Staff

Focused subject

Dear Lee,

Because our sales force spends so much time in the field, I recommend that we issue them tablets to increase their productivity, expand sales, and improve customer satisfaction. On the road, a tablet is much more practical than a laptop and more useful and powerful than a smartphone for these reasons:

Gets to point quickly

- Enables our sales force to attend online meetings more easily
- Offers wider screens for better client presentations
- Contains more powerful apps to store and retrieve documents
- Allows staff to create and edit documents with the tablet's large virtual keyboard.

Provides convincing reasons

I think buying tablets for the sales team is a necessary and cost-effective investment. With your approval, I will obtain more information from vendors to prepare a proposal so we can request bids.

Closes with plan and request

Thanks,

Trudy

work and the individuals in it, not to mention how you want your readers to see you. Your words should reflect a high degree of ethics and honesty, free from bias, offense, and stereotype. They need to be sensitive to the needs of your international audience as well (see pages 142–150).

Sexist language in particular offers a distorted view of a job force and discriminates in favor of one sex at the expense of another, usually women. It portrays men as having more powerful, higher-paying jobs than women do. Using sexist language offends and demeans female readers by depriving them of their equal rights and it may cost your company business as well. You can avoid gender bias by using inclusive language for women and men alike, treating them equally and fairly.

Sexist language is often based on stereotypes that depict men as superior to women. For example, calling politicians *city fathers* or *favorite sons* follows the stereotypical picture of seeing politicians as male. Such phrases discriminate against women who do or could hold public office at all levels of government. Never assume or imply a person's gender is based on his or her profession.

Sexist Language and Professional Titles   As these examples show, such language prejudiciously labels some professions as masculine and others as feminine. Keep in mind that sexist phrases assume engineers, physicians, and pilots are male (*he, his,* and *him* are often linked with these professions in descriptions), while social workers, nurses, administrative assistants, and secretaries are often portrayed as female (*she, her*), although members of both sexes work in all these professions. Sexist language also wrongly points out gender identities when such roles do not seem to follow biased expectations—*lady lawyer, male secretary, female surgeon,* or *male nurse.* Such offensive distinctions reflect prejudiced attitudes that you should eliminate from your writing.

Always prune the following sexist phrases: *every man for himself, gal Friday, little woman, lady of the house, old maid, women's intuition, the best man for the job, to man a desk* (or *post*), *the weaker sex, woman's work, working wives, a manly thing to do,* and *young man on the way up.*

Finally, don't assume all employees are male. Instead of writing, "All staff members and their wives are invited to attend," simply say, "All staff members and their guests are invited to attend."

Ways to Avoid Sexist Language

Here are five ways you can eliminate sexist writing from your work.

1. **Replace sexist words with neutral ones.** Neutral words do *not* refer to a specific sex; they are genderless. The sexist words on the left in the following list can be replaced by the neutral nonsexist substitutes on the right.

Sexist	Neutral	Sexist	Neutral
alderman	representative	chairman	chair, chairperson
assemblyman	representative	common man	average citizen
businessman	businessperson	congressman	representative
cameraman	photographer	craftsman	skilled worker

Sexist	Neutral	Sexist	Neutral
fireman	firefighter	manmade	synthetic, artificial
foreman	supervisor	manpower	strength, power
housewife	homemaker	man to man	candidly
janitress	custodian	policeman	police officer
landlord, landlady	owner	salesman	salesperson, clerk
maiden name	family name	spokesman	spokesperson
mailman, postman	mail carrier	weatherman	meteorologist
man-hours	work-hours	women's intuition	intuition
mankind	humanity	workman	worker

2. Watch masculine pronouns. Avoid using the masculine pronouns (*he, his, him*) when referring to a group that includes both men and women.

> *Every worker must submit his travel expenses by Monday.*

Workers may include women as well as men, and to assume that all workers are men is misleading and unfair to women. You can edit such sexist language in several ways.

   a. Make the subject of your sentence plural and thus neutral.

> *Workers must submit their travel expenses by Monday.*

   b. Replace the pronoun *his* with *the* or *a* or drop it altogether.

> *Every employee is to submit a travel expense report by Monday.*
> *Every worker must submit travel expenses by Monday.*

   c. Use *his or her* instead of *his*.

> *Every worker must submit his or her travel expenses by Monday.*

   d. Reword the sentence using the passive voice.

> *All travel expenses must be submitted by Monday.*

Moreover, in some contexts exclusive use of the masculine pronoun might invite a lawsuit. For example, you would be violating federal employment laws prohibiting discrimination on the basis of sex if you wrote the following in a help-wanted notice for your company.

> *Each applicant must submit his transcript with his application. He must also supply three letters of recommendation from individuals familiar with his work.*

The language of such a notice implies that only men can apply for the position.

   Keep in mind that international readers may find these guidelines on avoiding masculine pronouns confusing because many languages (e.g., French, Spanish) follow grammatical instead of natural gender. In French, the word for *doctor* is masculine, for example.

3. Avoid using sexist words that end in -ess or -ette. Use gender-neutral alternatives for words like *stewardess* (*flight attendant*), *poetess* (*poet*), *waitress* (*server*).

4. **Eliminate sexist salutations.** Never use the following salutations when you are unsure of who your readers are:

- Dear Sir
- Gentlemen
- Dear Madam

Any woman in the audience will surely be offended by the first two greetings and may also be unhappy with the pompous and obsolete *madam*. It is usually best to write to a specific individual, but if you cannot do that, direct your letter to a particular department or group: *Dear Warranty Department* **or** *Dear Selection Committee.*

Be careful, too, about using the titles *Miss, Mr.,* and *Mrs.* Sexist distinctions are unjust and insulting. It is preferable to write *Dear Ms. McCarty* rather than *Dear Miss or Mrs. McCarty.* A woman's marital status should not be an issue. Try to find out if the person prefers *Ms.* to another courtesy title (e.g., *Editor Hawkins, Supervisor Jones*). If you are in doubt, write *Dear Indira Kumar.* Chapter 4 shows acceptable salutations to use in your letters (see page 104).

5. **Never single out a person's physical appearance.** Sexist physical references negatively draw attention to a woman's gender. Sexist writers would not describe a male manager using physical terms as in the following sentence:

> *The manager is a tall blonde who received her training at Mason Technical Institute.*

Avoiding Other Types of Stereotypical Language

In addition to sexist language, avoid any references that stereotype an individual because of race, national origin, age, disability, or sexual orientation. Not only are such references almost always irrelevant in the workplace (except for Equal Employment Opportunity Commission reports or health care documentation), they are discriminatory, culturally insensitive, and ethically wrong.

To eliminate biased language in your workplace writing, follow these guidelines.

1. **Do not single out an individual because of race or national origin or stereotype him or her because of it.** Be especially sensitive when referring to someone's ethnic identity.

Wrong: Bill, who is African American, is one of the company's top sales reps.
Right: Bill is one of the company's top sales reps.

Wrong: The Chinese computer whiz was able to find the problem.
Right: The programmer was able to find the problem.

2. **Identify members of an international community accurately.** Not every native Spanish speaker is Latin American or Hispanic. Be sensitive to significant cultural differences among groups (Cuban Americans and Mexican Americans, for example).

3. **Avoid words or phrases that discriminate against an individual because of age.** For example, do not use *elderly, up in years, geezer, old-timer, over the hill, senior moment,* or the adjectives *spry* or *frail* when they are applied to someone's age: "a spry sixty-seven."

> Wrong: Jerry Fox, who will be fifty-seven next month, comes up with obsolete plans from time to time.
>
> Right: Some of Jerry Fox's plans have not been adopted.

4. Respect individuals who may have a disability. Do not discriminate against someone who has a disability. Keep in mind that the Americans with Disabilities Act (1990) prohibits employers from asking if a job applicant has a disability. Avoid derogatory words such as *amputee, crippled, handicapped, impaired*, or *lame* (physical disabilities) or *retarded* or *slow* (mental disabilities). Stay away from terms such as these because they identify the entire individual rather than just the aspects that the disability affects. Emphasize the individual instead of the physical or mental condition as if it solely determined that person's abilities.

> Wrong: Tom suffers from MS.
>
> Right: Tom is a person living with MS.

> Wrong: Sarah, who is crippled, still does an excellent job of keyboardivng.
>
> Right: Sarah's disability does not prevent her from keyboarding.

Also, do not use such phrases as *wheelchair-bound* or *confined to a wheelchair*, which wrongly and unfairly imply that a person in a wheelchair cannot move around on his or her job. Avoid using discriminatory expressions in your writing, such as a *crippled economy, lame excuse, mentally challenged*, or *mental midget*.

5. Don't stereotype based on sexual orientation. Avoid unnecessarily labeling a person by sexual orientation as if that is the only significant aspect of that person's life.

> Wrong: Paula Smith, a lesbian, hosts a successful daytime talk show.
>
> Right: Paula Smith hosts a successful daytime talk show.

In addition, avoid derogatory innuendos, comments, or jokes about gay men, lesbians, or bisexuals (e.g., "That's so gay"), and don't assume that all of your readers are heterosexual.

Collaboration Is Crucial to the Writing Process

In the world of work, writing skills, such as researching, planning, drafting, revising, and editing—just discussed in this chapter—are vital for your success. But you will often communicate as part of a team (including managers and co-workers) to write a report, a proposal, or even a letter successfully. A major survey estimates that 90 percent of all businesspeople spend some time writing as part of a collaborative team. Being a team player is one of the most prized skills you can possess in the world of work.

Over the next few sections of this chapter, we'll explore the advantages of the collaborative writing process, guidelines for effective group writing, and ways to help resolve conflicts in the group-writing process. Because an overwhelming majority of workplace collaborative writing takes place online, we'll also investigate how technology enhances the collaborative writing process and see how a document can be collaboratively created online.

Advantages of Collaborative Writing

Collaborative writing teams benefit both employers and employees. Specific advantages of collaboration include the following.

1. It builds on collective talents.
2. It allows for productive feedback and critique.
3. It increases productivity and saves time and money.
4. It ensures overall writing effectiveness.
5. It accelerates decision-making time.
6. It reduces corporate risk.
7. It boosts employee morale and confidence while decreasing stress.
8. It contributes to customer service and satisfaction.
9. It affords a greater opportunity to understand global perspectives.

Seven Guidelines for Successful Group Writing

To be successful, a collaborative writing team should observe the following seven helpful guidelines.

1. **Understand and agree on the purpose, audience, scope, organization, and deadlines for the report.** Everyone needs to be on the "same page" from start to finish.

2. **Establish group rules early on and stick to them.** Decide when and where the group will meet, how and when members are to communicate with each other (face-to-face, telephone, email, other online technologies).

3. **Put the good of the group ahead of individual egos.** Group harmony and productivity are essential if the report or proposal is to get done on time. Adopt a "we can get this done together" attitude.

4. **Agree on the group's organization.** The group can appoint a leader who keeps the team on task by being a coordinator, cheerleader, a scheduler, and a peacemaker who can resolve conflicts quickly, as well as a referee who knows when to call time-out.[1]

5. **Identify each member's responsibilities precisely.** There should be a fair distribution of labor so that each member can use his or her particular and proven skills. The entire group, however, needs to share responsibility for the overall preparation, design, writing, and proofing of the report.

6. **Provide clear and positive feedback at each meeting and for each part of the report the group prepares.** Members need to come to meetings prepared, raise important questions, and make thoughtful recommendations.

7. **Follow an agreed-on timetable, but leave room for flexibility.** The group should estimate a realistic time frame necessary to complete the various stages of their work—when drafts and revisions are due or when editing must be concluded.

---

[1]Adapted from Hendrie Wesigner, *Emotional Intelligence at Work* (New York: Jossey-Bass, 1997).

But remember: Projects always take longer than initially planned. New information may surface or you may need to do additional research.

Sources of Conflict in Group Dynamics and How to Solve Them

The success of collaborative writing depends on how well the team interacts. They have to meet and plan before they can even begin researching, set ground roles, decide on responsibilities, and work together on solving problems and come up with solutions. Discussion and criticism are essential to the process of creating any successful document—report, proposal, etc. "Conflict" in the sense of conflicting opinions—a healthy give-and-take—can be positive if it alerts the group to problems (inconsistencies, redundancies, incompleteness) and provides ways to resolve them. A conflict can even help the group generate and refine ideas, leading to a better organized and more carefully written document.

But when conflict translates into ego tripping and personal attacks, nothing productive emerges. Everyone in the group must agree beforehand on three iron-clad working policies of group dynamics: (1) individuals must seek and adhere to group consensus; (2) compromise may be advisable, even necessary, to meet a deadline; and (3) if the group decides to accept compromise, the group leader's final decision on resolving conflicts must be accepted.

Common Problems, Practical Solutions

Following are some common problems in group dynamics, with suggestions on how to avoid or solve them.

1. Resisting constructive criticism. No one likes to be criticized, yet criticism can be vital to the group effort. Be open to suggestions. Individuals who insist on "their way or no way" can become hostile to any change or revision, no matter how small.

> Solution: When emotions become heated, the group leader may wisely move the discussion to another section of the document or to another issue to allow for some cooling-off time. Negotiation is an essential job skill.

2. Giving only negative criticism. Do not saturate a meeting with nothing but negatives. You will block communication if you start criticizing the group's efforts with words such as "Why don't you try . . . ," "What you need is . . . ," "Don't you realize that . . . ," or "If you don't. . . ."

> Solution: When you criticize an idea, diplomatically remind the individual of the team's goals and point to ways in which revision (criticism) furthers those goals. Explain the problem, and offer a helpful, relevant revision. Never attack a group member. Mutual respect is everyone's right and obligation. For the sake of group harmony, be objective, constructive, and cooperative.

3. Dominating a meeting. The group process should stress sharing and responding to ideas, not about taking over. When one member dominates the discussion and becomes aggressive and territorial, the group process suffers.

> Solution: The leader should let the group know that the participation of all members is valued but then say, "We need to hear from the rest of the group." Some groups follow a three-minute rule—each member has three minutes to make comments and does not get the floor again until everyone has had a chance to speak. If one group member still continues to dominate, the leader may (in private) have to speak to him/her.

4. Refusing to participate. Withholding your opinions hurts the group efforts; identify what you believe are major problems, and give the group a chance to consider them.

> Solution: If you don't feel sure of yourself or your points, talk to another member of the group, a listening partner, before a meeting to "test" your ideas or to write down your suggestions before a meeting to share them with the group.

5. Interrupting with incessant questions. Some people interrupt a meeting so many times with questions that all group work stops. The individual may simply be unprepared or may be trying to exercise his or her control of the group.

> Solution: When that happens, a group leader can remark, "We appreciate your interest, but would you try an experiment, please, and attempt to answer your own questions?" or if the person claims not to know, the leader might then say, "Why don't you think about it for a while and then get back to us?"

6. Inflating small details out of proportion. Nitpickers can derail any group. Some individuals waste valuable discussion and revision time by dwelling on relatively insignificant points (e.g., an optional comma, the choice of a single word, etc.) or steer the group away from larger, more important issues (e.g., costs, schedules, etc.).

> Solution: If there is consensus about a matter, leave it alone and turn to more pressing issues. The leader should remind the group (without singling anyone out) about the bigger picture and caution them to stay on track.

7. Being overly deferential to avoid conflict. This problem is the opposite of that described in guideline 1. You will not help your group by being a "yes person" simply to appease a strong-willed member of the group.

> Solution: Feel free to express your opinions politely; if tempers begin to flare, call in the group leader or seek the opinions of others on the team. The leader needs to promote and protect meetings as a safe place to express ideas.

8. Not respecting cultural differences. You may have individuals from different countries or cultures on your team. Disregarding or misjudging the way they interact with the group can seriously threaten group success and harmony. Moreover, discrimination of any type—based on race, age, religious beliefs, sexual orientation, or nationality, for example—is unacceptable in a collaborative group or workplace.

> Solution: Some companies offer employees seminars on cultural sensitivity in the workplace. But a group leader must also ensure that diversity is honored and, if anyone does not, he/she may write that person up.

9. Violating confidentiality. Leaking confidential information about a personal issue, product, procedure, or operation is a serious violation in the world of work. Sometimes meetings are closed to everyone in the company except for those who are a part of the group.

> Solution: Violating confidentiality is often grounds for dismissal. At a preliminary meeting, and periodically during the writing process, the leader should emphasize the whys, hows, and whens of confidentiality.

10. Not finishing on time or submitting an incomplete document. Meeting established deadlines is the group's most important obligation to individual members and to the company. When some members are not involved in the planning stages or when they skip meetings or ignore group communications, deadlines are invariably missed. If you miss a meeting, get briefed by an individual who was there.

> Solution: The group leader can institute networking through email or other web-based systems to announce meetings, keep members updated, or provide for ongoing communication and questions. See page 60.

Computer-Supported Collaboration

To be successful writers, employees must be proficient in using multiple types of collaborative software systems, otherwise known as **groupware**. You will be expected to know—or at least be adaptable to learning—not only how to use email for collaborative coomunications but also how to navigate document tracking systems (such as Microsoft Word's Track Changes feature or Adobe Acrobat) as well as web-based collaboration systems (wikis, Google Docs).

Groupware does not, of course, completely eliminate the need for a group to meet in person to discuss priorities, clarify issues, or build team spirit. But face-to-face communications, although sometimes essential, are frequently accompanied by computer-supported collaboration via groupware.

Types of Groupware

There are essentially three types of groupware commonly used to produce collaboratively written documents in today's workplace: email, document tracking software, and web-based collaboration systems.

Email

Email is used for many jobs in the world of work, as you will see in Chapter 3. It has an important role to play in collaborative writing online as well. While email is not the place to create or revise a collaboratively written document (because edits and other changes are hard to incorporate and track), email nevertheless makes on-line collaboration possible for the following reasons:

1. It is used to send collaboratively written documents as text files or PDF files. Team members in the same office or from around the globe can then access the same document and share their feedback.
2. It can be used to make sure every member of the team is working on the same document by identifying each document by name and number in the "subject field" (*Report on Parking, Rev. 4* or *Proposal on Recycling, Draft 2*).
3. It saves the group time by decreasing the number of face-to-face meetings it must have. Email cannot take the place of a face-to-face exchange, however.

Document Tracking Software

Document tracking software, such as Microsoft Word's Track Changes feature or Adobe Acrobat, provides another way for collaborative writing teams to share, comment on, and revise their work online. Figure 2.8 shows an example of a collaboratively written document using Microsoft Word—the first draft of a section of a report on increasing parking spaces at a hospital—and how it has been revised and edited by several team members using the Track Changes feature.

Sent as an email attachment to every team member, Figure 2.8 uses the Track Changes feature in Word to preserve all the original text of Draft 1 while automatically showing and identifying comments from each individual. Team members can ask for and even supply new text, insert headings, clarify and verify factual data, and call for visuals. They can also edit sentences in the document, and Word will automatically track these changes. When a group member revises the next version of this section of the report, he or she can then accept or reject the tracked changes. But keep in mind that all changes must be agreed on by the group. This is where the dynamics of collaborative writing works for the good of the entire group in order to produce a careful document on time.

Web-Based Collaboration Systems

You can also use a wide variety of web-based applications to write collaboratively at work. These include wikis and online word-processing applications like Google Docs. With web-based collaboration systems, the text/report is automatically shared between you and your various collaborators—no emails or attachments are required. You and your collaborators can deposit files, meet to review one another's work, offer suggestions, send new text, and store files and revisions.

Web-based collaboration systems also make communication among more than two people much more efficient. Most systems consolidate all of the team's communications into a single site on the Web for each team member to view. In the workplace these systems help employees to manage complicated editing projects and to receive feedback from co-workers at different branches of a company.

FIGURE 2.8 Collaborative Editing Using a Document Tracking System

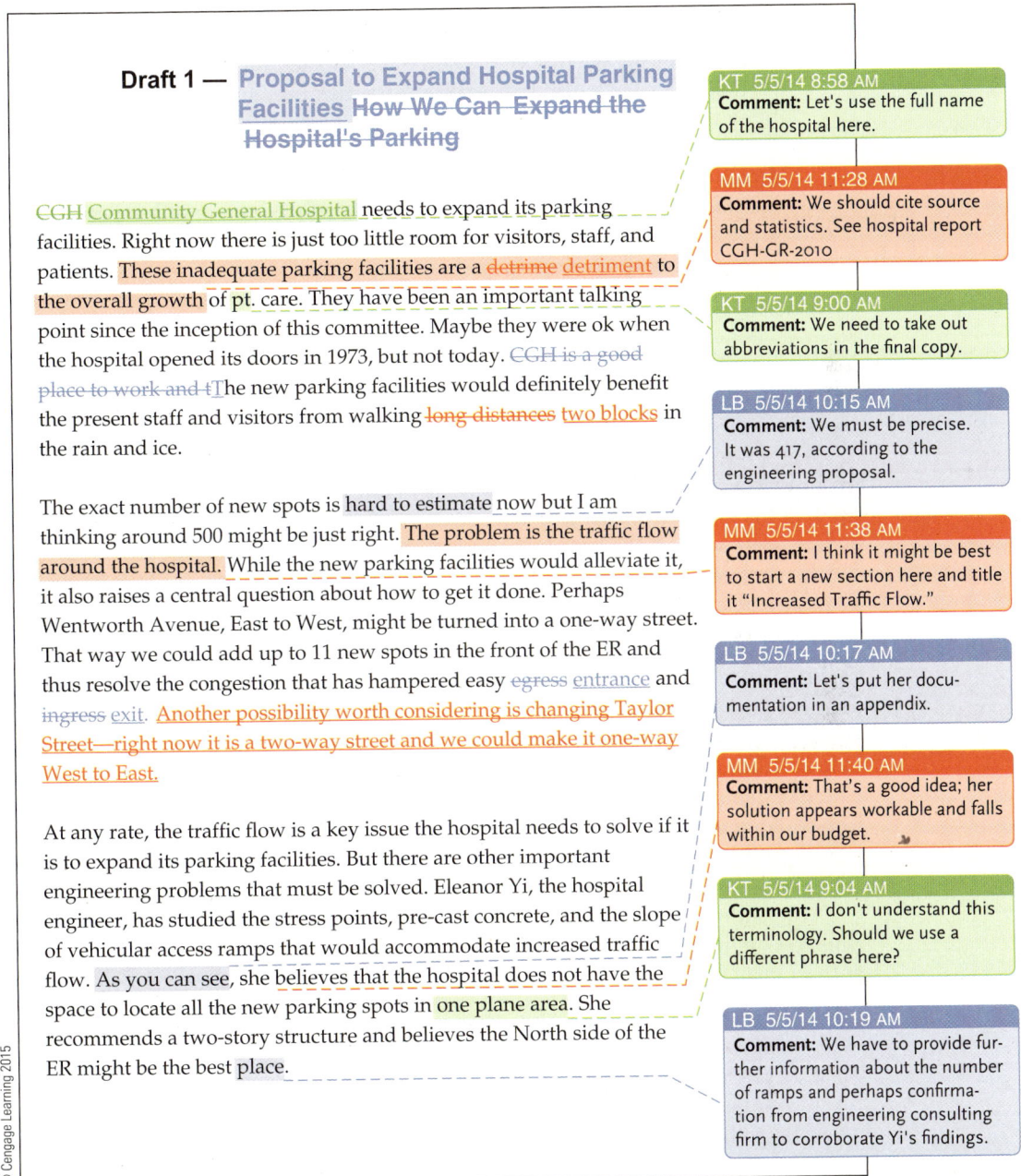

Draft 1 — Proposal to Expand Hospital Parking Facilities How We Can Expand the Hospital's Parking

CGH Community General Hospital needs to expand its parking facilities. Right now there is just too little room for visitors, staff, and patients. These inadequate parking facilities are a detrime detriment to the overall growth of pt. care. They have been an important talking point since the inception of this committee. Maybe they were ok when the hospital opened its doors in 1973, but not today. CGH is a good place to work and tThe new parking facilities would definitely benefit the present staff and visitors from walking long distances two blocks in the rain and ice.

The exact number of new spots is hard to estimate now but I am thinking around 500 might be just right. The problem is the traffic flow around the hospital. While the new parking facilities would alleviate it, it also raises a central question about how to get it done. Perhaps Wentworth Avenue, East to West, might be turned into a one-way street. That way we could add up to 11 new spots in the front of the ER and thus resolve the congestion that has hampered easy egress entrance and ingress exit. Another possibility worth considering is changing Taylor Street—right now it is a two-way street and we could make it one-way West to East.

At any rate, the traffic flow is a key issue the hospital needs to solve if it is to expand its parking facilities. But there are other important engineering problems that must be solved. Eleanor Yi, the hospital engineer, has studied the stress points, pre-cast concrete, and the slope of vehicular access ramps that would accommodate increased traffic flow. As you can see, she believes that the hospital does not have the space to locate all the new parking spots in one plane area. She recommends a two-story structure and believes the North side of the ER might be the best place.

KT 5/5/14 8:58 AM
Comment: Let's use the full name of the hospital here.

MM 5/5/14 11:28 AM
Comment: We should cite source and statistics. See hospital report CGH-GR-2010

KT 5/5/14 9:00 AM
Comment: We need to take out abbreviations in the final copy.

LB 5/5/14 10:15 AM
Comment: We must be precise. It was 417, according to the engineering proposal.

MM 5/5/14 11:38 AM
Comment: I think it might be best to start a new section here and title it "Increased Traffic Flow."

LB 5/5/14 10:17 AM
Comment: Let's put her documentation in an appendix.

MM 5/5/14 11:40 AM
Comment: That's a good idea; her solution appears workable and falls within our budget.

KT 5/5/14 9:04 AM
Comment: I don't understand this terminology. Should we use a different phrase here?

LB 5/5/14 10:19 AM
Comment: We have to provide further information about the number of ramps and perhaps confirmation from engineering consulting firm to corroborate Yi's findings.

Wikis

Wikis are similar to document-tracking systems, but they have a few crucially different characteristics:

- They are not included within a software package such as Microsoft Office. Instead, wikis are websites to which team members are given passwords, enabling them to check documents in and out of the site.
- They typically do not show tracked changes directly on the document as Microsoft Word does. Rather, each edited version is assigned a new version number. The team members can then easily compare different versions of the document, but these differences will not show up within a single version.

The advantage of wikis over tracked documents is that each wiki version is a clean document free of complicated tracked edits. When team members revise, they need to proofread only the latest draft rather than going through the time-consuming process of accepting or rejecting changes, deleting comments, or troubleshooting inconsistencies.

The disadvantage of wikis the lack of quality control. Because each group member's changes are not clearly tracked, it can be difficult for members to keep up with the number of changes. When using wikis, then, the team needs to establish a clear protocol outlining who may make changes to the document and when. To see an example of a wiki, go to http://en.wikipedia.org/wiki/Main_Page (the main English-language Wikipedia page).

Online Word-Processing Systems

Another popular web-based collaboration tool are online word-processing systems. Applications like Google Docs, Office 365, Adobe Buzzword, and Zoho Writer help collaborative teams share and edit a variety of documents easily on the Web. These systems are essentially online word processors that bundle file-sharing, online collaboration, word-processing, and document design features. Like wikis, writing and editing are done on websites. Unlike wikis, though, these systems also allow for tracking changes and document design.

One of the most widely used online systems is Google Docs, seen in Figure 2.9. This free application can be accessed and used through the Google site by anyone with a Gmail password. Google Docs offers the following benefits:

- It functions like a word processor, so the user can build publishable documents with it (a feature most wikis do not include).
- It safely stores documents in a secure space online, accessible from any computer.
- Is available free-of-charge.
- It allows team members to create, comment on, share, and revise documents on the Web.
- It records a complete revision history of any changes made to the document.
- It provides a chat window in the interface for real-time collaboration online.

FIGURE 2.9 Using Google Docs to Collaborate on a Document

Similar with Track Changes in MS Word, Google Docs highlights specific revisions made to the document. This is an earlier version of the document in the document window above. Notice how Google Docs has recorded the changes to the document.

Google Docs records a revision history of all changes made to the document in a chronological list, allowing you to easily access different versions.

Gmail Calendar **Documents** Photos Reader Sites Web more ▾   allenknutz@gmail.com ▾ ⚙

Google docs ☆   New Inventory Management   🔒 Private to me + 4 more   View only   Saved   💬 Comments ▾   Share ▾

File   Edit   View   Insert   Format   Tools   Table   Collaborate   Help

THE PROBLEM

Because of the continued growth of our business, our 1,500-square-foot warehouse is at capacity and ~~it is too expensive~~ we are spending $3,500 per month to rent ~~temporary~~ additional space ~~to store the overflow~~. We need to find a more permanent, long-term, and cost-effective storage solution. There are two possible locations available within one mile of the plant. Each one is 4,000 square feet with five-year leases of $0.68 and $0.71 per square foot, monthly. The lease improvements ~~are~~is comparable. Through the Christmas season and early spring we ~~will begin in just two months, with an~~ expected an inventory increase of 30%.

Revision history ✕

Today, 4:25 PM
■ allenknutz

Today, 4:21 PM
■ MegShao

Today, 4:18 PM
■ elenalemus66

Today, 4:15 PM
■ donrogers55

allenknutz   Document stats ↓
Don, please supply precise names of the possible storage facilities
Reply - Resolve

MegShao   4:21 PM Today ▾
Be more precise about expected inventory costs
Reply - Resolve

elenalemus66   4:18 PM Today ▾
Fix verb agreement; sentence should read: The lease improvements are
Reply - Resolve

donrogers55   4:15 PM Today ▾
Allen: supply exact space figures and costs
Reply - Resolve

Comments ▾   🔒 Share

▾ 2 other viewers

■ **donrogers55**
■ **MegShao**
■ **allenknutz**

donrogers55 has opened the document.
donrogers55: Looking at it now
MegShao: Thanks. Need to check some costs
me: Good research here

Chat window allows for real-time collaboration with editing partners.

Google Docs allows groups to edit collaboratively. A pop-up box (similar to the one above) will appear when comments are added.

Google Docs is used frequently in the workplace as a collaborative tool because it streamlines the editing process and bundles all revisions into a shared and secured space. Google Docs and other online word processors are especially helpful when you need a fast turnaround on collaboratively written and edited documents.

Avoiding Problems with Online Collaboration

Regardless of the online collaborative method your team uses, it must establish ground rules by which documents are created, posted, revised, protected, and submitted. By following these guidelines, your team can avoid common problems in any online collaboration:

1. Be sure that all team members have access and authorization.
2. Everyone in the group must be "in the loop."
3. Save the original draft and subsequent ones in separate files in case earlier drafts need to be revisited.
4. Link each revision with the individual who made it.
5. Maintain confidentiality to protect the document from unauthorized users.
6. Require all team members to sign off on and agree to the complete, final document.

Meetings

One of the most frequent ways to collaborate is through meetings, which can take the form of small group discussions or large, formal conferences. Whether it is regularly scheduled (a weekly staff meeting) or a special, unscheduled one, a meeting requires teamwork. Collective energy and goodwill will bear much fruit. To succeed in the workplace, you need to know how to plan a meeting, create an agenda, and write minutes for your group.

Planning a Meeting

As with a collaboratively written document, meetings have to be carefully planned. A group of individuals cannot simply gather and start a conversation; someone needs to help organize when and how the meeting will take place, to provide the focus for the meeting and set guidelines for how it will be conducted. If you have the responsibility of planning a meeting, be sure you can answer the following questions:

1. **What is the purpose of the meeting?** Determine why the meeting is necessary, what essential topics need to be discussed, and what results or outcomes the meeting hopes to accomplish.
2. **Who should attend the meeting?** Identify key people who need to be there, including managers, co-workers, colleagues from other departments, and any individuals outside your company (clients, vendors, etc.).
3. **What specific responsibilities do individuals in your group have?** Determine who will take minutes (see "Writing the Minutes" below), introduce the meeting, or deliver a PowerPoint or Prezi presentation, for example.
4. **When should the meeting take place?** There are good times and bad times to hold a business meeting, as the following schedule shows:

Good times	Bad times
1. Mid-morning or mid-afternoon	1. Early in the morning or late in the afternoon
2. Any time during the week except Monday morning or Friday afternoon, or immediately before or after a major holiday	2. Monday morning or Friday afternoon
	3. Immediately before or after a major holiday
3. After a major company celebration when morale is high	4. Same day as a long training session or long meeting

© Cengage Learning 2015

5. **Where should the meeting take place?** Select an appropriate space, one equipped with all the technology your group plans to use, e.g. speakerphones, SMART Boards, web-based conferencing systems.

Creating an Agenda

Out of your planning will come your **agenda**, a list of the topics to be covered at the meeting. An agenda is a one- or sometimes two-page outline of the main points to be covered at the meeting. The agenda should list only those items that your group, based on its work and interaction, regards as most crucial. Prioritize your action items so that the most important ones come first.

Writing the Minutes

The **minutes** are a summary of what happened at the meeting (see Figure 2.10, pages 67–68). Copies of minutes are kept on file—they are the official, permanent record of the group's deliberations and are regarded as legal documents. Minutes need to be clear, accurate, and impartial. If you are asked to take minutes, don't inject your own opinions of how well or poorly the meeting went; for example, "Once more Hicks got off the topic" is not appropriate. Plan on transmitting minutes 24 to 48 hours after the meeting has adjourned.

What to Include in Your Minutes

Minutes of a meeting should include the following information:

- date, time, and place of the meeting
- name of the group holding the meeting and why
- name of the person chairing the meeting
- names of those present and those absent
- the approval or amendment of the minutes of the previous meeting
- for each major point—the action items—indicate what was done:
    - what was discussed, suggested, or proposed
    - what was decided and the vote, including abstentions
    - what was continued (tabled) for a subsequent study, report, or meeting
    - the time the meeting officially concluded

Guidelines on Writing Minutes

To be effective, minutes must be concise and to the point. Here are a few guidelines to help you:

- Make sure of your facts; spell all names, products, and tests correctly.
- Concentrate on the major facts surrounding action items. Condense lengthy discussions, debates, and reports given at the meeting.
- Do not report verbatim what everyone said; readers will be more interested in outcomes—what the group did.
- List each motion (or item voted on) exactly as it is worded and in its final form.
- Avoid words that interpret (negatively or positively) what the group or anyone in the group did or did not do.

Figure 2.10 containing minutes of a meeting shows how these parts fit together.

Virtual Meetings

While face-to-face meetings are still very frequent in the workplace, technology has made virtual meetings a useful alternative. They allow a group to meet online even when a member may be traveling. Moreover, meetings in the world of work are increasingly conducted in part or entirely over the telephone or via the Web, as a convenience and to save money on travel costs.

Here are three ways technology can help you conduct a virtual meeting:

1. **Teleconferencing** allows for conference calls in which multiple participants at one's office, across the country, or around the globe can communicate with one another. But note that participants have to be notified of the call and given a password to participate in the conversation.
2. **Web conferencing** (such as Cisco's WebEx) combines the audio component of teleconferencing with the face-to-face interaction of a traditional meeting. The greatest advantage of web conferencing over teleconferencing is that individuals attending a web conference can view presentations and share documents electronically during a meeting.
3. **Dedicated videoconferencing** systems are primarily used for group-to-group conferences or one-way seminars in large rooms and auditoriums, bringing large groups of people together to share information without the expense and time of traveling.

Videoconferencing with Skype

Skype is a widely used software application that allows individuals to conduct videoconferences over the Internet without purchasing expensive videoconferencing systems. Workers can use Skype for one-on-one meetings or for videoconferences with a small group (up to 10 participants). Skype functions like a telephone call placed from one party to another. But it uses your computer's built-in or extended webcam to send video to your Skype partner(s). You can download the free software from www.skype.com.

FIGURE 2.10 Minutes from a Business Meeting

NewTech, Inc.   4300 Ames Boulevard, Gunderson, CO 81230-0999
303.555.9721   **www.newtech.com**

Minutes for Environmental Safety Committee (ESC) meeting on August 12, 2014, in Room 203 of Lab Annex Building at 10:00 a.m.

Members Present:

Thomas Baldanza, Grace Corlee (President), Virginia Downey, Victor Johnson, Roberta Koos, Kent Leviche (Secretary), Ralph Nowicki, Barbara Poe-Smith, Williard Ralston, Asah Rashid, Morgan Tachiashi, and Carlos Zandrillia

Supplies essential information on attendance, date, and place of meeting

Members Absent:

Paul Gordon (sick leave); Marty Wagner

Old Business:

The minutes from the previous meeting on July 8, 2014, were approved as read.

Refers to previous meeting to provide continuity

Reports:

(1) Morgan Tachiashi reported on the progress the Site Inspection Committee is making in getting the plant ready for the August 29 visit of the State Board of Examiners. All preparations are on schedule.

Concisely summarizes progress on ongoing business

(2) The proposal to study the use of biometric identification in place of employee ID badges is nearly complete, according to Asah Rashid.

New Business:

(1) Virginia Downey and Ralph Nowicki voiced concern about a computer virus that may strike the plant—Monkey. Disguised as a familiar email, the virus is contained in an attachment that destroys files. A motion was made by Barbara Poe-Smith, seconded by Virginia Downey, that management upgrade its antivirus protection software. The vote carried by 9 to 3.

Identifies key speakers

Records only main points of discussion and votes

FIGURE 2.10 (Continued)

Page 2

Includes other business to be continued

(2) Kent Leviche calculated computer downtime in the plant during the month of July—5 outages totaling 7.5 lost working hours—and asked the ESC to address this problem. After discussion, the ESC unanimously agreed to appoint a subcommittee to investigate the outages and determine solutions. Roberta Koos and Thomas Baldanza will chair the subcommittee and then present a survey report at next month's meeting.

Excellent morale builder

(3) Personnel in the Environmental Testing Lab were commended for their extra effort in ensuring that their department maintained the highest professional standards during the month of July.

(4) Grace Corlee adjourned the meeting at 11:41 a.m.

Signals end of meeting and date of next one

Next Meeting:

The next meeting of the ESC will be on September 9 at 1:00 p.m. in Room 203 of the Lab Annex Building.

© Cengage Learning 2015

Like other business meetings, you have to prepare for a Skype conference. Just because it is not as formal as other videoconferences does not release you from the responsibilities of doing your homework—planning, sharing information, and taking notes. Here are five guidelines to help make your Skype videoconference productive:

- Collaboration works best in Skype videoconferences when everyone has a fast Internet connection. But confirm with the participants before the meeting that their Internet connection will support a videoconference.
- Always test your camera to make sure it is working (and is in focus) before making a Skype call, and ask the other participants to check theirs, too. In your Skype contact list, click on "Echo/Sound Test Service" to test your audio settings.
- Look directly into your computer's webcam (and not at the keyboard) so that the participants can see you clearly.
- Be sure that any files you share during the meeting through Skype are relevant.
- Do not try to carry on another conversation on your cell phone or tweet or text during your Skype conversation.

✓ Revision Checklist

- [ ] Researched my topic carefully to obtain enough information to answer all my readers' questions—online searches, interviews, questionnaires, personal observations.
- [ ] Before writing, determined the amount and kinds of information needed to complete my writing task.
- [ ] Spent enough time planning—brainstorming, outlining, clustering, or a combination of these techniques. Produced substantial material from which to shape a draft. Documented sources.
- [ ] Prepared enough drafts to decide on the major points in my message to readers. Made major changes and deletions where necessary in my drafts to strengthen the document.
- [ ] Revised drafts carefully to successfully answer readers' questions about content, organization, and tone. Formatted the text to make it easy to follow.
- [ ] Made time to edit my work so that the style is clear and concise and the sentences are readable and varied. Checked punctuation, sentences, and words to make sure they are spelled correctly and are appropriate for my audience.
- [ ] Eliminated sexist and other biased language that unfairly stereotypes individuals because of race, ethnicity, disability, or sexual orientation.
- [ ] Followed the necessary steps of the writing process to take advantage of team effort and feedback.
- [ ] Attended all group meetings and understood and agreed to the responsibilities of the group and my own obligations.
- [ ] Finished the research, planning, and/or drafting expected of me as a group member.
- [ ] Shared my research, ideas, and suggestions for revision through constructive criticism.
- [ ] Participated honestly and politely in discussions with colleagues.
- [ ] Was open to criticism and suggestions for change.
- [ ] Took advantage of email, instant messaging, and groupware applications (e.g., document tracking systems, wikis, Google Docs) to communicate with my collaborative team.
- [ ] Investigated the research, drafting, revising, and editing benefits available with computer software.
- [ ] Answered questions and responded to requests promptly from the team leader and collaborative team members.
- [ ] Attached pertinent documents in emails to the collaborative team.
- [ ] Avoided technical problems with online collaboration by adhering to established policies.
- [ ] Respected confidentiality and used computer-assisted editing technologies responsibly and ethically.

☐ Prepared a clear agenda for the meeting and distributed it to members ahead of time.

☐ Wrote minutes that objectively reported what happened.

☐ Took notes that highlighted main points of the meeting for my collaborative team and boss.

☐ Participated in virtual meetings through teleconferencing or web conferencing or videoconferencing.

Exercises

1. Following is a writer's initial brainstormed list for a report on stress in the workplace. Revise the brainstormed list, eliminating repetition and combining related items.

— leads to absenteeism
— high costs for compensation for stress-related illnesses
— proper nutrition
— numerous stress-reduction techniques
— good idea to conduct interviews to find out levels, causes, and extent of stress in the workplace
— low morale caused by stress
— higher insurance claims for employees' physical ailments
— myth to see stress leading to greater productivity
— various tapes used to teach relaxation
— environmental factors—too hot? too cold?
— teamwork intensifies stress

— counseling
— work overload
— setting priorities
— wellness campaign
— savings per employee add up to $6,150 per year
— skills to relax
— learning to get along with co-workers
— need for privacy
— interpersonal communication
— employee's need for clear policies on transfers, promotion
— stress management workshops very successful in California
— physical activity to relieve stress
— affects management
— breathing exercises

2. Prepare a suitable outline from your revised list in Exercise 1 for a report to a decision maker on the problems of stress in the workplace and the necessity of creating a stress-management program.

3. From the revised brainstormed list in Exercise 1, write a one-page memo to a decision maker about how the problems of stress negatively affect workplace production.

4. Assume you have been asked to write a short report (two to three pages) to a decision maker (the manager of a business you work for or have worked for; the

director of your campus union, library, or security force; a city official) about one of the following topics. Write the report alone or as part of a collaborative team.

a. recruitment of more specialists in your field
b. Internet resources
c. security lighting
d. food service
e. health care plans
f. public transportation
g. sporting events/activities
h. team building/morale
i. greening the workplace/community
j. hiring more part-time student workers

Then do relevant research and planning about one of those topics and the audience for whom it is intended by answering the following questions:

- What is my precise purpose in writing to my audience?
- What do I know about the topic?
- What information will my audience expect me to know?
- Where can I obtain relevant information about my topic to meet my audience's needs?

5. Using one or more of the planning strategies discussed in this chapter (clustering, brainstorming, outlining), generate a group of ideas for the topic you chose in Exercise 4. Work on your planning activities for about 15–20 minutes or until you have about 10–15 items. At this stage, do not worry about how appropriate your ideas are or even if some of them overlap. Just get some thoughts down on paper.

6. The following paragraphs are wordy and full of awkward, hard-to-read sentences. Edit these paragraphs to make them more readable and user friendly by using clear and concise words and sentences.

   a. It has been verified conclusively by this writer that our institution must of necessity install more bicycle holding racks for the convenience of students, faculty, and staff. These parking modules should be fastened securely to walls outside strategic locations on the campus. They could be positioned there by work crews or even by the security forces who vigilantly and constantly patrol the campus grounds. There are many students in particular who would value the installation of these racks. Their bicycles could be stationed there by them, and they would know that safety measures have been taken to ensure that none of their bicycles would be apprehended or confiscated illegally. Besides the precaution factor, these racks would afford users maximized convenience in utilizing their means of transportation when they have academic business to conduct, whether at the learning resource center or in the instructional facilities.

   b. On the basis of preliminary investigations, it would seem reasonable to hypothesize that among the situational factors predisposing the Smith family toward showing pronounced psychological identification with the San Francisco Giants is the fact that the Smiths make their domicile in the

San Francisco area. In the absence of contrariwise considerations, the Smiths' attitudinal preferences would in this respect interface with earlier behavioral studies. These studies, within acceptable parameters, correlate the fan's domicile with athletic allegiance. Yet it would be counterproductive to establish domicility as the sole determining factor for the Smiths' preference. Certain sociometric studies of the Smiths disclose a factor of atypicality, which enters into an analysis of their determinations. One of these factors is that a younger Smith sibling is a participant in the athletic organization in question.

7. Following are very early drafts of memos that businesspeople have sent to their bosses or co-workers. Revise and edit each draft, referring to the checklist on pages 69–70. Turn in your revision and the final, reader-ready copy. As you revise, keep in mind that you may have to delete and add information, rearrange the order of information, and make the tone suitable for your readers. As you edit, make sure your sentences are clear and concise and your words are professional.

a.   CAMDEN COMPANIES

TO: All Employees
DATE: February 10, 2014
RE: Improving Our Recycling Program

An in-house study has shown that Camden sends approximately 26,000 pounds of paper to the landfill. The landfill charge for this runs about $2,240, which we could save by recycling. Camden Companies is conscious of our responsibility to save and protect the environment. Accordingly, starting March 1 we will begin a more intensive paper recycling program. Our program, like many others nationwide, will use the latest degradable technology to safeguard the air, trees, and water in our community. It has been estimated that of the 250 million tons of solid waste, three-quarters of goes to landfills. These landfills across the country are becoming dangerously overcrowded. Such a practice wastes our natural resources and endangers our air and drinking water. For example, it takes 10 trees to make 1 ton of paper, or roughly the amount of paper Camden uses in four weeks. If we could recycle that amount of paper, we could save those trees. Recycling old paper into new paper involves less energy than making paper from new trees. Moreover, waste sent to landfills can, once broken down, leach, seep into our water supply, and contaminate it. The dangers are great.

By enhancing our recycling, we will not be sending so much to the Springfield Landfill and so help alleviate a dangerous condition there. We will keep it from overflowing. Camden will also be contributing to transforming waste products into valuable reusable materials. Recycling paper in our own office shows that we are concerned about the environmental clutter. By having an improved paper recycling program, we will establish our company's reputation as an environmentally conscious industry and enhance our company's image.

Camden is primarily concerned with recycling paper. The 200 old phone books that otherwise would be tossed away can get our recycling program off to a good start.

We encourage you to start thinking about the additional kinds of paper around your office/workspace that needs to be earmarked for recycling. When you start to think about it, you will see how much paper we as a company use.

Starting the last week of February, paper bins will be placed by each office door inside the outer wall. These bins will be green—not unsightly and blending with our decor. Separate your waste paper (white, colored, and computer) and put it into these bins. You do not need to remove paper clips and staples, but you must remove rubber bands, tape, and sticky labels. They will be emptied each day by the clean-up crew. There will also be large bins at the north end of the hallway for you to deposit larger paper products. The crucial point is that you use these specially marked bins rather than your wastebasket to deposit paper.

Camden Companies will deeply appreciate your cooperation and efforts.
Thanks for your cooperation.

b. TO: All Employees
    FROM: George Holmes
    DATE: October 20, 2014
    RE: Travel

Every company has its policies regarding travel and vouchers. Ours strike me as important and fairly straightforward. Yet for the life of me I cannot fathom why they are being ignored. It is in everyone's best interest. When you travel, you are on company time, company business. Respect that, won't you. Explain your purpose, keep your receipts, document your visits, keep track of meals. Do the math.

If you see more than one client per day, it should not be too hard or too much to ask you to keep a log of each, separate, individual visit. After all, our business does depend on these people, and we will never know your true contributions on company trips unless you inform us (please!) of whom you see, where, why, when, and how much it costs you. That way we can keep our books straight and know that everything is going according to company policy.

8. The following sentences contain sexist and other biased language. Edit them to remove these errors.
   a. Every intern had to record his readings daily for the spokesman.
   b. Although Marcel was an amputee, he still could hunt and peck at the keyboard.
   c. She saw a woman doctor, who told her to take an aspirin every day.
   d. Our agency was founded to help mankind.

   e. John, who is a diabetic, has an excellent attendance record.

   f. Every social worker found her schedule taxing—not enough days in the week to help out man-to-man.

   g. Maria, who is Cuban, always adds spice to company events.

   h. To be a policeman, each applicant had to pass a rigorous physical and prove himself in the manly art of self-defense.

   i. It's a wise man who can rise to the top in this cutthroat, volatile stock market.

   j. Sandy Frain, a middle-aged Irish woman, came by this morning wanting an appointment about the new policies on energy efficiency.

   k. Mrs. Johnson is in change of safety issues.

   l. He made his PowerPoint presentation as emphatically as an Italian opera singer on stage.

   m. Sanji, a longtime member of the IT department, is naturally adept at crunching the figures.

   n. Team B tried to disable our proposal by introducing irrelevant references to the many foreigners living on the north side.

   o. The average consumer spends at least two to three hours a week before her computer looking for coupons and other bargains.

   p. How many of our customers don't speak English well?

9. A new manager will be coming to your office park in the next month, and you and five other employees have been asked to serve on a committee that will submit a report about safety problems at your office park and what should be done to solve them. You and your team must establish priorities and propose guidelines that you want the new manager to put into practice. After two very heated meetings, you realize that what you and two other employees have considered solutions, the other half of your committee regards as the problems. Here is a rundown of the leading conflicts dividing your committee:

- **Speed bumps**. Half the committee likes the way they slow traffic down in the office park, but the other half says they are a menace because they can damage a car's shock absorber system.
- **Sound pollution**. Half your team wants Security to enforce a noise policy preventing employees from playing loud music while driving in and out of the office park, but the other half insists that policy violates employee rights.
- **Van and sport utility vehicle parking**. Half the committee demands that vans and sport utility vehicles park in specially designated places because they block the view of traffic for any vehicle parked next to them; the other members protest saying that people who drive these vehicles will be singled out and be given less desirable parking places.

Clearly your committee has reached a deadlock and will be unproductive as long as those conflicts go unresolved. Based on this scenario, do the following:

   a. Have each person on the committee email the other five committee members suggesting a specific plan on how to proceed—how the group can resolve their conflicts. Prepare your email message and send it to the other five committee members and to your instructor. What's your plan to get the committee moving toward writing the report to the incoming manager?

b. Assume that you have been asked to convince the other half of the committee to accept your half's views on the three areas of speed bumps, noise control, and parking. Send the three opposition committee members an attachment via email persuading them to your way of thinking. Your message must assure them that you respect their point of view.

c. Assume that the committee members reach a compromise after seeing your plan put forth in part (a). Collaboratively draft a three-page report to the new manager.

CHAPTER 3

E-Communications at Work

A large and routine share of your writing at work will be through e-communications—emails, instant messages (IMs), text messages (or texts), and blogs. Other types of e-communications will be discussed in later chapters—using social networking (165–170) and writing for the web (256–261). Each of these e-communications helps a business manage the large flow of information it needs to be competitive. Through emails, IMs, texts, and blogposts, you can send and receive information quickly, forward documents and graphics, enhance collaboration, arrange schedules, and increase business opportunities for your company.

The Flow of Information through E-Communications

Because each of these e-communications is vital to the operation of any business, expect to use them—often in combination—in the course of the business day. It is common for information to flow from one type of e-communication to another because these mediums are often used collectively to develop, edit, or send information to people both internally and externally. Your reader's needs and the type of message will dictate which e-communication you use. How carefully you manage your emails and IMs, for instance, gives your employer a very good idea of how well you do your job. See how an employee's monthly activity report (see Figure 8.5, page 315) reflects, in part, the quality and quantity of work he/she has done through these various e-tools.

This chapter will give you practical information on (a) the benefits and differences among these various e-technologies, (b) when and how to write them, and (c) the ethical and legal obligations you have when you communicate in the digital workplace.

Differences Among E-Communications

While e-communications are the workhorse of business communication, there are key differences among them you need to know. Essentially, your workplace circumstances will also determine which one is the most practical. For example:

- When you need to write a longer message, or send documents to co-workers across the country or the globe, send an email with an attachment.
- If your team members (or your boss) need to see brief information right away because of a looming deadline, and they work in the same office, write an IM.
- When a team member is out in the field and away from the office/his or her desk, a text is an expedient way to ask or answer a question.
- When you want to quickly share news, information, or promote your products to your customers or the general public, a tweet may be appropriate.
- When you want to communicate in more detail with customers about a new product, service, or your company's views on a topic, write a blogpost.

E-Communications Are Legal Records

Employers own their e-communications systems as well as the PCs, smartphones, and tablets that employees use. As we saw in Chapter 1 (pages 21–22), employers have the right to monitor what you write and to whom. Any e-communication sent over a company server can be copied, archived, forwarded, and, most significantly, intercepted. Moreover, you can be fired for writing an angry or abusive email, IM, text, tweet, or blog. Your communications can easily be converted into an electronic paper trail. You never know who will receive and then forward them—to your boss, a customer, an attorney, a licensing board. Many companies issue disclaimers to protect themselves from legal action because of an employee's offensive workplace communication. In court, an email, IM, text message, tweet, or blog can carry the same weight as a printed letter or memo.

Legal/Ethical Guidelines to Follow in Writing E-Communications

Here are some guidelines to help you write and send ethical/legal business e-communications.

1. **Do not use them for personal messages.** Send emails, IMs, texts, tweets, and blogposts only to conduct appropriate company business.
2. **Always project your company's best image.** Do not make your employer look bad by undermining management or criticizing a vendor, customer, or even a competitor. And, of course, never attack a boss or co-worker.
3. **Be accurate.** Double-check your facts—contracts, prices, warranties, guarantees, model numbers, delivery dates, safety features, etc. If you give customers wrong or misleading information, your company can be legally liable.
4. **Respect your employer's confidentiality.** Guard company trade secrets. Do not send an e-communication about ongoing research, developing new or updated products and services, sales figures, marketing plans, or personnel issues.
5. **Never write a text message, tweet, IM, email, or blog post about a raise, a grievance, or a complaint about a co-worker.** Meet with your supervisor in person to discuss these issues.

6. **Be professional and conscientious.** Avoid posting stories or pictures unrelated to your job. Moreover, don't spread rumors, comment on company policies, or make political statements—all of which may be grounds for your dismissal.
7. **Deliver what you promise.** Answer e-communications promptly and courteously. If you IM or text someone that you will respond later, don't fail to do so. And always do the necessary research to give your reader(s) the information they need.
8. **Be familiar with and follow your company's policies on e-communication and on any company-specific apps.** Know your company handbook.
9. **Protect your business records from viruses, spam, worms, Trojan horses, and hackers by following your company's security procedures.** Review your firm's IT strategies about identifying and reporting cyberspace problems. Install and use virus protection software as your company instructs.
10. **Always follow company policy.** Find out what your company rules are about texting, formats, screen names, contact information, whether you can download documents or software, etc.

Pages 167–170 will give you advice on how to avoid ethical and legal problems when using social network sites.

Email: Its Importance in the Workplace

Email continues to be one of the most common forms of communication in the workplace. It is the lifeblood of every business or organization because it expedites communication within a firm as well as outside it. On their tablets, PCs, notebooks, or mobile devices, professionals in the world of work may receive between forty and one hundred emails each day from supervisors, co-workers, clients, and vendors worldwide. Email allows you to send short messages about routine matters that make business function smoothly. Some of the information you convey (or is conveyed to you) via email may need to be disseminated further via IM, texts, tweets, or blog posts; an important skill employers look for is the ability to move information across these media platforms without losing its meaning or coherence.

Email is an informal, relaxed type of business correspondence, far more informal than a printed memo, letter, short report, or proposal, though it is more complex than instant messaging (see pages 85–87). Think of your workplace email as a polite, informative, and professional conversation. It should always be to the point and accessible, as in Figure 3.1. Yet even though business email is a way of communicating, this does not mean you can forget about your responsibilities as a courteous and ethical employee, co-worker, and writer. Figure 3.2 (page 80) exemplifies an email used to communicate diplomatically with a collaborative team.

Business Email Versus Personal Email

The email you write on the job will require more effort than your personal email will. Don't assume you can write to your employer or a customer the way you would an old friend. In the world of work, you don't just dash off an email. You have to revise and review it before you click and send it. That means proofreading carefully and

FIGURE 3.1 An Email Sent to a Co-worker

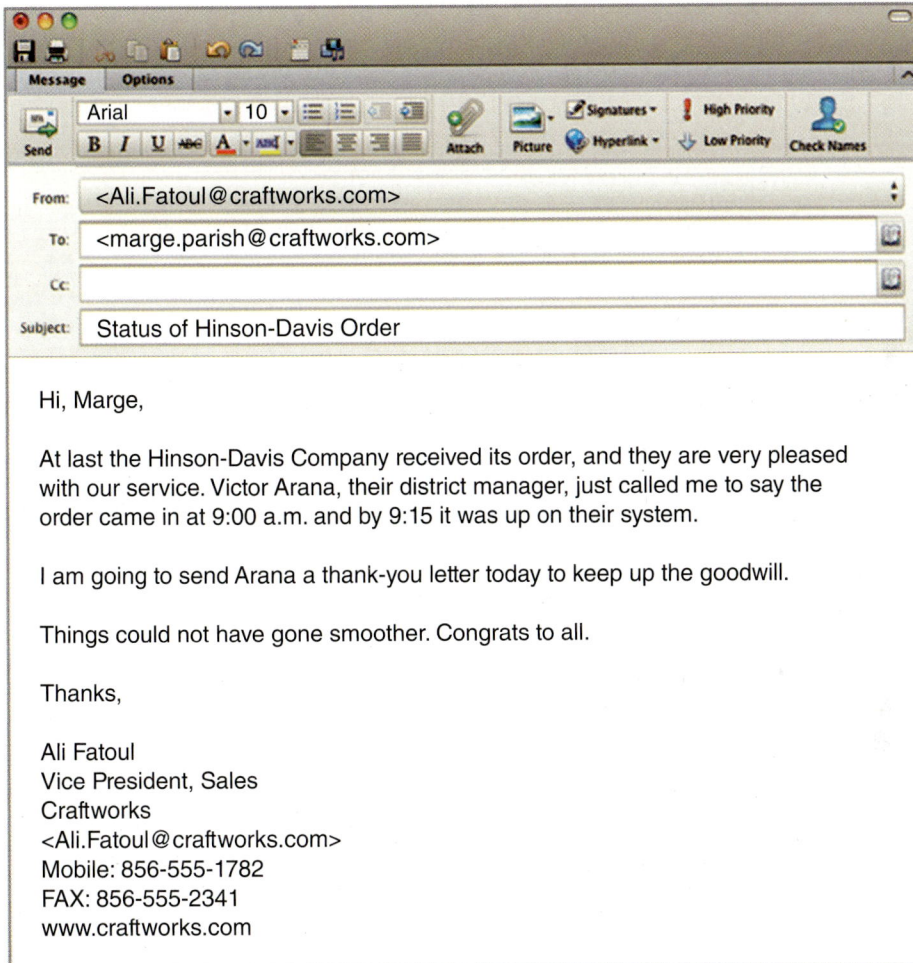

From:	<Ali.Fatoul@craftworks.com>
To:	<marge.parish@craftworks.com>
Cc:	
Subject:	Status of Hinson-Davis Order

Hi, Marge,

At last the Hinson-Davis Company received its order, and they are very pleased with our service. Victor Arana, their district manager, just called me to say the order came in at 9:00 a.m. and by 9:15 it was up on their system.

I am going to send Arana a thank-you letter today to keep up the goodwill.

Things could not have gone smoother. Congrats to all.

Thanks,

Ali Fatoul
Vice President, Sales
Craftworks
<Ali.Fatoul@craftworks.com>
Mobile: 856-555-1782
FAX: 856-555-2341
www.craftworks.com

Header contains all necessary information

Gives all necessary details concisely

Indicates follow-up

Uses informal yet professional tone

Gives contact information

© Cengage Learning 2015

following all the rules of proper spelling (avoid text-message spellings), punctuation, capitalization, and word choice, as well as the email guidelines on pages 80–83. The tone of your business email should also be much more professional than the instant messaging you may do with friends or the e-conversations you have in chat rooms.

Unlike with your personal email, you need to consider the impact your business email will have on your company and on your career. When you send a business email, you are representing more than yourself and your preferences, as in a personal email. You are speaking on behalf of your employer. Because your email must reflect your company's best image, make sure it is businesslike, carefully researched, and polite. Sarcasm, slang, an aggressive tone, name-calling, and inappropriate clip art do not belong in a company email. As we saw, Figures 3.1 and 3.2 illustrate effectively written business email. Notice that these emails are cordial without being unprofessional.

FIGURE 3.2 Email Sent to a Distribution List of Co-workers

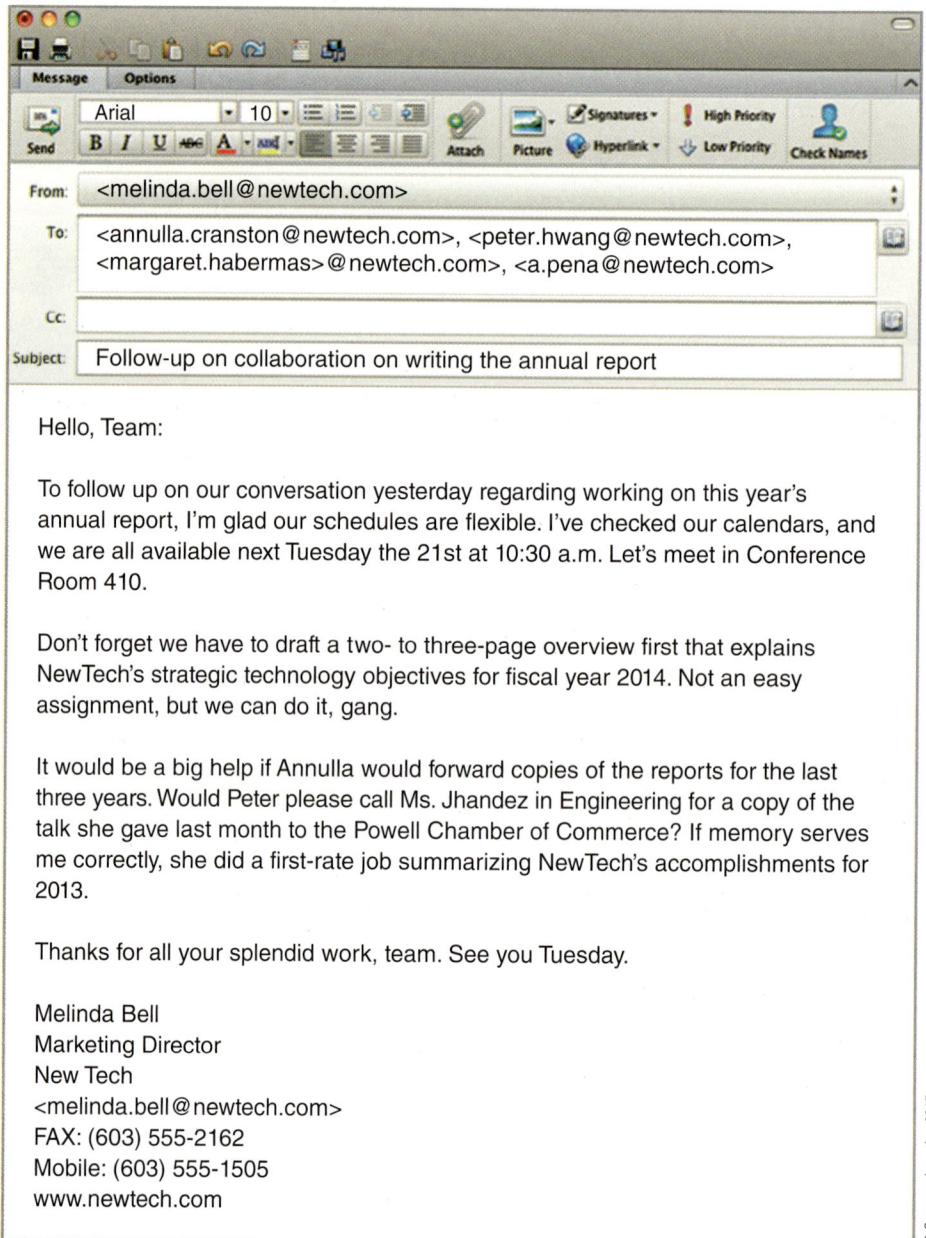

Message | Options

Arial | 10

Send | B I U ABC A ABC | Attach Picture Signatures Hyperlink High Priority Low Priority Check Names

From: <melinda.bell@newtech.com>

To: <annulla.cranston@newtech.com>, <peter.hwang@newtech.com>, <margaret.habermas>@newtech.com>, <a.pena@newtech.com>

Cc:

Precise subject line — Subject: Follow-up on collaboration on writing the annual report

Hello, Team:

Starts with context for and confirmation of meeting — To follow up on our conversation yesterday regarding working on this year's annual report, I'm glad our schedules are flexible. I've checked our calendars, and we are all available next Tuesday the 21st at 10:30 a.m. Let's meet in Conference Room 410.

Provides clear explanations and instructions — Don't forget we have to draft a two- to three-page overview first that explains NewTech's strategic technology objectives for fiscal year 2014. Not an easy assignment, but we can do it, gang.

Requests information politely — It would be a big help if Annulla would forward copies of the reports for the last three years. Would Peter please call Ms. Jhandez in Engineering for a copy of the talk she gave last month to the Powell Chamber of Commerce? If memory serves me correctly, she did a first-rate job summarizing NewTech's accomplishments for 2013.

Ends by building morale — Thanks for all your splendid work, team. See you Tuesday.

Provides contact information —
Melinda Bell
Marketing Director
New Tech
<melinda.bell@newtech.com>
FAX: (603) 555-2162
Mobile: (603) 555-1505
www.newtech.com

Guidelines for Using Email on the Job

When you prepare and organize your email message, always consider your reader's specific needs as well as those of your company. The guidelines set out here will help you to write effective business emails.

1. **Make sure your email is confidential and ethical.**

   ■ Avoid *flaming*, that is, using strong, angry language that mocks, attacks, or insults your employer, a colleague, a customer, a government agency, or a company, as in Figure 3.3 (see page 83). Abusive, obscene, or racially or culturally offensive language in an email constitutes grounds for dismissal.

   ■ Send nothing through email that you would not want to see on your company's website or that of your local newspaper.

   ■ Do not forward a co-worker's or an employer's email without that person's approval.

   ■ Do not change the wording of a message that you are expected to read and forward.

   ■ Never send an objectionable photo or file.

2. **Make your email easy to read.**

   ■ **Provide a clear, precise subject line**. Avoid one-word subjects like "Report" or "Meeting." Instead, write "Meeting to boost declining April sales." A subject line like "Bill" leaves readers wondering if your email is about a person or an unpaid account.

   ■ **Try to limit your emails to one screen**. Longer messages are better sent in an attachment rather than in the body of an email.

   ■ **Do not send emails written in all capital or all lowercase letters**. All capital letters look as if you are shouting. Conversely, emails in all lowercase imply you do not know how to capitalize, or may be seen as spam.

   ■ **Break your message into short paragraphs**. A screen filled with one dense block of text is intimidating. Make each paragraph no more than three to four lines long and always double-space between paragraphs. Do not indent your paragraphs.

   ■ **Provide hyperlink URLs for all websites you reference.** Do not make your reader look them up.

   ■ **Use plain text**. Because different email programs can garble your message, avoid overusing typefaces like italic, script, or decorative fonts, colored wallpaper, or complex formatting (such as long numbered and bulleted lists), and symbols (monetary, accents, etc.) within the body of an email. Use Times New Roman 12.

   ■ **Avoid long strings of emails**. Delete strings of previously answered emails when you reply.

3. **Observe the rules of "netiquette" (*Internet* + *etiquette*).**

   ■ **Respond promptly to an email**. Don't let emails pile up in your in-box. Check for new messages three to four times each day. If you will be offline for an extended period, use the out-of-office assistant to let readers know you are not available and when you will return. You can also have your emails forwarded to your mobile device (see page 78).

   ■ **Give your readers reasonable time to respond**. Consider time zone differences between you and your reader. It may be 2:00 a.m. when your email arrives for an international recipient.

   ■ **Do not keep sending the same email over and over**. This is discourteous and will only antagonize your recipient.

- **Avoid unfamiliar abbreviations, jargon, and emoticons**. Don't use abbreviations common in personal emails (*btw*, *lol*) or that are used in text messaging. Include only those abbreviations and jargon that your recipients will understand (e.g., *fyi*). Also, stay away from emoticons (smiley faces, sad faces, etc.) in your professional communications.
- **Don't use red flag words unnecessarily**. Stay away from words like "Urgent," "Crucial," or "Top Priority," along with accompanying red exclamation marks, in your subject line just to get your reader's attention. Your tactic will backfire, potentially upsetting readers or, worse yet, causing them to ignore any genuinely urgent messages you may send in the future.
- **Include a signature block**. A signature block, found at the end of your message, includes your name, title, and contact information (see Figures 3.1 and 3.2). Make it easy for others to contact you. Such information is crucial when you are part of a large organization.

4. **Adopt a professional business style**.

- **Use a salutation (greeting), but always follow your company's policy**. Use a comma before the party's name in a direct address.
   — to a colleague—Hi, Hello
   — to a customer—Dear Ms. Pietz, Dear Bio Tech
- **Get to the point right away**. Because readers receive a lot of email, they may look only at the first few lines you write. Start by briefly reminding readers why you are writing. Refer to a previous email. Fill in the background that explains the purpose of your message.
- **Keep your message concise**. Cut wordy phrases, and send only the information your reader needs. Exclude unnecessary details and chatter.
- **Don't turn your email into a telegram**. "Send report immediately; need for meeting" is rude, as is a reply only with "Yes," "No," or "Sure." Save words like "Nope," "Yeah," and "Huh" for your personal emails.
- **End politely**. Let readers know in your last sentence that you appreciate their help or cooperation and look forward to their reply (see Figure 3.2).
- **Use a complimentary close, but always follow your company's policy**.
   — to a colleague—Thanks, Later, Take care,
   — to a customer—Sincerely yours, Sincerely, Best regards,
- **Do not include your favorite quotation** at the bottom of your email. Your boss or customer may not agree with you. Remember, your email represents your company.
- **Proofread and spell-check** your email before you send it.

5. **Respect your international readers**.

- Use international English (see pages 4–6), which calls for short sentences, common words, and so on.
- Avoid using abbreviations, symbols, or measurements your reader may not know.
- Respect your reader's cultural traditions. For example, do not use first names unless the reader approves. Some cultures (East Asian, for instance) regard the use of abbreviations as discourteous.

- Always spell your reader's name, address, and country correctly, including the use of hyphens, accents, and capital letters.

6. **Ensure that your email is safe and secure.**

- **Use email antivirus software.** Always consult with your company's information technology (IT) department.
- **Don't be a victim of identity theft, or "phishing."** Companies you do business with will never ask for personal information, such as your bank account or Social Security number.
- **Create an email password that is not easy to guess.** Do not use a password such as "ABCDE" or "123456." Change your password regularly, and do not use the same password for all your accounts.
- **Back up important files, including emails.** Save your most important and current files in case your computer contracts a virus or crashes.

Figure 3.3 shows an example of a poorly written email that violates many of the preceding guidelines. Figure 3.4 contains an effective revision that reflects the professional and courteous way the writer and his company conduct business.

FIGURE 3.3 A Poorly Written Email Guilty of Flaming

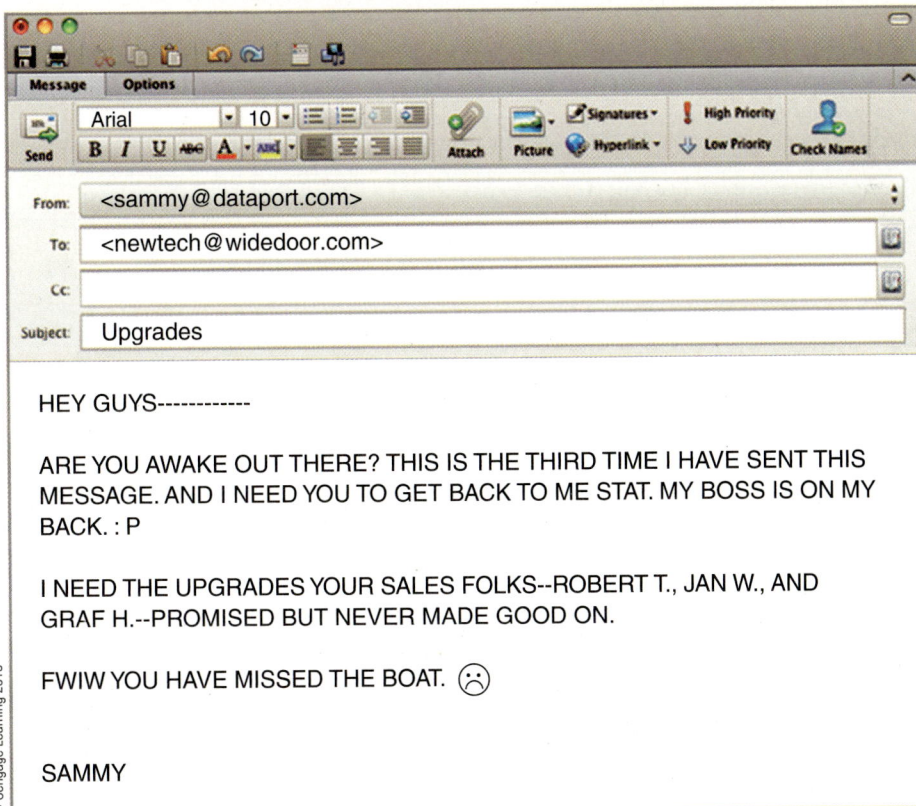

From: <sammy@dataport.com>
To: <newtech@widedoor.com>
Cc:
Subject: Upgrades

HEY GUYS------------

ARE YOU AWAKE OUT THERE? THIS IS THE THIRD TIME I HAVE SENT THIS MESSAGE. AND I NEED YOU TO GET BACK TO ME STAT. MY BOSS IS ON MY BACK. : P

I NEED THE UPGRADES YOUR SALES FOLKS--ROBERT T., JAN W., AND GRAF H.--PROMISED BUT NEVER MADE GOOD ON.

FWIW YOU HAVE MISSED THE BOAT. ☹

SAMMY

Vague subject line

Unprofessional greeting

Discourteous tone, flaming

All caps perceived as shouting

Insufficient information

Unclear abbreviation, unprofessional emoticon

No signature block

FIGURE 3.4 A Revised, Effective Version of the Poorly Written Email in Figure 3.3

Uses email address of specific person	**From:** <sammy@dataport.com>
	To: <MWood@widedoor.com>
	Cc:
Precise subject	**Subject:** Providing upgrades for service contract #4552
	📎 🔲 Service agreement.pdf

Polite salutation

Hello, Mary:

Gets to the point concisely but diplomatically

I would appreciate your delivering the upgrades for our service contract #4552 by Thursday afternoon, the 13th of November, if at all possible.

Provides explanation and documentation

We need to proceed to the next phase of our operation, and the upgrades are crucial to that task.

I am attaching a copy of our service agreement with Wide Door for your convenience.

Ends with clear-cut directions

If you run into any problems with the delivery date, please give me a call this afternoon or email me.

Professional close

Thanks,

Sammy

Includes signature block

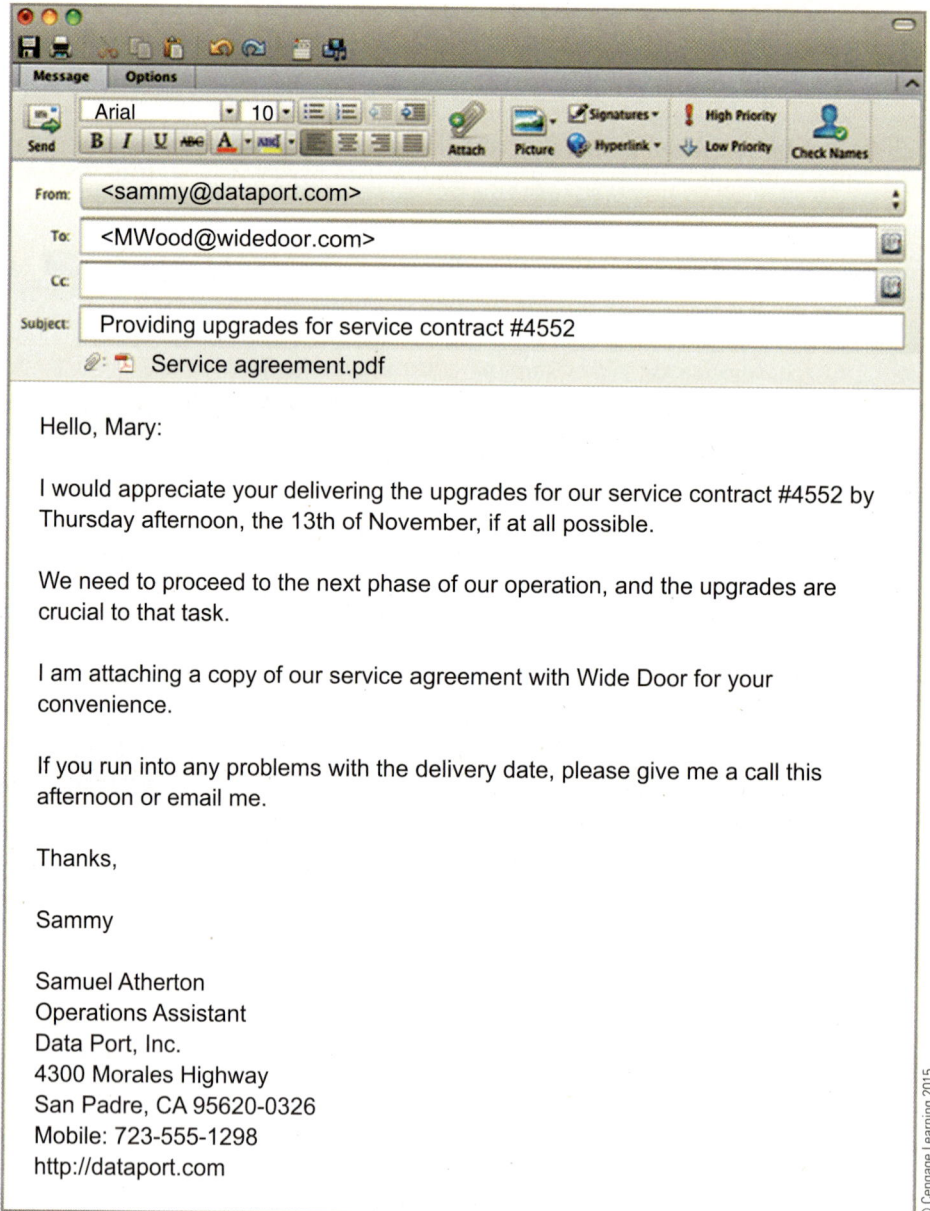

Samuel Atherton
Operations Assistant
Data Port, Inc.
4300 Morales Highway
San Padre, CA 95620-0326
Mobile: 723-555-1298
http://dataport.com

When Not to Use Email

Although email is convenient, easy to use, and appropriate for the routine business correspondence we have been discussing, be careful not to use it in the following situations:

- Send a formal letter rather than an email when you apply for a job and for any follow-up communication.
- When you make a new business contact or welcome a new client, write a formal letter, not an email. International readers, in particular, will expect this.
- Always acknowledge a business gift or courtesy by sending a handwritten thank-you note or formal letter rather than dashing off an email.
- Never send an email in place of a letter for any type of legal notification or financial statement.

Instant Messages (IMs) for Business Use

IMs are textual conversations that take place online over a PC, laptop, or tablet, and always in real time. They should not be confused with cell phone text messages, which occur in a different environment. Think of IMs as somewhere between a phone call and an email, or a chat with a colleague in the hallway of your office. IM conversations are almost as instantaneous as phone conversations, but at the same time they provide written records of communications as emails do. Keep in mind, though, that IMs are not just used for communication with your friends; they are also a vital part of workplace correspondence. In fact, researchers estimate that 90 percent of all businesses have used or will use IMs for routine workplace correspondence.

Exchanges through IM reflect the way people in the world of work connect and communicate with one another. IMs allow you to communicate with one or several co-workers and managers in the same office, at remote sites, or around the globe, all using the same system. Crossing time zones, IMs give you access to anyone around the world who is online and connected to the same service. Figure 3.5 (page 86) is an example of a professional workplace IM conversation.

When to Use IMs versus Emails

Like emails, IMs promote collaboration, provide a written record, and further global communication. But they are used for very different kinds of messages. Emails are more detailed than IMs. By answering the following questions, you will be better able to determine when to send an IM or an email:

1. **How quickly does my message need to be answered?** If you need information right away, use IM rather than an email because recipients will most likely reply at once if they are online.
2. **How long or complex is my message?** If you need to transmit a message that is, say, more than a line or two or that contains multiple points, send an email. But you can also use an IM to send attachments for immediate discussion.
3. If your message requires more time than a few brief back-and-forth communications, start an email exchange that can extend over several hours or days.

FIGURE 3.5   An IM Exchange Between Co-workers

IM user names are informal but appropriate

Messages are kept to 1–2 lines each

Message exchange sticks to a single topic

Clear language avoids "text speak"

Time stamp accompanies each message

Style is informal but polite

Writer lets co-worker know there will be a delay in responding so he can obtain the information

Writer confirms the necessary information has been received, signaling the end of the exchange

DanielleS   9:14 AM
I'm working on the second draft of the environmental impact report today.

JuanB   9:15 AM
So am I; let's talk.

DanielleS   10:01 AM
I just emailed my revision--OK or not?

JuanB   10:19 AM
Looks good, but not enough detail on the cost of implementation.

DanielleS   10:24 AM
I'll take another stab at it later today.

JuanB   10:31 AM
FYI, I'll fax you a copy of a similar short report so you have an idea of what they're looking for.

DanielleS   10:34 AM
Got it!

JuanB   10:49 AM
Let's confer after you've had a chance to read it over.

DanielleS   1:10 PM
I've just read the report. Do you have the latest figures on the expected implementation costs? Mine are from last quarter.

JuanB   1:18 PM
I don't have them either, but let me call Florence Ng; she should have them.

JuanB   1:25 PM
Florence said she'd send you the latest cost figures in an email.

DanielleS   1:36 PM
Got the cost figures, thanks. Great! They're just what we need.

© Cengage Learning 2015

Guidelines for Using IMs in the Workplace

IMs may be instantaneous and informal, but that does not mean that you can send them with little thought about their content, tone, and punctuation. Again, keep in mind that your company can monitor, trace, record, and archive your IM conversations just as it can with emails. In addition to the guidelines for writing workplace emails (pages 80–83), observe these rules for your IMs:

1. **Stay connected.** Always indicate your status—"Away," "Busy," "Offline." "Please email me at tjones@comcast.com." If you are away, tell individuals on your contact list when you will be back or give them alternate contact information, as in the preceding example.

2. **Always ask if the other person is available for IMing.** He or she may be in a meeting, on the road, etc. Don't keep sending messages if you haven't received a response. It is discourteous to have your query keep popping

up on the reader's screen. If the person is busy, inquire about a better time to chat.

3. **Keep your message short.** Get to the point right away. A sentence, or two at most, is enough for your IM. Ask your question and then wait for a reply. Don't inject unnecessary pleasantries; for example, "How was your weekend?"

4. **Write about one topic at a time.** Don't include information about two or three different subjects in one IM exchange. Keep the conversation flowing in one direction, not three.

5. **Avoid textspeak.** That may be acceptable in your personal texting, but avoid acronyms and abbreviations such as "CUL8R" for "See you later" or "B4" for "before," especially when writing to an international reader who may not understand them. Moreover, your boss might not appreciate a textspeak IM such as "np gtg ttyl" for "No problem. Got to go. Talk to you later."

6. **Be professional.** Make sure the style and tone of your message are polite and business-like. Your boss will expect you to be courteous to co-workers as well as management and customers.

7. **Choose an appropriate screen name, not "Go-Getter Pete" or "Party Animal."** Select one that is professional and reflects your job title and responsibilities.

8. **Use correct spelling and punctuation.** Just because IMs are streamlined, don't assume you can use slang, misspell words, or forget about punctuation.

9. **Don't bombard co-workers or your boss with IMs.** Send them only for brief, necessary work-related communications.

10. **Organize your contact lists into separate groups,** such as clients, co-workers, friends/family, and so on, so you do not embarrassingly send someone the wrong message.

Job-Related Tweets

Twitter is a social networking program that allows people to "tweet" information up to 140 characters at a time to both the public at large and to people who "follow" an individual or company. "Follow" someone means subscribing to his/her Twitter feed; his/her tweets will automatically come to you if you follow them. (You can sign up for Twitter—which is free of charge—at www.twitter.com.) An example of a tweet that a company might send out is shown here:

NewTech, Inc. @NewTech	8 Apr
Our new app Our Facilities is being released today; available at Apple & Android app stores.	
Expand	

Many companies use Twitter to communicate information about themselves quickly, promote their products, or share news about the company to potential customers and/or the public at large. When you write tweets on the job, follow these essential guidelines:

1. Do not share any confidential or otherwise proprietary information via Twitter.
2. Even though you can use only 140 characters, avoid textspeak as much as possible, as at times it is hard to decipher.
3. Although Twitter may seem to be an informal, casual way to "talk," don't forget that any e-communication that represents your company deserves careful, serious attention. Don't write something in a tweet you would not put in an official company email or say in a business telephone call.
4. If you have any questions about what company information you should post in a tweet, ask your supervisor to review your tweet before posting it.

Job-Related Text Messaging

Texting is the most casual, and among the shortest, form of business communication. Even so, text messaging plays an important role in the world of work:

- It is a quick and quiet way to send and receive information.
- It keeps employees who travel or telecommute in the loop.
- Used ethically, texting can be a valuable marketing tool, informing established clients about new services, product upgrades, etc.
- A text can be crucial for safety alerts and/or maintenance reminders.

Because individuals often carry their mobile devices with them, texting makes it easier to reach a co-worker or client than emailing or even calling them. In fact, you can arrange to have emails forwarded to your smartphone, and so not have to wait to use a PC to read and respond to them. Texting programs also make it possible to share multiple files, photos, videos, and graphics. A number of mobile apps will also help you to search, retrieve, send, and post information. One mobile app—Group ME—allows you to send a text to all the individuals in your office (for example, notifying staff that an employee will be out sick for two to three days or that the date of a meeting has been changed).

But the text messages you send from a company smartphone are very different from those that you write to a friend or family member. As with business emails and IMs, your texts must be ethical and legal (see pages 77–78). Pay close attention to tone, context, and spelling and always remember that what you write needs to reflect positively on you and your employer (see Figure 3.6).

Guidelines for Texting

While the guidelines for sending a text and IMing (see pages 86–87) are similar, here are a few especially relevant to texting.

1. Never text while driving a car or operating machinery.
2. Put your mobile phone on vibrate to avoid disturbing co-workers or clients at any meeting.

FIGURE 3.6 An Example of a Text Message Exchange Between Ali and Thomas, Two Public Works Employees

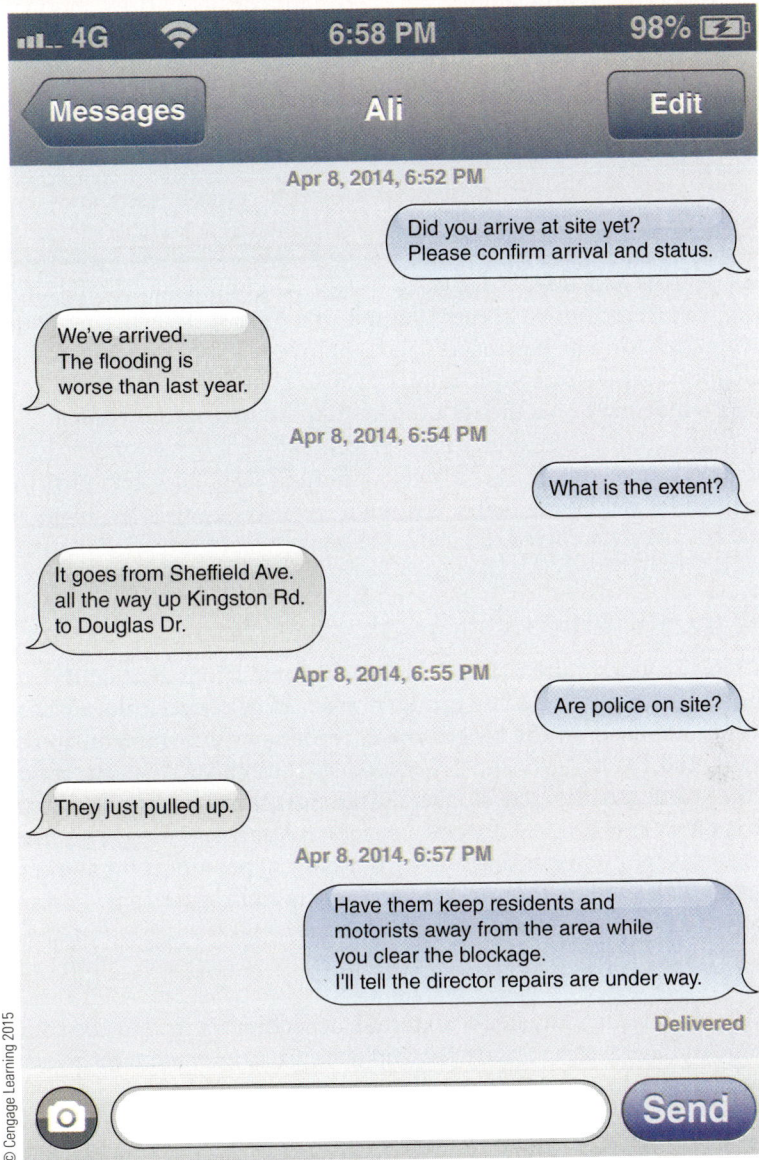

© Cengage Learning 2015

3. Do not text when you are at a business meeting or a class or when talking to a client, co-worker, or manager. It is unprofessional and discourteous.
4. Send texts only when they convey company business; never use them for your personal conversations.
5. Avoid textspeak, which often disregards proper spelling and punctuation.

6. Make sure any photos/videos you send are ethical and relevant to your job.
7. Textual harassment (for example, sending or forwarding sexual images or jokes; bullying a fellow employee) is grounds for being fired and maybe even prosecution. Again, don't put something in a text you would not put in an email or say in a telephone call.
8. Don't text excessively. Rather than sending a series of texts, focus on your precise message and then send only one text about it.

Blogs

Like emails and IMs, blogs (*web + logs*) are important digital tools for employees, managers, and customers. Think of a blog as an evolving website, or a daily newspaper for which managers and employees write regular short articles, or posts. Blogposts are short, conversational articles giving readers current and relevant news and commentary on a variety of issues important for your company, your organization, and your profession. Posts are generally a few paragraphs long and are often written two to three times a week, although some bloggers post their work more frequently, sometimes daily. Written in chronological order, blogs are dated, titled, and frequently archived. Figure 3.7 shows a blog (pages 93–94).

Blogs Are Interactive

A blog includes more than the blogger's views. Blogs are highly interactive, allowing for a two-way or often group conversation between the author and his or her online audience. In the blogosphere, readers write comments in response to blog posts, and the blogger and other readers can reply. This interaction is the key to a blog's success. In fact, bloggers often post the number of visitors who have left comments at the site. To write a successful business blog, you have to (1) attract readers, (2) build relationships with them, (3) promote and market products, services, or ideas, and (4) respond to comments and suggestions.

Internal/External Blogs

Blogs can be either **internal** or **external**, depending on the intended audience. **Internal blogs** are designed exclusively for employee readers. Employees can interact by posting their comments and asking questions, express their views on new policies, announce events and introduce new staff, and communicate up and down the corporate ladder.

External blogs allow companies to express their side of the story—their interpretation of events and their clarification of the issues—quickly and publicly. But besides being a forum for the company's viewpoints, external blogs are a fast way to announce and explain new or updated products and services, expanded locations, changes in technology, product recalls, efforts at greening an environment, community service, or just about anything related to a company's mission and activities. Read Figure 3.7 which contains an external blog about a company's reason for discontinuing one of its popular products but replacing it with a better alternative.

Guidelines for Writing a Business Blog

An external, or company, blog is your employer's official, and many times daily, publication. You may have to get your business blog approved by a blog administrator to make sure it meets your company's expectations. One way to make sure it is approved is by always honoring the confidentiality of company business. Moreover, keep your blog concise and make it readable.

Following the guidelines in this list will help you write an effective (external) business blog. As you read these guidelines, refer to Figure 3.7.

Target Your Audience

- **Know what your audience cares about.** Make sure your comments are relevant to their questions and needs. Be aware of their attitudes, likes, and dislikes. Read replies to previous blog posts, be open to suggestions, and acknowledge readers' insights. Tell readers how and why your blog will help them.
- **Write an attention-grabbing headline**. Attract readers with a title that tells them how and why they can profit from reading your blog, and encourage them to respond to your post; for example, "A Power Tool Even Better than the PH-450?" in Figure 3.7. Avoid vague, boring headlines, such as "Important News," "Something You Need to Know," or "Any Further Ideas?"
- **Determine if your blog will attract an international audience** as well as native English speakers (see pages 3–6). To accommodate a global readership, avoid jargon and unclear abbreviations.
- **Date every blog post so readers can follow a conversation**. Update your blog to make sure the information you give readers is current and accurate.
- **Make it easy for readers to respond to your post**. Welcome feedback. Tell readers where and how to reply. As in the blog in Figure 3.7, refer to customer posts to show how concerned you and your company are about readers' opinions. Build a relationship with them.

Make Your Blog Persuasive

- **Structure your blog so that your first paragraph comes to the point at once and tells readers what you are blogging about and why**. In the case study in Figure 3.7, Clay Denton-Tyler clearly states he has information on "why the PH-450 will not be available," a question his audience is eager to see him answer.
- **Provide firsthand information that shows readers you are knowledgeable and sincere.** Observe how Denton-Tyler expresses his views as an owner of the popular, but discontinued, PH-450 without in any way compromising his company's position or decision.
- **Highlight any new, improved, or special features.** Note how Denton-Tyler points to the benefits the new power tool offers customers. See how he gives his readers an incentive to buy the new model.

- **Use facts and statistics to develop your message or point of view.** Honest numbers sell products and services. Include units sold, costs, and so on. See how Denton-Tyler wisely cites a lower price to promote the new model SHP-1000 in Figure 3.7.

Write Concisely and Sincerely

- **Keep your posts short and easy to read.** Your blog needs to be simple and practical. Most blogs are no more than a few paragraphs. Don't turn yours into a report or a compilation of technical data.
- **Adopt a casual, conversational style.** Be personable and friendly. Sound authentic and upbeat. Emphasize your interest in your readers. Don't weigh them down with long, windy paragraphs that can bore or confuse your audience.

Document Your Sources, Including Visuals

- If you use someone else's statistics, surveys, illustrations, or ideas, get permission first from the individual or the company that owns the copyright.
- Quote accurately, but do not include an extended quote without obtaining permission.
- Include relevant documentation (and permission) if you use a visual you or your company did not create.

Case Study

Writing a Blog to Keep Customer Goodwill

Clay Denton-Tyler is an assistant sales manager for PowerHouse Inc., a company that sells a large line of power tools. The company recently decided to discontinue one of its most popular models, the PH-450, which had enjoyed wide brand recognition and high consumer ratings. Customers had been blogging PowerHouse to complain about the company's decision, and Denton-Tyler faced the difficult challenge of responding to customer posts. His blog in Figure 3.7 does that.

To respond successfully, he had to consider his audience's needs, as voiced in their posts to the PowerHouse blog. Because his readers were loyal customers, he did not want to lose their business and goodwill. But he had to acknowledge that they were understandably disappointed that a well-received product was being taken off the market. He also had to be credible, honest, and diplomatic in addressing their needs and expressing his company's continuing gratitude to its customers. He also had to convince them that the replacement model PowerHouse was offering was better and cheaper than the discontinued PH-450.

But in the interactive world of blogging, he recognized that he was also writing to potential customers, and he realized that his post would be a part of an ongoing public discussion about the new model and his company. He wanted to answer as many questions as he could while keeping the conversation going—all in a positive direction—and, ideally, attracting new customers around the globe.

FIGURE 3.7 An External Blog

PowerHouse, Inc.

About Us | Products | International | Jobs | Mobile | RSS

⊙ PowerBlog   ○ All of Powerhouse, Inc.   🔍 Search this site   **Go**

PowerBlog

| All | Company News | Product News | Distribution | Manufacturing |

<< Previous Post   >> Next Post

Today's Post (August 15, 2014):

>> **A Power Tool Even Better than the PH-450?**
by Clay Denton-Tyler, District Manager

© iStockPhoto.com/Prill
Mediendesign & Fotografie

Recent Posts:

International Dyanamics, SE CFO announces retirement.

PowerHouse announces the discontinuation of the PH-450.

PowerHouse opens new retail outlets in Dunedin, New Zealand and Tianjin, China.

International Dyanamics, SE acquires quality Swiss Home Products.

PowerHouse goes international.

More

Many of our loyal customers have disagreed with PowerHouse's decision to discontinue manufacturing the PH-450 All-in-One Power Tool. It is always great to hear from our customers and to receive their feedback, even when they believe we've done something wrong. To help our customers better understand our perspective, let me fill in some of the background about why the PH-450 will not be available.

Discontinuing the PH-450 was not an easy decision. After all, this was the product that first brought our company to national attention and widespread customer acceptance. Also, I know from many complimentary emails and replies to earlier posts, as well as from my personal experience as a proud owner of the PH-450, that customers have always applauded its price, compact design, durability, and all-weather usability. As one of you put it, "Why kill a popular product that has worked so well for 20 years?"

While all of these responses are helpful, the good news is that even though the PH-450 is being discontinued, our customers will now have a very similar but improved alternative. Recently, our parent company, International Dyanamics, SE, acquired a new multipurpose tool from Swiss

Right margin annotations:

Search engine and navigation links help readers find information

Additional links aid site navigation

Provides a clear and concise title and date

Writes to a general audience and avoids jargon

Thanks customers for feedback

Uses a conversational but professional tone

Acknowledges customers' disappointment

Attempts to persuade customer to switch to a new model

FIGURE 3.7 (Continued)

Describes benefits of new model and why it is being marketed

Home Products. The SHP-1000 is not only just as compact, durable, and weather-friendly as the PH-450, but it offers several additional features, such as a nail gun attachment and a lifetime limited warranty. And due to an excellent distribution deal negotiated between International Dyanamics, SE, and Swiss Home Products, we can sell it at less than 30 percent of the retail cost of the PH-450.

Sympathizes with readers but offers personal endorsement characteristic of bloggers at same time

I know it is hard to say goodbye to a reliable helper, but like many products in our increasingly technical age, the PH-450 is being replaced by a more efficient model. I will miss the old PH-450, but I have found that the SHP-1000 is even more effective in my home shop. Adapting to a new model has never come easier for me. Why not give it a try? Thanks. I would like to hear from you.

Tone is sincere and friendly

Comments: (21)
- Sign in to add a comment
- First time users, please register first, in order to add a comment

Comments link allows for further discussion

Conclusion

E-communications—emails, IMs, tweets, texts, and blogs—are a routine yet important part of every employee's job. These basic types of business communication keep crucial information flowing among co-workers, management, vendors, and others, so that a company can meet its day-to-day obligations. In addition, the information contained in these short messages often helps you to write longer documents.

By following the guidelines in this chapter, you will be better able to write clear, concise, and ethical e-communications for your audience. Your annual evaluations may in part depend on how well you research, draft, revise, and how promptly you send and respond to e-communications.

✔ Revision Checklist

☐ Understood the reader's need and the information that had to be transferred, and determined which e-communication to use.

☐ Distinguished the various types of e-communications and how they relate to one another.

Email

☐ Did not send unsolicited or confidential email.

☐ Sent to reader's correct address.

☐ Formatted email with acceptable margins and spacing.

☐ Observed netiquette; avoided flaming.

☐ Wrote a separate message rather than returning sender's message with a short reply.

☐ Kept paragraphs short but used full—not telegraphic—sentences.

☐ Avoided unfamiliar abbreviations or terms that would confuse a reader.

☐ Received permission to repeat or incorporate another person's email.

☐ Observed all legal obligations in using email.

☐ Safeguarded employer's confidentiality and security by excluding sensitive or privileged information.

☐ Included enough information and documentation for reader's purpose.

☐ Honored reader by observing proper courtesy.

☐ Began with friendly greeting; ended politely.

☐ Considered needs of international audience.

☐ Used antivirus program, did not forward or reply to spam.

Instant Messaging

☐ Used IM only for professional, job-related communications.

☐ Kept messages short—not over a line or two.

☐ Avoided "textspeak" in business IMs.

☐ Notified readers when IM was offline and back online.

☐ Did not send anything confidential through an IM exchange.

Tweeting

☐ Did not share any confidential or otherwise proprietary information via Twitter.

☐ Avoided textspeak as much as possible.

☐ Did not write something in a tweet that would not be put in an official company letter or email or said in a telephone call.

☐ When in doubt, had a colleague or superior review the tweet before posting it on behalf of the company, and edited/revised further as needed.

Texting

☐ Texted only for necessary business communications.

☐ Made sure text was courteous and professional.

☐ Kept messages short, but used correct spelling and punctuation.
☐ Took advantage of apps to communicate more efficiently on the job.

Blogs

☐ Posted nothing critical of employer or co-workers and nothing embarrassing, offensive, or confidential.
☐ Made posts conversational and informal, yet professional.
☐ Dated every blog.
☐ Targeted my audience.
☐ Included attention-grabbing headline.
☐ Posted only current and relevant information.
☐ Provided a place for readers to give feedback.

Exercises

1. Write an email requesting information from one of the following types of businesses. Submit a copy of your email request, along with the response, to your instructor.
   a. From an airline: an up-to-date schedule along a certain route and information about any bonus-mile or discount programs
   b. From a stock brokerage firm: free quotes or research about a particular stock
   c. From a resort: special rates for a given week
   d. From a professional organization to which you belong about any conferences to be held in your city or state

2. Write an email with one of the following messages, observing the guidelines discussed in this chapter on pages 80–83.
   a. You have just made a big sale, and you want to inform your boss.
   b. You have just lost a big sale, and you have to inform your boss.
   c. Inform a co-worker about a union or national sales meeting.
   d. Notify a company to cancel your subscription to one of its publications because you find it to be dated and no longer useful in your profession.
   e. Request help from a listserv about research for a major report you are preparing for your employer.
   f. Advise your district manager to discontinue marketing one of the company's brands because of low customer acceptance.
   g. Write to a friend studying finance at a German, Korean, or South American university about the biggest financial news in your town or neighborhood in the last month.

3. Rewrite the following email to your boss to make it more professional.

Hi—

This new territory is a pain. Lots of stops; no sales. Ughhhh. People out here resistant to change. Could get hit by a boulder and still no change. Giant companies ought to be up on charges. Will sub. reports asap as long as you care rec.

The long and short of it is that market is down. No news = bad news.

4. As a collaborative venture, join with three or four classmates to prepare one or more of the email messages for Exercise 2. Send each other drafts of your messages for revision. Email the final draft to your instructor.

5. Email your instructor about a project you are now working on for class, outlining your progress and describing any difficulties you are having.

6. You have just missed work or a class meeting. Email your employer or your instructor explaining the reason and telling how you intend to make up the work.

7. As a group activity, instant message two or three other members of your collaborative writing team on a project you are working on. Print out your IM exchanges during this time, and submit them to your instructor.

8. Revise the following unethical or poorly worded text messages.
   a. Y r u not here yet? Mtg starts in 5.
   b. If u don't have reprt on my desk by 5 heads will roll!!!!
   c. U rocked tht mtg thx 4 cing this thru ttyl
   d. GMAB u need 2 GOWI and meet the client F2F by COB 2moro

9. As a collaborative project, write three or four external blog posts about some aspect of your current job or a previous job. Share with readers news about your company's products or services, technology you are using, professional travel, community service, work with international colleagues, and so forth. Be sure that your posts show your company, department, or agency in a good light.

10. Send a short post (200–300 words) to your company's blog administrator about a recent accomplishment you or your office, department, or section achieved. Include a link to a relevant site for readers to visit for further information.

CHAPTER 4

Preparing Correspondence

Some Basics for Writing to Audiences Worldwide

Business correspondence includes letters and memos. Letters are among the most important writing you will do on your job. Businesses worldwide take letter writing very seriously, and employers will expect you to prepare and respond to your correspondence promptly and diplomatically. Your signature on a letter tells readers that you are accountable for everything in it. The higher up the corporate ladder you climb, the more letters you will be expected to write.

You can also expect to write memos, a more formal kind of internal company correspondence that may announce a new policy, alert staff to a problem, or give instructions to team members. Memos are discussed on pages 133–141. Because correspondence is so significant to your career, this chapter introduces you to the entire process, provides guidelines and problem-solving strategies, and shows you how to prepare the most frequently written types of correspondence. It also shows you how to write for international readers.

Letters in the Age of the Internet

Even in this age of the Internet, letters are still vital in the world of work. A professional-looking letter is one of the most significant symbols in the business world for the following reasons:

1. **Letters represent your company's public image and your competence**. A firm's corporate image is on the line when it sends a letter. Carefully written letters can create goodwill; poorly written letters can anger customers, cost your company business, and project an unfavorable image of you.

2. **Letters are far more formal—in tone and structure—than any other type of business communication**. Emails, IMs, texts, and tweets are the least formal communications.

3. **Letters constitute an official legal record of an agreement**. They state, modify, or respond to a business commitment. A signed letter constitutes a legally

binding contract (and will often be scanned to create an electronic record). Be absolutely sure that what you put in a letter about prices, guarantees, warranties, equipment, delivery dates, and/or other issues is accurate. Your readers can hold you and your company accountable for such written commitments.

4. **Unlike emails, many businesses require letters to be routed through channels before they are sent out.** Because they convey how a company looks and what it offers to customers, letters often must be approved at a variety of corporate levels.

5. **Letters are more substantial and secure than emails.** They provide a documented hard copy. Unlike emails that can be erased, letters are often logged in, filed, and bear a written, authorized signature.

6. **A letter is the official and expected medium through which important documents and attachments (contracts, specifications, proposals) are sent to readers.**

7. **A letter is still the most formal and approved way to conduct business with many international audiences.** These readers see a letter as more polite and honorable than an email for initial contacts and even for subsequent business communications.

8. **A hard-copy letter is confidential.** It is more likely to be delivered to the proper recipient in its sealed envelope and less likely to be forwarded to unintended readers, as an email might be.

Letter Formats

Letter format refers to the way in which you print a letter—where you indent and where you place certain kinds of information. Several letter formats exist. Two of the most frequently used business letter formats are full-block and modified-block, but you should also be familiar with a third format, the semi-block.

Full-Block Format

In full-block format all information is flush against the left margin, double spaced between paragraphs. Figure 4.1 (page 100) shows a full-block letter. Many employers prefer this format when your letter is on **letterhead stationery** (specially printed paper giving a company's name and logo, business and web addresses, fax and telephone numbers, and sometimes the names of its executives).

Modified-Block Format

In modified-block format (see Figure 4.2 on page 101), the writer's address (if it is not imprinted on a letterhead), the date, the complimentary close, and the signature are positioned at the center point and then keyed toward the right side of the letter.

FIGURE 4.1 Full-Block Letter Format with Appropriate Margins

Letterhead with company name and logo

NIRA Nevada Insurance Research Agency
7500 South Maplewood Drive, Las Vegas, NV 89152-0026
(702) 555-9876 **www.NIRA.org**

1"–1.25"   1"–1.25"

April 7, 2014

All text aligned on the left-hand margin

2 spaces

Ms. Molly Georgopolous, C.P.A.
Business Manager
Meyers, Inc.
3400 South Madison Road
Reno, NV 89554-3212

Uses professional, businesslike font

2 spaces

Dear Ms. Georgopolous:

2 spaces

As I promised in our telephone conversation earlier this afternoon, I am enclosing a study of the Nevada financial responsibility law. I hope that it will help you prepare your report.

2 spaces

Text of letter balanced on the page

Let me emphasize again that probably 95 percent of all individuals who are involved in an accident obtain reimbursement for medical bills and for damages to their automobiles. If individuals have insurance, they can receive reimbursement from their own carrier. If they do not have insurance and the other driver is uninsured and judged to be at fault, the Nevada Bureau of Motor Vehicles revokes that party's driver's license until all costs and damages are paid.

Generous margins on all sides of the letter

2 spaces

Please call me again if I can help you.

2 spaces

Sincerely yours,

Signature written in black ink

4 spaces

Carmen Tredeau

Carmen Tredeau, President

2 spaces

Encl. (1)

Names of agency's executives

Bradley Fuller, CPCU
Chairperson

Carmen Tredeau, CPCU
President

Theodore Kendrick
Vice President
Public Affairs

Iping Li, CPCU
Vice President
Research

Dora Salinas-Diego, CPCU
Vice President
Actuary

FIGURE 4.2 Modified-Block Letter Format

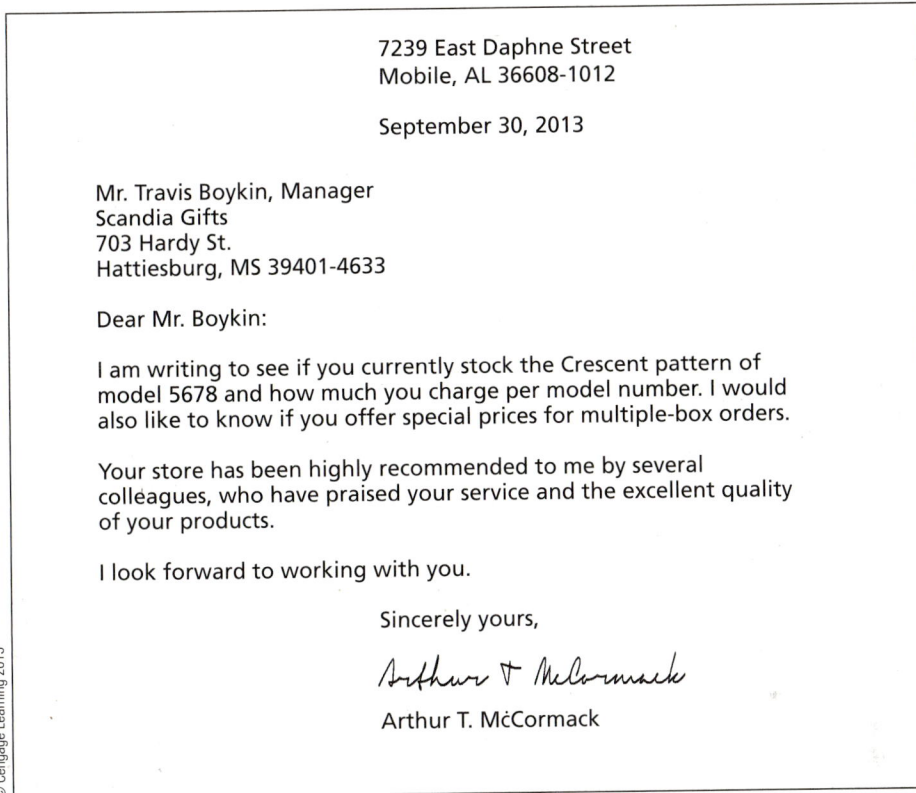

7239 East Daphne Street
Mobile, AL 36608-1012

September 30, 2013

Mr. Travis Boykin, Manager
Scandia Gifts
703 Hardy St.
Hattiesburg, MS 39401-4633

Dear Mr. Boykin:

I am writing to see if you currently stock the Crescent pattern of model 5678 and how much you charge per model number. I would also like to know if you offer special prices for multiple-box orders.

Your store has been highly recommended to me by several colleagues, who have praised your service and the excellent quality of your products.

I look forward to working with you.

Sincerely yours,

Arthur T. McCormack

Arthur T. McCormack

Date is indented at center point of letter

Inside address is single-spaced

Paragraphs can be indented or not indented

Complimentary close and writer's name are indented and aligned under date line

© Cengage Learning 2015

The date aligns with the complimentary close. The inside address, the salutation, and the body of the letter are flush against the left margin.

Semi-Block Format

The semi-block format (see Figure 4.7, page 114) looks just like the modified-block format in terms of aligning the date line with the complimentary close, signature, and any enclosures at the center point of the letter. But the paragraphs in the semi-block format are always indented five to seven spaces. Though not as frequently used as the full-block or modified-block formats, the semi-block format is a template an employer may ask you to use.

Continuing Pages

To indicate subsequent pages if your letter runs beyond one page, use one of these two conventions. Note the use of the recipient's name.

Jorge Vargas   2   April 7, 2014

1¼" above the continuing text of the letter

2
Bo Yates
September 30, 2013

Parts of a Letter

A letter contains many parts, each of which contributes to your overall message. The parts and their placement in your letter form the basic conventions of effective letter writing. Readers look for certain information in key places.

The parts of a letter discussed in the following sections will appear in every letter you write. Figure 4.3 is a sample letter containing all of the parts discussed here. Note where each part is placed in the letter.

Heading

The heading of a letter may be either your company's letterhead or your full return address. (See Figure 4.2 for an example of a full return address when letterhead is not used.)

Date Line

Try to leave four lines below the letterhead before the date line. Spell out the name of the month in full—"September" or "March" rather than "Sept." or "Mar." The date line is usually keyboarded this way: November 12, 2014. Different cultures express dates in different ways. Most countries, including those in Europe, list the day first, then the month, and then the year. See Figure 4.24 on page 149 for an example of how to correctly provide a date for international readers.

Inside Address

The inside address, the address of the recipient, is always placed against the left margin, two lines below the date line. It contains the name, title (if any), company, street address, city, state, and zip code of the person to whom you are writing. Single-space the inside address, and do not use any punctuation at the end of the lines.

FIGURE 4.3 A Sample Letter, Full-Block Format, with All Parts Labeled

Madison and Moore, Inc.
Professional Architects

7900 South Manheim Road
Crystal Springs, NE 71003-0092
Phone 402-555-2300 **www.mmi.com**

Heading (letterhead)

July 14, 2014

Date line

Ms. Paula Jordan
Systems Consultant
Broadacres Development Corp.
12 East River Street
Detroit, MI 48001-0422

Inside address with correct state abbreviation and zip code

Dear Ms. Jordan:

Salutation

Thank you for your letter of July 7, 2014. I have discussed your request with the staff in our planning department and have learned that the design modules we used for our Vestavia project are no longer available.

In searching the Internet, however, I came across some designs from a California firm that might be helpful to you. California Concepts offers plans very similar to the ones you are interested in, as you can tell from the design featured here: www.californiaconcepts.com/officemodule.

I hope this will help you, and I wish you every success in your project.

Body of letter

Sincerely yours,

Complimentary close

MADISON AND MOORE, INC.

Company name

William Newhouse

Signature

William Newhouse
Design Coordinator

Writer's name and title

cc: Planning Department

Enclosure Copy notation

© Cengage Learning 2015

Dr. Mary Petro
Director of Research
Midwest Laboratories
1700 Oak Drive
Rapid City, SD 56213–3406

Always try to write to a specific person rather than just "Sales Manager" or "President." To find out the person's name, check previous correspondence, email lists, or the company's or individual's website, or call the company. Make sure you use an abbreviated courtesy title (Ms., Mr., Dr., Prof.) before the recipient's name for the inside address (e.g., Capt. María Torres; Mr. A. T. Ricks; Rev. Siam Tau). Use Ms. when writing to a woman unless she has expressly asked to be called Miss or Mrs.

The last line of the inside address contains the city, state, and zip code.

Salutation

Two spaces below the inside address includes your salutation, or greeting. Begin with *Dear*, and then follow with a courtesy title, the reader's last name (unless you are on a first-name basis), and a colon (Dear Mr. Brown:). *Never use a comma for a formal letter.* Avoid the sexist "Dear Sir," "Gentlemen," or "Dear Madam" and the stilted "Ladies and Gentlemen" or "Dear Sir or Madam." (For a discussion of sexist language and how to eliminate it, see Chapter 2, pages 50–54).

Sometimes a first name does not reveal whether the reader is male or female. There are women named Stacy, Robin, and Lee, and men named Leslie, Kim, and Kelly. If you aren't certain, you can use the reader's full name: "Dear Terry Jones." Similarly, if your recipient uses just initials, write "Dear S.K. Holmes." Or if you know the person's title, you might write "Dear Credit Manager Jones."

Avoid casual salutations such as "Hello," "Hi," "Good Morning," "Greetings," or "Happy Tuesday"; these are best reserved for emails or IMs. And never begin a letter with "To Whom It May Concern," which is old-fashioned, impersonal, and trite.

Body of the Letter

The body of the letter, two spaces after the salutation, contains your message. Some of your letters will be only a few lines long, while others may extend to three or more paragraphs. Keep your sentences concise, and try to hold your paragraphs to less than seven lines. (Refer to pages 46–50 in Chapter 2.)

Complimentary Close

A close, two lines below the last line of your message, is the equivalent of a formal goodbye. For most business correspondence, use one of these standard closes:

Sincerely,

Respectfully,

Sincerely yours,

Capitalize only the first letter of the first word. The entire close is followed by a comma. If you and your reader know each other well, as in Figure 4.4, you can use

Cordially,

Best wishes,

Regards,

But avoid flowery closes, such as

> Forever yours,
>
> Devotedly yours,
>
> Faithfully yours,

These belong in a romance novel, not in a business letter.

Signature

Allow four spaces between the complimentary close and your typed name and title so that your signature will not look squeezed in. Always sign your name in black ink. An unsigned letter indicates carelessness or, worse, indifference toward your reader. A stamped signature tells readers you could not give them personal attention.

Some firms prefer using their company name along with the employee's name in the signature section. If so, type the company name in capital letters two line spaces below the complimentary close and then sign your name. Add your title underneath your typed name. Here is an example:

> Sincerely yours,
>
> THE FINELLI COMPANY
>
> *Helen Stravopoulos*
>
> Helen Stravopoulos
> Web Coordinator

Enclosure Line

The enclosure line informs the reader that additional materials (such as a brochure, diagram, form, contract, or proposal) accompany your letter.

> Enclosure (only one item is enclosed)
>
> Enclosures (2)
>
> Encl.: Spring Quarter Sales Report

Copy Notation

The abbreviation *cc:* —two c's followed by a colon—informs your reader that a copy of your letter has been sent to one or more individuals.

> cc: Service Dept.
>
> cc: Hannah Pittman-Jarzelski
>
>   Ivor Vas

Letters are copied and sent to third parties for two reasons: (1) to document a paper trail and (2) to indicate that other readers need the information contained in the letter. Unless your employer instructs you otherwise, tell your reader if others will receive a copy of your letter.

The Appearance of Your Letter

The way your letter looks can determine how readers will respond to your message. Here are some tips on how to format and print professional-looking letters:

- Use a letter-quality printer, and check ink or toner cartridge levels to avoid sending a fuzzy, faint, or messy letter.
- Stay away from fancy fonts and scripts. Use the business-like Times New Roman or Helvetica. (For a discussion of typography, see Chapter 6, pages 223–226.)
- Consider using letter wizards to help format and design your letters. Most word-processing programs, such as Microsoft Word or Corel Word Perfect, have them. Some organizations, however, may prefer not to use standard letter formatting. Always check with your company before using a letter wizard.
- Leave generous margins of at least 1 to 1¼ inches all around your message. For a shorter letter, as in Figure 4.6 (page 110), don't expand your margins to 2 inches or increase the font size, which will only make your letter look unprofessional.
- Leave double spaces between key parts of a letter—the date line, the salutation, copy notation, and enclosure—but leave four spaces between the letterhead and date as well as the complimentary close and your typed signature.
- Single-space within each paragraph, but double-space between paragraphs. The white space enhances the professional look of your letter and makes it easier to read.
- Avoid crowding too much text onto one page. Squeezing too many characters on a line by using overly small fonts will make your letter look cramped and be hard to read. Also, don't cram a long letter onto one page; instead, allow your letter to flow to a second page.
- Be careful about lopsided letters. Don't start a brief letter at the top of the page and then leave the lower three-fourths blank. Begin a shorter message near the center of the page.
- Use Print Preview to see an image of your letter before you print a hard copy so that you can make any necessary changes or corrections. Never print over your company's letterhead or any addresses or company logos printed across the bottom of the letter.
- Always print your letter on high-quality white bond paper (20-pound, 8½ × 11) and matching standard-size (#10) business envelopes. Avoid colored paper.

Organizing a Standard Business Letter

A standard business letter can be divided into an introduction, a body, and a conclusion, each section responding to or clarifying a specific issue for your recipient. These three sections can each be one paragraph long, as in Figures 4.1, 4.2, and 4.3, or the body of your letter can be two or more paragraphs, as in Figure 4.4.

FIGURE 4.4 Careful Organization of a Business Letter

Office Property Management Associates
2400 South Lincoln Highway
Livingston, NJ 07040-9990
(201) 555-3740   www.opma.com

Clear, professional letterhead with contact information

April 10, 2014

Mr. W. T. Albritton
Albritton & Sharp, CPA
Suite 400
Suburban Office Complex
Livingston, NJ 07038-2389

Accurate inside address

Dear Mr. Albritton:

Thank you for your recent suggestions on improving security at the Suburban Office Complex. You will be pleased to learn that at our March meeting OPMA has agreed to make the following improvements in services, which will go into effect within 45 days.

Introduction comes to point quickly and cordially by referencing reader's earlier request

Starting May 5, you will have an on-site manager, Thomas Vasquez, who will be happy to answer any questions you may have about the Complex and help you with any problems you may encounter. His ten years of experience in managing commercial office parks will benefit you and other businesses at the Suburban Office Complex.

Body describes changes with specific details

The new outdoor security system you asked for will be installed by May 19. It will give you and your employees greater protection through seven additional security cameras around the perimeters of the parking lot while movement sensors will monitor every outside door.

I want to reassure you that none of these changes will inconvenience the operation of your firm. We are honored to have Albritton & Sharp as residents. I welcome your comments as these changes are implemented as well as additional suggestions you may have.

Conclusion builds goodwill by promising reader what will be done and how

Best wishes,

Cheryl Hu

Cheryl Hu
Vice President

Four spaces left between complimentary close and typed name

To help readers grasp your message clearly and concisely, follow this simple plan for organizing your business letters:

- In your first paragraph start with a friendly opening and explain why you are writing and why your letter is important to the recipient. Acknowledge any relevant previous meetings, correspondence, or telephone calls early in the paragraph (as in Figures 4.1 and 4.3).
- Put the most significant point of each paragraph first to make it easier for the reader to find. Never bury important ideas in the middle or at the end of a paragraph.
- In the second (or subsequent) paragraph, develop the body of your message with factual support, key details, and descriptions your reader needs. For instance, note how Figure 4.4 refers to the specific changes to improve security that the reader had requested.
- In your last paragraph, thank readers and be very clear and precise about what you want them to do or what you will do for them. Let them know what will happen next, what you or they need to do (Figure 4.4), or any combination of these messages. Don't leave your readers hanging. End cordially and professionally.

Making a Good Impression on Your Reader

You have just learned about formatting and organizing your letters. Now we turn to the content of your letters—what you say (your message) and how you say it (your style and tone). Writing letters means communicating to influence your readers, not to alienate or antagonize them. Keep in mind that writers of effective letters are like successful diplomats; they represent both their company and themselves. You want readers to see you as courteous, well-informed, and professional.

First, put yourself in the reader's position. What kinds of letters do you like to receive: vague, impersonal, sarcastic, pushy, and condescending; or polite, business-like, and considerate? If you have questions, you want them answered honestly, courteously, and fully.

To send such effective letters, adopt the **"You Attitude,"** in other words, signal to readers that they and their needs are of utmost importance. Incorporating the "you attitude" means you should be able to answer "Yes" to these two questions:

1. Will my readers receive a positive image of me?
2. Have I chosen words that convey both my respect for the readers and my concern for their questions and comments?

Figures 4.5 and 4.6 (page 110) contain two versions of the same letter. Which one would you rather receive?

FIGURE 4.5 A Letter Lacking the "You Attitude"

Brown County • Office of the Tax Assessor

County Building, Room 200, Ventura, Missouri 56780-0101

712-555-3000

February 6, 2014

Mr. Ted Ladner
451 West Hawthorne Lane
Morris, MO 64507-3005

Dear Mr. Ladner:

You have written to the wrong office here at the County Building. There is no way we can attempt to verify the kinds of details you are demanding from Brown County.

Tone is sarcastic and uncooperative

Simply put, by carefully examining the 2013 tax bill you said you received, you should have realized that it is the Tax Collector's Office, not the Tax Assessor's, that will have to handle the problem you claim exists.

Use of "you" alone does not signal a positive image of reader

In short, call or write the Tax Collector of Brown County.

Thank you!

Insulting and curt ending and complimentary close

Tracey Kowalski
Tracey Kowalski

Does not list writer's job title

www.browncounty.gov

© Cengage Learning 2015

Achieving the "You Attitude": Four Guidelines

As you draft and revise your work, pay special attention to the following four guidelines for making a good impression on your reader.

FIGURE 4.6 A You-Centered Revision of Figure 4.5

Brown County • Office of the Tax Assessor

County Building, Room 200, Ventura, Missouri 56780-0101

712-555-3000

February 6, 2014

Mr. Ted Ladner
451 West Hawthorne Lane
Morris, MO 64507-3005

Dear Mr. Ladner:

Thanks reader and gives polite explanation

Thank you for writing about the difficulties you encountered with your 2013 tax bill. I wish I could help you, but it is the Tax Collector's Office that issues your annual property tax bill. Our office does not prepare individual homeowners' bills.

Helps reader solve problem with specific information

If you will kindly direct your questions to Paulette Sutton at the Brown County Tax Collector's Office, County Building, Room 100, Ventura, Missouri 56780-0100, I am sure that she will be able to assist you. Should you wish to call her, the number is 712-555-3455, extension 212. Her email address is **psutton@bctc.gov**. I hope this helps you.

Uses appropriate complimentary close

Respectfully,

Tracey Kowalski

Tracey Kowalski
Assistant Tax Assessor

Lists specific job title

www.browncounty.gov

© Cengage Learning 2015

1. Never forget that your reader is a real person. Avoid writing cold, impersonal letters that sound as if they were form letters or voicemail instructions. Let the readers know that you are writing to them as individuals. The following letter violates every rule of personal and personable communications.

> It has come to our attention that policy number 342q–765r has been delinquent in payment and is in arrears for the sum of $302.35. To keep the policy in force for the duration of its life, a minimum payment of $50.00 must reach this office by the last day of the month. Failure to submit payment will result in the cancellation of the aforementioned policy.

The example above displays no sense of one human being writing to another, of a customer with a name, personal history, or specific needs. Revised, this letter contains the necessary personal (and human) touch.

> We have not yet received your payment for your insurance policy (342q–765r). By sending us your check for $50.00 within the next two weeks, you will keep your policy in force and can continue to enjoy the financial benefits and emotional security it offers you.

The benefits to an individual reader are stressed, and the reader is addressed directly as a valued customer.

Don't be afraid of using "you" in letters. Readers will feel more friendly toward you and your message. Of course, no amount of "yous" will help if they appear in a condescending context, such as the letter in Figure 4.5.

2. Keep the reader in the forefront of your letter. Make sure the reader's needs control the tone, message, and organization of your letter—the essence of the "you attitude." Stress the "you," not the "I" or the "we." Below you can see a paragraph from a letter that forgets about the reader:

I-Centered Draft

> I think that our rug shampooer is the best on the market. Our firm has invested a lot of time and money to ensure that it is the most economical and efficient shampooer available today. We have found that our customers are very satisfied with the results of our machine. We have sold thousands of these shampooers, and we are proud of our accomplishment. We hope that we can sell you one of our fantastic machines.

3. Be courteous and tactful. Refrain from turning your letter into a punch through the mail. Don't inflame your letter or email audience; review Figures 3.3 and 3.4 on pages 83 and 84. When you capture the reader's goodwill, your rewards will be great. The following negative words can leave a bad taste in the reader's mouth.

it's defective	unprofessional (job, attitude, etc.)
I demand	your failure
I insist	you contend
we reject	you allege
that's no excuse for	you should have known
totally unacceptable	your outlandish claim

Compare the following discourteous sentences with the courteous revisions.

Discourteous	Courteous
We must discontinue your service unless payment is received by the date shown.	Please send us your payment by November 4 so that your service will not be interrupted.
You are sorely mistaken about the contract.	We are sorry to learn about the difficulty you experienced over the service terms in your contract.
The new iPad you sold me is third-rate and you charged first-rate prices.	Because the iPad is still under warranty, I hope you can make the repairs easily and quickly.
It goes without saying that your suggestion is not worth considering.	It was thoughtful of you to send me your suggestion, but, unfortunately, we are unable to implement it right now.

© Cengage Learning 2015

The last discourteous example begins with a phrase that frequently sets readers on edge. Avoid using *"It goes without saying"*—it can quickly set up a hostile barrier between you and your reader.

    4. Don't sound pompous or bureaucratic. Write to your reader as if you were carrying on a professional conversation. Your tone should be polite but natural and to the point. Make your letters reader-friendly and believable, not stuffy and overbearing. To do that, don't resort to using phrases that remind readers of *legalese*—language that some writers use to make themselves sound important, but that only alienates readers. It smells of contracts, deeds, and stuffy rooms.

    In the following list, the words and phrases on the left are pompous expressions that have crept into letters for years; the ones on the right are contemporary equivalents.

Pompous	Contemporary	Pompous	Contemporary
aforementioned	previously mentioned	herewith; heretofore; hereby	(drop these three *h*'s entirely)
as per your request	as you requested	immediate future	soon
I am in receipt of	I have received	in lieu of	instead of
attached herewith	enclosed	pursuant	concerning
be advised that	for your information	remittance	payment
due to the fact that	because	under separate cover	I'm also sending you
endeavor	try	this writer	I
henceforth	after this	we regret to inform you that	we are sorry that

© Cengage Learning 2015

The Five Most Common Types of Business Letters

The following section discusses the most frequently used types of business correspondence you will be expected to write on the job.

1. Inquiry letters
2. Cover letters

3. Special request letters
4. Sales letters
5. Customer relations letters

- Follow-up letters
- Complaint letters
- Adjustment letters

These letter types involve a variety of formats, writing strategies, and techniques. Business letters can be classified as **positive, neutral**, or **negative**, depending on their message and the anticipated reactions of your audience. Inquiry and special request letters are examples of neutral, routine letters. Letters can be positive or negative, depending on your message.

- Neutral letters request specific information about a product or service, place an order, or respond to some action or question.
- Sales letters promoting a product carry good news, according to the companies that spend millions of dollars a year preparing them.
- Customer relations letters can be positive (responding favorably to a writer's request or complaint) or negative (e.g., refusing a request, saying no to an adjustment, seeking payment, or critiquing poor performance).

Inquiry Letters

An inquiry letter asks for information about a product, service, or procedure. Businesses frequently exchange such letters. As a customer, you too may write a letter asking about a service or a special line of products, the price, the size, the color, delivery arrangements, or recent technological changes. The clearer your letter, the quicker and more helpful your answers are likely to be.

Figure 4.7 shows an inquiry letter from Michael Ortega to a real estate office managing a large number of apartment complexes. Note that it follows these five rules for writing an effective inquiry letter:

- states exactly what information the writer wants
- indicates clearly why the writer requests the information
- keeps questions short and to the point
- specifies when the writer must have the information
- thanks the reader

Had Michael Ortega simply written the following very brief letter to Hillside Properties, he would not have received information he needed about size, location, and price of apartments: "Please send me some information on housing in Roanoke. My family and I plan to move there soon."

Cover Letters

A cover letter accompanies a document (a proposal, a report, a catalog, a portfolio) that you send to your readers. It identifies the type of document you are sending and prepares your audience to read it. Figure 9.1 (page 366)

FIGURE 4.7 A Letter of Inquiry Written in Semi-Block Format

Ortega has designed his own letterhead to use

Michael Ortega
403 South Main Street
Kingsport, TN 37721-0217
mortega@erols.com

April 7, 2014

Mr. Fred Stonehill
Property Manager
Hillside Properties
701 South Arbor St.
Roanoke, VA 24015-1100

Dear Mr. Stonehill:

States precise request

Would you please let me know if you will have any two-bedroom furnished apartments available for rent during the months of June, July, and August. I did not see any short-term vacancies on your website, but I know such openings are not usually announced months in advance. I am willing to pay up to $850 a month plus utilities. My wife, one-year-old son, and I will be moving to Roanoke for the summer so I can take classes at Virginia Western Community College.

Explains need for information

Identifies area of interest

If possible, we would like to have an apartment that is within two or three miles of the college. We do not have any pets.

Specifies exact date when a reply is needed

I would appreciate hearing from you within the next two weeks. My email address is mortega@erols.com, or you can call me at home (606-555-8957) any evening from 6–10 p.m.

Offers to confer with and then thanks the reader

Should you have any suitable vacancies, we would be happy to drive to Roanoke to look at them and give you a deposit to hold an apartment. Thanks for your help.

Sincerely yours,

Michael Ortega

Michael Ortega

contains a cover letter sent with a copy of a long report. A cover letter should do the following:

- Provide a written record that you have transmitted a document.
- Tell readers why you are sending them the document.
- Briefly summarize what the document contains—number of sections, visuals, statistics, appendices, etc.
- Explain why the document is of interest to readers.
- Express a willingness to answer questions about the document.
- Thank readers for their time.

Special Request Letters

Special request letters make a special demand, not a routine inquiry. For example, these letters can ask a company for information that you as a student will use in a paper, an individual for a copy of an article or a speech, or an agency for facts that your company needs to prepare a proposal or sell a product.

Make your request clear and easy to answer. Supply readers with an addressed, postage-paid envelope, a URL (if necessary), an email address, and fax and telephone numbers in case they have questions.

Follow these seven guidelines when asking for information in a special request letter.

1. Address your letter to the appropriate person.
2. State who you are and why you are writing—e.g., student doing a paper, employee compiling information for a report, and so on.
3. Indicate clearly your reason for requesting the information. Mention any individuals who may have suggested you write for help and information.
4. Precisely and succinctly state your questions; list and number them.
5. Specify exactly when you need the information. Allow sufficient time—at least three weeks. Be reasonable; don't ask for the impossible.
6. Offer to forward a copy of your report, paper, or survey in thanks of the anticipated help.
7. Thank the reader for helping.

Figure 4.8 (page 116) gives an example of a letter that follows these guidelines.

Sales Letters

A sales letter is written to persuade the reader to buy a product, try a service, support some cause, or participate in some activity. No matter what profession you have chosen, there will always be times you have to sell a product, a service, a community or charitable program, a point of view, or yourself! In fact, an application letter for a job (see page 197–205) or an introductory letter to a new or prospective customer is a sales letter. Study the sales letters in Figure 4.9 on page 118 and to an international reader in Figure 4.22 on page 143.

FIGURE 4.8 A Special Request Letter

An example of a student-designed letterhead

1505 West 19th Street
Syracuse, NY 13206
315-555-1214   jkawatsu@webnet.com

October 4, 2013

Ms. Sharonda Aimes-Worthington
Research Director
Creative Marketing Associates
198 Madison Ave.
New York, NY 10016-0092

Dear Ms. Aimes-Worthington:

Explains reason for letter and how the writer learned about the firm

I am a junior at Monroe College in Syracuse, and I am writing a report on "Internet Marketing Strategies for the Finger Lakes Region of New York" for my Marketing 340 class. Several of my professors have spoken highly of Creative Marketing Associates, and in my own research I have learned a great deal from reading your blogs that posted last month.

Proves writer has done research

Acknowledges reader's expertise

Given your extensive experience in developing Internet sites to promote regional businesses and tourism, I would be grateful if you would share your responses to the following three questions with me:

1. What have been the most effective design components in websites for a regional marketplace such as the Finger Lakes?

Lists specific, numbered questions on the topic

2. How can area chambers of commerce and various municipalities help generate Web traffic to a regional marketplace website for the Finger Lakes area?

3. Which other regional area(s) do you see having the same or very similar marketing goals and challenges as the Finger Lakes?

As an incentive offers to send copy of report

Your answers to these questions would make my report much more authoritative and useful. I would be happy to send you a copy and will, of course, be honored to cite you and Creative Marketing Associates in my work.

Indicates when information is needed, and makes contact easy

Because my report is due by December 2, I would greatly appreciate having your answers within the next month so that I can include them. Would you kindly send your responses, or any questions you may have, to my email address, jkawatsu@webnet.com.

Thanks reader

Many thanks for your help.

Sincerely yours,

Julie Kawatsu

Julie Kawatsu

The Four A's of Sales Letters

Successful sales letters follow a time-honored and workable plan—what can be called the "Four A's":

1. It gets the reader's *attention*—with a question or a how-to statement (e.g., "We can show you how to save $100 on your next credit card purchase").
2. It highlights the product's or service's *appeal*—emotionally or financially, or both. Focus on benefits to the reader.
3. It shows the customer the product's or service's *application*—descriptions, special features, guarantees.
4. It ends with a specific request for *action*—call, visit, participate, register online. Motivate reader to act promptly.

These four goals can be achieved in fewer than four or five paragraphs. Look at the sales letter in Figure 4.9 (page 118) in which these parts are labeled.

Do I Mention Costs?

As a general rule, do not bluntly state the cost. Relate prices, charges, or fees to the benefits provided by the services or products you are selling. Let customers see how much they are getting for their money, as Cory Soufas does in paragraph 3 in Figure 4.9. Similarly, a dealer who installs steel shutters did not tell readers the exact cost but stressed that they will save money by buying them: "Your Reel Shutters also offer substantial savings in energy costs by reducing your heat loss through radiation by as much as 65% … and that lowers your utility bills by at least 35%."

Customer Relations Letters

Much business correspondence deals explicitly with establishing and maintaining friendly working relations. Customer relations letters show how you and your company regard the people with whom you do business. The letters should reveal your sensitivity to their needs. The first lesson to learn is that you cannot look at your letter only from your (the writer's) perspective. You have to see the letter from the reader's perspective and anticipate his/her needs and reactions. Customer relations letters send readers good news or bad news, acceptances or refusals. Good news tells customers one or more of the following:

- You agree with them about a problem they brought to your attention.
- You are solving their problem exactly the way they want.
- You are approving their loan or request for a refund.
- You are grateful to them for their business.

Thank you letters, congratulations letters, and adjustment letters saying "Yes" with these messages are all examples of good news messages.

Bad news messages, however, inform readers that:

- You do not like their work or the equipment/technology they sold you.
- You do not have the equipment or service they want or you cannot provide it at the price they want to pay.

FIGURE 4.9 A Sales Letter Sent to a Business Reader

Workwell Software
3700 Stewart Avenue   Chicago IL 60637-2210
Phone: (312) 555-3720   **Fax:** (312) 555-7601   **Email: sales@workwell.com**
www.workwell.com

August 13, 2014

Ali Jen, Office Manager
Circuit Systems, Inc.
7 Tyler Place
Oklahoma City, OK 73101-0761

Dear Ali Jen:

Do you know how much money your company loses from repetitive
strain injury (RSI)? Each year employers spend millions of dollars on
employee insurance claims because of back pains, fatigue, eye strain,
bursitis, and carpal tunnel syndrome injuries.

Workwell can solve your problems with its easy-to-use Exercise
Program Software, which automatically monitors the time employees
spend at their computers and also measures their keyboard activity. After
each hour (or the specified number of keystrokes), **Workwell** software
will take your employees through a series of brief exercises that will help
prevent carpal tunnel syndrome and muscle strains.

Workwell's Exercise Program Software will not interfere with your busy
schedule. Each of the 27 exercises is demonstrated on screen with audio
instructions. The entire program takes less than 3 minutes and is available

for Windows 7 and 8 as well as OS X 10.7 or higher. For only $1,499.00,
you can provide a networked version of this valuable software to all of Circuit
Systems' employees.

To help your employees stay at peak efficiency in a safe work environment,
please call us at 1-800-555-WELL or visit us at **www.workwell.com** to order
your software today.

Thank you. I hope to hear from you soon.

Cory Soufas

Cory Soufas
Sales Representative

- You cannot refund their purchase price or perform a service.
- You are raising their rent or not renewing their lease.

Bad news messages often come to readers through complaint letters, adjustment letters that say "No," and collection letters.

Being Direct or Indirect

Not every customer relations letter starts by giving the reader the writer's main point, judgment, conclusion, or reaction. Whether you are sending good news or bad news, determine what to say and where. *Where you place your main idea is determined by the type of letter you are writing.* Good news messages require one tactic; bad news ones, another.

Good News Message

If you are writing a good news letter, use the direct approach. Start your letter with the welcome, pleasant news that the reader wants to hear. Don't postpone the opportunity to put your reader in the right frame of mind. Then, provide any relevant supporting details, explanations, or commentary. Being direct is advantageous when you have good news to convey.

Bad News Message

If you have bad news to report, do *not* open your letter with it. Be indirect. Prepare your reader for the bad news; keep the tension level down. If you throw the bad news at your reader right away, you jeopardize the goodwill you want to create and sustain. Consider how you would react to a letter that begins with these slaps:

- Your order cannot be filled.
- Your application for a loan has been denied.
- It is our unfortunate duty to report …

Having been denied, disappointed, or even offended in the first sentence or paragraph, the reader is not likely to give you his or her attentive cooperation thereafter.

Case Study

Two Versions of a Bad News Message

Figures 4.10 and 4.11 illustrate two versions of a letter written by A. J. Griffin, the accounts representative of a large mall, to one of her tenants, Daniel Sobol, notifying him about an increase in rent. Notice how Griffin's bad news letter in Figure 4.10 curtly starts off with the bad news of a rent increase. Receiving such a letter, the owner of Flowers by Dan certainly could not be blamed for looking for a new place of business. Griffin was too direct when she should have been diplomatically indirect. She did not consider her reader's reaction; all she was concerned about was delivering her message.

Compare the curt version of Griffin's letter in Figure 4.10 with her revised message in Figure 4.11. In the revised version, she begins tactfully with pleasant, positive words designed to put her reader in a good frame of mind. Then Griffin gives some background information that the owner of Flowers by Dan can relate to. Griffin makes one more attempt to encourage Sobol to recall his good feelings about the mall—last year they did not raise rents—before introducing the bad news of a rent increase.

Griffin softens the blow by saying that the River Road Mall knows it is bad news. Her tactic here is to defuse some of the anger that Sobol will inevitably feel. In fact, Griffin words the bad news so that the tenant sees the mall as acting in the best interest of his flower shop. The mall will not lower or compromise on the services that the tenant has enjoyed and profited from in the past. Griffin then ends on a positive, upbeat note: a prosperous future for Flowers by Dan.

FIGURE 4.10 An Ineffective Bad News Letter

River Road Mall

December 3, 2013

Mr. Daniel Sobol
Flowers by Dan
Lower Level 107
River Road Mall

Dear Mr. Sobol:

Blunt opening disregards audience's needs and feelings

This is to inform you of a rent increase. Starting next month your new rent will be $3,500.00, resulting in a 15 percent increase.

Ends with a discourteously written demand

Please make sure that your January rent check includes this increase.

No attempt to help audience understand or accept message

Sincerely,

A. J. Griffin
Accounts Representative
ajg@rrmall.com

300 First Street
Canton, Ohio 44701
(216) 555-6700
www.RRMall.com

FIGURE 4.11 A Diplomatic Revision of the Bad News Letter in Figure 4.10

River Road Mall

December 3, 2013

Mr. Daniel Sobol
Flowers by Dan
Lower Level 107
River Road Mall

Dear Mr. Sobol:

It has been a pleasure to have you as a tenant at the Mall for the past two years, and we look forward to serving you in the future.

Over these last two years we have experienced a dramatic increase in costs at River Road Mall for security, maintenance, landscaping, pest control, utilities, insurance, and taxes. Last year we absorbed those increases and so did not have to raise your rent. We wish we could do it again, but, unfortunately, we must increase your rent by 15 percent, to $3,500.00 a month, effective January 1.

Although no one likes a rent increase, we know that you do not want us to compromise on the quality of service that you and your customers expect and deserve from River Road Mall.

Please let us know how we can assist you in the future. We wish you a very successful and profitable 2014. If you have any questions, please call or visit my office.

Cordially,

A. J. Griffin

A. J. Griffin
Accounts Representative
ajg@rrmall.com

300 First Street
Canton, Ohio 44701
(216) 555-6700
www.RRMall.com

Opens with positive association

Prepares reader for bad news to follow

States bad news in most concise, upbeat way

Links bad news to reader benefits

Does not apologize but ends respectfully

Friendly complimentary close suitable for a long-term client

Follow-Up Letters

A follow-up letter is sent by a company after a sale to thank the customer for buying a product or using a service and to encourage the customer to buy more products and services. A follow-up letter is a combination thank-you note and sales letter. The letter in Figure 4.12 (page 123) shows how an income tax preparation service attempts to obtain repeat business by doing the following:

1. begins with a brief and sincere expression of gratitude
2. discusses the benefits (advantages) the customer already knows about and then transfers the firm's dedication to the customer to a continuing sales area
3. ends with a specific request for future business

Complaint Letters

Each of us, either as customers or businesspeople, at some time has been frustrated by a defective product, inadequate or rude service, or incorrect billing. When we get no satisfaction from calling an 800 number and are routed through a series of menu options, our frustration level goes up. Usually our first response is to write a letter, dripping with juicy insults. But an angry letter, like a piece of flaming email (see Figure 3.3, page 83), rarely gets positive results and can hurt your company's image.

A complaint letter is a delicate one to write. First off, avoid the following:

- name calling
- sarcasm
- insults
- threats
- unflattering clip art
- using all captial letters

The key thing to keep in mind is that you can disagree without being disagreeable. Be rational, not hostile. Just to let off steam, you might want to write an angry letter but then tear it up, replacing all the heat with courteous and diplomatic language.

Establishing the Right Tone

A complaint letter is written for more reasons than just blowing off steam. You want some specific action taken. The "you attitude" is especially important here to maintain the reader's goodwill. Complaint letters that are professional and considerate are more likely to receive positive attention than letters bristling with angry words. An effective complaint letter can be written by an individual consumer or by a company. Figure 4.13 (page 124) shows Michael Trigg's complaint about a defective fishing reel; Figure 4.14 (page 125) expresses a restaurant's dissatisfaction with an industrial dishwasher.

Writing an Effective Complaint Letter

To increase your chances of receiving a speedy settlement, follow these seven steps in writing your letter of complaint. They will help you build your case.

FIGURE 4.12 A Follow-Up Letter to Encourage Repeat Business

Taylor Tax Service
Highway 10, North Jennings, TX 78326
(888) 555-9681 email taylor@aol.com
www.taylor.com

December 3, 2013

Ms. Laurie Pavlovich
345 Jefferson St.
Jennings, TX 78326

Dear Ms. Pavlovich:

Thank you for using our services in February of this year. We were pleased to help you prepare your 2012 Federal income tax return. Our goal is to save you every tax dollar to which you are entitled. If you ever have questions about your return, we are open all year long to help you.

We are looking forward to serving you again next year. Several new federal tax laws enacted this year will change the types of deductions you can declare. These changes might appreciably increase your refund. Our consultants know the new laws and are ready to apply them to your return.

Another important tax matter influencing your 2013 returns will be any losses you may have suffered because of the hailstorms and tornadoes that hit our area five months ago. Our consultants are specially trained to assist you in filing proper damage claims with your federal return.

To make using our services even more convenient, we file your tax return electronically to speed up any refund. Please call us at (888) 555-9681 or email us at **taylor@aol.com** as soon as you have received all your 2013 tax forms to set up an appointment. We are waiting to serve you seven days a week from 9:00 a.m. to 9:00 p.m.

Sincerely yours,

TAYLOR TAX SERVICE

Demetria Taylor

Demetria Taylor, CPA

Links business goal to customer advantage

Stresses reasons for customer to return for service

Makes it easy and profitable for customer to act soon

Ends with commitment to customer convenience

FIGURE 4.13 A Complaint Letter from a Consumer

17 Westwood Drive

Magnolia, MA 02171

mtrigg@roof.com

October 10, 2014

Identifies appropriate persons to resolve problem

Mr. Ralph Montoya
Customer Relations Department
Smith Sports Equipment
P.O. Box 1014
Tulsa, OK 74109-1014

Dear Mr. Montoya:

Documents all relevant details about the product

On September 21, 2014, I purchased a Smith reel, model 191, at the Uni-Mart Store on Marsh Avenue in Magnolia. The reel sold for $94.95 plus tax. The reel is not working effectively, and I am returning it to you under separate cover by first-class mail.

Explains politely what is wrong

I had made no more than five casts with the reel when it began to malfunction. The button that releases the spool and allows the line to cast would not spring back into position after casting. In addition, the gears made a grinding noise whenever I tried to retrieve the line. Because of these problems, I was unable to continue my participation in the Gloucester Fishing Tournament last week.

Clearly states what should be done

I request that a new reel be sent to me free of charge in place of the defective one I returned. I would also like to know what was wrong with the defective reel.

Specifies an acceptable timeframe

Thank you for processing my claim within the next two weeks.

Sincerely yours,

Michael Trigg

Michael Trigg

1. Sending your letter to the right person further ensures your success. But, as we saw, never address it "To Whom It May Concern." Do your homework—search the company's website or go to *Hoover's Business Directory* (www.hoovers.com) to get contact information. But don't send your letter to the CEO. Find the appropriate person or office that responds to customer problems.

FIGURE 4.14 A Complaint Letter from a Business

The Loft

Camerson and Dale
Sunnyside, California 91793-4116
213-555-7500

June 21, 2013

Ms. Priscilla Dubrow
Customer Relations Department
Superflex Products
San Diego, CA 93141-0808

Dear Ms. Dubrow:

On September 15, 2012, we purchased a Superflex industrial dishwasher, model 3203876, at the Hillcrest store at 3400 Broadway Drive in Sunnyside, for $5,000. In the last three weeks, our restaurant has had serious and repeated problems with this machine. Three more months of warranty remain on the unit.

The machine does not complete a full cycle; it stops before the final rinsing and thus leaves the dishes dirty. It appears that the cycle regulators are not working properly because they refuse to shift into the next necessary gear. Attempts to repair the machine by the Hillcrest service team on June 4, 11, and 14 have been unsuccessful.

The Loft has been greatly inconvenienced. Our kitchen team has been forced to sort, clean, and sanitize utensils, dishes, pans, and pots by hand, resulting in additional overtime. Moreover, our expenses for proper detergents have increased.

We want your main office to send another repair crew to fix this machine. If your crew is unable to do this, we want a discount worth the amount of the warranty life on this model to be applied to the purchase of a new Superflex dishwasher. This amount would come to $1,000, or 20 percent of the original purchase price.

So that our business is not further disrupted, we would appreciate your resolving this problem promptly within the next four to five business days.

Sincerely yours,

Emily Rashon

Emily Rashon
Co-Owner

▶ **Browse our menu, which changes daily, at www.theloft.com**

Writes to specific reader

Gives all product's facts and warranty information

Describes what happened and when

Documents problem and reason for adjustment

Provides clear description of how problem should be solved

Concludes politely with justification for prompt action

2. Be concise. Keep your letter to one page. Your reader wants essential details, not a saga of your troubles.

3. Begin with a detailed description of the product or service. Give the appropriate model and serial numbers, size, quantity, color, and cost, as Emily Rashon does in Figure 4.14. Indicate when, where (specific address), and how (through a vendor, the Internet, at a store) you purchased it and also the remaining warranty. If you are complaining about a service, give the name of the company, the date of the service, and the personnel providing it.

4. State exactly what is wrong with the product or service. Be factual. Precise information will enable the reader to understand and act on your complaint.

- How many times did the product work before it stopped?
- What parts were malfunctioning?
- What parts of a job were not done or were done poorly?
- When did all this happen? How many times?
- Where and exactly how were you inconvenienced?
- Was the service late, incomplete, rude?

Stating that "the brake shoes were defective" tells very little about how long they were on your car, how effectively they may have been installed, or what condition they were in when they ceased functioning safely. Michael Trigg specifies "no more than five casts" in Figure 4.13.

5. Briefly describe the inconvenience you have experienced. Show that your problems were directly caused by the defective product or service. To build your case, give precise details about the time and money you lost. Don't just say you had "numerous difficulties." Did you have to pay a mechanic to fix your car when it was stalled on the road? Did you have to buy a new printer or Blu-ray player? In Figure 4.14, Emily Rashon cites overtime her staff had to put in. Where appropriate, refer to any previous telephone calls, emails, or letters. Give the names of the people you have written to or spoken with and the dates.

6. Indicate precisely what you want done. Be realistic. Don't inflate costs or damages. And do not simply write that you "want something done." State precisely that you want one or more of the following:

- your purchase price refunded in full
- a credit made to your account
- a credit toward the purchase of another model (as in Figure 4.14)
- your exact model repaired or replaced (as in Figure 4.13)
- a new repair crew assigned to the job
- an apology from the company for discourteous or late service

If you are asking for damages, state your request in dollars and cents and always include copies of bills documenting your expenses related to the problem.

7. Ask for prompt handling of your claim. In your concluding paragraph, ask the reader to answer any question you may have (such as finding out where calls came from that you were billed for but did not make). Also specify a reasonable time by which you want to hear from the reader or need the problem fixed. Note how the writer does this in the last paragraph in Figure 4.14.

Adjustment Letters

Adjustment letters respond to complaint letters by telling customers dissatisfied with a product or service how their claim will be settled. Adjustment letters should reconcile the differences that exist between a customer and a company and restore the customer's confidence in that company.

Adjustment Letters That Tell the Customer "Yes"

It is easy to write a "Yes" letter if you remember a few useful suggestions. As with a good news message, start with the favorable news the customer wants to hear; that will put him or her in a positive frame of mind to read the rest of your letter. Let the customer know that you sincerely agree with him or her—don't sound as if you are begrudgingly honoring the request.

The two examples of adjustment letters saying "Yes" show you how to write this kind of correspondence. The first example, Figure 4.15 (page 128), says "Yes" to Michael Trigg's letter in Figure 4.13. Reread the Trigg complaint letter to see what problems Ralph Montoya faced when he had to write to Mr. Trigg. The second example of an adjustment letter that says "Yes" is in Figure 4.16 (page 129). It responds to a customer who has complained about an incorrect billing.

Guidelines for Writing a "Yes" Letter

The following four steps will help you write a "Yes" adjustment letter.

1. Admit immediately that the customer's complaint is justified and apologize. Briefly state that you are sorry and thank the customer for writing to inform you.

2. State precisely what you are going to do to correct the problem. Let the customer know that you will

- extend warranty coverage
- credit the account with funds, more air miles, or the like
- offer a discount on the next purchase
- cancel a bill or give credit toward another purchase
- repair damaged equipment
- enclose a free pass, coupon, or waiver
- upgrade a product or service

Do not postpone the good news the customer wants to hear. That way the rest of your letter will be much more appreciated and convincing. In Figure 4.15, Michael Trigg is told that he will receive a new reel; in Figure 4.16, Kathryn Brumfield learns she will not be charged for parts or service.

FIGURE 4.15 An Adjustment Letter Saying "Yes" to the Complaint Letter in Figure 4.13

Smith Sports Equipment
P.O. Box 1014   Tulsa, Oklahoma 74109-1014
(918) 555-0164 ▪ www.smithsport.com

October 20, 2014

Mr. Michael Trigg
17 Westwood Drive
Magnolia, MA 02171

Dear Mr. Trigg:

Thank you for alerting us in your letter of October 10 to your problems with one of our model 191 spincast reels. I am sorry for the inconvenience the reel caused you. A new Smith reel is on its way to you.

We have examined your reel and found the difficulty. It seems that a retaining pin on the button spring was improperly installed by one of our new soldering machines on the assembly line. We have thoroughly inspected, repaired, and cleaned this machine to eliminate the problem from happening again.

Since we began making quality reels in 1955, we have taken pride in helping loyal customers like you who rely on a Smith reel. We hope that your new Smith reel brings you years of pleasure and many good catches, especially next year at the Gloucester Fishing Tournament.

Thank you for your business. Please let me know if I can assist you again.

Respectfully,

SMITH SPORTS EQUIPMENT

Ralph Montoya

Ralph Montoya
Customer Relations Department

Side annotations:

Responds within time frame specified in complaint letter

Apologizes and announces good news

Explains what happened and why problem will not recur

Expresses respect for customer

Closes with friendly offer to help again

Signed, not stamped, signature

© Cengage Learning 2015

FIGURE 4.16 An Adjustment Letter Saying "Yes"

Brunelli Motors

Route 3A, Giddings, Kansas 62034-8100 (913) 555-1521

August 6, 2014

Ms. Kathryn Brumfield
34 East Main
Giddings, KS 62034-1123

Dear Ms. Brumfield:

We appreciate your notifying us, in your letter of July 30, about the problem you experienced with the warranty coverage on your new Phantom Hawk GT. The bills sent to you were incorrect, and I have canceled them. Please accept my apologies. You should not have been charged for a shroud or for repairs to the damaged fan and hose, since all those parts, and labor on them, are fully covered by your warranty.

Responds promptly

Thanks customer and complies with request

The problem was the result of an error in the way the charges were listed. Our firm has begun using new billing software to give customers better service, and the technician apparently entered the wrong code for your account. We have since programmed our system to flag any bills for vehicles still under warranty. We hope that this new procedure will help us serve you and our other customers more efficiently.

Explains why problem occurred and how it has been resolved

Thank you for taking the time to write to us. We value you as a customer at Brunelli Motors. When you are ready for another Phantom Hawk GT, take a virtual test drive at our website **www.brunelli.com**. Happy motoring!

Ends courteously and leaves reader with good feeling about the dealership

Sincerely yours,

Susan Chee-Saafir
Susan Chee-Saafir
Service Manager

Experience virtual reality: Drive a new Phantom at
http://www.brunelli.com

Provides company URL so customer can further explore product line

3. Tell customers exactly what happened. They deserve an explanation for the inconvenience they suffered. Note that the explanations in Figures 4.15 and 4.16 (pages 128 and 129) give only the essential details; they do not bother the reader with side issues or petty remarks about who was to blame. But assure customers that the mishap is not typical of your company's operations.

4. End on a friendly—and positive—note. Don't remind customers about their trouble. Leave customers with a positive feeling about your company. You want them to purchase your product or service again.

Adjustment Letters That Tell the Customer "No"

Writing to tell customers "No" is obviously more difficult than agreeing with them. You are faced with the sensitive task of conveying bad news, while at the same time convincing the reader that your position is fair, logical, and consistent. Do not bluntly start off with a "No." Do not accuse or argue. Avoid remarks such as the following that blame, scold, or remind customers of a wrongdoing:

- You obviously did not read the instruction manual.
- Our records show that you purchased the equipment after the policy went into effect.
- The company policy plainly states that such refunds are not allowed.
- You were negligent in running the machine.
- You claim that our scanner was poorly constructed.
- Your complaint is unjustified.

Guidelines for Saying "No" Diplomatically

The following five suggestions will help you say "No" diplomatically. Practical applications of these suggestions can be found in Figures 4.17 (page 131) and 4.18 (page 132). Contrast the refusal of Michael Trigg's complaint in Figure 4.17 with the favorable response to it in Figure 4.15.

1. Thank customers for writing. Open with a polite, respectful comment, called a buffer, to soften your reader's response before he or she sees your "No." Don't put them on the defensive by beginning with "We regret to inform you." The letter writers in Figures 4.17 and 4.18 use buffers to thank the customers for bringing the matter to their attention and sympathize with them about their inconvenience. As with other bad news letters, never begin with a refusal. Telling them "No" in the first sentence or two will negatively color their reactions to the rest of your letter. Use the indirect approach discussed earlier in this chapter (page 119), and avoid these reader-hostile openings:

- I was surprised to learn that you found our product unsatisfactory.
- We have been in business for years and nothing like this has ever happened.
- There is no way we could give you what you demand.

FIGURE 4.17 An Adjustment Letter Saying "No" to the Complaint Letter in Figure 4.13

Smith Sports Equipment

P.O. Box 1014   Tulsa, Oklahoma 74109-1014
(918) 555-0164 ■ www.smithsport.com

October 20, 2014

Mr. Michael Trigg
17 Westwood Drive
Magnolia, MA 02171

Dear Mr. Trigg:

Thank you for writing to us on October 10 about the trouble you experienced with our model 191 spincast reel. We are sorry to hear about the difficulties you had with the release button and gears.

Buffer— thanks and sympathizes with reader

We have examined your reel and found the difficulty. It seems that a retaining pin in the button spring was pushed into the side of the reel casing, thereby making the gears inoperable. The retaining pin is a vital yet delicate part of your reel. In order to function properly, it has to be pushed gently. Since our warranty does not cover pushing the pin forcibly, we cannot send you a replacement.

Explains problem without directly blaming the reader; gives firm decision

However, we want you to have many more hours of fishing pleasure, and so we would be happy to repair your reel for $19.98 and return it to you within 5–7 days. Please let us know your decision.

Turns a "No" into a "Yes" for customer

I look forward to hearing from you. Thank you for writing to us.

Ends politely without any reference to the problem

Respectfully,

SMITH SPORTS EQUIPMENT

Ralph Montoya

Ralph Montoya
Customer Relations Department

FIGURE 4.18 Another Adjustment Letter Saying "No"

Eye-catching and appropriate logo

Health AIR

4300 Marshall Drive
Salt Lake City, Utah 84113-1521
(801) 555-6028
www.healthair.com

August 28, 2014

Inside address and salutation list reader's title

Ms. Denise Southby, Director
Bradley General Hospital
Bradley, IL 60610-4615

Dear Director Southby:

Professional you-centered opening with buffer

Thank you for your letter of August 20 explaining the problems you encountered with our Puritan MAII ventilator. We were sorry to learn that you were unable to get the high-volume PAO_2 alarm circuit to work.

Justifies firm decision by explaining causes of problem and conditions of sale

Our ventilator is a high-volume, low-frequency unit that can deliver up to 40 cm of water pressure. The ventilator runs with a center of gravity attachment on the right side of the diode. The trouble you had with the high oxygen alarm system is due to an overload on your piped-in oxygen. Our laboratory inspection of the ventilator you returned indicated that the high-pressure system had blown a vital adapter in the MAII. An overload in an oxygen system is not covered by the warranty on the ventilator, and so we cannot replace it free of charge.

Provides practical alternative with financial incentive to keep customer's business

We would, however, be pleased to send you another model of the adapter, which would be more compatible with your system, as soon as we receive your order. The price of the adapter is $600, but because you are a valued customer, our service representative will install it at no charge to you.

Ends with goodwill

Please let me know your decision. I look forward to hearing from you.

Sincerely yours,

R. P. Gifford

R. P. Gifford
Customer Service Department

2. State the problem carefully to reassure the customer that you understand the complaint. You thereby prove that you are not trying to misrepresent or distort what the customer has told you.

3. Explain what happened with the product or service before you give the customer a decision. Provide a factual explanation to show the customer that he or she is being treated fairly. Rather than focusing on the customer's misunderstanding the instructions or a failure to observe details of a service contract, state the proper ways of handling a piece of equipment.

> **Poor:** By reading the instructions on the side of the paint can, you would have avoided the streaking condition that you claim resulted.
>
> **Revised:** Hi-Gloss Paint requires two applications, four hours apart, for a clear and smooth finish.

The revision reminds the customer of the right way to apply the paint without pointing an accusing finger. Note how the explanations in Figures 4.17 and 4.18 emphasize the appropriate way of using the product equipment.

4. Give your decision without hedging. Do not say, "Perhaps some type of restitution could be made later" or "Further proof would have been helpful." Indecision will infuriate customers who believe that they have already presented a sound, convincing case. Never apologize for your decision.

5. Leave the door open for better and continued business. Whenever possible, help customers solve their problem by offering to send them a new product or part, or installing or repairing a product free of charge or at a discount. Note how the second-to-last paragraphs in Figures 4.17 and 4.18 do that diplomatically.

Memos

Memorandum, usually shortened to *memo*, is a Latin word for "something to be remembered." The Latin meaning points to the memo's chief function: to record information of immediate importance and interest in the busy world of work. Memos are often brief but can contain official announcements that serve a variety of functions, including

- making an announcement
- giving instructions
- clarifying a policy, procedure, or issue
- changing a policy or procedure
- alerting staff to a problem
- sending recommendations
- providing a record of an important matter
- calling a meeting

Memos are usually written for an in-house audience, although the memo format can be used for documents sent outside a company, such as proposals or short reports (see Chapter 8) or for cover notes for longer reports (see Chapter 9).

Memos keep track of what jobs are done where, when, and by whom; they also report on any difficulties, delays, or cancellations and what your company or organization needs to do about correcting or eliminating them.

Memo Protocol and Company Politics

As with other business correspondence, memos reflect a company's image and therefore must follow the company's *protocol*—accepted ways in which in-house communications are formatted, organized, written, and routed. In addition to following your company's protocol, use these commonsense guidelines when writing memos:

1. Be timely. Don't wait until the day of the meeting to announce it.

2. Be professional. Just because a memo is an in-house piece of correspondence does not mean you can dash off a poorly organized, poorly written, or factually inaccurate document. Notice that in Figure 4.19, the memo to Lucy from Roger is professionally written, clearly organized, and properly spelled and punctuated.

3. Be tactful. Be polite and diplomatic, not curt and bossy. For example, in Figure 4.20 (page 136), Janet Hempstead adopts a firm tone regarding an important safety issue, yet she does not blame or talk down to her readers—the machine shop employees. Politeness and diplomacy count a lot at work.

4. Send memos to the appropriate individuals. Don't send copies of a memo (either via hard copy or as an attachment) to people who don't need to read them. It wastes time and energy. Moreover, don't send a memo to high-ranking company personnel in place of your immediate supervisor, who may think you are going over his or her head. For instance, in Figure 4.20, Janet Hempstead has sent her memo only to the machine shop workers, not to the upper management of the Dearborn Company.

Keep in mind, though, that memos are often sent up and down the corporate ladder. Employees send memos to their supervisors, and workers send memos to one another. Figure 4.19 shows a memo sent from one worker to another. Figure 4.20 contains a memo sent from the top down, and Figure 4.21 (page 137) illustrates a memo sent from an employee to management.

Sending Memos: Email or Hard Copy?

A memo can be sent as a printed hard copy, in the body of an email, or as an email attachment. Find out your company's policy. Increasingly, email is replacing printed memos, but there are times when a hard-copy memo is preferred.

Consider the level of importance and confidentiality of your memo. If your memo is an official document, such as the policy outlined in Figure 4.20, you

FIGURE 4.19 Standard Memo Format

MEMO

TO: Lucy
FROM: Roger
DATE: November 12, 2013
SUBJECT: Review of "Successful Website" Seminar

Memo parts

As you know, I attended the "How to Build a Successful Website" seminar on November 7 and learned the "rules and tools" we will need to redesign our own site.

Introduction provides background and tells reader what memo will do

Here is a review of the major topics covered by the presenter, Jackie Wei:

Preview

1. Keep your website content-based—identify your target audience.
2. Visualize and "map out" your site ahead of time.
3. Keep the design of your website simple and elegant; "busy" websites drive away potential customers.
4. Be sure your site is easy to navigate, especially for global readers.
5. Use keywords to maximize your website's search engine exposure.
6. Create hot links and image maps to move users from page to page.
7. Encourage customer interaction by including a comments section.
8. Complete your site with appropriate sound and animation.
9. Keep your site updated.

Numbered list in body helps readers follow information quickly

Could we meet in the next day or two to discuss recreating our website in light of these guidelines? I would really appreciate your suggestions about this project as well.

Conclusion asks for comments

Thanks.

will likely draft it on company letterhead or send it as an attachment. Printing your memo on company letterhead signals that a formal policy now in place. If your memo on company letterhead is confidential (e.g., an evaluation of a co-worker or vendor, or a message containing sensitive financial or medical information), you may not want to send it as an email because it could easily be forwarded to someone other than for whom it was intended. But when you send a routine message that must reach your readers quickly, use email (see Chapter 3, pages 78–85).

FIGURE 4.20 Memo on Letterhead with a Clear Introduction, Discussion, and Conclusion

DEC

Dearborn Equipment Company

Writer's initals verify message

To:	Machine Shop Employees
From:	Janet Hempstead, Shop Supervisor
Date:	September 26, 2014
Subject:	Cleaning Brake Machines Safely

Introduction explains purpose and importance of memo

During the past two weeks I have received several reports that the brake machines are not being cleaned properly after each use. Through this memo I want to explain and emphasize the importance of keeping these machines clean for the safety of all our employees.

Discussion states why problem exists and how to solve it

When the brake machines are used, the cutter chops off small particles of metal from brake drums. These particles then settle on the machines and create a potentially hazardous situation for anyone working on or near the machines. If the machines are not cleaned routinely before being used again, these metal particles could easily fly into an individual's face or upper body when the brake drum is spinning.

Safety message is boldfaced for emphasis

To prevent accidents like this from happening, please make sure you vacuum the brake machines after each use.

You will find two vacuum cleaners for this purpose in the shop—one of them is located in work area 1-A, and the other, a reserve model, is in the storage area. Vacuuming brake machines is quick and easy: It should take you no more than a few seconds, a small amount of time to make the shop safer for all of us.

Conclusion builds goodwill and asks for questions

Thanks for your cooperation. If you have any questions, please call or text me at (609) 555-9899, email me at jhemp@dearco.com, or come by my office.

204 South Mill St., South Orange, NJ 02341-3420 (609) 555-9848 www.dec.com

FIGURE 4.21 A Memo That Uses Headings to Highlight Organization

RAMCO TECHNOLOGIES
Where Technology Shapes Tomorrow

marketing@Ramco.com   www.Ramco.com

Company logo

TO:	Rachel Mohler, Vice President
	Harrison Fontentot, Public Relations
FROM:	Mike Gonzalez MG
DATE:	March 3, 2014
SUBJECT:	Three Ways to Increase Ramco's Community Involvement

Header

At our planning session in early February, our division managers stressed the need to generate favorable publicity for our new Ramco facility in Mayfield. Knowing that such publicity will highlight Ramco's visibility in Mayfield, I think the company's image might be enhanced in the following three ways.

Introduction supplies background and rationale

CREATE A SCHOLARSHIP FUND
Ramco would receive favorable publicity by creating a scholarship at Mayfield Community College for any student interested in a career in technology. A one-year scholarship would cost $7,600. The scholarship could be awarded by a committee composed of Ramco executives and staff. Such a scholarship would emphasize Ramco's enthusiastic support for the latest technical education at a local college.

Body offers concrete evidence (costs, personnel, location) that plan can work

OFFER SITE TOURS
Guided tours of the Mayfield facility would introduce the community to Ramco's innovative technology. These tours might be organized for academic, community, and civic groups. Individuals would see the care we take in protecting the environment in our production and equipment choices and the speed with which we ship our products. Of special interest to visitors would be Ramco's use of industrial robots working alongside our employees. Since these tours would be scheduled in advance, they should not conflict with our production schedules.

Boldfaced headings reflect organization

Relates plan to company mission and image

PROVIDE GUEST SPEAKERS
Many of our employees would be excellent guest speakers at civic and educational meetings in the Mayfield area. Possible topics include the advances Ramco has made in designing and engineering and how these changes have helped consumers as well as the local economy.

Closing emphasizes the plan's feasibility

Please reply via email with your comments as soon as possible. If we are going to put one or more of these suggestions into practice before the facility opens in mid-April, we'll need to act before the end of the month.

Ends with request for feedback and authorization

Memo Format

Memos vary in format and the way they are sent. Some companies use standard, printed forms (as in Figure 4.19), while others have their names (letterhead) printed on their memos (as in Figures 4.20 and 4.21). You can also create a memo by including the necessary parts in an email, as in Figures 3.1 and 3.2, which appear in Chapter 3.

As you can see from looking at Figures 4.19, 4.20, and 4.21, memos look different from letters. Because they are often sent to individuals within your company, memos do not need the formalities necessary in business letters, such as an inside address, a formal salutation or complimentary close, or a signature line, as discussed on pages 102–105).

Memo Parts

Basically, the memo consists of two parts: the *header*, or the identifying information at the top, and the *message* itself. This identifying information includes four easily recognized parts: *To, From, Date,* and *Subject* lines.

TO:	Aileen Kelly, Chief Computer Analyst
FROM:	Stacy Kaufman, Operator, Level II
DATE:	January 30, 2014
SUBJECT:	Progress report on the fall schedule

You can use a memo template, which automatically formats headers such as the following, to save time.

TO:	[Enter name]
FROM:	Linda Cowan
DATE:	[Enter date]
RE:	[Enter subject here.]

On the *To* line, write the name and job title of the individual(s) who will receive your memo. If you are sending your memo to more than one reader, make sure you list your readers in the order of their status in your company or agency, as Mike Gonzalez does in Figure 4.21 (according to company policy, the vice president's name appears before that of the public relations director). If you are on a first-name basis with the reader, use just his or her first name, as in Figure 4.19. Otherwise, include the reader's first and last names. Don't leave out anyone who needs the information.

On the *From* line, insert your name (use your first name only if your reader refers to you by it) and your job title (unless it is unnecessary for your reader). Some companies ask employees to handwrite their initials after their typed name to verify that the message comes from them and that they are certifying its contents, as in Figures 4.20 and 4.21.

On the *Date* line, do not simply name the day of the week. Give the full calendar date (June 2, 2014).

On the *Subject* line, key in the purpose of your memo. The subject line serves as the title of your memo; it summarizes your message. Vague subject lines, such as

"New Policy," "Operating Difficulties," or "Software," do not identify your message precisely and may suggest that you have not restricted or developed it sufficiently. Note how Mike Gonzalez's subject line in Figure 4.21 is so much more precise than just saying "Ramco's Community Involvement."

Questions Your Memo Needs to Answer for Readers

Here are some key questions your audience may ask and your memo needs to answer clearly and concisely:

1. When? When did it happen? Is it on, ahead of, or behind schedule? When does it need to be discussed or implemented? *When* is answered in Figures 4.19 ("November 14," "in the next day or two"), 4.20 ("during the past two weeks," "after each use"), and 4.21 ("in early February," "before the end of the month").

2. Who? Who is involved? Who will be affected by your message? How many people are involved? *Who* is answered in Figures 4.19 (Jackie Wei), 4.20 (all machine shop employees), and 4.21 (Ramco Technologies as a whole).

3. Where? Where did it take place or will it take place? *Where* is answered in Figures 4.19 (the website seminar), 4.20 (the brake shop), and 4.21 (the Mayfield facility).

4. Why? Why is it an important topic? *Why* is clearly answered in Figures 4.19 (because the website is being redesigned), 4.20 (because it's a safety issue), and 4.21 (because favorable publicity will help the company).

5. Costs? How much will it cost? Will the costs be lower or higher than a competitor's costs? Not every memo will answer financial questions, but in Figure 4.20, the injuries discussed cost the company money, and in Figure 4.21, the specific cost of an individual scholarship ($7,600) is an important issue.

6. Technology? What technology is involved? Is the technology current, able to be upgraded, safe for the environment? Note that Figures 4.19, 4.20, and 4.21 all especially refer to technological issues—website design, equipment safety, education, robots.

7. What's next? What are the next steps that should be taken as a result of the issues discussed in the memo? What are the implications for the product, service, budget, staff? A good example of this is in Figure 4.21 (the company needs to decide on how to implement the suggestions before the new plant opens).

Memo Style and Tone

The audience within your company will determine your memo's style and tone (for a review of identifying audience, see Chapter 1, pages 6–11). When writing to a co-worker whom you know well, you can adopt a casual, conversational tone. You want to be seen as friendly and cooperative. In fact, to do otherwise would make you look self-important, stuffy, or hard to work with. Consider the friendly tone appropriate for one colleague writing to another as in Roger's memo to Lucy in Figure 4.19. Note how he ends in a polite but informal way.

When writing a memo to a manager, though, you will want to use a more formal tone than you would when communicating with a co-worker or peer. Your boss will expect you to show a more respectful, even official, posture. See how formal yet conversationally persuasive Mike Gonzalez's memo to his bosses is in Figure 4.21. His tone and style are a reflection of his hard work as well as his respect for his employers. Here are two ways of expressing the same message, the first more suitable when writing to a co-worker and the second more appropriate for a memo to the boss.

Co-worker: I think we should go ahead with Marisol's plan for reorganization. It seems like a safe option to me, and I don't think we can lose.

Boss: I think that we should adopt the organizational plan developed by Marisol Vega. Her recommendations are carefully researched and persuasively answer the questions our department has about solving the problem.

When an employer writes to workers informing them about policies or procedures, as Janet Hempstead does in Figure 4.20, the tone of the memo is official and straightforward. Yet even so, Hempstead takes into account her readers' feelings (she does not blame) and safety, which are at the forefront of her rhetorical purpose.

Finally, remember that your employer and co-workers deserve the same clear and concise writing and attention to the "you attitude" (see pages 108–112) that your customers do. Memos, like letters, require the same care and should follow the same rules of effective writing discussed in Chapter 1.

Strategies for Organizing a Memo

Take a few minutes to outline and draft what you need to say and to decide in what order it needs to be presented. Organize your memos so that readers can find information quickly and act on it promptly. For longer, more complex communications, such as the memos in Figures 4.20 and 4.21, your message might be divided into three parts: (1) introduction, (2) discussion, and (3) conclusion. Regardless of how short or long your memo is, recall the three *P*'s for success: *plan* what you are going to say; *polish* your writing before you send it; and *proofread* everything.

Introduction

The introduction of your memo should do the following:

- Tell readers clearly about the problem, procedure, or question that prompted you to write.
- Explain briefly any background information the reader needs to know.
- Be specific about what you are going to accomplish in your memo.

Do not hesitate to come right out and say, "This memo summarizes the action taken in Evansville to reduce air pollution." See how clearly this is done in Figure 4.19.

Discussion

In the discussion section (the body) of your memo, help readers in these ways:

- State why a problem or procedure is important, who will be affected by it, and what caused it and why.
- Indicate why and what changes are necessary.
- Give precise dates, times, locations, and costs.

Notice Janet Hempstead's memo in Figure 4.20 carefully describes an existing problem and explains the proper procedure for cleaning the brake machines, and how Mike Gonzalez in Figure 4.21 offers carefully researched evidence on how Ramco can increase its favorable publicity in the community.

Conclusion

In your conclusion, state specifically how you want the reader to respond to your memo. To get readers to act appropriately, you can do one or more of the following:

- Ask readers to call you if they have any questions, as in Figure 4.20.
- Request a reply—in writing, over the telephone, via email, or in person—by a specific date, as in Figure 4.21.
- Provide a list of recommendations that the readers are to accept, revise, or reject, as in Figures 4.19 and 4.21.

Organizational Markers

Throughout your memo, use the following organizational markers, where appropriate:

- Headings organize your work and make information easy for readers to follow, as in Figure 4.21.
- Numbered or bulleted lists help readers see comparisons and contrasts readily and thereby comprehend your ideas more quickly, as in Figure 4.19.
- Underlining or boldfacing emphasizes key points (see Figure 4.20). Do not overuse this technique; draw attention only to main points and those that contain summaries or draw conclusions.

Organizational markers are not limited to memos; you will find them in email, letters, reports, and proposals as well. (See Chapter 6, pages 217–227).

International Business Correspondence

After emails, letters are the most frequent type of communication you are likely to have with international readers. Formal letter writing is a highly prized skill in the global marketplace. But as we saw in Chapter 1 (pages 2–6), you cannot assume that people in every culture write letters the way we do in the United

States. The conventions of letter writing—formats, inside addresses, salutations, dates, complimentary closes, signature lines—are as diverse as international audiences are.

Sometimes your international client may reside in the United States. Then you have to exercise the same diplomacy as you would when communicating with audiences living in other countries. For example, in Figure 4.22 restaurant owner Patrice St. Jacques writes an effective sales letter by zeroing in on his reader's (Etienne Abernathy's) ethnic pride and heritage. Although Abernathy's company is located in the United States, St. Jacques persuasively sees him from a much broader cultural perspective.

It would be impossible to provide information about how to write letters to each international audience. There are at least five thousand major languages representing diverse ethnic and cultural communities around the globe. But here are some of the most important culturally sensitive questions you need to ask about writing to readers whose cultures are different from yours:

- What is your relationship to your reader(s) (client, vendor, salesperson, or international colleague)?
- How should you format and address your letter?
- What is an appropriate salutation?
- How should you begin and conclude your letter?
- What types and amount of information will you have to give?
- What is the most appropriate tone to use?

To answer these and similar questions about proper letter protocol for your international readers, you need to learn about their culture by consulting a source such as www.cyborlink.com.

Ten Guidelines for Communicating with International Readers

The following eleven guidelines will help you communicate more successfully with an international audience and significantly reduce the chances of readers' misunderstanding you.

1. Use common, easily understood vocabulary. Write in basic, simplified English. Choose words that are widely understood. Whenever you have a choice, use the simpler word. For example, use *stop*, not *refrain*; *prevent*, not *forestall*; *happy*, not *exultant*.

2. Keep your sentences simple and easy to understand. Short, direct sentences will cause a reader whose native language is not English the least amount of trouble. A good rule of thumb is that the shorter and less complicated your sentences, the easier and clearer they will be for a reader to process. Long (more than fifteen words) and complex (multiclause) sentences can be so difficult for readers to unravel that they may skip over them or simply guess at your message. Do not, however, be insultingly childish, as if you were writing to someone in kindergarten. Also, always try to avoid the passive voice. It is one of the most difficult sentence patterns

FIGURE 4.22 A Sales Letter That Appeals to a Specific International Audience

ISLAND JACQUES

4700 Cyprus Avenue
Philadelphia, PA 19172

www.islandjacques.netdoor.com
856-555-3295

10 May 2013

Mr. Etienne Abernathy, President
Seagrove Enterprises
1800 S. Port Haven Road
Philadelphia, PA 19103-1800

Dear Mr. Abernathy:

Congratulations on winning the Hanover Award for Community Service. We in the Port Haven area of Philadelphia are proud that a business with Caribbean roots has received such a distinguished honor.

To celebrate your and Seagrove's success, as well as all your business entertaining needs (annual banquet, monthly meetings, etc.), I invite you to Island Jacques. We are a family-owned business that for 30 years has offered Philadelphia residents the finest Caribbean atmosphere and food west of the Islands. Our black pepper shrimp, reggae or mango chicken, and Steak St. Lucie—plus our irresistible beef and pork jerk—are the talk from here to Kingston. You and your guests can also see our original Caribbean art and enjoy our steel drum music.

Island Jacques can offer Seagrove a variety of dining options. With five separate dining rooms, we are small enough for an intimate party of 4 yet large enough to accommodate a group of 250. We can do early lunches or late dinners, depending on your schedule. And we even cater, if that's your style. Our chefs—Diana Maurier and Emile Danticat—will prepare a special calypso menu just for you. Also a benefit, our prices are competitive for the Philadelphia area.

Please call me soon so you can savor Island Jacques's unique hospitality. For your convenience, I am enclosing a copy of this week's menu delights. Check out our website, too, for a taste of Caribbean sound. We would love to feature Seagrove as Island Jacques's "Guest of the Week!"

Stay Cool, Mon.

Patrice St. Jacques

Patrice St. Jacques
Event Coordinator

Distinctive, functional letterhead and use of color

Compliments reader on award

Extends invitation

Appeals to reader's senses through art, music, and food

Describes special features, such as flexible hours and dining options

Ties costs to benefits

Ends by giving reader incentive to act soon

Uses an appropriate close for reader

for a non-native speaker to comprehend. Stick to the common subject-verb-object pattern as often as possible. See pages 46–48 and the "Writer's Brief Guide to Paragraphs, Sentences, and Words" (pages A-1–A-19).

3. Avoid ambiguity. Words that have double meanings force non-native readers to wonder which one you mean. For example, "We fired the engine" would baffle your readers if they were not aware of the multiple meanings of *fire.* Unfamiliar with the context in which *fire* means "start up," a non-native speaker of English might think you're referring to "setting on fire or inflaming," which is not what you intend. Or because *fire* can also mean "dismiss" or "let go," a non-native speaker of English might even suspect the engine was replaced by another model. Such misinterpretations are likely because most bilingual dictionaries list only a few meanings.

Be especially careful of using synonyms just to vary your word choice. For example, do not write *quick* in one sentence and then, referring to the same action, describe it as *rapid.* Your reader may assume you have two different things in mind instead of just one.

4. Be careful about technical vocabulary. While a reader who is a non-native speaker may be more familiar with technical terms than with other English words, make sure the technical word or phrase you include is widely known and not a word or phrase used only at your plant or office. Double-check by consulting the most up-to-date manuals in your field, but steer clear of technical terms in fields other than the one with which your reader is familiar. Be especially careful about using business words and phrases that an international reader may not know, such as *lean manufacturing*, *reverse mortgages*, *best practices, toxic assets*, and so forth.

5. Avoid idiomatic expressions. Idioms are the most difficult part of a language for an audience of non-native speakers to master. As with the example of *fire,* the following colorful idiomatic expressions will confuse and may even startle a non-native reader:

I'm all ears	think outside the box
throw cold water on it	sleep on it
hit the nail on the head	give a heads-up
new blood	land in hot water
easy come, easy go	touch and go
get a handle on it	pushed the envelope
right under your nose	it was a rough go

The meanings of those and similar phrases are not literal but figurative, a reflection of our culture, not necessarily your reader's. A non-native speaker of English will approach such phrases as combinations of the separate meanings of the individual words, not as a collective unit of meaning.

A non-native speaker of English—a potential customer in Asia or Africa, for example—might be shocked if you wrote about a sale concluded at a branch office this way: "Last week we made a killing in our office." Substitute the idiomatic expression with a clear, unambiguous translation easily understood in international

English. "We made a big sale last week." For "Sleep on it," you might say, "Please take a week to make your decision."

6. Delete sports and gambling metaphors. These metaphors, which are often rooted in U.S. popular culture, do not translate word for word for non-native speakers and so can interfere with your communication with your readers. Here are a few examples to avoid:

out in left field	a ballpark figure
strike out	out of bounds
drop the ball	make a pass
long shot	beat the odds
be in left field	win by a nose

Use a basic English dictionary and your common sense to find nonfigurative alternatives for these and similar expressions.

7. Don't use unfamiliar abbreviations, acronyms, or contractions. While these shortened forms of words and phrases are a part of U.S. business culture, they might easily be misunderstood by a non-native speaker who is trying to make sense of them in context or by looking them up in a foreign language dictionary. Avoid abbreviations such as pharm., gov., org., pkwy., rec., hdg., hr., mfg., or w/o. The following acronyms can also cause your international reader trouble: ASAP, PDQ, p's and q's, IRA, SUV, RV, DOB, DOT, SSN. If you have to use acronyms, define them. Finally, contractions such as the following might lead readers to mistake them for the English words they look like: I've (ivy), he'll (hell), I'll (ill), we'll (well), can't (cant), won't (wont, want).

8. Watch units of measure. Do not fall into the cultural trap of assuming that your reader measures distances in miles and feet (instead of kilometers and meters as most of the world does), measures temperatures on the Fahrenheit scale (instead of Celsius), buys gallons of gasoline (instead of liters), spends dollars (rather than euros, pesos, marks, rupees, or yen), tells time by a twelve-hour clock (many countries follow a twenty-four-hour clock), and records dates by month/day/year (most countries record dates by day/month/year).

9. Avoid culture-bound descriptions of place. For example, when you tell a reader in Hong Kong about the Sunbelt or a potential client in Africa about the Big Easy, will he or she know what you mean? When you write from California about the eastern seaboard, meaning the East Coast of the United States, the directional reference may not mean the same thing to a reader in India as it does to you. Moreover, referring to February as a winter month does not make sense to someone in New Zealand for whom it is a summer month.

10. Use appropriate salutations, complimentary closes, and signature lines. Find out how individuals in the recipient's culture are formally addressed in a salutation (e.g., Señor, Madame, Frau, Monsieur). Unless you are expressly asked to use a first name, always use your reader's surname and include proper titles and other honorifics (e.g., Doctor, Sir, Father). For a complimentary close, use an appropriately formal one, such as *Respectfully*, which is acceptable in almost any culture.

Respecting Readers' Nationality and Ethnic/Racial Heritage

Do not risk offending any of your readers, whether they are native speakers of English or not, with language that demeans or stereotypes their nationality or ethnic and racial background. Here are some precautions to take.

1. **Respect your reader's nationality.** Always spell your reader's name and country properly, which may mean adding diacritical marks (e.g., accent marks) not used in English—e.g. Muñoz. If your reader has a hyphenated last name (e.g., Arana-Sanchez), it would be rude to address him or her by only part of the name (e.g., only Arana or only Sanchez). In addition, be careful not to use the former name of your reader's country or city, for instance, the Soviet Union (now Russia), Calcutta (now Kolkata), Czechoslovakia (now the Czech Republic), or Bombay (now Mumbai). Not only is it rude, but it also demonstrates a lack of interest about your reader's nationality.

2. **Observe your reader's cultural traditions.** Cultures differ widely in the way they send and receive information and how they prefer to be addressed, greeted, and informed in a letter. Culture plays a major role in how you word your message. What is acceptable in one culture may be offensive in another. A sales letter to an East Asian business person, for example, needs to employ a very different strategy from one intended for an American reader. The best strategy for an American audience would be hard-hitting and to the point, stressing your product's strengths versus the competitor's weaknesses. But the East Asian way of drafting such a letter would be more subtle, indirect, and complimentary.

> **American:** Our Imaging 500 delivers much more extensive internal imaging than any of our competitors' models.
>
> **East Asian:** One of the ways we may be able to serve you is by informing you about our new Imaging 500 MRI (Magnetic Resonance Imaging) equipment.

The hard sell in the American example would be a sign of arrogance, suggesting inequality for a reader in China, Japan, Malaysia, or Korea who is more comfortable with a compliment or a wish for prosperity.

3. **Honor your reader's place in the world economy.** Phrases such as "third-world country," "emerging nation," and "undeveloped/underprivileged area" are derogatory. Using such phrases signals that you regard your reader's country as inferior. Use the name of your reader's country instead. Saying that someone lives in the Far East implies that the United States, Canada, or Europe is the center of culture, the hub of the business community. The word "Oriental," is insulting. Simply say "East Asia."

4. **Avoid derogatory stereotypes.** Expressions such as "oil-rich Arabs," "time-relaxed Latinos," and "aggressive foreigners" unfairly characterize particular groups. Similarly, prune from your communications any stereotypical phrase that

insults one group or singles it out for praise at the expense of another—"Mexican standoff," "Russian roulette," "Chinaman's chance," "Irish wake," "Dutch treat," "Indian giver." Also note that the word *Indian* refers to someone from India; use *Native American* to refer to the indigenous people of North America, who want to be known by their tribal affiliations (e.g., the Lakota).

5. **Be sensitive to the cultural significance of colors.** Do not offend your audience by using colors in a context that would be offensive. Purple in Mexico, Brazil, and Argentina symbolizes bad luck, death, and funerals. Green and orange have a strong political context in Ireland. In Egypt and Saudi Arabia, green is the color of Islam and is considered sacred. But in China, green can symbolize infertility or adultery. Also in China, white does not symbolize purity and weddings but mourning and funerals. Similarly, in India if a married woman wears all white, she is inviting widowhood. While red symbolizes good fortune in China, it has just the opposite meaning in Korea.

6. **Be careful, too, about the symbols you use for international readers**. Triangles are associated with anything negative in Hong Kong, Korea, and Taiwan. Political symbols, may have controversial implications as well (e.g., the hammer and sickle, a crescent). Avoid using the flag of a country as part of your logo or letterhead for global audiences. Many countries see this as a sign of disrespect, especially Saudi Arabia, whose flag features the name of Allah.

Case Study

Writing to Readers from a Different Culture

In 2014, two IT firms—one American, the other Argentinian—merged. The manager of the American company asked her assistant, Frank Sims, to write a letter of introduction to Antonio Mosca-Guzman, the manager of the Argentinian company, Technologia Canderas, explaining how much Pro-Tech was looking forward to the merger and was seeking help with the transition. The early draft of Sims's letter in Figure 4.23 violates the guidelines discussed earlier because it:

- used the incorrect format for the dateline
- misspelled the name of the reader's city
- left out important postal information
- contained U.S. idioms (e.g., *drop you a line*)
- included troubling abbreviations for the reader
- disregarded how the reader's culture records time and temperature

Even more disrespectful, Sims's overall tone is condescending (*south of the border*) and inappropriately casual. At the end of the second paragraph, for instance, he tells Señor Mosca-Guzman U.S. firm is superior to the Argentine company.

But after consulting relevant cultural guides and asking a fellow worker, originally from Argentina, to critique his draft, Sims revised his letter. Note how the revised letter in Figure 4.24, respects Señor Mosca-Guzman's cultural conventions because it

- spells and punctuates the reader's name and address correctly
- incorporates a clear date line
- uses an appropriate salutation and complimentary close

FIGURE 4.23 Frank Sims's Inappropriately Written Letter to His International Reader

Pro-Tech, Ltd. 452 West Main St. Concord, MA 01742 978-634-2756
www.protech.com

Misleading date line

5-9-14

Incorrect, misspelled address

Mr. Antonio Guzman
Canderas
Mercedes Ave.
Bunos Aires, ARG.

Salutation is too informal

Dear Tony,

Impolite opening disrespecting reader's status

I wanted to drop you a line before the merger hits and in doing so touch base and give you the lowdown on how our department works here in the good old U.S. of A.

Culturally condescending

None of us had a clue that Pro-Tech was going to go south of the border, but your recent meeting about the Smartboard T-C spoke volumes to the tech people who praised your operations to the hilt. So it looks like you and I both will be getting a new corp. name. Olé. I love moving from Pro-Tech, Ltd. to Pro-Tech International. We are so glad we can help you guys out.

Filled with American idioms and abbreviations

At any rate, I'm sending you an email with all the ins and outs of our department struc., layout, employees, and prod. eff. quotas. From this info, I'm hoping you'll be able to see ways for us to streamline, cooperate, and soar in the market. I understand that all of this is in the works and that you and I need to have a face-to-face and so I'd appreciate your reciprocating with all the relevant data stat.

Disregards time differences and reader's 24-hour clock

Consequently, I guess I'll be flying down your way next month. Before I take off, I would like to give you a ring. How does after lunch next Thursday (say, 1:00–1:30) sound to you? I hope this is doable.

Ignores differences between Fahrenheit and Celsius scales

We've had a spell of great weather here (can you believe it's in the low 80s today!). So, I guess I'll just sign off and wait 'til I hear from you further.

I send you felicitations and want things to go smoothly before the merger is a done deal.

Close sounds insincere

Adios,

Frank Sims

Frank Sims

FIGURE 4.24 Sims's Appropriately Revised Letter

Pro-Tech, Ltd. 452 West Main St. Concord, MA 01742 978-634-2756
www.protech.com

9 May 2014

Señor Antonio Mosca-Guzman
Director, Quality Assurance
Tecnología Canderas, S.A.
Av. Martin 1285, 4° P.C.
C1174AAB BUENOS AIRES
ARGENTINA

Dear Señor Mosca-Guzman:

As our two companies prepare to merge, I welcome this opportunity to write to you. I am the manager for the Quality Assurance division at Pro-Tech, a title I believe you have at Tecnología Canderas. I am looking forward to working with you both now and after our companies merge in two months.

Allow me to say that we are very honored that your company is joining ours. Tecnología Canderas has been widely praised for the research and production of your Smartboard T-C systems. I know we have much to learn from you, and we hope you will allow us to share our systems analyses with you. That way everyone in our new company, Pro-Tech International, will benefit from the merger.

Later this week, I will send you a report about our division. It describes how our division is structured and the quality inspections we make. It will also give you a brief biography of our staff so that you can learn about their qualifications and responsibilities.

The director of our new company, Dr. Suzanne Nknuma, asked me to meet with you before the merger to see how we might help each other. I would very much like to travel to Buenos Aires in the next month to visit you and take a tour of your company.

Would you please let me know by email when it may be convenient for us to talk so we might discuss the agenda for our meeting? I am in my office from 11:00 to 17:00 Buenos Aires time.

I look forward to working with and meeting you.

Respectfully,

Frank Sims

Frank Sims
Quality Assurance Officer

Clear date line

Includes appropriate title for reader

Complete and correct address

Uses courteous salutation

Clear and diplomatic opening

Respectful view of reader's company

Explains business procedures in plain English

Recognizes reader's time zone

Polite close

Gives business title

- is written in plain, international English
- recognizes that the reader uses a twenty-four-hour clock
- identifies the writer and makes the reader feel welcome and honored
- courteously informs the reader how the merger will affect his relationship with the writer
- strives to develop a spirit of cooperation and mutuality
- acknowledges the reader's position of authority in his company

Above all, though, Sims now honors his audience's culture and role in the business world and seeks to win the reader's confidence and respect, two invaluable assets in the global marketplace. Writing letters with the specific needs of your international audience in mind, as in Figure 4.24, is a crucial skill to have in the global world of work.

Sending Letter-Quality Messages: Final Advice to Seal Your Success

Judging your letters in light of the following guidelines will help you to draft, tailor, and evaluate the types of business correspondence you will be asked to write:

- **Identify your reader:** one individual; a group; a company or agency; a new customer or a longtime one; a native or non-native speaker
- **Pay special attention to an international reader's needs.** Research his or her cultural traditions to avoid writing anything offensive or confusing
- **Determine your purpose:** explanation; complaint; apology; sell product/service; build goodwill; express thanks
- **Determine reader's reason for writing:** complaint; request for information; make an adjustment; provide information or procedures
- **Organize information appropriately:** direct or indirect; begin with good news and save negative message for middle of the letter
- **Include essential information:** schedules; dates; places; prices and expenses; personnel; explanation of services, warranties, products; background information
- **Use professional style and tone:** courteous; concise and focused; sensitive to reader's needs
- **Make sure your letter looks professional**

Planning your letter carefully—its purpose, its organization, and its content—will help you to make sure your message begins, continues, and ends professionally and successfully for readers in the United States and around the globe.

✓ Revision Checklist

Audience Analysis and Research
- [ ] Made sure reader's name and job title are correct.
- [ ] Found out something about my audience—interests and background, well informed or unfamiliar with topic, former client or new one.
- [ ] Determined whether audience will be friendly, hostile, or neutral about my message.
- [ ] Did necessary research—in print, through online sources, in discussions with colleagues—to give readers what they need.
- [ ] Acknowledged previous correspondence.
- [ ] Spent sufficient time drafting and revising letter before printing final copy.

Letter Format and Appearance
- [ ] Followed one letter format (full-block, modified-block, semi-block) consistently.
- [ ] Used letter wizards with caution.
- [ ] Set left margins wide enough to make my letter look attractive and well proportioned.
- [ ] Included all the necessary parts of a letter for my purpose.
- [ ] Made sure that my letter looks neat and professional.
- [ ] Printed my letter on company letterhead or quality bond paper.
- [ ] Proofread my letter carefully and made sure each correction was made before printing final copy.
- [ ] Eliminated any grammatical and spelling errors.
- [ ] Signed my letter legibly in black ink.
- [ ] Informed reader that copies were sent to appropriate parties.
- [ ] Printed envelopes properly.

Memos
- [ ] Used appropriate and consistent format.
- [ ] Announced purpose of memo early and clearly.
- [ ] Organized memo according to reader's need for information, putting main ideas up front, providing necessary documentation, and supplying conclusion.
- [ ] Wrote clearly and concisely.
- [ ] Included bullets, lists, and underscoring where necessary to reflect logic and organization of memo and make it easier to read for the audience.
- [ ] Refrained from overloading reader with unnecessary details.

Style: Words, Tone, Sentences, Paragraphs
- [ ] Emphasized the "you attitude" by seeing things from the reader's perspective.
- [ ] Avoided being too casual or colloquial.
- [ ] Chose words that are clear, precise, and friendly.

☐ Cut anything sounding flowery, stuffy, or bureaucratic.

☐ Ensured that my sentences are readable, clear, and not too long (less than fifteen to twenty words).

☐ Wrote paragraphs that are easy to read, flow together, and are formatted correctly

Writing to International Readers

☐ Did appropriate research about the reader's culture—in print, through online sources, and with colleagues who are native speakers (as well as teachers)— especially about accepted ways of communicating.

☐ Adopted a respectful, not condescending, tone.

☐ Avoided anything offensive to my reader, especially references to politics, religion, or cultural taboos.

☐ Used plain and clear language that my reader would understand.

☐ Tested my sentences for length and active voice.

☐ Chose colors and symbols culturally appropriate for readers.

☐ Selected the right format, salutation, and complimentary close for my reader.

☐ Observed the reader's units of measurement for time, temperature, currency, dates, and numbers.

Exercises

1. Find two business letters and bring them to class. Be prepared to identify and comment on the various parts of a letter discussed in this chapter.

2. Correct the following inside addresses:

   a. Dr. Ann Clark, M.D.
   1730 East Jefferson
   Jackson, MI. 46759

   b. To: Miss Tommy Jones
   Secretary to Mrs. Franks
   Donlevey labs
   Cleveland, O. 45362

   c. Debbie Hinkle
   432 Parkway
   N. Y. C. 10054

   d. Mr. Charles Howe, Acme Pro.
   P.O. Box 675
   1234 S. e. Boulevard
   Gainesville, Flor. 32601

   e. Alex Goings, man.
   Pittfield Industries
   Longview, TEXAS 76450

   f. ATTENTION: G. Yancy (Mrs.)
   Police Academy
   1329 Tucker
   N. O., La. 3410–70122

   g. David and Mahenny
   Lawyers
   Dobbs Build.
   L.A. 94756

   h. Barry Fahwd
   Peninsular, Ltd.
   Arabia

3. Write appropriate inside addresses and salutations to (a) a woman who has not specified her marital status; (b) an officer in the armed forces; (c) a professor at your school; (d) an assistant manager at your local bank; (e) a member of the clergy; (f) a government worker.

4. Rewrite the following sentences to make them more personal.
   a. It becomes incumbent upon this office to cancel order #2394.
   b. Management has suggested the curtailment of parking privileges.
   c. ALL USERS OF HYDROPLEX: Desist from ordering replacement valves during the period of Dec. 20–30.
   d. The request for a new catalog has been honored; it will be shipped to same address soon.
   e. Perseverance and attention to detail have made this writer important to company in-house work.
   f. The Director of Nurses hereby notifies staff that a general meeting will be held Monday afternoon at 3:00 p.m. sharp. Attendance is mandatory.
   g. Reports will be filed by appropriate personnel no later than the scheduled plans allow.

5. The following sentences are discourteous, boastful, excessively humble, vague, or lacking the "you attitude." Rewrite them to correct those mistakes.
   a. Something is obviously wrong in your head office. They have once more sent me the wrong model number. Can they ever get things straight?
   b. My instructor wants me to do a term paper on safety regulations at a small plant. Because you are the manager of a small plant, send me all the information I need at once. My grade depends heavily on all this.
   c. It is apparent that you are in business to rip off the public.
   d. I was wondering if you could possibly see your way into sending me the local chapter president's name and address—if you have the time, that is.
   e. I have waited for my confirmation for two weeks now. Do you expect me to wait forever, or can I get some action?

6. Write a business letter to one of the following individuals.
   a. your mayor, asking for an appointment and explaining why you need one
   b. your college president, stressing the need for more parking spaces or for additional software at a library
   c. the local water department, asking for information about fluoride supplements and why you need such information
   d. an editor of an online or print magazine, asking permission to reprint an article in a company blog and indicating why
   e. a computer vendor, asking about costs and availability of a specific software package; explain your company's special needs

7. Write a letter of inquiry to a utility company, a safety or health care agency, or a business in your town requesting information on how its services to the community protects the environment. Be specific about your reasons for requesting the information.

8. Choose one of the following, and write a sales letter addressed to an appropriate audience on why they should
   a. work for the same company you do
   b. live in your neighborhood
   c. be happy taking a vacation where you did last year
   d. dine at a particular restaurant
   e. use a particular app
   f. have their cars repaired at a specific garage
   g. give their real estate business to a particular agency
   h. use your company's new technology when constructing their website

9. Rewrite the following sales letter to make it more effective. Add any details you think are relevant.

Dear Pizza Lovers:

Allow me to introduce myself. My name is Rudy Moore and I am the new manager of Tasty Pizza Parlor in town here. The Parlor is located at the intersection of North Miller Parkway and 95th Street. We are open from 10 a.m. to 11 p.m., except on the weekends, when we are open later.

I think you will be as happy as I am to learn that Tasty's will now offer free delivery to an extended service area. As a result, you can get your Tasty Pizza hot when you want it.

Please read your newspapers for our ad. We also are offering customers a coupon. It is a real deal for you.

I know you will enjoy Tasty's pizza and I hope to see you. I am always interested in hearing from you about our service and our fine products. We want to take your order soon. Please come in.

10. Send a follow-up letter to one of the following individuals:
   a. a customer who informs you that she will no longer do business with your company because your prices are too high
   b. a family of four who stayed at your motel for a week last summer
   c. a wedding party or professional organization that used your catering services last month
   d. a customer who exchanged a coat for the purchase price
   e. a customer who purchased a used car from you and who has not been happy with your service
   f. a company that bought software from you nine months ago, alerting them about updates

11. Write a bad news letter to an appropriate reader about one of the following:
   a. Your company has to discontinue Saturday deliveries because of rising labor and fuel costs.
   b. You are the manager of an insurance company writing to tell one of your customers that, because of reckless driving, his or her rates will increase.
   c. You have to refuse to send a bonus gift to a customer who sent in an order after the expiration date for qualifying for the gift.

d. You have to notify residents of a community that a bus route or hours of operation are being discontinued.

e. You represent the water department and have to tell residents of a community that they cannot water their lawns for the next month because of a serious water shortage in your town.

f. You cannot send customers a catalog—which your company formerly sent free of charge—unless they first send $10 for the cost of that catalog.

g. You cannot repair a particular piece of equipment because the customer still owes your company for three previous service visits.

12. Write a good news letter about the opposite of one of the situations listed in Exercise 11.

13. Write a complaint letter about one of the following:

   a. an error in your utility, mobile phone, credit card, or Internet provider bill

   b. discourteous service you received on an airplane, train, or bus

   c. a frozen food product of poor quality

   d. a shipment that arrived late and damaged

   e. an insurance payment to you that is $357.00 less than it should be

   f. a public television station's policy of discontinuing a particular series

   g. junk mail or spam that you are receiving

   h. equipment that arrives with missing parts

   i. misleading representation by a salesperson

   j. incorrect or misleading information given on a website

14. This exercise might be done as a collaborative project. You are a section manager at e-Tech. Your company has a service contract with Professional Office Cleaners (POC). However, each morning when you arrive at work you are disappointed with what they've done. POC has overlooked some essential tasks and done a poor job on others. Your staff is also disappointed and has emailed or spoken to you about problems with POC. Write the following:

   a. a memo or email to your boss, the vice president, about POC's shoddy work

   b. a complaint letter to POC that the vice president has asked you to write and to sign his name to it

   c. a letter to the vice president from the manager of POC who is responsible for your e-Tech section, apologizing for the problem and offering a solution

   d. a letter from POC to the vice president taking issue with the complaint made against his cleaning company, offering proof that the work was done according to contract specifications

   e. an email you send to your staff about what's happened with POC

15. Rewrite the following complaint letter to make it more precise, less emotional, and effectively persuasive.

Dear Sir:

We recently purchased a machine from your Albany store and paid a great deal of money for it. This machine, according to your website, is supposedly the best model in your line and has caused us nothing but trouble each time we use it. Really, can't you do any better with your technology?

We expect you to stand by your products. The warranties you give with them should make you accountable for shoddy workmanship. Let us know at once what you intend to do about our problem. If you cannot or are unwilling to correct the situation, we will take our business elsewhere, and then you will be sorry.

Sincerely yours,

16. Rewrite the following ineffective adjustment letter saying "No."

Dear Customer:

Our company is unwilling to give you a new toaster or to refund your purchase price. After examining the toaster you sent to us, we found that the fault was not ours, as you insist, but yours.

Let me explain. Our toaster is made to take a lot of punishment. But being dropped on the floor or poked inside with a knife, as you probably did, exceeds all decent treatment. You must be careful if you expect your appliances to last. Your negligence in this case is so bad that the toaster could not be repaired.

In the future, consider using your appliances according to the guidelines set down in warranty books. That's why they are written.

Since you are now in the market for a new toaster, let me suggest that you purchase our new heavy-duty model, number 67342, called the Counter-Whiz. I am taking the liberty of sending you some information about this model. I do hope you at least go to see one at your local appliance center.

Sincerely,

17. You are the manager of a computer software company, and one of your sales-people has just sold a large order to a new customer whose business you have tried to obtain for years. Unfortunately, the salesperson made a mistake writing out the invoice, undercharging the customer by $229. At that price, your company would not break even, and so you must write a letter explaining the problem so that the customer will not assume all future business dealings with your firm will be offered at such "below market" rates. Decide whether you should ask for the $229 or just "write it off" in the interest of keeping a valuable new customer.
   a. Write a letter to the new customer, asking for the $229 and explaining the problem while still projecting an image of your company as accurate, professional, and very competitive.
   b. Write a letter to the new customer, not asking for the $229 but explaining the mistake and emphasizing that your company is both competitive and professional.
   c. Write a letter to your boss explaining why you wrote letter a.
   d. Write a letter to your boss explaining why you wrote letter b.
   e. Write a letter to the salesperson who made the mistake, asking him or her to take appropriate action with regard to the new customer.

18. Write a memo to your boss saying that you will be out of town two days next week and three days the following week for one of the following reasons: (a) to inspect some land your firm is thinking of buying, (b) to investigate some claims, (c) to look at some new office space for a branch your firm is thinking of opening in a city 500 miles away, (d) to attend a conference sponsored by a professional society, or (e) to pay calls on customers. In your memo, be specific about dates, places, times, and reasons.

19. Send a memo to your public relations department informing it that you are completing a degree or work for a certificate. Indicate how the information could be useful for your firm's publicity campaign.

20. Write a memo to the director of your school's library asking for one of the following. Be sure you include specific reasons for such a change.
   a. extended weekend hours
   b. more vending machines
   c. more computers
   d. more group study rooms
   e. increased journal subscriptions in your field of study

21. Select some change (in policy, schedule, or personnel assignment) you encountered in a job you held in the last two or three years and write an appropriate memo describing that change. Write the memo from the perspective of your former employer explaining the change to employees.

22. Rewrite the following letters, making them appropriate for a reader whose native language is not English. Identify the intended reader's cultural heritage. As you revise the letters, pay attention to the words, measurements, and sentence constructions you employ. Be sure to consider the reader's cultural traditions and avoid cultural insensitivity.

a. Dear Mr. Wong,

It's not every day that you have the chance to get in on the ground floor of a deal so good you can actually taste it. But Off-Wall Street Mutual can make the difference in your financial future. Give me a moment to convince you.

By becoming a member of our international investing group for just under $250, you can just about ensure your success. We know all the ins and outs of long-term investing and can save you a bundle. Our analysts are the hot shots of the business and always look long and hard for the most propitious business deals. The stocks we select with your interests in mind are as safe as a bank and not nearly so costly for you. Unlike any of your undertrained local agents, we can save you money by investing your money. We are penny pinchers with our clients' initial investments, but we are King Midas when it comes to transforming those investments into pure gold.

I am enclosing a brochure for you to study, and I really hope you will examine it carefully. You would be foolish to let a deal like Off-Wall Street Mutual pass you by. Go for it. Call me by 3:00 today.

Hurriedly,

b. Dear Mr. Bafaloukos,

My firm is taking a survey of businesses in your part of the world to see if there is any likelihood of getting you on board our international computer network, and so I thought I would see if you might like to take the chance. In today's shaky world, business events can change overnight and without the proper scoop you could be left out in the cold. We can alleviate that mess.

Not only do we interface with major exchanges all around the globe, but we make sure that we get the facts to you pronto. We do not sit on our hands here at Intertel. Check out our website on who and how we serve and I have no doubts that you will email or ring us up to find out about joining up.

One last point: Can you really risk going out on a limb without first knowing that you have all the facts at your fingertips about worldwide business events? Intertel is there to save you.

Fondly,

23. Interview a student at your school or a co-worker who was born and raised in a non-English-speaking country about the proper etiquette in writing a business letter to someone from his or her country. Collaborate with that student to write a letter to an executive from that country—for example, a sales letter or a letter asking for information.

24. In a letter to your instructor, describe the kinds of adaptations you had to make for the international reader you wrote to in Exercise 23.

CHAPTER 5

How to Get a Job

Searches, Networking, Dossiers, Portfolios/ Webfolios, Résumés, Transitioning to a Civilian Job, Letters, and Interviews

Obtaining a job in today's tough market involves a lot of hard work. Before your name is added to a company's payroll, you will have to do more than simply walk into the human resources office and fill out an application form or send a résumé online. Finding the *right* job takes time in this highly competitive job market. And finding the right person to fill that job also takes time for the employer.

Steps an Employer Takes When Hiring

From the employer's viewpoint, the stages in the search for a valuable employee include the following:

1. Deciding what duties and responsibilities go with the job and determining the qualifications the future employee should possess
2. Advertising the job on the company website, on online job-posting sites, in newspapers, and in professional publications
3. Reviewing and evaluating résumés and letters of application
4. Having candidates complete application forms
5. Requesting further proof of candidates' skills (letters of recommendation, transcripts, portfolios/webfolios)
6. Interviewing selected candidates
7. Doing further follow-ups and selecting those to be interviewed again
8. Offering the job to the best-qualified individual

Sometimes the steps are interchangeable, especially steps 4 and 5, but generally speaking, employers go through a long and detailed process to select employees. Step 3, for example, is among the most important for employers (and the most crucial for job candidates). At that stage employers often classify job seekers into one of three groups: those they definitely want to interview, those they may want to interview, and those in whom they have no interest.

Chapter opening image: © dimitris_k/ShutterStock.com

Steps to Follow to Get Hired

As a job seeker, you will have to know how and when to give prospective employers the kinds of information the preceding eight steps require. You will also have to follow a definite schedule in your search for a job. Expect to go through the following eight procedures:

1. analyzing your strengths and restricting your job search
2. enhancing your image
3. looking in the right places for a job
4. assembling a dossier and a portfolio
5. preparing a résumé
6. writing a letter of application and filling out a job application
7. going to an interview
8. accepting or declining a job offer

Your timetable should match that of your prospective employer. This chapter shows you how to begin your job search, design an effective portfolio, prepare an appropriate résumé, write a persuasive letter of application, and prepare for an interview. It also contains information to help individuals to transition from their military assignment to the civilian workforce (see pages 186–189).

Analyzing Your Strengths and Restricting Your Job Search

Job counselors advise students to start planning for their careers several years before they graduate. The more you find out about what career path you want to take ahead of graduation, the better you will be able to target the jobs that are right for you. Individuals changing careers or transitioning from the military to the civilian sector also need to assess their experiences, skills, and job goals.

Before you apply for jobs, analyze your job skills, career goals, and interests. Here are some points to consider:

1. Make an inventory of your most significant accomplishments in your major or on the job—writing and speaking, working with people, organizing, and troubleshooting, managing money, speaking a second language, designing websites, working for a healthcare agency.
2. Decide which specialty within your chosen career appeals to you the most. If you are in a nursing program, do you want to work in a large teaching hospital, for a home health or hospice agency, or in a physician's office?
3. What types of working conditions most appeal to you—small groups, traveling, telecommuting, relocating overseas?
4. What most interests you about a position—travel, technology, international contacts, on-the-job training, helping people, being creative?

5. What are some of the greatest challenges you face in your career today—or will face in five years?
6. Which specific companies or organizations have the best track record in hiring and promoting individuals in your field? What qualifications will such firms insist on from prospective employees?

Once you answer these questions, you can avoid applying for positions for which you are either overqualified or underqualified. If a position requires ten years of related work experience and you are just starting out, you will only waste the employer's time and your own by applying. However, if a job requires a certificate or license and you are in the process of obtaining one, go ahead and apply.

Enhancing Your Professional Image

Whether you are looking for your first job in your career field, re-entering the job market, changing careers or transitioning to a civilian job, you can take several steps to help improve your chances of getting hired.

- Attend job fairs and interviewing workshops on campus as well as those sponsored by municipal, state, and federal agencies.
- Go to trade shows to learn about the latest products, services, and technologies in your profession and to meet contacts and even potential employers.
- Join and participate in student and professional organizations and societies in your area of interest.
- Apply for relevant internships and training programs to gain real-world experience and increase your networking contacts.
- If available, take a temporary job in your profession to gain some experience.
- Confer with your academic adviser regularly, not just once a semester.
- Find a mentor—someone in a field you might want to join.
- Do volunteer work to gain or enhance experience working in a group setting, preparing documents, and so on.
- Find out if your school or university offers *job shadowing* opportunities, where you can follow someone during his/her daily work routine to gauge whether or not a particular position or profession matches your skills and interests.

Looking in the Right Places for a Job

One way to search for a job is simply to send out a batch of letters and résumés to companies you want to work for. But how do you know what jobs, if any, those companies have available, what qualifications they are looking for, and what deadlines they might want you to meet? You can avoid these uncertainties by knowing where to look for a job and knowing what responsibilities a specific job entails. Consult the following resources for a wealth of job-related information. Use as many of them as you can.

1. Personal (face-to-face) networking. One of the most successful ways to land a job is through networking. In fact, most jobs come through consulting with other people. John D. Erdlen and Donald H. Sweet, experts on job searching, cite the following as a primary rule of job hunting: "Don't do anything yourself you can get someone with influence to do for you." Let your professors, co-workers, friends, classmates, neighbors, relatives, and even your clergy know you are looking for a job. They may hear of something and can notify you or, better yet, recommend you for the position. See how the job seekers in Figures 5.13 and 5.14 (pages 203–204) have successfully networked with people they know.

2. Your campus placement office. Counselors keep an online file of current available positions, and they also make your résumé available to recruiters when they come on campus to conduct interviews. Placement offices also have recruiting databases, allowing students access to a broad range of contacts and interview information. Counselors can help you locate summer and part-time work as well, both on and off campus, positions that might lead to full-time jobs. Most important, they will give you sound advice on your job search, including strategies for finding the right job, salary ranges, and interview tips. Many placement offices also sponsor career fairs to bring job seekers and employers together in specific professional fields. Finally, your placement office will help you set up and archive your dossier, or credentials (see pages 170–173).

3. Online job-posting sites. A majority of jobs can be found on the Internet. You can learn about jobs at a specific company or organization by visiting its website to see what vacancies it has and what the qualifications are for them. Also consult the *Riley Guide: Employment Opportunities and Job Resources* on the Internet (www. rileyguide.com). This invaluable resource surveys and classifies job openings on the Web by field, location, and category (private or public) and provides you with links for direct access. In addition, you might want to explore many of the job-posting sites, such as those in Table 5.1, which list positions and sometimes give you advice about applying for them.

4. Newspapers. Look at local newspapers as well as the Sunday editions of large city papers with a wide circulation, such as *The New York Times* (http://jobmarket .nytimes.com). The Careers section of *The Wall Street Journal* also lists jobs in different areas, including technical and managerial positions (online.wsj.com/public /page/news-career-jobs.html).

5. Federal and state employment offices. The U.S. government is one of the biggest employers in the country. During 2012 and 2013, for instance, the most active career site on the Web was operated by the federal government, with 2 million new hires. Counselors at federal and state employment centers also help

TABLE 5.1   Job-Posting Sites on the Web

Website	URL	Description
After College	www.aftercollege.com	Lists more than 200,000 entry-level jobs and internships; connects students, alumni and employers through faculty and career networks across the country
Career One Stop	www.careeronestop.com	Sponsored by the Department of Labor; offers employment services, job search sites, vocational trends ("What's Hot," "Green Jobs"), and help for military transitions
Career Builder	www.careerbuilder.com	Hosts the career sites for more than 9,000 websites, including 140 newspapers and broadband portals such as MSN and AOL
College Recruiter	www.collegerecruiter.com	Leading job board for college students searching for internships and recent graduates hunting for entry-level jobs and other career opportunities
College Grad	www.collegegrad.com	Targets college students and recent grads exclusively. Provides more entry-level job search content to job seekers and linked to more colleges and universities than any other career site
Diversity Employers	www.diversityemployers.com	Largest database of equal-opportunity employers committed to workplace diversity. Dedicated to providing career- and self-development information on careers, job opportunities, graduate/professional schools, internships/co-ops, and study-abroad programs
Monster	www.monster.com	Biggest commercial online job board; lists hundreds of thousands of openings; includes global postings; offers advice on the job-search process
Monster College	college.monster.com	Jobs posted for college graduates and internships
Net Temps	www.net-temps.com	Postings for temporary, temp-to-perm, and full-time employment through the staffing industry

job seekers find career opportunities. Consult USAJOBS (www.usajobs.gov) for listings of government jobs. Figure 5.1 shows the home page of USAJOBS, a U.S. government website. Veterans can also take advantage of My Next Move for Veterans (http://www.mynextmove.org/vets/) or Veterans Jobs Bank (https://www.nrd.gov/home/veterans_job_bank).

FIGURE 5.1 USAJOBS Website

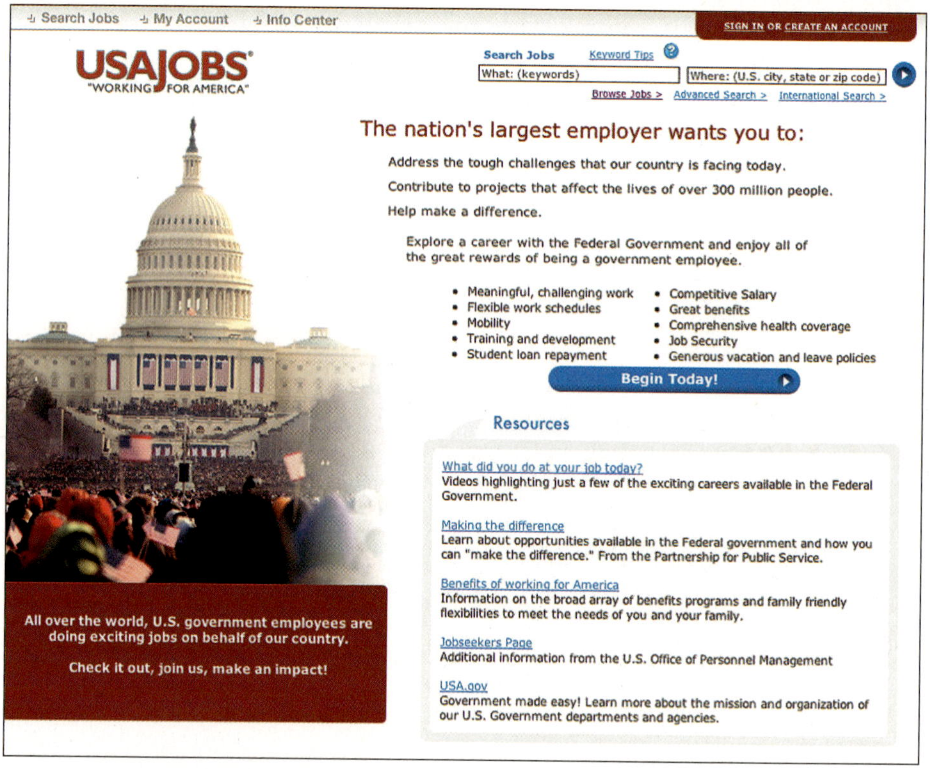

Courtesy of the United States Office of Personnel Management

6. Professional and trade journals and associations in your major. Identify the most respected periodicals (print and online) in your field and search their ads. Each issue of *Food Technology*, for example, features a section called "Professional Placement," a listing of jobs all over the country. Similarly, *CIO Magazine—Information Technology Professional Research Center* (itjobs.cio.com/a/all-jobs/list) can help you find jobs in the computer industry, engineering, and technology. Consulting the *Encyclopedia of Associations* (library.dialog .com/bluesheets/html/bl0114.html) is the quickest way to find out about professional organizations and the journals they publish in your field.

7. The human resources department of a company or an agency you would like to work for. Often you will be able to fill out an application even if there is not a current opening. But do not call employers asking about openings; a visit shows a much more serious interest.

8. A résumé database service. A number of online services will put your résumé in a database and make it available to prospective employers, who scan the database regularly to find suitable job candidates. Check to see if a professional society to which you belong (or might join) offers a similar service.

But be careful about posting personal information, such as your phone number or social security number. You never know who can gain access to this information. If your current boss finds out you are looking for another job, you risk being fired. (See page 173).

9. **Professional employment agencies.** Some agencies list jobs you can apply for free of charge (because the employer pays the fee), while others charge a stiff fee, usually a percentage of your first year's salary. Be sure to ask who pays the fee for this service. Because employment agencies often find out about jobs through channels already available to you, speak to someone at your campus placement center first.

Using Online Social and Professional Networking Sites in Your Job Search

Social networking sites (e.g., Facebook, Twitter, LinkedIn, and Google+) are essential tools to help you find a job and advance your career. Do not think of them only as personal media sites where you exchange news and photos with friends and family. These sites contain valuable information about the companies that might hire you.

Finding Jobs Through Networking Sites

Consulting these networks will alert you to job possibilities in your area. Facebook, for example, contains a "marketplace" where you can search for jobs by location and title in your network. Twit Job Search (**www.twitjobsearch.com**) is another site you may find useful as you begin your job search. If you follow businesses and organizations on Twitter, you can receive notifications from them about job openings. Facebook and Twitter also allow you to post your profile or a link to your blog, to your portfolio, or both, to attract potential employers.

Using Facebook to Start Your Network

Facebook can help you start your professional networking. Begin with former employers or co-workers on Facebook, for example, who know your work and who will say good things about your education, skills, and previous work experience. As you prepare to enter the job market, contact these people through Facebook and ask if they would write a reference for you. Also, be sure to "friend" former professors through Facebook, especially in your area of study and who liked your work. Your teachers are important professional contacts because many of them are plugged into professional networks themselves. Contact them to ask if they have heard about any jobs in your field. Moreover, with their permission, your instructors can become your professional references.

LinkedIn

LinkedIn (www.linkedin.com) is the most important social network for your job search. As the name implies, its purpose is to link, or connect, you to people who can help you professionally. As job counselors repeatedly advise, the best way to land a job is through networking—that is, one person helping another. LinkedIn is all about networking, making contacts who have inside information at a company and who may introduce (and maybe even recommend) you to the individual who makes the decision to interview applicants and eventually hire. More than 90 million companies and individuals belong to LinkedIn, including *Fortune* 500 companies such as Microsoft, McDonald's, Walmart, IBM, GM, and Pfizer, giving you valuable information about the company and allowing you to target people whom you may want to contact.

Benefits of Joining LinkedIn

Joining LinkedIn is easy and free. Not only will belonging to LinkedIn help you find a job, it will enhance your professional image and signal that you value teamwork. But networking entails more than someone helping you. You need to be prepared to help others through your contacts. Joining LinkedIn tells prospective network contacts and employers you are ready to do that.

Five Ways LinkedIn Can Help Your Job Search

LinkedIn can help you find a position in five key ways.

   1. LinkedIn allows you to search for a specific type of job by targeting a particular specialized field, company, job title, or even zip code. LinkedIn includes thousands of classified posts helping you to search the wider Internet more efficiently.

   2. LinkedIn gives you valuable information about a company, such as its mission statement, the names of the CEO and directors, its products and services, its locations, its awards, and even its competitors. Company profiles on LinkedIn provide the names and contact information for hiring managers and human resource professionals, the very individuals you want to reach and have reach you.

   3. LinkedIn helps you become part of a network and expand your list of contacts. The working principle behind LinkedIn is to assist you in joining a network and then finding out if someone in your network knows someone at the company you want to work for.

   4. LinkedIn improves your search by including short recommendations from people in your network. Recommendations praising your work will enhance your profile on LinkedIn, and give potential employers proof that you are a qualified, conscientious, and respected worker.

5. LinkedIn allows you to create a public profile that shows you are a professional. This profile will be one of the first pages that come up in a Google search when someone looks for you by name.

Establishing Your LinkedIn Network

When establishing your LinkedIn network, the first thing you need to do is identify as many individuals as possible who might be able to help you in your job search. Look for people who know you and like your work. Here are some of the individuals you might consider asking to be possible members of your network:

- Current and former instructors who have complimented your work
- Former bosses, managers, or co-workers who are willing to write a recommendation on your behalf—for example, "I have worked with Agnes Delancy for two years and always found her cooperative and efficient."
- Individuals who belong to a professional association or organization that you have joined, such as the National Society of Black Engineers, the National Student Nurses Association, or the Society of Marketing Specialists
- Community leaders you have worked for and who value what you have done
- Individuals in the military to whom you reported and can comment on your technical skills, cooperation, leadership ability, and so on
- People you do business with on a regular basis and who may have a wide circle of connections (e.g., current and former customers, suppliers)
- Alumni of schools you attended.

A Sample LinkedIn Profile

Figure 5.2 (pages 168–169) contains the LinkedIn profile of Daniel Ricks Solter. The profile lists such job-relevant categories as current and past positions he has held, education, and a brief summary of his accomplishments. It also indicates that Solter is interested in such LinkedIn categories as job inquiries, expertise requests, reference requests, and getting back in touch. And it includes important recommendations about him.

Promoting Your Best Image—Some Do's and Don'ts

Used effectively, networking sites allow you to publicize your qualifications through text, audio, video images, and podcasts. Hiring managers and recruiters check these social networks for potential job candidates as well as to screen applicants to interview and eventually hire. In fact, more than a million hiring managers, recruiters, and human resource professionals look for qualified candidates on LinkedIn alone. These individuals scout other social networking sites, too, and ask colleagues and other professionals to alert them to qualified job candidates.

But when you use these networks, make sure you enhance and don't jeopardize your chances with prospective employers. You have to be careful about your digital footprint (e.g. presence) and your online reputation. Success is all about

FIGURE 5.2   LinkedIn Profile

Includes recent, professional-looking photo

Linked in.   Account Type: Basic   Daniel Solter ▾   **Add Connections**

Home   **Profile**   Contacts   Groups   Jobs   Inbox **4**   Companies   News   More | People ▾ | Search... | 🔍 | Advanced

Edit Profile   **View Profile**

Daniel Ricks Solter

Assistant Coordinator, Employee Fitness Center, Savoy-Anderson, Inc.

Greater Philadelphia Area / Fitness, Wellness, Corporate Fitness Programs

Current	• Assistant Coordinator, Employee Fitness Center at Savoy-Anderson, Inc.
Past	• Fitness Instructor, Midtown Center for Wellness and Sports Medicine • Personal Trainer at Institute, Newark, DE • Intern, Cardiac Rehabilitation Program, St. Catherine's Hospital, Trenton, NJ • New Jersey National Guard
Education	• Monmouth University • Raritan Valley Community College
Connections	12 Connections
Website	Savoy-Anderson (company Website)
Public Profile	http://www.linkedin.com/in/daniel-solter/b/107/705

Supplies information about work, military, and educational background

People in Solter's network, many of whom are in a position to help his career

→ **Forward this profile to a connection**

Daniel's Activity   edit

Daniel Solter has a new profile photo
2 days ago - Like - Comment

See more **Activity** ⟩

Daniel's Connections (12)

Susan Dong
Coordinator, Employee Fitness Center, Savoy-Anderson

Laura Jankowski, RN
Head Nurse, Cardiac Unit, St. Catherine's Hospital

Bob Segura
Physical Therapist, Midtown Center for Wellness and Sports Medicine

See all **Connections** ⟩

Note: Currently your connections are **allowed** to view your connections list.

Recommendations for Daniel Ricks Solter

**Assistant Coordinator, Employee Fitness Center
Savoy-Anderson, Inc.**

Secured recommendations from current and former supervisors and co-workers praising his expertise, team spirit, and cooperative attitude, all qualities that hiring managers prize

"I have worked with Daniel for the last two years and he consistently ranks among the very best of Savoy-Anderson's staff. His immediate response to any request, whether from the administration or employees, is outstanding. He wants to help our employees get in shape and stay that way."

1ˢᵗ   **Jennifer Keller**, **Human Resource Director, Savoy-Anderson**

"Daniel is dynamic and knowledgable. He can build rapport and relationships quickly and is always available for individual counseling about fitness needs."

1ˢᵗ   **Buddy Rirerson**, **Client Relations Director, Savoy-Anderson, Inc.**

Fitness Instructor
Midtown Center for Wellness and Sports Medicine

Dan Vallero/LinkedIn. Photo, © iStockphoto.com/ranplett

FIGURE 5.2 (Continued)

"When he worked for MCWSM (Midtown Center for Wellness and Sports Medicine), Daniel Solter was a supportive and effective spokesperson for our facility. His group classes were among the most popular ones we offered, and he knows fitness programs extremely well."

1st   Joyce Hwang, **Assistant Director, Midtown Center for WSM**

Summary

Excel at providing fitness evaluations and exercise prescriptions and at teaching diverse classes—customized, group, and Web-based—in corporate settings. Help oversee in-house fitness center (400+ employees), including promoting and scheduling health/wellness events, offering health screenings, purchasing supplies and equipment, and supervising a staff of two part-time workers. Adept at organizational communication with employees and management. Helped draft sections of the company safety manual.

Concisely describes job responsibilities emphasizing technical leadership, and communication skills

Specialties
Employee Fitness, Managing Corporate Fitness Facilities

Uses incomplete sentences, the standard style for LinkedIn profiles; chooses strong active verbs

Additional Information

Coached 9th grade soccer at Boys and Girls Club, Trenton; and worked as physical fitness trainer for high school football players at South Trenton High School.

Volunteer work shows professional commitment

Groups and Associations

ASEP (American Society of Exercise Physiologists)
Young Professionals of Trenton Fitness

Strong link between job goals and community service

Groups from which Solter has built his network

Personal Information

Email	dsolterfitness@yahoo.com
Birthday	**February 19**
Marital status	**Married**

Contact Settings
Interested in

- job inquiries
- reference requests
- expertise requests
- getting back in touch

Identifies areas in which Solter wants to exchange information to further expand his network of professional contacts

© Cengage Learning 2015

Dan Vallero/LinkedIn

how you look online, including your social networking profile and what you post on your page and in your portfolio (see pages 173–174), in a blog, or on a website, whether it is your own or someone else's. To project your best professional image, employ the same care as you would in preparing other job-related documents, such as memos, letters, reports, and proposals.

In Table 5.2 (page 170), you will find some Do's and Don'ts when you create your profile on a social networking site.

TABLE 5.2   Do's and Don'ts When Creating Your Online Profile

Do's	Don'ts
Supply a current, professional picture showing how you want employers to see you at an interview.	Never use a profile photo taken at a party, a sports event, or on your vacation. Exclude photos with revealing clothing or compromising poses or gestures.
Choose appropriate "likes" and "activities" relating to your professional, community service, or charitable work. Mention the titles of current books related to your major or articles in *Time*, *US News & World Report*, or *Bloomberg Businessweek*.	Make sure that the hobbies or activities you list do not detract from your professional profile (e.g., playing computer games, gambling, etc.).
Highlight your strongest career accomplishments to demonstrate your knowledge of the industry where you want to work.	Do not give out someone's personal information (such as email addresses, phone numbers, or names) without first obtaining that person's permission.
Ensure that your tone, words, and comments are ethical.	Never use sexist, racist, or obscene language online. Steer clear of sensitive or inflammatory topics, such as politics and religion.
Respect all the ethical guidelines of your current or former employer (see pages page 22).	Refrain from giving out any privileged company information (e.g., names of clients, financial details, marketing plans, etc.). Never use your company email address when registering for social networking sites, and do not log onto them via your office computer.
Check other websites where you may appear or may be quoted to make sure you look and sound professional. Google yourself to find these and other links.	Avoid posting anything that makes you look unprofessional in dress, actions, or words.
Be careful when blogging; exclude anything embarrassing or damaging to your job search.	Avoid criticizing a former or current co-worker, employer, client, vendor, competitor, instructor, or government official or agency.
Keep all information up-to-date.	Do not bombard a potential employer with repeated small posts, queries, or updates.
Verify that all images and video clips are clear and professional.	Eliminate background noise or unnecessary background images.
Be discreet. Check your privacy/security settings to ensure that information about you is available only to those you want to have it, and adjust them if necessary. Contact website administrators if anything abusive has been posted about you, and request that the material is removed.	Don't forget that your profile is never as private as you think. Your current network of friends may include someone who has some type of connection to a prospective employer.

Dossiers and Letters of Recommendation

Dossiers play a major role in the job search. A *dossier*, French for "bundle of documents," provides a file of information about you and your work—recommendations and so on—that others have supplied.

Basically, your dossier contains the following documents:

- letters of recommendation
- letters that awarded you a scholarship, gave you an academic honor, or acknowledged your community service
- letters that praised your work on the job, notified you of a merit raise, promotion, or recognition ("Employee of the Month")
- your academic transcript(s)

A dossier collects important information about you that prospective employers will want to see to decide whether to interview you. You may ask your placement office to send your dossier to an employer, or employers may request it themselves if you have listed the placement office address on your résumé.

Obtaining Letters of Recommendation

Should You See Your Letters?

You have a legal right to see your recommendation letters, but some employers believe that if candidates read them, their references may be overly complimentary and more inclined to withhold information. Also, some of your references may refuse to write a letter of recommendation if they know you will read it. However, you may feel more comfortable knowing what your recommendation letters contain. But before you make any decisions about seeing your recommendation letters, get the advice of your instructors and placement counselors.

Whom Should You Ask?

Be careful about whom you ask. Whether your recommendation letters are confidential or not, they can sell you or sink your chances, so select your references carefully. Ask the following individuals to be your references and to write enthusiastically about your work qualifications and skills:

- previous employers (even for summer jobs or internships) who commended you and your work
- two or three of your professors who know and like your work, have graded your papers, or have supervised you in fieldwork or laboratory activities
- supervisors who evaluated and praised your work in the military
- community leaders or officials with whom you have worked successfully on civic projects

Recommendations from such individuals will be regarded as more objective—and more relevant—than letters from friends, neighbors, or members of the clergy.

Whoever you ask, make sure he or she is a strong supporter of yours, someone who has sincerely and consistently complimented your work and encouraged you in your career. Find out by asking if this person is willing to write a strong, enthusiastic letter on your behalf. Stay clear of individuals who are lukewarm about your work or who might be reluctant to recommend you for another reason. Figure 5.3 shows a letter requesting a letter of recommendation.

FIGURE 5.3 Request for a Letter of Recommendation

Student-designed letterhead

TADEUS MAJESKI • 5432 South Kenneth Avenue • Chicago, IL 60651

312-555-7733   **tmajeski@gatenet.com**

March 29, 2014

Mr. Sonny Butler, Manager
Empire Supermarket
4000 West 79th Street
Chicago, IL 66052-4300

Dear Mr. Butler:

Reviews employment history

I was employed at your store from September 2012 through August 2013. During my employment, I worked part time as a stock clerk and relief cashier, and during the summer I was a full-time employee in the produce department, helping to fill in while Bill Dirksen and Vivian Ho were on vacation.

Emphasizes skills learned on the job

I enjoyed my work at Empire, and I learned a great deal about the latest inventory tracking systems, ordering stock, calculating and helping to prevent merchandise shrinkage, and assisting customers.

Diplomatically requests strong letter of recommendation

This May, I will receive my A.A. degree from Moraine Valley Community College in retail merchandising and I have already begun preparing for my job search for a position in retail sales. Would you be willing to write an enthusiastic letter of recommendation for me describing what you regard as my greatest strengths as one of your employees? Having your endorsement would be a great help to me, for which I would be grateful.

Explains how letter will be used

To assist you, I can send you a letter of recommendation form from the Placement Office at Moraine Valley. Your letter would then become part of my permanent placement file.

Encloses copy of résumé and thanks reader

I look forward to hearing from you. I thought you might like to see the enclosed résumé, which shows what I have been doing since I left Empire. Thank you for the opportunity to work at your store.

Sincerely yours,

Tadeus Majeski

Tadeus Majeski

Encl.: Résumé

Always Ask for Permission

Always ask for permission before you list an individual as a reference. You could jeopardize your chances for a job if a prospective employer called one of your references and that person did not even know you were looking for a job or, worse yet, reveals that you did not have the courtesy to ask to use his or her name.

Should You Ask Your Current Boss?

Asking your current boss can be tricky. If your present employer is already aware that you are looking for work elsewhere (for instance, if your job is temporary or if your contract is about to run out) or you are working at a part-time job, by all means ask for a letter of recommendation. However, if you are employed full time and are looking for professional advancement and/or for a better salary elsewhere, you may not want your current employer to know that you are searching for another job. You may want to speak to a job counselor.

Career Portfolios/Webfolios

Like dossiers, career portfolios/webfolios play a major role in the job search. The documents they contain work together to support and supplement your résumé. Increasingly, job seekers are providing both a dossier and portfolio/webfolio to prospective employers. Unlike a dossier, which provides information about you and your work that others have written, a portfolio (or **webfolio** if it is submitted electronically) contains documents you have created or produced yourself.

For example, a portfolio would contain samples of your work—written or visual (plans, paintings, photos, slides)—to show to prospective employers.

Following is a sampling of the kinds of documents you might include in your career portfolio/webfolio.

- a mission statement (two or three paragraphs) that outlines your career goals and work skills
- an additional copy of your résumé
- scans of diplomas, certificates, licenses, internships, papers
- copies of awards (academic and job-related), promotion letters, or commendations (e.g., for protecting the environment)
- impressive examples of written work you did for college courses, such as reports or proposals (include any positive comments provided by instructors)
- newspaper or newsletter stories about your academic, community, or on-the-job successes
- pertinent examples of media presentations or other graphic work you have done, PowerPoint presentations you have created, or a USB flash drive of a website designed
- a list of your references with contact information

What Not to Include in a Career Portfolio/Webfolio

Be highly selective about what you include. Never include anything that would contradict or call into question information in your résumé or letter of application. Exclude the following types of documents from your career portfolio/webfolio:

- documents or scans of documents that show your memberships in clubs, fraternities/sororities, sports teams, and so on, unless directly relevant to the job (e.g., applying for a job at the national office for Sigma Sigma Kappa or with the Professional Golfers Association)
- links to or printouts from personal webpages, including Facebook, Twitter, and Tumblr pages (these may contain inappropriate personal information or portray you as unprofessional; see pages 167–170)
- pictures of your family, friends, pets, and the like
- scans of newspaper or newsletter stories about you that are not directly related to your job search, such as your winning a cruise or playing on a bowling team

Career Portfolio/Webfolio Formats

When you provide a prospective employer with your career portfolio, you can either mail it or send it electronically as a webfolio. If you submit a hard-copy portfolio, always make high-quality copies of each document. Never include originals. If you submit a webfolio, make sure that all of your scans are clean and clear. In addition, you can hyperlink parts of your career portfolio to your résumé, as Anthony Jones does in Figure 5.4, making it easy for a job recruiter or prospective employer to find evidence of your qualifications.

Preparing a Résumé

The résumé, sometimes called a *curriculum vitae (cv)*, may be the most important document you prepare for your job search. It merits doing some careful home-work. A résumé is not your life history or your emotional autobiography, nor is it a transcript of your college work. It is a factual and concise summary of your qualifications, convincing a prospective employer that you have the education and experience to do the job you are applying for. Regard your résumé as a persuasive ad for your professional qualifications. It is a billboard advertising you.

What you include—your key details, the wording, the ordering of informa-tion, and the formatting—are all vital to your campaign to sell yourself and land an interview. Employers want to see the most crucial and current details about your qualifications quickly. Accordingly, keep your print résumé short (preferably one page, never longer than two) and hard-hitting. The same thing goes for your digital résumés. See Figures 5.8–5.11 for examples of digital résumés. Everything on your résumé needs to convince an employer you have the exact skills and background he or she is looking for.

What Employers Like to See in a Résumé

Prospective employers will judge you and your work by your résumé; it is their first view of you and your qualifications. They will expect an applicant's résumé to be

- **Honest.** Be truthful about your qualifications—your education, experience, and skills. Distorting, exaggerating, or falsifying information about yourself in your résumé is unethical and could cost you the job. If you were a clerical assistant to an attorney, don't describe yourself as a paralegal. Always tell the truth.
- **Attractive.** The document should be pleasing to the eye, with generous margins, consistent punctuation, and suitable spacing, typeface, and use of boldface; it shows you have a sense of proportion and document design and that you are visually smart. The print should be clear and dark, not faded, on high-quality paper, and not so small it would be hard to read. Do not use gimmicks like clip art or excessive capitalization.
- **Carefully organized.** Arrange information so that it is easy to follow, logical, and consistent; the way you organize information shows you have the ability to process information and to summarize. Employers prize analytical thinking. Include plenty of white space to separate major sections, and use bullets to list and highlight key facts within each section, as in Figures 5.4 and 5.5 (pages 178–179).
- **Concise.** Make sure your résumé is to the point. Generally, keep your résumé to one page, as in Figure 5.4. However, depending on your education or job experience, you may want to include a second page. Résumés are written in short sentences that omit "I" and that use action-packed verbs, such as those listed in Table 5.3 on page 176.
- **Accurate.** Make sure your grammar, spelling, dates, names, titles, and programs are correct; typos, inconsistencies, and math errors say you didn't check your facts and figures.
- **Current.** All information needs to be up-to-date and documented, with no gaps or sketchy areas about previous jobs or education. Missing or incorrect dates or leaving key information out are red flags.
- **Relevant.** The information on your résumé must be appropriate for the job description and level. It must show that you have the necessary education and experience and must confirm that you can be an effective team player.
- **Quantifiable.** For instance, include specifics about how much revenue you generated for an employer (or how much money you saved, or how many times you performed a complex job).

Your goal is to prepare a résumé that shows the employer you possess the sought-after job skills. A résumé that is unattractive, difficult to follow, poorly written, filled with typos and spelling mistakes or that is sketchy, vague, boastful, or not relevant for the prospective employer's needs will not make the first cut.

TABLE 5.3   Action Verbs to Use in Your Résumé

accommodated	conducted	generated	operated	selected
accomplished	converted	guided	organized	served
achieved	coordinated	handled	oversaw	settled
adapted	created	headed	performed	sold
adjusted	customized	hired	persuaded	solved
administered	dealt in	implemented	planned	spearheaded
advocated	delivered	improved	posted	streamlined
analyzed	designed	increased	prepared	supervised
appraised	determined	informed	programmed	surveyed
arranged	developed	initiated	protected	taught
assembled	devised	inspected	provided	teamed up
assisted	directed	installed	purchased	tested
attended	discovered	instituted	ranked	tracked
awarded	drafted	instructed	reappraised	trained
bridged	earned	interpreted	received	transcribed
budgeted	economized	judged	reconciled	translated
built	edited	launched	recorded	tutored
calculated	elected	led	reduced	updated
chaired	established	logged	re-evaluated	upgraded
coached	estimated	maintained	reported	validated
collaborated	evaluated	managed	researched	verified
collected	excelled	mapped	reviewed	volunteered
communicated	expanded	monitored	saved	weighed
compiled	expedited	motivated	scanned	wired
completed	figured	navigated	scheduled	won
composed	founded	negotiated	searched	worked
computed	fulfilled	observed	secured	wrote

Create Several Versions of Your Résumé

It is to your advantage to prepare several versions of your résumé and then adapt each one you send out to the specific job skills a prospective employer is looking for. It pays to customize your résumé based on information you may have gathered about the job from researching the company (see page 205), through networking on sites such as LinkedIn (see pages 166–169), and from analyzing the keywords the employer used to describe the position. Following the process detailed in the next section will help you prepare any résumé.

The Process of Writing Your Résumé

To write an effective résumé, ask the following important questions:

1. What classes did you excel in?
2. What papers, reports, surveys, or presentations earned you your highest grades?
3. What computer skills have you mastered—languages, software, e-commerce, blog or website design, collaborative online editing?
4. What other technical skills have you acquired?
5. What relevant jobs have you had? For how long and where? What were your primary duties? Did you supervise other employees?

6. How did you open or expand a business market? Increase a customer base?
7. What did you do to earn a raise or a promotion in a previous or current job?
8. Do you work well with people? What skills do you possess as a member of a team working toward a common job goal (e.g., finishing a report)?
9. Can you organize complicated tasks or identify and solve problems quickly?
10. Have you had experiences or responsibilities managing money—collecting fees or receipts, preparing payrolls, conducting nightly audits, and so on?
11. Have you won any awards or scholarships or received a commendation or other recognition at work?

Pay special attention to your four or five most significant, job-worthy strengths, and work especially hard on listing them concisely and persuasively.

Although not everything you have done relates directly to a particular job, indicate how your achievements are relevant to the employer's overall needs. For example, supervising staff in a convenience store points to your ability to perform the same duties in another business context.

Balancing Education and Experience

If you have years of experience, don't flood your prospective employer with too many details. You cannot possibly include every detail of your jobs for the last ten or twenty years.

- Emphasize only those skills and positions most likely to earn you the job.
- Eliminate early jobs that do not relate to your present employment search.
- Combine and condense skills acquired over many years and jobs.
- Include relevant military schools or service.

Figure 5.6 (page 185) shows the résumé of an individual who has a great deal of experience to offer prospective employers.

Many job candidates who have spent most of their lives in school are faced with the other extreme: not having much job experience to list. The worst thing to do is to write "None" for experience. Any part-time, summer, or other seasonal jobs, as well as volunteer work, apprenticeships, and internships, show an employer that you are responsible and knowledgeable about the obligations of being an employee. Figure 5.4 contains a résumé from Anthony Jones, a student with little job experience; Figure 5.5 shows María López's résumé, a student with a few years of experience.

What to Exclude from a Résumé

Knowing what to exclude from a résumé is as important as knowing what to include. Because federal employment laws prohibit discrimination on the basis of age, sex, race, national origin, religion, marital status, or disability, do not include such information on your résumé. Here are some other details best left off your résumé:

- salary demands, expectations, or ranges
- preferences for work schedules, days off, or overtime
- comments about fringe benefits

FIGURE 5.4 Résumé from a Student with Little Job Experience

WEBSITE DEVELOPER
DESIGNER
GRAPHIC ARTIST

Anthony H. Jones
73 Allenwood Boulevard
Santa Rosa, CA 95401-1074
707-555-6390
ajdesigner@plat.com
www.plat.com/users/ajones/resume.html

Headlines major achievements and gives contact details

CAREER OBJECTIVE

Offers precise, convincing objective

Full-time position as a layout artist with a commercial publishing house using my training in state-of-the-art design technology.

EDUCATION

Starts with most important qualification— education

Santa Rosa Junior College, 2012–2014, A.S. degree to be awarded in 2014

Dean's List in 2013; GPA 3.25

Major: Commercial Graphics Illustration, with specialty in design layout

Related courses included:

- Digital Photography
- Graphics Programs: Illustrator, Photoshop, Dreamweaver
- Desktop Publishing: Adobe InDesign, QuarkXPress

Stresses job-related activities of internship

Internship, 2013–2014, McAdam Publishers

Major projects included:

- Assisting layout editors with page composition and photo archiving.
- Writing detailed assessment reports on digital photography, designs, and artwork used in *Living in Sonoma County* (www.sonomacounty.com) and *Real Estate in Sonoma County* (www.resc.net) magazines.

EXPERIENCE

Includes part-time work experience

Salesperson (part-time), 2011–2013, Buchman's Department Store

Duties included assisting customers in sporting goods and appliance departments, designing custom window displays each month for the main entrance, and helping to manage the inventory database.

COMPUTER SKILLS

Demonstrates skills in Web design software

Adobe InDesign, QuarkXPress, Illustrator, Photoshop, Dreamweaver, FinalCut Pro

RELATED ACTIVITIES

Relevant volunteer work

Designed website and three-fold brochure for the Santa Rosa Humane Society's 2013 fund drive; helped raise $5,600.

REFERENCES/WEBFOLIO

Credentials and webfolio document accomplishments

References and webfolio containing designs, photographs, and graphics are available at **www.plat.com/users/ajones/resume.html**

FIGURE 5.5 Résumé from a Student with Some Job Experience

María López

1725 Brooke Street   Miami, FL 32701-2121   (305) 555-3429   mlopez@eagle.com

Provides easy-to-find contact information

CAREER OBJECTIVE

Position assisting dentist in providing dental care, counseling, and preventive dental treatments, especially in pediatric dentistry

EDUCATION

A.S. in Dental Hygiene, Miami-Dade Community College
Aug. 2012–May 2014
GPA: 3.58 (Ranked in the top 10 percent of class)

Lists course and clinical work required for licensure and job

Major courses:

- Oral pathology
- Dental materials and specialties
- Periodontics
- Community dental health

- Experienced with procedures and instruments used with oral prophylaxis techniques
- Subject of major project was proper nutrition and dental health for preschoolers
- Will take American Dental Assisting National Board exams on June 2

Calls attention to career or professional skills that benefit employer and patients

Minor: Psychology (twelve hours in child and adolescent psychology)

EXPERIENCE

St. Francis Hospital
(Miami Beach, FL) April 2010–July 2012
Unit assistant on pediatric unit. Maintained medical supply levels using inventory tracking software, keyboarded all medical records into hospital-wide database, transcribed medical orders and surgical notes, greeted and assisted visitors

Emphasizes professional licensure qualifications

Highlights previous job responsibilities in health care setting

Murphy Construction Company
(Miami, FL) June 2009–April 2010
Office assistant-receptionist. Did data entry and filing, and assisted with billing and creating project schedules in a small office (5 employees)

City of Hialeah, FL
Summers 2007–2008
Lifeguard. Established safety procedures and tested pool chlorine levels

COMPUTER SKILLS

PowerPoint, DentiMax, Microsoft Office, FileMaker Pro

Includes career-relevant computer skills

LANGUAGE SKILLS

Fluent in Spanish

REFERENCES

Available on request

Calls attention to bilingual skills of value to employer and patients

- travel restrictions
- reasons for leaving your previous job
- your photograph (unless you are applying for a modeling or acting job)
- your Social Security number
- information about your family, spouse, or children
- height, weight, hair or eye color
- sexual orientation, religious and political affiliations
- hobbies, interests (unless relevant to the job you are seeking)

Save comments about salary and schedules for your interview (see pages 205–210). The résumé should be written to earn you that interview.

Parts of a Résumé

As with memos, letters, and reports, résumés consist of specific parts shown in boldface headings on the following pages. These parts—contact information, career objective, credentials (education and experience), related skills and achievements, and references/portfolios—need to be included in any résumé.

Contact Information

At the top of the page, provide your full name (do not use a nickname), address including your zip code, telephone number (use a cell phone number if you always have your phone with you), and email address. If your academic address is different from your home address, list and identify both. The contact information can either be centered on the page or flush left or right. Avoid unprofessional email addresses such as toughguy@netfield.com or sassygirl@techscape.com. Make sure your voice mail message is straightforward and professional as well. Also include a URL for your website and a fax number, if you have one.

Career Objective

One of the first things a prospective employer will read is your career objective statement, which specifies the exact type of job you are looking for and in what ways you are qualified to hold it. Create an objective that precisely dovetails with the prospective employer's requirements. Such a statement should be the result of your focused self-evaluation and your assessment of the job market. It will influence everything else you include on your résumé. Depending on your background and the types of jobs you are qualified for, you might formulate two or three different career or employment objectives to use with different versions of your résumé as you apply for various positions. Always try to incorporate keywords an employer lists in the job announcement on your résumé.

To write an effective career objective statement, ask yourself four basic questions:

1. What kind of job do I want?
2. What kind of job am I qualified for?
3. What capabilities do I possess?
4. What kinds of skills do I want to learn?

Avoid trite, vague, or self-centered goals, such as "Looking for professional advancement," "Want to join a progressive company," "Seeking high-paying job that brings personal satisfaction," or "Job where I can use my proven leadership abilities." Compare the vague objectives on the left with the more precise ones on the right.

Unfocused	Focused
Job in sales to use my aggressive skills in expanding markets	Regional sales representative using my proven skills in e-commerce and communication to develop and expand a customer base.
Full-time position as staff nurse	Full-time position as staff nurse on cardiac step-down unit to offer excellent primary care nursing and patient/family teaching.
Position in cable industry	Position as part of a service team to provide efficient cable repair service.

A career objective can help you when you are applying for a specific job opening. You need to tailor it to meet the needs of a prospective employer.

Credentials

The order of the next two categories—Education and Experience—can vary. Generally, if you have lots of work experience, list it first. However, if you are a recent graduate short on job experience, list education first, as Anthony Jones does in Figure 5.4. María López (Figure 5.5) also decided to place her education before her job experience because the job she was applying for required the formal training she recently received at Miami-Dade Community College.

Education Begin with your most recent education first, then list everything significant since high school. For each school, give the name, the dates you attended, and the degree, diploma, or certificate you earned. Don't overlook relevant military experience or major training programs (EMT, court reporter), institutes, internships, or workshops you have completed.

Remember, however, that a résumé is not a transcript. Simply listing a series of required courses will not set you apart from hundreds of other applicants taking similar courses across the country. Focus on courses that have specifically prepared you for the job. Avoid vague titles such as Science 203 or Nursing IV. Instead, concentrate on describing the specific skills you learned.

> 30 hours in planning and development courses specializing in transportation, land use, and community facilities; 12 hours in field methods of gathering, interpreting, and describing survey data in reports.

Completed 28 hours in major courses in business marketing, management, and materials in addition to 12 hours in information science, including web design and publishing.

Mention any special projects, experiments, or reports that bear directly on the job you are seeking. Note how María López (Figure 5.5) briefly references her major project on preschoolers' nutrition and dental health, a topic sure to interest her potential employer.

List your grade point average (GPA) only if it is 3.0 or above; otherwise, indicate your GPA in just your major or during your last year or term, again if it is above 3.0.

Experience   Your job history is the key category for many employers. It shows them that you have held jobs before and that you are responsible. Here are some guidelines about listing your experience.

1. Begin with your most recent position and work backward—in reverse chronological order. List the company or agency name, location (city and state), your job title, and dates of employment. Do not mention why you left a job.

2. For each job or activity, provide a short description (one or two lines) of your duties and achievements. If you were a work-study student, don't say that you helped an instructor teach a class. Emphasize your responsibilities; for example, you helped to set up a chemistry laboratory, ordering supplies and keeping an inventory of them. Rather than saying you were an administrative assistant, indicate that you wrote business letters and used various software programs, maintained records, designed a company website, prepared schedules for part-time help in an office of twenty-five people, or assisted the manager in preparing minutes, accounts, and presentations.

3. In describing your position(s), emphasize any responsibilities that involved handling money (for example, assisting customers, filing insurance claims, or preparing payrolls); managing other employees; working with customer accounts, services, and programs; or writing letters and reports. Prospective employers are interested in your leadership abilities, teamwork, financial responsibility (especially if you earned or saved your company money), tact in dealing with the public, and communications skills. They will also be favorably impressed by commendations "Earned Highest Sales Record"; recognized for "Exceptional Clinical Care" in serving geriatric patients), and promotions you have earned.

4. Include any relevant volunteer work you have done, as Anthony Jones did for an animal shelter in Figure 5.4. Note, too, how Dora Cooper Bolger's volunteer work translates into marketing skills an employer wants to see in a prospective employee's résumé in Figure 5.6 on page 185.

5. If you have been a full-time parent for ten years or a caregiver for a family member or friend, briefly note the management skills you developed while running a household and any community or civic service, as Dora Cooper Bolger does in her résumé. She skillfully relates her family and community accomplishments to the specific job she seeks.

Related Skills and Achievements

Not every résumé will have this section, but the following are all employer-friendly things to include:

- second or third languages you speak or write
- extensive travel
- certificates or licenses you hold
- memberships in professional associations (e.g., American Society of Safety Engineers, National Black Law Students Association, National Hispanic Business Association, Texas Executive Women)
- memberships in community service groups (e.g., Habitat for Humanity, Salvation Army, Big Brothers/Big Sisters); list any offices you held

Computer Skills   Knowledge of computers, software, word-processing programs, web design, and search engines is extremely valuable in the job market. Note how Anthony Jones and María López both inform prospective employers about their relevant technical competencies in Figures 5.4 and 5.5.

Honors/Awards   List any civic honors (mayor's award, community service award, cultural harmony award) and academic honors (dean's list, department awards, scholarships, grants, honorable mentions), and military awards or medals you have won. Memberships in honor societies in your major and technical/business associations also demonstrate that you are professionally accomplished and active.

References

As a rule, do not list references with personal contact information. Simply say they are available on request. But here is where networking can help you select references. Ask your instructors, previous employer, or individuals who have supervised your work. Always give the person providing the reference a copy of your current résumé, as Tadeus Majeski did in Figure 5.3.

Organizing Your Résumé

There are two primary ways to organize your résumé: chronologically and by function or skill area. You may want to prepare two versions of your résumé—one chronological and one by function or skill area—to see which sells your talents better. Don't hesitate to seek the advice of a placement counselor or instructor about which may work best for you.

Chronologically

The résumés in Figures 5.4 and 5.5 are organized chronologically, with most recent education and experience listed first. This is the traditional way to organize a résumé. It is straightforward and easy to read, and employers find it acceptable. The chronological sequence works especially well when you can show a clear continuity toward progress in your career through your employment and schoolwork or when you want to apply for a similar job with another company.

A chronological résumé is also appropriate for students who want to emphasize recent educational achievements.

By Function or Skill Area

Depending on your experiences and accomplishments, you might organize your résumé according to function or skill area. According to this plan, you would *not* list your information chronologically in the categories "Experience" and "Education." Instead, you would sort your achievements and abilities—whether from course work, jobs, extracurricular activities, military service, or technical skills—into two to four key skill areas, such as

- Sales
- Public Relations
- Training/Teaching
- Management
- Safety/Security
- Counseling
- Leadership
- Communication

- Network Operations
- People Skills
- Teamwork
- Troubleshooting
- Opening New Markets
- Multicultural Experiences
- Information Technology
- Problem-Solving Skills

Under each area you would list three to five points illustrating your achievements in that area. Functional and skills résumés are often called *bullet résumés* because they itemize the candidate's main strengths in bulleted lists. Some employers prefer the bullet résumé because they can skim the candidate's list of qualifications in a few seconds.

Note Dora Cooper Bolger's profitable use of a skills résumé format in Figure 5.6. She delayed attending college for several years because of family commitments, yet she uses the experiences she acquired during those years to her advantage in her résumé organized by "Skills." No gap of ten years interrupts her valuable marketable skills.

Preparing a Functional or Skills Résumé

When you prepare a functional or skills résumé, start with your name, address, telephone number, and career objective, just as in a chronological résumé. To find the best two or three functional areas to include, use the prewriting strategies (especially clustering and brainstorming) discussed in Chapter 2.

The following individuals would probably benefit from organizing their résumés by function or skill area instead of chronologically:

- nontraditional students who have had diverse job experiences
- people who are changing professions
- individuals who have changed jobs frequently
- ex-military personnel reentering the civilian marketplace

After you discover and suitably revise the information to be included in your categories, briefly list your educational and work experiences, as Dora Cooper Bolger in Figure 5.6.

FIGURE 5.6 Dora Cooper Bolger's Résumé Organized by Skills Areas

DORA COOPER BOLGER

1215 Lakeview Avenue
Westhampton, MI 46532
Cell: 616-555-4773
dcbplanner@aol.com

Objective	Seek full-time position as public affairs officer to promote the goals of a health care, educational, or charitable organization

Restricted objective

Skills   **Organizational Communication**
- Delivered 24 presentations to civic groups on educational issues
- Recorded minutes and helped formulate agenda as president of large, local PTA (800 members) for past 6½ years
- Possess excellent computer skills in Microsoft Word, Microsoft Dynamics CRM, and PowerPoint
- Updated and maintained computerized mailing lists for Teens in Trouble and Foster Parents' Association

Aptly features skill areas before education

Financial
- Spearheaded 3 major fund-raising drives (total of $225,000 collected)
- Prepared and implemented large family budget (3 children, 8 foster children)
- Planned budget, Foster Parents' Association
- Served as financial secretary, Faith United Methodist Church, for 4 years

Links achievements from volunteer and home-based activities most important to employer

Administrative
- Organized volunteers for National Kidney Foundation (last 5 years)
- Established and oversaw neighborhood carpool (17 drivers; more than 70 children) for 7 years
- Coordinated after-school tutoring program for Teens in Trouble; president since 2001
- Vice-president, Foster Parents' Association, 2012

Chooses strong, active verbs to convey image of a results-oriented professional

Honors   "Volunteer of the Year," (2013) Michigan Child Placement Agency

Education   Metropolitan Community College, A.A., 2010
Mid-Michigan College, B.S., expected May 2014
Major: Public Administration; Minor: Psychology
GPA: 3.55 | Dean's List: 2012–2014

Places education after skills; includes major and related minor plus strong GPA

Work Experience   Secretary, 2002–2009 (full- and part-time): Merrymount Plastics; Foley and Wasson; Westhampton Health Dept.; G & K Electric

Excludes details about least recent jobs

References   Available on request

Transitioning into the Civilian Workforce

Transitioning from the military into the civilian workforce is not easy. It may require you to greatly modify or adapt your military training or even to change careers altogether. Above all, you will have to ask yourself questions such as those on pages 160–161 to find out what skills you learned in the service—technical, communication, interpersonal—that might transfer to the civilian job market. Listing your skills will help you focus on the various kinds of jobs for which you can apply. Like other job seekers, you need to take advantage of networking sites such as LinkedIn and Facebook to find the latest information about jobs and to make contracts. In addition, though, consult the following sites especially created to assist veterans in finding civilian employment.

- **MyNextMove.org**: directory of civilian occupations based on specific military job and experience
- **NRD.gov**: the National Resource Directory's Veterans Job Bank lists postings from companies looking to hire veterans
- **Milicruit.com**; **Monster.com**: virtual career fairs geared toward veterans
- **Military.com**: resources for transitioning to civilian life
- **LinkedIn.com/veterans**: networking microsite for veterans with tips, tools, and webinars
- **SimplyHired.com**; **Taleo.com**; **Indeed.com**; **BranchOut.com**: jobs sites tagging positions specifically for veterans

Veterans bring a wealth of experiences and competencies that can improve their chances of landing a job in the civilian sector. The skills listed here, common to all branches and divisions of the armed services, appeal to employers who want to hire individuals who possess a strong work ethic and a sense of duty and loyalty that the military stresses. Capitalize on these when preparing your résumé and drafting your letter of application:

1. Offering leadership by training and example
2. Excelling in building teamwork and efficiency
3. Meeting deadlines under stressful conditions
4. Working respectfully with individuals from diverse cultures
5. Adapting quickly to change
6. Paying attention to detail
7. Troubleshooting and solving problems quickly
8. Receiving specialized technical training
9. Managing budgets, equipment, supplies and other resources
10. Maintaining equipment
11. Exhibiting self-discipline
12. Being physically fit

Illustrate your accomplishments in these categories with specific examples when you write your résumé or letter of application. The more you match your military competencies to your employer's needs, the better your chances of landing an interview. Make your military service work for you in the civilian sector. See how Sandy Meagher did this in Figure 5.7 (page 188).

Using a Civilian Résumé Format, Language, and Context

While it is to your advantage to showcase the experience and technical skills you gained in the service, keep in mind that not all military jobs automatically or even easily translate into civilian ones. You cannot prepare a resume for a civilian boss the way you would your superior in the service. Study Figure 5.7, which contains a résumé prepared by a veteran, Sandy Meagher, who was discharged after eight years of service in the Marine Corps. As you prepare your civilian resume, follow these guidelines:

1. Complete the Veterans Preference Document, and indicate that you have done so at the top of your résumé so that a prospective employer knows about your background, as Sandy Meagher has done in Figure 5.7.
2. When listing contact information, do not refer to yourself by your military rank, for example, Lance Cpl. Joseph Johns; Spec. E-3 Cathy Cookeston.
3. Avoid military abbreviations, and acronyms (Sitrep, FOB, LAV, MOS/MUC) that a civilian employer might not understand.
4. Provide a career objective consistent with the civilian job for which you are applying.
5. Describe your military job(s) in terms that an employer will easily understand. Rather than indicating you were a 1A2X1, simply say you were a cargo manager.
6. Whether you use a chronological or functional résumé depends on the types of jobs you did in the military. If the job you performed involved immediately transferable skills and competencies, a chronological résumé may work well. But if your duties were diverse or appreciably different from those expected in a civilian job (for example, infantry, explosive detonation, warehousing surplus parts), then a functional résumé, such as that used by Dora Cooper Bolger in Figure 5.6 or Sandy Meagher in Figure 5.7 is preferable. (Meagher had other jobs in the military before being assigned to the motor pool.) It allows you to avoid any gaps that a chronological résumé shows and to summarize your military training and accomplishments spread over several enlistments and at various duty stations.

As the résumés in Figure 5.6 and 5.7 do, quantify your accomplishments. Some possible skill/function categories from your tour(s) of duty you might use include:

Accounting/Finance	Maintenance
Administration	Public Information/Affairs
Communication	Purchasing
Criminal Justice	Recruiting
Cultural Diversity	Research
Engineering	Safety and Security
Health Care	Special skills (heavy equipment operations,
Human Resources	special truck/vehicle license, etc.)
Languages	Teamwork
Leadership	Training/Teaching

7. List your education, including any significant military training you received or schools you attended. Omit your high school or GED.

FIGURE 5.7 Sandy Meagher's Résumé Showing Transition from Military Service to Civilian Employment

Easy to see contact information

Sandy Meagher

301 65th St., Kansas City, KS 66083 • (703)-555-4309 • sandy.meagher@gmail.com

Completed Veterans Preference Document

Free from military jargon

Objective

A position in maintenance/vehicle repair for an urban mass transit system

Uses four skill areas that transfer military accomplishments to civilian workforce

Supervising/Training

• Supervised/managed staff of 9 mechanics and transportation technicians
• Performed high-quality inspections on military wheeled and track vehicles
• Helped coordinate and maintain a "just-in-time" inventory of parts and products
   Received high ratings (96%) for unit efficiency and team building

Technical

• Worked as a fully trained mechanic on military wheeled and track vehicles
• Operated state-of-the-art diagnostic technologies equipment
• Responsible for both routine and extended vehicle/equipment repairs

Helpfully organized with bulleted items

Recordkeeping/Communications

• Monitored administrative actions regarding staff (finance, work schedules, etc.)
• Initiated and oversaw ordering and inventorying parts and products
• Maintained detailed records on vehicles serviced from start to finish

Chose effective strong verbs

Safety and Security

• Coordinated safety checks for motor pool and safety drills for staff
• Lessened shop environmental hazards by enforcing strong safety standards
• Decreased loss of parts/supplies by adhering to strict security codes

Education

A.S. Garden City Community College, 2014
U.S. Army, Wheeled Vehicle Mechanic (91B), Track Vehicle Repairer (91H), Basic Non-Commissioned Officers School

Lists military honors to show dedication and service commitments

U.S. Decorations/Badges

Afghanistan Campaign Medal
Army Achievement Medal
Meritorious Service Medal

Employment

Walmart Auto Repair Technician, Kansas City, MO 2003–2004
U.S. Army, 2005–2013. Honorably discharged with rank of Sergeant First Class (E-5)
   Fort Riley, Kansas, 2005–2008
   Fort Benning, Georgia, 2009–2012
   Tour in Afghanistan, 2012–2013

References

Provided upon request

8. Briefly describe your computer skills (for example, Proficient in Windows 8) or any specialized military software you used, but only if it is relevant to the civilian job for which you are applying and in terms a civilian employer can understand.

9. Emphasize languages you know (and indicate level of competency). But if you know only a few words or phrases, skip this category; however, if you have conversational skills (for example, basic conversational Arabic) or reading knowledge, then certainly note that.

10. List military awards, medals, or promotions (for example, Commendation for Efficiency, Meritorious Service Medal, Exceptional Leadership; promoted to E-5).

11. Mention any affiliations relevant to your job search (for example, professional societies or military organizations in your area of expertise), but do not include political affiliations or clubs.

The Digital Résumé

In addition to drafting a hard copy of your résumé, expect to prepare multiple digital versions of it, including creating and posting it to the Web, formatting a scannable text, or emailing it. In today's highly competitive job market, where employers have differing requirements, it is to your advantage to use these various formats to attract the interest of prospective employers.

Things to Keep in Mind when Preparing a Digital Résumé

As you did with your hard copy résumé, your digital résumé has to be carefully organized and accurately written to meet a prospective employer's needs. But while the content of your résumé may remain the same when moving to a digital format, there are other things to keep in mind:

1. Always follow the employer's instructions when sending or posting your digital résumé.

2. Employers generally prefer submission of digital résumé as either Microsoft Word files or PDF files.

3. When preparing your digital résumé, be sure to use keywords from the job advertisement, so you can match your job skills with the ones employers are searching for when they review possible candidates.

Ways to Post, Email, Scan, or Video Capture Your Résumé

Your digital résumé may be the most important document in your job search because employers determine who will make their interview list based on what they see in a résumé. There are six basic ways to create and post your digital résumé to the web or to scan, email, or video capture it. But whether you post, scan, or email it, you must remember to make any changes in all versions of your résumé to be consistent. The following guidelines will help you prepare different versions of your résumé:

1. **Use the employer-provided application form.** Many employers have their own dedicated website where they accept applications for employment; this is one of the most widely used ways to get a prospective employer to look at your résumé. Applicants to these companies are asked to "paste" the text of their résumé into the online application form in order to submit it. In these situations, using a scannable version of a résumé, similar to the one in Figure 5.11 (page 195), is usually the best way to proceed.

2. **Post your résumé on the Web.** The Internet offers a variety of sites to disseminate your résumé. But regardless of where you post your résumé, the main advantage is that you will be reaching a large pool of potential employers. Here are some tips to help you post your résumé correctly for a potential employer.

   ■ Send it to one of the large job posting sites listed in Table 5.1 (page 163) to reach the maximum number of employers. Make sure you carefully follow all the directions listed on the site, and keep a log, too, of where you have posted your résumé.

   ■ Post your résumé directly on an employer's website where it can be indexed and stored. Follow the employer's instructions precisely or your application may be automatically deleted.

   ■ Include hyperlinks (e.g., Education, Experience, Honors) to your own website, to appropriate blogs you wrote, or to reviews of your professional work. If you include a webfolio, as in Figures 5.8 or 5.10 (page 194), hyperlinks will help an employer to access examples of your work quickly.

   ■ Employers often print out the résumés of job seekers they are interested in, so be sure your résumé can be downloaded easily and quickly.

   ■ If you post your résumé on your own website, do not provide more information than a prospective employer needs, and do not give out personal information. Protect your privacy by following the guidelines on pages 196–197.

3. **Send your résumé via an email attachment.** Many ads will ask you to email your résumé. To do so, prepare your résumé as a Word file and then save it as a read-only PDF file. A PDF file will automatically retain the format, fonts, and graphics in your document, ensuring that it will look as you want it to no matter where and when it is printed. If you are given the option, email your résumé as a PDF document. Here are some practical guidelines to follow when emailing your résumé.

   ■ Create your résumé as a Microsoft Word file and, unless the employer says not to, send it as a PDF attachment.

   ■ Include a short cover email, but also attach a longer application letter.

   ■ If either Word or PDF poses problems, you can always save your Word file as a rich text format (rtf) document. But make sure you use a plain and simple design. Avoid underlining, boldface, italics, or shadowing, which can garble the text of your résumé, making it almost impossible to read. Use all capital letters instead of bold or italics for emphasis and insert an asterisk (*) or a plus sign (+) in place of bullets.

FIGURE 5.8 A Scannable, Electronic Version of Anthony Jones's Hard-Copy Résumé in Figure 5.4

Anthony H. Jones
ajdesigner@plat.com
Phone: (707) 555-6390

KEYWORDS
Web designer, graphic designer, Illustrator, Photoshop, QuarkXPress, InDesign, fundraiser, budgets, sales, virus protection, team player

All lines aligned flush with the left margin

Keywords (for search engine readiness) go at the top of the digital résumé

OBJECTIVE
Position as layout artist with a commercial publisher using my training in state-of-the-art design technology

Objective appears in the body of the digital resume

EDUCATION
Santa Rosa Junior College, A.S. degree to be awarded in June 2014. Commercial Graphics Illustration major. GPA 3.45

All caps rather than bold, italics, or fancy fonts used to highlight skill categories

COMPUTER SKILLS
Excellent knowledge of computer graphics and design software: Adobe InDesign, QuarkXPress, Illustrator, Dreamweaver, Photoshop, and FinalCut Pro

EXPERIENCE
∗ Intern in layout and design department. Preparing page composition, photo archiving, and writing detailed assessment reports, McAdam Publishers, 8 Parkway Heights, Santa Rosa, CA
∗ Salesperson; display designer, Buchman's Department Store, Greenview Mall, Santa Rosa
∗ Designed website and three-fold brochure for successful fund drive, Santa Rosa Humane Society
∗ Web designer, graphic artist, display designer

Uses terminology appropriate for position

Chooses nouns rather than action verbs to increase employer matches

WEBFOLIO
www.plat.com/users/ajones/resume.html

REFERENCES
Available on request.

Asterisks rather than bullets mark beginning of lines

Webfolio is hyperlinked to make it easily accessible

- Stay away from hard-to-read, nonstandard, or fancy fonts. Instead, choose a font like Helvetica, Times New Roman, or Verdana that is easy to scan and does not mask letters.

4. Create a scannable résumé. Many companies scan hard copy résumés (such as those in Figures 5.8 and 5.9) into their databases so they can search for keywords (see page 196). An increasing number of employers are now asking job candidates to paste the text of their résumé into a special submission window. To be successful, format your résumé so that key information is easy to locate and stands out clearly

> **FIGURE 5.9** A Scannable, Electronic Version of Dora Cooper Bolger's Hard-Copy Résumé in Figure 5.6

Avoids giving personal information; uses P.O. box, not address

Dora Cooper Bolger
P.O. Box 3216
Westhampton, MI 46532
dcbplanner@aol.com

Uses many keywords taken from job description

KEYWORDS
Activity planner, budget coordinator, fund-raising, community service campaign, child advocacy, grant writer, public affairs, public speaking, interpersonal communication, management internal and external groups, team builder, strategic planner

Uses nouns to list accomplishments

OBJECTIVE
Position as public affairs officer for health care, educational, or charitable organization

RELEVANT EXPERIENCE
Presenter at 24 civic group functions
Fund raiser for 3 major campaigns, over $225,000 collected
President and coordinator, Teens in Trouble, a tutoring and mentoring program
Budget planner, Foster Parents' Association; also at large urban church

Summarizes experience concisely

VOLUNTEER WORK/AWARDS
Volunteer of the Year, Michigan Child Placement Agency, 2013
Volunteer Coordinator/Leader, National Kidney Foundation, 2010–2014
President and Secretary, local PTA, 2008–2014
Vice-president, Foster Parents' Association, 2012

Avoids any symbols, boldfacing, or italics that could garble text

EDUCATION
Metropolitan Community College, A.A., 2010
Mid-Michigan College, B.S., May 2014; Major: Public Administration
Minor: Psychology
GPA: 3.45. Dean's List: 2012–2014

Documents acquired computer skills

COMPUTER SKILLS
Microsoft Word; PeopleSoft; Microsoft Dynamics CRM; PowerPoint

REFERENCES
Available on request.

in the thirty to forty-second review of your credentials. Adhere to the following points when creating a scannable résumé:

- Follow all of the employer's instructions on formatting and submitting a résumé online. Otherwise, your application will be rejected.
- Where possible, make your scannable résumé longer than your hard copy version to increase the number of keywords or matches with the employer's job description.

- Use ample white space, which a scanner recognizes as separating one heading or section from another.
- If asked to submit a scannable hard copy résumé, use a high-quality laser printer and put your résumé on white or off-white paper.
- Avoid a script font. Use Times New Roman or Arial instead.
- Use at least 10- to 12-point type and allow a maximum width of 6½ inches to make your résumé easier to scan and read.
- Do not surround your résumé with a frame or border because this can lead to formatting difficulties.
- Do not staple or fold the pages.

5. Create an HTML version of your résumé. You can post your résumé on your own website, and you can link to an HTML version of your résumé from other websites or from an email you send to a potential employer. HTML is the computer language used to create much of the content on the Internet. Because employers are always impressed by job candidates with some HTML knowledge or web design experience, be sure to list this skill on your résumé. It may be one of your most powerful assets in your job search.

6. Send a video résumé. Video résumés are growing in popularity with prospective employers. A video résumé allows them to see and hear you, thus displaying your communication skills and dedication to your professional goals. You can post a video résumé on YouTube and other sites, as well on the Web. You can also include it as part of your LinkedIn profile (see pages 166–169). But make sure you prepare your presentation carefully before you record it and ask an instructor or someone at your job placement center to critique it.

Case Study

Creating a Digital Résumé for a Job Search

Beth Pryor has just earned her B.S. in marketing at Southern Ohio University. She realizes that the competition for jobs is fierce and that she has to prepare a persuasive résumé as well as a cover letter to go with it.

She quickly discovered that she would have to create more than one type of résumé. Some companies wanted job applicants to send their résumé as a Word or PDF document attached to an email. Others required applicants to paste a text résumé into a submission form on their human resources website. And many employers asked candidates to submit digital portfolios of their work. The most useful advice she received from a former teacher was to: "Make certain your résumé emphasizes the skills that a marketing manager will want to have—teamwork, leadership, enthusiasm, creativity, and most of all your strong sense of visual design and thinking."

She created a Word version of her résumé first, and then saved it as a PDF file (Figure 5.10 on page 194). To prepare a scannable version of her résumé, she removed the formatting from her Word résumé. Note that Beth's scannable résumé seen in Figure 5.11 on page 195 does not contain any boldface, italics, or indentations because these elements might prevent a scanner from capturing her information. To accompany her résumé, Beth developed a webfolio to display logo designs and advertising artwork plus copies of documents from her college marketing courses and an internship.

FIGURE 5.10 A PDF File of Beth Pryor's Résumé

Phone number not given because résumé posted on Web

Beth Pryor

PO Box 5112, Oxford, OH 45056
bethpryor@hotmail.com

Objective
A position with marketing firm emphasizing analysis, management, and leadership skills

Education
Southern Ohio University, Jamesville, OH
B.S. in Marketing; Minor: Spanish
Graduation: June 2014 — GPA in major: 3.36

PDF file retains all formatting— boldface, bullets, etc.

Relevant Areas of Study
- Buyer Behavior
- e-Business Ethics
- Management: Leadership and Learning
- Marketing Analysis
- Collaborating in the Workplace
- International Business

Study Abroad, Summer 2013, Southern Ohio University
Business Administration Program in Santiago, Chile
- Completed 10-week program
- Developed second-language skills in Spanish

Information chunked into logically divided sections

Business Internship
Archer Media Associates, Marketing Assistant, Spring 2012
- Drafting marketing copy for Archer's largest client, Techsure, Ltd.
- Led a team that created a marketing plan for 3 Amazon.com clients
- Prepared 8 major press releases for clients in health care, food service management, IT
- Tracked media coverage for clients
- Participated in corporate training seminars

Information is easy to access for employer through bulleted lists

Retail Experience
The Boutique, Sales Representative, 2010–2012
- Promoted to "key holder" (opened and closed store; supervised store short-term, Summer 2012)
- Helped train staff of 4 in weekly meetings
- Chaired 2-3 weekly meetings per quarter
- Implemented goal-oriented management strategies

Software Skills
- Lotus Notes, Access, Adobe InDesign, Illustrator, Photoshop, Excel

Hyperlinks allow employer to access further relevant information about candidate

Profiles
- LinkedIn: www.linkedin.com/in/bethpryor
- MarketingEdge: www.ms.marketingedge.com/profiles/bpryor

Webfolio
www.bethpryor.com/portfolio

Memberships
Student Marketing Association, Southern Ohio University
- Treasurer (senior year)
- Public Relations Committee (2 years)

References
Available on request.

FIGURE 5.11 A Scannable Version of Beth Pryor's Résumé

BETH PRYOR
PO Box 5112
Jamesville, OH 45056
bethpryor@hotmail.com

KEYWORDS
Marketing analyst, marketing management, e-business, business ethics, international clients, marketing plans, team spirit, media coverage writer, motivator

EDUCATION
Southern Ohio University
B.S. in Marketing; Minor: Spanish
Graduation: June 2014 — GPA in major: 3.36

RELEVANT AREAS OF STUDY
Buyer Behavior
e-Business Ethics
International Business
Management: Leadership and Learning
Marketing Analysis
Collaborating in the Workplace
Promotional Strategies

STUDY ABROAD, Summer 2013
Southern Ohio University Business Administration Program in Santiago, Chile
Graduate of 10-week program
Reader, speaker, intermediate Spanish

BUSINESS INTERNSHIP, Archer Media Associates, Spring 2012
Team marketing planner, amazon.com client
Writer, press releases and copy for clients in health care, food service, IT
Researcher, media coverage and visual designs
Participant, corporate training seminars

SALES MANAGEMENT EXPERIENCE, The Boutique, 2010-2012
Sales Representative
Key holder, 2011-2012
Staff trainer, 4 employees
Chair, 2-3 weekly meetings per quarter
Developer, goal-oriented management strategies

SOFTWARE
Lotus Notes, Access, Adobe InDesign, Illustrator, Photoshop, Excel

PROFILES
LinkedIn: www.linkedin.com/in/bethpryor
MarketingEdge: www.ms.marketingedge.com/profiles/bpryor

WEBFOLIO
www.bethpryor.com/portfolio

PROFESSIONAL MEMBERSHIP
Student Marketing Association

REFERENCES
Available on request

Omits personal details

Simple text easily scanned into company's HR database, which will search for keywords

Does not use boldfacing, italics, etc.

All text formatted flush left for easy scanning

Key sections are separated with extra spacing and all caps

Uses numbers instead of words when quantifying achievements

Supplies hyperlinks to profiles and individual website

Making Your Digital Résumé Search-Engine Ready

The most important section of your digital résumé contains the keywords you use. Prospective employers scan résumés to find the keywords they most want to see in the job seeker's description of his or her experience, education, and interpersonal skills. The more matches, or hits, they find between appropriate keywords in your résumé and those on their list, the better your chances are of being interviewed. List keywords throughout your résumé in appropriate places. Keywords should highlight your technical expertise, training and education, knowledge of a field, leadership ability, teamwork, writing/speaking skills, sales experience, and so on.

Here are a few tips to help you select and use appropriate keywords:

1. Provide a keyword section at the top of your résumé to give employers an immediate snapshot of your skills, as in Figures 5.8, 5.9, and 5.11.
2. Include the descriptive keywords found in the employer's ad and website in sections on education and experience to increase your chances of landing an interview.
3. Do not be afraid of using the shoptalk (or jargon) of your profession. An employer will expect you to be familiar with current terminology.
4. Use keywords to connect sections or categories of your résumé. Keyword headers will help you emphasize your job strengths and make it easy for employers to scroll back to an appropriate section of your résumé.
5. Replace the action verbs found in conventional résumés (on the left in the following list) with keyword nouns in digital résumés. Here are some examples:

Conventional Résumé	Digital Résumé
Wrote business report	Business report writer
Performed laboratory tests	Laboratory technician
Solved consumer complaints	Consumer advocate
Responsible for managing accounts	Accounts manager
Won three awards	Award winner
Edited company newsletter	Newsletter editor
Solved software problem	Software specialist

© Cengage Learning 2015

Making Your Résumé Cybersafe

Whether you use a database service or post your résumé on your own website, protect your identity and your current job. Be careful about revealing personal information.

- Post your résumé only on legitimate sites. Avoid those that say they will flood the market. You don't know where your résumé will end up.
- Do not put personal information in your résumé—home address, phone number, Social Security number, birthday, health status, or photograph.
- You may want to use an anonymous email address rather than your personal one if you are concerned about sharing personal information. Consider a

generic email address that includes a word or phrase that identifies your area of expertise.

- Never put the names of your references or their contact information online. Simply say, "References available on request."
- Never use your present employer's company name or business email address.

Testing, Proofreading, and Sending Your Digital Résumé

Never underestimate the negative impact of errors in your résumé, email, or application letter. Many prospective employers will discard a résumé if they spot a typo.

1. Test your formatting. Send your résumé to a friend to be sure your file is readable and formatted correctly.
2. Print out your résumé and proofread the hard copy carefully. Do not rely on spell-check alone. It is easy to overlook mistakes if you only proofread what is on your computer screen.
3. Don't just put "resume" as the subject of your email when sending your résumé to an employer. List the title, number, or code of the position for which you are applying.
4. Simply posting your résumé online is not enough. Also send a scannable hard copy and a letter of application (discussed next) to prospective employers. Do not fold or staple your résumé. Send it, along with your letter, in a large envelope ($8\frac{1}{2} \times 11$ inches).
5. Always keep a log of where you have posted your résumé online.

Letters of Application

Along with your résumé, you must send your prospective employer a letter of application, one of the most important pieces of correspondence you may ever write. Its goal is to get you an interview and ultimately the job. Letters you write in applying for jobs should be *personable*, *professional*, and *persuasive*—the three *P*'s. Knowing how the letter of application and résumé work together and how they differ can give you a better idea of how to compose your letter.

How Application Letters and Résumés Differ

The résumé is a persuasive record of dates, important achievements, skills, names, places, addresses, and jobs. As noted earlier, you may prepare several different résumés, depending on your experience and the job market.

Your letter of application, however, is much more personal. It introduces you to a prospective employer. Because you must write a new, original letter to each prospective employer, you may write (or adapt) many different letters. Each letter of application should be tailored to a specific job. It should respond precisely to the qualifications the employer seeks.

The letter of application is a sales letter that emphasizes and applies the most relevant details (of education, experience, and talents) in your résumé. In short, the résumé contains the raw material that the letter of application transforms into a finished and highly marketable product—you.

Résumé Facts to Exclude from Letters of Application

The letter of application should not simply repeat the details listed in your résumé. In fact, the following details that you would include in your résumé should *not* be restated in the letter:

- personal data, including license or certificate numbers
- specific course numbers
- names and addresses of your references

Writing the Letter of Application

The letter of application, such as those in Figures 5.12, 5.13, and 5.14 can make the difference between your getting an interview and your being eliminated early from consideration. It should convince a prospective employer that you will use the experience and education listed on your résumé in the job he or she is hoping to fill. You want your letter to be placed in the "definitely interview" category. As you prepare your letter, use the following general guidelines.

1. **Follow the standard conventions of letter writing.** Print your letter on good-quality, white 8½ × 11 inch paper. Proofread meticulously; a spelling error, typo, or grammatical mistake will make you look careless. As with your résumés, don't rely only on your spell checker.

2. **Supply all contact information as part of your heading.** Include home address, phone numbers, email address, and your website, if you have one. (see pages 101–102.)

3. **Make sure your letter looks attractive.** Use wide margins, and don't crowd information onto your page. Keep your paragraphs short and readable—no more than four or five sentences each.

4. **Send your letter to a specific person.** Never address an application letter "To Whom It May Concern," "Dear Sir or Madam," or "Dear Director of Human Resources." Get an individual's name from the company's website or by calling the company's main office, and be sure to verify the spelling of the person's name and his or her title.

5. **Don't send a form letter to every potential employer.** Stay away from generic application letter templates. Customize your letter to make sure you address the employer's specific needs.

6. **Be concise.** A one-page letter is standard in today's job market unless you have years of experience.

7. Emphasize the "you attitude." (See pages 109–112.) See yourself as an employer sees you. Focus on how your qualifications meet the employer's needs, not the other way around. Employers are not impressed by vain boasts ("I am the most efficient and effective safety engineer"). Convince prospective employers that you will be a valuable addition to their organization—a team player, a problem solver, an energetic representative, a skilled professional. (See pages 108–112.)

8. Don't be tempted to send out your first draft. Write and rewrite your letter of application until you are convinced it presents you in the best possible light. Getting the job may depend on it. A first or even second draft rarely sells your abilities as well as a third, fourth, or even fifth revision does.

The sections that follow give you some suggestions on how to prepare the various parts of an application letter successfully.

Your Opening Paragraph

The first paragraph of your letter of application is your introduction. It must get your reader's attention by answering four questions:

1. Why are you writing?
2. Where or how did you learn of the vacancy, the company, or the job?
3. What is the specific job title for which you are applying?
4. What is your most important qualification for the job?

Begin your letter by stating directly that you are writing to apply for a job. Don't say that you "want to apply for the job"; such an opening raises the question, "Why don't you, then?"

Avoid an unconventional or arrogant opening: "Are you looking for a dynamic, young, and talented accountant?" Do not begin with a question; be more positive and professional.

If you learned about the job through a newspaper or journal, make sure you italicize its title.

> I am applying for the food service manager position you advertised in the May 10 edition of the *Los Angeles Times* online.

Because many companies announce positions on the Internet, check there first to see if their position is listed online, as Anthony Jones did in Figure 5.12 (page 200).

If you learned of the job from a professor, a friend, or an employee at the firm, indicate that. Take advantage of a personal (networking) contact who is confident that you are qualified for and interested in the position, as María López (Figure 5.13, page 203) and Dora Cooper Bolger (Figure 5.14, page 204) did. But first confirm that your contact gives you permission to use his or her name.

You have to attract the reader's attention quickly and persuasively. In a sentence or two, tell the reader how your education and experience qualify you for the job. Use keywords from the job announcement.

The Body of Your Letter

The body of your letter, comprising one or two paragraphs, cites evidence from your résumé to prove you are qualified for the job. You might want to spend one

FIGURE 5.12 Letter of Application from Anthony Jones, a Recent Graduate with Little Job Experience

Clear and professional–looking letterhead

WEBSITE DEVELOPER
DESIGNER
GRAPHIC ARTIST

Anthony H. Jones
73 Allenwood Boulevard
Santa Rosa, CA 95401-1074
707-555-6390
ajdesigner@plat.com
www.plat.com/users/ajones/resume.html

May 16, 2014

Writes to a specific person

Ms. Jocelyn Nogasaki
Human Resources Manager
Megalith Publishing Company
1001 Heathcliff Row
San Francisco, CA 94123-7707

Dear Ms. Nogasaki:

Identifies position and source of ad

I am applying for the layout editor position advertised on your website, which I accessed on May 14. Early next month, I will receive an A.S. degree in commercial graphics illustration from Santa Rosa Junior College.

Applies education directly to employer's business

With a special interest in publishing, I have successfully completed more than 40 credit hours in courses directly related to layout design and gained experience using Adobe InDesign, QuarkXPress, Illustrator, and Photoshop. You might like to know that many Megalith publications were used as design and layout models in my graphics communications and digital photography courses.

Convincingly cites related job experience

My studies have also given me practical experience at McAdam Publishers as part of my Santa Rosa internship program. While working at McAdam, I was responsible for assisting the design department in page composition and archiving photos. Other related experiences I have include creating a website and brochure for the Santa Rosa Humane Society and designing and executing custom window displays at Buchman's Department Store. As the enclosed résumé indicates, a list of my references and a webfolio are available at **www.plat.com/users/ajones/resume.html.**

Refers to résumé/ webfolio

Asks for an interview and thanks employer

I would welcome the opportunity to discuss my qualifications in graphic design with you. My phone number, email address, and website are listed above. After June 8, I will be available for an interview at any time convenient for you.
Thank you for considering my application.

Sincerely yours,

Anthony H. Jones

Anthony H. Jones
Encl.: Résumé

paragraph on your education and one on your experience or combine your accomplishments into one paragraph.

Follow these guidelines for the body of your letter:

1. Keep your paragraphs short and readable—four or five sentences. Avoid long, complex sentences. Use the active voice to emphasize yourself as a doer. Review the action verbs in Table 5.3 (page 176) and, again, use keywords found in the employer's ad.

2. Don't begin each sentence with "I." Vary your sentence structure. Write reader-centered sentences, even those beginning with "I."

3. Concentrate on seeing yourself as a potential employer sees you. Prove that you can help an employer's sales and service, promote an organization's mission and goals, and be a reliable team player.

4. Highlight your qualifications by citing specific accomplishments. Tell your reader exactly how your education and job experience qualify you to perform and advance in the job advertised. Show how you can make a positive contribution to the employer's company. Don't simply say you are a great salesperson. Demonstrate your accomplishments by stressing that you increased the sales volume in your department by 15 percent within six months, you won an award or received a promotion for customer service, or you reduced costs by 10 percent. Prove you saved a lab money by comparison shopping equipment. Employers are not impressed by boasting or arrogance. They want hard facts to prove you are the right person for the job.

5. Mention you are enclosing your résumé. Put an "Encl." notation at the bottom of your letter.

Education   Recent graduates with little work experience, such as Anthony Jones in Figure 5.12, will, of course, spend more time discussing their education. Emphasize why and how your most significant educational accomplishments—course work, degrees, certificates, licenses, training—are relevant for the particular job. Mention significant extracurricular activities if they relate to the job description. Employers want to know which specific skills from your education translate into benefits for their company.

Simply saying you will graduate with a degree in criminal justice does not explain how you, unlike all the other graduates of such programs, are best suited for a particular job. Ask yourself which classes you took are most relevant for the employer. Consider grouping classes to show how and why you are the best qualified applicant for the job. For example, when you indicate that you have completed 36 credit hours in software security and have another 12 credit hours in global business, you prove you have an expertise other job candidates may not have. Note how Anthony Jones in Figure 5.12 and María López in Figure 5.13 (page 203) establish their educational qualifications with specific details about their training. Be sure to also mention internships or clinical training, as Jones and López do.

Experience   After you discuss your educational qualifications, turn to your job experience. But if your experience is your most valuable and extensive qualification for the job, put it before education and stress any previous experience similar to what a new position calls for. Be sure to stress any promotions or other leadership roles you have had. If you are switching careers or returning to a career after years away from the workplace, (because of military service, for example), start the body of your letter with your experience or your community and civic service, as Dora Cooper Bolger does in Figure 5.14 (page 204). Her volunteer work convincingly demonstrates she has the organizational and communication skills her prospective employer seeks. Never minimize such contributions.

Relate Your Education and Experience to the Job   Link your education and experience as benefits to the particular job you apply for. Persuasively show a prospective employer how your previous accomplishments, especially teamwork and responsibility, have prepared you for future success on the job. Relate your course work in computer science to being an efficient programmer. Indicate how your summer work for a local park district reinforced your exemplary skills in customer service. Connect your background to the prospective employer's company. Any homework you can do about the company's history, goals, or structure will pay off.

- By citing Megalith publications as a model in his courses, Anthony Jones stresses he is ready to start successfully from the first day on the job (Figure 5.12).
- Note how María López links her major school project and her work on a hospital pediatric unit to Dr. Henrady's specialty (Figure 5.13).
- Dora Cooper Bolger likewise proves that she is familiar with and can contribute to Tanselle's programs in community mental health though her extensive volunteer work and public speaking experience (Figure 5.14).

Closing

The purpose of your last paragraph is clear-cut—to convince the reader to call or email you for an interview. Keep your closing paragraph short—about two or three sentences—but be sure it fulfills the following four important functions:

1. briefly emphasizes once again your major qualifications
2. asks for an interview or a phone call
3. indicates when you are available for an interview
4. thanks the reader

End gracefully and professionally. Be straightforward. Don't leave the reader with a single weak, vague sentence: "I would like to have an interview at your convenience." That does nothing to sell you. Say that you would appreciate talking with the employer further to discuss your qualifications, as María López does in Figure 5.13. Then mention your chief talent. If you are applying for an international job or one far from home, you might request a phone call instead of an in-person interview. You might also express your willingness to relocate if the job requires it.

After indicating your interest in the job, give the times you are available for an interview and specifically tell the reader where you can be reached. If you are going

FIGURE 5.13 Letter of Application from María López, a Recent Graduate with Some Job Experience

1725 Brooke Street
Miami, FL 32701-2121
(305) 555-3429 • mlopez@eagle.com

May 15, 2014

Dr. Marvin Henrady
Medical/Dental Plaza, Suite 34
839 Causeway Drive
Miami, FL 32706-2468

Dear Dr. Henrady:

Mr. Mitchell Pelbourne, my clinical instructor at Miami-Dade Community College, informs me you are looking for a dental hygienist to work in your northside office. My education and experience qualify me for that position. This month I will graduate with an A.S. degree in the dental hygienist program, and I will take the American Dental Assisting National Board exams in early June.

I have successfully completed all course work and clinical programs in oral hygiene, anatomy, and prophylaxis techniques. During my clinical training, I received intensive practical instruction from several local dentists, including Dr. Pia Gutiérrez. Since your northside office specializes in pediatric dental care, you might find the subject of my major project—proper nutrition and dental care for preschoolers—especially relevant.

My related job experience working with children in a health care setting would be both relevant for and helpful to your office. For over two years, I was a unit assistant on the pediatric unit at St. Francis Hospital, and am experienced in greeting patients, transcribing medical orders and surgical notes, and assisting the nursing staff. An additional job strength I would bring to your office is my bilingual (Spanish/English) communication skills. You will find more detailed information about my accomplishments in the enclosed résumé.

I would appreciate the opportunity to talk with you about the position and my interest in pediatric dental care. I am available for an interview any time after 2:00 pm until June 9th, but after that date I could come by your office at any time at your convenience. Thank you for your consideration.

Sincerely yours,

María López

María López

Encl. Résumé

Uses professional-looking letterhead with contact information

Begins with personal contact

Verifies she will have necessary licensure

Links training to job responsibilities; demonstrates knowledge of employer's office

Relates previous experience to employer's needs; refers to résumé

Ends with a polite request for an interview and thanks reader

FIGURE 5.14 Letter of Application from Dora Cooper Bolger, a Job Candidate with Years of Community and Civic Experience

Email address emphasizing professional achievement

DORA COOPER BOLGER

1215 Lakeview Avenue
Westhampton, MI 46532
Cell: 616-555-4773
dcbplanner@aol.com

February 10, 2014

Dr. Lindsay Bafaloukos, Director
Tanselle Mental Health Agency
4400 West Gallagher Drive
Tanselle, MI 46932-3106

Dear Dr. Bafaloukos:

Begins with contact made at professional meeting, highlighting her qualifications

At a recent meeting of the County Services Council, a member of your staff, Homer Steen, told me that you will soon be hiring a public affairs coordinator. Because of my extensive experience in and commitment to community affairs, I would appreciate your considering me for this opening. I expect to receive my B.S. in Public Administration from Mid-Michigan College later this year.

Relates proven past successes to employer's needs; gives concrete examples of her skills

For the past ten years, I have organized community groups with outreach programs similar to Tanselle's. I have held administrative positions in the PTA and the Foster Parents' Association and served as president of Teens in Trouble, a volunteer group providing assistance to dysfunctional teens. My responsibilities with Teens have included coordinating counseling activities with various school programs, scheduling tutorials, and representing the organization before local and state governmental agencies. I have been commended for my organizational and communication skills. My twenty-four presentations on foster home care and Teens in Trouble also demonstrate that I am an effective speaker, a skill I could put to work for Tanselle immediately.

Encourages reader to see her as best-prepared candidate; includes résumé

Because of my work at Mid-Michigan as well as for Teens and Foster Parents, I have the practical experience in communication and psychology to promote Tanselle's goals successfully. The enclosed résumé provides details about my experience, education, and honors I have received.

Requests interview and thanks reader

I would appreciate an opportunity to discuss my work with Teens and other organizations I represented and how I might assist Tanselle with its programs. I am available for an interview at your convenience. Thanks for considering my interest in and qualifications for your public affairs coordinator position.

Sincerely yours,

Dora Cooper Bolger

Dora Cooper Bolger

Encl. Résumé

to a professional meeting that the employer might also attend, or if you are visiting the employer's city soon, say so.

The following samples show how *not* to close your letter and explain why.

> **Pushy:** I would like to set up an interview with you. Please phone me to arrange a convenient time. [That's the employer's prerogative, not yours.]
>
> **Too Informal:** I do not live far from your office. Let's meet for coffee sometime next week. [Say instead that because you live nearby, you will be available for an interview.]
>
> **Introduces New Subject:** I would like to discuss other qualifications you have in mind for the job. [How do you know what the interviewer might have in mind?]

Note that the closing paragraphs in Figures 5.12, 5.13, and 5.14 avoid these errors.

Going to an Interview

There are various ways for a prospective employer to conduct an interview. It might be a one-on-one meeting—you and the interviewer—or you may visit with a group of individuals or even with several groups from different divisions in the company to decide if you would fit in. You could have an interview over the telephone, or through a videoconference, or via Skype.

Preparing for an Interview

Before you go to an interview, prepare by doing the following:

1. Do your homework about the company. Show you are interested in the company by learning as much as you can about it. Imagine how embarrassing it would be if an employer asked you what you know about the firm and you could not reply with a relevant answer. Click on "About Us" and other links on the corporate or agency website to find out who founded the company, who the current CEO is, if it is a local firm or a subsidiary, its chief products or services, how many years it has been in business, how many employees it has, where its main office and plants are, and who its major clients and competitors are. Find the company's profile on LinkedIn. Read company websites, blogs, and brochures to get a sense of the corporate culture. Also look for recent stories about the company in leading business publications, such as the following:

- *The Wall Street Journal*—www.online.wsj.com
- *The New York Times*—www.nytimes.com
- *USA Today*—www.usatoday.com
- *Bloomberg Businessweek*—www.businessweek.com
- *Fast Company*—www.fastcompany.com
- *Fortune*—www.fortune.com
- *Forbes*—www.forbes.com

2. Review the job description carefully. Research the job—what does it entail? What skills do you have that relate directly to the job?

3. Prepare a one- or two-minute summary of your chief qualifications. You will most likely be asked to summarize your education, experience, teamwork, and professional goals during the job interview. In doing so, identify how specific classes, course projects, jobs you have held, or community service have equipped you for the position the company wants to fill. Provide examples.

4. Take your portfolio, including three or four extra copies of your résumé, with you. Also bring a notepad and a pen (or your tablet) to write down essential details.

5. Practice your interview skills with a friend or job counselor. Be sure that this person asks tough questions about your education and experience so that you will get practice answering these questions realistically and convincingly.

6. Brush up on business etiquette. Silence your phone before your interview. Remember the name(s) of the interviewer(s) and others you may meet. Always be polite and respectful, saying "Thank you," "You're welcome," and so on. Pay special attention to acceptable ways of communicating with international audiences if your interview is with a multinational company or with a non-native speaker of English.

7. Bring your photo ID and Social Security card. Also bring any licenses or certificates you may be asked to present to a human resources office. If you are not a U.S. citizen, bring your work visa.

Questions to Expect at Your Interview

The following questions are typical of those you can expect from interviewers, with advice on how to answer them.

- **Tell us something about yourself.** Emphasize achievements that show you are responsible (e.g., working to pay for your tuition), conscientious (participating in a community or service activity), and eager to contribute to and learn more about your profession and potential employer.
- **Why do you want to work for us?** Recall any job goals you have and apply them specifically to the job under discussion.
- **What qualifications do you have for the job?** Point to educational achievements and relevant work experience, especially IT skills.
- **What could you offer us that other candidates do not have? Why should we hire you?** Say enthusiasm, being a team player, problem-solving skills, ability to meet deadlines under stress. Emphasize that you are diplomatic yet goal oriented.
- **Why did you attend this school?** Be honest—location, costs, programs.
- **Why did you major in "X"?** Do not simply say financial benefits; concentrate on professional goals and interests.
- **Why did you get a grade of C in a course?** Don't say that you could have done better if you'd tried. Explain what the trouble was, and mention that you corrected it in a course in which you earned a B or an A.

- **What extracurricular activities did you participate in while in high school or college?** Indicate any responsibilities you had—managing money, preparing minutes, coordinating events. If you were unable to participate in such activities, tell the interviewer that a part-time job or community or church activities prevented you from participating. Such answers sound better than saying that you did not like sports or clubs in school.

- **Did you learn as much as you wanted from your course work?** This is a loaded question. Indicate that you learned a great deal but now look forward to the opportunity to gain more practical skills, to put into practice the principles and procedures you have learned.

- **What is your greatest strength?** Say being a team player, planning and organizing tasks efficiently, concerned about the environment, being cooperative and willing to learn, having the ability to grasp difficult concepts easily, wanting to find a more efficient or economical way of doing something, being proficient at managing time or money, taking criticism easily, and profiting from it.

- **What is your greatest shortcoming?** Be honest here and mention it, but then turn to ways in which you are improving. Don't say something deadly like, "I can never seem to finish what I start" or "I hate being criticized." You should neither dwell on your weaknesses nor keep silent about them. Saying "None" to this kind of question is as inadvisable as rattling off a list of faults.

- **How do you handle conflict with a co-worker, supervisor, or customer?** Stress your ability to be courteous and honest and to work toward a productive resolution. State that you avoid language, tone of voice, or gestures that interfere with healthy dialogue. Describe a specific situation where you resolved a problem with maturity and grace. Indicate what you learned that helped you on the job.

- **Why did you leave your last job?** Say "I returned to school full time" or "I moved from Jackson to Springfield," or say that you changed professions. *Never attack your previous employer.* That only makes you look bad.

- **Why would you leave your current job?** Again, never attack an individual or an organization. Say your current job has prepared you for the position you are now applying for. Emphasize your desire to work for a specific company because of its goals, work environment, and opportunities.

- **What are your career goals over the next three to five years?** State your career objectives in terms of what you would like to accomplish for the company, your profession, the community, and yourself. Be confident, not cocky.

What Do I Say About Salary?

Find out what the salary range is for your professional level in your area. Consult the U.S. Bureau of Labor Statistics' *Occupational Outlook Handbook* at www.bls.gov/ooh as well as www.salary.com. You can also ask your instructors or individuals you know who work for the company or call your professional organization for information. If the issue of salary comes up, ask if the company has established a salary range for the position and where you stand in relationship to that range. However, because many companies set fixed salaries for entry-level positions, it may be unwise to try to negotiate.

If you are asked what salary you expect for the job, do not give an exact figure. You may undercut yourself if the employer has a higher figure in mind. By doing your homework on salary ranges, you will have a better feel for the market when the employer does mention salary.

Factor other benifits into your salary calculations—health insurance, day care, housing, uniform/clothing allowances, product or service discounts, opportunities for travel and language instruction, and tuition reimbursement.

Questions You May Ask the Interviewer(s)

You will have a chance to ask the interviewer(s) questions. Watch for appropriate cues, and be prepared to say more than "No, I don't have any questions," which suggests either indifference or lack of preparation on your part. Here are some legitimate questions you can ask interviewers:

1. Will there be any safety, security, or proficiency requirements I will need to meet?
2. When is the starting date?
3. Is there a probationary period? If so, how long?
4. How often will my work be evaluated (monthly, quarterly, semiannually) and by whom (immediate superior, committee)?
5. What types of on-the-job training are required or offered?
6. Are there any mentoring programs in place?
7. Is there any support for continuing my education to improve my job performance?
8. What is the next step in your hiring process?

Also, ask questions about the company's products and services, including a dedication to greening the environment.

What Interviewer(s) Can't Ask You

Federal and state laws limit the questions an interviewer can ask you. Questions about your age, marital status, the number or names of any children, religion, race, national origin, disabilities, or sexual orientation violate equal opportunity employment laws. Even so, some employers may disguise their interest in those subjects by asking you indirect questions about them. A question such as "Will your husband care if you have to work overtime?" or "How many children do you have?" could probe into your personal life. Confronted with such questions, it is best to answer them positively ("My home life will not interfere with my job," "My family understands that overtime may be required") rather than bristling defensively, "It's none of your business if I'm married."

Ten Interview Do's and Don'ts

Keep in mind these other interview do's and don'ts:

1. Be on time. In fact, show up about fifteen minutes early in case the interviewer or human resources office wants you to complete some forms.
2. Turn off your cell phone and any other media device! The last thing you want is for your phone to ring or receive a text message during your interview. Never text during an interview.
3. Dress appropriately for the occasion and be well groomed. Avoid using strong perfume or cologne. Men: Wear a dark solid-color or pinstripe suit and tie. Women: Wear a suit (pants or skirt) or other equally business-like attire.
4. Be careful about tattoos. Job counselors warn that visible tattoos can hurt a job seeker's chance for success.
5. Greet the interviewer with a friendly and firm, but not vicelike, handshake. Don't be a wimp, either, with a limp, fishy handshake. Thank the interviewer for inviting you.
6. Don't sit down before the interviewer does. Wait for the interviewer to invite you to sit and to indicate where.
7. Speak slowly and distinctly; do not nervously hurry to finish your sentences, and never interrupt or finish an interviewer's sentences. Avoid one- or two-word answers, which sound unfriendly or unprepared. Do not use slang (e.g., "Awesome!" or "Chill") or overly casual language ("Like…" "You know?"). Don't monopolize the discussion by talking too much and always about yourself. And don't act arrogantly as if the job is yours already. Show a keen interest in the company and its products, services, employees, contributions to the environment.
8. Do not chew gum, click a ballpoint pen, fidget, twirl your hair, or tap your foot against the floor, a chair, or a desk.
9. Maintain appropriate eye contact with the interviewer; do not sheepishly stare at the floor or the desk. If you are interviewed by a group of individuals, make eye contact with each one of them. Body language is equally important. Don't fold your arms—a signal that you are closed to the interviewer's suggestions and comments. Sit up straight; do not slouch. Smile; it shows you are confident.
10. When the interview is over, thank the interviewer(s) for considering you for the job, and say you look forward to hearing from him or her.

The Follow-Up Letter

Within a week after the interview, it is wise to send a follow-up letter, not an email, thanking the interviewer for his or her time and interest in you. In your letter, reemphasize your qualifications for the job by showing how they apply to the requirements described by the interviewer. You might also ask for further information to show your interest in the job and the employer. The sample follow-up letter in Figure 5.15 on page 210 accomplishes all of these things.

FIGURE 5.15 A Follow-Up Letter

2739 EAST STREET
LATROBE, PA 17042-0312

610-555-6373
mlb@springboard.com

September 22, 2014

Mr. Jack Fukura, Director
Human Resources Dept.
Global Tech
1334 Ridge Road N.E.
Pittsburgh, PA 17122-3107

Dear Mr. Fukura:

Expresses gratitude for an interview and singles out main company feature

I enjoyed talking with you last Wednesday and learning more about the security officer position available at Global Tech. It was especially helpful to take a tour of the plant's north gate to see the challenges it presents for the security officer stationed there.

Reemphasizes qualifications

As you noted at the interview, my training in surveillance electronics has prepared me to operate the sophisticated equipment Global Tech has recently installed. Please thank Ms. Turner for me for taking time to demonstrate this technology.

Asks for newsletter to express future interest

I look forward to receiving the handbook about Global Tech's employee services. Would you also kindly email me a copy of the newsletter from last quarter that introduced the new security equipment to your employees?

Ends politely by thanking interviewer

Thank you, again, for interviewing me for the position and your hospitality. Please let me know if you have any other questions. I look forward to hearing from you.

Sincerely yours,

Marcia Le Borde

Marcia Le Borde

Accepting or Declining a Job Offer

If you accept a job, send the employer a letter within a week of the offer. Accepting verbally on the phone is not enough, and never accept or decline a job offer through an email, text, or tweet. Your letter will make your acceptance official and will probably be included in your permanent personnel file. Accepting a job is easy. Make the communication with your new employer a model of clarity and diplomacy.

Refusing a job requires tact. You are obligated to inform an employer why you are not taking the job. But do not bluntly begin with the refusal. Instead, prepare the reader for bad news by finding something about the company or agency to compliment—its products, the friendly work environment, the interview process, etc. Then move to your refusal and supply an honest but not elaborate explanation of why you are not taking the job. Many students cite educational opportunities, work schedules, geographic preference, or additional professional opportunities. End on a friendly note because you may be interested in working for the company in the future and do not want to leave any bad feelings.

Searching for the Right Job Pays

As we saw, finding the right job takes a lot of hard work (researching, organizing, networking, and writing). But all your efforts will pay off with your first and subsequent checks. May all your letters, résumés, portfolios/webfolios, and applications be models of successful writing at work.

✔ Revision Checklist

- ☐ Enhanced my professional image to apply for jobs for which I am qualified.
- ☐ Looked for relevant jobs on social and professional networking sites.
- ☐ Created a professional profile for Facebook and LinkedIn.
- ☐ Joined groups on LinkedIn to increase my network.
- ☐ Did not put personal information on a job board/the Internet.
- ☐ Prepared a dossier at school placement office, including supporting letters from professors, employers, and community officials.
- ☐ Identified places where relevant jobs are advertised.
- ☐ Networked with instructors, friends, relatives, and individuals who work for the companies I want to join; notified them that I am looking for a job.
- ☐ Researched the companies I am interested in—on the Internet, through printed sources, and by networking with current employees.
- ☐ Inventoried my strengths carefully to prepare résumé.
- ☐ Wrote a focused and persuasive career-objective statement.
- ☐ Determined the most beneficial format of résumé to use—chronological, functional, or both.

☐ Investigated creating a website for my job search–related documents.

☐ Prepared a portfolio/webfolio that includes documents demonstrating my professional skills and achievements relevant for the job.

☐ Made résumé attractive and easy to read, with logical and persuasive headings and descriptive keywords.

☐ Made sure résumé contains neither too much nor too little information.

☐ Proofread résumé to ensure everything is correct, consistent, and accurate.

☐ Adapted military experience for a civilian employer's job listing.

☐ Created properly formatted digital résumé to send to prospective employers.

☐ Wrote a letter of application that shows how my specific skills and background meet an employer's exact needs.

☐ Prepared a short oral presentation about myself and my accomplishments for an interview.

☐ Researched prospective employer's company or organization and salary range.

☐ Sent prospective employer a follow-up letter within a few days after interview to thank the interviewer and show interest in position.

Exercises

1. Using at least four different sources, including LinkedIn, compile a list of ten employers for whom you would like to work. Get their names, street and email addresses, phone numbers, and the names of the managers or human resources officers. Then select one company and profile it—locations, services, kinds of products or services offered, number of employees, clients served, awards, contributions to the community or environment, and any other pertinent facts.

2. Create an appropriate professional profile for LinkedIn.

3. Write a letter to a former employer, a community leader, or an instructor requesting a letter of recommendation.

4. Which of the following would belong on your résumé? Which would not belong? Why?
   a. your student ID number
   b. your driver's license number
   c. the zip codes of your references
   d. a list of all your English courses in college
   e. the section numbers of the courses in your major

    f. a statement that you are recently divorced

    g. subscriptions to journals in your field

    h. the titles of stories or poems you published in a high school literary magazine or newspaper

    i. your GPA for each year you were in college

    j. foreign languages you studied

    k. years you attended college

    l. the date you were discharged from the service

    m. names of the neighbors you are using as references

    n. your religion

    o. job titles you held

    p. your summer job waiting tables

    q. your telephone number

    r. the reason you changed schools

    s. your current status with the National Guard

    t. the URL of your website or blog

    u. your volunteer work for the Red Cross

    v. the number of hours per week you spend reading science fiction

    w. the title of your last term paper in your major

    x. the name of the agency or business where you worked last

5. Indicate what is wrong with the following career objectives, and rewrite them to make them more precise and professional.

    a. Job in a lawyer's office

    b. Position with a safety emphasis

    c. Desire growth position in a large department store

    d. Am looking for entry position in health sciences

    e. Position in sales with fast promotion rate

    f. Want a job working with semiconductor circuits

    g. Desire a good-paying job, hours: 8–4:30, with time and a half for overtime. Would like to stay in the Omaha area

    h. Insurance work

    i. Working with media

    j. Job with preschoolers

    k. Full-time position with hospitality chain

    l. I want a career in nursing

    m. Police work, particularly in a suburb of a large city

    n. Any position for a qualified dietitian

    o. Although I have not made up my mind about which area of forestry I shall go into, I am looking for a job that offers me training and rewards based upon my potential

6. As part of a team or on your own, revise the following poor résumé to make it more precise and persuasive. Include additional details where necessary and exclude any details that would hurt the job seeker's chances. Also correct any inconsistencies.

RÉSUMÉ OF

Powell T. Harrison
8604 So. Kirkpatrick St.
Ardville, Ohio
345 37 8760
614 234 4587
harrison@gem.com

PERSONAL	Confidential
CAREER OBJECTIVE	Seek good paying position with progressive Sunbelt company.
EDUCATION	
2012–2014	Will receive degree from Central Tech. Institute in Arch. St. Earned high average last semester. Took necessary courses for major; interested in systems, plans, and design development.
2010–2012	Attended Ardville High School, Ardville, OH; took all courses required. Served on several student committees.
EXPERIENCE	None, except for numerous part-time jobs and student apprenticeship in the Ardville area. As part of student app. worked with local firm for two months.
HOBBIES	Surfing the Net, playing Nintendo DSi, Member of Junior Achievement.
REFERENCES	Please write for names and addresses.

© Cengage Learning 2015

7. Determine what is wrong with the following sentences in a letter of application. Rewrite them to eliminate any mistakes, to focus on the "you attitude," or to make them more precise.
   a. Even though I have very little actual job experience, I can make up for it in enthusiasm.
   b. My qualifications will prove that I am the best person for your job.
   c. I would enjoy working with your other employees.
   d. This email résumé is my application for any job you now have open or expect to fill in the near future.

e. Next month, my family and I will be moving to Detroit, and I must get a job in the area. Will you have anything open?

f. If you are interested in me, then I hope that we make some type of arrangements to interview each other soon.

g. I have not included a résumé because all pertinent information about me is in this letter.

h. My GPA is only 2.5, but I did make two B's in my last term.

i. I hope to take state boards soon.

j. Your company, or so I have heard through the grapevine, has excellent fringe benefits. That is what I care about most, so I am applying for any position that you may advertise.

k. I am writing to ask you to kindly consider whether I would be a qualified person for the position you announced in the newspaper.

l. I have made plans to further my education.

m. My résumé speaks for itself.

n. I could not possibly accept a position that required weekend work, and night work is out, too.

o. In my own estimation, I am a go-getter—an eager beaver, so to speak.

p. My last employer was dead wrong when he let me go. I think he regrets it now.

q. When you want to arrange an interview time, give me a call. I am home every afternoon after 4:00.

8. Explain why the following letter of application is ineffective. Rewrite it to make it more precise and appropriate.

Apartment 32

Jeggler Drive

Talcott, Arizona

Monday

Grandt Corporation

Production Supervisor

Capital City, Arizona

Dear Sir:

I am writing to ask you if your company will consider me for the position you announced online recently. I believe that with my education (I have an associate degree) and experience (I have worked four years as a freight supervisor), I could fill your job.

My schoolwork was done at two junior colleges, and I took more than enough courses in business management and information technology.

In fact, here is a list of some of my courses: Supervision, Materials Management, Work Experience in Management, E-commerce, Safety Tactics, Introduction to Software Analysis, Art Design, Contemporary Business Principles, and Small Business Management. In addition, I have worked as a loading dock supervisor for the last two years, and before that I worked in the military in the Quartermaster Corps.

Please let me know if you are interested in me. I would like to have an interview with you at the earliest possible date, since there are some other firms also interested in me, too.

Eagerly yours,

George D. Milhous

© Cengage Learning

9. In the weekend edition of your local newspaper or in one of the other sources discussed on pages 161–165, find notices for two or three jobs you believe you are qualified to fill, and then write a letter of application for one of them.

10. Write a chronological résumé to accompany the letter you wrote for Exercise 9.

11. Write a functional résumé to accompany your application letter in Exercise 9.

12. Bring the two résumés you prepared for Exercises 10 and 11 to class to be critiqued by a collaborative writing team. After your résumés are reviewed, revise them. Write an email to your instructor about the revisions you made, and explain why they will help you in your job search. Attach your résumé to the email.

13. Prepare a digital version of the résumé you prepared in either Exercise 10 or Exercise 11.

14. Write a letter to a local business inquiring about summer employment. Indicate that you can work only for three months because you will be returning to school by September 1. Include an appropriate résumé.

CHAPTER 6

Designing Successful Documents, Visuals, and Websites

The success of your document depends as much on how it looks as on what it says. You will be expected to design professional-looking memos, letters, instructions, and reports; to create blogs and websites; and to provide appropriate visuals to support these documents. This chapter gives you practical advice for making your work more reader-friendly and visually appealing. It also surveys the kinds of visuals you will encounter most frequently and shows you how to read, construct, and write about them.

Characteristics of Effective Design

In designing documents and websites, you need to project a positive, professional image of yourself, your company, and your product or service. A report or website filled with nothing but thick, unbroken long paragraphs crowded to the margins, with no visual clues to break them up or to make information stand out, is sure to intimidate readers and turn them away. They will conclude that your work is too complex and not worth their effort or time. Your company, too, will win or lose points because of your design choices. A visually appealing document or website will enhance a company's reputation and improve its sales. A poorly designed one will not.

Make your documents look user-friendly—clear and logical—by signaling to your audience that your message is

- easy to read
- easy to follow and understand
- easy to recall

Organizing Information Visually

Today's web-based culture prizes visual thinking when you design all kinds of documents. The way you organize and visualize information can help readers move quickly and clearly through your document. Take a quick look at Figures 6.1

Chapter opening image. © dimitris_k/ShutterStock.com

and 6.2 (pages 219–222). The same information is contained in each figure. Which visually appeals to you more? Which do you think would be easier to read? Which is better designed? As the two figures show, design or layout plays a crucial role in an audience's overall acceptance of your work.

Figure 6.2 exemplifies the effective design characteristics (on the left) while Figure 6.1 displays the ineffective ones (on the right).

<table>
<tr><td>

Effective Design

- visually appealing
- logically organized
- clear
- accessible
- varied
- relevant

</td><td>

Ineffective Design

- crowded
- disorganized
- hard to follow
- difficult to read
- boring, repetitive
- inconsistent

</td></tr>
</table>

Study the annotations to these figures to see how the errors in Figure 6.1 are corrected in Figure 6.2. By modeling your written work after the document in Figure 6.2, you can guarantee that your readers will appreciate your layout.

The ABCs of Print Document Design

The basic elements of effective document design are

- page layout
- typography, or type design, including using color
- graphics, or visuals

The proper arrangement and balance of type, white space, and graphics involve the same level of preparation that you would spend on your research, drafting, revising, and editing. Just as you do research to find information, you have to research and experiment in order to adopt the most effective design for your document.

Page Layout

Each of your pages needs to coordinate space and text pleasingly. Too much or too little of one or the other can jeopardize the reader's acceptance of your message. To design an effective page layout, pay attention to the following elements.

   1. White space. White space (blank space), which refers to open areas on a page, such as margins and space around images, is free of text and visuals. It can help you increase the impact and tone of your message. Skimping on white space by packing too much print on the page only distracts the reader from the message you want to convey. White space, on the other hand, can entice, comfort, and appeal to the reader's "psychology of space" by

- attracting the reader's attention
- assuring the reader that information is presented logically
- announcing that information is easy to follow

FIGURE 6.1 A Poorly Designed Document

The results for the recent cholesterol screening at *our company's Health Fair* were distributed to each employee last week. Many employees wanted to know more about cholesterol in general, the different types of cholesterol, what the results mean, and the foods that are high or low in cholesterol.

We hope the information provided below will help employees better answer their questions concerning cholesterol and our cholesterol screening program.

High cholesterol, along with high blood pressure and obesity, is one of the primary risk factors that may contribute to the development of coronary heart disease and may eventually lead to a heart attack or stroke. Cholesterol is a fatty, sticky substance found in the bloodstream. Excessive amounts of the bad type of cholesterol can deposit on the walls of the heart arteries. *This deposit is called plaque, and over a long period of time plaque can narrow or even block the blood flow through the arteries.*

Total cholesterol is divided into three parts—LDL (low-density lipoprotein), or bad cholesterol; HDL (high-density lipoprotein), or good cholesterol; and VLDL (very low-density lipoprotein), a much smaller component of cholesterol you don't have to worry about. Bad (LDL) cholesterol forms on the walls of your arteries and can cause a lot of damage. Good cholesterol, on the other hand, functions like a sponge, mopping up cholesterol and carrying it out of the bloodstream.

You should have received *three cholesterol numbers.* One is for your HDL (or good cholesterol) and the other is for your LDL, or bad cholesterol, reading. These two numbers are added to give you the third, or composite, level of your total cholesterol.

As you can see, a total cholesterol reading of below 200 is considered safe. Continue what you have been doing. If your reading falls in the moderate risk range of 200–239, you need to modify your diet, get more exercise, and have your cholesterol checked again in six months. *If your reading is above 240, see your doctor.* You may need to take cholesterol-lowering medication, if your doctor prescribes it. Reducing your total cholesterol by even as little as 25% can decrease your risk of a heart attack by 50%.

The Surgeon General recommends that your LDL, or bad cholesterol, should be below 130; and your HDL, or good cholesterol, needs to be at least above 36. Ideally, the ratio between the two numbers should not be greater than 5 to 1. That is, your HDL should be at least 20% of your LDL. The higher your HDL is, the better, of course. So even if you have a high LDL reading, if your HDL is correspondingly high you will be at less risk.

One of the easiest ways to decrease your cholesterol is to modify your diet. Cholesterol is found in foods that are high in saturated fat. *Saturated fat comes from animal sources and also from certain vegetable sources.* Foods high in bad cholesterol that you should restrict or avoid, include whole milk, red meat, eggs, cheese, butter, shrimp, oils such as palm and coconut, and avocados. Generally, food groups low in cholesterol include fruits, vegetables, and whole grains (assorted wheat breads, oatmeal, and certain cereals), *lean meats (fish, chicken)*, and beans.

The goal of our cholesterol screening is to help each employee lower his or her cholesterol level and eventually reduce the risk of heart disease. **Besides the advice given above**, you can do the following: get regular aerobic exercise—bicycling, brisk walking, swimming, rowing—for at least 30 minutes 3–4 times a week. But get your doctor's approval first. *Eat foods low in cholesterol* but high in dietary fiber (beans, oatmeal, brown rice). Maintain a healthy weight for your frame to lower your body fat. Minimize stress, which can increase cholesterol. Learn relaxation techniques.

No title

Single-spacing makes document difficult to read

Lack of headings in color or boldface makes it hard for readers to organize material

Arbitrary font changes confuse readers

Uneven presentation of numbers

Lack of adequate margins makes document look dense and complex

Unnecessary italics are confusing

Inconsistent use of italics and boldfacing

© Cengage Learning

FIGURE 6.2 An Effectively Designed Document with the Same Text as Figure 6.1

Title clearly set apart from text with capitalization, larger font, and use of color

Text is double-spaced with more ample margins, making it more readable

Headings in color and larger font divide material into easy-to-follow units for readers

Consistent use of one font for text

Only key words being defined are boldfaced

Page does not look cluttered

Types of cholesterol are helpfully labeled with numbers

Cholesterol Screening

The results for the recent cholesterol screening at our company's Health Fair were distributed to each employee last week. Many employees wanted to know more about cholesterol in general, the different types of cholesterol, what the results mean, and the foods that are high or low in cholesterol. We hope the information provided below will help employees better answer their questions concerning cholesterol and our cholesterol screening program.

Determining Risk Factors

High cholesterol, along with high blood pressure and obesity, is one of the primary risk factors that may contribute to the development of coronary heart disease and may eventually lead to a heart attack or stroke. Cholesterol is a fatty, sticky substance found in the bloodstream. Excessive amounts of the bad type of cholesterol can deposit on the walls of the heart arteries. This deposit is called **plaque** and over a long period of time plaque can narrow or even block the blood flow through the arteries.

Separating Types of Cholesterol

Total cholesterol is divided into three parts: (1) **LDL** (low-density lipoprotein), or bad cholesterol; (2) **HDL** (high-density lipoprotein), or good cholesterol; and (3) **VLDL** (very low-density lipoprotein), a much smaller component of cholesterol you don't have to worry about. Bad (LDL) cholesterol forms on the walls of your arteries and can cause a lot of damage. Good cholesterol, on the other hand, functions like a sponge, mopping up cholesterol and carrying it out of the bloodstream.

1

FIGURE 6.2 (Continued)

Understanding Your Cholesterol Results

You should have received three cholesterol numbers. One is for your **HDL** (or good cholesterol), and the other is for your **LDL** (or bad cholesterol) reading. These two numbers are added to give you the third, or composite, level of your total cholesterol.

Cholesterol levels can be classified as follows:

Minimal Risk	Moderate Risk	High Risk
below 200	200–239	above 240

As you can see, a total cholesterol reading of below 200 is considered safe. You are doing fine. Continue what you have been doing. If your reading falls in the moderate risk range of 200–239, you need to modify your diet, get more exercise, and have your cholesterol checked again in six months. If your reading is above 240, see your doctor. You may need to take cholesterol-lowering medication, if your doctor prescribes it. Reducing your total cholesterol by even as little as 25% can decrease your risk of a heart attack by 50%.

Knowing the Relationship Between Bad and Good Cholesterol

The Surgeon General recommends that your **LDL**, or bad cholesterol, be below 130. And your **HDL**, or good cholesterol, needs to be at least above 36. Ideally, the ratio between the two numbers should not be greater than 5 to 1. That is, your **HDL** should be at least 20% of your **LDL**. The higher your **HDL** is, the better, of course. So even if you have a high **LDL** reading, if your **HDL** is correspondingly high you will be at less risk.

Recognizing Food Sources of Cholesterol

One of the easiest ways to decrease your cholesterol is to modify your diet. Cholesterol is found in foods that are high in saturated fat. Saturated fat

Concise paragraph provides clear opening for new section

Emphasizes range of risk categories by setting them apart in a shaded box

Paragraph clearly defines and distinguishes numbers

Includes additional space between sections

Paragraphs are neither too long nor too short

Functional use of boldface, not overdone

Headings consistently formatted

Page is numbered in footer

FIGURE 6.2 (Continued)

comes from animal sources and also from certain vegetable sources. Foods high in bad cholesterol that you should restrict include:

1. whole milk
2. red meat
3. eggs
4. cheese
5. butter
6. shrimp
7. oils such as palm and coconut
8. avocados

Generally, food groups low in cholesterol include fruits, vegetables, and whole grains (wheat breads, oatmeal, and certain cereals), lean meats (fish, chicken), and beans.

Realizing It Is Up to You

The goal of our cholesterol screening program is to help each employee lower his or her cholesterol level and eventually reduce the risk of heart disease. Besides the advice given above, you can do the following:

- Get regular aerobic exercise—bicycling, brisk walking, swimming, rowing—for at least 30 minutes 3–4 times a week. But get your doctor's approval first.
- Eat foods low in cholesterol but high in dietary fiber (beans, oatmeal, brown rice).
- Maintain a healthy weight for your frame to lower your body fat.
- Minimize stress, which can increase cholesterol. Learn relaxation techniques.

3

A double-spaced, numbered list helps readers easily identify foods with bad cholesterol

Easy-to-follow examples of foods low in cholesterol in parentheses

Heading signals conclusion

Bulleted list serves as both conclusion and plan for future action

Source: Thanks to Sgt. Mannie E. Hall of the U.S. Army for his advice in drafting this document

- assisting the reader to organize information visually
- allowing the reader to highlight important information

Again, compare Figures 6.1 and 6.2. Which document shows that it was designed by someone who understands the importance of white space?

2. Margins. Use wide margins, usually 1 to 1 ½ inches, to "frame" your document with white space surrounding text and visuals. Margins prevent your document from looking cluttered or overcrowded. If your document requires binding, you may have to leave a wider left margin (2 inches).

3. Line length. Most readers find a text line of 10 to 14 words, or 50 to 70 characters (depending on the type size you choose), comfortable and pleasing to read. Excessively long lines that bump into the margins signal that your work is difficult to read. In the following example, note how the extra-long lines unsettle your reading and tax your eye movement; they signal rough going.

To succeed in the world of business, workers must brush up on their networking skills. The network process has many benefits that you need to be aware of. These benefits range from finding a better job to accomplishing your job more easily and efficiently. Through networking you are able to expand the number of contacts who can help you. Networking means sharing news and opportunities. The Internet is the key to successful networking.

Conversely, do not print a document with overly short or extremely uneven lines.

> To succeed in the world of
> business, workers must
> brush up on their networking skills. The
> network process has many
> benefits you need to be
> aware of.

Readers will suspect your ideas are incomplete, superficial, or even simple-minded.

4. Columns. Document text can be organized in either single-column or multi-column formats. Memos, letters, and reports are usually formatted without columns, whereas documents that intersperse text and visuals (such as newsletters and magazines) work better in multicolumn formats.

Typography

Typography consists of font (also called *typeface*), font size, font styles, justification, heads and subheads. Take a look at Figure 6.3, which illustrates different typefaces and sizes.

Font

The readability of your text is crucial. Select a font, therefore, that ensures your text is

- legible
- attractive
- functional
- appropriate for your message
- complementary with accompanying graphics

FIGURE 6.3 Sample Typefaces and Type Sizes

Helvetica 8 point	Georgia 8 point
Helvetica 10 point	Georgia 10 point
Helvetica 12 point	Georgia 12 point
Helvetica 14 point	Georgia 14 point
Helvetica 18 point	Georgia 18 point
Verdana 8 point	Times New Roman 8 point
Verdana 10 point	Times New Roman 10 point
Verdana 12 point	Times New Roman 12 point
Verdana 14 point	Times New Roman 14 point
Verdana 18 point	Times New Roman 18 point

© Cengage Learning 2015

Fonts are also characterized as *serif* (the short cross-lines at the ends of some letters) or *sans serif* (without the serifs). The font you use can make your document look businesslike or too casual. Avoid using a font that looks like script, and don't mix and switch fonts. The result makes your work look amateurish and disorganized, as in Figure 6.1.

Font Size

Font size options are almost unlimited. Font size is measured in units called *points*. There are 72 points to the inch. The larger the point size, the larger the type. Never print your letter or report in 6- or 8-point type, like a print newspaper ad, or in a size larger than 12-point type.

Font Styles

Font styles include roman, boldface, italics, underlining, and small caps.

Roman
Boldface
Italics
Underlining
SMALL CAPS

Avoid overusing boldface and italics. Use them only when necessary and not just for decoration. Do *not* underline the text unless absolutely necessary. Not only will too many special visual effects make your work harder to read, but you will also lose the dramatic impact these features have to distinguish and emphasize key points that rightfully deserve to be set in boldface or italic type.

Justification

Sometimes referred to as *alignment*, justification consists of left, right, full, and centered options. Left-justified (also called *unjustified* or *ragged right*) text is preferred because it allows the space between words to remain constant, making the text easier to read. In full-justified text (both left and right margins are aligned) the word spacing varies from line to line. Left justification gives a document a less formal look than full justification. Narrow columns of text should be set left-justified to avoid awkward gaps between words and excessive hyphenation.

Our website offers consumers a mall on the Internet. It gives shoppers access to our products and services and makes buying easy and fun.

Left-justified text

Our website offers consumers a mall on the Internet. It gives shoppers access to our products and services and makes buying easy and fun.

Right-justified text

Our website offers consumers a mall on the Internet. It gives shoppers access to our products and services and makes buying easy and fun.

Full-justified text

Our website offers consumers a mall on the Internet. It gives shoppers access to our products and services and makes buying easy and fun.

Centered text

Heads and Subheads

Heads and subheads are brief descriptive phrases that signal starting points or major divisions in your document. They provide helpful road signs for readers charting their course through a document, as in Figure 6.2. Heads divide, or chunk, your document into its major parts, sections, or segments. Note how many of the figures in this book include heads and subheads. Heads immediately attract attention and quickly inform readers about the function, scope, purpose, or contents of your document and its individual sections. Moreover, they help readers prioritize information by emphasizing the main points they need to look for and remember. Without heads and subheads your work will look unorganized and cluttered.

How to Write Heads and Subheads

It takes time to write appropriate heads and subheads and determine where to place them in your document. Following the writing process described in Chapter 2, first map out what you want to say. By carefully outlining your work and then revising it, you can determine how many sections you will need and what kinds of information each should contain. In your final copy, every major section will require a head; and each subdivision will use a subhead. Look at the table of contents (page 351) to see how the writer logically divided her work.

How to Format Heads and Subheads

To design a document with logical heads and subheads, follow these guidelines.

1. Insert white space between the sections to make room for the head. Leave at least two additional spaces above and below a head to set it off from a previous section.
2. Be consistent in the way you print each type of head—that is, center each head or align it flush with the left margin.
3. Use larger type size for heads and subheads than for text; major heads should be larger than subheads. If your text is in 10-point type, your heads may be in 16-point type and your subheads in 12- or 14-point type.
4. To further differentiate heads from subheads, use all capital letters, initial capital letters (capitalize the first letter of each important word), boldface, or italics.
5. If you are using a color printer, consider using a second color for major heads.

Note how the long report in Chapter 9 illustrates these principles.

Lists

Placing items in a list helps readers by dividing, organizing, and ranking information. Lists emphasize important points and contribute to page design that is easy to read. Lists can be numbered (as in Figure 6.2), lettered, or bulleted. Take a look at Figures 4.19 (page 135), 8.9 (pages 330–334), and 9.2 (pages 367–380) that effectively use lists.

Using Color

Using color in workplace documents is a good way to enhance readability, break up long segments of text, and tie important ideas together. Tastefully done, color can help sell ideas more effectively than black and white alone. You can use color for borders and graphic accents, headings, titles, keywords, Internet addresses, sidebars, rules, and boxes that link related facts, figures, or information. But first determine if using color serves a functional purpose, as in Figure 6.2, or if it is merely a decoration. If it is window-dressing, stick with black and white.

Guidelines on Using Color Effectively

Here are some guidelines to follow when you use color in your documents or websites:

- Estimate how the color will look on the page—colors look different on the screen than they do on a sheet of paper. Print a sample page to get a clear idea.
- Make sure text colors contrast sharply with background colors in both print and web-based documents.
- Use no more than two or three colors on a page or screen unless there are photographs, illustrations, or graphics.
- Too many bright colors overwhelm the eye, so use them sparingly—only to call attention to important elements.
- Select "cool" colors, such as blue, turquoise, purple, and magenta, for backgrounds. However, avoid light blue text, which is hard to read against a dark background, or yellow text on a light blue background.
- Use colors that respect an international reader's cultural heritage. See pages 147 and 255.

The Purpose of Visuals

Visuals are essential in the world of work. They are vital to the success of reports, proposals, instructions, PowerPoint presentations, websites, blogs, and many other documents. Even your company logo reveals a great deal about your firm's or organization's image and mission. Here are several reasons visuals can improve your work; each point is graphically reinforced in Figure 6.4 (page 228).

1. **Visuals condense and summarize a large quantity of information into a relatively small space.** They can record data in far less space than it would take to describe those facts in words alone. Note how in Figure 6.4 a simple graph summarizes and documents the market shares of two different businesses.

2. **Visuals can simplify concepts.** A visual shows ideas while a verbal description only tells about them. Visuals help readers more clearly see and understand percentages, trends, comparisons, and contrasts. Figure 6.4, for example, shows at a glance the growth of online computer sales.

3. **Visuals arouse a reader's immediate interest.** They catch the reader's eye quickly by setting important information apart and giving relief from having to wade through a page of only sentences and paragraphs. Visuals also have tremendous sales appeal, persuading readers to buy a product or service or accept your point of view.

FIGURE 6.4 A Line-and-Bar Chart Comparing Market Share of Online Computer Purchases with Those Purchased at Brick-and-Mortar Stores

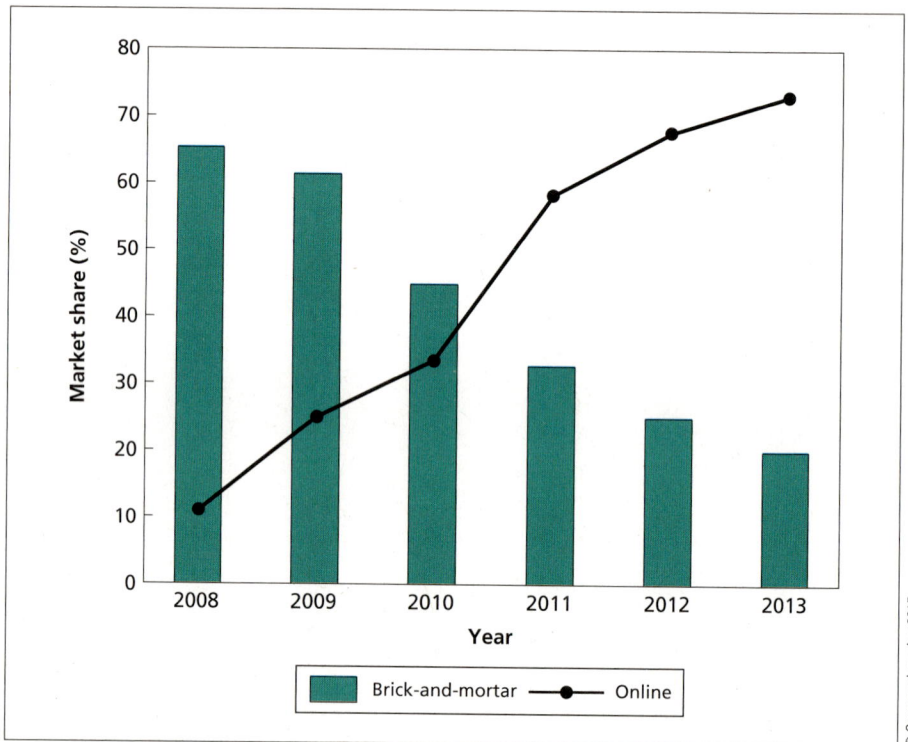

© Cengage Learning 2015

Choosing Effective Visuals

Select your visuals carefully. Here are some suggestions that will guide you when choosing a visual:

1. Supply a visual only when it is relevant for your purpose and audience. Never include a visual simply for decoration. A short report on fire drills does not need a picture of a fire station.

2. Don't include more detail in your visual than your reader needs. Unnecessary details complicate and slow down any process.

3. Use visuals in conjunction with—not as a substitute for—your written work. Visuals do not take the place of words. Giving readers a set of illustrations or a table alone may not meet their need for a summary or recommendations. See how the visual of an MRI, along with a description of its function in Figure 6.5, makes the procedure easier to understand for a general audience.

4. Visuals should not simply repeat what is in your text. If your text is clear and concise without a visual, don't include one.

FIGURE 6.5 A Visual Used in Conjunction with Written Work

A PICTURE FROM THE INSIDE OUT

At the heart of the magnetic resonance imager is a large magnet that is big enough for you to lie inside. Look at the picture below. The **magnet** directs radio signals to surround sections of your body. When the signals pass through your body, they **resonate** (release a signal). Then your body's response is picked up by a receiver and sent to a computer. The computer analyzes the signal and converts it into a visual **image** of your tissues on a video screen.

1. **The MR Imager** surrounds your body with a harmless **magnetic** field and radio signals that safely pass through your body.

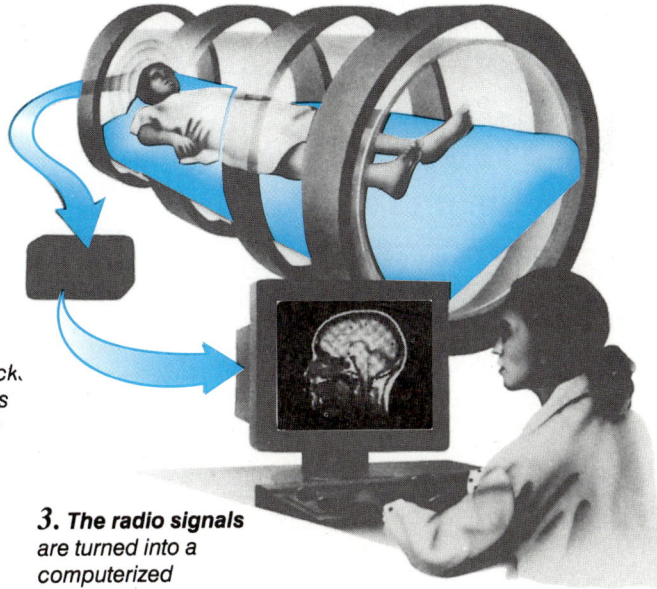

2. **A receiver** pick, up and measures the radio signals that leave, or **resonate** from, your body.

3. **The radio signals** are turned into a computerized picture—or **image**—of your body's tissues.

Source: Krames Communications.

5. **Size your visuals carefully.** Do not try to cram a visual onto a page or allow it to spill over the text or margins. Also do not resize an image so that it becomes hard to read or distorted.

Generating, Scanning, and Uploading Visuals

Here are three ways to incorporate a visual into your work.

1. You can easily generate charts, graphs, or tables through the templates in your word-processing software, such as Microsoft Word. By selecting, for instance, Insert Chart or Insert Table, you can insert your raw numerical data into the appropriate template and then add titles, labels, and color-coded keys, etc. This

software also shows visuals from different perspectives, adds shading or three-dimensional effects, etc., and can help you insert the visual in your text.

2. With a scanner you to produce a high-resolution digital copy of an image, or a document, and then use it online and archive it. Scanners also help you incorporate visuals that are unavailable in digital form, such as older photographs, diagrams, etc.

3. You can upload visuals into documents or presentations, often with just a few short clicks, with the right software. But always make sure when uploading a file with a visual that you've selected the highest-quality version available. That way, the visual is clear and sharp.

Regardless of how you incorporate a visual, always request permission if you did not create the visual yourself. Otherwise, you are guilty of plagiarism.

Inserting and Writing About Visuals: Some Guidelines

Using a visual requires more of you as a writer than simply inserting it into your written work. You need to use visuals in conjunction with what you write. The following guidelines will help you to (1) identify, (2) cite, (3) insert, (4) introduce, and (5) interpret visuals for your readers.

Identify Your Visuals

Give each visual a number and caption (title) that indicates the subject or explains what the visual illustrates. An unidentified visual is meaningless. A caption helps your audience interpret your visual—to see it with your purpose in mind. Tell your readers what you want them to look for by doing the following:

- Use a different typeface (**bold**) and size in your caption than what you use in the visual itself.
- Include key words about the function and the subject of your visual in a caption.
- Make sure any terms you cite in a caption are consistent with the units of measurement and the scope (years, months, seasons) of your visual.

Tables and figures should be numbered separately throughout the text—Table 1 or Figure 3.5, for example. (In the latter case, Figure 3.5 is the fifth figure to appear in Chapter 3.)

Cite the Source for Your Visuals

If you use a visual that is not your own work, give credit to your source (newspaper, magazine, textbook, company, federal agency, individual, or website). If your paper or report is intended for publication, you must first obtain permission to reproduce copyrighted visuals from the copyright holder.

Insert Your Visuals Appropriately

Because many of the images you use will come from other sources, especially the Web, you have to incorporate them clearly and in appropriate places in your written work.

Here are some guidelines to help you incorporate the visuals in the most appropriate places for your readers.

- Never introduce a visual *before* a discussion of it; readers will wonder why it is there. Include a sentence or two to introduce your visuals.
- Always mention in the text of your paper or report that you are including a visual. Tell readers where it is found—"on the following page," "to the right," "at the bottom of page 17."
- Place visuals as close as possible to the first mention of them in the text. Try not to put a visual more than one page after the discussion of it. Never wait two or three pages to present it. By inserting a visual near the beginning of your discussion, you help readers better understand your explanation.
- Center your visual and, if necessary, box it. But leave at least 1 inch of white space around it. Squeezing visuals toward the left or right margins looks unprofessional.
- Never collect all your visuals and put them in an appendix. Readers need to see them at those points in your discussion where they are most pertinent.

Introduce Your Visuals

Refer to each visual by its number, and if necessary, mention the title as well. In introducing the visual, though, do not just insert a reference to it, such as "See Figure 3.4" or "Look at Table 1." Relate the visual to the text it illustrates or helps explain. Here are two ways of writing a lead-in sentence for a visual.

> **Poor:** Our store saw a dramatic rise in the shipment of electric ranges over the five-year period as opposed to the less impressive increase in washing machines. (See Figure 3.)

This sentence does not tie the visual (Figure 3) into the sentence where it belongs. The visual just trails insignificantly behind.

> **Better:** As Figure 3 shows, our store saw a dramatic rise in the shipment of electric ranges over the five-year period as opposed to the less impressive increase in washing machines.

Mentioning the visual in this way alerts readers to its presence and function in your work and helps them to more easily understand your message.

Interpret Your Visuals

Help readers understand your visual by telling them what to look for and why. Let them know what is most significant about the visual. Mention any distinctive features, major parts, or crucial relationships. Do not expect the visual to explain itself. Inform readers what the numbers or images in your visual mean, how they make or prove a key point. What conclusions do you want readers to reach after seeing your visual?

In a report on the benefits of vanpooling, the writer supplied the following visual, a table:

TABLE 14   Travel Time (in minutes): Automobile versus Vanpool

Individual Automobile	Vanpool
25	32.5
30	39.0
35	45.5
40	52.0
45	58.5
50	65.0
55	71.5
60	78.0

Source: U.S. Department of Transportation. *Increased Transportation Efficiency Through Ridesharing: The Brokerage Approach* (Washington, D.C., DOT-OS—40096): 45.

To interpret the table, the writer called attention to it in the context of a discussion on transportation efficiency.

> Although, as Table 1 suggests, the travel time in a vanpool may be as much as 30 percent longer than in an automobile (to allow for pickups), the total trip time for the vanpool user can be about the same as with an automobile because vanpools eliminate the need to search for parking spaces and to walk to the employment site entrance.[1]

Two Categories of Visuals: Tables and Figures

Visuals can be divided into two categories—tables and figures. A *table* arranges information—numbers and/or words—in parallel columns and rows for easy comparison of data. Any visual that is not a table is considered a figure. *Figures* include graphs, circle charts, bar charts, organizational charts, flow charts, pictographs, maps, photographs, drawings, and infographs. Expect to use both tables and figures in your work.

Tables

Tables contain parallel columns and rows of information organized and arranged into categories to show, in a compact space, changes in time, distance, cost, employment, or some other distinguishable or quantifiable variable. Tables

---

[1] James A. Devine, "Vanpooling: A New Economic Tool," *AIDC Journal.*

also summarize material for easy recall—causes of wars; provisions of a law; or differences between a common cold, flu, and pneumonia. See how Table 6.1 on sources of protein condenses much information and arranges it in quickly identifiable categories.

Parts of a Table

To use a table properly, you need to know the parts that constitute it. Refer to Table 6.1 (page 234), which labels these parts, as you read the following:

- The main *column* is "Amount Needed to Satisfy Minimum Daily Requirement," and the *subcolumns* are the protein sources for which the table gives data.
- The *stub* is the first column on the left-hand side, below the column heading "Source." The stub lists the foods for which information is broken down in the subcolumns.
- A *rule* (or line) across the top of the table separates the title from the column headings and the column headings from the body of the table.

Guidelines for Using Tables

When you include a table in your work, follow these guidelines.

- Number the tables according to the order in which they are discussed (Table 1, Table 2, Table 3). Tables should be numbered separately from figures (charts, graphs, photos) in your text.
- Keep the table on the page where it is most appropriate. It is hard for readers to follow a table spread across different pages.
- Give each table a concise and descriptive title to show exactly what is being represented or compared.
- Use words in the stub (a list of items about which information is given), but put numbers under column headings.
- Supply footnotes, often indicated by small raised letters ([a], [b]), if something in the table needs to be qualified, for example, the number of cups of milk in Table 6.1 (page 234), Then put that information below the table.
- List items in alphabetical, chronological, or other logical order.
- Arrange the data you want to compare vertically, not horizontally; it is easier to read down a column than across a series of rows.
- Place tables at the top (preferable) or bottom of the page, and center them on the page rather than placing them up against the right or left margin.
- Don't use more than five or six columns; tables wider than that are more difficult for readers to understand.
- When possible, round off numbers in your columns to the nearest whole number to assist readers in following and retaining information.
- Always credit the source (the supplier of the statistical information) on which your table is based.

TABLE 6.1   Parts of a Table

Table number →

TABLE 1	Efficiency of Some Protein Sources in Meeting an Adult's Minimum Daily Requirements			
			Amount Needed to Satisfy Minimum Daily Requirement	
Source	Percent of Protein	Percent of Amino Acids	(grams)	(ounces)
Cheese[a]	27	70	227	7.2
Corn	10	50	860	30.0
Eggs	11	97	403	14.1
Fish[a]	22	80	244	8.5
Kidney beans	23	40	468	16.4
Meat[a]	25	68	253	8.8
Milk	4	82	1,311	45.9[b]
Soybeans	34	60	210	7.3

← Title
← Rule
← Column head
← Sub

Stub {

Source: From Starr/Taggart, Biology: *The Unity and Diversity of Life*, 4E. © 1987 Cengage Learning.   ← Origin of d

[a] = Average value
[b] = Equivalent of 6 cups   } *Footnotes*

Figures

As we saw, any visual that is not a table is classified as a figure. The types of figures we will examine next are

- graphs
- circle, or pie, charts
- bar charts
- organizational charts
- flow charts
- pictographs
- maps
- photographs
- drawings
- clip art
- infographics

Graphs

Graphs transform numbers into pictures with shapes, patterns, and shading. They take statistical data presented in tables and put them into rising and falling lines or steep or gentle curves. The three types of graphs are (1) simple line graphs, (2) multiple-line graphs, and (3) area graphs.

Functions of Graphs

Graphs vividly portray information that changes, such as

- sales
- costs
- trends
- distributions
- employment
- energy levels
- temperatures
- population
- tourism/travel

Graphs not only describe past and current situations but also forecast trends.

Simple Line Graphs

Basically, a simple graph consists of two sides—a **vertical** or **y-axis** and a **horizontal** or **x-axis**—that intersect to form a right angle, as in Figure 6.6. The space between the two axes contains the picture made by the graph—the amount of snowfall in Springfield between November 2013 and April 2014. The vertical line represents the **dependent variable** (the snowfall in inches); the horizontal line, the **independent variable** (time in months). The dependent variable is influenced most directly by the independent variable, which almost always is expressed in terms of time or distance. The vertical axis is read from bottom to top; the horizontal axis from left to right.

Multiple-Line Graphs

The graph in Figure 6.7 (page 236) contains only one line per category. But a graph can have multiple lines to show how a number of dependent variables (conditions, products) compare with one another.

The six-month sales figures for three salespeople can be seen in the graph in Figure 6.7. The graph contains a separate line for each of the three salespersons. At a glance, readers can see how the three compare and how many dollars each salesperson generated per month. Note how the line representing each person is clearly differentiated from the others by symbols and colors. Each line is clearly tied to a **legend** (an explanatory key below the graph) specifying the three salespersons.

FIGURE 6.6 A Simple Line Graph Showing the Amount of Snowfall in Springfield from November 2013 and April 2014

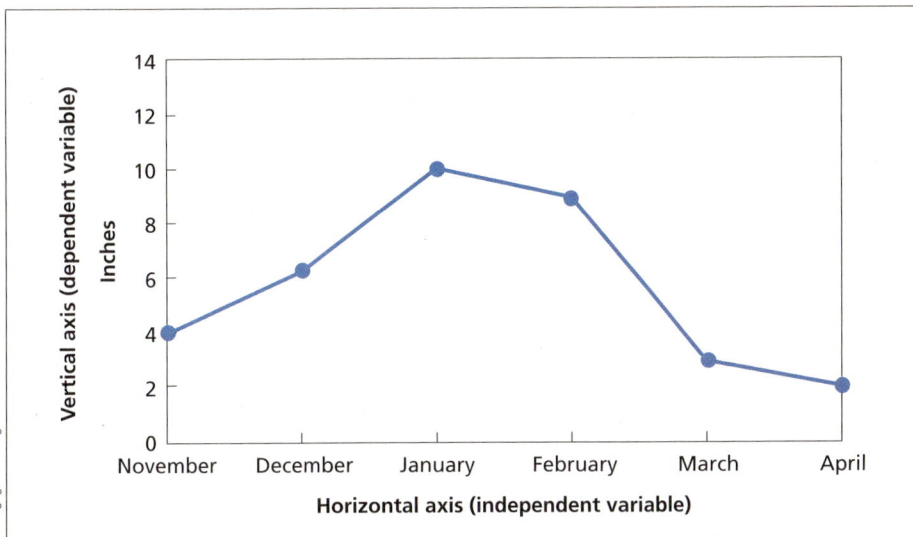

Graph is easy to read and follow

Variables clearly labeled

© Cengage Learning 2015

FIGURE 6.7   A Multiple-Line Graph Showing Sales Figures for the First Six Months of 2014 for Three Salespeople

Graph is easy to read and follow; lines are distinct

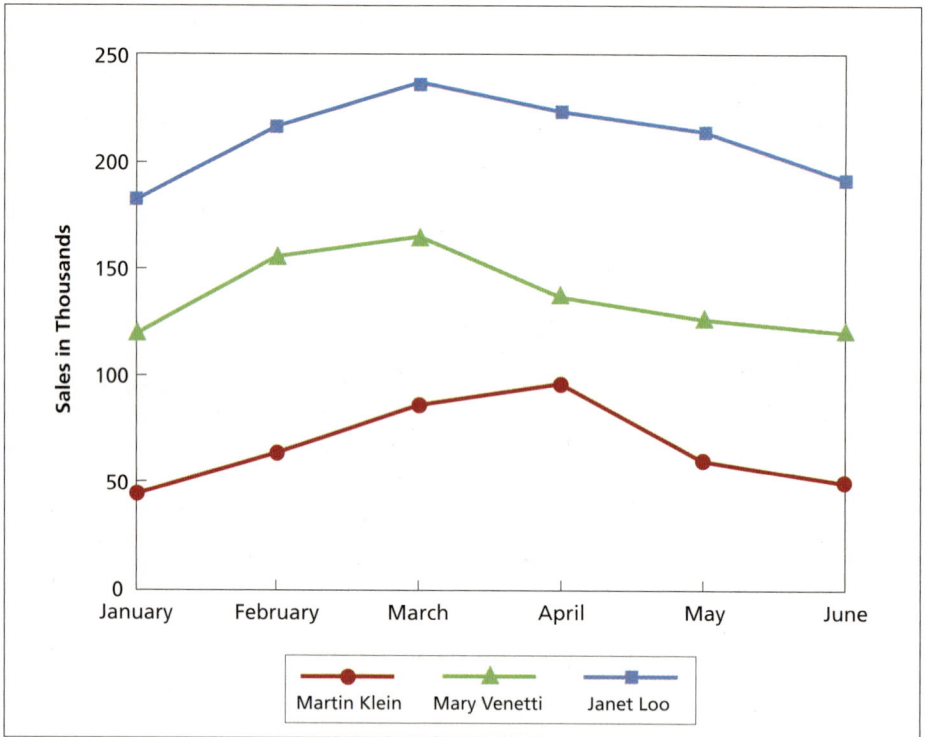

Legend explains what different symbols and colors represent

© Cengage Learning 2015

Guidelines for Creating Graphs

1. Use no more than three lines in a multiple-line graph, so readers can interpret the graph more easily. If the lines run close together, use a legend to identify individual lines.
2. Label each line to identify what it represents for readers. Include a key, or legend, as in Figure 6.7.
3. Keep each line distinct in a multiple-line graph by using different colors, dots or dashes, or other symbols. Note the different symbols in Figure 6.7.
4. Make sure you plot enough points to show a reasonable and ethical range of the data. Using only three or four points may distort the evidence. See pages 250–251 on unethical uses of graphics.
5. Keep the scale consistent and realistic. If you start with hours, do not switch to days or vice versa. If you are recording annual rates or accounts, do not skip a year or two in order to save time or be more concise.

Charts

Among the most frequently used charts are (1) pie, or circle, charts, (2) bar charts, (3) organizational charts, and (4) flow charts.

Pie Charts

Pie charts are also known as **circle charts**, a name that descriptively points to their construction and interpretation. Tables are more technical and detailed than pie charts. Figure 6.8 shows an example of a pie chart used in a government document. A table or graph with a more detailed breakdown of, say, a city's budget would be much more appropriate for a technical audience (auditors, budget and city planners).

The full circle, or pie, represents the whole amount (100 percent or 360 degrees) of the data being represented; the entire budget of a company or a family, a population group, an area of land, the resources of an organization or institution. Each slice or wedge represents a percentage or portion of the whole.

A pie chart effectively allows readers to see two things at once: the relationship of the parts to one another and the relationship of the parts to the whole.

Preparing a Pie Chart

Follow these seven rules to create and present your pie chart.

1. Make sure the individual slices total 100 percent, or 360 degrees. Check your math.

2. Put the largest slice first, at the 12 o'clock position, and then move clockwise with proportionately smaller slices. Schools occupy the largest slice in Figure 6.8 because they receive the biggest share of taxes.

FIGURE 6.8   A Three-Dimensional Pie Chart Showing the Breakdown by Department of a Proposed City Budget for 2014

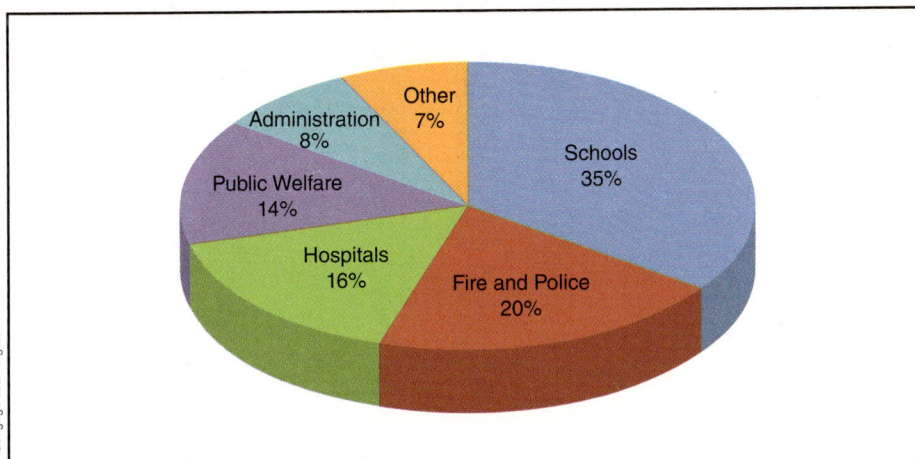

Other 7%

Administration 8%

Public Welfare 14%

Hospitals 16%

Schools 35%

Fire and Police 20%

Puts largest slice first

Size of slice determined by percentage; totals 100%

Uses a different, easily contrasted color for each category

© Cengage Learning 2015

3. Do not divide a circle, or pie, into too few or too many slices. If you have only three wedges, use another visual to display them (a bar chart, for example, discussed next). If you have more than seven or eight wedges, you will destroy the dramatic effect. Instead, combine several slices of small percentages (2 percent, 3 percent, 4 percent) into one slice labeled "Other," "Miscellaneous," or "Related Items."

4. Label each slice of the pie horizontally. Do not put in a label upside down or slide it in vertically. If the individual slice of the pie is small, draw a connecting line from the slice to a label positioned outside the pie.

5. Shade, color, or cross-hatch slices of the pie to further separate and distinguish the parts. Note how Figure 6.8 effectively uses color. But be careful not to obscure labels and percentages; also make certain that adjacent slices can be distinguished readily from each other. Do not use the same color or similar colors for two adjacent slices.

6. Give percentages for each slice to further assist readers, as in Figure 6.8.

Bar Charts

A bar chart consists of a series of vertical or horizontal bars that indicate comparisons of statistical data. For instance, in Figure 6.9, vertical bars depict increases in

FIGURE 6.9 A Vertical Bar Chart

Bars are evenly spaced and clearly labeled

Length of bar determined by the percentages listed on the left-hand side of visual

Years clearly marked at bottom of columns

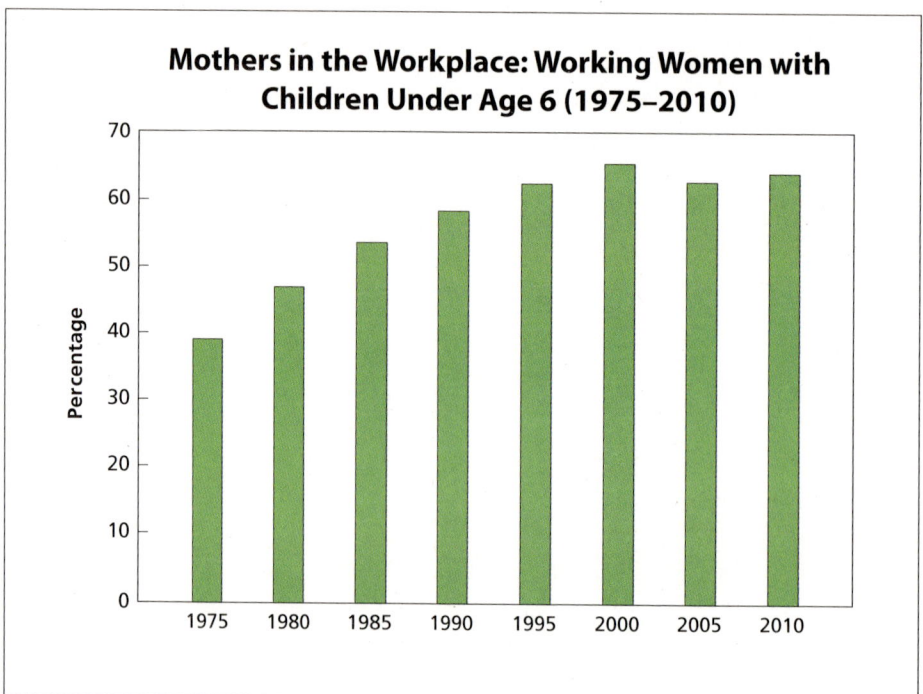

Mothers in the Workplace: Working Women with Children Under Age 6 (1975–2010)

Source: U.S. Bureau of Labor Statistics. Women in the Labor Force: A Databook (2013 Edition)

the number of working mothers. Figure 6.10 uses horizontal bars to depict the nation's top 20 metropolitan areas in 2013. The length of the bars you present is determined according to a scale that your computer software can easily calculate. In a figure like Figure 6.10, readers appreciate having numbers after each bar listing specific population figures.

Organizational Charts

An *organizational chart* pictures the chain of command in a company or agency, with the lines of authority stretching down from the chief executive, manager, or administrator to the assistant manager, department heads, or supervisors to the workforce of employees. Figure 6.11 (page 240) shows a hospital's organizational chart for its nursing services.

Organizational charts have these functions:

- to inform employees and customers about the makeup of a company
- to depict the various offices, departments, and units
- to show where people work in relationship to one another in a business

---

FIGURE 6.10 A Horizontal Bar Chart

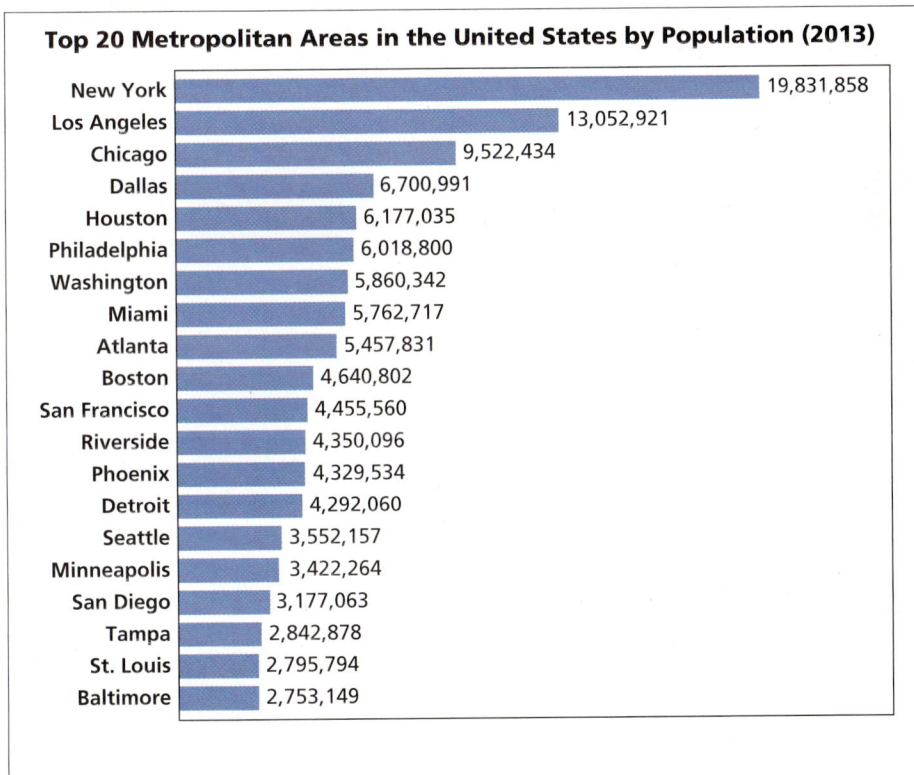

Top 20 Metropolitan Areas in the United States by Population (2013)

New York	19,831,858
Los Angeles	13,052,921
Chicago	9,522,434
Dallas	6,700,991
Houston	6,177,035
Philadelphia	6,018,800
Washington	5,860,342
Miami	5,762,717
Atlanta	5,457,831
Boston	4,640,802
San Francisco	4,455,560
Riverside	4,350,096
Phoenix	4,329,534
Detroit	4,292,060
Seattle	3,552,157
Minneapolis	3,422,264
San Diego	3,177,063
Tampa	2,842,878
St. Louis	2,795,794
Baltimore	2,753,149

Arranges bars in decreasing order

Name of city precedes bar for easier reference

Provides exact numbers after each bar

Visual summarizes a large amount of information concisely

Source: U.S. Census Bureau

FIGURE 6.11 An Organizational Chart Representing Critical Care Nursing Services at Union General Hospital

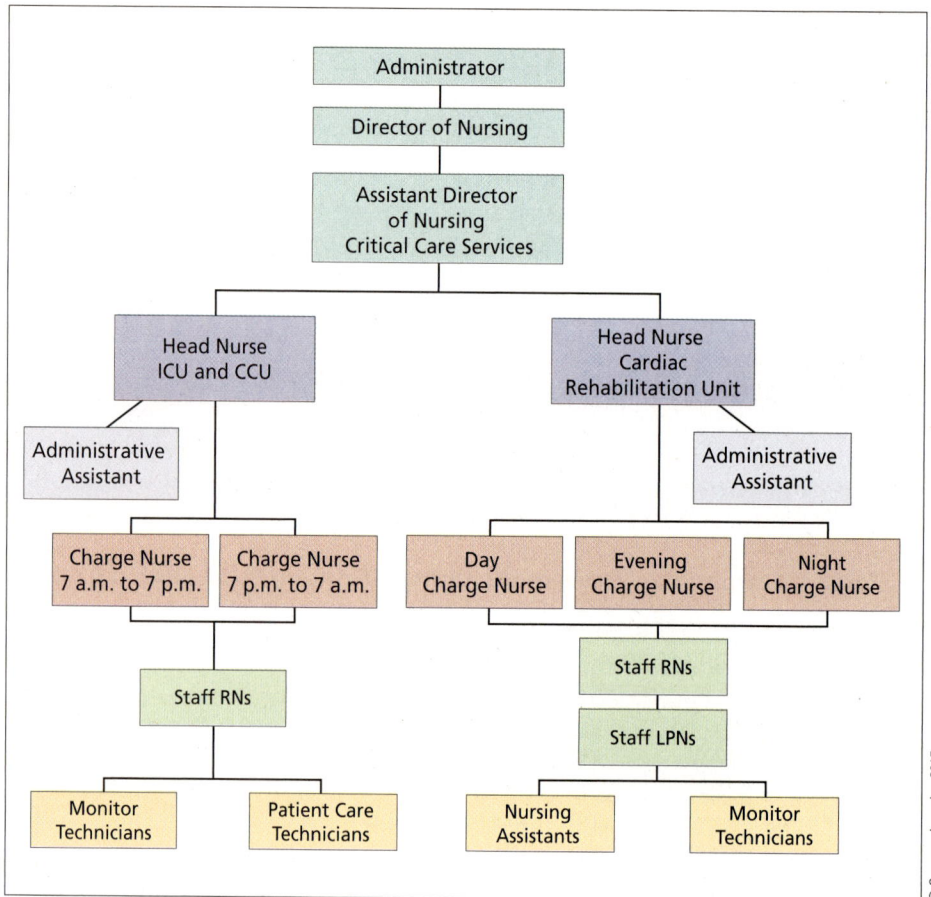

© Cengage Learning 2015

Flow Charts

A **flow chart** displays the stages in which something is manufactured, is accomplished, develops, or operates. Flow charts are highly effective in showing the steps of a procedure.

Flow charts often proceed from left to right and back again, as in the one appearing here, showing the steps students must take to graduate

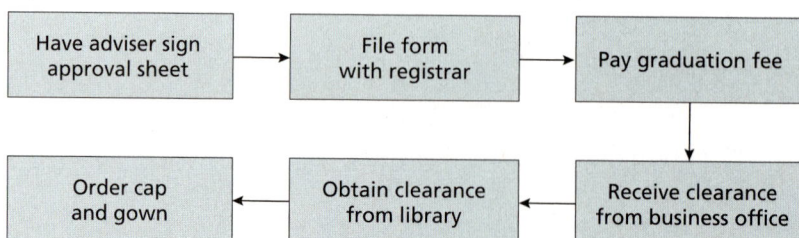

© Cengage Learning

Flow charts can also be constructed to read from top to bottom. Computer programming instructions often are written that way. See, for example, Figure 6.12, which like a computer programming chart lists the steps that an employee must follow when ordering products online.

Pictographs

A **pictograph** uses picture symbols (called **pictograms**) to represent differences in statistical data, as in Figure 6.13 on page 242. Each symbol or icon stands for a specific number, quantity, or value.

When you create a pictograph, follow these three guidelines:

1. Choose an appropriate symbol for the topic—such as a smartphone icon to represent the increase in the number of sales of iPhones.
2. Always indicate the precise quantities involved by placing numbers after the pictures or at the top of the visual.

FIGURE 6.12 A Flow Chart for Ordering Products Online

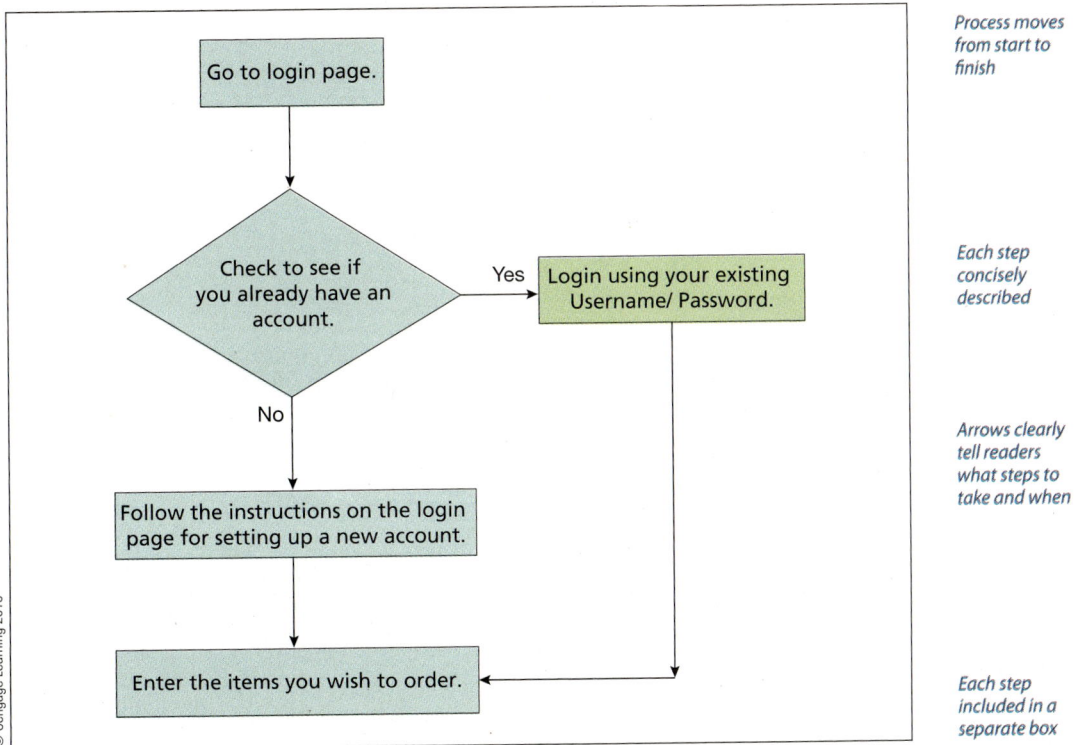

Process moves from start to finish

Each step concisely described

Arrows clearly tell readers what steps to take and when

Each step included in a separate box

© Cengage Learning 2015

FIGURE 6.13 A Pictograph Showing Financial Details from One Pension Fund

Provides financial context/history to better understand visual

Specifies what each pictograph stands for

Uses easily recognized pictographs

Increases number, not size, of pictograph

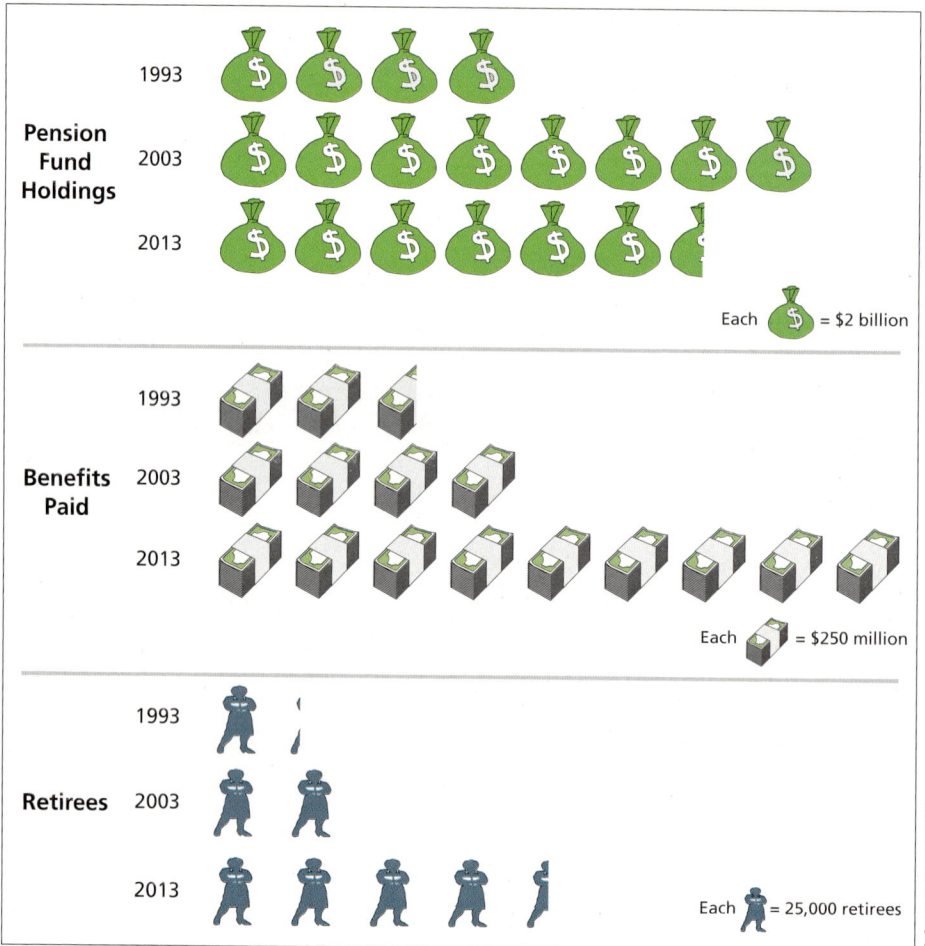

© Cengage Learning 2015

3. Increase the number of symbols rather than their sizes because differences in size are often difficult to construct accurately and harder for readers to interpret.

Maps

The maps you use on the job may range from highly sophisticated and detailed geographic tools to simple sketches such as the map in Figure 6.14, which shows the location of a town's water filter plants and pumping stations.

You may have to construct your own map, like the one in Figure 6.14, or scan one in a printed source or on the Internet. If you scan a map, be sure to obtain permission to use it from the copyright holder.

FIGURE 6.14 A Map Showing the Location of Smithville Water Department's Water Filter Plants and Pumping Stations

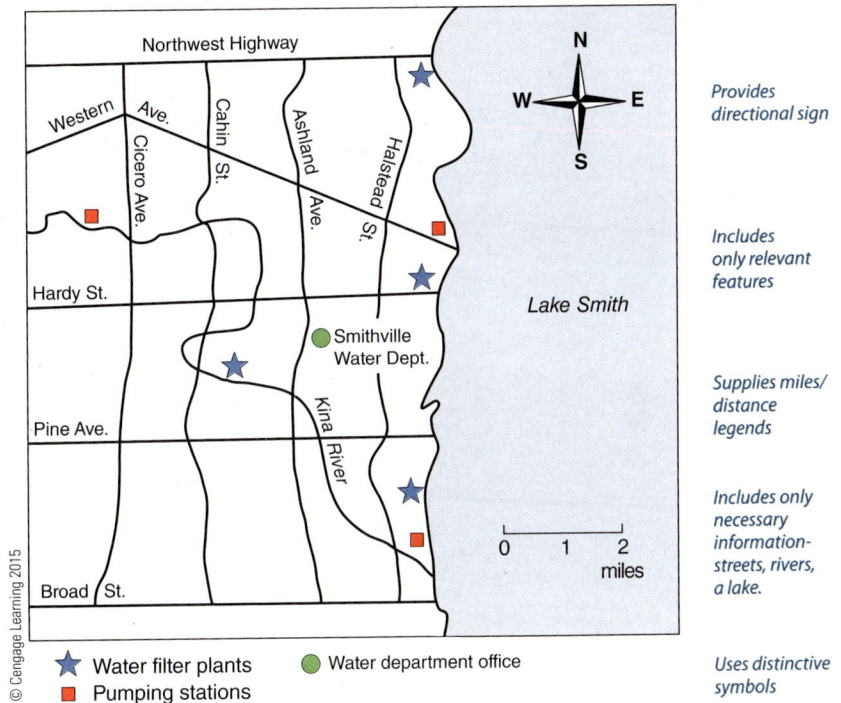

Provides directional sign

Includes only relevant features

Supplies miles/ distance legends

Includes only necessary information- streets, rivers, a lake.

Uses distinctive symbols

★ Water filter plants   ● Water department office

■ Pumping stations

© Cengage Learning 2015

Guidelines for Creating a Map

Follow these steps when you create a map:

1. Always acknowledge your source if you did not construct the map yourself.
2. Use distinct lines, colors, symbols, and shading to indicate features.
3. Include a legend, or map key, explaining dotted lines, colors, shading, and symbols, as in Figure 6.14.
4. Exclude features (rivers, elevations, county seats) that do not directly relate to your topic. For example, a map showing the crops grown in two adjacent counties need not show all the roads and highways in those counties.

Photographs

Correctly taken or scanned, photographs are an extremely helpful addition to job-related writing. A photograph's chief virtues are realism and clarity, as Figure 6.15 (page 244) illustrates. Among its many advantages, a photo can

- show what an object looks like
- demonstrate how to perform a certain procedure

FIGURE 6.15 A Photo Showing How to Perform a Procedure and Comparing Relative Sizes and Shapes of Objects

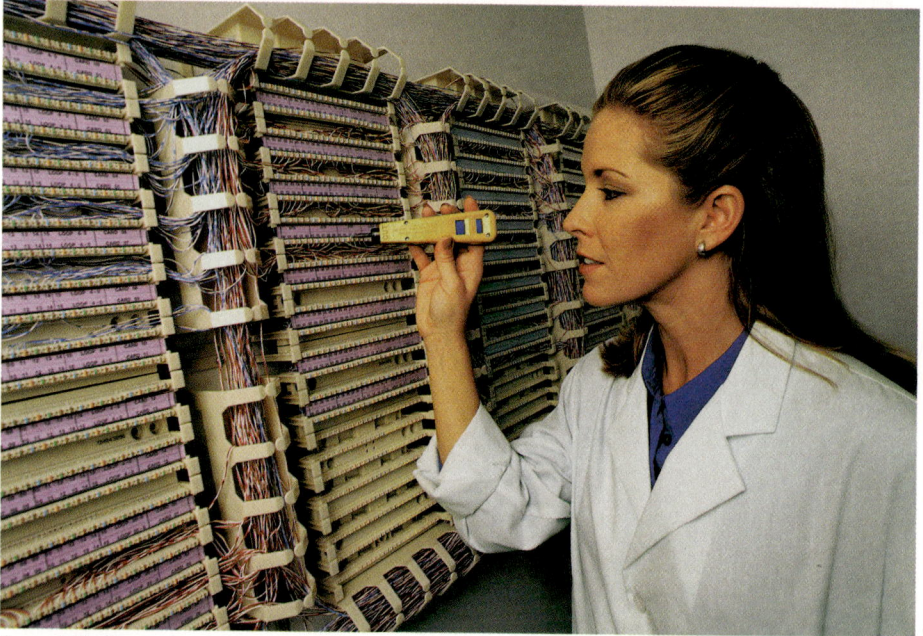

Source: ©Corbis

- compare relative sizes and shapes of objects
- compare and contrast scenes or procedures

Digital cameras and smartphones allow you to supply professional-looking, customized photos easily with your written work. Digital photography offers the following benefits in the global marketplace:

- Shows conditions or sites right away so you can include a photo in an incident or credit report—you do not need to wait for film to be developed.
- Gives you more than one opportunity to take a picture—helps you select, highlight, and edit.
- Allows you to send photographs easily and quickly over the Internet, store them on your computer or on a CD, and upload them to a website.
- Allows you to edit photographs for color, sharpness, contrast, brightness, size, and resolution—you can also use retouching software to edit out unnecessary details, and eliminate "red eye." The original photo in Figure 6.16 was changed to remove cars and bags of trash, to show the affects of a downtown beautification effort more clearly.

FIGURE 6.16 Removing Unnecessary Details from a Photograph

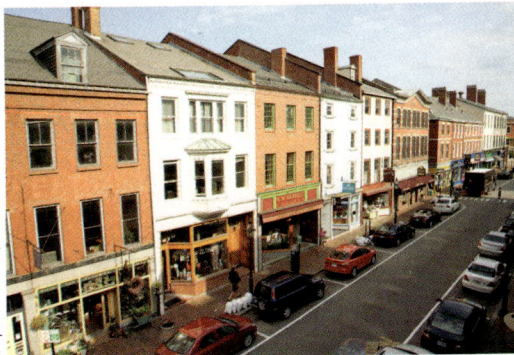

Before

After

Drawings

Drawings can show where an object is located, how a tool or machine is put together. A drawing can be simple, such as the one in Figure 6.17 (page 246), which shows readers exactly where to place smoke detectors depending on the size of their homes.

A more detailed drawing can reveal the interior of an object. Such sketches are called **cutaway drawings** because they show internal parts normally concealed from view. Figure 6.18 (page 247) is a cutaway drawing of an extended-range electric vehicle, the Chevrolet Volt.

Another kind of sketch is an **exploded drawing**, which blows the entire object up and apart, as in Figure 6.19 (page 248), to show how the individual parts are arranged. An exploded drawing comes with most owner's guides to computers and uses **callouts**, or labels, to identify the components.

Guidelines for Using Drawings

1. Include only as much detail as your reader will need to understand what to do, be it to assemble or to operate a mechanism.
2. Clearly, label all parts so that your reader can identify and separate them.
3. Decide on the most appropriate view of the object to illustrate—aerial, frontal, lateral, reverse, exterior, interior—and indicate in the title which view it is.

Clip Art

Clip art (or icons) refers to ready-to-use electronic images. These small cartoon-style representations and photographs, such as the ones shown in Figure 6.20 (page 248), depict almost any workplace subject. Free clip art and photo-illustration

FIGURE 6.17 A Simple Drawing Showing Where to Place Smoke Detectors in a House

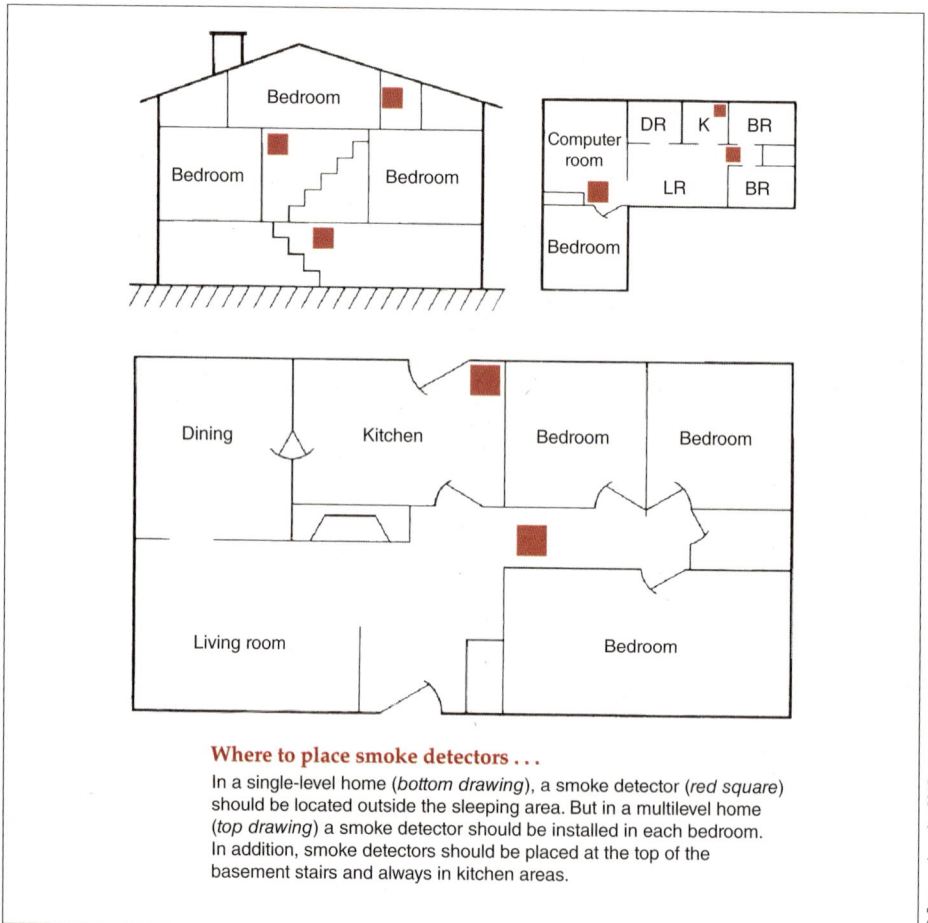

Where to place smoke detectors . . .
In a single-level home (*bottom drawing*), a smoke detector (*red square*) should be located outside the sleeping area. But in a multilevel home (*top drawing*) a smoke detector should be installed in each bedroom. In addition, smoke detectors should be placed at the top of the basement stairs and always in kitchen areas.

© Cengage Learning 2015

databases can be found at the following websites (among others): www.wpclipart .com; www.reusableart.com; and freerangestock.com.

When you use clip art, follow these guidelines:

1. **Choose simple, easy-to-understand icons.** Select an image that conveys your idea quickly and directly. Avoid using an icon of an unfamiliar object or of a drawing or silhouette that might confuse your audience, especially a global one.

2. **Use clip art functionally.** Do not insert clip art as decorations. Including too many will make your work look unprofessional.

FIGURE 6.18 Cutaway Drawing of an Electric Car

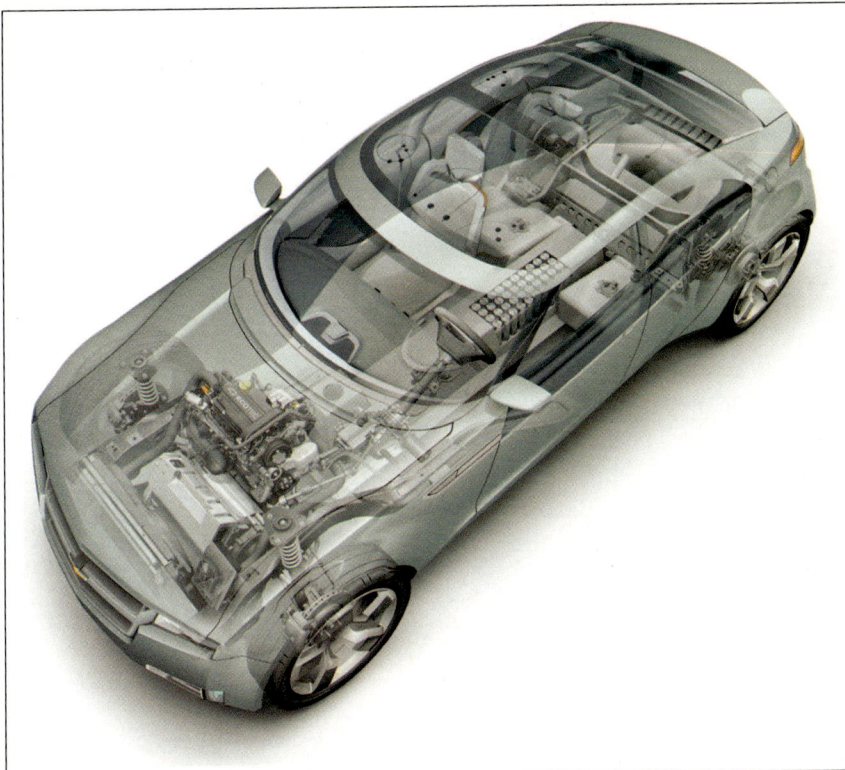

Source: General Motors Corporation. Used with permission, GM Media Archives.

3. **Make sure your clip art is professional.** Some clip art is humorous, even silly, which may not be appropriate for a professional business report or proposal.

Infographics

An **infograph** (*information* plus *graphic*) combines a variety of visuals (for example, bar charts, graphs, icons, photographs) with numerical data (for example, statistics) to give readers an easy-to-understand overview or timeline of a complex process. Influenced by the Web, an infograph such as the one in Figure 6.21 (page 249) summarizes information that otherwise would require many visuals and pages of text to explain. As with the other visuals discussed in this chapter, use only the highest-quality graphics, and make sure text and image work together, not in opposition to each other; words, numbers, and visuals all need to reinforce your message.

FIGURE 6.19 Exploded Drawing of a Notebook Computer

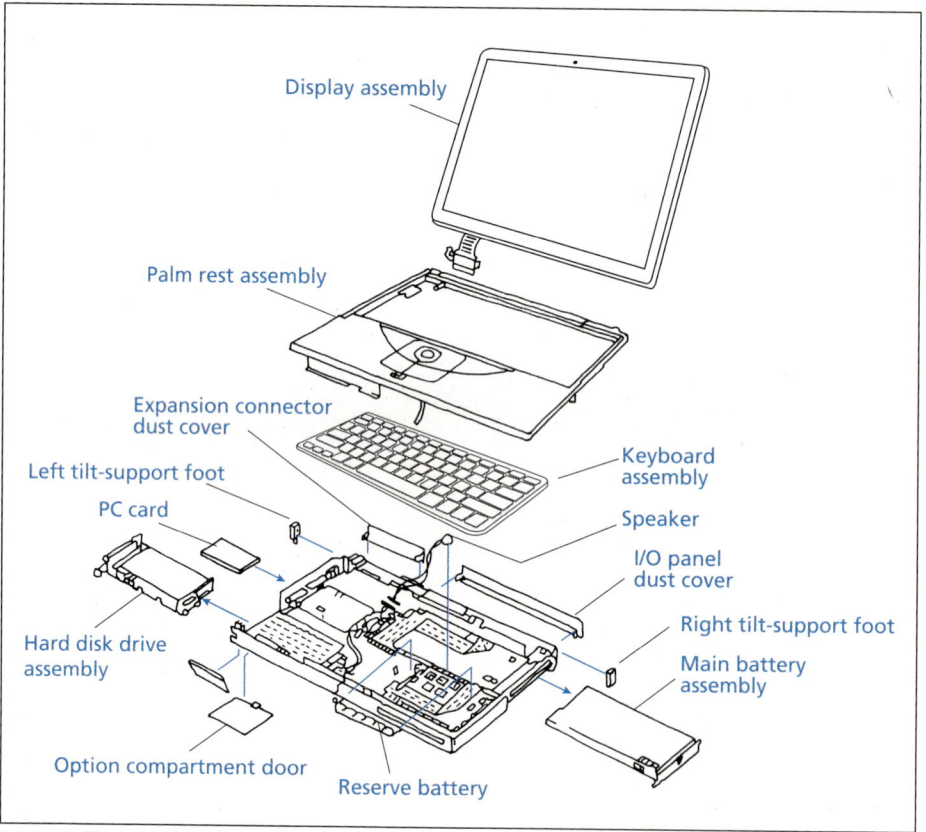

Display assembly

Palm rest assembly

Expansion connector
dust cover

Left tilt-support foot

PC card

Keyboard
assembly

Speaker

I/O panel
dust cover

Hard disk drive
assembly

Right tilt-support foot

Main battery
assembly

Option compartment door

Reserve battery

FIGURE 6.20 Examples of Clip Art

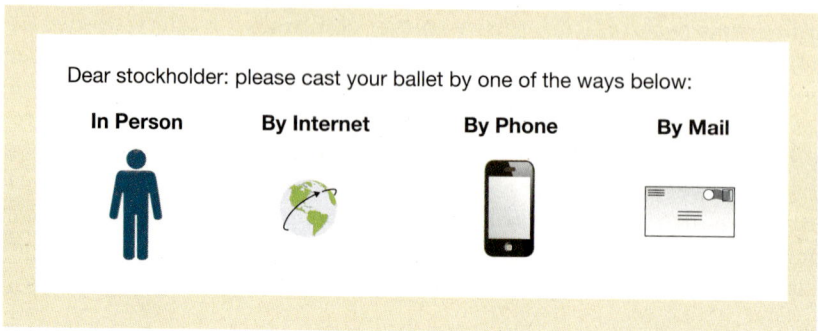

Dear stockholder: please cast your ballet by one of the ways below:

In Person   **By Internet**   **By Phone**   **By Mail**

FIGURE 6.21 Example of an Infograph

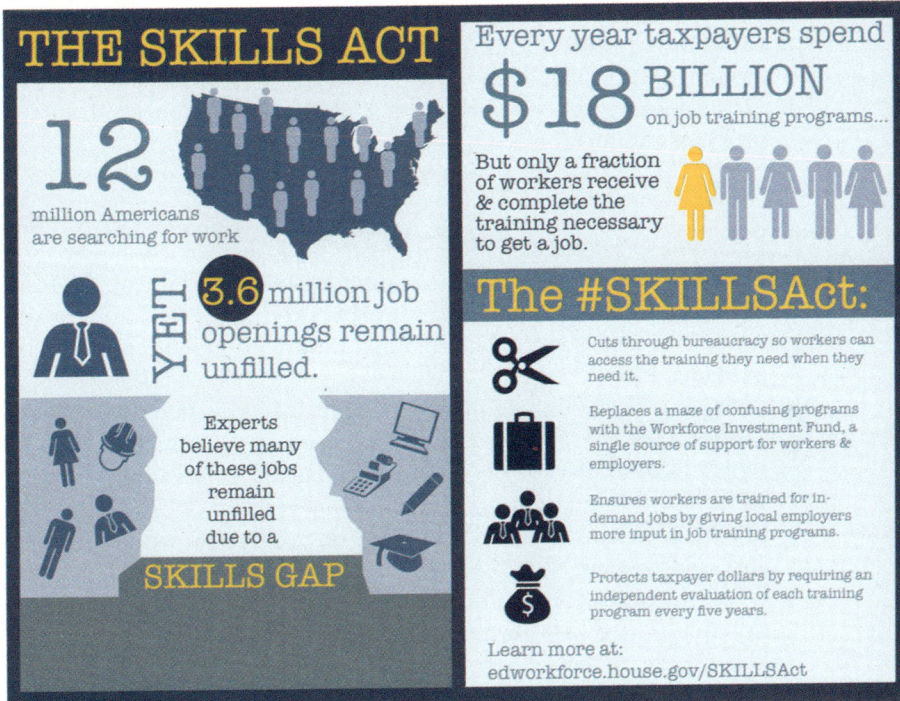

THE SKILLS ACT

12 million Americans are searching for work

YET **3.6** million job openings remain unfilled.

Experts believe many of these jobs remain unfilled due to a SKILLS GAP

Every year taxpayers spend $18 BILLION on job training programs...

But only a fraction of workers receive & complete the training necessary to get a job.

The #SKILLSAct:

Cuts through bureaucracy so workers can access the training they need when they need it.

Replaces a maze of confusing programs with the Workforce Investment Fund, a single source of support for workers & employers.

Ensures workers are trained for in-demand jobs by giving local employers more input in job training programs.

Protects taxpayer dollars by requiring an independent evaluation of each training program every five years.

Learn more at: edworkforce.house.gov/SKILLSAct

Courtesy of the Education & the Workforce Committee, U.S. House of Representatives.

Using Visuals Ethically

Make sure your visuals, whether you create or import them, are ethical. Ethical visuals convey and interpret statistical information and other types of data, products and equipment, locations, and even individuals without misinterpretation. Ethical visuals should be:

- accurate
- honest, fair
- complete
- appropriate
- easy to read
- clearly labeled
- uncluttered
- consistent with conventions

Guidelines for Using Visuals Ethically

To ensure that your visuals are ethical, honest, accurate, and easy to read, avoid the following unethical practices no matter what type of visual you use.

Photos

- Don't distort a photo by omitting key details or by misrepresenting dimensions, angles, sizes, or surroundings or by superimposing one image over another.

- Don't take a photo of your most expensive, top-of-the-line product/model but then place the cost of your lowest-priced product/model under it.
- Don't misrepresent location—for example, taking a photo in a "doctored" or off-site location, studio, or lab and then claiming it as an "actual" location shot.
- Don't counterfeit or subtly alter a company's logo to sell, distribute, or promote an imitation as the real thing.

Graphs

- Don't distort a graph by plotting it in misleading or unequal intervals—for example, omitting certain years or dates to hide a decline in profits. Contrast Figure 6.22, and its misleading interpretation, with the ethical revision in Figure 6.23.
- Include information in correct chronological sequence along the horizontal axis. Note how Figure 6.22 omits key years.
- Don't switch the type of information usually given along the vertical axis with the horizontal axis.
- Don't project any growth or increase on your graph without having reliable and valid reasons.
- Don't misrepresent data or trends by making increments along the vertical axis too limited, leaving a much smaller (and incomplete) area to represent. When data are plotted wrongly this way, readers are unethically led to misinterpret the numbers—to read that there was little loss in revenue, or no change in sales, for example. For instance, if the horizontal axis begins at $5 and advances to $6 a share, you leave only an intentionally small and misleading area to measure. If stocks fell below $5 a share, your graph would unethically not represent those declines.

Bar Charts

- Don't use color or shading to mislead or distort—for example, shading one bar to make it more prominent than the others.
- Make sure the height and width of each bar truthfully represents the data it purports to. That is, don't make one of the bars larger to maximize the profits, products, or sales in any one year.
- Show bars for every year (or other sales period) covered. Note how the unethical bar chart (and accompanying text) in Figure 6.24 (page 252) violates this rule, but the chart in Figure 6.25 (page 252) ethically represents the data.

Pie Charts

- Don't use 3-D to distort the thickness of one slice of the pie and thereby misleadingly deemphasize other slices.

FIGURE 6.22 An Unethical Graph and Misleading Interpretation

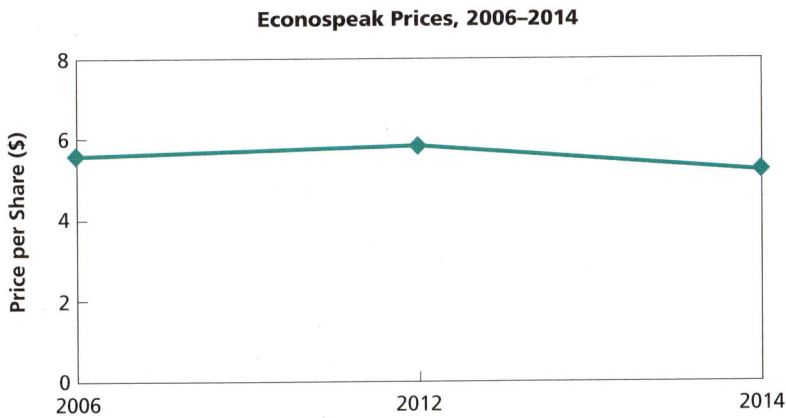

Econospeak Prices, 2006–2014

Econospeak's stock prices during 2006–2014 have been stable, resting securely at about $5.60. The graph above illustrates the stability of Econospeak's stock. Given our steady market, we believe shareholders will be confident in our recent decision to proceed with Econospeak's further expansion into global markets.

FIGURE 6.23 An Ethical Revision of Figure 6.22

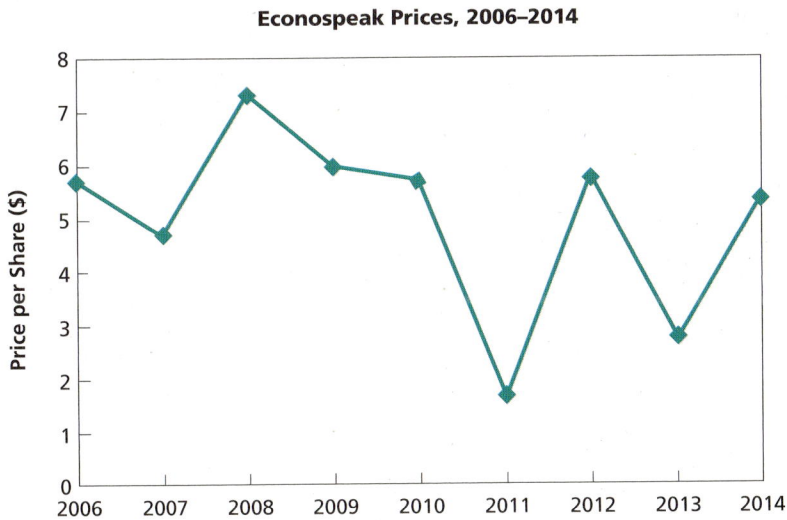

Econospeak Prices, 2006–2014

Econospeak's stock prices have not been as stable over 2006–2014 as we would have liked. The graph above illustrates the challenges the company has faced in the market in the past decade, resulting in fluctuation of prices. We believe, however, that Econospeak's further expansion into global markets will increase dividends by 2015.

FIGURE 6.24 An Unethical Bar Chart

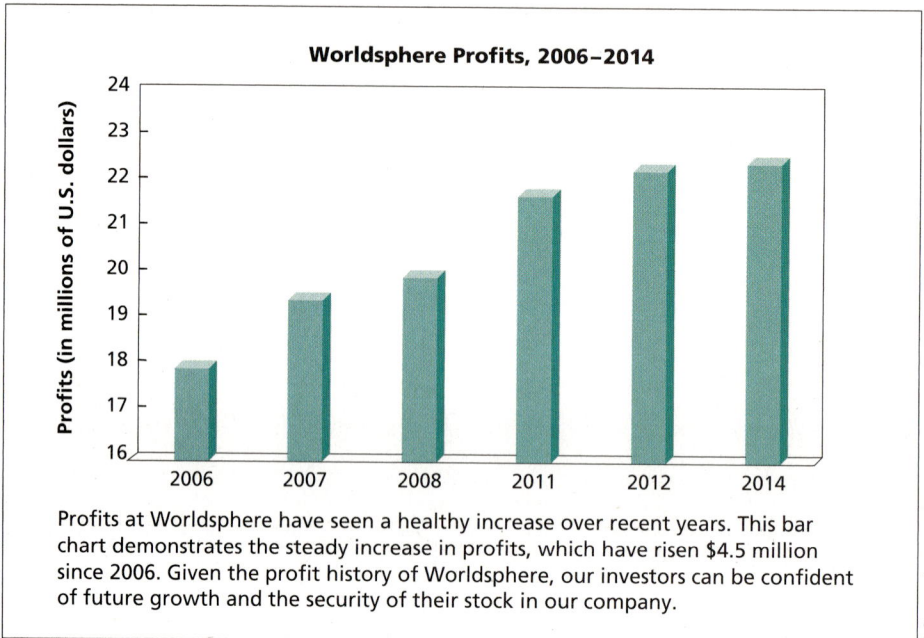

Worldsphere Profits, 2006–2014

Profits at Worldsphere have seen a healthy increase over recent years. This bar chart demonstrates the steady increase in profits, which have risen $4.5 million since 2006. Given the profit history of Worldsphere, our investors can be confident of future growth and the security of their stock in our company.

© Cengage Learning 2015

FIGURE 6.25 An Ethical Revision of Figure 6.24

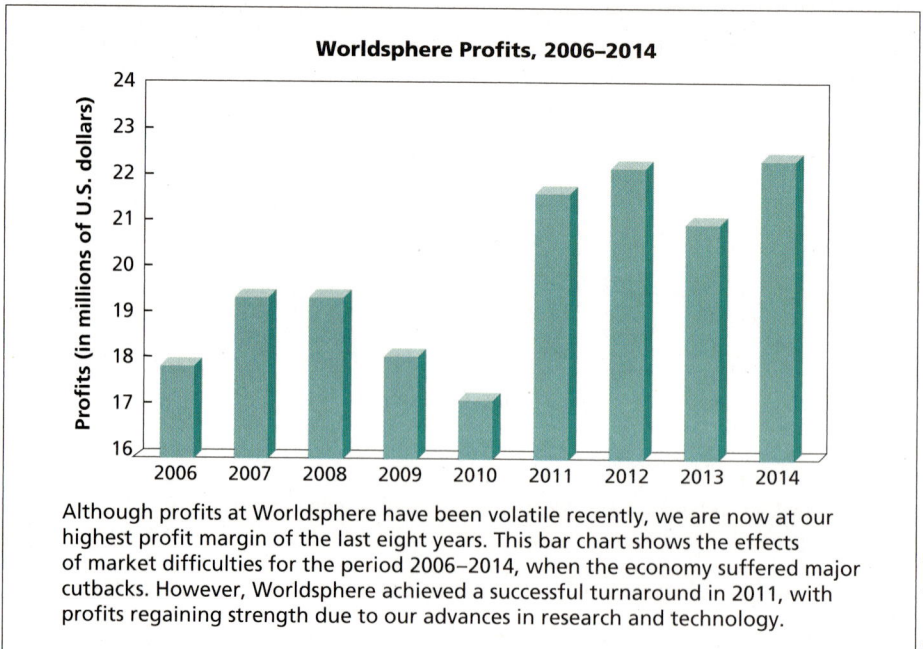

Worldsphere Profits, 2006–2014

Although profits at Worldsphere have been volatile recently, we are now at our highest profit margin of the last eight years. This bar chart shows the effects of market difficulties for the period 2006–2014, when the economy suffered major cutbacks. However, Worldsphere achieved a successful turnaround in 2011, with profits regaining strength due to our advances in research and technology.

© Cengage Learning 2015

- Avoid concealing negative information (losses, expenses, etc.) by including the information in another category, or slice, or lumping it into a category marked "Other" or "Miscellaneous."
- Make sure percentages match the size of the slices of the pie chart. Study Figures 6.26 and 6.27 (on page 254). Note how a larger expense for guest speakers (35 percent of budget) is unethically misrepresented in Figure 6.26 by using a smaller-sized wedge, while the expenses for venue rental (14 percent) are actually less than for guest speaker expenses but are drawn larger to misrepresent costs.

Using Appropriate Visuals for International Audiences

Whether you are writing for an expanding international business community in India or China, or for multicultural readers in the United States, you will have to prepare numerous documents that require visuals. These can range from instructions containing warning and caution statements to tables, graphs, charts, and photos included in proposals, reports, and online presentations.

Visuals Do Not Always Translate from One Culture to Another

While there are internationally recognized icons, such as those in Figure 6.28 (page 255), visuals do not automatically transfer from one culture to another. Visuals and other graphic devices may have one meaning or use in the United States and a radically different one in other countries around the world. To avoid confusing or offending an international audience, consult a native speaker from your audience's country to see if your visuals are culturally acceptable.

Guidelines for Using Visuals for International Audiences

To communicate appropriately and respectfully with international readers through visuals and other graphics, follow these guidelines:

1. **Do not use images that ethnically or racially stereotype your readers.** Depicting Native Americans through clip art images of red-faced chiefs is insulting. Rather than using an ethnic or racial pictograph, use neutral stick figures or nonbiased clip art. See, for example, the human figure in Figure 6.20.

2. **Be respectful of religious symbols and images.** Portraying a smiling Buddha to sell products is considered disrespectful to residents in Southeast Asia.

3. **Avoid using culturally insensitive or objectionable photographs.** A photograph portraying men and women eating together at a business conference is

FIGURE 6.26 An Unethical Pie Chart

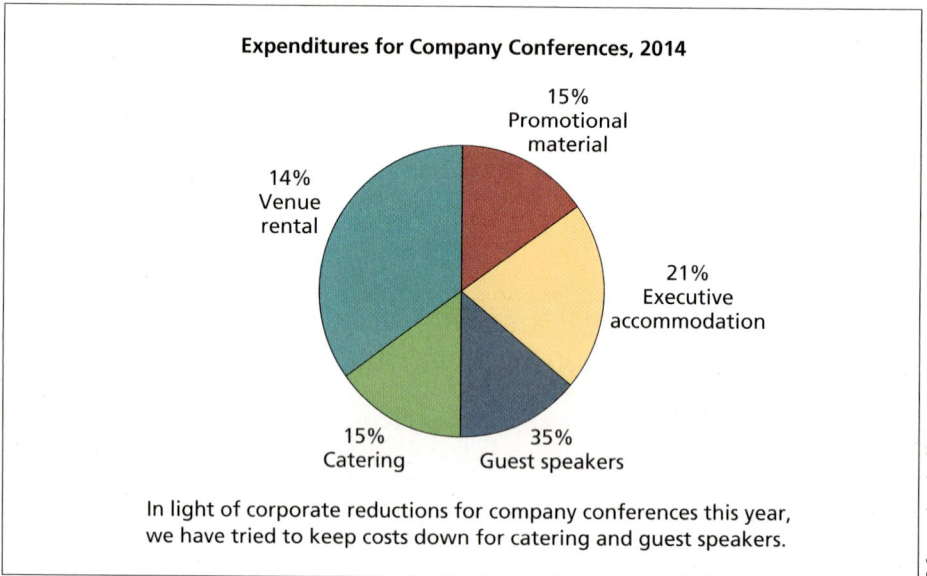

Expenditures for Company Conferences, 2014

15%
Promotional
material

14%
Venue
rental

21%
Executive
accommodation

15%
Catering

35%
Guest speakers

In light of corporate reductions for company conferences this year,
we have tried to keep costs down for catering and guest speakers.

© Cengage Learning 2015

FIGURE 6.27 An Ethical Revision of Figure 6.26

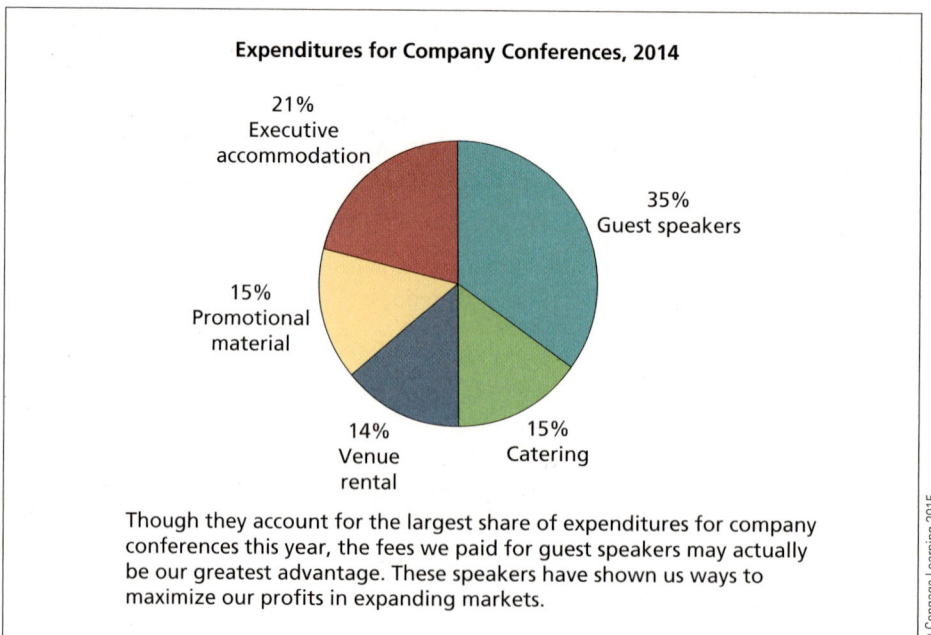

Expenditures for Company Conferences, 2014

21%
Executive
accommodation

35%
Guest speakers

15%
Promotional
material

14%
Venue
rental

15%
Catering

Though they account for the largest share of expenditures for company
conferences this year, the fees we paid for guest speakers may actually
be our greatest advantage. These speakers have shown us ways to
maximize our profits in expanding markets.

© Cengage Learning 2015

FIGURE 6.28 Internationally Recognized Icons

© Cengage Learning

unacceptable in Saudi Arabia. Moreover, sitting with one leg crossed over the other is regarded as a disrespectful gesture in many countries in the world.

4. Avoid icons or clip art that international readers would misunderstand. In the United States, an owl can stand for wisdom, thrift, and memory while in Japan Romania, and some African countries it is a symbol for death. A software program showing an icon of a mailbox (shown here) to represent email confused readers in other countries who thought the icon represented a birdhouse. A better alternative would be an icon of an envelope.

© Cengage Learning

Similarly, the Apple icon for "trash" (a garbage can) confused some international readers because not all garbage cans look alike.

5. Be cautious about using images or photos with hand gestures, especially in manuals or other instructional materials. Many gestures are culture-specific; they do not necessarily mean the same thing in other countries that they do in the United States. Table 6.2 lists cultural differences around the globe for some common gestures.

6. Don't offend international readers by using colors that are culturally inappropriate. Red in China symbolizes happiness while yellow in Saudi Arabia signifies strength. Green is regarded as a sacred color in Saudi Arabia.

Always research (on the Internet or by consulting a representative from the audience you want to reach) if the color scheme you have chosen is appropriate for your target audience. For example, purple is the color of death and mourning in Thailand as white is in China. Although orange is the symbolic color of Northern Ireland, avoid using it when writing to readers whose culture does not value that color.

7. Be careful when using directional signs and shapes. While road signs tend to be fairly recognizable throughout the world—for example, the octagon is generally

TABLE 6.2   Different Cultural Meanings of Various Gestures

Gesture	Meaning in the United States	Meaning in Other Countries
OK sign (index finger joined to thumb in a circle)	All right; agreement	Sexual insult in Brazil, Germany, Russia; sign for zero, worthlessness in France
Thumbs-up	A winning gesture; good job; approval	Offensive gesture in Muslim countries
Waving or holding out open palm	Stop	Obscene in Greece—equivalent to throwing garbage at someone
Pointing with the index finger	This way; pay attention; turn the page	Rude, insulting in Japan, Sri Lanka, and Venezuela; in Saudi Arabia used only for animals, not for people
Nodding head up and down	Agreement, saying yes	Greek version of saying "no"; in China means "I understand," not "I agree"

© Cengage Learning 2015

understood as the shape for the stop sign—there are country-specific signs and code books. For instance, a pennant-shaped sign, signaling a no-passing zone on American highways, may not have the same meaning in Nigeria or India. The following symbol points to a railroad crossing for American readers but would baffle an audience in the Czech Republic.

© Cengage Learning

Writing for and Designing Websites*

In the global marketplace, you need to apply the skills you have just learned in designing documents and visuals to an online environment (websites, blogs, etc.). In fact, companies often ask their employees to write for and prepare visuals for a corporate website, and while you may not be expected to construct a website on your own, you will likely be part of a team of specialists in information technology, graphics, and marketing responsible for your firm's web presence. To be a helpful member of this team, you have to keep up with the latest features of website design and information on how your company can incorporate them. You may also be

---

* I am grateful to Michael Tracey, of Bay St. Louis, Mississippi, for his invaluable advice on designing websites.

asked to critique a competitor's website or to assist a client in preparing his/her website. This section of the Chapter 6 stresses the principles and guidelines you need to follow to

- help readers navigate your website quickly, moving from one part to another easily
- ensure that your site is current
- make your site user friendly (for global readers as well as English-speaking audiences)
- create a visually attractive site
- keep your design and content ethical

Web Versus Print Readers

To help design and write for the web, you need to recognize how webpages are read differently from the way print documents are.

1. Readers do not generally go through a website word for word hunting for information, carefully studying each sentence. They want to find information at a glance. On the average, web readers spend ten to eighty seconds scanning a page. If they don't find what they need, they'll click to another site.

2. Web readers want articles, news stories, and features to be more condensed, and more strategically arranged. They want only essential information.

3. A web audience will not necessarily read your entire website. Because they may not have even begun their search at your site, your web audience may not navigate through your pages in any predetermined order, or even read all of its parts.

4. Web readers will expect navigational cues that readers of a print source do not have. A web audience will be looking for visual markers such as highlighted keywords to click on or bulleted lists, different colored text, commands such as *search, click here, go to, go back, contact us,* arrows and crosses, or hyperlinks of other sites to visit. Note how these cues are incorporated into the website in Figure 6.29 on page 258.

Preparing a Successful Home Page

Successful homepages catch a visitor's attention and sell a product or service, or introduce your organization clearly and effectively. For example, students applying for financial aid can find it a daunting process, but the design of the FinAid homepage, Figure 6.29, keeps things upbeat and easy to follow. Even the image of the student "jumping for joy" contributes to the site's user-friendliness. The writing style and tone, for example, are appropriately conversational, friendly, and helpful—"Find everything from grants to . . . tuition payment plans"; "Beware scholarship scams." The FinAid homepage also provides clear links to the other related websites.

FIGURE 6.29 A Well-Designed Home Page

Spare, simple design avoids using unnecessary visuals and images

Page is carefully organized, visually balanced, and uncluttered

Left column headers use appropriate icons

Uses concise and clear language

Links arranged by audience needs

Additional links to content on the website are provided at the bottom of the home page

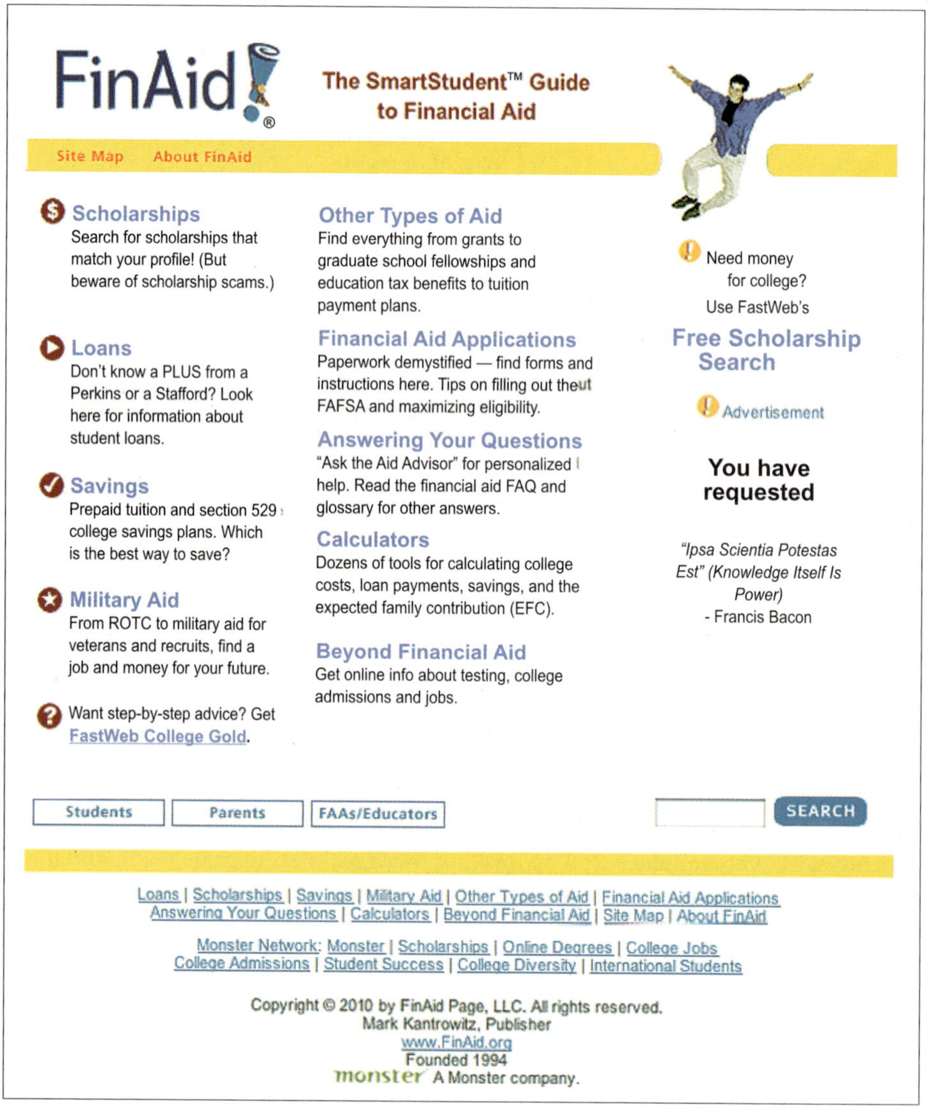

Designing and Writing for the Web: Eight Guidelines

By adhering to the following eight guidelines, you can create an effectively designed and written website that will capture your audience's attention.

1. **Make your site easy to find.**

   ■ Choose a professional domain name that clearly and quickly tells readers what you do. Avoid cute spellings and fanciful names, e.g., happihouse.com.

Instead, use a clear, easy-to-remember name, e.g., toledohousepainters. com. A good place to start is the InterNIC website (www.internic.net) which provides updated information on domain name registrations.

- Submit your website to the various search engines and directories to make sure the largest possible audience can find your site. Google, for instance, gives helpful tips to do this.
- To optimize your chances of being listed by search engines, use keywords that sell your business or organization. Use Google's AdWords' Keyword Tool (https://adwords.google.com/o/KeywordTool) for help in choosing terms that will increase traffic to your site. Make sure you cross-link to relevant pages on your website as well.

2. Make your site easy to navigate.

- Help your visitors find their way easily through your site with logical and effective navigation tools such as

hyperlinks	search engines
navigation bars	button links
indexes and menus	rollover icons
site maps and tables of contents	previous, next, and back links

Provide multiple navigation aids such as clearly labeled sections, each illustrated with icons, and links to multimedia and tools, as in Figure 6.29 and Figure 5.1 (page 164).

- Test every link to make sure it is current, that it works, and that it connects to related sites.
- Track visitors to your site to build a customer database.
- Insert tabs on every page back to your homepage.
- Don't overload your page with images, making it look crowded. Note how the FinAid website in Figure 6.29 uses a single image, six smaller icons, and boxes at the bottom left of the home page to help readers.

3. Make your site informative.

- Provide essential information on or through your home page, including your company's name, address, zip code, email, phone number, and corporate blog, as well as such key links as "Contact," "About," and "Menu." The more helpful your site is, the more likely it will draw repeat visitors.
- Tell visitors what products or services you offer. Figure 6.29 offers tailor-made services to students, parents, and educators.
- Indicate what type of information can be obtained through your website, including links to your customer service and technical support. The FinAid website in Figure 6.29 provides information quickly on scholarships, savings, military aid, and more.
- Offer readers different types of interaction—FAQs, bulletin boards, animated product demonstrations, and free email subscriptions. For example, the FinAid site offers dozens of useful "Calculators."

4. **Make your site easy to read for both native English speakers and international readers.**

   - Keep text short because of screen size coupled with the problem of glare. Avoid squeezing lots of text, clip art, and images onto a webpage.
   - Put the most important point first in a seven- to eight-word headline (e.g., "The Smart Student Guide to Financial Aid").
   - Get to the point right away. Don't begin with background information.
   - Write short descriptions of content—no more than three to four lines, as in the FinAid site in Figure 6.29.
   - Provide headings with attention-grabbing keywords, bulleted lists, and numbered lists to help readers locate information quickly, (e.g., Scholarships, Loans, Military).
   - Include plenty of white space between sections.
   - Insert scannable terms and hyperlinks; always highlight them to make them stand out.
   - Select fonts that are easy to read (see pages 223–224). Use larger fonts than you would for a print document.
   - Select background colors that make your text easy to read. For example, don't use dark green lettering on a black background.

5. **Keep your site updated.**

   - New information is vital for selling your product or service on a company website. Feature a blog, updates about your business, or preproduction information on products, services, community projects, and environmental efforts. Build in hyperlinks to product reviews, conferences, awards, and so on.
   - Revise the design of your home page if your company offers a new product or service or a new promotion. Clearly, your site does not need a major design overhaul every week, but a new or revised home page alerts customers to the latest products and services.
   - Indicate when your site was last updated so readers will know your information is kept current.

6. **Use images and icons effectively.**

   - Arrange images and photos so they do not interfere with text. Proportion is important for achieving a balance between different page elements.
   - Choose appropriate icons or images to illustrate menus and page sections. See how Figure 6.29 uses easy-to-recognize icons for money and military assistance.
   - Be conservative in using animations or anything that might be viewed as a gimmick because they may distract readers from other content on your page.
   - Keep images proportional so that they are neither too big nor too small for the page.

7. **Encourage visitor interaction by soliciting feedback.**

   ■ Ask readers to email you about your product, service, or website. Alert them to any relevant blog entries. And make sure a procedure for handling that feedback is developed within your organization.

   ■ Include a feedback form or survey with specifically targeted questions—including multiple-choice, pull-down menus, and comment boxes—about your website to encourage visitors to leave useful comments.

8. **Make sure your website is ethical.**

   ■ Never post confidential or proprietary information.

   ■ Never post anything insulting or harassing, and never attack a competitor, a colleague, another department in your company, or a government agency.

   ■ Do not plagiarize from another web (or print) source. If you include any information from another site—including quotations, visuals, or statistics—obtain permission, and acknowledge the source on your site.

   ■ Do not use sexist, racist, or other biased forms of language. Moreover, do not offend an international audience by using terms, names, or visuals that are insulting, stereotypical, or condescending. (See pages 253–256.)

   ■ Never make false or exaggerated claims. Be honest and accurate. Earn your readers' and employer's trust.

✔ Revision Checklist

Printed Documents

☐ Arranged information in the most logical, easy-to-grasp order.

☐ Left adequate, eye-pleasing white space in text and margins to frame document.

☐ Maintained pleasing, easy-to-read line length and spacing.

☐ Chose appropriate typeface for message and type of document.

☐ Did not mix typefaces.

☐ Inserted heads and subheads to organize information for reader.

☐ Used effective type size, neither too small (under 10 points) nor too large (over 12 points) for the body of the text.

☐ Used lists, bullets, numbers to divide information for readers.

☐ Chose colors carefully to make sure they look professional.

Visuals

☐ Selected most effective type of visual (table, chart, graph, drawing, photograph, infograph) to represent information the audience needs.

☐ Drafted and edited visual until it met readers' needs.

☐ Included right amount of detail to include in visual.
☐ Made sure every visual is attractive, clear, complete, and relevant.
☐ Gave each visual a number, a title, and, where necessary, a legend and callouts.
☐ Inserted visual close to the description or commentary accompanying it—on
☐ the same or facing page.
☐ Inserted page number where visual can be found.
☐ Introduced and interpreted each visual in appropriate place in report or proposal.
☐ Made sure every photograph is clear and relevant.
☐ Acknowledged sources for any copyrighted visuals and gave credit to individuals whose statistical data are the basis of a visual.
☐ Used and interpreted visuals ethically and appropriately.
☐ Selected visuals, colors, and images that respect the cultural traditions of my international readers.
☐ Did not distort or skew any visual to misrepresent data.

Websites

☐ Designed website so that it is easy to find on major search engines.
☐ Made sure navigation is clear and logical, not overly complex.
☐ Provided identification for all pages either with headings or text that explains the purpose of each page.
☐ Ensured that the site is informative and relevant, and that the content is current.
☐ Kept the site current by revising it frequently and including most recent research.
☐ Used headings, subheadings, and white space to break information into readable chunks.
☐ Encouraged visitor interaction by soliciting feedback.
☐ Provided ways for reader to interact with the site, whether via email, a feedback page, or a blog where comments can be posted.
☐ Did not crowd images and text on the same page.
☐ Chose appropriate background colors so text is clear and easy to read.
☐ Strove to make sure the site is ethical.

Exercises

1. Find an ineffectively designed print document—a form, a set of instructions, a brochure, a section of a manual, a catalog, a newsletter—and assume that you are a document design consultant. Write a sales letter to the company or agency that prepared and distributed the document, offering to redesign it and any other documents they have. Stress your qualifications and include a sample of your work. You will have to be convincing and diplomatic—precisely and professionally persuading your readers that they need your services to improve their corporate image, customer relations, and sales or services.

2. Redesign the following handwashing document to make it conform to the guidelines specified in this chapter—reformat; add headings, spacing, and visual clues; include appropriate clip art; and provide short introduction.

WHY SHOULD YOU WASH YOUR HANDS?

Bacteria and viruses (germs) that cause illnesses are spread when you don't wash your hands.

If you don't wash your hands, you risk acquiring:

The common cold or flu

Gastrointestinal illnesses Shigella or hepatitis A

Respiratory illnesses

Should you wash your hands?

You need to wash your hands several times every day. Some important times to wash your hands are:

BEFORE

Preparing or eating food.

Treating a cut wound.

Tending to someone who is sick.

Inserting or removing contacts

After

Using the bathroom.

Changing a diaper or helping a child use the bathroom (don't forget the child's hands)

Handling raw meats/poultry/eggs

Touching pets, especially reptiles

handling garbage

Sneezing or blowing your nose, or helping a child blow his/her nose

Touching any body fluids like blood or mucus

Being in contact with a sick person

Playing outside or with children and their toys

WHEN SHOULD YOU WASH YOUR HANDS?

There is a right way to wash your hands.

Follow these steps and you will help protect yourself and your family from illness.

Like any good habit, proper hand washing must be taught.

Take the time to teach it to your children and make sure they practice.

© Cengage Learning

---

3. One government agency supplied statistics on the world production of oranges (including tangerines) in thousands of metric tons for the following countries during the years 2010–2014: Brazil, 2,098, 2,132, 2,760, 2,872; Israel, 909, 1,076, 1,148, 1,221; Italy, 1,669, 1,599, 1,766, 1,604; Japan, 2,424, 2,994, 2,885, 4,070; Mexico, 937, 1,405, 1,114, 1,270; Spain, 2,135, 2,005, 2,179, 2,642; and the United States, 7,658, 7,875, 7,889, 9,245. Prepare a table with that information and then write a paragraph in which you introduce and refer to the table and draw conclusions from it.

4. Write a paragraph introducing and interpreting the following table for a publication aimed at general readers.

Year	Soft Drink Companies	Bottling Plants	Per Capita Consumption (Gallons)
1945	750	750	10.3
1950	578	611	12.5
1955	457	466	18.6
1960	380	407	17.2
1965	231	292	15.9
1970	171	229	15.4
1975	118	197	16.0
1980	92	154	18.7
1985	54	102	21.1
1990	43	88	23.1
1995	45	82	25.3
2000	37	78	27.6
2005	34	72	30.1
2010	31	70	32.3
2015	30	69	31.4

© Cengage Learning 2015

5. According to a municipal study in 2014, the distribution of all companies classified in each enterprise in that city was as follows: minerals, 0.4 percent; selected services, 33.3 percent; e- and brick-and-mortar sales, 36.7 percent; wholesale trade, 6.5 percent; manufacturing, 5.3 percent; and construction, 17.8 percent. Make a pie chart to represent the distribution, and write a one- or two-paragraph interpretation to accompany (and explain the significance of) your visual.

6. Make an organizational chart for a business or an agency you worked for recently. Include part-time and full-time employees, but indicate their titles or functions with different kinds of shapes or lines. Then write a brief letter to your employer explaining why your organizational chart should be distributed to all employees. Focus on the types of problems that could be avoided if employees had access to such a visual.

7. Prepare a flow chart for one of the following activities:
   a. jumping a "dead" car battery
   b. giving an injection
   c. making a reservation online
   d. using an iPhone to check the status of a flight
   e. checking your credit online
   f. putting out an electrical fire
   g. changing your email password
   h. preparing a visual using a graphics software package
   i. putting your blog online
   j. joining a chat group
   k. filing for an extension to pay state taxes
   l. any job you do

8. Prepare a drawing of one of the following simple tools, and include appropriate callouts with your visual.
   a. high-definition TV
   b. iPod
   c. pliers
   d. stethoscope
   e. swivel chair
   f. Galaxy S4
   g. Compact fluorescent lightbulb
   h. Makita circular saw

9. Prepare appropriate visuals to illustrate the data listed in parts (a) and (b). In a paragraph immediately after the visual, explain why the type of visual you selected is appropriate for the information.

    a. Life expectancy is increasing in the United States. This growth can be dramatically measured by comparing the number of teenagers with the number of older adults (over age 65) in the United States during the last few years and then projecting those figures. In 1970, there were approximately 28 million teenagers and 20 million older adults. By 1990 the number of teenagers climbed to 30 million, and the number of older adults increased to 25 million. In 2000, there were 27 million teenagers and 31 million older adults. In 2010, the number of teenagers had leveled off to 23 million, but the number of older adults soared to more than 36 million.

    b. Researchers estimate that for every adult in the United States 3,985 cigarettes were purchased in 1990; 4,100 in 1995; 3,875 in 2000; 3,490 in 2005; 2,910 in 2010; and 2,720 in 2015.

10. Following are two examples of poorly prepared visuals with brief explanations of how they were intended to be used. Redo one of the visuals to make it easier to read by re-organizing information. Supply a paragraph to introduce your new visual.

    a. To accompany a report on problems that pilots have encountered with a particular model of jet engine.

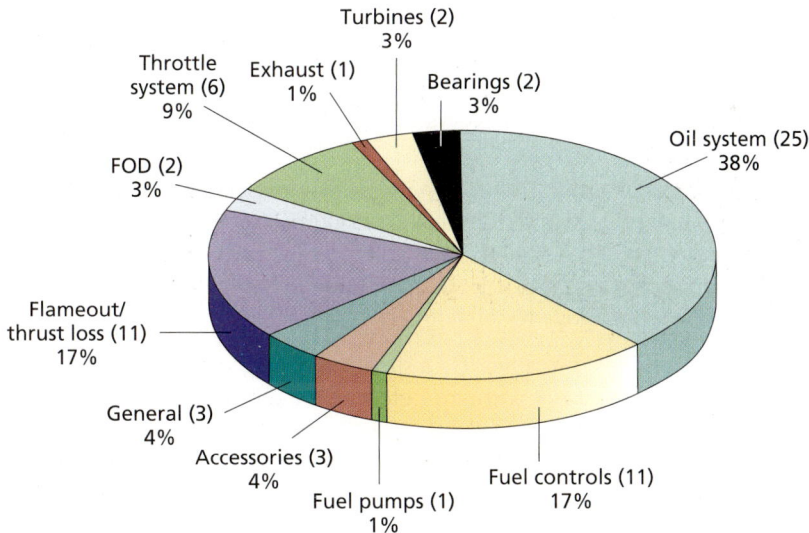

    b. To show that a hiking trail is compatible with wheelchair access laws.

11. You have been asked to create a logo, including a visual, for one of the following new businesses opening in your town. Explain your design and why you think it is effective.
   a. landscaping firm
   b. home health care company
   c. studio offering musical instrument lessons
   d. outdoor apparel manufacturer
   e. toxic waste removal company
   f. math and science tutor

12. Explain why the following would be inappropriate in communicating with an international audience and how you would revise the document containing such visuals/graphics symbols:
   a. clip art showing a string tied around an index finger
   b. picture of a man with a sombrero on a website for Pronto Quick Check Cashing Service
   c. clip art/drawing of a light bulb and logo "Smart Ideas" from a CPA firm
   d. clip art showing someone crossing the middle finger over the index finger (wishing sign)
   e. drawing of a cupid figure for a caterer
   f. a sales brochure showing a white and blue flag for a French audience
   g. an advertisement showing a woman's track and field team used to advertise a brand of footware to an Arabic-speaking audience
   h. a satisfied customer making the gesture of OK in an ad aimed at a Japanese audience
   i. an image of a rabbit on a website for an automobile manufacturer to stress how fast its cars can accelerate
   j. a photograph of a roll of Scotch tape to show international readers that your company can solve problems quickly and economically
   k. a photograph of a baseball umpire holding his hands up to ask international readers to repeat a step in a set of instructions
   l. an icon of a white glove to sell home and carpet cleaning

13. Locate two webpages that advertise a similar product, service, industry, or other topic. Analyze some of the webpage elements each one uses, comparing the strengths and weaknesses of each site. Write a one-page memo to your instructor explaining which is the more effective site and why

14. Find a webpage that you believe is ineffective. Using the four keys to effective writing (see Chapter 1, pages 6–15), as well as your knowledge of webpage elements, write a one-page assessment of the site, discussing three or four changes you think would make it more effective. Attach a printed hard copy of the webpage with your assessment.

Summarizing Information at Work

A summary is a brief restatement of the main points of a book, report, website, article, laboratory test, PowerPoint presentation, meeting, or convention. A summary saves readers hours of time because they do not have to study the original work or attend a conference. A summary can reduce a report or an article by 85 to 95 percent (or even more) and can capture the essential points of a three-day convention in a one-page memo. Moreover, a summary can tell readers whether they should even be concerned about the original; it may be irrelevant for their purposes. Finally, since only the most important points of a work are included in a summary, readers will know they have been given the crucial information they need.

Access chapter-specific interactive learning tools, including quizzes and more in your English CourseMate, accessed through www.cengagebrain .com.

Summaries in the Information Age

Thanks to the Web and other communication technologies, we have an abundance of information. It would be impossible to locate, classify, understand, and assess all this information without the help of summaries. They can be found all around you.

- Google, one of the most frequently used search engines, retrieves positive "hits" by looking for keywords that summarize a source and help users determine whether the material is relevant for their purpose.
- A home page on the Web is in essence a summary of the various pages to which it is connected.
- Television and radio stations regularly air one- or two-minute "news breaks" that summarize in a few paragraphs the major stories of the day, such as CNN (www.CNN.com).
- Blogs, such as those shown in Figures 4.10 and 4.11 (pages 156–157 and 161–162) frequently summarize the results of many weeks of research and decision making.
- Today's e-communication technologies, such as IMs and text messages, require you to summarize information concisely for readers who have small screens and tight schedules.

The Importance of Summaries in Business

Summaries are vital in the world of work. They get to the main points—the bottom line—right away for busy readers, giving them the big picture.

On the job, writing summaries for employers, co-workers, and customers is a regular and important responsibility. Chapter 14 discusses a variety of reports—periodic, sales, progress, trip, test, and incident—whose effectiveness depends on a faithful summary of events. You may be asked to summarize a week-long business trip in one or two pages or a two-hour teleconference in just a few paragraphs. You may have to condense a proposal to fit a one-page format for an organization. A busy manager may ask you to read and condense a ninety-page report so that she or he will have a knowledgeable overview of its contents. Or you may be asked to summarize the main features of a competitor's product or a new model you saw at a trade show. You may be asked to write a news release—another type of summary vital for your organization's image (pages 444–451)—for your employer's website.

Figure 9.1 is a summary of a long report evaluating child-care facilities. Note how it concisely identifies the main purpose and conclusions of the report.

FIGURE 9.1 A Summary of a Long Report on Child-Care Facilities

HIGH MARKS FOR ON-SITE CARE

The best place to find high-quality child care may be your workplace, according to a new study by Burud & Associates, a California-based work/life benefits consulting firm. The study of 205 work-site child-care programs found that such centers are eight times more likely than other facilities to meet the high standards set by the National Association for the Education of Young Children (NAEYC).

Forty-one percent of work-site centers open at least two years are NAEYC-accredited—compared to only 5 percent of all child-care centers. Other key findings include:

- Ninety-two percent of work-site centers offer infant care.
- Workplace centers provide "substantially better" employee benefits—which help the centers recruit and retain high-quality caregivers.
- One in four centers is open past seven p.m. and one in seven is open before six a.m. and/or offers weekend care.

© Cengage Learning 2013

Source: First appeared in *Working Mother*, May 1999. Reprinted by permission.

Contents of a Summary

The chief problem in writing a summary is deciding what to include and what to omit. Determine what is most relevant for your audience and its purpose. As we have seen, a summary is a streamlined review of *only* the most significant points. You will not save your readers time if you simply rephrase large sections of the original. That will simply supply readers with another report, not a summary.

Make your summary lean and useful by briefly telling readers the main points: purpose, scope, conclusions, and recommendations. A summary should straightforwardly and accurately answer readers' two most important questions:

1. What are the findings of the report or meeting?
2. How do the findings apply to my business, research, or job?

Note how the summary in Figure 9.1 successfully answered those two questions by indicating to working mothers where the best child care is likely to be found and why.

How long should a summary be? While it is hard to set down precise limits about length, effective summaries are generally no more than 5 to 10 percent of the length of the original. The complexity of the material being summarized and your audience's exact needs can help you to determine an appropriate length. The following suggestions will guide you on what to include and what to omit in your summary.

What to Include in a Summary

1. **Purpose.** A summary should indicate why the article or report was written or why a hearing meeting was held. Your summary should give readers a brief introduction (even one sentence will do) indicating the main purpose of the report or event.
2. **Essential specifics.** Include only the names, costs, titles, places, or dates essential to understanding the original.
3. **Conclusions or results.** Emphasize what the final vote was, the result of the tests, or the proposed solution to the problem.
4. **Recommendations or implications.** Readers will be especially interested in important recommendations — what they are, when they can be carried out, and why they are necessary, or why a plan will not work. They may look to your summary to determine what action needs to be taken.

What to Omit from a Summary

1. **Opinion.** Avoid injecting opinions — your own, the author's, or the speaker's. You distract readers from grasping main points by saying that the report was too long or missed the main point, that a salesperson from Detroit monopolized the meetings, or that the author digressed to blame the Land Commission for failing to act properly. A later section of this chapter (pages 438–442) will deal with evaluative summaries.

2. **New data.** Stick to the original article, report, book, or meeting. Avoid introducing comparisons with other works or conferences; readers will expect an unbiased digest of only the material being summarized.
3. **Irrelevant specifics.** Do not include biographical details about the author of an article that might be included in "Notes on Contributors." This information plays no role in the reader's understanding of your summary.
4. **Examples.** Illustrations, explanations, and descriptions are unnecessary in a summary. Readers will want to know outcomes, results, and recommendations, not the illustrative details supporting or elaborating on those results.
5. **Background.** Material in introductions to articles, reports, and conferences can usually be excluded from a summary. Such "lead-ins" prepare the reader for a discussion of the subject by presenting background information, not the big picture readers expect to see in a summary.
6. **Jargon.** Technical definitions or jargon in the original document may confuse rather than clarify the essential information for general readers.
7. **Reference data.** Exclude information found in footnotes, bibliographies, appendixes, tables, or graphs.

Preparing a Summary

To write an effective summary, you need to proceed through a series of steps. Basically, you will have to read the material carefully, making sure that you understand it thoroughly, to identify the major points, and, finally, to put the essence of the material into your own words. Follow these steps to prepare a concise, useful summary.

1. **Read the material once in its entirety to get an overall impression of what it is about.** Become familiar with large issues, such as the purpose and organization of the work and the audience for whom it was written. See if there are visual cues—headings, subheadings, words in italic or boldface type, sidebars—that will help you to classify main ideas. Also look for a conclusion and any mini-summaries within the article or report.

Tech Note

Using Software to Summarize Documents

Your word-processing software can help you prepare your summary. First, download and open an existing digital file of the material (article, report, technical paper) you need to summarize. Then, "save as" a new file with a new filename. If all you have is hard copy, do an OCR scan so you can create a digital file to edit. As you read through it on your screen, cut nonessential material. The first time through, it is easier to cut what you don't want than it is to select exactly what you do want. Using this method of editing, you can delete single sentences or several paragraphs at a time. Also, highlight key points as you read through the original material. Highlighting during the first pass can guide you on your second reading as you attempt to include only relevant material for your summary.

2. Reread the material. Read it a second time or more if necessary. Locate all of the main points, and underline them. (If the work is a book or in a journal that belongs to your library, work with a photocopy so you can underline.) To spot the main points, pay attention to the key transitional words, which often fall into predictable categories:

- Words that enumerate: *first, second, third, initially, subsequently, finally, next, another*
- Words that express causation: *accordingly, as a result, because, consequently, subsequently, therefore, thus*
- Words that express contrasts and comparisons: *although, by the same token, despite, different from, furthermore, however, in comparison, in contrast, in addition, less than, likewise, more readily, more than, not only . . . but also, on the other hand, the same is true for, similar, unlike*
- Words that signal essentials: *basically, best, central, crucial, foremost, fundamental, important, indispensable, in general, leading, major, obviously, principal, significant*

Pay special attention to the first and last sentences of each paragraph. Often the first sentence of a paragraph contains the topic sentence, and the last sentence summarizes the paragraph or provides a transition to the next paragraph.

Also be alert for words signaling information you do *not* want to include in your summary, such as the following:

- Words announcing opinion or inconclusive findings: *from my personal experience, I feel, I admit, in my opinion, might possibly show, perhaps, personally, may sometimes result in, has little idea about, questionable, presumably, subject to change, open to interpretation*
- Words pointing out examples or explanations: *as noted in, as shown by, circumstances include, explained by, for example, for instance, illustrated by, in terms of, learned through, represented by, such as, specifically in, stated in*

3. Collect your underlined material or notes and organize the information into a draft summary. At this stage do not be concerned about how your sentences read. Use the language of the original, together with any necessary connective words or phrases of your own. Key the draft into your computer. *Expect to have more material here than will appear in the final version.* Do not worry; you are engaged in a process of selection and exclusion. Your purpose at this stage is to extract the principal ideas from the examples, explanations, and opinions surrounding them.

4. Read through and revise your draft(s) and delete whatever information you can. As you revise, see how many of your underlined points can be condensed, combined, or eliminated. You may find that you have repeated a point. Check your draft against the original for accuracy and importance. Be sure to be faithful to the original by preserving its emphases and sequence. Put quotation marks around any direct quotations. But try to avoid direct quotation wherever possible at this stage.

5. Now put the revised version into your own words. Again, make sure that your reworded summary has eliminated nonessential words. Connect your sentences with words that show relationships between ideas in the original (*also, although, because, consequently, however, nevertheless, since*). Compare this version of your summary with the original material to double-check your facts.

6. Do not include remarks that repeatedly call attention to the fact that you are writing a summary. You may want to indicate initially that you are providing a summary, but avoid such remarks as "The author of this article states that water pollution is a major problem in Baytown" and "On page 13 of the article three examples, not discussed here, are found."

7. Edit your summary to make sure it is fair, clear, and concise. Compare your summary with the original to make sure you have captured the key points, especially those in the conclusion and recommendation sections. Check as well that your summary is coherent. Tell the reader how one point flows into another. Proofread your summary carefully.

8. Identify the source you have just summarized. Include pertinent bibliographic information in the title of your summary or in a footnote or an endnote. This gives proper credit to the original source and informs your readers where they can find the complete text if they want more details.

Case Study

Summarizing an Original Article

Figure 9.2, a 2,500-word article entitled "Virtual Reality: The Future of Law Enforcement Training," appeared in the *FBI Law Enforcement Bulletin* and hence is of primary interest to individuals in law enforcement administration. Assume you have been asked to write a summary of the FBI article for your boss, a police chief in a medium-sized city who would be interested in incorporating virtual reality segments into the police academy training program.

By following the steps outlined above, you would first read the article carefully two or three times, underscoring or highlighting the most important points, signaled by key words. Note what has been underscored in the article. Also study the comments in the margins to see why certain information is to be included or excluded from the summary.

After you have identified the main points, extract them from the article and, still using the language of the article, join them into a coherent working draft summary, as in Figure 9.3. Then shorten and rewrite the working draft in your own words to produce the compact final version of your summary, as shown in Figure 9.4. Only 154 words long, the final summary is 6 percent of the length of the original article and records only major conclusions relevant to the audience for the article.

FIGURE 9.2 An Original Article with Important Points Underscored for Use in a Summary

Virtual Reality: The Future of Law Enforcement Training

Jeffrey S. Hormann

A late night police pursuit of a suspected drunk driver winds through abandoned city streets. The short vehicle chase ends in a warehouse district where the suspect abandons his vehicle and continues his flight on foot. Before backup arrives, the rookie patrol officer exits his vehicle and gives chase. A quick run along a loading dock ends at the open door to an apparently unoccupied building. The suspect stops, brandishes a revolver, and fires in the direction of the pursuing officer before disappearing into the building. The officer, shaken but uninjured, radios in his location and follows the suspect into the building.

> *Omit scenario— example of background; an opener*

Did the officer make a good decision? Probably not by most departments' standards. Whether the officer's decision proves right or wrong, the training gained from this experience is immeasurable, that is, provided the officer lives through it. Fortunately for this officer, <u>the scenario occurred in a realistic, high-tech world called virtual reality</u>, where <u>training</u> can have <u>a real-life impact without the accompanying risk</u>.

> *Include important observation*

Traditional Training Limitations

Experience may be the best teacher, but in real life, police officers may not get a chance to learn from their mistakes. To survive, they must receive training that prepares them for most situations they might encounter on the street. <u>However</u>, because <u>many training programs</u> emphasize repetition to produce desired behaviors, they <u>may not achieve the intended results</u>, especially after students leave the training environment. Thus, the more realistic the training, the <u>greater the lessons</u> learned.

> *Major distinction*

<u>Additionally</u>, even some in law enforcement may fall prey to the effects of what has come to be termed "The MTV Generation." As products of this generation, today's young officers purportedly have short attention spans requiring new, nontraditional training methods. The key to teaching this new breed is to provide fast-paced, <u>attention-getting instruction</u> that is <u>clear, concise, and relevant</u>.

> *Omit explanation and example*
>
> *Include significant qualification*

Training with Virtual Reality

<u>Virtual reality</u> can <u>provide</u> the type of <u>training that today's law enforcement officers need</u>. By completely immersing the senses in a computer-generated environment, the <u>artificial world becomes reality to users</u> and greatly enhances their training experiences.

> *Emphasize author's main point*

<u>Although</u> considerable research and development have been conducted in this field, <u>only a limited amount has applied directly to law enforcement</u>. The apparent reason simply is that, for the most part, <u>law enforcement has not asked for it</u>.

> *Important reason for its neglect by law enforcement*

<u>Because virtual reality</u> technology is <u>relatively new</u>, most <u>law enforcement administrators know little about it</u>. They know even less about what it can do for

> *Restatement of main point above*

(Continued)

FIGURE 9.2 (Continued)

Note parallel items with key words signaling important applications

their agencies. By <u>understanding what virtual reality is, how it works,</u> and <u>how</u> it <u>can benefit them,</u> law enforcement administrators can become significantly involved in the development of this important new technology.

What Is Virtual Reality?

Include definition

<u>Simply stated, virtual reality</u> is <u>high-tech illusion</u>. It is a computer-generated, three-dimensional environment that engulfs the senses of sight, sound, and touch. Once entered, it becomes reality to the user.

Important explanation

Within this virtual world, users travel among, and interact with, objects that are wholly the products of a computer or representations of other participants in the same environment. Thus, the limits of this virtual environment depend on the sophistication and capabilities of the computer and the software that drives the system.

How Does Virtual Reality Work?

Significant phrase

Omit specific pieces of equipment

Based on data entered by programmers, computers create virtual environments by generating <u>three-dimensional images</u>. Users usually view these images through a head-mounted device, which, for instance, can be a helmet, goggles, or other apparatus that restricts their vision to two small video monitors, one in front of each eye. Each monitor displays a slightly different view of the environment, which gives users a sense of depth.

Omit example

<u>Another device</u>, called a position tracker, monitors users' physical positions and provides input to the computer. This information instructs the computer to change the environment based upon users' actions. <u>For example</u>, when users look over their shoulders, they see what lies behind them.

<u>Because</u> virtual reality users remain stationary, they use a <u>joy stick</u> or trackball to move through the virtual environment. Users <u>also</u> may wear a special glove or use other devices to manipulate objects within the virtual environment. <u>Similarly,</u> they can employ virtual weapons to confront virtual aggressors.

Omit further examples

Major conclusion

To enhance the sense of reality, some researchers are experimenting with tactile feedback devices (TFDs). TFDs transmit pressure, force, or vibration, providing users with a simulated sense of touch. <u>For example</u>, a user might want to open a door or move an object, which in reality, would require the sense of touch. A TFD would simulate this sensation. At present, <u>however</u>, it is important to remember that these devices are <u>crude</u> and somewhat <u>cumbersome to use</u>.

Uses for Virtual Reality

In <u>today's competitive business environment</u>, organizations continuously strive to accomplish tasks faster, better, and inexpensively. This especially holds true in training.

Major value to audience of administrators

Virtual reality is <u>emerging rapidly</u> as a <u>potentially unlimited</u> method for providing <u>realistic, safe</u>, and <u>cost-effective training</u>. <u>For example</u>, a firefighter can battle the flames of a virtual burning building. A police officer can struggle with virtual shoot/don't shoot dilemmas.

Emphasize significant advantages in training

Within a virtual environment, <u>students</u> can <u>make decisions</u> and act upon them <u>without risk</u> to themselves or others. By the same token, <u>instructors</u> can critique

FIGURE 9.2 (Continued)

students' actions, enabling students to review and learn from their mistakes. This ability gives virtual reality a great <u>advantage over most conventional training methods</u>.

The Department of Defense <u>(DOD) leads public and private industry</u> in <u>developing virtual reality training</u>. <u>Since</u> the early 1980s, DOD has actively researched, developed, and implemented virtual reality to <u>train members</u> of the <u>armed forces</u> to fight effectively in combat.

<u>DOD's current approach</u> to virtual reality training <u>emphasizes team tactics</u>. Groups of military personnel from around the world engage in combat safely on a virtual battlefield. Combatants never come together physically; <u>rather</u>, simulators located at various sites throughout the world transmit data to a central location, where the virtual battle is controlled. Basically, it costs less to move information than people. Consequently this form of training has proven quite cost-effective.

An <u>additional benefit</u> to this <u>type of training</u> is that <u>battles</u> can be <u>fought under varying conditions</u>.

Virtual battlefields <u>re-create real-world locations</u> with <u>interchangeable characteristics</u>. To explore "what if" scenarios, participants can modify enemy capabilities, terrain, weather, and weapon systems.

Virtual reality <u>also can re-create actual battles</u>. Based on information from participants, the Institute for Defense Analyses re-created the 2nd Armored Cavalry Regiment Offensive conducted in Iraq during Operation Desert Storm. The success of the virtual re-creation became apparent when, upon viewing the simulations, soldiers who had fought in the actual battle reported the extreme accuracy of the event's depiction and the feeling of reliving the battle. <u>Clearly, virtual reality holds great potential</u> for accurate review and analysis of <u>real-world situations</u>, which would be <u>difficult to accomplish</u> by <u>any other method</u>.

Preliminary studies, for instance, show that military units perform better following virtual reality training. <u>Even though</u> virtual environments are only simulations, the complete immersion of the senses literally overwhelms users, totally engrossing them in the action. <u>This realism</u> presumably plays a <u>major role</u> in the <u>program's success</u> and <u>likely</u> will prove positive in future endeavors. <u>In fact</u>, due to its success in training multiple participants in group combat situations, DOD plans to train infantry personnel individually with virtual reality fighting skill simulators.

Law Enforcement Training
While virtual reality has proven its value as a training and planning tool for the military, <u>applications for this technology reach far beyond DOD</u>. In varying but key ways, many military uses can <u>transfer to law enforcement</u>, including training in firearms, stealth tactics, and assault skills.

Unfortunately, few organizations have dedicated resources to developing virtual reality for law enforcement. <u>According</u> to a recently published resource guide, more than <u>100 companies</u> currently are <u>developing and/or selling virtual reality hardware or software</u>. However, <u>none</u> of these firms <u>mentioned law enforcement uses</u>.

<u>Further</u>, a review of relevant literature revealed numerous articles on virtual reality technology, but only a few addressed law enforcement applications. <u>Yet</u>,

Use only main points relevant to target audience of administrators

Note main military advantage

Omit examples

Major conclusion signaled by key word "clearly"

Omit example

Key word "major" signals relevant idea for audience

Omit military application

Significant parallel points

Omit statistics

Subordinate idea

(Continued)

FIGURE 9.2 (Continued)

Restatement of major point

virtual reality <u>clearly offers law enforcement benefits</u> in a number of areas, including pursuit driving, firearms training, high-risk incident management, incident recreation, and crime scene processing.

Pursuit Driving

Include application but omit examples

<u>Pursuit driving</u> represents one area in which <u>virtual reality application</u> has become <u>reality for law enforcement</u>. Law enforcement personnel identified a need and provided input to a well-known private corporation that developed a driving simulator equipped with realistic controls.

Omit specific mechanism and explanation of operation of screen mechanism

The simulator provides users with realistic steering wheel feedback, road feel, and other vehicle motions. The screen possesses a 225-degree field of view standard, with 360-degree coverage optional. <u>As noted in demonstrations</u>, simulations can involve one or more drivers, and environments can alternate between city streets, rural back roads, and oval tracks. The vehicle itself can change from a police car to a truck, ambulance, or a number of others.

Note cost efficiency again

Virtual reality driving simulators provide police departments invaluable training at a <u>fraction of the long-term cost of using actual vehicles</u>. In fact, the simulator is being used by a number of police departments around the country.

Include major advantage but exclude specific example

During the past year, for example, the Los Angeles County Sheriff's Office Emergency Vehicle Operations Center (EVOC) has used a four-station version of the driving simulator to train its officers. The simulators help students develop judgment and decision-making skills, while providing an environment free from risk of injury to students or damage to vehicles. Still, as the EVOC supervisor cautions, <u>virtual reality training</u> should <u>complement, not replace</u>, actual behind-the-wheel instruction.

Note major distinction for training purpose

Firearms Training

New subtopic; include advantage but omit examples

In another way, virtual reality could <u>greatly enhance</u> shoot/don't shoot <u>training simulators</u> currently in use, such as the Firearms Training System, a primarily two-dimensional approach that possesses limited interactive capabilities. A <u>virtual reality system</u> would <u>allow officers</u> to enter any <u>three-dimensional environment</u> alone or as a member of a team and confront computer-generated aggressors or other virtual reality users.

Include significant points on advantages

Evaluators could specifically observe the <u>training from any perspective</u>, including that of the officers, or the criminal. The <u>training scenarios</u> could involve actual building floor plans or local city streets, and criteria <u>such as</u> weather, number of participants, or types of weapons could be altered easily.

High-Risk Incident Management

Next three reasons to use virtual reality signaled by keywords: in addition, also, and likewise

<u>In addition</u> to weapons training, virtual reality <u>could prove invaluable for SWAT team members</u> before <u>high-risk tactical assaults</u>. Floor plans and other known facts about a structure or area could be entered into a computer to create a virtual environment for commanders and team members to analyze prior to action.

Incident Re-creation

Law enforcement agencies could <u>also collect data</u> from victims, witnesses, suspects, and crime scenes <u>to re-create traffic accidents</u>, shootings, and other crimes.

FIGURE 9.2 (Continued)

The virtual environment created from the data could be used to refresh the memories of victims and witnesses, to solve crimes, and ultimately, to prosecute offenders.

Crime Scene Processing
Virtual reality crime scenes could <u>likewise</u> be used to <u>train both detectives and patrol officers</u>. First, students could search the site and retrieve and analyze evidence <u>without ever leaving the station</u>. Then, actual crime scenes could be recreated to add realism to training or to evaluate prior police actions.

Omit examples

Is Virtual Reality Virtually Perfect?
<u>Though</u> virtual reality may appear to be the <u>ideal law enforcement tool</u>, as with any new technology, <u>some drawbacks exist</u>. <u>Currently</u>, areas of concern range from cumbersome equipment to negative physical and psychological effects experienced by some users. Fortunately, <u>however</u>, the <u>field is evolving and improving constantly</u>, and as <u>virtual reality gains widespread use</u>, most <u>major concerns should be dispelled</u>.

Crucial qualification and justification for using virtual reality in law enforcement training

Physical Limitations and Effects
<u>Because</u> computers currently are <u>not fast enough</u> to process large amounts of graphic information in real time, <u>some observers</u> describe virtual environments as "<u>slow-moving</u>." The human eye can process images at a much faster rate than a computer can generate them. In a <u>virtual environment</u>, frames are displayed at a rate of about 7 per second, an extremely slow speed when compared to television, which generates 60 frames per second. Users find the resulting choppy or slow graphics less than appealing.

Omit examples of limitations/ effects

Source: Adapted from FBI Law Enforcement Bulletin, 64/no. 7: 7–12.

Make Sure Your Summary Is Ethical

Your supervisor will expect your summary to be honest, fair, and accurate, identifying the most crucial points of the article. Figure 9.5 on page 434 contains an unethical summary of Figure 9.2 that distorts the meaning and intention of the original by leading the reader to conclude that virtual reality is not valuable for law enforcement administrators—the very opposite point the author makes.

You can write an ethical summary by doing the following:

- Make sure your summary agrees with the original.
- Emphasize the main points the author makes.
- Do not omit key points.
- Be fair in expressing the author's conclusions/recommendations.
- Do not dwell on minor points to the exclusion of major ones.
- Do not let your own opinions distort or contradict the message of the original document.

FIGURE 9.3 A Working Draft Summary of the "Virtual Reality" Article in Figure 9.2

Law enforcement officers put their lives on the line every day, yet their training does not fully allow them to anticipate what they will find on the streets. Virtual reality will give them realistic, high-tech benefits of encountering criminals without any risks. Traditional training methods, which work through repetition, cannot equal the advantages of virtual reality when it comes to teaching officers the lessons they must learn to survive in the field. This new breed of officers is demanding the attention-getting, highly realistic training that virtual reality affords them. Virtual reality translates the artificial world of the computer into the real world. Yet even though much research has been done on virtual reality, it is new to law enforcement officials. Moreover, manufacturers have not marketed their technology to them. It is essential that these administrators know how virtual reality works and what it can do for them. Virtual reality has been defined as high-tech illusion through the computer user's perceived interaction with the real world. Working through sophisticated software, virtual reality gives users a three-dimensional (hearing, feeling, and seeing) view of the things and people around them. Virtual reality requires specific equipment including goggles/headsets, a tracker, a trackball, and special gloves. But these devices do have problems; at present, they are crude and can be cumbersome. Even so, virtual reality provides cost-effective and life-saving benefits for law enforcement administrators. Thanks to this technology, new officers will be able to make quicker and better decisions in the field. Virtual reality has already been tried by the Department of Defense; the armed forces have used it to re-create battlefield conditions, helping the troops better understand the enemy and its position. Yet virtual reality holds great appeal for other real-world applications, especially law enforcement. Unfortunately, the 100 companies that manufacture virtual reality equipment have neglected these law enforcement applications. Yet virtual reality easily accommodates law enforcement instruction. Driving simulators help officers prepare for high-speed chases. In Los Angeles County, such simulators complement more traditional training. Virtual reality can help officers in a variety of training missions—firearms, high-risk incidents, re-creating crimes, understanding the crime scene. Using virtual reality, officers never have to leave the station. Admittedly, virtual reality has drawbacks, but as this new technology improves, users should face fewer problems.

FIGURE 9.4   A Final, Effective Summary of the Article in Figure 9.2

Virtual reality offers benefits for law enforcement training that traditional methods cannot provide. This computer-generated technology simulates and re-creates real-life crime scenes without placing officers at risk. Thanks to virtual reality's three-dimensional world of sight, sound, and touch, officers enter the criminals' world to gain invaluable experience interacting with them. Because virtual reality has not been marketed for law enforcement use, administrators may not know about it. Yet it provides a cost-effective, realistic way to enhance training programs. The applications of virtual reality far exceed its military use of simulating battlefield conditions. Virtual reality allows administrators to give trainees hands-on experience in pursuit driving, firearms training, SWAT team assaults, incident re-creation, and crime scene processing. Officers can investigate a crime without ever leaving the station. Although virtual reality is an emerging technology with limitations, it is quickly improving and rapidly expanding. Administrators need to incorporate it into their curriculum to give officers field-translatable experiences.

© Cengage Learning 2013

Executive Summaries

An executive summary, found at the beginning of a proposal (Chapter 13) or a long report (Chapter 15), is usually one or two pages long (four to six concise paragraphs) and condenses the most important points from the proposal or report for a busy manager—the executive. Your employer wants bottom-line conclusions, not all the technical details. An executive summary is written to help the reader reach a major decision based on the report or proposal. Your job, in an executive summary, then, is to concisely tell your employer what findings the report includes, what those findings mean for the company or organization, and what action, if any, needs to be taken. Figure 9.6 (page 436), an executive summary of a report on software for a safety training program, directly advises a decision maker to purchase a safety software package. Managers use executive summaries so they will *not* have to wade through entire reports. An effective executive summary is like a report itself—self-contained and able to stand on its own.

What Managers Want to See in an Executive Summary

Executive readers are most concerned with managerial and organizational issues—the areas over which they have supervisory control. These readers will look for information on costs, profits, resources, personnel, timetables, and feasibility. Your

FIGURE 9.5   An Unethical, Misleading Summary of the Article in Figure 9.2

Nonessential introductory material

Distorts article

Dwells on specific virtual reality equipment at the expense of the main advantages

Reverses chronology of events; misrepresents the role of virtual reality

Deletes unit's name

Deletes specifications

One-sided; omits success of simulation

Focuses on limits rather than usefulness

Does not subordinate flaws

A rookie police officer makes many mistakes in pursuing subjects. Training can cover many realistic situations, but young officers in the MTV Generation have short attention spans. Given the research so far on virtual reality, it holds little promise for law enforcement use. Virtual reality has too many limitations, but it works interestingly through gloves, helmets, and goggles, and with a position tracker users can see over their shoulders. It even has a joy stick (like those in an amusement park) and a crude device—a TFD—that simulates touch (nice to have in a horror movie). Instructors can gain much from virtual reality because they can better criticize their trainees. In the early 1980s, the DOD used virtual reality to duplicate battlefield conditions. The 2nd Armored Cavalry Regiment Offensive won the Iraqi War because of virtual reality. But companies manufacturing virtual reality technology are not interested in law enforcement applications, another indication of its limitations. The Los Angeles Sheriff's EVOC used a driving simulator—offering a 225-degree field of view but it can be ordered with a 360-degree field—but expressed their caution about it. There have been limited interactions in the use of virtual reality for firearms training, though floor plans might have helped SWAT teams. Witnesses may need to refresh their memories with virtual reality. Again drawbacks exist. Computers are not as fast as the human eye in processing information.

summary must supply key information on the executive's four *E*'s: evaluation, economy, efficiency, and expediency. Executive readers will expect you to summarize large, complex subjects into easy-to-read, easy-to-understand information that they can act on confidently.

Organization of an Executive Summary

An executive summary must be faithful to the report while giving readers what they need (Figure 9.6). First, read the report carefully, plan what you want to include, and then draft and revise using valuable connective words (page 68). Clearly, you cannot write an executive summary of your report until after you have written the report itself.

FIGURE 9.6 An Executive Summary

A Report on Providing Better Training at Techtron Sites

Management has commissioned this report to investigate ways to prepare for the OSHA audits scheduled between February and June 2012, at our seven regional Techtron plants. Most directly, this report focuses on our ability to complete Phase One of ISO 14001 certification.

Starts with purpose of report

Currently, the Techtron safety training programs are inadequate; they are neither comprehensive nor up-to-date. We lack necessary software to instruct employees about the EPA and OSHA regulations and requirements that apply to hazardous materials or procedures used in our company. Consequently, safety violations have occurred with lockouts, confined spaces, fall protection, and the "Right to Know Law" concerning labeling of chemicals.

Identifies problem the report investigates and why it is important

Exploring better ways to conduct our training sessions, we purchased a copy of the software program **EPA/OSHA Trainer**, regarded as the best on the market (available from EDI @ $800 per copy). The **Trainer** offers effective guidelines on developing safety meetings and giving demonstrations. It also includes instructions, written in clear, nontechnical language, on how to identify, collect, and document hazardous materials. Additionally, the **Trainer** supplies the full text of EPA/OSHA regulations, with updates issued quarterly.

Explains the solution tested

Highlights benefits of trainer

To test the effectiveness of the **Trainer** software, we scheduled an internal audit at our Hendersonville site last month. After progressing through the **Trainer** module, a core group of employees interviewed by management successfully completed all required regulatory training. Subsequently, employees who had undergone such training were able to instruct and monitor the performance of other employees in the program.

Verifies effectiveness of solution

To ensure the safety of our employees and to compete in a global marketplace, Techtron must pass the OSHA 14001 certification. Purchasing seven additional copies of the **EPA/OSHA Trainer** software (7 @ $800 = $5,600) in the next month is a wise and necessary investment.

Ends by stressing action to be taken and by when

Follow this organizational plan when you write an executive summary:

1. **Begin with the purpose and the scope of the report.** For example, a report might be written to study new marketing strategies, to identify obsolete software, or to relocate a branch store.
2. **Relate your purpose to a key problem.** Identify the source (history) and seriousness of the problem.

3. **Identify in nontechnical language the criteria used to solve the problem.** Be careful not to include too much information or too many details.
4. **Condense the findings of your report.** Relate what tests or surveys revealed.
5. **Stress conclusions and possible solutions.** Be precise and clear.
6. **Provide recommendations.** For example, buy, sell, hire more personnel, relocate, or choose among alternative solutions. You may also indicate when a decision needs to be made.

The order of information in an executive summary does not have to follow strictly the order of the report itself. In fact, some executive summaries start with recommendations. Find out your boss's preference.

Evaluative Summaries

To write an evaluative summary, also called a *critique*, follow the guidelines below. As with executive summaries, you will be expected to provide a commentary on the material (that is, give your opinion).

Your employer may often ask you to summarize and assess what you have read. For example, you may have to condense and judge the merits of a report, paying special attention to whether its recommendations should be followed, modified, or ignored. Your company or agency may also ask you to write short evaluative summaries of job candidates, applications, sales proposals, or conferences.

Guidelines for Writing a Successful Evaluative Summary

To write a careful evaluative summary, follow these guidelines:

- Keep the summary short—5 to 10 percent of the length of the original.
- Blend your evaluations with your summary; do not save your evaluations for the end of the summary.
- Place each evaluation near the summarized points to which it applies so readers will see your remarks in context.
- Include a pertinent quotation from the original to emphasize your recommendation.
- Comment on both the content and the style of the original.

Evaluating the Content

Answer these questions on content for your readers:

1. **How carefully and completely is the subject researched?** Is the material accurate and up-to-date? Are important details missing? Exactly what has the writer left out? Where could the reader find the missing information? If the material is inaccurate or incomplete, is the whole work affected or just part of it?
2. **Is the writer or speaker objective?** Are conclusions supported by evidence? Is the writer or speaker following a particular theory, program, or school of

thought? Is that fact made clear in the source? Has the writer or speaker emphasized one point at the expense of others? What are the writer's qualifications and background?

3. **Does the work achieve its goal?** Is the topic too large to be adequately discussed in a single talk, article, or report? Is the work sketchy? Are there digressions, tangents, or irrelevant materials? Do the recommendations make sense?

4. **Is the material relevant to your audience?** How would the audience use it? Is the entire work relevant or just part of it? Why? Would the work be useful for all employees of your company or only for those working in certain areas? Why? What answers offered by the work would help to solve a specific problem you or others have encountered on the job?

You may want to review pages 375–378 on evaluating websites.

Evaluating the Style

Answer these questions on style for the readers of your evaluative summary:

1. **Is the material readable?** Is it well written and easy to follow? Does it contain helpful headings, careful summaries, and appropriate examples?

2. **What kind of vocabulary does the writer or speaker use?** Are there too many technical terms or too much jargon? Is it written for the layperson? Is the language precise or vague? Would readers have to skip certain sections that are too complicated?

3. **What visuals are included?** Charts? Graphs? Photographs? How are they used? Are they used effectively? Are there too many or too few?

Figures 9.7, 9.8, and 9.9 (pages 440–442) contain evaluative summaries. Note how the writers' assessments are woven into the condensed versions of the originals. Figure 9.7 is a student's opinion of an article summarized for a class in information management. Figure 9.8 is an evaluative summary in memo format collaboratively written by two employees who have just returned from a seminar. They have divided their labor, one writing the opening paragraph and the summary of "Techniques of Health Assessment" and the other doing the summaries of "Assessment of the Heart and Lungs" and "Assessment of the Abdomen." Together they drafted and revised the "Recommendations" and prepared the final copy of the memo.

Another kind of evaluative summary—a book review—is shown in Figure 9.9. Many journals and websites carry book reviews to inform their professional audience about the most recent studies in their field. Reviews condense and assess books, reports, government studies, websites, blogs, films, and other materials. The short review in Figure 9.9 comments on why the book is useful for the intended audience, analyzes the style, provides clarifying information, and explains how the book is developed. The Web contains numerous sites that run book reviews, including

FIGURE 9.7 An Evaluative Summary of an Article

Abbasi, Sami M., Kenneth W. Hollman, and Robert Hayes. "Bad Bosses and How Not to Be One." *Information Management Journal* 42.1 (2008): 52–56.

Identifies purpose of article

According to this practical and convincing article, the way employees are managed determines a company's success. The authors helpfully begin by describing the new twenty-first-century workplace where power has shifted from a top-down authoritative management style to one respecting employees as "knowledge workers" whose professional contributions are essential in a digital culture. The article then turns to a classification of six types of difficult bosses, ranging from incompetents, crooks, and bullies to dodgers, know-it-alls, and "walking policy manual[s]" who stick to a policy, however dated or contradictory. These bad bosses use intimidation, manipulation, blame, conflict, and cover-ups to exert or protect their power. Effective bosses, on the other hand, remove fear from the workplace, build trust, encourage feedback, and act as advocates for their employees with upper management. Although aimed at information managers, the guidelines in this readable article apply to anyone who wants to be a good—or better—boss.

Comments on style and organization

Indicates why and how article is useful to diverse audiences

www.amazon.com	Editorial and reader reviews and publisher-supplied abstracts on over 100,000 business books
www.barnesandnoble.com	"Business Books" Web page offers direct links to over twenty-five subcategories, e.g., accounting, management and leadership, and women in business. Each individual book's page includes an overview, Barnes and Noble editorial review, and reader ratings (one to five stars)
www.businessbookreview.com	Detailed one-paragraph summaries on thousands of business books plus over 700 expertly written, eight-page summaries of top best business books
www.getabstract.com	Site dedicated to only business book summaries by industry-expert writers; abstracts focus on the main points of the book

A book review includes the most important and useful information—to a key audience—about a book or report. Reviews are also important for the kinds of information that they do *not* include: details and irrelevant (for the audience) information that would only clog a summary. For example, the review in Figure 9.9 indicates that the book is an excellent guide to team building, but it does not go into detailed descriptions of the author's recommended tips, strategies, and instruments.

FIGURE 9.8 A Collaboratively Written Evaluative Summary of a Seminar

SABINE MEMORIAL HOSPITAL

7200 Medical Blvd.
Sabine, TX 77231-0011
512-555-6734   www.sabinememorial.org

TO: Mohammed Lau, M.S.N.   SUBJECT: Evaluation of Physical
        Director of Nurses   Assessment Seminar

FROM: Elena Roja, R.N.   DATE: September 13, 2012
        Lee Schoppe, R.N.

On September 7, Doris Fujimoto, R.N., and Rick Poncé, R.N., both on the
staff of Houston Presbyterian Hospital, conducted a practical and beneficial
seminar on physical assessment. The one-day seminar was divided into three
units: (1) **Techniques of Health Assessment**, (2) **Assessment of the Heart
and Lungs**, and (3) **Assessment of the Abdomen**.

Gives overall structure of seminar

Techniques of Health Assessment
Four procedures used in physical assessment—inspection, percussion,
palpation, and auscultation—were defined and demonstrated. Return demonstrations, used throughout the seminar, meant we did not have to wait until we
went back to work to practice our skills. The instructors stressed the proper
use of the stethoscope and the ways of taking a patient's medical history. We
were also asked to take the medical history of the person next to us.

Describes and evaluates each part of seminar

Assessment of the Heart and Lungs
After we inspected the chest externally, we covered the proper placement of
hands for percussion and palpation and the interpretation of various breath
sounds. The instructors helped us find areas of the lung and identify heart
sounds. However, the film, "Cardiopulmonary Feedback," on examining the
heart and lungs was ineffective because it included too much information.

Explains why one part was unsuccessful

Assessment of the Abdomen
The instructors warned that the order of examination of the abdoman differs
from that of the chest cavity. Auscultation, not percussion, follows inspection
so that bowel sounds are not activated. The instructors clearly identified how
to detect bowel sounds and how to locate the abdomen and palpate organs.

Continues to emphasize practical benefits of seminar

Recommendations
We strongly recommend a seminar like this for all nurses whose expanding
role in the health care system requires more physical assessments. Although
the seminar covered a wealth of information, the instructors admitted that
they discussed only basics. In the future, however, it would be better to offer
follow-up seminars on specific body systems (e.g., chest cavity, abdomen,
central nervous system) instead of combining topics because of the amount
of information involved and the time required for demonstrations.

Ends with endorsement by offering suggestions for improving seminar

FIGURE 9.9 A Book Review

Book Review

Team Troubleshooting: How to Find and Fix Team Problems
By ROBERT W. BARNER
Davies-Black Publishing, Palo Alto, Calif.
Representation: Anita Halton Associates, (949) 494-8564, 326 pages, $32.95

Overall Recommendation

Quantifies rating

DON'T BOTHER	BORROW	BUY

Engaging: 4   Innovative: 4   Usefulness: 5   Visual Aids: 4

Begins with purpose and scope of book

Discusses organization

Highlights main points of book

Praises book and gives specific reasons

Team building with a twist: While most books on the subject limit themselves to talk about getting a new team up and running or fixing a team after it breaks, Robert W. Barner deals with both and then goes a step farther. *Team Troubleshooting* promotes the concept of maintaining a healthy team through anticipating problems, performing regular team tune-ups and taking proactive measures to head off trouble before it begins. High points: strategies to foresee and develop plans for dealing with change, rather than becoming a victim of it; how-to tips to extend beyond the team itself to the problems of creating, maintaining and mending external relationships; ideas to cope with the fact that the team is not an isolated, independent entity, but is part of a bigger system and may be at the mercy of management and other forces.

The unusually user-friendly format makes the book truly serve as a guide.

Useful organization, clear chapter headings and cross-referencing help the reader find information quickly. Barner also does more than just name problems and offer quick fixes—he helps to assure accurate problem diagnosis by clearly describing both symptoms and underlying causes. Dozens of new instruments—not just the same tired old quizzes that appear in so many other teamwork books—lead both team leaders and members (and trainers or consultants involved in the "team" business) through exercises. They include scripting out scenario forecasts, identifying early warning signs of trouble, performing stakeholder analyses, and mapping relationships. It's been a long time since anything new has been said about teams— Barner's book deserves a space on the shelf of anyone truly interested in making a team work.

—Jane Bozarth

Source: *The Human Side of Business* by Jane Bozarth. Copyright 2001 by Nielsen Business Media. Reproduced with permission of Nielsen Business Media in the format Textbook via Copyright Clearance Center.

Abstracts

In addition to writing summaries, your employer may ask you to write abstracts. Abstracts are found in several key documents in the world of work and are a staple of the Internet.

Differences Between a Summary and an Abstract

The terms *summary* and *abstract* are often used interchangeably, resulting in some confusion. That problem arises because there are two distinct types of abstracts: *descriptive abstracts* and *informative abstracts*. An informative abstract is the same as a summary; it indicates what research was done, what conclusions were reached, and what recommendations were made. Look at the summary in Figure 9.4. It explains why virtual reality should be included in law enforcement training: because virtual reality gives officers field-translatable training. Informative abstracts are found at the beginning of long reports. Descriptive abstracts, however, do not give conclusions.

All abstracts share two characteristics: the writer never uses "I" and avoids footnotes.

Writing an Informative Abstract

An informative abstract is not as long as an executive summary, which gives more supporting details. As a part of your course work or your job, you will probably have to write informative abstracts for long reports (Chapter 15).

One way to approach writing the abstract of a report is to think of it as a table of contents in sentence form. A table of contents is, in effect, a final outline; it is easily fleshed out into an abstract, as Figure 9.10 (page 444) shows. On the left is a table of contents, and on the right is the abstract written from that outline.

This system works only if your table of contents is neither too detailed nor too skimpy. Starting off with a good outline of an article or a report provides the best beginning for your abstract. Make sure your sentences are complete and grammatical. Do not omit verbs, conjunctions, or articles (*the*, *a*, *an*). Proper subordination is essential. You should expect to condense a whole paragraph of the original to a sentence, an individual sentence to a phrase, and a phrase to a single word.

Writing a Descriptive Abstract

Unlike an informative abstract, a descriptive abstract is usually only a few sentences long; it does not go into any detail or give conclusions. As the name implies, a descriptive abstract provides information on what topics a work discusses but not how or why they are discussed. Busy readers rely on a descriptive abstract to decide whether they need to consult the work itself. Here is a descriptive abstract of the article summarized in Figure 9.4:

> Virtual reality can be used to teach law enforcement officers firearms training, SWAT team assaults, incident re-creation, and crime location processing. This training technology will be of interest to law enforcement administrators.

Figure 9.11 (page 445) reproduces two descriptive abstracts from the reference work *Information Science Abstracts* as well as two abstracts from the *Journal of Interactive Marketing*, a publication that includes abstracts as a way to help readers learn about research in this specialized discipline.

FIGURE 9.10 An Abstract Written from a Table of Contents

Table of Contents	Abstract

Need for Genetic Counseling
   Definition of Genetic Counseling
   Statistics on Genetic Counseling
	Genetic counseling is a service for people with a history of hereditary disease. One in 17 births contains some defect; one-fourth of the patients in hospitals are victims of genetic diseases (including diabetes, mental retardation, and anemia). One of every 200 children born has chromosome abnormalities.

Purpose of Genetic Counseling	Genetic counseling offers advice to parents who may give birth to children with genetic diseases and assistance to those with children already afflicted.

The Counseling Process
   Evaluating the Needs of the
   Counselees
   Taking a Family History
   Estimating the Risks
   Counseling the Family
	The first step in counseling is to evaluate the needs of the parents. A family history is prepared and risks of future children being afflicted are evaluated. The life expectancy and possible methods of treatment of any afflicted child also can be determined. Alternatives are presented.

Determination of a Genetic Disorder
   Amniocentesis
   Karyotyping
   Fluorescent Banding
   Staining
	Four prenatal tests are used to determine if a genetic disorder is present: amniocentesis, karyotyping, fluorescent banding, and staining.

Advantages of Genetic Screening
   Lower Cost
   Increased Availability
	The development of these four relatively simple methods has lowered the cost of genetic counseling and increased its availability.

Source: Reprinted by permission of Professor Mary Scotto.

Writing Successful News Releases

A *news release*, sometimes called a *press release* or *media release*, is another type of on-the-job document that requires you to summarize key information for a variety of readers. Basically, a news release is an announcement (usually one page or a single screen on the Web) about your company's or agency's specific product, services, or personnel. It should be crisp and highlight only the most important and relevant facts clearly and straightforwardly, as the other summaries you have studied in this chapter do.

Such releases are frequently posted on a company's or agency's website, as well as sent in the mail, as a fax, or automatically to your computer or smartphone through an RSS feed (if you have clicked on "Subscribe to RSS" at the company's website). They inform readers—the news media, potential and current customers, other agencies—of newsworthy events that promote the professional accomplishments of a company. Because your company's image can be enhanced or tarnished by the release you write, double-check all your facts, particularly names, dates, places, and any warranty or sales conditions. The best releases project a professional, customer-centered, and quality-focused corporate or agency image.

Figures 9.12 and 9.13 (pages 446–447) contain sample news releases. The release shown in Figure 9.12 was distributed over the Web, and the release in Figure 9.13

FIGURE 9.11 Descriptive Abstracts of Journal Articles

2002-01577

Mann, Charles C **Electronic paper turns the page.** *Technology Review* **104**(2): 42–48 (March 1, 2001) (ISSN: 1099-274X) In English.
Journal URL: http://www.techreview.com

Reports that the key to enabling electronic books to revolutionize the publishing industry is the development of electronic paper. Draws a parallel between the general availability of paper and the development of the first moveable-type printing press, noting that the technology to create the printing press existed for 100 years before the widespread use of ordinary paper provided the means to make the press practical. Notes that several companies are engaged in research and development of electronic paper, adding that at least one working prototype already exists. Indicates that the recent discovery of electrical conducting properties in plastic will enable researchers to overcome the issues of flexibility and cost that have slowed development in the past.

28680312

Murphy, Jeannette **Globalization: Implications for health information professionals.** *Health Information & Libraries Journal* **25**(1): 62–68 (March 2008) (ISSN: 1471-1834) (DOI:10.1111/j.1471–1842.2007.00761.x)

The article discusses how globalization processes may affect health information personnel. The author notes how globalization has led to a global economy and global culture through the transmission of services and information and the creation of international organizations and policies. She suggests that international organizations such as the World Bank and the World Health Organization will affect international health governance through the influence of health librarians. Information technology in fact may improve health education and communication of health information. Globalization has also led to outsourcing of health care services such as information processing. Medical tourism and physician mobility have increased.

Informs readers about which topics are discussed, but not how or why

Source: Reprinted with permission from *Information Science Abstracts*, Vol. 37, No. 4. Copyright © Information Science and Technology Abstracts.

Strategic and Ethical Considerations in Managing Digital Privacy

Ravi Sarathy and Christopher J. Robinson (August 2003), *Journal of Business Ethics*, 46(2), pp. 111–126.

Information about customers and prospects is readily available through a variety of digital sources. The questions a marketer must answer is how much of this available data should be used for commercial purposes and how much should remain privileged and off limits. In this paper the authors develop a model of the factors influencing privacy strategy. This model incorporates external, ethical, and firm-specific factors that impact customer privacy protection strategy formulation. The model is then applied to various scenarios to determine the firm's most likely customer privacy strategy. International implications of the model are also discussed.

Scovotti. (8, 13)

The Professional Service Encounter in the Age of the Internet: An Exploratory Study

Gillian Hogg, Angus Laing, and Dan Winkelman (2003), *The Journal of Services Marketing*, 17(5), pp. 476–495.

The Internet, by providing access to an unprecedented amount of healthcare-related information, is changing the balance of power in the relationship between healthcare consumers and professionals. Patients play a more active role in the relationship, interacting with healthcare professionals and other consumers to understand their illnesses. This situation changes the nature of the doctor/patient relationship—where the doctor becomes only one of the *advisors* in the service encounter. The implications of this research extend to other types of service encounters, where consumers may be engaging in virtual, parallel service encounters.

Short, 3-4 sentence paragraph

Uses objective language

Source: Journal of Interactive Marketing 18/1 (Winter 2004): 84, 87. Copyright © 2004. Reprinted with permission of John Wiley & Sons, Inc.

was distributed in hard-copy form. The various parts of a news release, which are discussed on pages 449–451, are labeled on both figures.

Subjects Appropriate for News Releases

News releases should be written only about newsworthy subjects, such as these:

1. **New products, services, or publications**
   - a new or improved model, line of equipment, or website
   - new or expanded technical or customer-friendly services
   - the entrance of your company into a different market
   - the application of the latest technology in creating a product

2. **New policies or procedures**
   - acquisition of new technologies to lower production costs
   - changes in production to improve safety, delivery, accuracy
   - cooperation and collaboration between two agencies or branches

3. **Personnel changes and awards**
   - appointments
   - promotions or recognition for winning an award
   - new hires
   - retirements

4. **New construction and developments**
   - plant or office openings
   - new satellite, branch, or overseas offices
   - expansion of an existing site

5. **Financial and business news**
   - company reorganization: merger, acquisition
   - stock reports
   - quarterly earnings and dividends
   - sales figures

6. **Ecofriendly (green) news**
   - energy conservation
   - water/air quality improvement
   - organic farming techniques
   - protection of endangered species
   - preservation of environmentally sensitive sites
   - policies or products for the office, home, etc.

7. **Special events**
   - training seminars
   - demonstrations of new equipment
   - community service programs
   - charity benefits
   - visits of national speakers
   - dedications

FIGURE 9.12 A News Release from the Web

CDC Home

CDC **Centers for Disease Control and Prevention**
CDC 24/7: Saving Lives, Protecting People, Saving Money through Prevention.

SEARCH

A-Z Index A B C D E F G H I J K L M N O P Q R S T U V W X Y Z #

Media Relations

Newsroom Home
African-American Media Resources
Audio/Video Resources
Autism Spectrum Disorders Resources
Calendar Resources
Contact Us
Executive Leadership & Expert Bios
EID Summaries
CDC Fast Facts
Formatted Articles
Frequently Asked Questions
Have You Heard?
Hispanic Media Resources
Hookup to Health
Media Kit
MMWR Summaries
Newsroom Image Library
Press Release Archive
▶ Press Release
Resources
Story Ideas

March 18, 2008
Contact: CDC, Jennifer Marcone

(404) 639-3286
http://bookstore.phf.org

Press Release

CDC Releases New Interactive Website for
Health Information for International Travel **(The Yellow Book)**

ATLANTA—The Centers for Disease Control and Prevention (CDC) unveiled a re-designed, interactive website of one of CDC's most widely disseminated publications, *Health Information for International Travel,* commonly dubbed "The Yellow Book." The Yellow Book is considered by many health care providers, travel professionals, airlines, cruise lines, and humanitarian institutions to be the gold standard for health recommendations for international travel.

The Yellow Book and companion website **www.cdc.gov/travel/yb** are published biennially by CDC's Division of Global Migration and Quarantine as a reference for those who advise international travelers of health risks.

The key to the new, interactive website is the use of drop-down menus for all of the major subjects in the Yellow Book, including vaccination information, yellow fever requirements, malaria information, geographic distribution, and health hints. Users can obtain customized reports for individual travel plans and locate particular subjects or destinations in the text without having to search through unrelated topics.

"International travelers will find the interactive Yellow Book website to be very helpful," said CDC Director Jeffrey P. Koplan, MD, MPH. "The new features make it easier to find information about preventive measures travelers can take to protect their health."

The handy, interactive design of the Yellow Book website incorporated many comments and suggestions from the public and health care providers seeking more customized information in a user-friendly format. CDC encourages users to submit comments about the new website through the "comments section" on the site's homepage.

30

http://bookstore.phf.org

Slug emphasizes importance of topic

Lead answers who, where, how, and what, and why

Body emphasizes benefits for audience

Quotation from expert endorses new design and features

Conclusion invites reader interaction

Number 30 signals end of release

Centers for Disease Control and Prevention (CDC).

FIGURE 9.13 A News Release Circulated in Hard Copy

NEWS RELEASE
United States Department of Commerce • 1401 Constitution Avenue, NW •
Washington, DC 20230 • Web: http://www.commerce.gov

Release No. 0150.01

Cheryl Mendonsa
Cheryl.Mendonsa@technology.gov
202-482-8321

Contact information

Marjorie Weisskohl
Marjorie.Weisskohl@technology.gov
202-482-0149

Slug

U.S. Department of Commerce Announces Website Focused on Resources for Tech-Based Economic Development (TBED)

Lead, or hook

Under Secretary of Commerce Phillip J. Bond today announced a new resource that will help communities working to encourage the growth of technology companies and build tech-based economies. A new website, the TBED Resource Center (**http://www.tbedresourcecenter.org**), gives users the chance to learn from others' experiences and to benefit from the latest research on creating a tech-based economy.

Body

The TBED Resource Center categorizes and provides links to more than 1,300 research reports, strategic plans, best practices and impact analyses from state and federal government, university researchers, and foundations. The website is a result of a cooperative project of the U.S. Department of Commerce's (DOC) Office of Technology Policy and State Science and Technology Institute, based in Westerville, Ohio.

Quote from authority

"This website will be an invaluable tool to anyone involved in economic development," said Under Secretary Bond. "Access to information on what has worked in various communities will help policymakers and business people make efficient use of valuable time and resources, and provide productive ideas and contacts that others might find useful." Bond made the announcement via live telecast hosted by Commerce's Economic Development Administration and the National Association of Regional Councils.

Emphasizes benefits

The user-friendly search options allow for easy navigation with abundant topics spanning a wide field of interests. Users can search for reports based upon geography, topic, type, or keyword with the option of selecting multiple fields. Numerous international reports also are included, offering a globally diverse perspective in tech-based economic development.

Appropriate positive tone

Reports fall into one of the 35 topics, such as brain drain, education, entrepreneurship, innovation, research and development, and work force.

To keep current with TBED trends, the website is continually updated as new reports are released.

Symbol # signals end of release

\#

Source: Material reprinted from the United States Department of Commerce.

News Releases About Bad News

While the topics above focus on a company's or organization's achievements—the positive contributions a firm or an agency makes to its customers and its community—not all the news you may be asked to announce is pleasant. At times you may have to report on events that are difficult: product recalls, work stoppages or strikes, layoffs, plant closures, limited availability or unavailability of products or parts, fires, computer viruses, alerts, higher prices, declining enrollment, or canceled events.

Even when you have to write releases about such unpleasant events, portray your company honestly and in the most professional and conscientious light. Regardless of the news, be accurate, ethical, honest and straightforward, and available.

Topics That Do Not Warrant a News Release

Not every event or change at your company or agency will warrant a news release. Releases about events that have already happened are old, tired news. Keep in mind, too, that it is unethical to write about some subjects (see pages 29–42 in Chapter 1). Following are topics that hold little or no interest or about which you should *not* write a release:

1. **Well-known products or services.** Don't repeat the obvious.
2. **Products or services still in the planning stages.** Not only would such news be premature, but releasing it ahead of time might meet with your boss's severe disapproval, not to mention your competition's delight.
3. **Controversial events or company problems.** Refrain from writing a news release on these subjects unless your boss instructs you to do so.
4. **A history of your department, division, or company.** Save remarks about your firm's history for the annual report to stakeholders.
5. **An obviously padded tribute to your boss, your company, or your customers.**

Organization of a News Release

The following sections contain guidelines for organizing and writing the different parts of your news release. Note how these various parts flow together in the news releases in Figures 9.12 and 9.13.

The cardinal rule in writing a news release is to put the most important piece of news first. Don't bury it in the middle or wait until the end. Everything in a news release should be arranged in descending order of importance so that your first paragraph contains only the most significant facts and ideas. Think of your release as an inverted pyramid with the top summarizing only the most crucial points.

The Three Parts of a News Release
The three components of a news release are the slug (headline), lead, and body.

The Slug, or Headline   One of the most crucial parts of your release is the headline, or *slug*. It should announce a specific subject for readers and draw them into it. Write a slug that entices or grabs your readers, but also informs them quickly and clearly. Note how the slugs in Figures 9.12 and 9.13 point readers to the main idea in the first sentence and use keywords to help readers track the subject.

The Lead   The first (and most significant) sentence of a news release is called the *lead*. It introduces and aptly summarizes your topic, sets the tone, and continues to keep readers' attention. For that reason it is also called the *hook*. See how the leads in Figures 9.12 and 9.13 grab readers' attention. The best leads easily answer the basic questions *Who? What? When? Where? Why?* — the five *W*'s — and *How?* (or *How much?*). Not every lead will answer all these questions, but the more of them you do answer, the better your chances will be of capturing your audience's attention. Here are some effective leads that answer these crucial questions:

> *who*   *when*
> Massey Labs announced today that the FDA has approved the marketing
>
> *what*   *why*
> of its vaccine—Viobal—to retard recurrent lesions of herpes simplex.

> *who*   *what*
> Maryville Engineering, Inc., has been awarded a contract by Aerodynamics, Inc.,
>
> *why*
> to develop an acoustical system to measure and monitor stress levels at the
>
> *where*   *when*
> Knoxville aircraft plant, district manager Carmelita Stinn, P.E., announced today.

Misleading leads that deviate substantially from the guidelines just discussed annoy readers and risk losing their interest. Resist the temptation to start off with a question or with folksy humor.

Feeble humor:	Slap, slap, scratch, scratch, itch. This is how millions of people will handle their mosquito problems this summer.
Boastful start:	If you thought 2011 was great, you ain't seen nothin' yet!
Undirected question:	Does the thought of hypothermia send chills up your spine?
Exaggeration:	I bet you wonder how you ever did without the new Fourier scanner.

The Body   What kinds of information should you give readers in the second and subsequent paragraphs of your release? If the five *W*'s are answered in your lead, the following paragraphs fill in only the most necessary supporting details. Regard your lead as a summary of a summary. The body of your release then amplifies the *Why?* and *How?* and may also get into the *So what?*

But avoid filling your news release with unnecessary technical details, such as scientific formulas or intricate speculations. Instead, relate your product or service to your targeted audience's needs by emphasizing the benefits to them without loading your news release with hype.

Use quotations selectively to clarify and highlight, not to apple-polish. Use a quotation only to report vital facts or to cite an authority. Do not turn your release into an interview with your employer or favorite customer.

Style and Tone of a News Release

The tone of your news release needs to be objective and take into account your audience's background. Keep your style simple and to the point. Here are some suggestions that will help you:

1. Write concisely. Use easy-to-read paragraphs of three to five sentences, and keep your sentences short. Under twenty words is ideal. Avoid long, convoluted sentences and fillers that start off with such phrases as "It has been noted that. . . ."

2. Emphasize benefits to the reader. Use graphic, understandable language that applies to the reader's life. Avoid unfamiliar jargon—it's deadly. A news release summarizing the benefits of a hospital counseling center will lose potential seminar participants by describing it in jargon: "Milford Hospital is pleased to offer an adventure-intensive counseling workshop that incorporates trust sequencing; high-element activities; and quantifiable decision modules."

3. Keep your tone upbeat, easygoing, and direct; stress the human side. But stay away from adjectives dripping with a pushy sell: *incomparable, fantastic, incredible*. Note how Figures 9.12 and 9.13 emphasize benefits to travelers and to communities interested in technology-based economic development, respectively.

As with other types of summaries described in this chapter, news releases give readers essential, useful information quickly and concisely. They provide the "big picture." And by doing so, they capture the reader's interest and emphasize the goals and contributions of the company or agency at the same time.

Conclusion

Summaries are a vital part of workplace writing, and knowing how to summarize a document—a report, proposal, or presentation—and select only the most important and relevant points for your audience is a prized job skill. Busy managers, clients, and even co-workers will depend on your summaries to give them the big picture, the bottom-line conclusions and recommendations they need to get the job done. Your summaries must be accurate, concise, relevant, and ethical. The process presented in this chapter for summarizing information will help you to write different kinds of summaries: As this chapter has also stressed, you need to be familiar with *executive summaries* that assist a manager in making a decision, *evaluative summaries* that summarize and assess what you have read, *informative abstracts* that let readers know what a report covers and the conclusions and recommendations it reaches, and *descriptive abstracts* that tell readers what topics a document covers but not how or why. A *news release* is another type of essential workplace summary that informs a large group of readers about important projects and accomplishments, as well as bad news subjects of crucial concern to your company's or organization's image and mission.

✓ Revision Checklist

- ☐ Read and reread the original thoroughly to gain a clear understanding of the purpose and scope of the work.
- ☐ Underlined key transitional words, main points, significant findings, applications, solutions, conclusions, and recommendations.
- ☐ Separated main points clearly from minor ones, background information, illustrations, and inconclusive findings.
- ☐ Omitted examples, explanations, and statistics from summary or abstract.
- ☐ Deleted information not useful to the audience because it is too technical or irrelevant.
- ☐ Changed language of original to my own words so I am not guilty of plagiarism.
- ☐ Made sure that emphasis of summary matches emphasis of original.
- ☐ Determined that sequence of information in the summary follows sequence of original.
- ☐ Added necessary connective words that accurately convey relationships between main points in original.
- ☐ Edited summary to eliminate wordiness and repetition.
- ☐ Cited source of original correctly and completely.
- ☐ Avoided phrases that draw attention to the fact that I am writing a summary or an abstract.
- ☐ Summarized material in informative summary objectively without adding commentary.
- ☐ Commented on both content and style in an evaluative summary.
- ☐ Interspersed evaluative commentary throughout the summary so that assessments appear near relevant points.
- ☐ Included a direct quotation in the evaluative summary or news release to illustrate or reinforce my recommendation.
- ☐ Ensured that descriptive abstract is short and to the point and does not offer a judgment.
- ☐ Prepared news release that projects a professional image of my employer.
- ☐ Summarized only essential information in news release.
- ☐ Arranged information from top down, with most important information first.
- ☐ Wrote clear, crisp slug and lead and concise body for news release.
- ☐ Saved word-processing file in document folder on computer.
- ☐ Sent news release on newsworthy topic to appropriate publications, organizations, and audiences.

Exercises

1. Summarize a chapter of a textbook you are now using for a course in your major field. Provide an accurate bibliographic reference for that chapter (author of the textbook, title of the chapter, title of the book, place of publication, publisher's name, date of publication, and page numbers of the chapter).

2. Summarize a lecture you heard recently. Limit your summary to one page. Identify in a bibliographic citation the speaker's name, the date, and the place of delivery.

3. Listen to a television network evening newscast and to a later news update on the same station. Select one major story covered on the evening news and indicate which details from it were omitted in the news update.

4. Write a summary of the marketing report in Chapter 8 (pages 398–413) or the business report in Chapter 15 on non-native speakers of English in the workforce (pages 701–719).

5. Bring to class an article from *Reader's Digest* and the original material it condensed, usually an article in a journal or magazine published six months to a year earlier. In a paragraph or two indicate what the *Digest* article omits from the original. Also point out how the condensed version is written so that the omitted material is not missed and how the condensation does not misrepresent the main points of the article.

6. Assume that you are applying for a job and that the human resources manager asks you to summarize your qualifications. In two or three paragraphs, indicate how your background and interests make you suited for the job. Mention the job by title at the beginning of your first paragraph.

7. Write a summary of one of the following articles.
   a. "Microwaves," in Chapter 1 (pages 47–49)
   b. "Protecting Personal Information," below

Protecting Personal Information: A Guide for Businesses

Small Business Administration

Companies keep sensitive personal information in their files—names, social security numbers, credit card or other account data—that identifies customers or employees. This information often is necessary to fill orders, meet payroll, or perform other necessary business functions. However, if sensitive data falls into the wrong hands, it can lead to fraud, identity theft, or similar troubles. Given the high cost of a security breach—losing your customers' trust and perhaps even defending yourself against a lawsuit—it is just plain good business to safeguard personal information.

Protect the Information That You Keep

What's the best way to protect the sensitive, personal information your company needs to keep? It depends on the kind of information and how it's stored. The most effective data security plans deal with four key elements: physical security, electronic security, password management, and employee training, all of which are discussed below.

Physical Security

Many data compromises happen the old-fashioned way—through lost or stolen paper documents. Often, the best defense is a locked door or an alert employee. Here are some helpful ways to protect information from falling into the wrong hands:

First of all, store paper documents or files, as well as CDs, floppy disks, Zip drives, tapes, and backups containing personally identifiable information, in a locked room or in a locked file cabinet. Limit access to employees with a legitimate business need. Control who has a key, and the number of keys. Then require that files containing personally identifiable information be kept in locked file cabinets except when an employee is working on the file. Remind employees not to leave sensitive papers out on their desks when they are away from their workstations, to put files away, log off their computers, and lock their file cabinets and office doors at the end of the day.

Next, implement appropriate access controls for your building. Tell employees what to do and whom to call if they see an unfamiliar person in the office or elsewhere on the premises. If you maintain off-site storage facilities, limit employee access to those with a legitimate business need. Know if and when someone accesses the storage site. For example, if you ship sensitive information using outside carriers or contractors, encrypt the information and keep an inventory of the information being shipped. Also, use an overnight shipping service that will allow you to track the delivery of your information.

Electronic Security

Computer security isn't just the realm of your IT staff. Make it your business to understand the vulnerabilities of your computer system, and follow the advice of experts in the field. To do this, identify the computers or servers where sensitive personal information is stored. Make sure, too, that you identify all connections to the computers where you store sensitive information. These may include the Internet, electronic cash registers, computers at your branch offices, computers used by service providers to support your network, and wireless devices like inventory scanners or cell phones.

Moreover, encrypt all sensitive information that you send to third parties over public networks (like the Internet), and consider encrypting sensitive information stored on your computer network or on disks or portable storage devices used by your employees. It is a smart idea to encrypt e-mail transmissions as well—within your company if they contain personally identifying information. In addition, regularly run up-to-date anti-virus and anti-spyware programs on individual computers and on servers on your network. Check expert websites (such as **www.sans.org**) and your software vendors' websites regularly for alerts about new threats and to learn about implementing new policies for installing vendor-approved patches to correct problems.

Most important of all, scan the computers on your network to identify and profile the operating system and open network services. If you find services that you don't need, disable them to prevent hacking or other potential security problems. For example, if e-mail service or an Internet connection is not necessary on a certain computer, close the ports to those services on that computer to prevent unauthorized access to that machine. When you receive or transmit credit card information or other sensitive financial data, use Secure Sockets Layer (SSL) or another secure connection that protects the information in transit.

Pay particular attention to the security of your Web applications—the software used to give information to visitors to your website and to retrieve information from them. Web applications may be particularly vulnerable to a variety of hacker attacks. In one variation called an "injection attack," a hacker inserts malicious commands into what looks like a legitimate request for information. Once in your system, hackers transfer sensitive information from your network to their computers. Be on guard against these attacks by more closely scrutinizing requests.

Password Management

Also essential to any business's security is password protection. You can control access to sensitive information by requiring your employees to use "strong" passwords. Technical security experts advise that the longer the password, the better. Because simple passwords—like common dictionary words—can be easily guessed, insist that your employees choose passwords with a mix of letters, numbers, and characters. Require an employee's user name and password to be different, and insist on frequent changes in passwords. Lock out users who don't enter the correct password within a designated number of log-on attempts. Password-activated screen savers can lock employee computers after a period of inactivity.

Another wise move is to warn employees about possible calls from identity thieves attempting to deceive them into giving out their passwords by impersonating members of your IT staff. Let employees know that calls like this are always fraudulent, and that no one should be asking them to reveal their passwords. Set up clear and effective procedures through which employees can communicate with IT staff.

When installing new software, make sure your company immediately switches vendor-supplied default passwords to a more secure strong password and cautions employees against transmitting sensitive personally identifying data—social security numbers, passwords, account information—via e-mail. Unencrypted e-mail is not a secure way to transmit any information.

Employee Training

Your data security plan may look great on paper, but it's only as strong as the employees who implement it. Take time to explain the rules to your staff, and train them to spot security vulnerabilities. Periodic training emphasizes the importance you place on data security practices. A well-trained work force is a company's best defense against identity theft and data breaches.

You can also create a "culture of security" by implementing a regular schedule of employee training. Update employees as you find out about new risks and vulnerabilities. Make sure training extends to employees at satellite offices and to temporary help and seasonal workers as well. If employees don't attend, consider blocking their access to the network. If you train employees to recognize security threats, you can cut down on the risks such thefts pose. Tell your employees how to report suspicious activity and publicly reward employees who alert you to vulnerabilities.

Finally, ask every new employee to sign an agreement to follow your company's confidentiality and security standards for handling sensitive data. Make sure these most recent members of your work force understand that abiding by your company's data security plan will be an essential part of their duties. And regularly remind all employees of your company's policy—and any legal requirement—to keep customer information secure and confidential.

Source: Federal Trade Commission, *Protecting Personal Information: A Guide for Businesses.* Washington, DC: GPO, 2008.

8. Write a descriptive abstract of the article you selected in Exercise 7.

9. Below are two sloppily written news releases that are poorly organized, unethical, and incorrectly formatted. Reorganize and rewrite them according to the guidelines presented in this chapter and those in Chapter 1 (pages 29–42) on making sure your writing is ethical.

a.   Friday   Alan Bowerstock

Metropolitan State University is a four-year urban institution of higher education offering majors in many fields. Located two miles west of Taylorsville Tech Park, MSU currently boasts more than 7,000 undergraduate students, more than our rival, Central Tech.

Among the many student services currently available at MSU is the Division of Career Placement; this division is located in the Student Services Building, Room 301, just across the hall from the Department for Greek Life.

In the last year, the Division has assisted more than 2,000 MSU students to find part-time jobs. Full-time jobs, too.

The goal of the Division is to help students earn money for their college expenses. The Division also wants to assist local businesses in contacting MSU qualified undergraduates.

The MSU family is well represented on the homepage. Every department from the University has been encouraged to report on only its most favorable activities. The Division of Career Placement is also on the homepage.

Counselors at the Division can help MSU students prepare a four- or five-line ad about their qualifications. The Division will run these ads in their homepage. The university will also run ads looking for job candidates from the state employment agency and the greater Taylorsville area.

b.   For General Information   Frank Day

J. T. Bushart, CEO of Bonnetti and Blount Construction for the last three years, asserted today that the company is devoted to progress and change. Bushart came to B & B Engineering after several years working for Capitol City Engineering, a less progressive firm.

Bonnetti and Blount is a leading firm of contractors and has worked for both national and international corporations.

The firm specializes in construction projects that require special expertise because of their challenges in difficult terrains.

B & B has just been awarded a contract to work on the 10 million dollar renovation of two major Fairfax dams. The firm anticipates hiring more than 200 new workers. These new employees will work on the dams that present dangerous conditions to residents.

When completed, the two new dams will further assist residents of Fairfax and Hamilton Counties receive all the necessary irrigation and hydroelectric energy they need.

Engineering sketches and blueprints are in the works.

10. Write an appropriate news release on one of the following newsworthy topics to be included on your company's website:
    a. hiring a new webmaster
    b. premiering a new product or service
    c. acquiring a smaller firm whose products and services are very different from those of your company
    d. providing an environmentally sensitive service that enhances life in the community in which your employer's headquarters is located
    e. promoting an employee who has been with your company for at least five years
    f. offering highly competitive warranties on a new line of products
    g. protecting a section of wetlands adjoining one of your company's construction sites

11. Write a news release on one of the following unpleasant topics, while still projecting a positive image of your company:
    a. inconveniences because of recent construction
    b. a temporary power outage in a neighborhood or city
    c. the temporary failure of one of your company's servers
    d. a change in the hours of operation of a store or plant
    e. an increase in insurance premiums
    f. a reduction in the number of times trash is picked up per week
    g. an order page is down on a frequently visited e-business site because of a computer virus
    h. a sports injury that has benched a star player on a local team for the next month
    i. a boil-water notice issued for a subdivision that depends on a local reservoir for its water supply

CHAPTER 8

Writing Effective Short Reports and Proposals

This chapter shows you how to write short reports and proposals, which are among the most important and frequent types of business communications you may be called upon to prepare. Short, informal reports give up-to-date information (and sometimes what it means and what should be done about it) to help a company or organization run smoothly, efficiently, and profitably. These reports, which cover a wide range of topics, can help a company fulfill its obligations and plan for its future. Proposals are used to keep current business clients as well as attract new ones, or to make recommendations for changes within a company or organization. Both are crucial to day-to-day operations of any company or organization, and both are designed for an audience of busy decision makers.

Why Short Reports Are Important

A short report can be defined as an organized presentation of relevant data on any topic—money, travel, time, technology, personnel, service equipment, weather, the environment—that a company or agency tracks in its ongoing operations. Short reports are practical and to the point. They show that work is being done, and they also show your boss that you are alert, professional, and reliable. Short reports are written to co-workers, employers, vendors, and clients. When they are intended for individuals within your organization, these reports are most often sent as memos or as emails. But, for clients, you will usually send your reports out as letters.

Businesses cannot function without short written reports. Reports tell whether

- schedules are being met
- costs have been contained
- sales projections are being met
- trips or conferences have been successful
- locations have been selected
- problems have been solved

You may write an occasional report in response to a specific question, or you may be required to write a weekly or monthly report about routine activities. For example, a short report can update your manager or client about the status of a project, provide feedback about a customer survey, prove you followed the regulations of a state or federal agency, or assess your own or someone else's accomplishments at work.

Types of Short Reports

To give you a sense of some of the topics you may be required to write about, here is a list of short reports common in the business world.

appraisal report	incident report	production report
audit report	inventory report	progress/activity report
budget report	investigative report	recommendation report
compliance report	laboratory report	sales report
construction report	manager's report	status report
design report	medicine/treatment	survey report
employee activity report	error report	test report
evaluation report	operations report	travel report
experiment report	periodic report	
feasibility report		

This chapter concentrates on six of the most common reports you are likely to encounter in your professional work.

1. periodic reports
2. sales reports
3. progress reports
4. employee activity/performance reports
5. trip/travel reports
6. incident reports

Although there are many short reports, they all are written for readers who need factual information so that they can get a job accomplished. Never think of the reports you write as a series of casual notes jotted down for *your* convenience.

Seven Guidelines for Writing Short Reports

Although there are many short reports, the following seven guidelines will help you write any type of short report successfully.

1. Anticipate How an Audience Will Use Your Report

Knowing who will read your report and why is crucial to your success as a writer. Consider how much your audience knows about your project and what types of information they need most. A co-worker or someone else in your field may be familiar with technical information. But managers, who will constitute the largest audience for your report, may not always understand or be interested in such technical information. Instead, they will want bottom-line details about costs, personnel, and schedules, for example. Similarly, audiences outside of your company (clients, media, community agencies, etc.) will likely not be interested in technical information. Rather, they want information that helps them understand your company, how it works or serves customers, and how to interact with it.

All audiences, however, want clear and concise information. For more information on how to make your reports concise and easy to follow, see pages 305–306.

2. Do the Necessary Research

An effective short report needs the same careful research that goes into other on-the-job writing. Your research may be as simple as instant messaging, emailing, or leaving a voicemail for a colleague or checking a piece of equipment. Or you may have to test or inspect a product or service or assess the relative merits of one plan over another. Some frequent types of research you can expect to do on the job include:

- verifying data in reference manuals or code books
- searching online archives and databases for recent discussions of a problem or procedure
- comparing and contrasting competitor's products or services
- reading background information in professional and trade journals
- reviewing and updating a client's file
- testing equipment
- performing an experiment or procedure
- conferring with or interviewing colleagues, managers, vendors, or clients
- visiting and describing a site
- attending a conference or workshop

Never trust your memory to keep track of all the details that go into making a successful short report. Take notes, either by hand or on your notebook or tablet. Collect all the relevant data you will need—names, model numbers, costs, places, technology, etc.—and organize this information carefully into an outline, which will help you interpret these facts for your readers.

3. Be Objective and Ethical

Your readers will expect you to report the facts objectively and impartially—locations, costs, sales, weather conditions, eyewitness accounts, observations, statistics, test measurements, and descriptions. Your reports should be truthful, accurate, and complete. Here are some guidelines to follow:

- Avoid guesswork. If you don't know or have not yet found out, say so and indicate how, where, and when you'll try to find out.
- Do not substitute impressions or unsupported personal opinions for careful research.
- Be ethical. Don't use biased, skewed, or incomplete data. Provide a balanced, straightforward, and honest account; don't exaggerate or minimize. Don't omit key facts. If a project is over budget or late, state so but indicate why and what might be done to correct the problem.

- Make sure your report is relevant, accurate, and reliable. Double-check your details against other sources, and make sure you have sufficient information to reach your conclusions or provide recommendations.

Review the discussion of ethics in business writing in Chapter 1 (pages 21–29).

4. Organize Carefully

Organizing a short report effectively means including the right amount of information in the most appropriate places for your audience. Make your report easy to read and to follow. Many times a simple chronological or sequential organization is best. Regardless of how you organized your report, readers will expect your report to contain information on such topics as **purpose, findings, conclusions,** and, in many reports, **recommendations,** as described in the following sections.

Purpose

Always begin by telling readers why you are writing (your purpose) and by alerting them to what you will discuss and why it is significant. Give your readers a summary of key events and details at the beginning to help them follow the remainder of the report quickly. Essential background information alerts readers to the importance of your report. When you establish the scope (or limits) of your report, you help readers zero in on specific times, costs, places, or problems.

Findings

This should be the longest part of your report and contain the data (the results) you have collected—facts about prices, personnel, equipment, events, locations, incidents, or tests. Gather the data from your research, site visits, interviews, or discussions with co-workers, employers, or clients. Again, choose only those details that have the greatest importance and relevance to your reader. Separate major points from minor ones.

Conclusion

Your conclusion tells readers what your data mean. It can summarize what has happened; review what actions were taken; or explain the outcome or results of a test, a visit, or a program. Be aware, though, that readers are skeptical and may ask why you didn't reach a different conclusion. Anticipate possible objections and explain why other conclusions are unworkable.

Recommendations

A recommendation informs readers what specific actions you think your company or client should take, e.g., market a new product, hire more staff, institute safety measures, select among alternative plans or procedures, and so on. Recommendations must be based on the data you collected, the resources (budget) and schedule that your company or department follows, and the conclusions you have reached. They need to show persuasively how all the pieces fit together.

Note how the periodic report in Figure 8.1 (page 307) fails to help readers see and understand the organization and importance of the information. But the revised version of the report, Figure 8.2 (page 308–309), clearly illustrates effective report writing.

5. Write Clearly and Concisely

Writing clearly and concisely is essential in all business reports. Ask your boss or experienced co-workers about the appropriate style your company prefers. Also look at previous, similar reports to get a sense of your company's style and tone.

Here are a few guidelines to help you write clearly and concisely.

- **Use an informative title or subject line that gets to the point right away.** "Software Options" is not as clear as "Most Economical Options for Spreadsheet Software."
- **Write in plain English.** Make every word count, avoid jargon, and keep your writing simple and straightforward. Prune business clichés such as "at the end of the day" or "to put a fine point on it."
- **For global readers, make sure you use international English.** Keep your sentences short, and write in the active voice. Do not use U.S. idioms, slang, or abbreviations. (See pages 4–6.)
- **Adopt a professional yet personal tone.** Avoid being overly formal or too casual—strike a balance between these two extremes. Don't sound arrogant by adopting a tone that suggests you alone have the final authority.
- **Keep your report as concise as possible to give readers essential information.** Don't burden them with lengthy project histories when all they ask for is a quick update on a project, and don't pad the report with unnecessary details to sound important. A short report is usually no longer than two to three pages.

6. Create a Reader-Centered Design

The appearance of your report will influence how your readers will respond to it and to you. Here are some useful guidelines. (You may also want to review Chapter 7 on visuals and document design.)

- **Help readers locate and digest information quickly.** Use headings, subheadings, bullets, and numbered lists to guide readers through your report. Doing this, you break large portions of text into easy-to-read parts. Your headings and subheadings give readers the big picture at a glance. Many reports in this chapter demonstrate how headings and bulleted or numbered lists assist readers. For instance, see Figures 8.2, 8.3, and 8.4.
- **Make your report look professional, readable, and easy to follow.** Don't flood your report with color. Avoid using flashy color or fancy fonts that are hard to read. Also, don't try to squeeze too much text onto the page. Always leave comfortable margins.
- **Be consistent in your design and format.** Use the same font throughout the text of your report and a consistent typeface for headings and subheadings.

- **Include only the most essential visuals.** Use visuals only if they make the reader's job easier, reinforcing or summarizing key data quickly, as the table in Figure 8.2 and the map in Figure 8.5 do. Keep visuals simple and relevant, e.g., a picture or drawing to illustrate a major point.
- **Make sure that you place your visual as close as possible to the text it will help to explain or illustrate.**

7. Choose the Most Appropriate Format

Depending on your audience, you can send your short report as an email, a memo, or a letter. For routine reports to your boss or others inside your company, you will likely use a memo format, as in Figures 8.2, 8.3, and 8.6. Note that with a memo format your readers will not expect you to include an inside address or formal salutation and complimentary close. Depending on your company's policy, you might also send a short report in the body of an email, as in Figure 8.5, or as an attachment to an email. Incident reports, however, are often submitted as hard-copy memos for legal reasons; they can also be written as a memo, as in Figure 8.7, or by completing a special form. When writing to clients and other readers outside your company or organization, it is best to send your report as a formal letter (including a salutation and complimentary close, as in Figure 8.4).

Periodic Reports

Periodic reports, as their name signifies, provide readers with information at regularly scheduled intervals—daily, weekly, bimonthly (twice a month), monthly, or quarterly. They help a company or an agency monitor the quantity and quality of the services it provides and the amount and types of work done by employees. Information in periodic reports helps managers plan schedules; hire, train, assign, and reassign staff; budget funds; determine needs and goals; and fulfill a corporate mission. The following case study shows a poor draft of a periodic report (Figure 8.1) and a successful revision (Figure 8.2).

Case Study

A Poor and an Effective Short Report

Sergeants Daniel Huxley, Jennifer Chavez, and Ivor Paz of the Springdale Police Department were responsible for writing a monthly periodic report for the second quarter of 2014 for Captain J.T. Martin, their boss. Confronted with a mass of data about various crimes and misdemeanors, they had to organize, compare, and contrast this data as well as draw conclusions and make recommendations. Figure 8.1, an early draft of their report, does not follow the guidelines on pages 302–306. But Figure 8.2, a revised version of Figure 8.1, does. Read through both reports, keeping in mind the following differences:

- **Research.** Although Figure 8.1 includes statistics, it does not explain or provide recommendations based on them. Figure 8.2, however, provides explanations, supplies more detail, and gives concrete recommendations.

Springdale Police Department

Emergency 555-1000   **Administration** 555-1001   **Traffic** 555-1002

www.springdalepd.gov

TO: Captain J. T. Martin
FROM: Sergeants Daniel Huxley, Jennifer Chavez,
             and Ivor Paz
SUBJECT: Crimes
DATE: July 11, 2014

Vague subject line

This report will let you know what happened this quarter as opposed to what happened last quarter as far as crimes are concerned in Springdale. This **report is based on statistics** the department has given us over the quarter.

Introduction doesn't give overall picture

   Here we'll let the facts speak for themselves. From Jan.–Mar. we saw 126 robberies while from Apr.–June we had 106. Home burglaries for this period: 43; last period: 36. 33 cars were stolen in the period before this one; now we have 40. Interestingly enough, **last year at this time we had only 27** thefts. Four of them involved heirlooms.

Throws facts out without any sense of reader's needs

Includes irrelevant detail

Homicides were 4 this time versus 5 last quarter; assault and battery charges were 92 this time, 77 last time. Carrying a concealed weapon, 11 (10 last quarter). We had 47 arrests (55 last quarter) for charges of possession of **a controlled substance**. Rape charges were 8, **1 less than last quarter**. 319 citations this time for moving violations: **speeding** 158/98, and failing to observe the signals 165/102 last quarter. DUIs this quarter—only 45, or 23 fewer than last quarter.

No analysis or commentary

Gives undigested numbers

Poor, inconsistent format

   Misdemeanors this quarter: disturbing the peace 53; vagrancy/public drunkenness 8; violating leash laws 32; violating city codes 39, including **dumping trash**. Last quarter the figures were **48, 59, 21, 43**.

Hard-to-follow comparisons and contrasts

We believe this report is **complete and up-to-date**. We further hope that this report has given you all the facts you will need.

Conclusion provides no summary or recommendations

FIGURE 8.2 A Well-Prepared Report, Revised from Figure 8.1

Springdale Police Department

Emergency 555-1000   **Administration** 555-1001   **Traffic** 555-1002

www.springdalepd.gov

TO: Captain J. T. Martin
FROM: Sergeants Daniel Huxley, Jennifer Chavez, and Ivor Paz
SUBJECT: Crime rate for the second quarter of 2014
DATE: July 11, 2014

From April 1 to June 30, 852 crimes were reported in Springdale, representing a 5 percent increase over the 815 crimes recorded during the previous quarter.

TYPES OF CRIMES

The following report, based on the table below, discusses the specific types of crimes, organized into four categories: **robberies and theft**, **felonies**, **traffic**, and **misdemeanors**.

Table 1 Comparison of the 1st and 2nd Quarter Crime Rates in Springdale

Category	1st Quarter	2nd Quarter
ROBBERIES AND THEFT		
Commercial	63	75
Domestic	36	43
Auto	33	40
FELONIES		
Homicide	5	4
Assault and battery	77	92
Carrying a concealed weapon	10	11
Poss. of a controlled substance	55	47
Rape	9	8
TRAFFIC		
Speeding	165	197
Failure to observe signals	102	118
DUI	78	65
MISDEMEANORS		
Disturbing the peace	48	53
Vagrancy	40	48
Public drunkenness	19	40
Leash law violations	21	32
Dumping trash	43	39
Other	8	12

Robberies and Theft

The greatest increase in crime was in robberies, 20 percent more than last quarter.

Left margin annotations:
Precise subject line

Begins with concise overview of report

Organizes crimes into categories

Supplies easy-to-follow visual

Table is boxed, making it easier to read

Uses clear headings to show organization of report

FIGURE 8.2 (Continued)

Page 2

occurred on May 21 at Paterson's Jewelers, when three armed robbers stole more than $217,000 in merchandise. (Suspects were apprehended two days later.) Home burglaries accounted for 43 crimes, though the thefts were not confined to any one residential area. We also had 40 car thefts reported and investigated.

Documents effective actions

Felonies
Homicides decreased slightly from last quarter—from 16 to 13. Charges for battery, however, increased—15 more than we had last quarter. Arrests for carrying a concealed weapon were nearly identical this quarter to last quarter's total. But the 47 arrests for possession of a controlled substance were appreciably down from the first quarter. Arrests for rape for this quarter also were less than last quarter's. Three of those rapes happened within one week (May 6–12) and have been attributed to the same suspect, now in custody.

Provides essential background and statistical information and comparative analyses

Traffic
Traffic violations were higher (9 percent) than those last quarter—380 as opposed to 345. Most of the citations were issued for speeding (158) or for failing to observe signals (98). Officers issued 45 citations to motorists for DUIs, a significant decrease from the 78 DUIs issued last quarter. The new state penalty of withholding a driver's license for six months of anyone convicted of driving while under the influence appears to have been an effective deterrent.

Easy-to-read sentences

Draws logical conclusion

Misdemeanors
The largest number of arrests in this category were for disturbing the peace—53. Compared to last quarter, this is an increase of 10 percent. There were 88 arrests for vagrancy and public drunkenness, an increase from the 59 charges made last quarter. We issued 32 citations for violations of leash laws, which represents a sizable increase over last quarter's 21 citations. Thirty-seven citations were issued for dumping trash at the Mason Reservoir.

Includes only data reader needs

CONCLUSION
Overall, while the crime rate has decreased for traffic violations (especially DUIs) and possession of controlled substances this quarter, we have seen a marked increase in arrests for robberies and battery.

Summarizes findings of report

RECOMMENDATIONS
To help deter robberies in the downtown area, we recommend the following:
- increasing surveillance units to 15 rather than the 10 now in the area
- offering businesses our workshop on safety and security precautions, as we did during the first quarter

Historically, battery arrests have risen during the second quarter. Our recommendations to counter this trend include:
- continuing to work closely with the Springdale Anti-Crime League
- providing more foot and bicycle patrols in the neighborhoods with the highest incidence of battery complaints

Offers specific actions/ changes based on conclusion of report in bulleted lists

Recommendations are realistic and valid

- **Audience analysis.** Figure 8.1 simply throws facts at the reader. Figure 8.2, however, consistently takes the reader's needs into account by focusing on how Captain Martin will use the statistical information about the crime rate during the second quarter of the year. To help Captain Martin, Figure 8.2 presents the most important information first, then explains and analyzes the numbers for her and provides realistic and direct recommendations.
- **Objectivity/ethics.** In Figure 8.1, details have not been checked against any other sources, so the report is incomplete and possibly inaccurate. Figure 8.2, however, eliminates the guesswork and, more ethically, offers solutions, careful analysis, and a variety of relevant sources.
- **Organization.** Figure 8.1 makes no attempt to organize the report in a reader-friendly manner. It contains three dense and disorganized paragraphs and does not summarize the facts. But Figure 8.2 supplies a clear purpose statement, organizes and summarizes the facts concisely, and helpfully groups recommendations.
- **Writing style and tone.** Figure 8.1 is just an accumulation of numbers, making it hard for Martin to access or understand their importance. The tone is smug and arrogant. Figure 8.2, on the other hand, is easy to follow and to understand. It uses helpful connective words and phrases ("compared to last quarter," "overall") and includes important contexts ("were less than last quarter").
- **Format and visuals.** Figure 8.1 lacks headers, bullets, visuals, or consistent paragraph indentation. Figure 8.2 instead supplies clear heads, breaks the text into easy-to-digest subheads, places numerical data in visual form (Table 1), and uses bulleted lists.

Sales Reports

Sales reports provide businesses with a necessary and ongoing record of accounts, online and mail purchases, losses, and profits over a specified period of time. They help businesses assess past performance and plan for the future. As a financial record, sales reports list costs per unit, discounts or special reductions, and subtotals and totals. Sales reports also show gains and losses. They may also provide statistics for comparing two quarters' sales.

Sales reports are also a managerial tool because they help businesses make both short- and long-range plans. The restaurant manager's sales report illustrated in Figure 8.3 guides the owners to decide which popular entrées to highlight and which unpopular ones to modify or delete. Note how the recommendations follow logically from the figures manager Sam Jelinek gives to Gina Smeltzer and Alfonso Zapatta, the owners of The Oaks. Because readers are familiar with the subject of the report, Jelinek did not have to supply background information on the entire offerings.

Progress Reports

A progress report informs readers about the status of an ongoing project. It lets them know how much and what type of work has been done by a particular date, by whom, how well, and how close the job is to being completed. A progress report

FIGURE 8.3 A Sales Report

Dayton, OH 43210 • (813) 555-4000 • (813) 555-4100 fax
www.theoaks.com

THE OAKS

TO: Gina Smeltzer
       Alfonso Zapatta, Owners
FROM: Sam Jelinek S J
       Manager

DATE: June 25, 2014

SUBJECT: Analysis of entrée sales,
         June 9–13 and June 16–20

Restricted subject line

As we agreed at our monthly meeting on June 3, here is my analysis of entrée sales for two weeks to assist us in our menu planning. Below is a record of entrée sales for the weeks of June 9–13 and June 16–20 that I compiled and put in the table for easier comparisons.

Begins with purpose and scope of report

	Portion Size	June 9–13 Amount	June 9–13 Percentage	June 16–20 Amount	June 16–20 Percentage	Both Weeks Amount	Both Weeks Percentage
Cornish Hen	6 oz.	238	17	307	17	545	17
Stuffed Young Turkey	8 oz.	112	8	182	10	294	12
Broiled Salmon Steak	8 oz.	154	11	217	12	371	13
Brook Trout	12 oz.	182	13	252	14	434	9
Prime Rib	10 oz.	168	12	198	11	366	11
Lobster Tails	2–4 oz.	147	10	161	9	308	10
Delmonico Steak	10 oz.	56	4	70	4	126	4
Moroccan Chicken	6 oz.	343	25	413	23	756	24
		1,400	**100**	**1,800**	**100**	**3,200**	**100**

Organizes findings of the report in helpful table

Boldfaces totals

Recommendations
Based on the figures in the table above, I recommend that we do the following:

1. Order at least 100 more pounds of prime rib each two-week period to be eligible for further quantity discounts from the Northern Meat Company.
2. Remove the Delmonico Steak entrée because of its low acceptance.
3. Introduce a new chicken or fish entrée to take the place of the Delmonico Steak; I would suggest grilled lemon chicken to accommodate those patrons interested in a tasty, low-fat, lower-cholesterol, reduced sodium entrée.

Offers precise and relevant recommendations

Please give me your responses within the next week. It shouldn't take more than a few days to implement these changes. Thank you.

Requests authorization to implement recommendations

emphasizes whether you are

- specifying what work has been done
- keeping your schedule
- staying within your budget
- using the proper technology/equipment
- making the right assignments
- responding to unexpected problems
- making adjustments in schedules, personnel, and so on
- specifying what work remains to be done
- completing the job efficiently, correctly, and according to codes

Audience for Progress Reports

A progress report is intended for people who generally are not working alongside you but who need a record of your activities to coordinate them with other individuals' efforts and to learn about problems or changes in plans. For example, because supervisors may not be in the field or branch office or at a construction site, they will rely on your progress report for crucial information. Customers, such as a contractor's clients, expect reports on how carefully their money is being spent. That way they can adjust schedules or alter specifications if there is a risk of going over budget.

The length of the progress report will depend on the complexity of the project. Contractor Dale Brandt's assessment of the progress his contractor company is making in renovating Dr. Burke's clinic is given in a letter in Figure 8.4 (page 314). A shorter report, such as one on organizing a workshop on time management, or one providing employees with a status report on a project (as in Figure 3.2), however, might require only a short email.

Frequency of Progress Reports

Progress reports can be written daily, weekly, monthly, quarterly, or annually. Your specific job and your employer's needs will dictate how often you have to keep others informed of your progress. Contractor Brandt determined that three reports, spaced four to six weeks apart, would be necessary to keep Dr. Burke posted. Figure 8.4 is the second of those reports.

Parts of a Progress Report

Progress reports should contain information on (1) the work you have done, (2) the work you are currently doing, and (3) the work you will do.

How to Begin a Progress Report

In a brief introduction, cover the following:

- indicate why you are writing the report
- provide any necessary project titles or codes and specific dates
- help readers recall the job you are doing for them

If you are writing an initial progress report, supply brief background information in the opening. But, if you are submitting a subsequent progress report, your introduction should only remind the reader about where your previous report left off and where the current one begins. Note how Dale Brandt's first paragraph in Figure 8.4 calls attention to the successful continuity of his work for Dr. Burke.

How to Write the Body of a Progress Report

The body of the report should provide significant details about costs, materials, personnel, and times for the major stages of the project.

- Emphasize completed tasks, not false starts. If you report that the carpentry work or painting is finished, readers do not need an explanation of paint viscosity or geometrical patterns.
- Describe in the body of your report any snags you encountered that may affect the work in progress (see Dale Brandt's section on electrical problems in Figure 8.4). It is better for the reader to know about trouble early in the project so that appropriate changes or corrections can be made.

How to End a Progress Report

The conclusion should give a timetable for the completion of duties or submission of the next progress report. Give the date by which you expect work to be completed. Be realistic; do not promise to have a job done in less time than you know it will take. Readers will not expect miracles, only informed estimates. Even so, any conclusion must be tentative. Note that the good news Dale Brandt gives Dr. Burke about moving into her new clinic is qualified by the words "If everything stays on schedule." He is also well aware of the "you attitude" by thanking Dr. Burke again for her business.

Employee Activity/Performance Reports

An employee activity/performance report informs your boss about what you did during a specified period (weekly, monthly, quarterly). He/she will expect you to explain how you managed your time and fulfilled the requirements of your job. Accountability is a major objective in the world of work and, as we saw in Chapter 1 (see pages 21–22), employers closely monitor employees, even online. An activity report is a vital indication of an employee's performance. Your supervisor or manager will want to know about the specific tasks you accomplished, how many of them, when, and why, as well as any ongoing projects in which you are involved. Activity reports will play a role in assessing your job performance and determining whether you should be promoted.

Figure 8.5 (on page 315) shows an employee activity report written by Carey Lewis, an administrative assistant, for his supervisor, Beth-Anne Prohaska. Note how he classifies his accomplishments into four major categories and provides an honest, objective, and concise explanation of what he has done and why. Each of Lewis's accomplishments squares with his job responsibility.

FIGURE 8.4 The Second of Three Progress Reports from a Contractor to a Customer

Brandt Construction Company

"Building a Greener Tomorrow"

Halsted at Roosevelt, Chicago, Illinois 60608-0999 • 312-555-3700 • Fax: 312-555-1731

www.brandtcon.com

Professional-looking letterhead emphasizing ecology

April 28, 2014

Dr. Pamela Burke
1439 Grand Avenue
Mount Prospect, IL 60045-1003

Dear Dr. Burke:

Begins with key information: project status

Here is my second progress report about the renovation work being done at your new clinic at Hacienda and Donohue. I am pleased to report that work proceeded satisfactorily in April according to the plans you had approved in March.

Recaps activities for background

Review of Work Completed in March
As I informed you in my first progress report on March 31, we tore down the walls, pulled the old wiring, and removed existing plumbing lines. All the gutting work was finished in March.

Summarizes current accomplishments

Work Completed During April
By April 7, we had laid the new pipes and connected them to the main septic line. We also installed the two commodes, four standard sinks, and a utility basin. The heating and air-conditioning ducts were installed by April 11. From April 14–18, we erected soundproof walls in the four examination rooms, the reception area, your office, and the laboratory. Throughout your clinic we used environmentally safe (green) materials. To further conserve energy, we installed solar panels on the roof, as you requested.

Attention to greening the building

Problems with the Electrical System
We had difficulty with the electrical work, however. The outlets and the generator for the laboratory equipment required extra-duty power lines that Con Edison and Cook County inspectors had to approve, which slowed us down by three days. Also, Midtown Electric failed to deliver the recessed lighting fixtures by April 25. Those fixtures and the generator are now installed. Nevertheless, the cost of those fixtures increased the material budget by **$5,288.00**. But the overall cost for labor remains as we had projected—**$94,550**.

Identifies problems, how they were solved

Work Remaining
The finishing work is scheduled for May. By May 9, the floors in the examination rooms, laboratory, washrooms, and hallways should be tiled and the reception area and your office carpeted. By May 12, the reception area and your office should be paneled and painted. If everything stays on schedule, touch-up work is planned for May 12–16. You should be able to move into your new clinic by May 19.

Specifies work remaining

Projects successful completion

You will receive a third and final progress report by May 12. Thank you again for the confidence you have placed in our company.

Promises to keep reader informed

Sincerely yours,

Dale Brandt

Dale Brandt

FIGURE 8.5 An Employee Activity Report Sent as an Email with Attachments

From: Carey Lewis (clewis@wdynamics.com)

To: Beth-Anne Prohaska (baprohaska@wdynamics.com)

Cc: Gloria Arrelo (garrelo@starinstruments.com)

Subject: Monthly Activity Report for August

📎: 🔲 Purchase Orders   🔲 Workflow

Dear Ms. Prohaska:

During the past pay cycle (August 1–August 31), I worked on several projects that I believe helped to ensure, and even increase, the efficiency of our department. Below I have categorized my accomplishments (all of which are specified in my job description), included completion dates for major tasks, and attached relevant documentation.

Oversaw Day-to-Day Management of Office
- Maintained adequate office supplies (see attachment: "Purchase Orders")
- Researched costs and features of new all-in-one printer and priced models for purchase
- Submitted recommendation for all-in-one printer (August 8)
- Trained two new interns (Loretta Bauer, Scott Chu)

Prepared and Delivered Documents
- Edited and posted the monthly newsletter to the company's website (August 17)
- Compiled, printed, and distributed monthly sales report (August 22)
- Updated, archived, and retrieved records

Planned Schedules
- Managed office calendar of events and meetings and posted it to the website
- Arranged travel plans for 4 staff on sales visits; two of these were overseas trips
- Coordinated workflow charts (see attachment: "Workflow")
- Logged staff timesheets in master file

Organized Meetings
- Presented short report (15 minutes) at HR meeting on August 8 about our department's successes in marketing new products
- Created—with assistant manager Richard Fleming—and distributed agenda for monthly staff meeting (August 27)
- Took minutes for monthly meeting and shared them on company intranet (August 29)

For the coming month I will continue to fulfill my ongoing responsibilities as well as meet our department's goals for any new assignments. I look forward to any comments you may have about my past or current performance.

Sincerely,

Carey Lewis
Administrative Assistant

Includes attachment

Gives background and briefly summarizes purpose of report

Uses boldfaced headings to group activities

Uses strong verbs to convey type of work

Provides key dates

Describes job duties clearly

References attachment

Specifies length and topic of presentation

Acknowledges collaboration

Promises continuity and politely requests feedback

© Cengage Learning 2015

Trip/Travel Reports

Reporting on the trips you take is an important professional responsibility in the world of work. Basically, you are on a fact-finding mission. In documenting what you did and saw, trip reports (also called travel reports) keep readers informed about your efforts and how they affect ongoing or future business, as Figure 8.6 shows. Moreover, such reports help you better understand your job and develop your networking skills. Trip reports also should be written after you attend a convention or sales meeting or call on customers.

Questions Your Trip/Travel Report Needs to Answer

Specifically, a trip report should answer the following questions for your readers:

- Where did you go?
- When did you go?
- Why did you go?
- What did you see?

- Whom did you see?
- What did they tell you?
- What did you do about it?
- Do you have any recommendations?

For a business trip, you are also likely to have to inform readers how much it cost and to supply them with receipts for all of your business expenses.

Common Types of Trip/Travel Reports

Trip reports can cover a wide range of activities and are called by different names to characterize those activities. Most likely, you will encounter the following three types of trip reports.

   1. Site inspection reports. These reports inform managers about conditions at a branch office or plant, a customer's business, or the advisability of relocating an office or other facility. After visiting the site, you will determine whether it meets your employer's (or customer's) needs. Site inspection reports can provide information about the physical plant, the environment (air, soil, water, vegetation), safety, IT, or financial operations.

   Figure 8.6, which begins with a recommendation, is a report written to a district manager interested in acquiring a new site for a fast-food restaurant.

   2. Field trip reports. These reports, often assigned in a course, are written after a visit to a laboratory, hospital, detention center, or other location to show what you have learned about the operation of a facility. (Such visits might even be done via "virtual tours" on the Internet.) You will be expected to describe how an institution is organized, the technical procedures and/or equipment it uses, pertinent ecological conditions, or the ratio of one group to another. The emphasis in such reports is on the educational value of the trip. For example, a student nurse may write, "From my visit to Water Valley, I learned a great deal about the health care delivery system at an extended care facility, which will help me during my internship next term."

FIGURE 8.6 A Site Inspection Report Using a Map

VAIL's
Chicken House

"Chicken with Style"

TO: Pretha Bandi *B.A.R.*
FROM: Beth Armando-Ruiz
Development Department

DATE: March 28, 2014
SUBJECT: New Site for Vail's #7

Recommendation

To follow up on our discussions earlier this month, I think the best location for the new Vail's Chicken House is the vacant Dairy World restaurant at the northeast corner of Smith and Fairfax Avenues—1701 Fairfax. I inspected this property on March 19 and 20 and also talked to Kim Shao, the broker at Crescent Realty **(kims@crescent.org)**, representing the Dairy World Company. The location, parking facilities, and building at the Dairy World site all present the best opportunity for future growth and increased sales for Vail's.

The Location

Please refer to the map below. Located at the intersection of the two busiest streets on the southeast side of the city, the property will allow us to take advantage of the traffic flow to attract customers. Being only one block west of the Cloverleaf Mall should also help increase our business.

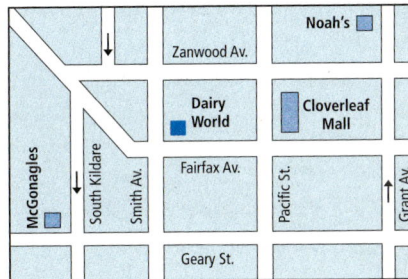

Another benefit is that customers will have easy access to our location. They can enter or exit the Dairy World site from either Smith or Fairfax Avenues. Left turns onto Smith are prohibited from 7 a.m. to 9 a.m., but since most of our business is done after 11 a.m., the restriction poses few problems.

Denver, CO 87123   (303) 555-7200   www.vails.com

Begins with most important details about the writer's recommendation

Gives essential contact information

Provides necessary background details

Includes map and traffic flow information essential for reader's purpose

Clearly transitions to another advantage

(Continued)

FIGURE 8.6 (Continued)

Pretha Bandi
March 28, 2014
Page 2

Area Competition

Assesses the location, in light of the competition

Only two other fast food establishments are within a one-mile vicinity. McGonagles, 1534 South Kildare, specializes in hamburgers; and Noah's, 703 Grant Ave., serves primarily seafood entrées. Their offerings will not directly compete with ours. The closest fast-food restaurant serving chicken is Johnson's, 1.8 miles away.

Parking Facilities

Gives only the most essential facts audience needs on parking, seating capacity, and alterations

The parking lot has space for 25 cars, and the area at the south end of the property (38 feet × 37 feet) could accommodate 14–15 more vehicles. The driveways and parking lot were paved with asphalt last July and appear to be in excellent condition. We will also be able to use the drive-up window on the north side of the building.

The Building

Writer has done research on equipment

The building has 3,993 square feet of heated and cooled space. The four air-conditioning units and heating units were installed within the last fifteen months and seem to be in good working order; nine more months of transferable warranty remain on all these units.

Paragraphs are easy to follow with precise topic sentences

The only major changes we must make are in the kitchen. To prepare items on the Vail's menu, we need to add at least three more exhaust fans (there is only one now) and to expand the grill and cooking areas by 80 square feet. The kitchen also has three relatively new sinks and offers ample storage space in the 16 cabinets.

Does not overwhelm reader with petty details

The restaurant has a seating capacity of up to 34 persons; 10 booths are covered with red vinyl and are comfortably padded. A color-coordinated serving counter could seat 8 to 10 patrons. The floor does not need to be retiled, but the walls will have to be painted to match Vail's decor.

3. Home health or social work visits. Nurses, social workers, and probation officers, for instance, report routinely on their visits to patients and clients. Their reports describe clients' lifestyles, assess needs, and make recommendations based on a variety of sources—clients, health care professionals, charitable organizations, and the like. These reports are often divided into Purpose of the Visit, Description of the Visit, and Action Taken as a Result of the Visit.

How to Gather Information for a Trip/Travel Report

Regardless of the kind of trip report you have to write, your assignment will be easier and your report better organized if you follow these suggestions.

1. Before you leave on the site inspection, field trip, or other business trip, be sure you are prepared:
    a. Obtain all necessary names; street, email, and website addresses; and relevant telephone, cell, fax numbers, and URLs.
    b. Check files for previous correspondence, case studies, warranties, or contracts or agreements.
    c. Download work orders, instructions, or other documents pertinent to your visit, for example, websites and ads.
    d. Bring a laptop, tablet, or notebook with you. Keep a journal of what you saw and heard.
    e. Locate a map of the area and get the directions you'll need beforehand. (Both maps and directions can be obtained easily at **www.mapquest.com, maps.yahoo.com,** and **maps.google.com**).
    f. Keep a record of appointment times and locations as well as the names and job titles of the people whom you expect to meet.
    g. Save all receipts.
    h. Bring a videorecorder, camera, audio recorder, smartphone, laptop, or tablet, if necessary, to record important data. You may be asked to post photographs from your trip on your company's website.

   When you return from your trip, keep the following hints in mind as you compile your report:

    a. Write your report promptly. If you put it off, you may forget important details.
    b. When a trip takes you to two or more widely separated places, note in your report when you arrived at each place and how long you stayed.
    c. Exclude irrelevant details, such as whether the trip was enjoyable, what you ate, or how delighted you were to meet people. Concentrate on the information your reader needs to make a decision, meet a goal, or receive a timely update.
    d. Be objective about what you saw and heard. Indicate when you quote someone as part of an interview.
    e. Offer to answer any questions your reader may have about the trip and its outcomes.

Incident Reports

The short reports discussed thus far in this chapter have dealt with routine work. They have described events that were anticipated or supervised. But every business or agency runs into unexpected trouble that delays routine work, damages equipment or property, or may result in personal injury. These circumstances need to be documented in an incident (or accident) report. The audience for an incident report can be within your organization or outside it, or both. Employers use incident reports to make changes so that the problem does not occur again or so that a job can be done more effectively and safely. On some occasions, government inspectors, insurance agents, and attorneys must be informed about those events that have interfered with or threatened normal, safe operations.

When to Submit an Incident Report

An incident report is submitted when there is, for example,

- an accident—fire, automobile, physical injury
- a law enforcement offense
- an environmental danger
- a computer virus
- a machine breakdown
- a delivery delay
- a cost overrun
- a production slowdown

Figure 8.7 is an incident report about a train derailment submitted by the engineer on duty. This report is in memo format, but some companies or agencies require you to fill out a special form. Because it can contain legally sensitive information needed in hard copy, an incident report should not be sent as an email.

Parts of an Incident Report

Include the following information in your incident report. Note how Figure 8.7 includes precise and accurate information for each of these parts.

1. Identification details. Specify who and what was involved, and gather all relevant data—names, contact information, model/serial numbers, and so on. Record titles, department, and employment identification numbers. Indicate if you or your fellow employees were working alone. For customers or victims, record home addresses, phone numbers, and places of employment. Insurance companies will also require policy numbers.

2. Type of incident. Briefly identify the incident—personal injury, fire, burglary, equipment failure. Identify any part(s) of the body precisely. "Eye injury" is not enough; "injury to the right eye, causing bleeding" is better. "Dislocated right shoulder" or "punctured left forearm" is descriptive and exact. A report on damaged equipment should list make and model numbers.

3. Time and location of the incident. Include precise date (not "Thursday") and time (a.m. or p.m.).

FIGURE 8.7 An Incident Report in Memo Format

THE GREAT HARVESTER RAILROAD
Des Moines, IA 50306-4005
www.ghrr.com

TO: Angela O'Brien, District Manager
                James Hwang, Safety Inspector
FROM: Nick Roane, Engineer *Nick Roane*
DATE: October 6, 2014
SUBJECT: Derailment of Train 26 on October 6, 2014

Signs report to verify account of incident

Type of Incident
Two grain cars went off the track while I was driving Engine 457 of Train 26 on October 6, 2014. There were no injuries to the crew.

Begins with most important details

Description of Incident
At 7:20 a.m., I was traveling north at a speed of 30 miles an hour on the single main line track four miles east of Ridgeville, Illinois. Weather conditions and visibility were excellent. Suddenly, the last two grain cars, 3022 and 3053, jumped the track. The train automatically went into emergency braking and came to a stop. But it did not stop before both grain cars turned at a 45° angle. After checking these cars, I found that half the contents of their loads had spilled. The train was not carrying any hazardous chemicals or other environmentally damaging shipments.

Gives precise time, location

Describes what happened

I notified Supervisor Bill Purvis at 7:40 a.m., and within 45 minutes he and a section crew arrived at the scene with rerailing equipment. The crew removed the two grain cars from the track, put in new ties, and made the main line track passable by 11:25 a.m. At 1:25 p.m. a vacuum car arrived with Engine 372 from Hazlehurst, Illinois, and its crew proceeded with the clean-up operation. By 3:25 p.m. all the spilled grain was loaded onto the cars brought by the Hazlehurst train. Bill Purvis notified Barnwell Granary that their shipment would be at least eight hours late.

Explains what was done

Causes of Incident
Supervisor Purvis and I checked the stretch of train track where the cars derailed and found it to be heavily worn. We believe that a fisher joint slipped when the grain cars hit it, and the track broke. You can see the location of the cracked fisher joint in the graphic below.

Determines likely cause

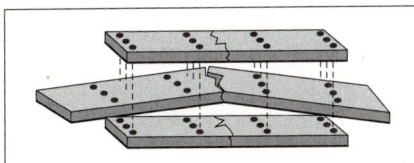

Supplies easy-to-follow exploded visual

(Continued)

FIGURE 8.7 (Continued)

Angela O'Brien
James Hwang
October 6, 2014
Page 2

Records precise steps taken

Actions Taken

We performed the following procedures after the accident:

1. Checked the section of track for 8 miles on either side of Ridgeville for any signs of defective fisher joints.
2. Repaired at once any defective joints we saw.
3. Instructed all engineers to slow down to 5 to 10 mph over this section of the track until the rail check is completed for 20 miles on either side of the accident site.

© Cengage Learning 2015

4. Description of what happened. This section is the longest part of the report. Let readers know exactly what took place and why, how it occurred, and what led up to the incident.

5. What was done after the incident. Describe the action you took to correct conditions, how things got back to normal, and what was done to treat the injured, make the environment safer, speed a delivery, or repair damaged equipment.

6. What caused the incident. Make sure your explanation is consistent with your description of what happened. Pinpoint the trouble. In Figure 8.7, for example, the defective fisher joint is listed under the heading "Causes of Incident."

7. Actions taken. Specify any actions taken to prevent the problem from recurring. They may involve repairing any broken parts, as in Figure 8.7, calling a special safety meeting, asking for further training, adapting existing equipment, doing emergency planning, or modifying schedules.

Protecting Yourself Legally

An incident report can be admitted as legal evidence, and it then becomes part of a permanent legal record that can be used by law enforcement and attorneys in court to establish negligence and liability on your and your company's part. It can also be used by an employer to determine employee responsibility. An incident report frequently concerns the two topics over which powerful legal battles are waged—health and property. You could lose a case in court if your report is not written competently, clearly, accurately, and completely.

You have to be very careful about collecting and recording details. Make sure your report is not sketchy, confusing, or incomplete. To avoid these errors, you may have to interview employees or bystanders; travel to the incident site; check manuals, code books, or other guides; consult safety experts; collect and describe evidence; or research records/archives.

To ensure that what you write is legally proper, follow these guidelines:

1. **Submit your report promptly, and sign or initial it.** Any delay might be seen as a cover-up. Send your report to the appropriate parties immediately after you have gathered the necessary information and had it reviewed by your supervisor. You may have to post photographs as well.

2. **Double-check your spelling (individuals' names, pieces of equipment, etc.), your math, and your punctuation.** An error here calls the accuracy and validity of your whole report into question.

3. **Be accurate, objective, and complete.** Give readers sufficient information to know exactly what happened and the order in which it occurred. Never omit or distort facts; the information may surface later, and you could be accused of a cover-up. Do not simply write "I do not know" for an answer. If you are not sure, state why. Also be careful that there are no discrepancies or inconsistencies in your report.

4. **Give facts, not opinions.** Provide a factual account of what actually happened, not a biased interpretation of events or one based on speculation or hearsay. Vague responses such as "I guess," "I wonder," "apparently," "perhaps," or "possibly" weaken your objectivity. Indicate who discovered, reported, or witnessed the incident. But stick to details you witnessed or that were seen by eyewitnesses. Identify witnesses or victims by giving complete names, addresses, places of employment, and so on. Keep in mind that stating what someone else saw is regarded as hearsay and therefore is not admissible in a court of law. State only what *you* saw or heard. When you describe what happened, avoid drawing uncalled-for conclusions. Consider the following statements of opinion versus fact:

> **Opinion:** The patient seemed confused and caught himself in his IV tubing.
> **Fact:** The patient caught himself in his IV tubing.

> **Opinion:** The equipment was defective.
> **Fact:** The bolt was cracked.

Be careful, too, about blaming someone. Statements such as "Baxter was incompetent" or "The company knew of the problem but did nothing about it" are libelous remarks.

5. **Do not exceed your professional responsibilities.** Answer only those questions you are qualified to answer. Do not presume to speak as a first responder, a detective, an inspector, a physician, a supervisor, or a judge. Do not represent yourself as an attorney or a claims adjuster in writing the report. And don't take sides.

Writing Winning Proposals

A proposal is a detailed plan of action submitted to a reader or group of readers for approval. The readers are usually in a position of authority—supervisors, managers, department heads, company buyers, elected officials, military or civic leaders—to endorse or reject the plan. Your proposal must convince these readers that your plan will help them improve their business, save them money, enhance their image, improve customer satisfaction, make the environment safer, or all of these.

Proposals are written for many purposes and many different audiences. You can write an internal proposal, for example, to your boss, seeking authorization to hire staff, change a procedure, or purchase new equipment or software. Or you can write a sales proposal to potential customers, offering a product or a service (such as providing training with new, special firefighting gear or selling an office manager a line of ergonomically designed furniture).

Depending on the job, proposals can vary greatly in size and in scope. A formal proposal can be a very long and complex document running into hundreds of pages. A proposal to your employer, however, about redesigning the company website could easily be conveyed in a few pages, the length of a short report. To propose doing a small job for a prospective client—for example, establishing an electronic record retrieval system—a letter with information on costs, materials, and a timetable might suffice. The sales letter in Figure 4.9 (page 118) illustrates a short proposal in letter format. Proposals can be *unsolicited*—that is, they originate with you—or they can be *solicited*, requested by a company or organization, as in Figure 8.10 (pages 337–339).

Proposals Are Persuasive Plans

Proposals, whether large or small, must be highly persuasive to succeed. Without your audience's approval, your plan will never go into effect, however accurate and important you think it is. Your enthusiasm is not enough; you have to supply hard evidence. Your proposals must convince readers that your plan is relevant, practical, based upon careful research, and designed to benefit the reader and his or her company.

Every proposal you write must exhibit a "can do" attitude, putting the reader and his or her company's needs at the center of your work. Show readers how approving your plan will save them time and money, increase productivity, enhance corporate image, improve employee morale, or attract new business. The tone of your proposal should be "Here is what I can do for you." Yates Engineering has won millions of dollars of business through its reader-centered proposals. Its slogan is "On time… within budget … to your satisfaction." Time, budget, and your readers' satisfaction and convenience are among the key ingredients of a winning proposal. Customize your proposal by personalizing it. Advertisements such as the ones in Figure 1.6 (page 19) and the figure with Exercise 8 on page 33 often contain mini-proposals appealing to a customer's need for a more economical and efficient way to do things. Notice how the advertisement in Figure 8.8 encourages potential clients to purchase a security package based on a variety of available options from motion detection systems to video surveillance to well-trained officers.

Proposals Frequently Are Collaborative Efforts

Like many other examples of business and technical writing, proposals often are the product of teamwork. Even a short in-house proposal, such as the one in Figure 8.9, is often researched and put together by more than one individual in the company or agency.

CPS Security/www.cpssecurity.com

Many times, individual employees will pull together information from their separate areas (such as graphics and design, finance, marketing, technology, transportation, and even legal) and put it into a proposal that each member of the team then reads and revises until the team agrees that the document is ready to be released.

Eight Guidelines for Writing a Successful Proposal

The following guidelines will help you persuade your audience to approve your plan. Refer to these guidelines and Figures 8.9 and 8.10 both before and while you formulate your plan.

   1. Approach writing a proposal as a problem-solving activity. Your purpose should reflect your ability to identify and solve problems. Convince your audience that you know what their needs are and that you will meet them, as Alissa Bond and Stacy Holton do in Figure 8.9, and as Neelow Singh and Jack Rosen do in Figure 8.10.

   2. Regard your audience as skeptical. Even though you offer a plan that you think will benefit readers, do not be overconfident that they will automatically accept it as the best and only way to proceed. Brainstorm, alone or with your collaborative team, to anticipate and answer your readers' questions and objections. To determine whether your proposal is feasible, readers will study it carefully. If your proposal contains errors or inconsistencies, omits information, or deviates from what they are looking for, your readers will reject it.

3. Research your proposal topic thoroughly. A winning proposal is *not* based on a few well-meaning, general suggestions. To provide the detailed information necessary and to convince readers, you will have to do your homework. Research your topic by studying the latest technology in the field (as Alissa Bond and Stacy Holton do in Figure 8.9), shopping for the best prices, comparing your prices and services with what the competition offers, verifying schedules, visiting customers, making site visits, and interviewing key individuals. Make sure that any technology or equipment you use or sell complies with all codes, specifications, and standards.

4. Scout out what your competitors are doing. Become familiar with your competitors' products or services, have a fair idea about their market costs, and be able to show how your company's work is better overall. Provide examples; offer a demonstration. Read competitors' websites and print publications very carefully. Let readers know you have done your homework on their behalf. See how the employees who wrote the internal proposal in Figure 8.9 researched the industry average for losses due to unsold inventory and inventory discounts. Note, too, how the writers in Figure 8.10 prove that their product and service are superior to those of their competitors.

5. Prove that your proposal is workable. The bottom-line question from your readers is "Will this plan work?" Your proposal should contain no statements that say, "Let's see what happens if we do X or Y." Analyze and test each part of your proposal to eliminate any quirks and to revise the proposal appropriately before readers evaluate it. What you propose should be consistent with the organization and capabilities of the company and should respect its corporate mission and culture. See how Alissa Bond and Stacy Holton argue how relevant, user friendly, and compatible Inventech is for their sporting goods company. For instance, recommending that a small company of eighteen employees triple its workforce to implement your plan would be foolish and risky.

6. Be sure your proposal is financially realistic. "Is it worth the money?" is another bottom-line question you can expect from your readers. For example, recommending that your company spend $20,000 to solve a $2,000 problem is just not feasible. Note how Figure 8.9 details both the cost of inaction and the amount needed to correct the problem and how Figure 8.10 stresses that the costs are in line with what the customer wants to spend. Above all, make readers believe that the benefits are worth the costs.

7. Be ethical. Your proposal needs to follow all the guidelines for ethical conduct on pages 21–29. You must be trustworthy and truthful about all the claims you make about products, services, and contracts and that you will be professional and respond to any questions or problems your readers voice.

8. Package your proposal attractively. Make sure that your proposal is well presented (professional looking, inviting, and easy to read) and that all visuals are clear and appropriately placed. The visual appearance of your proposal can contribute greatly to whether it is accepted.

Internal Proposals

The primary purpose of an internal proposal, such as the one shown in Figure 8.9, is to offer a realistic and constructive plan to help your company run its business more efficiently and economically.

On your job you may discover a better way of doing something or a more efficient way to correct a problem. You believe that your proposed change will save your employer time, money, or further trouble. (Note how Alissa Bond and Stacy Holton indentified and researched a more effective and efficient way for Challenger Sports to manage its inventory and to satisfy its customers in Figure 8.9.) Or your department head, manager, or supervisor may call your attention to a problem and ask you for specific ways to solve it.

Regardless of who identifies the problem, your proposal, generally speaking, will be an informal, in-house message. A brief (one- to three- or five-page) memo, as in Figure 8.9, or even a shorter email, should be appropriate.

Some Common Topics for Internal Proposals

An internal proposal can be written about a variety of topics, including the following:

- purchasing new or more advanced equipment to replace obsolete or inefficient computers, appliances, vehicles, and the like, or upgrading equipment technology
- obtaining new software and offering training sessions to show employees how to use it
- recruiting new employees or retraining current ones on a new technique or process
- eliminating a dangerous condition or reducing an environmental risk to prevent accidents—for employees, customers, or the community at large
- cutting costs—for services, supplies, transportation, advertising, etc.
- improving technology/communication within or between departments of a company or agency
- expanding work space or making it greener, more private, ergonomically comfortable and efficient for employees, or more inviting to customers
- providing better safety and security, safeguarding a company's records

As this bulleted list shows, internal proposals cover almost every activity or policy that can affect the day-to-day operations of a company or an agency.

Following the Proper Chain of Command

Writing an internal proposal requires you to be sensitive to office politics. It may be wise first to meet with your boss to see if she or he has already identified the problem or has specific suggestions on how to solve it. If given the go-ahead, then you and your team need to provide your boss with a draft and ask for feedback.

But do not assume that your readers will automatically agree that there is a problem or that your plan is the only way to tackle it. Remember that your employer will expect you to be very convincing about both the problem you say exists and the changes you are advocating in the workplace under his or her supervision. Don't rock the corporate boat by going over your supervisor's head, questioning his or her authority, or suggesting a plan that is too costly.

Ethically Anticipating and Resolving Corporate Readers' Problems

When you prepare an internal proposal, you need to be aware of the ethical obligations you have and the ways to meet them. Here are some important guidelines:

1. Consider the company-wide implications of your plan. The change you propose (transfers, new budgets or technology, new hires) may have sweeping and potentially disruptive implications for another office or division in your company.

2. Do not discount the possible impact of your change on co-workers from cultural traditions other than your own. In addition to speaking to your employer, consult your human resources or cultural diversity director.

3. Find out whether your proposed plan is within your company's budget. How much can your department, branch, or office spend (e.g., on hardware, software, updates)? Check with your boss, and always monitor the price of your company's stock orders to make sure any expenditures are likely to be approved.

4. Keep in mind that your boss may have to take your proposal farther up the organizational ladder for commentary and approval. You cannot disregard the chain of command at your company or organization.

5. Never rely on someone else to supply the specific details on how your proposal will work. For example, do not write an internal proposal that says the marketing, technical support, or human resources department could supply the necessary details for your proposal to work. That unfairly pushes the responsibility onto others.

Case Study

Drafting an Internal Proposal to Create a Mobile App for a Health Food Store

Jaclyn Tan, an evening shift supervisor for a small chain of health food stores, realized from conversations with staff and customers, as well as from marketing surveys conducted through the company website, that her employer was missing many opportunities for sales by not having a free mobile app available for customers.

Tan sent a memo to her boss, district manager Arnold Maddox, identifying some of the benefits to the company in having its own app and requested permission to investigate more formally the options and costs involved in building the app, testing it, and making it available on the company website. After several discussions with Maddox, in person and online, Tan received permission to draft an internal proposal and to locate the best qualified mobile tech consultants to create it. Brainstorming with her fellow employees from day and evening shifts, she identified the key information to be disseminated through the app, such as allowing customers to check the availability of favorite products, to pre-order/pre-pay for items that were difficult to keep in stock, and to alert them to sales and new products, and charge account status. She also found that customers would benefit from information on relevant FDA and USDA reports, special events such as the store hosting speakers and sponsoring healthy cooking classes, and community events where her company's products might be promoted.

Armed with this information, she began contacting several mobile app consultants to investigate the time and costs involved in creating an app. Given the company's history and customer needs, Tan learned that, on average, these IT consultants charged $75 per hour and that it would take 150 hours of work to create the app and link it to the store's website—for a total of $11,250. Because her company's competitors already offered an app for customers and that m-commerce revenue had increased by 15 percent in her market area (*Chamber of Commerce*, *Report for 2013*), there were many advantages in creating a customized app for her company.

Having gathered relevant technical and financial information, she shared her findings with her co-workers, and finally secured her boss's approval. She was then ready to write an internal proposal that respected her employer's chain of command and that would better promote her company's products and services.

Organization of an Internal Proposal

A short internal proposal follows a relatively straightforward plan of organization, from identifying the problem to solving it. Internal proposals usually contain four parts, as shown in Figure 8.9: *purpose*, *problem*, *solution*, and *conclusion*. Refer to the figure as you read the following discussion.

Purpose

Begin your proposal with a brief statement as Alissa Bond and Stacy Holton do to their supervisor: "I propose that . . ." State right away why you think a specific change is necessary now. Then succinctly define the problem and emphasize that your plan, if approved by the reader, will solve that problem.

Problem

In this section, prove that a problem exists. Document its importance for your boss and your company; as a matter of fact, the more you show, with concrete evidence, how the problem affects your boss's work (and area of supervision), the more likely you are to persuade him or her to act.

Here are some guidelines for documenting a problem:

- Avoid vague (and unsupported) generalizations such as these: "We're losing money each day with this procedure." "Costs continue to escalate." "The trouble occurs frequently in a number of places." "Numerous complaints have come in." "If something isn't done soon, more problems will result." Figure 8.9 focuses on an inventory tracking system.

FIGURE 8.9 An Internal Unsolicited Proposal to Purchase Updated Inventory Software

www.challengersports.com
Waveland 591-727-6079
Addison 591-650-2362
Turnersville 591-936-2290

Date: October 1, 2013
To: Michael Sapientia, Owner
From: Alissa Bond and Stacy Holton
RE: A proposal to purchase and implement new inventory-tracking software within the next 30 days

Purpose

Clearly states why proposal is being sent

We propose a cost-effective solution for what has become a growing problem at our stores: the lack of an accurate, easy-to-use inventory tracking system. We propose that you approve the purchase and installation, within the next month, of the Inventech software program as well as the necessary computer hardware to make the system operable. Our company will thereby benefit from an up-to-date inventory system that will better serve our customers and help us regain lost revenue because of inadequate inventory procedures.

Acknowledges company's stated goals and projects outcome of adopting their recommendation

The Problem with Current Inventory Systems

Identifies problem by giving reader essential background information based on primary research

Since we expanded last year from just our Waveland store to two additional locations, our inventory ordering methods have not accurately reflected customer demand. Up until now, we have relied on our experienced employees to gauge ordering needs, but because of our recent expansion, the sales force we had last year at our sole Waveland store (10 full- and 3 part-time employees) is now divided among all three Challenger stores. To staff all our locations, we added 15 part-time employees, most of whom are new to the retail sporting goods business. Consequently, our sales force is less experienced in predicting and maintaining adequate inventory needs.

Divides the problem into parts: financial and customer service

The problem of effectively tracking and ordering adequate inventory was compounded by assuming that the two new stores would mirror the purchasing decisions of customers at the Waveland site. Instead, our records show that customer demands differ greatly from store to store, and often by a disturbingly large amount. For example: The Addison store sells far more football-related jerseys and gear than Waveland does, while Turnersville sells far more fishing-related items than either the Waveland or Addison stores do. As a result of being stocked exactly as like Waveland, the Addison and Turnersville locations fell short of meeting customer demand during key selling seasons. Moreover, even when employees referred customers to one of our other two stores, we often lost business to competitors. Research shows that when consumers

FIGURE 8.9 (Continued)

have a negative buying experience the first time they try a new business, more than half of them will not give this business "a second chance to make a first impression" (Maynard et al., 2011).*

Cites important research

But having too much inventory is as unprofitable as stocking too little. A surplus of merchandise takes up costly warehouse and showroom space, while stocking too few items can drive our customers elsewhere. But whatever the case, we are losing business and revenue because of the dated and inefficient ways we purchase and stock merchandise. The table below, based on a detailed internal audit (made on September 16th in preparation for the 2013 tax year), breaks down the losses we have incurred since January 2013 due to overstocking in all three stores. *Revenue Loss from Discounting* represents the loss we actually experienced when we sold these items at a deep and necessary discount as opposed to their full retail prices. *Revenue Loss from Unsold Inventory* documents the revenue forfeited when the inventoried items did not sell at all:

Accumulates important financial information in easy-to-read table

Sport	Revenue Loss from Discounting	Revenue Loss from Unsold Inventory	Total Loss
Golf	$17,835	$7,715	$25,550
Football	$16,545	$4,455	$21,000
Fishing	$8,355	$11,390	$19,745
Soccer	$9,650	$3,850	$13,500
Cycling	$8,625	$3,570	$12,195
Baseball	$5,225	$3,730	$8,955
Basketball	$4,010	$4,715	$8,725
Swimming	$7,110	$890	$8,000
Hockey	$5,135	$2,680	$7,815
TOTAL	$82,490	$42,995	$125,485

Lost revenue comes from discounting plus unsold inventory. Our total losses amount to 12.6% of our expected revenue from all these items, or $125,485 across the three stores. In our metropolitan sales area, competing sporting goods stores lost only 6.6% of expected revenue, as opposed to our 12.6%, because of unsold inventory or deep discounting. Our inventory problems surfaced when we opened the two new stores.

Diplomatically identifies cause of the problem without assigning blame

The explanation for such losses is our not having a comprehensive inventory tracking system. This not only hurts Challenger's prestige in the marketplace; it will cumulatively mean greater losses this coming fiscal

(Continued)

* To save space the references section has been omitted.

FIGURE 8.9 (Continued)

Michael Sapientia
October 1, 2013
Page 3

year. Deep discounting undermines our marketing strategy of being a premiere sporting goods store that gives customers a one-stop-shopping experience. It also jeopardizes our long-term goal to expand our customer base effectively through the two new stores in Addison and Turnersville.

A Solution to the Problem

Purchasing and installing a comprehensive inventory tracking system will allow Challenger to reclaim a sizable percentage of the revenue we have lost by upgrading our inventory procedures and considerably reducing discounting and carrying unsold inventory. A relevant study of small businesses by Lapka and Harper (2012) found that when businesses began using a tracking system, they were able to reclaim almost 33% of revenue losses due to inventory issues in the first year. We believe that by switching to an updated, comprehensive inventory tracking system our company will benefit in several ways:

- Based on the study above (Lapka and Harper, 2012), we could conservatively reclaim 28% of the revenue lost this year due to our inventory problems
- We could make maximum use of display room and warehouse space.
- Eliminating a large percentage of surplus stock, we would reduce a lower profit margin from discount sales.
- We would provide better possibilities for each store to specialize based on sales/customer needs.
- We would be better positioned to expand and maintain our customer base at all three locations.

Feasibility of Installing New Inventory Tracking Software

We researched several tracking software programs and believe that Inventech Inventory Tracking (www.inventech.com/inventory) offers the best and most cost-effective software for Challenger's inventory problems. Inventech will allow us to track, record, and calculate our merchandise efficiently and be in a better position to project orders in fiscal year 2014.

A further benefit is that Inventech is compatible with our existing and outdated Reventrax system (which only tracks the cash flow/net receipts generated by each register), thus allowing us to retain historical sales data and to perform many inventory audits that we are currently unable to perform such as:

- Track inventory for each item from each store at the end of every business day.
- Project required inventory levels for the next 7 days based on historical sales data and current inventory levels.
- Automatically place orders for items that we are low on with suppliers who can promise delivery with only a 2-day lead.

Emphasizes possible future problems

Problem is clearly stated before giving reader supporting evidence

Relates solution to both parts of the inventory problem

Bulleted list makes benefits and recommendations easy to follow

Shows problem can be solved and how

© Cengage Learning 2015

FIGURE 8.9 (Continued)

Michael Sapientia
October 1, 2013
Page 4

- Generate daily recommended transfers of items from high-inventory locations to low-inventory ones, again based on historical sales data and current inventory levels.
- Assist us through customized software to grow and expand as we increase our stores in the future.

Training for all 6 full-time employees can begin as soon as the software is purchased, the necessary hardware and network upgrades are implemented, and the software installed. Another benefit of going with Inventech is that they offer on-site, 6-hour training programs at a cost of $240 per employee; these programs can be scheduled at our convenience with 1 week's notice—in plenty of time for holiday shopping. Given Inventech's solid reputation for training (which we verified by checking with several of their references), the system can be fully in-place within the next 30 days.

Provides an overview of the steps required to implement the proposal, and a timeline for carrying it out

Costs

The costs of implementing our proposal are as follows:

Itemizes costs

Site license and IT Service Plan for Inventech (Version 7.1)	$1,047.00 ($349.00 per year per store × 3 stores)
6-hour training for all full-time staff (6 employees)	$1,440.00 ($240 each × 6 employees)
New external hard drives for each store to run software and keep secure inventory records	$1,797.00 ($599 each × 3 stores)
Installation of software and increasing the capacity of the computer network for the company	$3,200.00
TOTAL $7,484.00	

There are other financial advantages in purchasing the new Inventech software. We would also be able to amortize, for tax purposes, the cost of the installation of the inventory tracking software ($7,484) over 5 years. Our annual expenses would, therefore, actually be:

Interprets costs for the reader

$6,437 ($1,440 for training + $1,797 for hard drives
+ $3,200 for network upgrades) ÷ 5 years = $1,287.40
 + $1,047.00 (annual site license)
 $\overline{\text{$2,334.40 per year}}$

Compared with the **$125,485** we lost in revenue last year because of insufficient inventory procedures, the amount of annual depreciated costs

(Continued)

FIGURE 8.9 (Continued)

Michael Sapientia
October 1, 2013
Page 5

Proves change is cost effective; provides specific financial evidence

for the new Inventech system is significantly smaller and well worth our investment. Using the Inventech software will allow us to recoup 28% of the revenue lost due to inventory problems, which means that purchasing the Inventech system will also bring in additional revenue of at least **$35,136** for 2014.

Conclusion

Succinctly recaps all major benefits of buying the updated software

Purchasing the Inventech software is necessary, feasible, and cost effective for Challenger. By approving our proposal, the company can realistically expect to generate at least **$35,136** in additional revenue annually and also increase customer satisfaction and patronage at all three stores. We will be happy to discuss this proposal with you at your convenience, and look forward to answering any questions. Thank you.

Thanks reader

© Cengage Learning 2015

- Provide quantifiable details about the problem, such as the amount of money or time a company is actually losing per day, week, or month. Document the financial trouble so that you can show in the next section how your plan offers an efficient and workable solution. See the table in Figure 8.9.
- Indicate how many employees (or work-hours) are involved or how many customers are inconvenienced or endangered by a procedure or condition. The writers in Figure 8.9 researched industry standards for losses related to inventory and used this information to document the importance of the problem.
- Verify how widespread a problem is or how frequently it occurs by citing specific occasions.
- Relate the problem to an organization's image, corporate reputation, or influence (where appropriate). Pinpoint exactly how and where the problem lessens your company's effectiveness or hurts its standing in the market. Indicate who is affected and how the problem affects your company's business, as the writers do especially well in the second and third paragraph of the problem statement in Figure 8.9 on pages 330–331.

Solution or Plan

In this section, describe the change you propose and want approved. Tie your solution (the change) directly to the problem you have just documented. Each part of your plan should help eliminate the problem or should help increase the productivity, efficiency, or safety you think is possible.

Your reader will again expect to find factual evidence. Be specific. Do not give merely an outline of your plan or say that details can be worked out later. Supply details that answer the following questions: (1) Is the plan workable? and (2) Is it cost-effective? See how the writers of the proposal in Figure 8.9 do that.

To get the reader to say "Yes" to both questions, supply the facts you have gathered as a result of your research. For example, if you propose that your firm buy new software or equipment, do the necessary homework to find the most efficient and cost-effective model available, as the proposal writers in Figure 8.9 do.

- Supply the vendors' names, the costs, major conditions of service and training contracts, and warranties.
- Describe how your firm could use the equipment or technology to obtain better or quicker results.
- Document specific tasks the new equipment can perform more efficiently at a lower cost than the equipment now in use.

A **proposal to change or establish new procedures** must address the following questions:

- How does the new (or revised) procedure work?
- How many employees or customers will be affected by it?
- When can it go into operation?
- How much will it cost the employer to change procedures?
- What delays or losses in business might be expected while the company switches from one procedure to another?
- What employees, equipment, technology, or locations are already available to accomplish the change?

Beyond a doubt, costs will be of utmost importance to your decision-maker reader. Make sure you supply a careful and accurate budget. Moreover, make the costs attractive by emphasizing how inexpensive they are compared with the cost of not making the change, as Bond and Holton do persuasively in the section labeled "Costs." Link costs to savings and other benefits. And always be sure to double-check your math.

It is also wise to raise alternative solutions before the reader does—and to discuss their disadvantages.

Conclusion

Your conclusion should be short—a paragraph or two at the most. Remind readers that (1) the problem is ongoing and serious, (2) the reason for change is justified and beneficial to your organization, and (3) action needs to be taken. Reemphasize the most important benefits as Bond and Holton do in their proposal in Figure 8.9. Also indicate that you are willing to discuss your plan with the reader and want his or her feedback, a necessity in arguing for a corporate change at any level.

Sales Proposals

A sales proposal is the most common type of external proposal. Its purpose is to sell your company's products or services for a set fee. Whether short or long, a sales proposal is a marketing tool that includes a sales pitch as well as a detailed description of the work you propose to do. Figure 8.10 on pages 337–339 is an example of sales proposals.

Knowing Your Audience and Meeting Its Needs

Your audience will usually be one or more executives who have the power to approve or reject a proposal. Your audience for a sales proposal may be even more skeptical than readers of an internal proposal, because they may not know you or your work. But you can increase your chances of success by trying to anticipate their questions, such as:

- Does the writer's firm understand our problem?
- Can the writer's firm deliver what it promises?
- Can the job be completed on time?
- Is the budget reasonable and realistic?
- Will the job be done exactly as we proposed?
- Has the writer demonstrated his or her qualifications and trustworthiness?

Answer each of these questions by demonstrating how your product or service is tailored to the customer's needs.

Be sure, too, that your proposal has a competitive edge. Your proposal has to convince readers that the product or service your company offers is more reliable, economical, efficient, and up-to-date than another company's. Whenever relevant, stress that your company offers state-of-the-art technology, exemplary service, and after-the-sale assistance and warranty. Here is where your homework will pay off. See how Neelow Singh and Jack Rosen emphasize the range of advantages their flooring offers a prospective customer in Figure 8.10.

Being Ethical and Legal

In addition to the guidelines in Chapter 1, here are some ways to make sure your sales proposal follows the highest ethical standards:

- **View your proposal as a contract.** If you omit information, misrepresent claims, or minimize risks, you can be taken to court and sued for damages.
- **Submit a complete, accurate, and fair budget.** Break down all costs in your budget. Indicate if your fees are by the job, weekly, or hourly. Always alert readers to any possible additional charges (e.g., the fees for permits, an increase in the price of materials).

FIGURE 8.10 A Sales Proposal in Response to a Request from a Company

Reynolds Interiors

250 Commence Avenue • Edison, NJ 08837-2129
www.reynolds.com • 732-777-8733 • Fax: 732-777-8833

FOLLOW US ON FACEBOOK (www.facebook.com/reynoldsinteriors)
AND TWITTER (@reynoldsinteriors)

January 20, 2014

Mr. Floyd Tompkins, Manager
General Appliances
140 Kilmer Road
Edison, NJ 08817-7639

Dear Mr. Tompkins:

In response to your request for bids #GA01012012 posted on your
website for an appropriate floor covering at your new showroom,
Reynolds Interiors is pleased to submit the following proposal to meet
your specific needs. We appreciated the opportunity to visit your
showroom on January 14 in order to gather information to prepare this
proposal.

After carefully reviewing your requirements for a floor covering and
inspecting your new facility, we believe that **Armstrong Classic Corlon
900** is the most suitable choice. We are enclosing a few samples of the
Corlon 900 so you can see how carefully it is constructed and
aesthetically designed.

Corlon's Advantages

Guaranteed against defects for a full three years, Corlon is one of the finest
and most durable floor coverings manufactured by Armstrong. It is a
heavy-duty commercial floor 0.085-inch thick for protection and
durability. Twenty-five percent of the material consists of interface backing;
the other 75 percent is an inlaid wear layer that offers exceptionally high
resistance to the heavy, everyday traffic your showroom will see.

Traffic tests conducted by the independent Contemporary Flooring
Institute have repeatedly proved the superiority of Corlon's construction
and resistance. Please go to the Institute's website (www.cfi.org) for a
demonstration of how durable and versatile Classic Corlon flooring is.

Another important feature of Corlon is the size of its rolls. Unlike other
leading brands of commercial flooring—Remington or Treadmaster—Corlon
comes in 12-foot-wide rather than 6-foot-wide rolls. This extra width will
significantly reduce the number of seams on your floor, thus increasing its
attractiveness and eliminating the dangers of splitting or bulging.

Letterhead
advertises
company's
presence
on social-
networking
sites

Begins with
a reference
to company's
request for bids

Acknowledges
site visit

Identifies best
solution

References
sample

Describes
product
features that
will benefit
reader

Cites an
independent
source to
corroborate the
benefits of the
product

Distinguishes
product from
competitors'

(Continued)

FIGURE 8.10 (Continued)

Mr. Floyd Tompkins
January 20, 2014
Page 2

Explains how job is done professionally

Installation Procedures

The Classic Corlon 900 requires an inlaid seaming process, a technical procedure requiring the skill of a highly trained floor mechanic. Herman Goshen, our certified chief floor mechanic, has more than eighteen years of experience working with the inlaid seam process. His professional work and keen sense of layout and design have been consistently praised by our customers.

Gives realistic timetable

Installation Schedule

We can install the Classic Corlon 900 on your showroom floor during the first week of March, which fits the timetable specified in your request. The material will take 3½ days to install but will be ready to walk on immediately. Be assured that your floor will be installed no later than March 7th. We recommend, though, that you do not move heavy equipment onto the floor for 24 hours after installation.

Costs

The following costs include the Classic Corlon floor, labor, and taxes:

Itemizes all costs based on market conditions and reader's bid

750 sq. yards of Classic Corlon at $23.50/sq. yd.	$17,625.00
Labor (28 hrs @ $18.00/hr.)	$ 504.00
Sealing fluid (10 gals. @ $15.00/gal.)	$ 150.00
Subtotal	$18,279.00
Sales tax (7 percent)	$ 1,279.53
GRAND TOTAL	**$19,558.53**

Points out proposal comes in under budget— always a major consideration for buyers

Our costs are more than $300.00 below those specified in your bid.

Reynolds' Qualifications

Establishes history of service and provides documented evidence of quality work

Reynolds Interiors has been in business for more than 28 years. In that time, we have installed more than 2,500 commercial floors in Trenton and its suburbs. In the last year alone, we have served more than 60 satisfied customers, including the new multipurpose Tech Mart facility in downtown New Brunswick. Our designs have also been included in several commercial properties that have won awards from the New Jersey

FIGURE 8.10 (Continued)

Architectural Review Board and have been showcased in such publications as *New Jersey Homes* and *Best Housing Plans, 2012–2013*. Reynolds has also repeatedly received high commendations from our many customers, and we would be happy to furnish you with a list of our references.

Thank you for the opportunity to submit this proposal to General Appliances. We are confident that you will be pleased with the appearance and durability of the Armstrong Classic Corlon 900 floor and our installation process. If we can provide you with further information about our service or Corlon flooring, or if you have any questions, please call us at 732-777-8733 or visit us at our website or on Facebook.

Thanks reader and encourages him to accept the proposal

Sincerely yours,

Neelow Singh

Neelow Singh
Sales Consultant

Jack Rosen

Jack Rosen
Installation Supervisor

© Cengage Learning 2015

- **Estimate a realistic timeframe to do the work.** It would be unethical to say a job takes more time than necessary so you can then charge more.
- **Stipulate precisely what your product can (or cannot) do and what a service contract includes and excludes.** Don't make false claims. Always identify exceptions, limitations, and restrictions.

Organization of a Sales Proposal

Most sales proposals include the following elements: introduction, description of the proposed product or service, timetable, costs, qualifications of your company, and conclusion.

Introduction

The introduction to a sales proposal can be a single paragraph in a brief proposal or several pages in a more complex one. Basically, your introduction should persuasively prepare readers for everything that follows in your proposal. The introduction itself may contain the following sections, which sometimes may be combined.

1. Statement of purpose and subject of proposal. Tell readers why you are writing, and identify the specific subject of your work. Refer to the request for proposals or bids the reader has issued, as the writers in Figure 8.10 do. Briefly define the solution you propose. Tell readers exactly what you propose to do for them. Be clear about what your plan covers and, if there could be any doubt, what it does not.

2. Background of the problem you propose to solve. Show readers that you are familiar with their problem and why it is important. In a solicited proposal like the one in Figure 8.10, this section is usually unnecessary because the potential client has already identified the problem and wants to know how you would address it. In that case, just point out how your company would solve the problem, mentioning your superiority over your competitors (see the section "Corlon's Advantages" in Figure 8.10).

In an unsolicited proposal, you need to describe the problem in convincing detail, identifying the specific trouble areas. Depending on the type of proposal you submit, you may want to focus briefly on the dimensions of the problem—when it was first observed, who/what it most acutely affects, and the specific organizational/community/environmental context in which the problem is most troubling.

Description of the Proposed Product or Service

This section is the heart of your proposal. Before spending their money, customers will demand hard, factual evidence of what you claim can and should be done. Here are some points that your proposal should cover.

1. Carefully show potential customers that your product or service is right for them. Stress particular benefits of your product or service most relevant to your reader. Blend sales talk with descriptions of hardware. Note how the proposal in Figure 8.10 references the results of an independent testing agency—the Contemporary Flooring Institute—to stress the benefits of the product it sells.

2. Describe your work in appropriate detail. Specify what the product looks like; what it does; and how consistently and well it will perform in the readers' office, plant, hospital, or agency. You might include a brochure; picture; diagram; or, as the writers of the proposal in Figure 8.10 do, a few samples of your product for customers to study.

3. Stress any special features, maintenance advantages, installation or warranty benefits. Convince readers that your product is the most up-to-date and efficient one they could select. Highlight features that show the quality, consistency, or security of your work. See how Neelow Singh and Jack Rosen in Figure 8.10 demonstrate why and how Corlon is the best choice for the heavy traffic of the General Appliances showroom. For a service, emphasize the procedures you use, the terms of the service, the quality assurance tests you run, and especially any state-of-the-art equipment.

Timetable

A carefully planned timetable assures readers that you know your job and that you can accomplish it in the deadline set forth in the call for proposals or bids. Your dates should match any listed in a company's proposal request. Provide specific dates to indicate

- when the work will begin
- how the work will be divided into phases or stages
- when you will be finished
- whether any follow-up visits or services are involved

For proposals offering a service, specify how many times—an hour, a week, a month—customers can expect to receive your help; for example, spraying three times a month if your company offers exterminating services. The proposal writers in Figure 8.10 assure their reader that installation will be done by a specified date.

Costs

Make your budget accurate, complete, and convincing. But give customers more than merely the bottom-line cost. Show exactly what readers are getting for their money so that they can determine if everything they need is included. Itemize costs for

- specific services
- equipment and materials
- labor (by the hour or by the job)
- transportation/travel
- training

To further persuade readers to accept their proposal, the writers in Figure 8.10 point out how their work comes in under the specified budget.

If something is not included or is considered optional, say so—additional hours of training, replacement of parts, upgrades, and the like. If you anticipate a price increase, let the customer know how long current prices will stay in effect. That information may spur them to act favorably now.

Qualifications of Your Company

Emphasize your company's accomplishments and expertise in providing similar services and/or equipment. Mention the names of a few local firms for whom you have worked that would be able to recommend you and cite any awards or commendations, as the writers do in Figure 8.10, e.g., the Tech Mart facility.

Conclusion

This is the "call to action" section of your sales proposal. Encourage your reader to approve your plan by stressing its major benefits. Offer to answer any questions the reader may have. And take the opportunity to refer the reader to any samples, visuals, or sites on social media. Some proposals end by asking readers to sign and return a copy of the proposal indicating their acceptance, as the proposal in Figure 8.10 does.

✓ Revision Checklist

Short Reports

- [ ] Had a clear sense of how my readers will use my short report.
- [ ] Provided significant, relevant information about costs, materials, personnel, locations, environmental conditions, and times so readers will know that my work consists of facts, not impressions.
- [ ] Double-checked all data—names, costs, figures, dates, places, equipment numbers, and so forth.
- [ ] Kept report concise, to the point, and readable.
- [ ] Used headings wherever feasible to organize and categorize information.
- [ ] Began report with statement of purpose that clearly described the scope and significance of my work.
- [ ] Incorporated tables, maps, graphs, and other pertinent visuals to display data whenever appropriate.
- [ ] Explained clearly what the data mean in a conclusion section.
- [ ] Determined that recommendations logically follow from the data and are realistic.
- [ ] Adhered to all ethical and legal requirements in writing an incident report.

Proposals

- [ ] Identified a realistic problem in my proposal—one that is restricted and relevant to my audience's needs.
- [ ] Incorporated the scope and importance of the problem.
- [ ] Effectively convinced audience that the problem exists and that it needs to be solved; adopted the "you attitude" throughout.
- [ ] Persuasively emphasized benefits of solving the problem according to the proposal.
- [ ] Offered a solution that can be realistically implemented—that is, it is both appropriate and feasible, economically and strategically, for audience.
- [ ] Used specific figures about costs, personnel, technology, and concrete details to show how proposal will save time and money.
- [ ] *For internal proposals*: Demonstrated how proposal benefits my company and my supervisor; followed the chain of command by discussing proposal with co-workers and/or supervisors who may be affected.
- [ ] *For sales proposals*: Related my product or service to prospective customer's needs; showed a clear understanding of those needs.
- [ ] Prepared a comprehensive, realistic, and ethical budget; accounted for all expenses; itemized costs of products and services.
- [ ] Linked costs to benefits.
- [ ] Provided a timetable with precise dates for implementing proposal.

Exercises

1. Assume that you are a manager of a large apartment complex (300 units). Write a periodic report based on the following information—26 units are vacant, 38 soon will be vacant, and 27 soon will be leased (by June 1). Also add a section of recommendations to your supervisor (the head of the management company for which you work) on how vacant apartments might be leased more quickly and perhaps at increased rents. Consider important information such as decorating, advertising, installing a new security system, providing Internet access, amenities such as pool, fitness center, clubhouse, and first-month discounts.

2. Assume you work for a household appliance store. Prepare a sales report based on the information contained in the following table. Include a section on recommendations for your manager.

Product	Number Sold	
	October	November
Kitchen Appliances		
Refrigerators	72	103
Dishwashers	27	14
Freezers	10	36
Electric Ranges	26	26
Gas Ranges	10	3
Microwave Ovens	31	46
Laundry Appliances		
Washers	50	75
Dryers	24	36
Air Treatment		
Room Air Conditioners	41	69
Dehumidifiers	7	2

© Cengage Learning

3. Submit a progress report to your writing instructor on what you have learned in his or her course so far this term, specifying which formatting and writing skills you want to develop in greater detail, and how you propose doing so. Mention specific memos, emails, letters, instructions, reports, websites and blogs, or proposals you have written or will soon write.

4. Prepare a site inspection report on any part of the college campus or plant, hospital, office, store, or other facility in which you work that might need remodeling, expansion, rewiring, or new or additional air-conditioning, plumbing, and/or heating work.

5. Write a report to an instructor in your major or to an employer about a trip you have taken recently—to a museum, laboratory, health care agency, correctional facility, radio or television station, plant or factory, or office. Indicate why you took the trip, name the individuals (with their job titles) you met on the trip, and stress what you learned and how that information will help you in course work or on your job. Include a relevant visual as part of your report.

6. Write an incident report about one of the following problems. Assume that it has happened to you. Supply relevant details and visuals in your report. Identify the audience for whom you are writing and the agency you are representing or trying to reach.
   a. After hydroplaning, your company car hits a tree and has a damaged front fender.
   b. You have been the victim of an electrical shock because an electrical tool was not grounded.
   c. You twist your back lifting a bulky package in the office or plant.
   d. A virus has infected your company's intranet, and it will have to be shut down for 12 hours to debug it.
   e. The crane (or other piece of equipment) you are operating breaks down, and you lose a half-day's work.
   f. The vendor shipped the wrong replacement part for your computer, and you cannot complete a job without buying a more expensive software package.
   g. An electrical storm knocked out your computer; you lost 1,000 mailing label addresses and will have to hire additional help to complete a mandatory mailing by the end of the week.
   h. A scammer has stolen some sensitive files (documents) about a new product your company hoped to launch next month.
   i. An irate customer threatens one of your sales staff, but there was no physical violence though the daily routine of your business was disrupted and several other customers walked out.

7. As a collaborative writing project, prepare a short internal proposal, similar to that in Figure 8.9 (pages 330–334), recommending to a company or a college a specific change in procedure, technology, training, safety, personnel, or policy. Make sure your team provides an appropriate audience (college administrator, department manager, or section chief) with specific evidence about the existence of the problem and your solution to it. Possible topics include:
   a. providing more and safer parking/lighting
   b. instituting a job share for mothers
   c. purchasing new office or laboratory equipment or software
   d. hiring more faculty, student workers, or office help
   e. allowing employees to telecommute
   f. changing the lighting/furniture in a student or company lounge to make it more eco-friendly
   g. increasing the number of weekend, night, or online classes in your major
   h. adding more health-conscious offerings to the school or company cafeteria menu

    i. converting existing clients over to using new smart chip credit cards

    j. installing wireless routers and signal enhancers to boost the range of the company's wireless network

    k. develop an app that lets customers order goods and services remotely

8. Write a sales proposal as a collaborative group, similar to the one in Figure 8.10 (pages 337–339), on one of the following services or products you intend to sell or on a topic your instructor approves:

    a. providing exterminating or trash removal service to a store or restaurant

    b. supplying a hospital with rental laptops for patients' rooms

    c. designing websites or blogs

    d. obtaining temporary office help or nursing care

    e. supplying landscaping and lawn care work

    f. testing for noise, air, or water pollution in your community or neighborhood

    g. furnishing transportation for students, employees, or members of a community group

    h. offering technical consulting service to save a company money

    i. digging a septic well for a small apartment complex

    j. supplying insurance coverage to a small firm (5 to 10 employees)

    k. cleaning the parking lot and outside walkways at a shopping center

    l. selling a content management system (CMS) to a business

    m. making a work area safer or greener

    n. preparing a technology seminar or training program for employees

    o. increasing donations to a community or charitable fund

    p. offering discounted memberships at a fitness center

9. Write a proposal in letter format (similar to Figure 4.22) for a business you manage to attract new international clients. As part of your letter, stress any new equipment or services you offer and provide any background/history about your business that might appeal to a particular group's international customers.

CHAPTER 9

Documenting and Writing Effective Long Reports

This chapter introduces you to long reports—and how and why they are written, organized, and documented. It is appropriate to discuss long reports in one of the last chapters of *Successful Writing at Work* because they require you to use and combine many of the writing skills and research strategies you have already learned. In the world of global business, a long report can be the culmination of many weeks or months of hard work on an important company project.

Characteristics of a Long Report

The following sections explain some of the key elements in a long report. You will find a model long report (Figure 9.2) at the end of the chapter (pages 367–380).

Scope

A long report is a major study that provides an in-depth view of a key problem or idea. It might be eight to twenty pages long or even much longer, depending on the scope of the subject. The implications of a long report are wide-ranging for a business or organization—relocating a plant, adding a new network, changing a programming operation, or adapting the workplace for multinational employees, as in Figure 9.2.

Long reports examine a major problem in detail while short reports cover just one part of the problem. Unlike a short report, a long report may discuss not just one or two current events but, rather, the continuing history of a problem or an idea (and the background information necessary to understand it in perspective).

The titles of some typical long reports suggest their extensive (and in some cases exhaustive) coverage:

- A Master Plan for the Recreation Needs of Dover Plains, New York
- The Transportation Problems in Kingford, Oregon, and the Use of Rapid Transit
- Promoting More Effective E-Commerce and E-Tailing at TechWorld Inc.

- Virtual Reality Attractions in Theme Parks in Jersey City, New Jersey
- Expanding Health Care Delivery Systems in Tate County
- Internet Medicine in Providing Health Care in Rural Areas: Ways to Serve Southern Montana

Research

A long, comprehensive report requires much more extensive research than a short report does. Information can be gathered over time from primary and secondary research—Internet searches, listservs, books, articles, blogs, social media, government documents, laboratory experiments, on-site visits and tests, conferences with your boss and co-workers, interviews, and the writer's own observations. For a course report, you will have to do a great deal of research and possibly interviewing to track down relevant background information and to discover what experts have said about the subject and what they propose should be suggested or have even done. Make sure all your sources are accurate, current, and relevant.

For a report for class, you will be asked to identify a major problem or topic, while in the business world the topic and even your approach to it will more than likely be dictated to you by your boss and company policy, as the cover letter (see Figure 9.1, page 366) to the long report in Figure 9.2 indicates.

Format

A long report is too detailed and complex to be adequately organized in a memo or letter format. The product of thorough research and analysis, the long report gives readers detailed discussions and interpretations of large quantities of data. To present the information in a logical and orderly fashion, the long report contains various parts, sections, headings, subheadings, documentation, and supplements (appendices) that would never be included in a short report. Look at the sections of a report in the Table of Contents (page 368) for the long report in Figure 9.2. Also, note how this long report gives readers a variety of visuals, including charts, a graph, and even a multicultural calendar.

Timetable

A long report is generally commissioned by a company or an agency to explore with extensive documentation a subject involving personnel, locations, technology, costs, safety, or the environment. Many times a long report is required by law—for example, investigating the feasibility of a project that will affect the ecosystem. When you prepare a long report for a class project, select a topic that really interests you and/or your collaborative group, because you will spend a good portion of the term working on it. Here is a possible timeline for a long report to give you a sense of the process of preparing one.

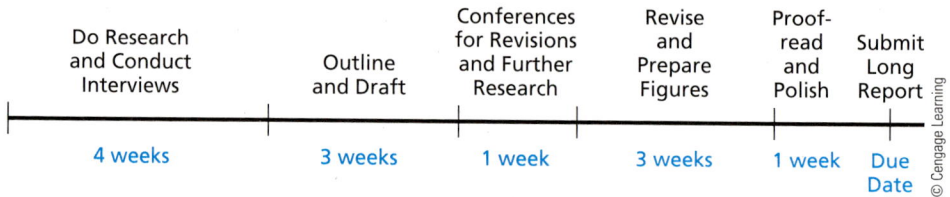

Do Research and Conduct Interviews		Outline and Draft		Conferences for Revisions and Further Research		Revise and Prepare Figures		Proof-read and Polish		Submit Long Report
4 weeks		3 weeks		1 week		3 weeks		1 week		Due Date

© Cengage Learning

Audience

The audience for a long report usually consists of individuals in the top levels of management—presidents, vice presidents, superintendents, directors, heads of departments—who make executive, financial, and organizational decisions. These individuals are responsible for long-range planning, or seeing the big picture, so to speak. A long report written about a campus issue or problem may at first be read by your instructor and then sent to an appropriate decision maker, such as a dean of students, a business manager, a director of athletics, or the head of campus security.

Collaborative Effort

Like many short reports, the long report in the world of business may be a collaborative effort, the product of a committee or team whose work is reviewed by a main editor to make sure that the final text is consistently and accurately written. Individuals in many departments within a company—IT, document design, engineering, sales, transportation, legal affairs, public relations, safety—may cooperate in planning, researching, drafting, revising, and editing a long report.

The team should estimate a realistic timeframe necessary to complete the various stages of their work—when drafts are due and when editing must be concluded, for example. A project schedule based on that estimate should then guide a writing team's work. But remember: Projects almost always take longer than initially planned. Prepare for a possible delay at any one stage. The team may have to submit written progress reports (see pages 310–313) to its members, as well as to management.

To be successful, a collaborative writing team (such as Teri Smith Ruckel's team in Figure 9.2) should observe the guidelines and procedures for collaborative writing in Chapter 2.

The Process of Writing a Long Report

Because work on a long report will be spread over many weeks, you need to see it not as a series of static or isolated tasks but as an evolving project. Before you embark on that project, review the information on the writing process in Chapter 2. The following guidelines will also help you plan and write a long report.

1. Identify a significant topic. While you won't usually get to choose the topic of your long report, when you write one for a class, make sure you select a topic that is important and worth exploring in detail. After all, you can expect to spend a lot of time researching and writing about it. Choose a topic/problem that is relevant for your audience, whether it is a group of college administrators or community leaders, and something that will help them better understand or even solve a problem.

2. Conduct research. You'll have to do some preliminary research—widespread reading, online searching, conferring with and interviewing experts, and possibly making site visits–to get an overview of key ideas and individuals involved, and the implications for your company and/or community. Note the kinds of research Terri Smith Ruckel and her collaborative team did for their long report (see Figure 9.2, pages 367–380). As they did, expect to search a variety of print and Internet sources, to read and evaluate them, to interview experts in the field, and to incorporate this research into your work.

3. Expect to confer regularly with your supervisor and team members. In these meetings, be prepared to ask pertinent and researched questions to pin down exactly what your boss wants and how your writing team can accomplish this goal. Focus your questions on the company's use of your report, how it wants you to express certain ideas, and the amount of information it needs. Your supervisor may want you to submit an outline before you draft the report and may expect several more drafts for approval before you write the final version.

4. Revise your work often. Be prepared to work on several outlines and drafts. Your revisions may sometimes be extensive, depending on what your boss or collaborative team recommends or what your research uncovers. You may have to consult new sources or delete older ones.

5. Keep the order flexible at first. Even as you work on your drafts and revisions, remember that a long report is not written in the order in which the parts will finally be assembled. You cannot write in "final" order—abstract to recommendations. Instead, expect to write in "loose" order to reflect the process in which you gathered information and organized it for the final copy of the report. Usually, the body of the report is written first and the introduction later so that the authors can make sure they have not left anything out. The abstract (see page 369), which appears very early in the report, is always written after all the facts have been recorded and recommendations are made or conclusions drawn.

6. Prepare both a day-to-day calendar and a checklist. Keep both posted where you do your work—above your desk or computer, or use your computer's built-in calendar program, if available—so that you can track your progress. The calendar should mark **milestones**—that is, dates by which each stage of your work must be completed. Match the dates on your calendar with the dates your instructor or employer may have given you to submit an outline, progress report(s), drafts, and then the final copy. Your checklist should list the major parts of the long report. As you complete each section, check it off. Before assembling the final copy of your report, use the checklist to make sure you have not omitted something.

Parts of a Long Report

A long report may include some or all of the following 12 parts, which form three categories: *front matter* (letter of transmittal, title page, abstract, table of contents, list of illustrations), *report text* (introduction, body, conclusion, recommendations), and *back matter* (glossary, references cited, any appendices).

Numbering the Pages of a Long Report

You will use two sets of numbers for the pages of your long report, one for the front matter and another for the text and back matter of your report. See Figure 9.2 for an example of proper pagination in a long report. Use lowercase Roman numerals (e.g., i, ii, iii, iv) for the front matter. The title page counts as page i, but do not number it. Instead, start with the table of contents as page ii. Then number the list of illustrations as page iii and the abstract, if it appears on a separate page as in Figure 9.2, as page iv. Format all front matter page numbers as footers.

For the text and back matter of your report, use consecutive Arabic numerals in the headers, that is, in the upper right-hand side of each page. Keep in mind, though, that your instructor or employer may prefer you to use APA (American Psychological Association) or MLA (Modern Language Association) style, or for you to use a different placement for the page numbers—for example, putting all report page numbers in footers or in headers.

Front Matter

As the name implies, the front matter of a long report consists of everything that precedes the actual text of the report. Such elements introduce, explain, and summarize to help the reader locate various parts of the report.

Letter of Transmittal

This three- or four-paragraph (usually only one-page) letter states the purpose, scope, and major recommendation of the report. It highlights the main points of the report that will most interest your readers. If written to an instructor, the letter should additionally note that the report was done as a course assignment. (See Terri Smith Ruckel's letter on page 366 for a sample letter of transmittal for a business report.)

Title Page

Find out what your boss or instructor prefers. Basically, your title page should contain the full title of your report and how you have restricted it in time, space, or method. Avoid titles that are vague, too short, or too long.

Vague Title: A Report on the Internet: Some Findings
Too Short: The Internet
Too Long: A Report on the Internet: A Study of Social Media Companies and Their Relationship with Consumer Preferences and Identity Protection Within the Past Five Years

Also include the date you submitted the report, and the person(s) for whom you prepared the report. For a report for a class assignment, give your instructor's name and the specific course for which you prepared the report. For most other long reports, the title page needs

- the name(s) of the report writer(s)
- the date of the report
- the name of the firm or individual for whom the report was prepared

Table of Contents

The table of contents lists the major headings and subheadings of your report and tells readers on which pages they can be found. Make sure that your table of contents exactly matches the order and wording of your main headings and subheadings. It reveals the scope of your report and helps readers identify the parts of your report that are of most interest to them.

List of Illustrations

A list of all the visuals indicates where they can be found in your report. Note the variety of visuals found in Figure 9.2—a circle chart, a bar chart, a graph, a calendar.

Abstract

An abstract summarizes the report, presenting a brief overview of the problem and conclusions. An informative abstract is far more helpful to readers of a report than is a descriptive one, which gives no conclusions or results. Abstracts may be placed at various points in long reports—on the title page, on a separate page preceding or following the table of contents, or as the first page of the report text.

Not every member of your audience will read your entire report, but almost everyone will read the abstract. For example, the president of the corporation or the director of an agency may use the abstract as the basis for approving the report and passing it on for distribution. Thus, the abstract may be the most important part of your report. See how the abstract Terri Smith Ruckel and her team prepared for their readers on page 369 succinctly provides conclusions, or findings.

Begin your abstract with a sentence that identifies the subject, purpose, scope, and importance of your report. Then concentrate on the main points your report covers, briefly comment on the results and outcomes you reached, and clearly pinpoint your major recommendations. Your abstract needs to emphasize the major sections of your report.

Some information does not belong in an abstract. Do not give readers a detailed description of the methods you used or try to squeeze in every minor point. Don't worry about describing the visuals accompanying your report, such as maps or graphs. It is also unnecessary to repeat who commissioned the report and why. And never include information in your abstract that is not found in your report.

When you write your abstract, use complete sentences with keywords. Appropriate keywords make it easy for search engines to find your report if it is posted on the Web or if it will be archived on, say, a company intranet.

Text of the Report

The text of a long report consists of an introduction, the body, a conclusion, and sometimes recommendations.

Introduction

The introduction may constitute as much as 10 or 15 percent of your report, but usually it is not any longer. If it were, the introduction would be disproportionate to the rest of your work, especially the body. The introduction is essential because it tells readers why your report was written and thus helps them to understand and interpret everything that follows. See how Terri Smith Ruckel and her team emphasize the importance of their research for their employer, RPM Technologies, in the introduction to Figure 9.2 on pages 370–372. But make sure you do not put your findings, conclusion, or recommendations in your introduction.

Do not regard the introduction as one undivided block of information. It includes the following related parts, which should be labeled with subheadings. Keep in mind, though, that your employer may ask you to list these parts in a different order.

1. **Background.** To understand why your topic is significant and hence worthy of study, readers need to know about its history. This history may include information on such topics as who was originally involved, when, and where; how someone was affected by the issue; what opinions have been expressed on the issue; and what the implications of your study are. Note how the long report in Figure 9.2 provides useful background information on why multinational employees are a growing and important segment of the U.S. workforce.

2. **Problem.** Identify the problem or issue that led you to write the report. Your problem needs to be significant enough to warrant a long report. Because the problem or topic you investigated will determine everything you write about in the report, you need to state it clearly and precisely. That statement may be restricted to a few sentences. Here is a problem statement from a report on how earlier construction designs have not taken into account the requirements of Americans with disabilities:

Every builder since the late 1990s has paid attention to codes on meeting needs of disabled residents. In the past, however, the building industry had not sufficiently met the needs for accessible workplaces and homes for all age and physical ability groups. The industry had too often relied on expensive and specialized plans to modify existing structures rather than creating universally designed spaces that were accessible to everyone.

 3. Purpose statement. The purpose statement, crucial to the success of the report, tells readers why you wrote the report and what you hope to accomplish or prove. It expresses the goal of all your research. In explaining why you gathered information about a particular problem or topic, indicate how such information might be useful to a specific audience, company, or group. Like the problem statement, the purpose statement does not have to be long or complex. A sentence or two will suffice. You might begin simply by saying, "The purpose of this report is. . . ."

 4. Scope. This section informs readers about the specific limits—number and type of issues, time, money, locations, personnel, and so forth—you have placed on your investigation. You inform readers about what they will find in your report or what they won't through your statement about the scope of your work. The long report in Figure 9.2 concentrates on adapting the U.S. workplace to meet the communication and cultural needs of a workforce of multinational employees, not on trends in the international employment market—two completely different topics.

Body

More than half of your long report will be devoted to the body or *discussion*. Everything in this and all the other sections of your report grows out of your purpose and how you have limited your scope. The body contains statistical information, details about the environment, and physical descriptions, as well as the various interpretations and comments of the authorities whose work you consulted or the individuals whom you have interviewed as part of your research. The body can also identify and describe the range of options you surveyed and earmark the most appropriate. In Figure 9.2 (pages 372–377), the body of the report spells out precisely what specific changes RPM must make to recruit and retain multinational employees—from offering cross-cultural training to making sure corporate documents are written in plain English.

What to Include in the Body of a Report   The body of your report should

- be carefully organized to reveal a coherent and well-defined plan
- separate material into meaningful parts to identify the major issues as well as minor issues in your report
- clearly relate the parts to one another
- use headings to help your reader identify major sections more quickly

Headings   Your organization is reflected in the different headings and subheadings included in your report. Use them to make your report easy to follow. Organizational headings will also enable someone skimming the report to find

specific information quickly. The headings, of course, will be included in the table of contents. (Note how Figure 9.2 is carefully organized into sections.)

Transitions   In addition to headings, use transitions to reveal the organization of the body of your report. At the beginning of each major section of the body, tell readers what they will find in that section and why. Summary sentences at the end of a section will tell readers where they have been and prepare them for any subsequent discussions. The report in Figure 9.2 does an effective job of providing internal summaries, e.g., on pages 372 and 374.

Conclusion

The conclusion should tie everything together for readers by presenting the findings of your report. Findings, of course, will vary depending on the type of research you do. For a research report based on a study of sources located through various reference searches, the conclusion should summarize the main viewpoints of the authorities whose works you have cited. For a report done for a business, you must spell out the implications for your readers in terms of costs, personnel, products, location, and so forth.

Regardless of the type of research you do, your conclusions should

- be based on the information and documentation in the body of the report
- corroborate the evidence/information you gave in the body of your report
- grow out of the work you describe in the body of the report
- stick to the areas that your report covers, and not stray into areas it does not

Recommendations

The recommendation(s) section tells readers what should be done about the findings recorded in the conclusion. Your recommendation(s) tells readers how you want them to solve the problem your report has focused on. Readers will expect you to advise them on a specific course of action—what new technology to purchase, when and where to expand a market, how to improve and safeguard a web presence, or who to recruit, hire, train, and retain multinationals for your company, as in Figure 9.2.

Back Matter

Included in the back matter of the report are all of the supporting data that, if included in the text of the report, would bog the reader down in details and cloud the main points the report makes.

Glossary

The glossary is an alphabetical list of the specialized vocabulary used in a long report and the definitions. A glossary might be unnecessary if your report does not use a highly technical vocabulary, as in Figure 9.2, or if *all* members of your audience are familiar with the specialized terms you do use.

References Cited

Any sources cited in your report—websites, books, articles, television programs, interviews, reviews, blogs, graphics, podcasts, webinars—are usually listed in this section. Always ask your instructor or employer how he or she wants information to be documented, that is, what method of documentation to follow (see page 357). Note that the long report in Figure 9.2 follows the American Psychological Association (APA) system of documentation (see www.apastyle.org).

Appendix

An appendix contains supporting materials for the report—tables and charts too long to include in the discussion, sample questionnaires, budgets and cost estimates, correspondence about the preparation of the report, case histories, transcripts of telephone conversations, copies of relevant letters and documents upon which the report is based, etc.

Documenting Sources

Documentation is at the heart of all the research you will do on the job. To document means to furnish readers with information about the print and electronic sources you have used for the factual support of your statements, including books, journals, newspapers, surveys, reports, websites, and other resources such as listservs and email.

Documentation is an essential part of any research you do for at least four reasons:

1. It demonstrates that you have done your homework by consulting experts on the subject and relying on the most authoritative sources to build your case persuasively.
2. It shows that you are aware of the latest research in your field, thus lending credibility and authority to your conclusions and recommendations.
3. It gives proper credit to those sources and avoids plagiarism (see page 356). Citing works by name and date is not a simple act of courtesy; it is an ethical requirement and, because so much material is protected by copyright, a point of law.
4. It informs readers about specific books, articles, surveys, blogs, or websites you used so they can locate your source and verify your facts or quotations.

The Ethics of Documentation: Determining What to Cite

As a researcher, you have to be sure about what information you must cite and what information you do not need to cite. Before you start consulting sources, you have to be very clear about the ethical standards involved in documentation. The following sections will give you a useful overview to make the documentation process more understandable and easier to follow.

What Must Be Cited

To ensure that your business report avoids plagiarism and maintains high ethical and professional standards, follow these guidelines:

- If you use a source and take something from it, document it. Document any direct quotations, even a single phrase or keyword.
- Stay away from *patchworking*—using bits and pieces of information and passing them off as your own—which is also an act of plagiarism. Always put quotation marks around anything you take verbatim, and document it.
- If any opinions, interpretations, and conclusions expressed verbally or in writing are not your own (e.g., you could not have reached them without the help of another source), you must document them.
- Even if you do not use an author's exact words but still get an idea, concept, or point of view from a source, document that work in your report.
- Never alter any original material to have it suit your argument. Changing any information—names, dates, times, test results—is a serious offense.
- If you use statistical data you have not compiled yourself, document them.
- Always document any visuals—photographs, graphs, tables, charts, images downloaded from the Internet (and if you construct a visual based on someone else's data, you must acknowledge that source, too).
- Never submit the same research paper for one course that you wrote for another course without first obtaining permission from the second instructor.
- Do not delete an author's name when you are citing or forwarding an Internet document. You are obligated to give the Internet author full credit.

What Does Not Need to Be Cited

Be careful not to distract readers with unnecessary citations that only demonstrate your lack of understanding of the documentation process and can undercut the professionalism of your report. There is no need to cite the following:

- Common-knowledge scientific facts and formulas, such as "The normal human body temperature is 98.6 degrees Fahrenheit" or "H_2O is the chemical formula for water."
- Readily available geographical data, such as elevation of mountains; depths of lakes, rivers, etc.; population; mileage between two places; and so on.
- Well-known dates, such as the date of the first moon landing in 1969.
- Factual historical information, such as "George W. Bush was the 43rd President of the United States."
- Proverbs from folklore, such as "The hand is quicker than the eye."
- Well-known quotations, such as "We hold these truths to be self-evident ...," although it may be helpful to the reader if you mention the name of the person being quoted.
- The Bible, the Koran, or other religious texts, but provide a reference to the text and to the portion of the text quoted in parentheses (for instance, *New Jerusalem Bible*, Exod. 2.3).

- Classic literary works, but again reference the original author and the name of the work parenthetically—for instance, Mark Twain, *The Adventures of Huckleberry Finn* (Chapter 4), or Shakespeare, *The Merchant of Venice* (5.3.15). Indicate, though, from which edition you took the quotation.

Parenthetical Documentation

Two frequently used systems of parenthetical documentation are MLA (Modern Language Association) and APA (American Psychological Association):

- *MLA Handbook for Writers of Research Papers,* 7th ed. (New York: Modern Language Association, 2009), **www.mla.org/style**
- *Publication Manual of the American Psychological Association,* 6th ed. (Washington, DC: American Psychological Association, 2010), **www .apastyle.org**

MLA is used primarily in the humanities while APA is used in psychology, nursing, social sciences, and several technological/scientific fields. In business, however, your employer will determine whether you will follow MLA or APA. Because MLA and APA are the most well-known and accessible documentation styles, many businesses prefer to rely on one or the other, or they adapt or modify these methods to suit the company's needs and those of its clients. Both MLA and APA use parenthetical, or in-text documentation. That is, the writer tells readers directly in the text of the report what source is being quoted or referenced.

> **MLA:** "Creating an interactive website was among the top three priorities businesses have had over the last two years" (Morgan 203).
>
> **APA:** "Creating an interactive website was among the top three priorities businesses have had over the last two years" (Morgan, 2014, p. 203).

The MLA citation "(Morgan 203)" or the APA "(Morgan, 2014, p. 203)" informs readers that the writer has borrowed information from a work by Morgan, specifically from page 203. APA also includes the year Morgan's work was published. Such a source (author's last name, year, and page number) obviously does not supply complete documentation. Instead, the parenthetical reference points readers to an alphabetical list of works that appears at the end of the report. The list, called "Works Cited" in MLA or "References" in APA, contains full bibliographic data—titles, dates, web addresses, publishers, page numbers, and so on—about each source cited in your report.

Every work that appears in your report must be listed in your references section. (The only exceptions are personal communications such as emails and texts or well-known works like the Bible; these do not have to appear in an APA-style References section.) To provide accurate parenthetical documentation for your readers, first carefully prepare your Works Cited or References list (discussed on page 358) so that you know which sources you are going to cite in the right form and at the right place in your text.

Keep your documentation brief and to the point so that you do not interrupt the reader's train of thought. In most cases, all you will need to include is the author's last name, date, and appropriate page number(s) in parentheses, usually at the end of sentences. When you mention the author's name in your sentence, though, MLA and APA both advise that you do not redundantly cite it again parenthetically; for example:

MLA: Moscovi claims that "tourism has increased 21 percent this quarter" (76).

APA: Moscovi (2012) claims that "tourism has increased by 21 percent this quarter" (p. 76).

For unsigned articles, use a shortened title in place of an author's name parenthetically.

MLA: Shrewd bosses know that "chain-of-command meetings provide the opportunity to pass information up as well as down the administrative ladder" ("Working Smarter" 33).

APA: Shrewd bosses know that "chain-of-command meetings provide the opportunity to pass information up as well as down the administrative ladder" ("Working Smarter," 2013, p.33).

Similarly, if you list the title of a reference work in the text of your paper, do not repeat it in your documentation.

MLA: According to the *Encyclopedia Britannica*, Cecil B. DeMille's *King of Kings* was seen by nearly 800,000,000 individuals (3: 458).

APA: According to the *Encyclopedia Britannica* (2014), Cecil B. DeMille's *King of Kings* was seen by nearly 800,000,000 individuals (3, p. 458).

The first number in parentheses in both versions refers to the volume number of the *Encyclopedia Britannica*; the second is the page number in that volume.

Preparing MLA Works Cited and APA References Lists

Whether you follow MLA or APA, you will need to list your sources at the end of your report, on a new page, under the title of "Works Cited" or "References" at the top and then arrange the list alphabetically by authors' last names (except when no author is listed). Both MLA and APA advise that you begin each citation flush to the left margin (but indent subsequent lines one-half inch) and that you double-space within and between the entries. But, as Table 9.1 points out, there are major differences between the MLA and APA guidelines on where to place information, punctuation, the use of italics and quotation marks, and capitalization. The following sections provide examples, following both MLA and APA, of some of the references you are most likely to include.

Sample Entries in MLA Works Cited and APA References Lists

Book by One Author

MLA: Spinello, Richard. *Cyberethics: Morality and Law in Cyberspace*. Burlington: Jones & Bartlett, 2013. Print.

APA: Spinello, R. (2013). *Cyberethics: Morality and law in cyber space*. Burlington, MA: Jones & Bartlett.

TABLE 9.1   Basic Differences Between Preparing an MLA Works Cited List and an APA References List

	MLA	**APA**
Author	• List author's last name first, followed by a comma, and then first name and (if applicable) middle name or initial. • For two or three authors, invert only the first author's name (e.g., Smith, John, and Jose Alvarez), and connect the last two authors' names with *and*. • For more than three authors, cite just the first author listed on the work (Smith, John) and add *et al.* ("and others"), or you can provide all names in full in the order in which they appear on the title page or byline.	• List author's last name first, followed by a comma, and then cite only the first initial and middle initial (if known). • For multiple authors, invert all authors' names, separate the last two names with an ampersand (&), and still use only an initial for first names of authors. • For more than seven authors, invert the first six authors' names, insert an ellipsis (. . .) and then list the name of the last author (also inverted).
Title	• Italicize the full title of the book, newspaper, journal, or magazine, including any subtitles. • Capitalize all words in the title except for prepositions, articles, and coordinating conjunctions, unless the book or journal begins or ends with one of these. • Enclose titles of journal, newspaper, and magazine articles in double quotation marks. • Capitalize all words in the journal, newspaper, or magazine article title except for prepositions, articles, and coordinating conjunctions, unless the book or journal begins or ends with one of these.	• For a book, italicize the full title, and capitalize only the first word of the title and any proper names. If there is a subtitle, place it after the main title, followed by a colon, and capitalize only the first word of the subtitle. • For articles in newspapers, journals, or magazines, the title is not italicized. • Do not enclose titles of newspaper, journal, or magazine articles in quotation marks. • Capitalize only the first word of the article title (even if it is a preposition) and any proper nouns.
Volume and Page Numbers	• For articles, cite the volume and the issue number (separated by a period), followed by the year in parentheses: 52.1 (2014). For newspapers and magazines, use only the date—12 Aug. 2014. Then include page numbers **without** a "p." or "pp.": 91–100.	• Put the volume number of the journal or magazine in italics, with the issue number (not in italics) in parentheses immediately following, without a space. Then insert a comma and include page numbers: *12*(3), 87–102.

(Continued)

TABLE 9.1   (Continued)

	MLA	APA
Publication	• For books, give the city of publication. Then, after a colon, supply the publisher's name, followed by a comma, the year of publication, and a period. • Include the publication medium for all entries (e.g., Print, PDF, DVD, Radio, etc.) at the end of the publication information.	• Place the date of publication in parentheses immediately after the author's name. Then add a period after the closing parenthesis. • For books, provide the city and two-letter abbreviation for the state, and then include the publisher's name after a colon—for example, Detroit, MI: MegaPress.
Web Sources (Websites, Blogs, etc.)	• You do not need to include URLs, but indicate the website name, sponsor or publisher, date of publication, and medium of publication, followed by the date of access.	• Insert URLs in place of page numbers with the following designation: Retrieved from [and then list the URL]. • If a DOI (digital object identifier) has been assigned to the source, provide the DOI instead of the URL, as follows: doi:xxxxx
Personal Interview	• Provide the name of the person interviewed (last name first), followed by the type of interview that was conducted (email; in person) and the date.	• Interviews, conversations, and personal communications such as email are not included in APA reference lists, but you must still cite them within your paper.

Book by Two Authors

MLA: Wu, Melody, and Tren Tucker. *China's Role in the Global Economy.* Denver: Tradevision P, 2011. Print.

APA: Wu, M., & Tucker, T. (2011). *China's role in the global economy.* Denver, CO: Tradevision Press.

Book by Three Authors

MLA: Barsh, Joanna, Cranston, Susie, and Geoffrey Lewis. *How Remarkable Women Lead: The Breakthrough Model for Work and Life.* New York: Crown, 2011. Print.

APA: Barsh, J., Cranston, S., and Lewis, G. (2011). *How remarkable women lead: The breakthrough model for work and life.* New York, NY: Crown.

Book by Four or More Authors (MLA)

MLA: Del Guidice, Manlio, et al. *Cross-Cultural Management: Fostering Innovation and Collaboration Inside the Multicultural Enterprise.* New York: Spring, 2012. Print.

Book by Eight or More Authors (APA)

APA: Berkowitz, H. A., Barner, P. L., Choi, D. G., Osler, T. O., Ruiz, J., Rowell, C. F., . . . Emmons, W. D. (2014). *Collaborating effectively and efficiently: A case study*. Los Angeles, CA: Ridgeway.

Electronic Version of a Printed Book

MLA: Martin, Dick. *OtherWise: The Wisdom You Need to Succeed in a Diverse World.* AMA COM, 2012. Books 24×7. Web. 19 Mar. 2013.

APA: Martin, D. (2012). *OtherWise: The wisdom you need to succeedin a diverse world.* [Books 24×7 version]. Retrieved from http://library.books24×7.com.logon.lynx.lib.usm.edu/toc.aspx?site=PB3FH&bookid=45534

Edited Collection of Essays

MLA: Yang, Harrison Hoa, and Shuyan Wang, eds. *Cases on E-Learning Management: Development and Implementation.* Hershey: Information Science Research, 2013. Print.

APA: Yang, H.H., & Wang, S. (Eds.). (2013). *Cases on e-learning management: development and implementation.* Hershey, PA: Information Science Research.

Work Included in a Collection of Essays

MLA: Maque, Isabelle, et al. "Profiting from Diversity in the Bank Sector." *Lessons on Profiting from Diversity.* Ed. Gloria Moss. New York: Palgrave Macmillan, 2012. 186–212. Print.

APA: Maque, I., Becuwe, A., Prim-Allaz, I., & Garnier, A. (2012). Profiting from diversity in the bank sector. In Gloria Moss (Ed.), *Lessons on profiting from diversity* (pp. 186–212). New York, NY: Palgrave Macmillan.

Book by a Corporate Author

MLA: African Development Bank. *African Economic Outlook: 2012.* Washington: Organisation for Economic Co-Operation and Development, 2012. Print.

APA: African Development Bank (2012). *African economic outlook: 2012.* Washington, D.C., Organisation for Economic Co-Operation and Development.

Article in a Professional Journal

MLA: Freeman, Douglas C. "Veterans in Corporate America: A New Source of World Class Diverse Talent." *Black Enterprise* 43.5 (2012): 82-84. Print.

APA: Freeman, D.C. (2012). Veterans in corporate America: A new source of world class diverse talent. *Black Enterprise, 43*(5), 82-84.

Article in a Print Magazine

MLA: Kurowska, Teresa. "Is the Boss Watching Every Keystroke You Make?" *Today's Workplace* Oct. 2011: 47+. Print.

APA: Kurowska, T. (2011, October). Is the boss watching every keystroke you make? *Today's Workplace, 47,* 72–73.

Article in a Professional Online Journal

MLA: Sayburn, Anna. "Health Campaigns that Have Changed Public Understanding." *British Medical Journal Online* 344 (2012). Web. 25 April 2012.

APA: Sayburn, A. (2012, April 25). Health campaigns that have changed public understanding. *British Medical Journal Online, 344.* doi: 10.1136/bmj. e2866

Article in a Print Newspaper

MLA: Korkki, Phyllis. "Finding a Job by Starting a Business." *New York Times* 31 Jan. 2010: BU2. Print.

APA: Korkki, P. (2010, January 31). Finding a job by starting a business. *New York Times,* p. BU2.

Online Encyclopedia Article

MLA: Kling, Arnold. "International Trade." *Concise Encyclopedia of Economics.* 2nd ed. Library of Economics and Liberty, 2008. Web. 27 Mar. 2010.

APA: Kling, A. (2008). International trade. In *Concise encyclopedia of economics* (2nd ed.). Retrieved March 27, 2010, from http://www.econlib.org/library/CEE/html

Online Unsigned Encyclopedia Article

MLA: "Link Sharing." *Small Business Encyclopedia.* Entrepreneur, 2013. Web. 20 Sept. 2013.

APA: Link Sharing. (2013). In *Small business encyclopedia.* Retrieved from http://www.entrepreneur.com/encyclopedia/

Unsigned Article in a Print Magazine or Newspaper

MLA: "The Green Machine." *Economist* 13 Mar. 2010: 7–8. Print.

APA: The green machine. (2010, March 13). *Economist,* 7–8.

Article in an Online Newspaper or Magazine

MLA: King, David Lee. "Revamping Social Media for 2013." *Business Review USA.* 6 Nov. 2012. Web. 20 Mar. 2013.

APA: King, D.L. (2012, November 6). Revamping social media for 2013. *Business Review USA*. Retrieved from http://www.businessreviewusa. com/marketing/social-media/revamping-social-media-for-2013

Government Document

MLA: Committee on Banking, Housing, and Urban Affairs. *Greener Communities, Greater Opportunities: New Ideas for Sustainable Development and Economic Growth.* Washington: GPO, 2010. Web. 12 Dec. 2010.

APA: Committee on Banking, Housing, and Urban Affairs (2010). *Greener communities, greater opportunities: New ideas for sustainable development and economic growth.* (Publication No. 1035-E online). Washington, D.C.: U.S. Government Printing Office.

Website

MLA: Natl. Council of La Raza. Home Page, 2013. Web. 17 May 2013.

APA: When referencing an *entire* website, APA style is to provide the URL in the body of the text and not list it in the References section.

Radio

MLA: "What Do Employers Really Want from College Grads." Reporter Amy Scott. *Marketplace*. American Public Media. WHYY, Philadelphia, 4 Mar. 2013. Radio.

APA: Scott, A. (Reporter). (2013, March 4). What do employers really want from college grads [Radio]. In *Marketplace.* Philadelphia, PA: WHYY American Public Media.

Television

MLA: "How Will Employment Change as U.S. Job Market Recovers?" Prod. Russ Clarkson. *NewsHour*. PBS. 8 Mar. 2013. Television.

APA: Clarkson, R. (Producer). (2013, Mar 8). How will employment change as U.S. job market recovers? [Television series episode.] In *NewsHour.* Arlington, VA: PBS.

Podcast

MLA: Coughlin, Chrissy, host. "60: Why climate change is a matter of policy for insurers." *Nature of Business Radio.* GreenBiz Group. 11 Nov. 2012. Web. 17 May 2013.

APA: Coughlin, Chrissy (Host). (2012, November 25). *Why climate change is a matter of policy for insurers* [Audio podcast]. Retrieved from http:// www.greenbiz.com/blog/2012/11/25/why-climate-change-matter-policy-insurers

Blogs

MLA: Hamilton, Tina. "How to Really Make Twitter Work for Your Business." *Successful Blog*. N.p., 8 Mar. 2013. Web. 20 Mar. 2013.

APA: Hamilton, T. (2013, March 8). How to really make Twitter work for your business [Blog post]. Retrieved from http://www.successful-blog .com/1/how-to-really-make-twitter-work-for-your-business/

Personal Interview

MLA: Alvarez, José. E-mail interview. 15 Oct. 2014.

APA: Interviews, conversations, and presentations are not included in APA Reference lists, but you must still cite them within your paper as fol lows: (J. Alvarez, personal communication, October 15, 2014).

Email

MLA: Frazer, Tim. "Site Inspection Report for Landsdowne Corners." Message to the author. 12 July 2013. Email.

APA: Emails are not included in the References list. They are cited in the text as a personal communication.

Brochure

MLA: Gao, Hubert. *Coping with Carpal Tunnel Syndrome.* New York: Beth Israel Hospital, 2012. Print.

APA: Gao, H. (2012). Coping with carpal tunnel syndrome [Brochure]. New York: NY: Beth Israel Hospital.

Survey

MLA: Guttierez, Joseph. "Market Survey for Duron, Inc." Survey. n.p. 10 Apr. 2014. Print.

APA: Surveys are unpublished personal communications not included in the References list.

Lecture or Speech

MLA: Phillips-Ricks, Jonathan. National Association of Black Business Leaders Conference. New York, 15 Aug. 2012. Lecture.

APA: Phillips-Ricks, J. (2012, August 15). Lecture presented at the National Association of Black Business Leaders Conference, New York, NY.

Press Release

MLA: American Council of Organic Farmers. *New Ways to Eliminate Chemicals from Home Gardens.* Omaha: ACOF, 31 Mar. 2011. Print.

APA: American Council of Organic Farmers. (2011, March 31). *New ways to eliminate chemicals from home gardens* [Press release]. Retrieved from aaof.org

Map

MLA: Fineberg, Donald. *Sonoma, California*. Map. Sonoma: Professional Maps, 2014. Print.

APA: Fineberg, D. (2014). *Sonoma, California* [Map]. Sonoma: Professional Maps.

Motion Picture

MLA: *Understanding Diabetes: From Diagnosis to Cure*. Dir. Jayne T. Cahill. Healthcare Videos. 2010. DVD.

APA: Cahill, J. T. (Director). (2010). *Understanding diabetes: From diagnosis to cure* [DVD]. Allentown, PA: Healthcare Videos.

A Model Long Report

The long report in Figure 9.2 (starting on page 367) was written by a senior training specialist, Terri Smith Ruckel and her collaborative team, for the vice president of human resources who commissioned it. Note that only Ruckel's name appears on the report, according to her company's policy. The main task facing Ruckel and her team was to demonstrate what RPM Technologies had to do to meet the needs of multinational workers and thus promote diversity in the workplace. She gathered relevant data from both **primary research** (interviews, direct observations, site visits, and tests) and **secondary research** (consulting and commenting at times on sources already available, such as books, websites, journal articles, reference works, government documents, and even RPM in-house publications.

Figure 9.2 contains all the parts of a long report discussed in this chapter except a glossary and an appendix. Intended for a decision maker interested in learning more about the problems multinational workers face, the report does not contain the technical terms and data that would require a glossary or an appendix. Note how the cover letter (Figure 9.1) introduces the report and spells out its significance for RPM Technologies while the abstract succinctly identifies only the main points of the report.

FIGURE 9.1 Transmittal Letter for a Long Report

RPMTechnologies

4500 Florissant Drive   St. Louis, MO 63174

314.555.2121   www.rpmtech.com

May 6, 2013

Jesse Butler
Vice President, Human Resources
RPM Technologies

Dear Vice President Butler:

Begins with major recommendation of report

With this letter I am enclosing the report my team and I prepared on effective ways to recruit and retain a multinational workforce for RPM Technologies, which you requested we submit by early May. The report argues for the necessity of adapting the RPM workplace to meet the needs of multinational employees, including promoting cultural sensitivity and ensuring that our written business communications are easily understood by this audience.

Presents findings of report

Multinational workers undoubtedly will continue to play a major role in U.S. businesses and at RPM as well. With their technical skills and homeland contacts, these employees can help RPM Technologies successfully compete in today's global marketplace.

Alerts reader to major ways to solve problems

But businesses like RPM need to recruit qualified multinational workers more aggressively and then provide equal opportunities for them in the workplace. We must also be sensitive to cultural diversity and communication demands of such an international workforce. By including cross-cultural training—for native and non-native English-speaking employees alike—RPM can more effectively promote cultural sensitivity. Plain English or translated versions of key corporate documents can further improve the workplace environment for our multinational employees.

Offers to answer questions

I hope you find this report helpful in recruiting and retaining additional multinational employees for RPM Technologies. If you have any questions or want to discuss any of our recommendations or research findings, please call me at extension 5406 or email me. I look forward to receiving your suggestions.

Sincerely yours,

Terri Smith Ruckel

Terri Smith Ruckel
Senior Training Specialist

Enclosure notation specifies report is attached

Enclosure: Report

FIGURE 9.2 A Long Report

Adapting the RPM Workplace for Multinational Employees

Title page is carefully formatted and uses boldface

Terri Smith Ruckel

Identifies writer and job title

**Senior Training Specialist
RPM Technologies**

Ruckel presents report from entire staff— writing for another's signature

Prepared for

**Jesse Butler
Vice President, Human Resources**

RPM executive who assigned the report

May 6, 2013

Date submitted

Title page is not numbered

(Continued)

FIGURE 9.2 (Continued)

While APA does not include a table of contents, individual employers such as RPM may require one

Major divisions of report in all capital letters

Subheadings indicated by indentations and italics

Page numbers included for major sections of report

No subsections needed here

Table of Contents

FIGURE 9.2 (Continued)

List of Illustrations

iii

Identifies each figure by number, title, and page number

Provides a title for each visual

© Cengage Learning 2015

Abstract

This report investigates how U.S. businesses such as RPM must gain a competitive advantage in today's global marketplace by recruiting and retaining a multinational workforce. The current wave of immigrants is in great demand for their technical skills and economic ties to their homeland. Yet many companies like ours still operate by policies designed for native speakers of English. Instead, we need to adapt RPM's company policies and workplace environment to meet the cultural, religious, social, and communication needs of these multinational workers. To do this, we need to promote cultural sensitivity training, both for multinationals and employees who are native speakers of English. Additionally, as other U.S. firms have successfully done, RPM should adapt vacation schedules and daycare facilities for an expanding multicultural workforce. Equally important too, RPM needs to ensure, either through translations or plain-English versions, that all company documents can be easily understood by multinational workers.

iv

Concise, informative abstract that states purpose of report and why it is important for audience

Uses helpful transitional terms such as "additionally" and "equally important"

Footer uses Roman numerals for front matter pages

© Cengage Learning 2015

(Continued)

FIGURE 9.2 (Continued)

1

Introduction

Background

APA requires the first line of every paragraph to be indented

The U.S. workforce has been undergoing a remarkable revolution. The U.S. Bureau of Labor Statistics predicts that by 2015 the labor force in the United States will comprise 162 million workers who must fill 167 million jobs (2009).

Gives convincing statistical evidence about the importance of topic

The most dramatic effect of filling this labor shortage will be in hiring greater numbers of highly skilled multinational employees, including those joining RPM. Currently, "one of every five IT specialists [and] one of every six persons in engineering or science occupations . . . is foreign born" (Keshevi & Foley, 2011,

APA cites year of publication

p. 211). This new wave of immigrants will make up 37 percent of the labor force by 2015 and continue to soar afterward. By 2025 the number of international

Cites various sources to validate projections

residents in the United States will rise from 26 million to 42 million, according to the U.S. Chamber of Commerce (2010). As Alexa Quincy aptly put it, "The United States is becoming the most multiculturally diverse country in the global economy" (2012, p. 5).

Explains potential impact of immigrants on RPM's business

Unlike earlier generations, immigrants today actively maintain ties with their native countries. These new immigrants travel back and forth so regularly they have become global citizens, exercising an enormous influence on the success of a business like RPM. They provide business contacts with other markets, enhancing [a company's] ability to trade and invest profitably abroad. Figure 1

Introduces figure to illustrate argument

below identifies these major groups. Undeniably, many immigrants today often

Provides number and title for figure

3-D pie chart reveals differences in immigrant workers

Figure 1
**Major Ethnic Groups
Immigrating to the United States (2000–2010)**

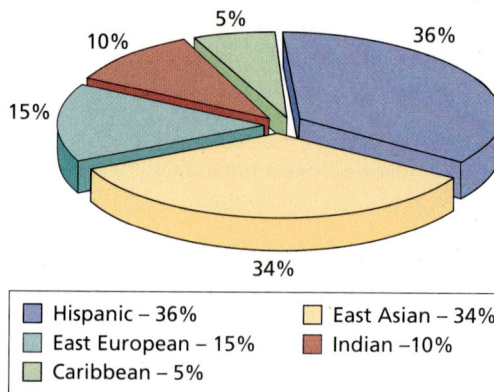

Provides key for visual

■ Hispanic – 36%	■ East Asian – 34%
■ East European – 15%	■ Indian –10%
■ Caribbean – 5%	

Cites source for visual

Source: Brown, P. (2012, February). *History of U.S. immigration.* Retrieved from http://immigration.ucn.edu

© Cengage Learning 2015

FIGURE 9.2 (Continued)

2

possess advanced levels of technical expertise. A report by the Kaiser Foundation found that California's Silicon Valley had significantly benefited from the immigrants who have arrived with much needed technical training. East Asian, Indian, Pakistani, and Middle Eastern scientists and engineers, who have relocated from a number of countries, now hold more than 40 percent of the region's technical positions ("Immigrants Find," 2012, p. 37). Figure 2 below indicated the leading countries of origin for Silicon Valley's immigrants in 2012 and records the percentage for each nationality.

Problem

RPM, like other e-companies, is experiencing a critical talent shortage of IT and other professionals, making the recruitment of a multinational workforce a vital priority for us. Meeting the cultural and communication demands of these workers, however, poses serious challenges for RPM. The traditional workplace has to be transformed to respect the ways multinational employees communicate about business. Native English-speaking employees will also have to be better prepared to understand and to appreciate their international co-workers.

Identifies a major problem and explains why it exists

Figure 2
Immigration to Silicon Valley in 2012

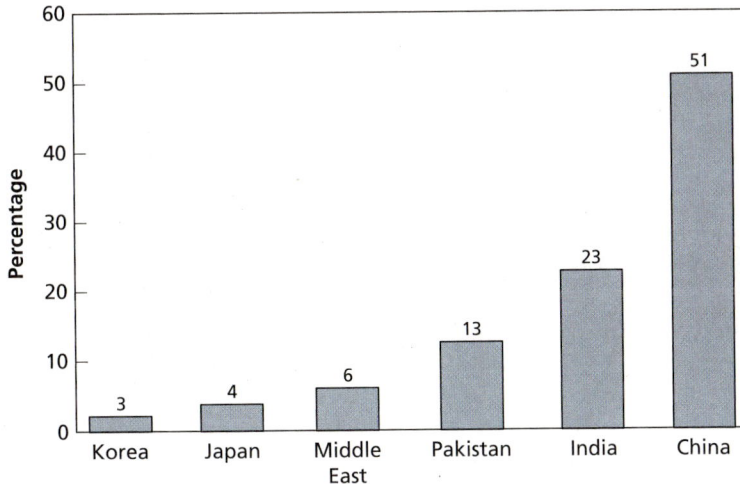

Bar chart identifies and quantifies major groups of immigrants

Relevant visual in appropriate place in text

Source: Immigrants find the American dream in California's Silicon Valley. (2012, March). *Silicon Valley News*, p. 37.

(Continued)

FIGURE 9.2 (Continued)

3

Unfortunately, many corporate policies and programs at RPM, and at other U.S. companies as well, have been created for native-born, English-speaking employees (Morales, 2011; Reynolds, 2012). Rather than rewarding multinational workers, such policies unintentionally punish them.

Two separate, corroborating sources

Purpose

The purpose of this report is to show that because of the need to increase the number of multicultural employees in the workplace, RPM must adapt its business environment to recruit and retain this essential and diverse labor force. This report spells out specific steps RPM must take to accommodate this new multinational workforce.

Concisely states why the report was written

Scope

This report explores cultural diversity in the current U.S. workplace and suggests ways for RPM to compete successfully in the global marketplace by providing equal employment opportunities for multinational workers. By doing this, we will foster cross-cultural literacy and improve training in intercultural communication at our firm.

Informs reader that report will focus directly on RPM's needs

Discussion

Providing Equal Workplace Opportunities for Multinational Employees

Discussion is organized into three main sections, each with subsections

Aggressive Recruitment of IT Professionals from Diverse Cultures

A multilingual workforce is essential if RPM wants to compete in a culturally diverse global market. But firms such as ours must be prepared to adapt or modify hiring policies and procedures to attract these multinational employees, beginning with rethinking our recruitment and retention policies. Routine visits to U.S. campuses by company recruiters or "specialized international recruiters" can help us identify and hire highly qualified multinational job candidates (Hamilton, 2012, p. 36).

Emphasizes recruiting multinational workers and suggests how to do so

Moreover, RPM should visit universities abroad with distinguished IT programs to attract talented multinational employees. We should encourage students and recent graduates from these universities to apply for a 1-J visa to learn more about RPM through an internship program here. As Catherine Bolgar reported, "Boeing went to Russia for specialist software engineers it couldn't find in the U.S." (2007, Human Capital section, para. 3). These searches, along with articles on our website and executive blogs, should emphasize RPM's commitment to globalization. Lobbying more actively to increase the number of H1-B visas for skilled workers will also help RPM.

FIGURE 9.2 (Continued)

4

Capitalizing on a diverse workforce, RPM can more effectively increase our multicultural customer base worldwide. Logically, customers buy from individuals they can relate to culturally. RPM might take a lead from Visions Bank of California, a business serving a diverse population, especially its Asian and Hispanic customers. The bank has a successful recruitment history of hiring employees with language skills in Hindi, Vietnamese, Korean, and Spanish. In fact, Visions Bank ranked fourth as an employer of minorities (Visions Bank of California, 2012). Figure 3 charts the increase in multinational employees hired by Visions Bank over an 8-year period.

Identifies specific benefits for RPM

Another highly competitive business, Darden Restaurants, Inc., selected Richard Rivera, a Hispanic, to serve as president of Red Lobster, the nation's largest full-service seafood chain with 680 restaurants nationwide. Under Rivera's leadership, Red Lobster has hired more international employees—totaling more than 35 percent of its workforce—than it had in previous years. Many top Fortune 500 companies, such as Cisco and Intel, can also claim that 40% or more of their workforce is comprised of multinationals ("100 Best Companies," 2010). Closer to RPM in St. Louis, Whitney Abernathy—manager of Netshop, Inc.—found that contracts from Indonesia increased by 17 percent after she hired Jakarta native Safja Jacoef (personal communication, April 2, 2013).

Personal communications (such as interviews and emails) not included in APA References list

Figure 3
Visions Bank of California
Growth in Percentage of Multinational Employees

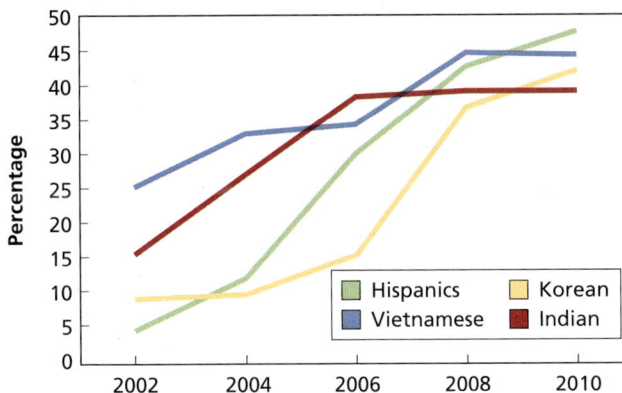

Tracks key information in a clear and concise graph

Supplies necessary legend

Source: Hamilton, B. E. (2012). Diversity is the answer for today's work force. *Journal of Business Diversity, 10* (38), 35–37.

Provides source

(*Continued*)

FIGURE 9.2 (Continued)

5

Commitment to Ethnic Representation

Many companies have mission statements on diversity and multinational employees in the workplace. G.E., American Airlines, IBM, and Walmart promote multinationals as mentors and interpreters. Eastman Kodak has eight employee cultural network groups, including the Hispanic Organization for Leadership and Advocacy, or HOLA, which is "committed to foster excellence and leadership among Hispanics by providing personal growth and development opportunities through informal mentoring, training, and interaction with management" ("Employee Networks," 2013, para. 6). Such a proactive program, which we might incorporate at RPM, recognizes the leadership abilities of multinational employees. Moreover, "glass ceilings," which in the past have prevented women and ethnic employees from moving up the corporate ladder, are being shattered. Tesfaye Aklilu, Vice President at United Technologies, astutely observes:

> In a global business environment, diversity is an ... imperative. Diversity of cultures, ideas, perspectives, and values is the norm of today's international companies. The exchange of ideas from different cultural perspectives gives a business additional, valuable information. Every employee can see his/her position from a global vantage point. (Aklilu, 2010, para. 1)

RPM would also do well to follow the lead of one of our chief competitors, Ablex Polymers. Ablex recently won an award from the International Business Foundation for hiring more Hispanic American women managers ("Ablex Wins Award," 2012).

Promoting and Incorporating Cultural Awareness Within the Company

Cross-cultural Training

Many of RPM's competitors have created cultural awareness programs for international employees as well as native speakers. Committed to diversity, Aetna offers online courses on ethnicity (e.g., "A Bridge to Asia") to "promote an atmosphere of openness and trust" (Aetna, 2008, p. 14) while Johnson & Johnson conducts Diversity University "to help employees . . . understand and value differences and the benefits of working collaboratively . . . to meet business

goals" (2013, Diversity University section, para. 1). Employees find it easier to work with someone whose values and beliefs they understand, while employers benefit from collaboration. Such a program could have prevented the problem RPM experienced when a non-native English-speaking employee was offended by a cultural misunderstanding ("RPM First Quarter," 2011). We may want to model our programs after those at American Express, which has a workforce representing 40 nations, or those at Extel Communications with its large percentage of Hispanic and Vietnamese employees. United Parcel Service (UPS) profitably pairs a native English-speaking employee with someone from another cultural group to improve on-the-job problem solving and communication

FIGURE 9.2 (Continued)

6

skills. For instance, Jamie Allen, a UPS employee since 2001, found her work with Lekha Nfara-Kahn to be one of the most rewarding experiences of her job (Johnson, 2012).

Although they need to encourage cultural sensitivity training, U.S. firms like RPM should also be cautious about severing international workers' cultural ties—a delicate balance. When management actively promotes bonds among employees from similar cultures, workers are less fearful about losing their identity. Encouraging such contacts, Globe Citizens Bank has long mobilized culturally similar groups by asking workers of shared ethnic heritages to network with each other (Gordon & Rao, 2011). Employees of Turkish ancestry from Globe's main New York office go to lunch twice a month with Turkish-born employees from the Newark branches. Globe hosts these luncheons and in return receives a bimonthly evaluation of the bank's Turkish and Middle Eastern policies (Hamilton, 2012).

Relevant source on topic of immigration

Offers two examples RPM could follow

Cultural education must go both ways, though. The U.S. business culture has conventions, too, and few international employees would want to ignore them, but they need to know what those conventions are (Johnson, 2012). A frequent problem with U.S. corporations such as RPM is that we assume everyone knows how we do things and how we think—it never occurs to us to explain ourselves. For example, native speakers of English are typically comfortable within a space of 1.5 to 2 feet for general personal interactions in business. But workers from Taiwan or Japan, who prefer a greater conversational distance, feel uncomfortable if their desks are less than a few feet away from another employee's workspace (Quincy, 2012; "Taiwanese Business Culture," 2012).

Another clear transitional sentence

Identifies key RPM problem

Gives cultural example

Promotion of Cultural Sensitivity

Corporate efforts to validate diverse cultures might also include the recognition of an ethnic group's holidays. RPM has just begun to do this by hosting cultural events, including Cinco de Mayo and Chinese New Year celebrations. Many companies honor National Hispanic Heritage Month in September, coinciding with the independence celebrations of five Latin American countries (U.S. Equal Employment Opportunity Commission, 2008). Emphasizing their "long-standing relationship with the Chinese community," Wells Fargo participates "every year in San Francisco's Chinese New Year parade" by featuring "a 200-foot-long Golden Dragon" (Babal, 2008, para. 2). GRT Systems sends New Year's greetings at Waisak (the Buddhist Day of Enlightenment) to its employees who are Buddhist. Techsure, Inc., allows Muslim employees to alter their schedules during Ramadan, (M. Saradayan, personal communication, February 28, 2012). Figure 4 (on page 7) provides a helpful multicultural calender that RPM needs to follow in developing our cultural sensitivity policies.

Spells out precise ways RPM can incorporate cultural sensitivity into the workplace

Includes valuable information from official corporate blogs

Includes appropriate calendar of ethnic holidays

Successful U.S. firms have been sensitive to the needs of their English-speaking employees for decades. Flexible scheduling, telecommuting options, daycare, and preventive health programs have become part of corporate benefit plans. Many of

(Continued)

FIGURE 9.2 (Continued)

7

Figure 4
A Multicultural Calendar

December 2012						
◀ Nov 2012						Jan 2013 ▶
Sun	**Mon**	**Tue**	**Wed**	**Thu**	**Fri**	**Sat**
						1
2 Advent begins (Christian)	3	4	5	6 Feast of St. Nicholas (European countries)	7	8 Bodhi Day (Rohatsu-Buddhism) Hanukkah begins (Jewish) (ends Dec. 16)
9 Uthpatti/ Utpanna Enkadashi (Hindu)	10	11	12 Feast of Our Lady of Guadalupe (Catholic)	13	14 Muharram ends (Muslim) (began Nov. 14)	15
16 Las Posadas begins (Hispanic) (endsDec. 24)	17	18	19	20	21 Winter Solstice (various Pagan)	22
23 Gita Jayanti (Hindu)	24 Noche Buena (Hispanic)	25 Christmas (Christian)	26 Kwanzaa begins (Interfaith) (ends Jan. 1)	27 Datta Jayanti (Hindu)	28	29
30	31 New Year's Eve (Western)					

Source: Johnson, V. M. (2012). Growing multinational diversity in business sparks changes. *Business Across the Nation, 23*(7), 43–48.

Major visual with a great deal of detail merits three-quarters of a page to make it readable

Pays attention to major world holidays

Visual helps to convince RPM to adopt similar policy

Identifies current RPM programs and how they could be easily modified to assist multinational workers

these options and benefits have been in place at RPM. But an international workforce presents additional cultural opportunities for RPM management. For example, our company cafeterias might easily accommodate the dietary restrictions of vegetarian workers or those who abstain from certain foods, such as dairy products. At GlobeTech, for example, soybean and fish entrees are always available (Reynolds, 2012). Adding ethnic items at RPM would express our cultural awareness and respect for multicultural employees.

Day care remains a key issue in hiring and retaining skilled employees, whether they are native or non-native speakers of English. RPM's child care facilities at our offices in St. Louis and San Luis Obispo have brought us much positive publicity

FIGURE 9.2 (Continued)

8

over the past eight years ("RPM Day Care Facilities," 2012). But by modifying child care that reflects our workers' culturally diverse needs, RPM can give a multinational workforce greater peace of mind and better enable them to do their jobs. A pacesetter in this field is DEJ Mobile, which insists that at least two or three of its daycare workers must be fluent in Korean or Hindi (Parker, 2011). One of our competitors, ITCorp, hires Hispanic and East Asian bilingual day care workers and tries to serve foods the children customarily eat at home (Gordon & Rao, 2011).

Making Business Communication More Understandable for Multinational Employees

Translation of Written Communications

Among the essential documents causing trouble for multicultural readers are company handbooks, insurance and health care obligations, policy changes, and OSHA and EPA regulations (Hamilton, 2012). To ensure maximum understanding of these documents by a multinational workforce, RPM should provide a translation, or at least a plain English version, of them. To accomplish this, RPM could solicit the help of employees who are fluent in the non-native English speakers' languages as well as contract with professional translators to prepare appropriate work-related documents.

Workplace signs in particular, especially safety messages, must consider the language needs of international workers. In the best interest of corporate safety, RPM could have these signs translated into the languages represented by multinationals in the workplace and/or post signs that use global symbols. Unquestionably, we need to avoid signs that workers might find hard or even impossible to decipher. For example, a capital **P** for "parking" or an **H** for "hospital" might be unfamiliar to non-native speakers of English (Parker, 2011).

Language Training Must Be Reciprocal

But language training has to be reciprocal—for native as well as non-native speakers—if communication is to succeed. A recent international survey of executive recruiters showed that being bilingual is critical to success in the international world of business ("Developing Foreign Language Skills," 2011). Sadly, even though second language instruction is on the rise, "fewer than 1 in 8 students at U.S. colleges major in [a] foreign language" (Cicorone, 2011, p. 19). Unfortunately, this is the case with RPM's native-speaking employees. However, many of the international workers RPM needs to recruit are bi- or even trilingual. In India, Israel, or South Africa, for example, the average worker speaks two or more languages every day to conduct business.

Since RPM needs to recruit such workers, we have to learn more about the cultures and languages of these global employees. RPM management should consider contracting with one of the companies specializing in language instruction for businesspeople (www.selfgrowth.com/foreignlanguage.html). We also need to network with international employee groups to solicit their help and advice.

Sidenotes:

Cites company publication showing research within the organization

APA lists blogs in references

Third major section of discussion

Turns to written communication and multinational workers

Offers practical solution

Gives examples of what to avoid and why

Cites business survey to confirm the necessity of change at RPM

Argues that reader must consider both sides

Includes helpful link to assist reader

(Continued)

FIGURE 9.2 (Continued)

9

Conclusion

To compete in the global marketplace, RPM must emphasize cultural diversity much more in its corporate mission and throughout the workplace. Through its policies and programs, RPM should aggressively recruit and retain an increasing number of technologically educated and experienced multinational workers. Such workers are in great demand today and will be even more so over the next ten to twenty years. They can help RPM increase our international customer base and advance the state of our technology. But the workplace must be sensitive to their cultural, religious, dietary, and communication needs. Providing equal opportunities, diversity training and networking, and easy-to-understand business documents will also keep RPM globally competitive in recruiting and retaining these essential employees.

Recommendations

By implementing the following recommendations, based on the conclusions reached in this report, RPM Technologies can succeed in hiring and promoting the IT multinational professionals our company needs for future success in today's global economy.

1. Recruit multinational workers more effectively through our website, international hiring specialists, and visits to college and university campuses here and abroad.
2. Work more closely with the Immigration and Naturalization Service (INS) to retain multinationals.
3. Establish a mentoring program to identify and foster leadership abilities in multinational employees, resulting in retaining and promoting these workers.
4. Promote cultural sensitivity and networking groups comprising both multinationals and native English-speaking employees.

5. Encourage a group's cultural ties by actively supporting such work-related organizations as the Hispanic Organization for Advocacy and Leadership (HOLA).
6. Develop educational materials for employees who are native speakers of English about the cultural traditions of their multinational co-workers.

7. Reassess and adapt RPM's day care facilities to more effectively meet the needs of children of multinational employees.
8. Supply relevant translations and plain-English versions of company hand-books, manuals, new regulations, insurance policies, safety codes, and other human resource documents.
9. Support second-language training programs to enhance communication and collaboration between multinational and native speaker employees at RPM.

FIGURE 9.2 (Continued)

10

References

100 best companies to work for, 2010. (2010, February 8). *Fortune 500*. Retrieved from http://money.cnn.com/magazines/fortune/bestcompanies/2010/minorities/

Ablex wins award. (2012, February). Retrieved from http://www.ablexinter.org

Aetna, Inc. (2008, March). *Diversity annual report: The strength of diversity*. Retrieved from http://www.aetna.com/about/aetna/diversity/data/AetnaEnglish_2008.pdf

Aklilu, T. (2010). *Diversity at UTC*. Retrieved from http://www.utc.com/careers/diversity/index4.htm

Babal, M. (2008, January 26). The year of the ox [Web log post]. Retrieved from http://blog.wellsfargo.com/wachovia/2009/01/the_year_of_the_ox.html

Bolgar, C. (2007, June 18). Corporations need a global mindset to succeed in today's multipolar business world. *Wall Street Journal Online*. Retrieved from http://www.accenture.com/global/highperformancebusiness_business/multipolarbusinessworld.htm

Brown, P. (2012, February). *History of U.S. immigration*. Retrieved from http://immigration.ucn.edu

Cicorone, M. (2011). The importance of foreign languages to success in the world of work. *Language Instruction, 51*(3), 18–27.

Developing foreign language skills is good business. (2011, February 3). *Business World*. Retrieved from http://www.businessworld.ca/article.cfm/newsID/7109.cfm

Employee Networks (Resource Groups). (2013, May). Retrieved from http://www.kodak.com/ek/US/en/Global_Sustainability/Global_Diversity/Employee_Networks.htm

Gordon, T., & Rao, P. (2011). Challenges ahead for American companies. *National Economics Review, 11*(3), 38–42, 56.

Hamilton, B. E. (2012). Diversity is the answer for today's work force. *Journal of Business Diversity, 10*(38), 35–37.

Immigrants find the American dream in California's Silicon Valley. (2012, March). *Silicon Valley News*, p. 37.

Johnson & Johnson. (2013). *Programs and activities*. Retrieved from http://www.jnj.com/connect/about-jnj/diversity/programs

Includes only sources actually cited in report

Double-spaces between entries

Arranges all entries by author's last name or (if no author) by first word of title excluding articles ("a," "an," "the")

Specifies date of publication for every entry after author's name (or title, if author's name not given)

Capitalizes only first word and proper nouns in title

Provides page numbers for print sources

Indents second and subsequent lines ½ inch

FIGURE 9.2 (Continued)

11

Johnson, V. M. (2012). Growing multinational diversity in business sparks changes. *Business Across the Nation, 23*(7), 43–48.

Keshevi, T. & Foley, B. (2011). The contributions of high-skilled immigrants. In B. Foley (Ed.), *Immigration and U.S. technology* (pp. 210–214). Washington, DC: International Policy Institute.

Morales, J. (2011). *Immigration News & Notes*. Retrieved from http://www.immigrationnewsandnotes.com

Parker, M. (2011, May 26). Multinational hires—advice and advocacy [Blog post]. Retrieved from http://parkeronimmigration.blogspot.com/2011/05/26/multinational_hires-advice_and_advocacy.php

Quincy, A. (2012). Multiculturalism makes for a good business. *Workforce, Inc., 14*(2), 5–8.

Reynolds, P. (2012, February 3). Serving up culture [Web log post]. Retrieved from http://www.culture.org/2011/02/serving_up_culture

RPM day care facilities rated high. (2012, November 15). *RPM News*. Retrieved from http://www.rpm.com/rpmnews/01_15_2012/rpm_daycare_facilities_rated_high

RPM first quarter activity report. (2011). *RPM Internal Reports*. Retrieved from http://www.rpm.com/internalreports/2011_firstquarter

Taiwanese business culture. (2012). *Executive Planet*. Retrieved from http://www.executiveplanet.com/business-culture-in/132438266669.html

U.S. Bureau of Labor Statistics. (2009). *Overview of the 2008–18 projections*. Retrieved from http://www.bls.gov/oco/oco2003.htm

U.S. Chamber of Commerce. (2010). *Immigration issues*. Retrieved from http://www.uschamber.com/issues/index/immigration/default

U.S. Equal Employment Opportunity Commission, Federal Hispanic Work Group. (2008). Report on the *Hispanic employment challenge in the federal government*. Retrieved from http://www.eeoc.gov/federal/reports/hwg

Visions Bank of California. (2012, June 23). Federation magazine ranks Visions Bank one of the best companies for minorities. Retrieved from http://www.vboc.com/about/main/0,3250,2485_11256_502261585,00.html

References blog posts with proper APA citations

Gives full Web addresses for verification and to make source easy to find

Cites material available on company intranet

Italicizes title of government report

Government documents provide valuable statistics

Article about a company included on company website

Final Words of Advice About Long Reports

Perhaps no piece of writing you do on the job carries more weight than the long report. You can simplify your job and increase your chances of success by following these guidelines for scheduling, researching, and collaborating:

1. Plan and work early. Do not postpone work until a deadline draws near.
2. Confer often and carefully with others in your group office.
3. Do a thorough search among Internet, print, and other resources.
4. Consult with specialists in other fields both in your company and in other organizations, including government officials.
5. Divide your workload into meaningful units. Reassure yourself that you do not have to write the report or even an entire section of the report in one day.
6. Set up mini-deadlines for each phase of your work, and then meet them.

✓ Revision Checklist

- [ ] Concentrated on a major problem—one with significant implications for my school, neighborhood, city, or employer.
- [ ] Identified, justified, and described the significance of the main problem.
- [ ] Did sufficient research—in the library, on the Internet, or through interviewing, personal observation, or testing.
- [ ] Anticipated how various managers and other decision makers will use and profit from my report for their long-range planning.
- [ ] Adhered to all specified schedules for completing various stages of the long report.
- [ ] Divided and labeled the parts of the long report to make it easy for readers to follow and to show a careful plan of organization.
- [ ] Supplied an informative abstract that leaves no doubt in readers' minds about what the report deals with and why.
- [ ] Designed an attractive title page that contains all the basic information—title, date, for whom the report is written, my name.
- [ ] Gave my readers all the necessary introductory information about background, problem, purpose of report, and scope.
- [ ] Included in the body of the report the research—the facts, statistics, interview comments, and descriptions—that my readers need.
- [ ] Included subheadings to reflect the major divisions into which I have organized the research that forms the nucleus of the text.
- [ ] Wrapped up the report in a succinct conclusion. Told readers what the findings of my research are and accurately interpreted all data.
- [ ] Supplied a recommendations section (if required) that tells readers concretely how they can respond to the problem using the data. Offered recommendations that are realistic and practical and related directly to the research and topic.

☐ Included in the final copy of the report all the parts listed in the table of contents.

☐ Supplied a one-page transmittal letter informing readers why the report was written and describing its scope and findings.

Exercises

1. Send an email to your instructor describing how one of the short reports in Chapter 8 could be useful to someone who has to write a long report.

2. What kinds of research did Terri Smith Ruckel and her team need to do to write the long report in Figure 9.2? As part of your answer, include the titles of any specific reference works you think the writer may have consulted.

3. Study Figure 9.2 and answer the following questions based on it:
   a. Why can the abstract be termed informative rather than descriptive?
   b. How have Ruckel and her team successfully limited the scope of the report?
   c. Where have Ruckel and her team used internal summaries especially well?
   d. Where and how have the writers adapted their technical information for their audience (a general reader)?
   e. What visual devices do the writers use to separate parts of the report?
   f. How do the writers introduce, summarize, and draw conclusions from the expert opinions in order to substantiate the main points?
   g. How have the writers documented information?
   h. What functions does the conclusion serve for readers?
   i. How do the recommendations follow from the material presented in the report? How are they both distinct and interrelated?

4. Come to class prepared to discuss a major community problem suitable for a long report (e.g., traffic, crime, air and water pollution, housing, transportation). Then write a letter to an appropriate agency or business requesting a study of the problem and a report.

5. Write a report outline for the problem you selected in Exercise 4. Use major headings. Include a cover letter with your outline.

6. Have your instructor approve the outline you prepared for Exercise 5. Then write a long report based on the outline, either on your own or as part of a collaborative writing team.

CHAPTER 10

Making Successful Presentations at Work

Almost every job requires employees to have and to use carefully developed speaking skills. In fact, to get hired, you have to be a persuasive speaker at your job interview. And to advance up the corporate ladder, you must continue to be a confident, well-prepared, and persuasive speaker. Some jobs may require you to deliver as many as three or four presentations a week.

The world of work receives and shares much of its information through informal briefings, collaborative discussions, PowerPoint or Prezi presentations, videoconfering, webinars, and formal presentations. Your employer will expect your oral communication skills in all these situations to be as effective and professional as your writing skills. The goal of this chapter is to help you be a more successful speaker on the job.

Writing a Document Versus Making a Presentation

Writing a document and delivering a report both require you to (1) research your topic, (2) plan your organization, and (3) choose your language and visuals carefully. There are, nevertheless, some fundamental differences between these two ways of communicating in the world of work. When you make a presentation, you must focus on these additional items:

- Your appearance—how you dress, stand, move, and gesture
- Your delivery—whether you can be heard, your tone of voice, whether you sound confident or nervous
- The complexity of your subject—your talk must be informative yet concise and easily understood the first (and likely only) time the audience hears it
- The amount of time you have been allotted
- Your audience's attention span—usually not more than fifteen or twenty minutes
- Your introduction—who you are and what you will talk about
- The layout of the room—lighting, capacity, acoustics, etc.
- The equipment necessary for your presentation—screen, monitors, computers, whiteboards, Skype, microphones

Chapter opening image: © dimitris_k/ShutterStock.com

383

- Your visuals—they must be clear and easily seen, even from the back of the room
- Your interaction with the audience—questions, comments, and nonverbal responses including laughs, frowns, puzzled looks

Types of Presentations

You will make numerous presentations on the job that will vary in the amount of preparation they require, the time they last, and the audience and occasion for which they are intended. Here are some presentations you can expect to make frequently before different audiences in the world of work.

For Your Customers or Clients

- sales appeals stressing how and why your company's products or services meet your listeners' needs
- scenarios about why your company is better than the competition
- demonstrations of your products or services
- a persuasive overview of your company's contributions to technology, the community, the environment

For Your Boss

- progress or status reports on how a project is going
- an assessment of your job accomplishments
- a justification of a budget, your own position, or your department or division
- a summary of a conference or meeting you attended

For Your Co-Workers

- an end-of-shift report, such as those made by police officers and nurses
- an explanation of a new or revised company policy
- a training session on job safety, operating equipment, new software
- a briefing on new job assignments and tasks

For Community Leaders or Groups

- appeals before elected officials
- an explanation of your company's decision or activity
- an update on completing a public works project
- tours of a company facility

Informal Briefings

If you have ever given a book report or explained laboratory results in front of a class, you have given an informal briefing. Such reports are a routine part of many jobs. They usually last between ten and twenty minutes and are given to a small group of co-workers and possibly your boss. Other topics for such briefings often focus on training, motivating a workforce, reviewing sales activities, and so on.

Whatever the topic, informal briefings bring people up-to-date by supplying them with key information. Figure 10.1 (page 386) contains an outline for an informal briefing to the staff of a bank.

When you have to make an informal briefing, follow these guidelines:

1. **Prepare.** Confer with your boss, individuals in human resources, collaborative team members. Never speak off-the-cuff.

2. **Decide on your main points.** Write down a few key items you want to cover, and keep this list or outline before you as you speak. Highlight key names, terms, dates, or places.

3. **Avoid information overload.** Do not crowd too many points into one briefing.

4. **Arrange your points in a logical sequence.** Put the main point first, or try using a cause-and-effect or chronological organization.

5. **Be clear.** Don't use unfamiliar terms or complex explanations. Include concrete examples that your audience will easily understand and apply to solve a problem or clarify a work-related issue.

6. **Be concise.** Your audience may be on a strict timetable and have obligations to fulfill later in the day.

7. **Don't rush your delivery.** Speak calmly and deliberately so that your audience can clearly absorb your message or even take notes.

8. **Stay positive.** Even when you have unpleasant news to impart (e.g., a project delay), resist blaming or lecturing your audience. Instead, focus on the positive steps needed to resolve the problem.

9. **Use appropriate visuals to clarify a point.** But do not overwhelm your listeners with numerous graphs, charts, and photos. Target only two or three points to illustrate.

10. **End on time.** Be sure to allow time at the end of your briefing for questions, comments, and suggestions. Thank listeners for their time and cooperation.

Note how the speaker's outline and slide in Figure 10.1 identifies key points, illustrates them with examples, inserts appropriate visuals (slides) in the most effective places, and makes sure the briefing is audience-focused and runs on schedule.

FIGURE 10.1 An Outline of Speaking Points for an Informal Briefing

Clearly focused topic

Crime Alert Briefing: People's National Bank, Millersville, May 8, 2014

Topic of briefing: Crime alert about the increasing number of counterfeit $20 and $50 bills in the Millersville area.

Uses short outline of main points to stress at briefing

I. **Introduction**
   A. Area banks have been asked to be on the lookout for an increased number of counterfeit $20 and $50 bills in circulation
   B. Our customers trust in us to protect their financial security
   C. We have a responsibility as tellers/bank officers to identify counterfeit bills and to keep them out of circulation

Motivates audience

II. **Identifying Counterfeit Bills**
   A. Be especially vigilant of $20's and $50's left in our night depository
   B. Make sure you compare any suspected fraudulent bills with real currency
   C. Here are some telltale signs to look for:
      1. No watermark is visible when the bill is held up to the light
      2. The portrait is not off centered as in legitimate $20 and $50 bills
         SHOW SLIDE 1 (enlarged photo of counterfeit $20 bill)
      3. There are blurred lines and fuzzy scrolls along the border (edges) of each counterfeit bill

Includes a relevant slide to help tellers identify counterfeit currency

Gives precise directions

III. **Conclusion**
   A. Thank you for your help
   B. If you have any questions, call a bank officer
   C. Review bank policy on reporting counterfeit currency (distributed to staff via email)

Supplies bank policy to staff via e-distribution.

© Cengage Learning 2015

Formal Presentations

Whereas an informal briefing is likely to be short, generally conversational, and intended for a limited number of people, a formal presentation is much longer, far less conversational, and perhaps intended for a wider audience. It involves much more preparation.

Expect to spend several days preparing your presentation. You cannot just dash it off. Just as you did with an informal briefing you will have to do the following; only more extensively and over a longer period of time:

- research the subject
- interview key resource individuals

- prepare, time, and sequence visuals
- coordinate your talk with presentations by your co-workers or boss
- rehearse your presentation

Many of us are uncomfortable in front of an audience because we feel frightened or embarrassed. Much of that anxiety can be eased if you know what to expect. The two areas you should investigate thoroughly before you begin to work on your presentation are (1) who will be in your audience and (2) why they are there.

Analyzing Your Audience

The more you learn about your audience, the better prepared you will be to give your listeners what they need. Just as you do for your written work, for your oral presentation you will have to do some research about the audience, emphasizing the "you attitude" and establishing your own credibility.

Consider Your Audience as a Group of Listeners, Not Readers

While audience analysis pertains both to readers of your work and to listeners of your presentation, there are several fundamental differences between these two groups. Unlike readers of your report, the audience for your presentation

- is a captive group of listeners
- has a shorter attention span
- may have only one chance to get your message
- has less time to digest what you say
- can't always go back to review what you said or jump ahead to get a preview
- is more easily distracted—by interruptions, chairs being moved, people coughing, outside noise, and so on
- cannot absorb as much as in a written report

Take all of these differences into account as you plan your presentation and assess who constitutes your audience.

Guidelines for Analyzing Your Audience

Here are seven key questions to ask when analyzing your audience.

1. **How much do they know about your topic?**

   - consumers with little or no technical knowledge
   - technical individuals who understand terms, jargon, and background
   - business managers looking only for the bottom line

2. **What unites them as a group?**

   - members of the same profession
   - customers using the same products
   - employees of the company you work for

3. **What do they want to receive from your presentation?**

   - a quick overview
   - bottom-line financial details
   - technical details on materials, methods, and conclusions (results)

4. **What is their interest or stake in your topic?**

   - friendly and interested
   - neutral—waiting to be informed, entertained, or persuaded
   - uncooperative, antagonistic, or likely to challenge you

5. **What do you want them to do after hearing your presentation?**

   - buy a product or service
   - adopt a plan
   - change a schedule
   - learn more about your topic
   - sign a petition
   - follow a new policy (e.g., safety procedures)

6. **What questions are they likely to raise?**

   - about money, profits, expenses, salary
   - about personnel, hiring, training
   - about transfers, mergers, promotions
   - about new job responsibilities, accountability
   - about locations, new, remodeled, domestic, overseas
   - about schedules/timetables, effect on quotes, salary

7. **What considerations should be given to a multinational audience?**

   - use common, easily understood vocabulary
   - use simple sentences
   - don't use unfamiliar abbreviations, acronyms, contractions, or metaphors
   - use appropriate salutations, complimentary closes, and signature line

The Parts of Formal Presentations

As you read this section, refer to Marilyn Claire Ford's PowerPoint presentation in Figure 10.2 (pages 389–392). Note how effectively she used the PowerPoint format to convince a potential client, GTP Systems, to purchase a service contract provided by World Tech, her employer. Her presentation consists of seven slides that contain relevant images and concise text.

FIGURE 10.2 A Sample PowerPoint Presentation

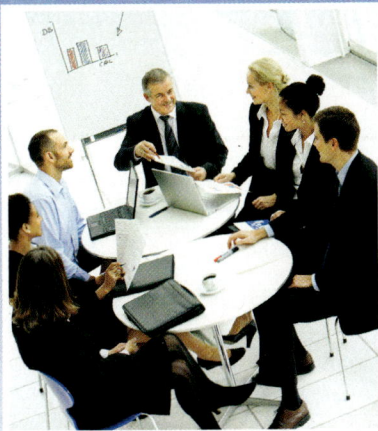

Slide 1

Clear, persuasive title

Background color contrasts well with text

Introduces speaker, provides reason for presentation and date

Type size and font make slide easy to read

Slide 2

Uses short title for each slide

Includes relevant visual emphasizing networking

Succinctly lists benefits in short, easy-to-read bulleted points

(Continued)

FIGURE 10.2 (Continued)

Slide 3

First of four slides that make up the body of the presentation

Relevant visual does not mask text

Develops first key sales feature

Easy to Use

With a simple phone call, you can

- Arrange a meeting with colleagues at multiple sites
- Use your computer to access World Tech's
- conferencing system
- See, hear, and talk with all participants

EastWest Imaging/Fotolia LLC

© Cengage Learning 2015

Slide 4

Second point gives only essential facts

Chooses verbs that emphasize cost savings

Does not overwhelm listeners with numbers

Cost Effective

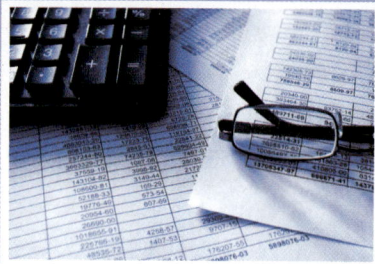

- Dramatically reduces costs for travel
- Upgrades current computer system for less than the cost of buying a new computer
- Cuts data-processing expenses by 60%

© istockphoto.com/George Peters

© Cengage Learning 2015

FIGURE 10.2 (Continued)

Slide 5

Third sales feature appropriately describes specific technology

Leaves generous margins

Explains how product can increase efficiency

Visual shows benefits of staff interacting

Slide 6

Stresses worldwide benefits

Visual reinforces global marketplace

Bulleted points all focus on single topic

(Continued)

FIGURE 10.2 (Continued)

Slide 7

Title signals end of presentation

Summarizes key advantages

Issues a call to action

Makes contact easy through website, email, and telephone

Conclusion

- Recap technology benefits
- Please sign up today—it is easy
- Just log on to **www.worldtech.com**
- Thank you for considering World Tech
- Any questions?

mcf@worldtech.com
1-800-271-5555

© Cengage Learning 2015

The Introduction

The most important part of a presentation is the introduction. Capture your audience's attention by answering these questions: (1) Who are you? (2) What are your qualifications? (3) What specific topic are you speaking about? and (4) How is the topic relevant to the audience?

Your first and most immediate goal is to establish rapport with your listeners, win their confidence, and elicit their cooperation. Because your listeners are probably at their most attentive during the first few minutes of your presentation, they will pay close attention to everything about you and what you say. Seize the moment and build momentum.

An effective introduction should be proportional to the length of the presentation. A ten-minute speech requires no more than a sixty-second introduction; a twenty-minute speech needs no more than a two- or three-minute introduction. Notice how in slides 1 and 2 of Figure 10.2, Ford introduces herself, her company, and its benefits for GTP.

How to Begin   You can begin by introducing yourself, emphasizing your professional qualifications and interests. (A self-introduction is unnecessary if someone else has introduced you or if you know everyone in the room.) Never apologize— for being nervous, unprepared, unqualified—or complain about the time or location for the presentation. Always ask if your audience can hear you clearly.

Give Listeners a Road Map   Indicate what your topic is and how you have organized what you have to say about it, for instance,

> My presentation today on greening the workplace last about 20 minutes. I have divided it into three linked parts. First, I will outline briefly recent software changes. Second, I will give a detailed review of how those changes directly affect our company. Third, I will show how our company can profitably implement those changes. At the end of my presentation, there will be time for your questions and comments.

The most informative presentations are the easiest to follow. Restrict your topic to ensure that you will be able to organize it carefully and sensibly—for example, a tasty diet under 1,000 calories a day or a course in learning InDesign or another software package.

Capture the Audience's Attention   Use any of the following strategies to get your audience to "bite the hook":

- Ask a question. "Did you know that every 15 minutes a foreign-owned business opens in China?" or "Do you know what's in your bottled water besides water?"
- Start with a quotation. "Winston Churchill said, 'We get things to make a living but we give things to have a life.'" (Consult *Bartlett's Familiar Quotations* online at www.bartleby.com/100)
- Use a relevant and memorable statistic. "In 2014, two million heart attack victims will live to tell about it." (Go to the *Information Please Almanac* at www.infoplease.com to find something relevant to your presentation topic.)

Be careful about using humor in a business talk. It could backfire; the audience may not get the point or may even be offended by it.

The Body

The body is the longest part of your presentation, just as it is in a long report. It should constitute about 60 to 70 percent of your presentation. Make it persuasive and relevant to your audience by (1) explaining a process, (2) describing a condition, (3) solving a problem, (4) arguing a case, or (5) doing all of these. See how the body of Marilyn Claire Ford's presentation in Figure 10.2 is organized around the benefits of GTP's switching to desktop videoconferencing. In slides 3 through 6 she outlines how easy, economical, and efficient such technology is to use in the global marketplace.

To get the right perspective, recall your own experiences as a member of an audience. How often did you feel bored or angry because a speaker tried to overload you with details or could not stick to the point?

Ways to Organize the Body   Here are a few helpful ways you can present and organize information in the body of your presentation. When you write a report, you design your document to help readers visually, supplying headings, bullets, white space, and headers and footers (see pages 218–227). In a presentation, you need to switch from those purely visual devices to aural ones, such as the following:

1. **Give signals to show where you are going or where you have been.** Enumerate your points: *first*, *second*, *third.* Emphasize cause-and-effect relationships with *subsequently*, *therefore*, *furthermore.* When you tell a story, follow a chronological sequence and use signposts: *before*, *following*, *next*, *then.* (See Appendix: A Writer's Brief Guide, Table A.1, page A-3.)

2. **Comment on your own material.** Tell the audience if some point is especially significant, memorable, or relevant. "This next fact is the most important one I'll give you today."

3. **Provide internal summaries.** Spending a few seconds to recap what you have just covered will reassure your audience that you want them to be clear about what you have covered thus far.

   We have already discussed the difficulties in creating a secure app that our sales force can use when in the field. Now we will need to turn to the options we recommend, from the most basic to those more complex.

4. **Anticipate any objections or qualifications your audience is likely to have.** Address potential objections with relevant facts about costs, personnel, or equipment in your presentation.

The Conclusion

Plan your conclusion as carefully as you do your introduction. Stopping with a screeching halt is as bad as trailing off in a fading monotone. An effective conclusion should leave the audience feeling that you and they have come full circle and accomplished what you promised. Let readers know you are near the end of your presentation.

What to Put in a Conclusion   A conclusion should contain something memorable. Never introduce a new subject or simply repeat your introduction. A conclusion can contain the following:

- a fresh restatement of your three or four main points
- a call to action, just as in a sales letter—to buy, to note, to agree, to volunteer
- a final emphasis on a key statistic (for example, "The installation of the stainless steel heating tanks has, as we have seen, saved our firm 32 percent in utility costs because we no longer have to run the heating system all day.")

End your presentation, as Marilyn Claire Ford does in slide 7, with a concise summary of the main points, and urge listeners to invest in your product or service.

Mean It When You Say, "Finally"   When you tell your audience you are concluding, make sure you mean it. Saying, "In conclusion," and then talking for another ten minutes frustrates listeners and makes them less receptive to your message. When you finish, thank your audience for their time and, if the schedule allows, invite questions.

Always Leave Time for Questions   Make sure you budget your time to give the audience an opportunity to ask questions, offer suggestions, or make comments.

Presentation Software

As Marilyn Claire Ford's presentation in Figure 10.2 demonstrates, business presentations very frequently rely on **PowerPoint** or other software such as **Corel Presentation**, **Apple's Keynote**, or the web-based **Prezi** (prezi.com). Knowing how to use these graphics packages is a crucial skill your employer will expect you to have. Presentation software enables you to create an electronic slide show with concise text and carefully chosen visuals that can be created on any computer. They allow you to plan, write, and add visuals to your slides.

Presentation Software Capabilities

With PowerPoint, Prezi, Corel Presentation, and Keynote, you can

- format and edit text
- import visuals, photos, digital art, clip art
- incorporate a variety of shapes and symbols—arrows, asterisks, bullets, cylinders, pyramids, flow charts, pictograms, infographs
- offer animation, sound bites, video clips
- design and insert logos and letterheads
- reuse and revise your presentation anytime

With the web-based presentation software such as Prezi, you can do all of the things listed here, as well as

- show a cohesive, complete presentation all at once, "zooming" into each key area as you make your presentation
- format your presentation into a "mental map" that you explore "slide-by-slide" in an animated, dynamic way
- help you work more easily with a group, using Prezi's web-based platform

Presentation software can also help you as a speaker. For instance, in PowerPoint you can keyboard your notes so that they scroll at the bottom of your computer screen. These notes are not projected for the audience, but they are available if you need to glance at them. You also can print parts of your presentation or your entire program in color or gray scale (black and white) to reinforce your presentation with professional-looking handouts.

Editing with presentation software allows you to customize any text or visual for any audience. You can copy, move, alter, and delete text, graphics, or sound bites. For example, you could edit the number of categories (bars, lines of a graph, items in a table) of an imported visual for a consumer audience that does not need much detail, or you could change the levels and positions of an organizational chart to suit your agency's needs. You can also change the color or texture of a background, saving you time and effort in re-creating a visual.

Organize the Presentation

Map out your presentation before you actually create your slides. Prepare an outline (see pages 38–41) to help you discover and develop the ideas you want to discuss. Following this outline, you can organize your presentation carefully, which is as important as the details you show your audience.

1. Identify the main points you want to cover, as Ford did in presenting information to save GTP time and money, increase staff efficiency, and help the company compete in a global economy. Then you can organize your topics logically and persuasively.
2. Divide your presentation into major sections that best accomplish your objective, whether to inform, to persuade, or to document.
3. Include only those supporting details that relate directly to your topic and to your audience's needs. These key points should help you determine the number of slides and visuals to use.
4. Don't overwhelm audiences with too much information. Note that Ford used only seven slides in Figure 10.2.
5. Choose your visuals carefully. Resist the temptation to dazzle your audience with electronic special effects. Your goal is not to create a glitzy show but to represent your company professionally.

Test the Technology

Find and eliminate any bugs at the rehearsal stage. Call in advance to confirm the room and any equipment you may need. Save and preview your presentation in the format in which you will be giving it. Bring your own computer to the meeting, and set up the projector and your notebook in advance. Make sure your software is compatible with the equipment you will use. Be sure any web links you plan to use are relevant and functioning, not broken links.

Prepare Transparencies and Handouts

It's always wise to have backup transparencies or handouts with you in case your equipment malfunctions before or during your presentation. Transparencies of your presentation will enable you to project your slides while you speak. Handouts of your slides (make sure you keep a copy for yourself) will allow you to continue with your presentation, and they will also help your audience follow your presentation and take notes about it while you speak. Make sure your handouts match your presentation exactly by providing your audience with a printout of each slide.

Do not distribute any handouts ahead of time. Wait until you are ready to use them. Otherwise, they may divert your audience's attention from your presentation.

Guidelines on Using Presentation Software Effectively

Here are some tips to ensure the best design and organization of your presentation, whether you use PowerPoint, Prezi, Keynote, or any other program. Refer to Figure 10.2 as you study these guidelines.

Readability

- Make sure each slide is easy to read—clear, concise, and uncluttered.
- Use a type size that is easy to see, even from a distance. For a small presentation on your notebook, use 24- to 28-point type or larger. Increase your type size for headings and titles to 32 point, as in Figure 10.2.

- Keep your type style consistent. Don't switch from one font to another.
- Avoid ornate and script fonts, and do not put everything in boldface, italics, or all capital letters. Marilyn Claire Ford used boldface (and white type against a blue background) for only the headings in Figure 10.2.

Text

- Keep your text short and simple. Use easy-to-recall names, words, and phrases. Your audience will not have the time to read long, complex messages.
- Use bulleted lists instead of unbroken paragraphs. But put no more than five bulleted lines on a slide, and limit each line to seven or eight words. Don't squeeze words on a line. Include no more than forty words per slide.
- Double-space between bulleted items, and leave generous margins on all sides.
- Title each slide using a question, a statement, or a key name or phrase, as in Figure 10.2.

Sequencing Slides

- Keep your slides in the order in which you need to show them.
- Retain the same transition (cover left or straight right) from slide to slide to avoid visual confusion.
- Spend about sixty to ninety seconds per slide, but don't read each slide verbatim. Summarize main ideas or concisely expand them while looking at your audience, not the slide.
- Time your slides so your audience can read them. Never continue to show a slide after you have moved on to a new topic.
- If you invite audience participation and interaction, build in extra time between your slides. Leave time for questions.

Background/Color

- Find a pleasant contrasting background to make your text easy to read. Avoid extremely light or dark backgrounds that may obscure your text. Stay away from stark backgrounds, such as using cold white images on a black screen.
- Use the same background for each slide, as in Figure 10.2.
- Avoid shadowing your text for "decorative" visual effect.
- Use color sparingly, and make sure it is professionally appropriate. Don't turn each slide into a sizzling neon sign. Avoid hot red, pink, etc.

Graphics

- Keep graphics clear, simple, and positioned appropriately on the slide.
- Make certain all graphics are at a high-enough resolution that they will not seem "blurry" or "pixilated" when projected on a larger screen.
- Be sure visuals do not cover or shadow text.

- Show only those visuals that support your main points. Not every slide requires a visual. For example, slides 1 and 7 in Figure 10.2 do not use visuals.
- Include no more than one graphic per slide; otherwise, your text will be more difficult to read.
- Include easy-to-follow graphs and charts instead of complicated tables, elaborate flow charts, or busy diagrams.
- Stay away from clip art; it can make your product or services look unprofessional.
- Incorporate animation, sound effects, or video clips only when they are persuasive, relevant, and undeniably professional.
- Don't bother with borders; they do not make a slide clearer.

Quality Check

- Be sure your spelling, grammar, names, dates, costs, and sources are correct.
- Double-check all math, equations, and percentages.

Noncomputerized Presentations

On the job you can expect to use a variety of visuals besides those included in PowerPoint presentations. There will be situations in which you may have to use a conventional chalkboard, a flip chart, a slide projector, or an overhead projector to make a presentation instead of your notebook. You will almost surely be asked to prepare handouts that include text, visuals, or a combination to distribute before or during your talk.

Regardless of the medium you use, make sure your visuals are

- easy to see
- easy to understand
- appropriately sized
- relevant
- accurate
- professional looking

Getting the Most from Your Noncomputerized Visuals

The following practical suggestions will help you get the most from your visuals when time and space may prohibit using computer setups.

1. Do not set up your visuals before your talk. The audience will wonder how you are going to use the graphics and so may not give you their full attention. When you are finished with a visual, put it away.

2. Firmly anchor any maps or illustrations. Having a map roll up or a picture fall off an easel during a presentation is embarrassing.

3. Never obstruct the audience's view by standing in front of your visuals. Use a pointer or a laser pointer to direct the audience's attention to your visual.

4. Avoid crowding too many images onto one visual. Use no more than one visual per page.

5. Do not put much writing on a visual. Elaborate labels or wordy descriptions are hard to read. Enlarge any writing on a visual so your audience can read it quickly and easily.

Rehearsing Your Presentation

All presentations require rehearsal. Don't skip rehearsing your presentation thinking it will save you time. Rehearsing will actually help you become more familiar with your topic and overall message, building your confidence. Rehearsing will also help you acquire more natural speech rhythms—pitch, pauses, and pacing. Here are some strategies to use as you rehearse your talk.

- Know your topic and the various parts of your presentation.
- If possible, practice in the room where you will make your presentation.
- Speak in front of a full-length mirror or before a friend or colleague for at least one rehearsal to see how an audience might view you.
- Talk into an audio recorder to determine whether you sound friendly or frantic, poised or pressured. You can also catch and correct yourself if you are speaking too quickly or too slowly. A rate of about 120 to 140 words a minute is easy for an audience to follow.
- Time yourself so that you will not exceed your allotted time or fall far short of your audience's expectations.
- Practice with the presentation software, visuals, equipment, or projector that you intend to use in your speech for valuable hands-on experience.
- Monitor the types of gestures (neither too many nor too few) you use for clarity and emphasis in your talk.
- Check the room where you will make your presentation, if possible, to find out about acoustics, lighting, seating, and available equipment.
- Video-capture your final rehearsal and show it to a colleague or instructor for feedback.

Delivering Your Presentation

A poor delivery can ruin a good presentation. You will be evaluated not only on what you say but on your style of presentation and the image you project: how you look, how you talk, and how you move (your body language). Do you mumble into your notes, never looking at the audience? Do you clutch the lectern as if to keep it in place? Do you shift nervously from one foot to the other? Do you shuffle through your notes? All those actions betray your nervousness and detract from your presentation.

First impressions are crucial. Research shows that people decide what they think of you in the first two or three minutes of your presentation. The way you dress is important, but so is your body language. Your nonverbal signals you send affect how an audience will judge your leadership abilities, your sales performance, even your sincerity. Pay attention to gestures, hand movements, how you stand, and so on. No matter how many hours you have worked to get your presentation ready, if your nonverbal presentation is misleading or inappropriate, the impact of what you say will be lost.

The following suggestions on how to deliver a presentation will help you be a well-prepared, poised speaker.

Settling Your Nerves Before You Speak

Being nervous before your presentation is normal—a faster heartbeat, cold, sweaty palms, shaking. But don't let your nerves stop you from delivering a highly successful talk.

Here are some ways you can calm yourself before you deliver your presentation:

- Give yourself plenty of time to get there. The more you have to rush, the more anxious you will be.
- Don't bring anything with you that is likely to spill, such as coffee, tea, or a soft drink.
- Avoid caffeine for a few hours before your talk if it makes you jittery.
- Take some deep breaths, and then hold your breath while you count to ten. Exhale. This will slow your heart rate and lower your blood pressure.
- Get away for a minute or two. Walk down a hall to get a drink of water or just to get a little exercise. It will help you reduce some anxiety and organize your thoughts.
- Remind yourself that you have spent hours preparing. Think positive. Your hard work will pull you through.
- Try to chat with one or two members of the audience ahead of time to relax. See your audience as friends—people who can help your career.

Guidelines for Making Your Presentation

Everyone is nervous before a talk. Accept that fact and even allow a few seconds of "panic time." Then put your nervous energy to work for you. Chances are, your audience will have no idea how anxious you are; they cannot see the butterflies in your stomach. Again, see your audience as friends, not enemies. Remember to do the following:

1. Establish eye contact with your listeners. Look at as many people in your audience as possible to establish a relationship with them. Never bury your head in your notes or keep your eyes fixed on a screen or keyboard. You will only signal your lack of interest in the audience or your fear of public speaking. Even during an informal presentation, try to establish rapport with each person in the room.

2. Repond to audience feedback. Watch your listeners' reactions and respond appropriately to them—nodding to agree, pausing a moment, paraphrasing to clarify a confusing point. Know your material well so that if someone asks you a question or wants you to return to a point, you are not fumbling through your notes or trying feverishly to locate the right screen.

3. Speak in a friendly and confident tone. Let the audience know that you are happy they are there and that you are enthusiastic. Speak in a natural, pleasant voice, but avoid verbal tics ("you know," "I mean") and fillers ("um," "ah," "er") repeated several times each minute. Such nervous habits will make your audience nervous and your speech less effective. Use pauses instead.

4. Vary the rate of your delivery. Vary your rate and inflection to help you emphasize key points and make transitions. Talk slowly enough for your audience to understand you, yet quickly enough so that you don't sound as if you are belaboring or emphasizing each word.

5. Adjust your volume appropriately. Talking in a monotone, never raising or lowering your voice, will lull your audience to sleep or at least inattention. Talk loudly enough for everyone to hear, but be careful if you are using a microphone. Your voice will be amplified, so if you speak too loudly, you will boom rather than project. Every word with a *b*, *p*, or *d* will sound like an explosive in your listeners' ears. Watch out for the other extreme—speaking so softly that only the first two rows can hear you.

6. Watch your posture. Don't shift from one foot to another. But do not slouch or look wooden either. If you stand motionless, looking as if *rigor mortis* has set in, your speech will be judged cold and lifeless, no matter how lively your words are.

7. Use appropriate body language. Be natural and consistent. Do not startle an audience by suddenly pounding on the lectern or desk for emphasis. Avoid gestures that will distract or alienate your audience. For example, don't fold your arms as you talk, a gesture that signals you are unreceptive (closed) to your audience's reactions. Also, avoid nervous habits that can divert the audience's attention: clicking a ballpoint pen, scratching your head, twirling your hair, pushing up your glasses, fumbling with your notes, or tapping your foot. Nor do you have to remain still or step with robotlike movements. The remote control for a PowerPoint or Prezi presentation allows you to casually walk around the room as you click and change screens.

8. Dress professionally. Do not wear clothes or clanking jewelry that call attention to themselves. Follow your company's dress code. Unless it specifies otherwise (e.g., "casual Fidays"), wear clothes that are the business norm. Women should wear a businesslike dress or suit; men should choose a dark suit or sports coat, a white or blue shirt, and a tasteful tie.

Handling Interruptions

Be diplomatic if someone interrupts your presentation with a question. Thank the individual by saying, "That's a good question. I'll be happy to answer it at the end of the presentation when there'll be time for questions." If someone is disruptive during your talk or a question-and-answer session and wants to debate with you, offer to meet with him or her after the session to discuss the point in question. Moreover, if you cannot answer a particular question, say you'll be glad to get back to the person, and go on to other questions.

When You Have Finished

Don't just sit down, walk back to your place on the platform or in the audience, or, worse yet, march out of the room. Thank your listeners for their attention and stay at the lectern or at your laptop for audience applause or questions. If appropriate, give the person who introduced you a chance to thank you while you are still in front of the group. And be sure to thank that person for his/her introduction.

If a question-and-answer session is to follow your speech, anticipate questions your audience is likely to ask. But it's a good idea to give your audience a time limit.

For example, you might say, "I'll be happy to answer your questions now before we break in ten minutes for lunch." By setting limits, you reduce the chances of a lengthy debate with members of the audience, and you can then politely leave after your time elapses.

Evaluating Presentations

This chapter has given you information on how to construct and deliver both an informal and formal business presentation. As a way of reviewing that advice, study Figure 10.3 below—an evaluation form similar to those used by instructors in colleges and universities. Note that the form gives equal emphasis to the speaker's performance or delivery and to the organization, content, and sequence of the presentation.

FIGURE 10.3 An Evaluation Form for a Presentation

Name of Speaker: _____   Date: _____

Title of Presentation: _____   Length: _____

PART I: THE SPEAKER'S DELIVERY
Circle the appropriate number using a 1 (lowest) to 5 (highest) scale.

1. Appearance	1 unprofessional	2	3	4	5 well-groomed
2. Eye contact	1 poor	2	3	4	5 effective
3. Tone of voice	1 monotonous	2	3	4	5 varied
4. Diction	1 slurred	2	3	4	5 clear
5. Posture	1 poor	2	3	4	5 natural
6. Gestures	1 distracting	2	3	4	5 appropriate
7. Self-confidence	1 nervous	2	3	4	5 poised
8. Interaction with audience	1 minimal	2	3	4	5 engaging

PART II: THE PRESENTATION ITSELF
Circle the appropriate number: 1 = poor; 5 = superior.

1. Made sure topic was relevant to audience	1	2	3	4	5

FIGURE 10.3 (Continued)

2. Began with clear statement of purpose	1	2	3	4	5
3. Followed logical organization	1	2	3	4	5
4. Gave audience cues to look for transitions between sections	1	2	3	4	5
5. Matched content to technical knowledge of audience	1	2	3	4	5
6. Provided convincing supporting evidence	1	2	3	4	5
7. Did not digress	1	2	3	4	5
8. Concluded with a summary of main points	1	2	3	4	5
9. Stayed within time limits	1	2	3	4	5
10. Allowed time for questions	1	2	3	4	5

PART III: USE OF VISUALS (SLIDES OR OTHER GRAPHICS)
Again, circle the appropriate number: = 1 poor; 5 = superior.

1. Used right number of visuals	1	2	3	4	5
2. Ensured all visuals were relevant	1	2	3	4	5
3. Carefully timed the sequence of visuals	1	2	3	4	5
4. Made sure audience could see visuals clearly	1	2	3	4	5
5. Selected visuals that clarified or simplified a point	1	2	3	4	5
6. Referred to visuals and indicated why they were important	1	2	3	4	5
7. Credited the source of visuals	1	2	3	4	5

✓ # Revision Checklist

- [ ] Anticipated my audience's background, interest, and even potential resistance, as well as questions about the message of both informal and formal presentations.
- [ ] Organized an informal briefing to make it easy to understand and to incorporate it into the work routine.
- [ ] Prepared an outline and identified and corrected any weak or redundant areas.
- [ ] Drafted an introduction to provide a "road map" of the presentation and to arouse audience interest.
- [ ] Started with interesting and relevant statistics, a question, an anecdote, or a similar "hook" to capture audience attention.
- [ ] Limited the body of my presentation to the main points.
- [ ] Sequenced the main points logically and made connections among them.
- [ ] Used supporting examples and illustrations appropriate to my audience and message.
- [ ] Made sure my conclusion contains a summary of the main points of my presentation and a specific call to action.
- [ ] Designed visuals that are clear, easy to read, and relevant for my audience.
- [ ] Experimented successfully with presentation software before using it for my presentation.
- [ ] Used an appropriate number of slides and made sure they were readable.
- [ ] Showed slides in the correct, carefully timed sequence.
- [ ] Prepared transparencies and handouts in case of equipment trouble.
- [ ] Rehearsed my presentation thoroughly to become familiar with its content, organization, and visuals.
- [ ] Monitored my volume, tone, and rate to vary my delivery and to emphasize my major points.
- [ ] Rehearsed my gestures to make them relevant and nonintrusive.
- [ ] Timed my presentation, complete with visuals, to run close to the allotted time.

Exercises

1. Prepare a three- to five-minute presentation explaining how a piece of equipment that you use on your job works. If the equipment is small enough, bring it with you to class. If it is too large, prepare an appropriate visual or two for use in your talk. Submit an outline similar to that in Figure 10.1.

2. You have just been asked to talk about the students at your school or the employees where you work. Narrow the topic and submit an outline to your instructor, showing how you have limited the topic and gathered and organized evidence.

Incorporate two or three appropriate visuals (photographs, maps, charts, icons, or even videos) in your PowerPoint presentation. Follow the format of the presentation in Figure 10.2.

3. Prepare a ten-minute presentation on a controversial topic that you would present before a civic group—the PTA, the local chapter of an organization, a post of the Veterans of Foreign Wars, a synagogue, a mosque, or a church club.

4. Using the information contained in the internal unsolicited proposal in Chapter 8 (pages 330–334) or in the long report on multinational workers in Chapter 9 (pages 367–380), prepare a short presentation (five to seven minutes) for your class.

5. Deliver a formal presentation on one of the following topics. Restrict your topic, and divide it into four key issues, as in Figure 10.2. Use at least three visuals with your talk. Submit an outline to your instructor.
   a. new equipment at work
   b. Using the Internet to provide interactive health care in rural areas
   c. a major change in housing or traffic control in your city
   d. a paper or report you wrote in school or on your job
   e. "greening" your school's or company's vistor's center
   f. the budget or spending cuts planned for your department or your town's school district for a given year
   g. applying for and receiving financial aid

6. Using the evaluation form in Figure 10.3, evaluate a speaker—a speech class student, a local politician, or a co-worker delivering a report at work. Specify the time, place, and occasion of the speech. Pay special attention to any visuals the speaker uses.

Newsletters[1]

Before the internet and before social media, organizations communicated via newsletters, and they still do. Newsletters provide an important piece of any organization's communication program.

FIGURE 11.1: What is a newsletter?

What is a newsletter?

• Regularly published news and information about an organization – in print and/or online

In the past, newsletters were print documents, handed out or mailed. Today's organizations have even more choices for their newsletters, including PDF documents emailed and/or available to download from websites or even embedded in websites themselves. Some organizations use all these formats to reach their readers.

In WR 214 at Oregon State, we introduce you to newsletters because they are so common in a wide range of workplaces you may encounter in your future. Your skill in preparing these communication documents can help you advance in your career.

We begin with a look at key components of any rhetorical situation. In other words, to plan, we can use the traditional **5W's and an H**: *Who, why, what, when, where, and how.* Let's look at each of them.

- **WHO:** **Readers / audience**
- **WHY:** **Message / purpose**
- **WHAT:** **Content / information**
- **WHEN:** **Context / frequency**
- **WHERE:** **Delivery method**
- **HOW:** **Format / visual design /writing**

---

[1] This chapter is written expressly for the 2014 Oregon State University Custom version of *Successful Writing at Work* by Sara Jameson, Assistant Director of Writing at OSU.

WHO: Readers

Organizations, which include businesses and non-profits, maybe even families, may have more than one newsletter for different groups of readers. These readers might be internal or external. Organizations might have multiple newsletters for communicating internally to staff, employees or volunteers as well as others for communication externally to clients, donors, taxpayers, potential staff and volunteers, or the general public.

For a public non-profit such as Oregon State University, reader groups might include students or prospective students, staff, or faculty. Each department and school in OSU might also have its own newsletter. We will look at some samples below.

In addition to a primary audience, such as OSU students, faculty, and staff, there might be secondary audiences, such as Oregon taxpayers and legislators, research funding agencies, and members of other Oregon colleges and universities.

As you can see, each group of readers will have different needs, so the newsletter must reflect that. Once the "who" is identified, next the "why" or message is decided.

WHY: Message

Why create a newsletter at all? Organizations want to communicate to remind readers of important messages. The first of these is to let readers know about the organization's existence, remind them of its mission and values, and inform them of any news. But newsletters can and should target specific readers. In all cases, the overall purpose is to create and maintain goodwill.

The purpose of an employee newsletter might be to congratulate workers on achievements, remind workers of safety tips, announce upcoming events, or provide news about the industry.

Whereas, the purpose of a client newsletter might be to advertise new services or products, applaud achievements, announce upcoming events, or provide news about the industry. So, as you see, there can be some overlap. The purpose or goal of the newsletter determines the content or information, the "what." What does the organization want to achieve with this newsletter for these readers?

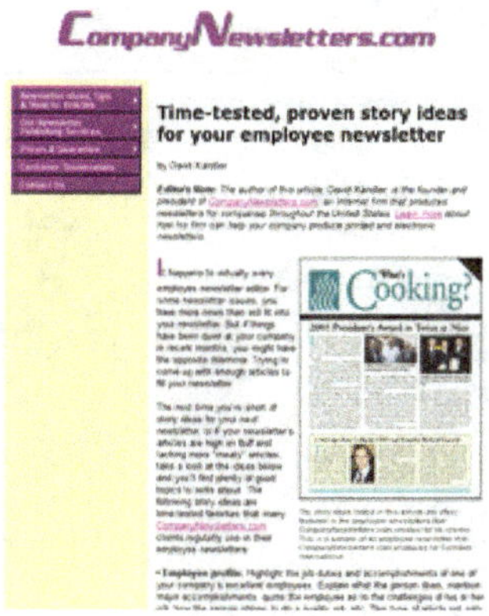

What?
Story Ideas include:

- Profile of employee or donor or person of interest (your INTO OSU Partner)
- Health tips and employee wellness
- Safety reminders and tips
- Related local or global news
- Upcoming events
- Seasonal items
- Philanthropies – charity events and volunteer activities

\+ Advertisements?

http://www.companynewsletters.com/storyideasemployeenews.htm

FIGURE 11.2: Sample story ideas for a newsletter prepared for INTO OSU, an international student program at OSU

WHAT: Content

The information included in a particular issue of a newsletter depends on the purpose of communicating with this particular set of readers, at this time. What do these readers want or need to know? Usually, an organization has more information to share than it has space or than readers will pay attention to, especially in these busy times of information overload and short attention span. Choices must be made about what goes in each issue, and what information could be provided later or in a different way.

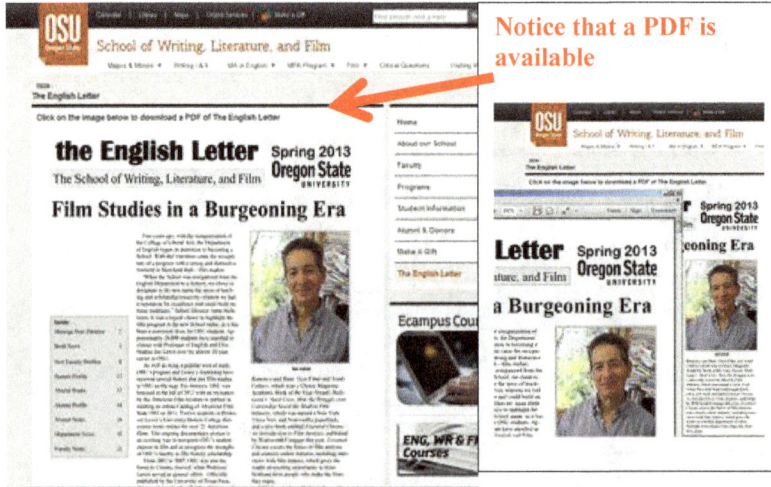

FIGURE 11.3: The English Letter at Oregon State University

WHEN: Context

Typically newsletters are issued on a regular basis, whether once a year, once a season, once a month, or once a week. With the schedule in mind, the newsletter editor can apportion the upcoming news and events to various issues.

At OSU, the School of Writing, Literature, and Film puts out an annual newsletter called **The English Letter,** sharing news of faculty and undergraduate and graduate students, including alumni/ae and any achievements over the past year.   It comes out in print and also via PDF on the web page. http://oregonstate.edu/cla/wlf/english-letter   See below.

By contrast, OSU's College of Forestry publishes a weekly newsletter for undergraduate students, also with a downloadable PDF, shown below. http://studentservices.forestry.oregonstate.edu/fernhopper-newsletter.   Naturally a weekly newsletter will have different information than an annual one.

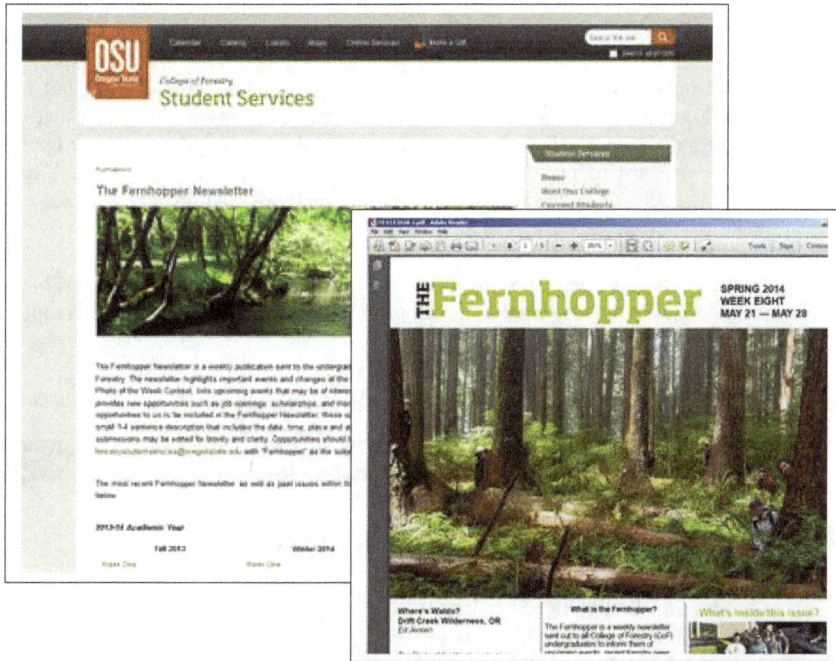

FIGURE 11.4: The Fernhopper at Oregon State

Some organizations might also create a special issue on a theme of particular interest. As we will see below, one WR 214 class at OSU created an internationally themed issue for **The Fernhopper.**

WHERE: Delivery Method

As we have just seen, newsletters today come out not only in print but also digitally, in order to best reach all their readers.   If an organization's readers do not primarily use email or the internet, then hard copy might be a better choice, despite the cost of printing and postage. However, today, many readers have online access, so organizations can use other methods. Ultimately the goal is to make the newsletter easy to find and read.

A document designed in a word processing program can be made available in print or PDF relatively easily. A webpage requires other software and computer programming skills.

HOW: Format, Visual Design, and Writing

Assuming the project involves a traditional print format, then decisions must be made about the format, visual design, and writing. To create your own design, review **Chapter 6: Designing Successful Documents, Visuals, and Websites** for essential document design and layout ideas.   In addition, sample newsletter templates are widely available for Microsoft Office and Microsoft Publisher, in Figures 11.5 a & b.

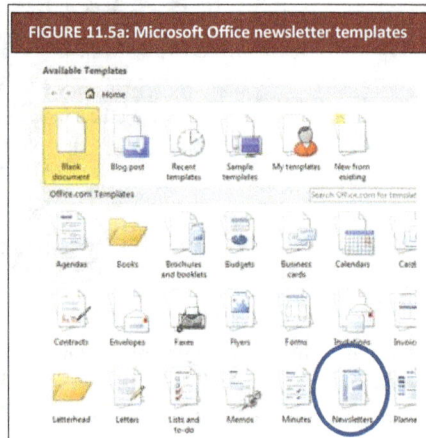

FIGURE 11.5a: Microsoft Office newsletter templates

Be sure to use a design that matches the graphic designs of other organizational documents, with the same colors, font styles, logos, images, etc. Check that the color contrast is accessible for readers with any visual disability and works well in print and online formats.

The newsletter should also align well in tone and content. Slogans and sayings need to match the organization's image, vision, and mission to maintain congruence and stay in character.

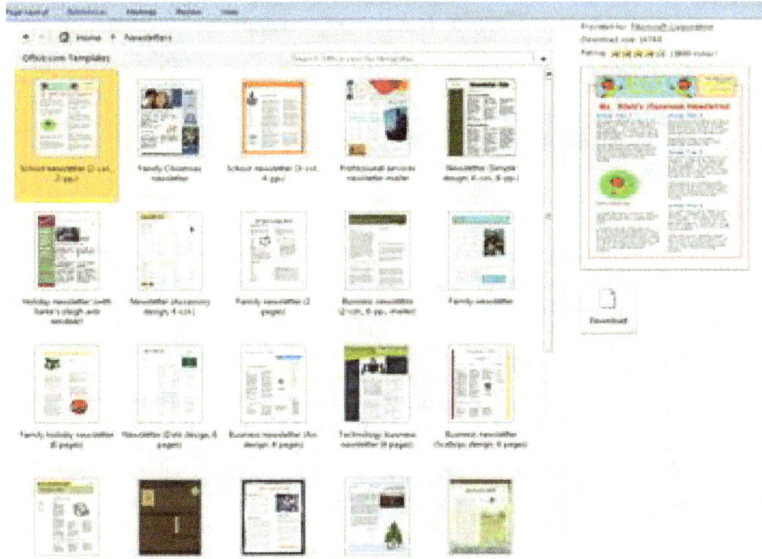

FIGURE 11.5b: Microsoft Office newsletter templates

CASE STUDY

Now that we have looked at some general concepts for newsletters, let's get started with this Case Study analysis. Following your instructor's directions, individually or in small groups, locate and share (in print or online) sample newsletters to analyze. For online classes, you can post links in your discussion forum and then analyze and reply.

Your analysis should answer the following questions about the samples you brought, and you should be ready to present your findings to the class in some way.

Sample Newsletter Analysis

BASICS
- Organization providing the newsletter
- Target audience of readers being addressed
- Demographics
  - Use research to be specific about demographics, since that information is essential for an effective document. Demographics include general age, likely gender, education level, socio-economic level, geographic region (including rural / urban), even possibly political leanings.

CONTENT & WRITING STYLE:
- What is the issue? Is there a theme? If yes, what is the theme?
- How many articles? What kinds? How many of each kind?
- What is the content? Informative? Educational? Entertaining?
- What writing style is used? Formal? Friendly? Humorous?
- How does it build goodwill for the organization?

VISUALS:
- How many pictures and/or graphics? Color or black and white?
- Graphs, charts or tables? Organizational logos? Cartoons?

PAGE DESIGN
- Font(s) and sizes? Color schemes?
  - Amount of white space? Use of principles of proximity, alignment,   contrast, and repetition?

ETHICS
- Are people and groups represented fairly?
- Is the document accessible to anyone with any disability in terms of font size and color contrast?
- Is the document provided in any language other than English?

EFFECTIVENESS
Based on these categories, analyze the newsletter for its overall effectiveness for its target audience and message.
- What is done well?
- Where could they improve?

FIGURE 11.6: Sample Newsletter Analysis

PROPOSING A NEWSLETTER

If an organization does not have a newsletter, you might propose one. Typically, you would write a proposal to present to your supervisor. A formal proposal document which will accomplish several major goals:

Research:
To create a proposal, you must start with research. Here is some of what you need to know to write a persuasive proposal:
- the organization's history and values
- its projects
- its organization style
- its message or purpose (mission statement)
- its style of communication
- the organization's audience for this newsletter

Analysis:
Next, apply critical thinking to the research to decide what contents to propose and how the newsletter will benefit the readers and create good will for the organization.

Persuasion:
To be persuasive, your proposal should be professionally formatted and show that you understand the organization.

In addition to explaining what you will create, you should probably also include a projected timeline so that the organization will know how long each step will take.

A budget might also be needed. Even if you are volunteering your time, it's good to factor in the hours that will be spent on the research, writing, revising, and formatting. The cost of labor is often the most expensive part of any project. When people are working on a newsletter, they are not doing other jobs.

Your budget should also estimate costs for paper, printing, any specialized editing software, and any other supplies. Even if the newsletter will be delivered digitally, it is often necessary to print sample pages for review.

The proposal document should also include information on the specifics, such as what articles will be included, who will write them, and what format is suggested. Check **Chapter 8** for information on proposals, and see sample Figure 11.8 below. Of course the writing should be clear, correct, and concise.

Sometimes you might create a PowerPoint presentation (see Fig 11.7 below) as part of your "pitch" to have the project approved. You may need to persuade the organization as to how this newsletter will benefit them. Check **Chapter 10** for information on successful, persuasive presentations. Be ready to tell the audience – whether the actual organization leaders, or your class and instructor – how this newsletter or special issue will benefit them and add goodwill.

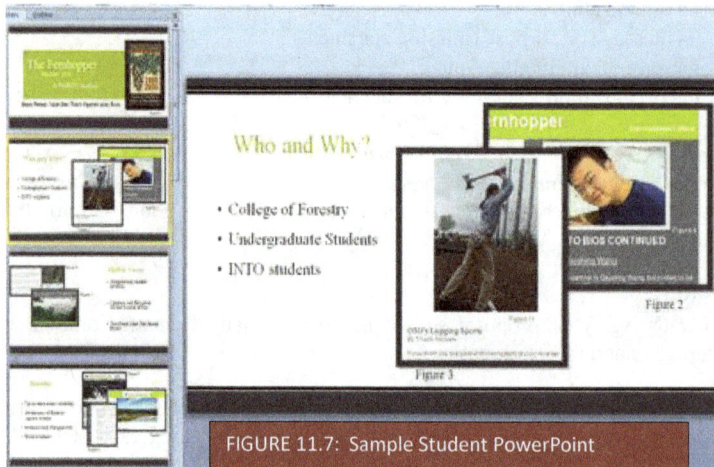

FIGURE 11.7: Sample Student PowerPoint

For a proposal memo, you would use the standard memo format to answer all the questions an organization might have. You might even compare the proposed newsletter to others put out by peer or rival organizations to demonstrate your knowledge of the field.

Planning this memo will help you (and your group, if you are working in teams) decide on effective processes, schedules, and technological compatibility.

October 20, 2014

TO: Mary Jones, Director, Happy Student Organization
FROM: Student Support Team
SUBJECT: Proposed "Year in Review" Issue of the *HSO News*

Because the quarterly *HSO News* keeps us all informed and connected, our Student Support Team proposes a special "Year in Review" issue for January, to showcase all our members' achievements and look ahead to special events in the coming year. Students are happier when their hard work is recognized, and issuing a special "Year in Review" will come at just the right time to start the new year. This special issue can also be used to recruit new members.

Please review the proposal below. We hope you will approve our project and lend your encouragement.

PROJECT
We propose to create a six page, two-sided, four-color special issue of the *HSO News*, including three long feature articles, several shorter articles, a calendar of seasonal events, and photos of our award-winning students. We hope you would provide a "Letter from the Director" to add a personal touch. We will use the HSO color scheme and logo, just as in the regular issues of the *HSO News*.

FORMAT
We will create the document as a collaborative team project in Google Drive and convert it to a PDF for easy emailing and attaching on the HSO Website.

TIMELINE
We plan to meet twice a week with our self-delegated team roles so that the first draft can be delivered for your approval by November 15, and the final draft will be ready by December 10. If you would like to see a more detailed timeline, please ask.

BUDGET
Because we will create this newsletter in Google Drive, we will only need to print drafts occasionally. However, these will be in color. Also, we need to download one student version of Microsoft Office Suite, available with our student ID for $10. And although we are donating our time, we want to be aware of the true cost of such a project, so we have factored in our hours at $10/hour. You can then use our donated project for an "in kind" component in the larger budget. Below is our brief estimated budget.

Item	Quantity	Unit cost	Subtotal
Color printing	36 pages	0.50	18.00
Microsoft Office Suite	1 student download	10.00	10.00
Student work hours	4 students @ 20=80	10.00	800.00
	TOTAL		828.00

REQUEST APPROVAL
We hope this project can be approved. Please let us know if there are other details you need.

FIGURE 11.8: Sample Newsletter Memo Style Proposal

Collaboration

Sometimes you might write a newsletter by yourself, but more often you will work in groups which share a common interest. As you saw in **Chapter 2: The Writing Process and collaboration at Work**, not only is collaboration common in the workplace, but also it is effective. Use the guidelines from that chapter for tips on how to communicate, set mini deadlines and goals, and resolve conflicts. Your instructor may also ask you to evaluate your team members at the end for their contributions. **Chapter 8** has information on employee performance reports which you could adapt for this.

Once you have the approval to start your newsletter, have some planning sessions where your group decides on the template and theme. You will need to divide the work fairly among group members. See Figure 11.9 below for a sample way to allocate the writing, the contents and the formatting.

Your group will need to meet regularly to keep in touch. If you are working online, then you could try Google hangouts for a synchronous work session. If your schedules do not permit synchronous meetings, you could use a wiki or an online course site for an asynchronous version of chat. Collaborating in an online format such as wikis or Google Drive helps ensure that everyone is always working on the newest version and there is no confusion over fonts and styles. Saving your drafts with multiple backups will avoid any frustration if a computer crashes.

OSU students have access to RemoteApps to use OSU software and OSU cloud storage. https://remoteapps.oregonstate.edu/RDWeb/Pages/en-US/login.aspx

Making an agenda for each meeting and keeping minutes can be extremely helpful to document your progress and keep on track. Your instructor may assign these documents during the term. See **Chapter 2** for tips on holding effective meetings.

FIGURE 11.9: Sample Division of Newsletter Jobs					
Group Members	Feature Articles	Short Articles	Short Fillers	Formatting	Other Roles
Joseph	1	2	2	Table of contents	Editor
Maria	2	1	1	Citations	Reporter
Sarah	2	2	0	Photos	Reporter
Travis	1	3	2	Masthead	Proofreader

Student Sample Newsletter

In Fall 2013, a group of students had great success with their Fernhopper newsletter, creating a custom version of the weekly student newsletter from OSU's College of Forestry. After a thorough analysis of the Fernhopper website and Week 8 PDF materials seen in Fig. 11.4, they effectively adapted it to make their own special project for an international issue, drawing on the same design and keeping the student-centered focus.

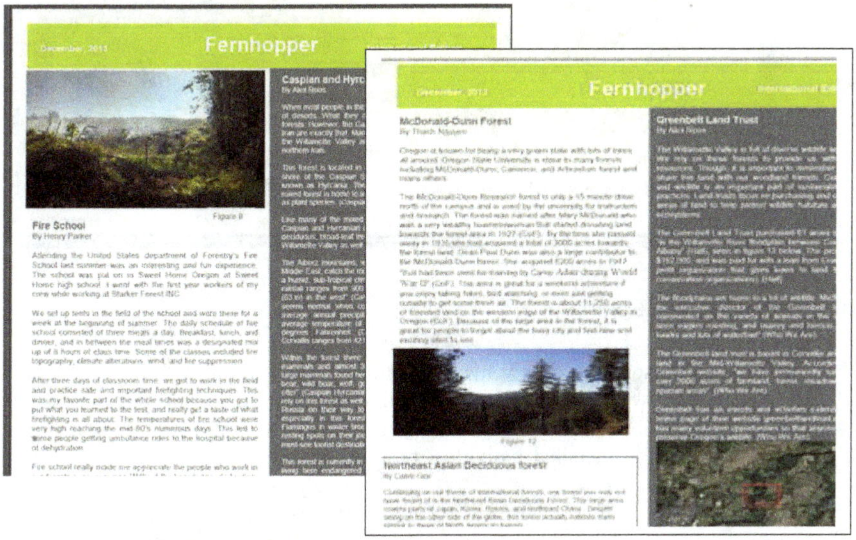

FIGURE 11.10: Student Fernhopper Newsletter

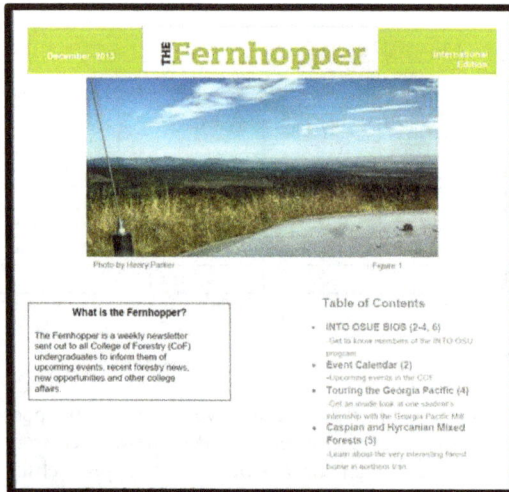

Each team member wrote several feature and filler articles for their forestry classmates, and they added notices about upcoming events of interest to Forestry Majors.

FIGURE 11.11: The Fernhopper Team's Original Newsletter and Presentation

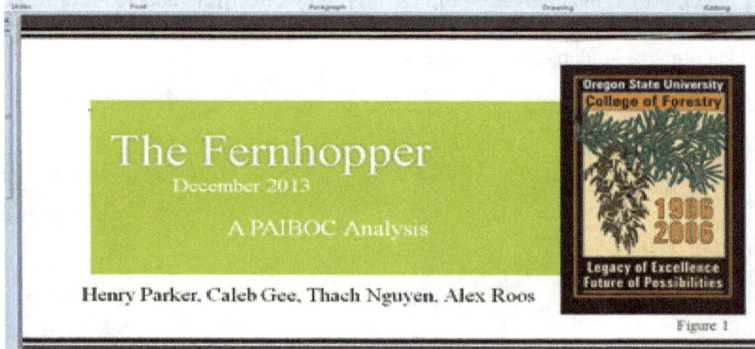

Progress Reports

Your supervisor or instructor may want to know how your project is coming and whether you will meet the deadline. Some managers just want to hear that the project is "fine," while others want a full report.   Here is a sample assignment for a thoroughly detailed individual progress report.   See other progress report samples in **Chapter 8.**

Fall 2014	FIGURE 11.10: Sample Assignment for an Individual Progress Report

To: WR 214 Interns
RE: **Newsletter Individual Progress Report**
DUE: Monday November 24

PURPOSE:
To practice a typical workplace document that brings a supervisor up to date on a project. The goal is to be thorough, with specific details, yet concise. Think about benefits to you and to me, possible objections, and context.

FORMAT
- Standard memo format
- Date/To me/From you/Subject Newsletter Project Individual Progress Report
- 12 pt. Times Roman, single space (0 pt. before and after)
- Small paragraphs and bullet lists are helpful
- Sub-headers
- Page number header or footer (if header, then not showing on page 1)

CONTENT
- Introduction paragraph explains which team you are on and your general contribution
- Separate body paragraphs explain:
- Progress on your research to date – interviews and/or online research to get needed information
- Progress on your OSU student profile article and what you still need to do with it
- Progress on your two shorter articles and what you still need to do with them
- Your part of the project dealing with any other filler articles
- Your part of the project dealing with templates – masthead, table of contents, works cited, etc. – what you are responsible for, how far along you are.
- Your part of the project dealing images – which ones are you responsible for, what have you found so far, etc.
- Your part of the PowerPoint document – what content and formatting you are responsible for.
- Your role in the Oral Presentation – what aspects of the project will you discuss in your portion of the time.
- Anything else you are doing with the project
- Your successes so far – what you are proud of accomplishing so far
- Your concerns at the moment – what questions you might have
- Your estimate with positive emphasis of your successful completion on time (how many hours have you invested to date?)
- Conclusion paragraph sums up your overall progress on this project

Final Words of advice about newsletters

Newsletters provide an organization with a great way to stay in touch with important audience groups – employees, clients, donors, or the public – and build good will. As you enter the workplace, you can rely on a regular update from the organizations you work with to keep people in touch.

1. Get a good start on the project and meet mini deadlines
2. Meet often with your group and share information
3. Do your share of the project on time
4. Use multiple drafts to adjust the content, format, and writing to fit the organization
5. Use workshop and peer review for effective revision.
6. Polish the final product to make it professional work you can be proud of

---

✔ **Revision Checklist**

⌘ Represented the organization's mission and values
⌘ Targeted a specific audience related to that mission
⌘ Did sufficient research to provide news and updates that advance the organization's credibility and built good will
⌘ Wrote interesting articles to meet the readers' needs
⌘ Used engaging and relevant images
⌘ Portrayed all people ethically and fairly
⌘ Used inclusive language
⌘ Aligned document colors and designs for readers with visual disabilities
⌘ Made sure the document was easily accessible visually and electronically
⌘ Used writing that is clear, correct, and compatible with the organization's style of communication
⌘ Created a positive image of the organization

Appendix:
A Writer's Brief Guide to Paragraphs, Sentences, and Words

To write successfully, you must know how to create effective paragraphs, write and punctuate clear sentences, and use words correctly. This guide succinctly explains some of the basic elements of clear and accurate writing.

Paragraphs

Writing a Well-Developed Paragraph

A paragraph is the basic building block for any piece of writing. It is (1) a group of related sentences (2) arranged in a logical order (3) supplying readers with detailed, appropriate information (4) on a single important topic.

A paragraph expresses one central idea, with each sentence contributing to the overall meaning of that idea. The paragraph does that by means of a *topic sentence*, which states the central idea, and *supporting information*, which explains the topic sentence.

Supply a Topic Sentence

The topic sentence is the most important sentence in your paragraph. Carefully worded and restricted, it helps you generate and control your information. An effective topic sentence also helps readers grasp your main idea quickly. As you draft your paragraphs, pay close attention to the following three guidelines.

1. **Make sure you provide a topic sentence.** In their rush to supply readers with facts, some writers forget or neglect to include a topic sentence. The following paragraph, with no topic sentence, shows how fragmented such writing can be.

No topic sentence: Sensors found on each machine detect wind speed and direction and other important details such as ice loading and potential metal fatigue. The information is fed into a microprocessor in the nacelle (or engine housing). The microprocessor then automatically keeps the blades turned into the wind, starts and stops the machine, and changes the pitch of the tips of

Chapter opening image: © dimitris_k/ShutterStock.com

the blades to increase power under varying wind conditions. Should any part of the wind turbine suffer damage or malfunction, the microprocessor will immediately shut the machine down.

Only when a suitable topic sentence is added—"The MOD-2 wind turbine features the latest technology"—can readers understand what the technical details have in common.

2. Put your topic sentence first. Place your topic sentence at the beginning of your paragraph because the first sentence occupies a commanding position. Burying the key idea in the middle or near the end of the paragraph makes it harder for readers to comprehend your purpose or act on your information.

3. Be sure your topic sentence is focused and discusses only one central idea. A broad or unrestricted topic sentence leads to a shaky, incomplete paragraph for two reasons:

- The paragraph will not contain enough information to support the topic sentence.
- A broad topic sentence will not summarize or forecast specific information in the paragraph.

The following example of a carefully constructed paragraph contains a clear topic sentence in an appropriate position (*italicized*) and adequate supporting details.

Fat is an important part of everyone's diet. It is nutritionally present in the basic food groups we eat—meat and poultry, dairy products, and oils—to aid growth or development. The fats and fatty acids present in those foods ensure proper metabolism, thus helping to turn what we eat into the energy we need. Those same fats and fatty acids also act as carriers for important vitamins like A, D, E, and K. Another important role of fat is that it keeps us from feeling hungry by delaying digestion. Fat also enhances the flavor of the food we eat, making it more enjoyable.

Three Characteristics of an Effective Paragraph

Effective paragraphs have *unity*, *coherence*, and *completeness*.

Unity

A unified paragraph sticks to one topic without wandering. Every sentence and every detail supports, explains, or proves the central idea. A unified paragraph includes only relevant information and excludes unnecessary or irrelevant comments.

Coherence

In a coherent paragraph, all sentences flow smoothly and logically to and from each other like the links of a chain. Use these three techniques to achieve coherence.

1. Use transitional words and phrases. Some useful transitional, or connective, words and phrases, grouped according to the relationships they express, are listed in Table A.1.

TABLE A.1   Transitional, or Connective, Words and Phrases

Addition	additionally	besides	moreover
	again	first, second, third	next
	along with	furthermore	together with
	also	in addition	too
	and	many	what's more
	as well as	numerous	
Cause/effect	accordingly	consequently	on account of
	and so	due to	since
	as a result	hence	therefore
	because of	if	thus
Comparison/ contrast	but	in contrast	on the other hand
	conversely	in the same way	similarly
	equally	likewise	still
	however	on the contrary	yet
Conclusion	all in all	in brief	on the whole
	altogether	in conclusion	to conclude
	as we saw	in short	to put into perspective
	at last	in summary	to summarize
	finally	last	to wrap up
Condition	although	granted that	provided that
	depending	if	to be sure
	even though	of course	unless
Emphasis	above all	for emphasis	of course
	after all	indeed	surely
	again	in fact	to repeat
	as a matter of fact	in other words	to stress
	as I said	obviously	unquestionably
Illustration	for example	in other words	that is
	for instance	in particular	to demonstrate
	in effect	specifically	to illustrate
Place	across from	below	over
	adjacent to	beyond	there
	alongside of	here	under
	at this point	in front of	where
	behind	next to	wherever
Time	afterward	formerly	previously
	at length	hereafter	soon
	at the same time	later	simultaneously
	at times	meanwhile	subsequently
	beforehand	next	then
	currently	now	until
	during	once	when
	earlier	presently	while

Paragraph with connective words: Advertising a product on the radio has many advantages over using television. *For one thing*, radio rates are much cheaper. *For example*, a one-time 60-second spot on local television can cost $5,000. *For that money*, advertisers can purchase nine 30-second spots on the radio. *Equally attractive* are the low production costs for radio advertising. *In contrast*, television advertising often includes extra costs for actors and voice-overs. *Another* advantage radio offers advertisers is immediate scheduling. *Often* the ad appears during the same week a contract is signed. *On the other hand*, television stations are *frequently* booked up months in advance, so it may be a long time *before* an ad appears. *Furthermore*, radio gives advertisers a greater opportunity to reach potential buyers. *After all*, radio follows listeners everywhere—in their homes, at work, and in their cars. *Although* television is very popular, it cannot do that.

2. Use pronouns and demonstrative adjectives. Words like *he*, *she*, *him*, *her*, *they*, *their*, and so on, contribute to paragraph coherence and improve the flow of sentences.

Paragraph with pronouns: Traffic studies are an important tool for store owners looking for a new location. *These* studies are relatively inexpensive and highly accurate. *They* can tell owners how much traffic passes by a particular location at a particular time and why. Moreover, *they* can help owners determine what particular characteristics the individuals have in common. Because of *their* helpfulness, *these* studies can save owners time and money and possibly prevent financial ruin.

3. Use parallel (coordinated) grammatical structures. Parallelism means using the same form of the word, phrase, clause, or sentence to express related concepts.

Orientation sessions accomplish four useful goals for trainees. First, they introduce trainees to key personnel in accounting, IT, maintenance, and security. Second, they give trainees experience logging into the database system, selecting appropriate menus, editing core documents, and getting off the system. Third, they explain to trainees the company policies affecting the way supplies are ordered, used, and stored. Fourth, they help trainees understand their ethical responsibilities in such sensitive areas as computer security and use.

Parallelism is at work on a number of levels in the preceding paragraph, among them these:

- The four sentences about the four goals start in the same way grammatically (". . . they introduce/give/explain/help . . .") to help readers categorize the information.
- Within individual sentences, the repetition of *present participles* (logg*ing*, select*ing*, edit*ing*, gett*ing*) and of *past participles* (order*ed*, us*ed*, stor*ed*) helps the writer coordinate information.
- Transitional words—*first*, *second*, *third*, *fourth*—provide a clear-cut sequence.

Completeness

A complete paragraph provides readers with sufficient information to clarify, analyze, support, defend, or prove the central idea expressed in the topic sentence. The reader feels satisfied that the writer has given necessary details.

Skimpy paragraph: Farmers are turning their crops and farm wastes into cost-effective fuels. Much that is grown on the farm is being converted to energy. This energy can have many uses and save farmers a lot of money in operating expenses.

Fully developed paragraph: Farm crops and wastes are being turned into fuels to save farmers operating costs. Alcohol can be distilled from grain, sugar beets, and corn. Converted to ethanol (90 percent gasoline, 10 percent ethanol), this fuel runs such farm equipment as irrigation pumps, feed grinders, and tractors. Similarly, through a biomass digestion system, farmers can produce methane from animal or crop wastes as a natural gas for heating and cooking. Finally, cellulose pellets, derived from plant materials, become solid fuel that can save farmers money in heating barns.

Sentences

Constructing and Punctuating Sentences

The way you construct and punctuate your sentences can determine whether you succeed or fail in the world of work. Your sentences reveal a lot about you. They tell readers how clearly you can convey a message. And any message is only as effective and as thoughtful as the sentences of which it is made.

What Makes a Sentence

A sentence is a complete thought, expressed by a subject and a verb that can make sense standing alone.

subject	verb	
Websites	sell	products.

The Difference Between Phrases and Clauses

The first step toward success in writing sentences is learning to recognize the difference between phrases and clauses. A *phrase* is a group of words that does not contain a subject and a verb; phrases cannot make sense standing alone. Phrases cannot be sentences.

in the park	No subject:	Who is in the park?
	No verb:	What was done in the park?
for every patient in intensive care	No subject:	Who did something for every patient?
	No verb:	What was done for every patient?

A *clause* does contain a subject and a verb, but *not every clause is a sentence.* Only *independent* (or *main*) *clauses* can stand alone as sentences. Here is an example of an independent clause that is a complete sentence.

subject	verb	object
The president	closed	the college.

A *dependent* (or *subordinate*) *clause* also contains a subject and a verb, but it does not make complete sense and cannot stand alone. Why? A dependent clause contains a subordinating conjunction—*after, although, as, because, before, even though, if, since, unless, when, where, whereas, while*—at the beginning of the clause. Such conjunctions subordinate the clause in which they appear and make the clause dependent for meaning and completion on an independent clause.

After
Before
Because   } the president closed the college
Even though
Unless

"After the president closed the college" is not a complete thought but a dependent clause that leaves us in suspense. It needs to be completed with an independent clause telling us what happened "after."

dependent clause (not a sentence)	subject	verb	phrase
After the president closed the college,	we	played	in the snow.

Avoiding Sentence Fragments

An incomplete sentence is called a *fragment*. Fragments can be phrases or dependent clauses. They either lack a verb or a subject or have broken away from an independent clause. A fragment is isolated: It needs an overhaul to supply missing parts to turn it into an independent clause or to glue it back to an independent clause to have it make sense.

To avoid writing fragments, follow these rules. *Note that incorrect examples are preceded by a minus sign, correct revisions by a plus sign.*

1. Do not use a subordinate clause as a sentence. Even though it contains a subject and a verb, a subordinate clause standing alone is still a fragment. To avoid this kind of sentence fragment, simply join the two clauses (the independent clause and the dependent clause containing a subordinating conjunction) with a comma—*not* a period or semicolon.

- Unless we agreed to the plan. (What would happen?)
- Unless we agreed to the plan; the project manager would discontinue the operation. (A semicolon cannot set off the subordinate clause.)
+ Unless we agreed to the plan, the project manager would discontinue the operation.
- Because safety precautions were taken. (What happened?)
+ Because safety precautions were taken, ten construction workers escaped injury.

Sometimes subordinate clauses appear at the end of a sentence. They may be introduced by a subordinate conjunction, an adverb, or a relative pronoun (*that, which, who*). Do not separate these clauses from the preceding independent clause with a period, thus turning them into fragments.

- An all-volunteer fire department posed some problems. Especially for residents in the western part of town.

+ An all-volunteer fire department posed some problems, especially for residents in the western part of town. (The word *especially* qualifies *posed*, referred to in the independent clause.)

2. Every sentence must have a subject telling the reader who does the action.

– Being extra careful not to spill the solution. (Who?)
+ The technician was being extra careful not to spill the solution.

3. Every sentence must have a complete verb. Watch especially for verbs ending in *-ing*. They need another verb (some form of *to be*) to make them complete.

– The machine running in the computer department. (Did what?)

You can change that fragment into a sentence by supplying the correct form of the verb.

+ The machine *is running* in the computer department.
+ The machine *runs* in the computer department.

Or you can revise the entire sentence, adding a new thought.

+ The machine running in the computer department processes all new accounts.

4. Do not detach prepositional phrases from independent clauses. Prepositional phrases (beginning with *at, by, for, from, in, to, with,* and so forth) are not complete thoughts and cannot stand alone. Correct the error by leaving the phrases attached to the sentence to which they belong.

– By three o'clock the next day. (What was to happen?)
+ The supervisor wanted our reports by three o'clock the next day.

Correcting Comma Splices

Fragments occur when you use only bits and pieces of complete sentences. Another common error that some writers commit involves just the reverse kind of action. They weakly and wrongly join two complete sentences (independent clauses) with a comma as if those two sentences were really only one sentence. Such an error is called a *comma splice*. Here is an example:

– Gasoline prices have risen by 15 percent in the last month, we will drive the car less often.

Two independent clauses (complete sentences) exist:

+ Gasoline prices have risen by 15 percent in the last month.
+ We will drive the car less often.

A comma alone lacks the power to separate independent clauses.

As the preceding example shows, many pronouns—*I, he, she, it, we, they*—are used as the subjects of independent clauses. A comma splice will result if you place a comma instead of a semicolon or period between two independent clauses where the second clause opens with a pronoun.

– Maria approved the plan, she liked its cost-effective approach.
+ Maria approved the plan; she liked its cost-effective approach.

However, relative pronouns (*who*, *whom*, *which*, *that*) are preceded by a comma, not a period or a semicolon, when they introduce subordinate clauses.

- − She approved the plan. Which had a cost-effective approach.
- + She approved the plan, which had a cost-effective approach.

Four Ways to Correct Comma Splices

1. Remove the comma separating two independent clauses and replace it with a period. Then capitalize the first letter of the first word of the new sentence.

- + Gasoline prices have risen by 15 percent in the last month. We will drive the car less often.

2. Insert a coordinating conjunction (*and*, *but*, *or*, *nor*, *so*, *for*, *yet*) after the comma. Together, the conjunction and the comma properly separate the two independent clauses.

- + Gasoline prices have risen by 15 percent in the last month, so we will drive the car less often.

3. Rewrite the sentence. If it makes sense to do so, turn the first independent clause into a dependent clause by adding a subordinate conjunction; then insert a comma and add the second independent clause.

- + Because gasoline prices have risen by 10 percent in the last month, we will drive the car less often.

4. Delete the comma and insert a semicolon.

- + Gasoline prices have risen by 15 percent in the last month; we will drive the car less often.

Of the four ways to correct the comma splice, sentences 3 and 4 are equally suitable, but sentence 3 reads more smoothly and so is the better choice.

The semicolon is an effective and forceful punctuation mark when two independent clauses are closely related—that is, when they announce contrasting or parallel views, as the two following examples reveal:

- + The union favored the new legislation; the company opposed it. (contrasting views)
- + Night classes help the college and the community; students can take more credit hours to advance their careers. (parallel views)

How *Not* to Correct Comma Splices

Some writers mistakenly try to correct comma splices by inserting a conjunctive adverb (*also*, *consequently*, *furthermore*, *however*, *moreover*, *nevertheless*, *then*, *therefore*) after the comma.

- + Gasoline prices have risen by 15 percent in the last month, consequently we will drive the car less often.

Because the conjunctive adverb (*consequently*) is not as powerful as the coordinating conjunction (*and*, *but*, *for*), the error is not eliminated. If you use a conjunctive adverb—*consequently*, *however*, *nevertheless*—you still must insert a semicolon or a period before it, as the following examples show:

+ Gasoline prices have risen by 15 percent in the last month; consequently, we will drive the car less often.
+ Gasoline prices have risen by 15 percent in the last month. Consequently, we will drive the car less often.

Avoiding Run-on Sentences

A *run-on sentence* is the opposite of a sentence fragment. The fragment gives the reader too little information, the run-on too much. A run-on sentence forces readers to digest two or more grammatically complete sentences without the proper punctuation to separate them.

Run-on: The Internet has become a primary source of information and students and other researchers are right to call it a virtual library this library is not like the collections of hard-copy books and magazines that are carefully shelved, waiting for students to check and recheck them out too often a website disappears, is under construction, or changes considerably and without a backup file or a hard copy of the site, the researcher has no document to quote from and no exact citation to prove that he or she consulted an authentic source.

Revised: The Internet has become a primary source of information. Students and other researchers are right to call it a virtual library, although this library is not like the collections of hard-copy books and magazines that are carefully shelved, waiting for students to check and recheck them out. But too often a website disappears, is under construction, or changes considerably. Without a backup file or a hard copy of the site, the researcher has no document to quote from and no exact citation to prove that he or she consulted an authentic source.

As the revision shows, you can repair a run-on sentence (1) by dividing it into separate, correctly punctuated sentences and (2) by adding coordinating conjunctions (*and*, *but*, *yet*, *for*, *so*, *or*, *nor*) between clauses.

Making Subjects and Verbs Agree in Your Sentences

A subject and a verb must agree in number. A singular subject takes a singular verb, whereas a plural subject requires a plural verb.

Singular Subject	Plural Subject
the engineer calculates	engineers calculate
a report analyzes	reports analyze
a policy changes	policies change

You can avoid subject-verb agreement errors by following eight simple rules.

1. Disregard any words that come between the subject and its verb.

Faulty: The customer who ordered three parts want them shipped this afternoon.
Correct: The customer who ordered three parts wants them shipped this afternoon.

2. A compound subject takes a plural verb. (A compound subject has two parts connected by *and*.)

> Faulty: The engineering department and the safety committee prefers to develop new guidelines.
> Correct: The engineering department and the safety committee prefer to develop new guidelines.

3. When a compound subject contains *neither . . . nor* or *either . . . or*, the verb agrees with the subject closer to it.

> Faulty: Either the residents or the manager are going to file the complaint.
> Correct: Either the residents or the manager is going to file the complaint.
> Correct: Either the manager or the residents are going to file the complaint.

4. Use a singular verb after collective nouns when the group functions as a single unit. (Collective nouns are words like *committee, crew, department, group, organization, staff, team*.)

> Correct: The crew was available to repair the machine.
> Correct: The committee asks that all recommendations be submitted by Friday.

However, in this situation:

> Correct: The staff were unable to agree on the best model. (The staff acted as individuals, not a unit, so a plural verb is required.)

5. Use a singular verb with indefinite pronouns. (Indefinite pronouns are words such as *anybody, anyone, each, everyone, everything, no one, somebody, something*.)

> Each of the programmers has completed the seminar.
> Somebody usually volunteers for that duty.

Similarly, when *all*, *most*, *more*, or *part* is the subject, it requires a singular verb.

> Most of the money is allocated.
> Part of the equipment was salvageable.

6. Words like *scissors* and *pants* are plural when they are the true subject.

> Faulty: A pair of trousers were available in his size. (*Pair* is the true subject, and it is a singular noun.)
> Correct: The trousers were on sale.

7. Some foreign plurals always take a plural verb. Examples include *curricula, data, media, phenomena, strata, syllabi*.

> The data conclusively prove my point.
> The media are usually the first to point out a politician's weak points.

8. Use a singular verb with fractions.

> Three-fourths of her research proposal was finished.

Writing Sentences That Say What You Mean

Your sentences should say exactly what you mean, without double talk, misplaced humor, or nonsense. Sentences are composed of words and word groups that influence each other.

Writing Logical Sentences

Sentences should not contradict themselves or make outlandish claims. The following example contains an error in logic; note how easily the suggested revision solves the problem.

Illogical: Steel roll-away shutters make it possible for the sun to be shaded in the summer and to have it shine in the winter. (The sun is far too large to shade; the writer means that a room or a house could be shaded with the shutters.)

Revision: Steel roll-away shutters make it possible for owners to shade their living rooms in the summer and to admit sunshine during the winter.

Using Contextually Appropriate Words

Sentences should use the combination of words most appropriate for the subject.

Inappropriate: The members of the Nuclear Regulatory Commission saw fear radiated on the faces of the residents. (The word *radiated* is obviously ill advised in this context; use a neutral term.)

Revision: The members of the Nuclear Regulatory Commission saw fear reflected on the faces of the residents.

Writing Sentences with Well-Placed Modifiers

A *modifier* is a word, phrase, or clause that describes, limits, or qualifies the meaning of another word or word group. A modifier can consist of one word (a *blue* car), a prepositional phrase (the man *in the toll booth*), a relative clause (the woman *who won the marathon*), or an -*ing* or -*ed* phrase (*walking three miles a day*, the student was in good shape; *seated in the first row*, we saw everything on stage).

A *dangling modifier* is one that cannot logically modify any word in the sentence.

− When answering the question, his calculator fell off the table.

One way to correct the error is to insert the right subject after the -*ing* phrase.

+ When answering the question, he knocked his calculator off the table.

You can also turn the phrase into a subordinate clause.

+ When he answered the question, his calculator fell off the table.
+ His calculator fell off the table as he answered the question.

A *misplaced modifier* illogically modifies the wrong word or words in the sentence. The result is often comical.

− Hiding in the corner, growling and snarling, our guide spotted the frightened cub. (Is the guide growling and snarling in the corner?)
− All travel requests must be submitted by employees in red ink. (Are the employees covered in red ink?)

The problem with both of those examples is word order. The modifiers are misplaced because they are attached to the wrong words in the sentence. Correct the error by moving the modifier to where it belongs.

+ Hiding in the corner, growling and snarling, the frightened cub was spotted by our guide.
+ All travel requests by employees must be submitted in red ink.

Misplacing a relative clause (introduced by relative pronouns like *who, whom, that, which*) can also lead to problems with modification.

− The salesperson rang up the merchandise for the customer that the store had discounted. (The merchandise was discounted, not the customer.)
− The salesperson rang up the merchandise that the store had discounted for the customer. (The salesperson rang up the discount for the customer; the store did not discount the customer.)
+ The salesperson rang up for the customer the merchandise that the store had discounted.

Always place the relative clause immediately after the word it modifies.

Using Pronoun References Correctly

Sentences will be vague if they contain a faulty use of pronouns. When you use a pronoun whose *antecedent* (the person, place, or object the pronoun refers to) is unclear, you risk confusing your reader.

Unclear: After the plants are clean, we separate the stems from the roots and place them in the sun to dry. (Is it the stems or the roots that lie in the sun?)

Revision: After the plants are clean, we separate the stems from the roots and place the stems in the sun to dry.

Unclear: The park ranger was pleased to see the workers planting new trees and installing new benches. This will attract more tourists. (The trees or the benches or both?)

Revision: The park ranger was pleased to see the workers planting new trees and installing new benches, because additional trees and benches will attract more tourists.

Words

Spelling Words Correctly

Your written work will be judged in part on how well you spell. A misspelled word may seem like a small matter, but on an employment application, an email, an incident report, a letter, a short or long report, a Prezi presentation or a PowerPoint slide, it can make you look careless or, even worse, uneducated to a client or a supervisor. Readers will inevitably question your other skills if your spelling is incorrect.

The Benefits and Pitfalls of Spell-Checkers

Spell-checkers can be handy for flagging potential problem words. But beware! Spell-checkers recognize only those words that have been listed in them. A proper name or a new, infrequently used word may be flagged as an error even though the word is spelled correctly. Moreover, a spell-checker cannot differentiate between such homonyms as *too* and *two* or *there* and *their*. A spell-checker identifies only misspelled words, not misused words. In short, do not rely exclusively on a spell-checker to solve all your spelling and word-choice problems.

Consulting a Dictionary

Always have a dictionary handy. Two useful online dictionaries to consult are *Merriam-Webster OnLine* (**www.merriam-webster.com**) and *Dictionary.com* (**www.dictionary.com**).

Using Apostrophes Correctly

Apostrophes cause some writers special problems. Basically, apostrophes are used for three reasons: (1) contractions, (2) possessives, and (3) plurals of some abbreviations and letters used as nouns. The following guidelines will help you sort out these uses.

1. In a *contraction*, the apostrophe takes the place of the missing letter or letters: *I've = I have*; *doesn't = does not*; *he's = he is*; *it's = it is.* (*Its* is a possessive pronoun—the dog and *its* bone—not a contraction. There is no such form as *its'*.)

2. To form a *possessive*, follow these rules.

   a. If a singular or plural noun does not end in an -*s*, add *'s* to show possession.

Mary's locker	the woman's jacket
children's books	the women's jackets
the staff's dedication	the company's policy

   b. If a singular noun ends in -*s*, add *'s* to show possession.

the class's project	the boss's schedule

   c. If a plural noun ends in -*s*, add just the *'* to indicate possession.

employees' benefits	computers' speed
lawyers' fees	stores' prices

   d. If a proper name ends in -*s*, add *'s* to form the possessive.

Jones's account	Keats's poetry
Jill Williams's house	James's contract

   e. If it is a compound noun, add an *'* or *'s* to the end of the word.

my brother-in-law's business	Ms. Melek-Patel's order

   f. To indicate shared possession, add *'s* to just the final name.

Rao and Kline's website	Juan and Anne's major

   g. To indicate separate possession, add *'s* to each name.

Juan's and Tia's transcripts	Shakespeare's and Byron's poetry

3. For abbreviations with periods and for lowercase letters used as nouns, form the plural by adding *'s.*

his *p*'s and *q*'s   Q and A's   Ph.D.'s

To form the plural of numbers and capital letters used as nouns, including abbreviations without periods, just add *s*. To avoid misreading some capital letters, however, you may need to add an apostrophe.

during the 1980s   all perfect 10s
their SATs   several local YMCAs
the 3 R's   straight A's

Inserting Hyphens Properly

Use a hyphen (-, as opposed to a dash, —) for

- **compound words**
  four-part lecture   heavy-duty machine   long-term prospects

- **most words beginning with** *self*
  self-starting   self-defense   self-regulating   self-governing

- **fractions used as adjectives**
  at the three-quarter level   two-thirds majority

Using Ellipses

Sometimes a sentence or passage is particularly useful, but you may not want to quote it fully. You may want to delete some words that are not really necessary for your purpose. An omission is indicated by using an *ellipsis* (three spaced dots within the sentence to indicate where words have been omitted). Here is an example:

Full Quotation: "Diet and nutrition, which researchers have studied extensively, significantly affect oral health."

Quotation with Ellipsis: "Diet and nutrition . . . significantly affect oral health."

Using Numerals Versus Words

Write out numbers as words rather than numerals in these situations:

- **to begin a sentence**

Nineteen ninety-nine was the first year of our recruitment drive.

- **to indicate the first number when two numbers are used together**

The company needed eleven 9-foot slabs.

But use numerals, not words, in these situations:

- **with abbreviations, percentages, symbols, units of measurement, dates**

17 percent   11:30 a.m.   70 ml
December 3, 2012 $250.00   50 K

- **for page references**

pp. 56–59

- **for large numbers**

3,000,000   23,750   1,714

Use both numerals and words when you want to be as precise as possible in a contract or a proposal.

> We agreed to pay the vendor an extra twenty-five dollars ($25.00) per hour to finish the job by May 18.

Matching the Right Word with the Right Meaning

The words in the following list frequently are mistaken for one another. Some are true homonyms; others are just similar in spelling, pronunciation, or usage. The part of speech is given after each word. Make sure you use the right word in the right context.

accept (v) to receive, to acknowledge: *We accept your proposal.*
except (prep) excluding, but: *Everyone attended the meeting except Neelou.*

advice (n) a recommendation: *I should have taken Xi's advice.*
advise (v) to counsel: *Our lawyers advised us not to sign the contract.*

affect (v) to change, to influence: *Does the detour on Route 22 affect your travel plans?*
effect (n) a result: *What was the effect of the new procedure?*
effect (v) to bring about: *We will try to effect a change in company policy.*

allot (v) to distribute, to assign: *The manager allotted the writing team two weeks to complete the report.*
a lot (n) a quantity: *They bought a lot of supplies for the trip.*

all ready (adj) two-word phrase *all + ready*; to be finished; to be prepared: *We are all ready for the inspector's visit.*
already (adv) previously, before a given time: *Our webmaster had already updated the site.*

altar (n) central place of worship: *The bride met the groom at the altar.*
alter (v) to change, to amend: *The tailor altered the trousers.*

ascent (n) upward movement: *We watched the space shuttle's ascent.*
assent (n) agreement: *She won the teacher's assent.*
assent (v) to agree: *The committee asked the company to assent to the new terms.*

attain (v) to achieve, to reach: *We attained our sales goal this month.*
obtain (v) to get, to receive: *You can obtain a job application on their website.*

cite (v) to document: *Please cite several examples to support your claim.*
site (n) place, location: *They want to build a parking lot on the site of the old theater.*
sight (n) vision: *His sight improved with bifocals.*

coarse (adj) rough: *The sandpaper felt coarse.*
course (n) subject of study: *Sharonda took a course in calculus this fall.*

complement (v) to add to, enhance: *Her graphs and charts complemented my proposal.*
compliment (v) to praise: *The customer complimented us on our courteous staff.*

continually (adv) frequently and regularly: *This answering machine continually disconnects the caller in the middle of the message.*
continuously (adv) constantly; without stopping: *The air-conditioning is on continuously during the summer.*

council (n) government body: *The council voted to increase salaries for all city employees.*
counsel (n) advice: *She gave the trainee pertinent counsel.*

defer (v) To put off until later: *His student loan was deferred while he finished his degree.*
differ (v) to disagree, to be different: *The committee differed among its members about the bond issue.*

discreet (adj) showing respect, being tactful: *The manager was discreet in answering the complaint letter.*
discrete (adj) separate, distinct: *Put those figures into discrete categories for processing.*

dual (adj) double: *That report serves a dual purpose.*
duel (n) a fight, a battle: *The argument almost turned into a duel.*

eminent (adj) prominent, highly esteemed: *Dr. Felicia Rollins is the most eminent neurologist in our community.*
imminent (adj) about to happen: *A hostile takeover of that company is imminent.*

envelop (v) to surround: *The major feared that fog would envelop the city.*
envelope (n) container for a letter: *Always send letters in an envelope with our company logo on it.*

fair (n) convention, exhibition: *The technology fair featured a home theater with five satellite speakers.*
fair (adj) honest: *Their price was fair.*
fare (n) cost for a trip: *She was able to get a discount on a round-trip fare.*
fare (n) food: *They ate East Asian fare.*

foreword (n) preface to a book: *The foreword outlined the author's goals in her study of new global markets.*

forward (adv) toward a time or place; in advance: *We moved the time of the visit forward on the calendar so we could meet the overseas manager.*
forward (v) to send ahead: *We forwarded her email to her new server.*

imply (v) to suggest: *The supervisor implied that the mechanics had taken too long for their lunch break.*
infer (v) to draw a conclusion: *We can infer from these sales figures that the new advertising campaign is working.*

it's (pronoun + verb) contraction of *it* and *is*: *Do you think it's too early to tell?*
its (adj) possessive form of *it*: *That old printer is on its last legs.*

knew (v) (past tense of *know*): *She knew the new regulations.*
new (adj) never used before: *The subwoofer was new.*

lay/laid/laid (v) to put down: *Lay aside that project for now. He laid aside the project. He had already laid aside the project twice before.*
lie/lay/lain (v) to recline: *I think I'll lie down for a while. He lay there for only a few minutes before the firefighter rescued him. She has lain out in the sun too often.*

lean (adj) thin, skinny: *She asked for a lean slice of roast.*
lean (v) to rest against: *The shovel leaned against the fence.*
lien (n) a claim against: *There was a lien against his property for back taxes.*

lose (v) to misplace, to fail to win: *Be careful not to lose my calculator. I hope I don't lose my seat on the planning board.*
loose (adj) not tight: *The printer ribbon was too loose.*

miner (n) individual who works in a mine: *His uncle was a miner in West Virginia.*
minor (n) someone under legal age: *The law forbids the sale of tobacco to minors.*

overdo (v) to exceed, to do in excess: *The coach did not want her players to overdo their practice time.*
overdue (adj) past due: *The quarterly bill was overdue by three weeks.*

pare (v) to cut back: *Sandoval pared the skin from the apple.*
pair (n) a couple: *They offered a pair of resolutions.*
pear (n) a fruit: *Alphonso ate a pear with lunch.*

passed (v) went by (past tense of *pass*): *He passed me in the hall without recognizing me.*
past (n) time gone by: *We've never used their services in the past.*

peace (n) absence of war or conflict: *Joaquin enjoyed the peace he found in his new job.*
piece (n) a fragment, portion: *Each daycare child received a piece of Wanda's birthday cake.*

personal (adj) private: *The manager closes the door when she discusses personal matters with one of her staff.*

personnel (n) staff of employees: *All personnel must participate in the 401(k) retirement program.*

perspective (n) viewpoint: *From the customer's perspective, we are an honest and courteous company.*

prospective (adj) expected, likely to happen or become: *Email the prospective budget to district managers.*

plain (adj) simple, not fancy: *He ate plain food.*

plane (n) airplane: *The plane for Dallas leaves in an hour.*

plane (v) to make smooth: *The carpenter planed the wood.*

precede (v) to go before: *A presentation will precede the open discussion.*

proceed (v) to carry on, to go ahead: *Proceed as if we had never received that letter.*

principal (adj) main, chief: *Sales of new software constitute their principal source of revenue.*

principal (n) the head of a school: *She was a high school principal before she entered the business world.*

principal (n) money owed: *The principal on that loan totaled $32,800.*

principle (n) a policy, a belief: *Sales reps should operate on the principle that the customer is always right.*

quiet (adj) silent, not loud: *He liked to spend a quiet afternoon surfing the Net.*

quite (adv) to a degree: *The officer was quite encouraged by the recruit's performance.*

stationary (adj) not moving: *Miguel rides a stationary bicycle for an hour every morning.*

stationery (n) writing supplies, such as paper and envelopes: *Please stop off at the stationery store and buy some more address labels.*

than (conj) as opposed to (used in comparisons): *He is a faster keyboarder than his predecessor.*

then (adv) at that time: *First she called the vendor; then she summarized their conversation in an email to her boss.*

their (adj) possessive form of *they*: *All the lab technicians took their vacations during June and July.*

there (adv) in that place: *Please put the printer in there.*

they're (pronoun + verb) contraction of *they* and *are*: *They're our two best customer service representatives.*

to (prep): *They invited us to their new facility.*

too (adv) also, excessive: *The painters put too much enamel on the railings.*

two (n) the number: *Two new notebooks arrived today.*

waiver (n) intentional relinquishment of a right, claim, or privilege: *The company issued a waiver so that additional liability insurance would not have to be secured.*

waver (v) to shake, to move: *Our company would not waver in its commitment to safety.*

who's (pronoun + verb) contraction of *who* and *is*: *Who's up next for a promotion?*
whose (adj) possessive form of *who*: *Whose idea was that in the first place?*

you're (pronoun + verb) contraction of *you* and *are*: *You're going to like their decision.*
your (adj) possessive form of *you*: *They agree with your ideas.*

Index

© dimitris_k/ShutterStock.com